Dirk Ge

HOLISTIC DETECTIVE AGENCY

BIG HOLISTIC GRAPHIC NOVEL

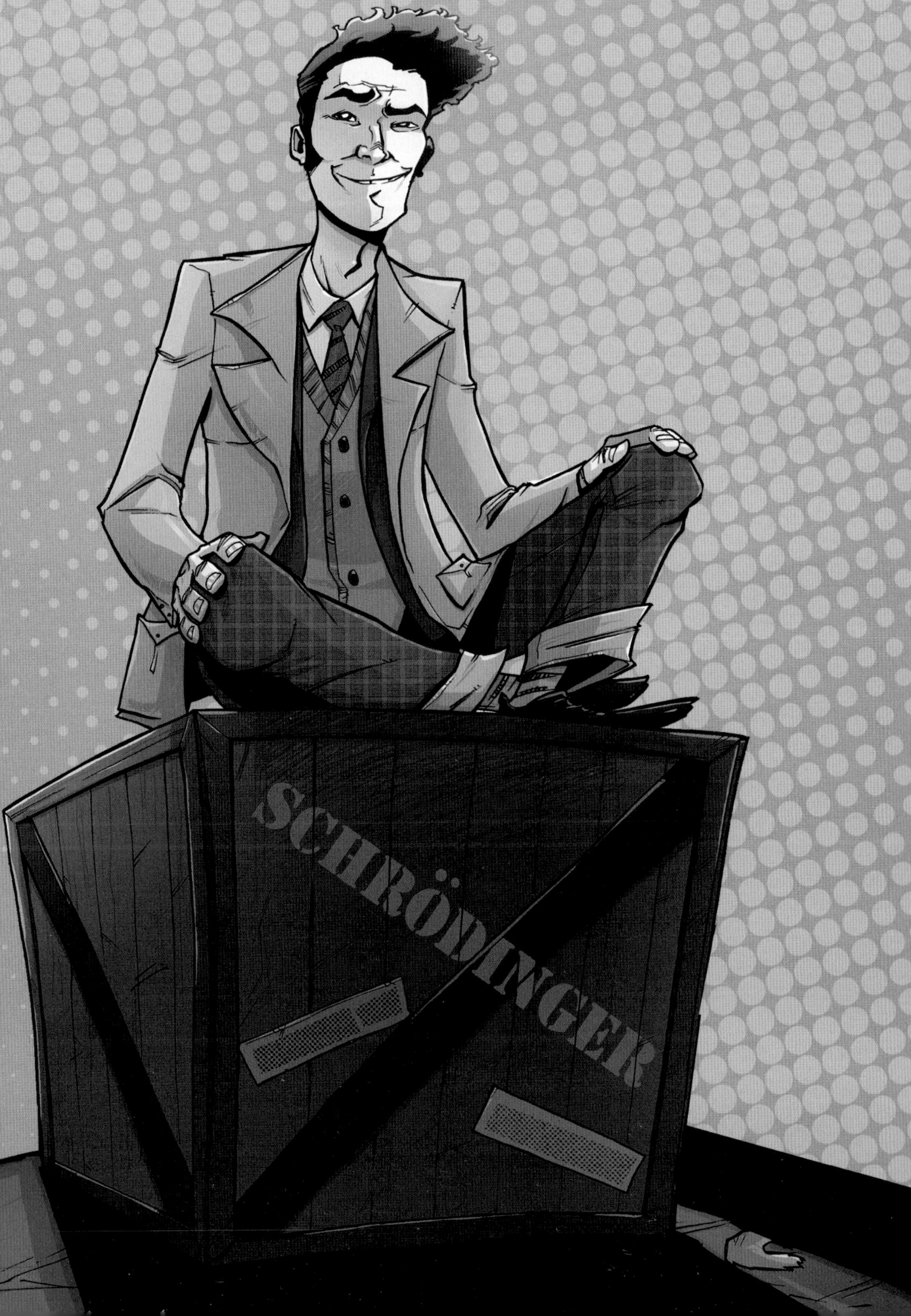
SCHRÖDINGER

COVER BY
ROBERT HACK

COVER COLORS BY
STEPHEN DOWNER

COLLECTION EDITS BY
JUSTIN EISINGER
& ALONZO SIMON

COLLECTION DESIGN BY
CLAUDIA CHONG

PUBLISHER:
TED ADAMS

Special Thanks to Ted Adams, Ed Vickor, Max Landis, James Goss, Mike Carey, Devon Byers, Ed Victor, Bruce Vinokour, Maggie Phillips, Charlie Campbell, Polly Adams & Dedicated with love to Douglas Noel Adams, who came to see a stude

IDW®
www.IDWPUBLISHING.com

Dirk Gently created by **Douglas Adams.**

PRESENTED IN ASSOCIATION WITH
iDEATE MEDIA

Ted Adams, CEO & Publisher
Greg Goldstein, President & COO
Robbie Robbins, EVP/Sr. Graphic Artist
Chris Ryall, Chief Creative Officer/Editor-in-Chief
Laurie Windrow, Senior VP of Sales & Marketing
Matthew Ruzicka, CPA, Chief Financial Officer
Dirk Wood, VP of Marketing
Lorelei Bunjes, VP of Digital Services
Jeff Webber, VP of Licensing, Digital and Subsidiary R
Jerry Bennington, VP of New Product Development

Facebook: **facebook.com/idwpublishing** • Twitter: **@idwpublishing**
YouTube: **youtube.com/idwpublishing** • Instagram: **instagram.com/idwpublishing**

Originally published as DIRK GENTLY'S HOLISTIC DETECTIVE AGENCY: THE INTERCONNECTEDNESS OF ALL KINGS issues #1–5 and DIRK GENTLY'S HOLISTIC DETECTIVE AGENCY: A SPOON TOO SHORT issues

Dirk Gently's
HOLISTIC DETECTIVE AGENCY
BIG HOLISTIC GRAPHIC NOVEL

A SPOON TOO SHORT

WRITTEN BY **Arvind Ethan David**
ART BY **Ilias Kyriazis**

COLORS BY **Charlie Kirchoff**
LETTERS BY **Robbie Robbins** & **Shawn Lee**
EDITS BY **Denton J. Tipton** & **Chi-Ren Choong**
EXECUTIVE PRODUCER **Max Landis**

THE INTERCONNECTEDNESS OF ALL KINGS

WRITTEN BY **Chris Ryall**
PENCILS BY **Tony Akins** & **Ilias Kyriazis**

INKS BY **John Livesay**
COLORS BY **Leonard O'Grady**
LETTERS BY **Robbie Robbins** & **Shawn Lee**
EDITS BY **John Barber** & **Arvind Ethan David**

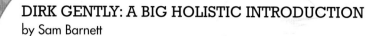

DIRK GENTLY: A BIG HOLISTIC INTRODUCTION

by Sam Barnett

I can't remember when I first encountered Dirk Gently, but when my audition for the TV s came up, I realized I knew the name. Perhaps it's one of those things that is in the collec unconscious, a bit like *Hitchhiker's Guide to the Galaxy*. But as soon as I mentioned to pe that I was auditioning for the show, I experienced an outpouring of love from almost every I spoke to for the novels. My sister had read them at school, friends of mine had read t — it seemed that most people I know had encountered the books or the BBC TV version, I felt somewhat out of the loop.

To be fair, my Dirk is very different to the Dirk in the novels — is very different to the Di the comics — is very different to… and off we go down the rabbit hole. But whatever ver you are looking at, the essence of all the Dirks i same. There are certain character traits ideas behind Dirk and the world in whic operates that are essential to a g portrayal of Dirk, such as his beli interconnectedness and a total deni any psychic power. Certainly the sp that Douglas Adams wrote where explains how he works as a holistic detectiv never been bettered in any other medium, indeed is so good that it's used pretty much wor word in all the incarnations of Dirk so far.

Physically, all the Dirks are very different. W first read the novels, knowing I was auditionin Dirk, I thought, "Well there's no way I'm right fo role, he's meant to be in his mid-forties, short, p and slightly curmudgeonly." The comic book makes him rather handsome, dashing,

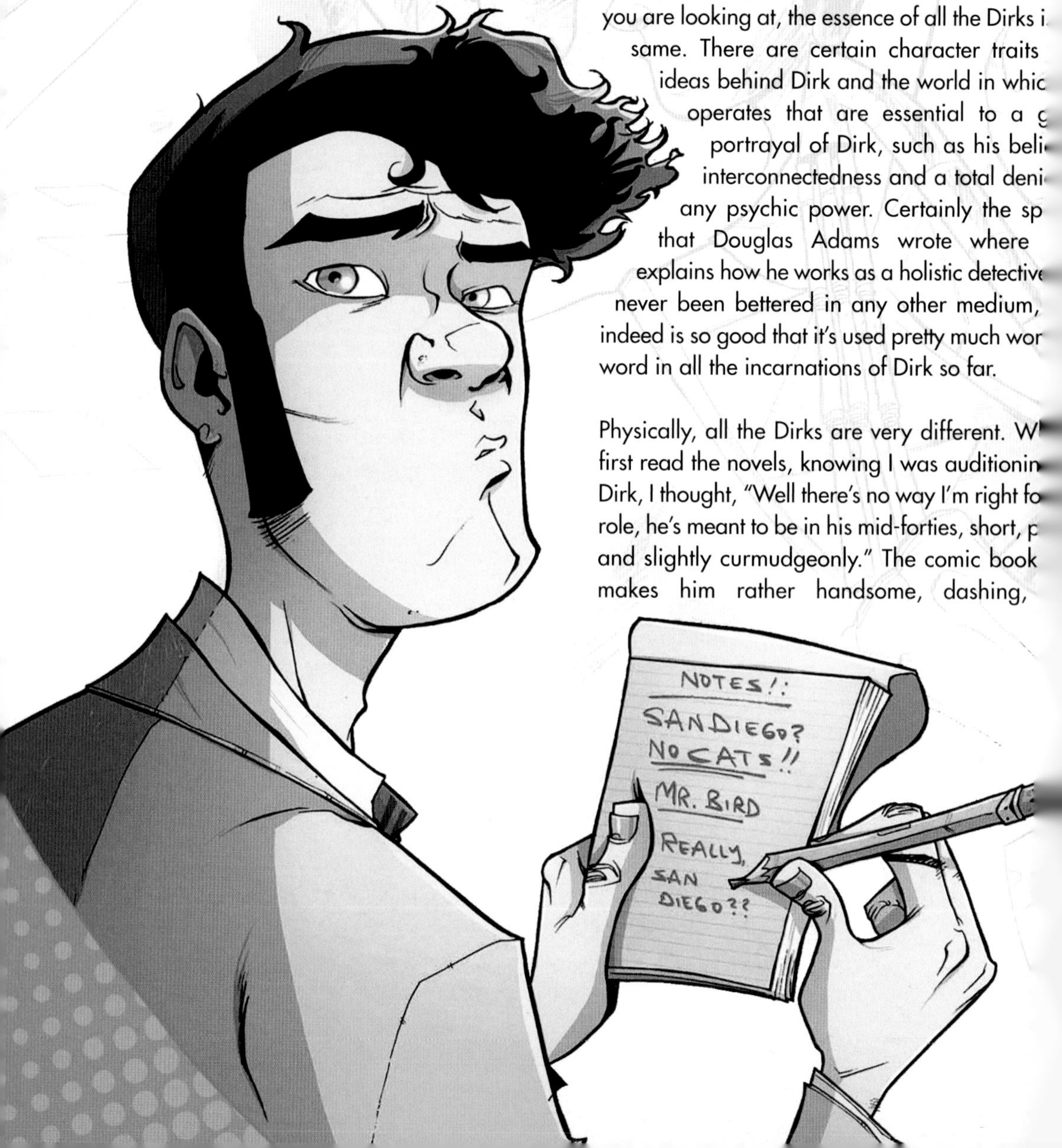
NOTES!:
SANDIEGO?
NO CATS!!
MR. BIRD
REALLY, SAN DIEGO??

getic I think, especially with all that fantastic hair the clothing, whereas my Dirk is young, slim, has a penchant for a primary-colored leather r jacket. But what they all have in common is a like awe of the world, an openness and curiosity so many adults grow to lack, and a belief that ything is connected, nothing is wasted, all things to the same place ultimately.

ain't broke, etc… Dirk works as a character use the original novels were so strong.

d comics as a child and reading the *Dirk* comics rekindled my love for them again! I faithfully and collected copies of *The Beano* and *The ly* for years and now I'm doing the same with *Dirk* issues. I'd forgotten how much pleasure I get reading a comic. It is such a unique art form. a book, not a movie, something in-between. I was reminded, reading the *Dirk* stories, how ordinary it is that so much information, acter, plot, and feeling can be conveyed with vely few images and words. Comics engage the ination in a unique way that forces the er/viewer to engage. And I guess that's the — you are both reading and viewing at the time, and the imagination fills in the gaps en the images. It is an active participation that

takes place. You don't sit back and get the picture fed to you like you do at the movies, and you don't get every word and thought and feeling spelled out for you like you do in books. You become part of the process of storytelling when reading a comic. And that is why I love them.

Which brings me to the hair. When I saw Dirk's hair in the comics, I immediately thought "I hope that's what they do to me in the TV show." But alas, no. I have my own hair, well, a little darker than my own color, but no fantastically towering like the comic book Dirk's hair, which I think is a great shame. I've seen the comic book version of my Dirk and it's SO COOL. And kinda weird, seeing myself but not myself because it's Dirk and Dirk's costume and Dirk's hair color. But on me. Weird. But very, very awesome.

Working with Max (Landis) and Arvind (Ethan David) is fantastic because Max has an encyclopedic knowledge of the entire first and second seasons of *Dirk Gently,* so anything I need to know, he is my go-to guy. And Arvind has grown up nurturing and living in the world of Dirk Gently since he was a boy, so he is the authority on all things Dirk. Between them, I feel in very safe hands.

l Barnett plays Dirk Gently in the new series. He was born in Whitby, England, and trained London Academy of Music and Dramatic Art. He is a two-time Tony Award nominee for ge performances in The History Boys and Twelfth Night on Broadway, as well as a Desk Award and WhatsOnStage Award recipient for The History Boys. TV work es Penny Dreadful (Showtime), John Adams (HBO), Alexander Hamilton (PBS), Twelve, Desperate Romantics, Beautiful People, Crooked House, Strange, Inspector (BBC), Endeavour, Vicious, Marple (ITV) and, Not Safe For Work (Channel 4). Stage include The History Boys, Twelfth Night, Richard III, His Dark Materials, Women e Women, The Beaux' Stratagem, Dealer's Choice, Rosencrantz And Guildenstern ad, When You Cure Me, The Whisky Taster, The Man, and The Way Of The World. nclude Jupiter Ascending, The Lady In The Van, Brightstar, The History Boys ominee), Mrs Henderson Presents, and Love Tomorrow.

CHAPTER
ONE

A Spoon Too Short

Cover Art by **ILIAS KYRIAZ**

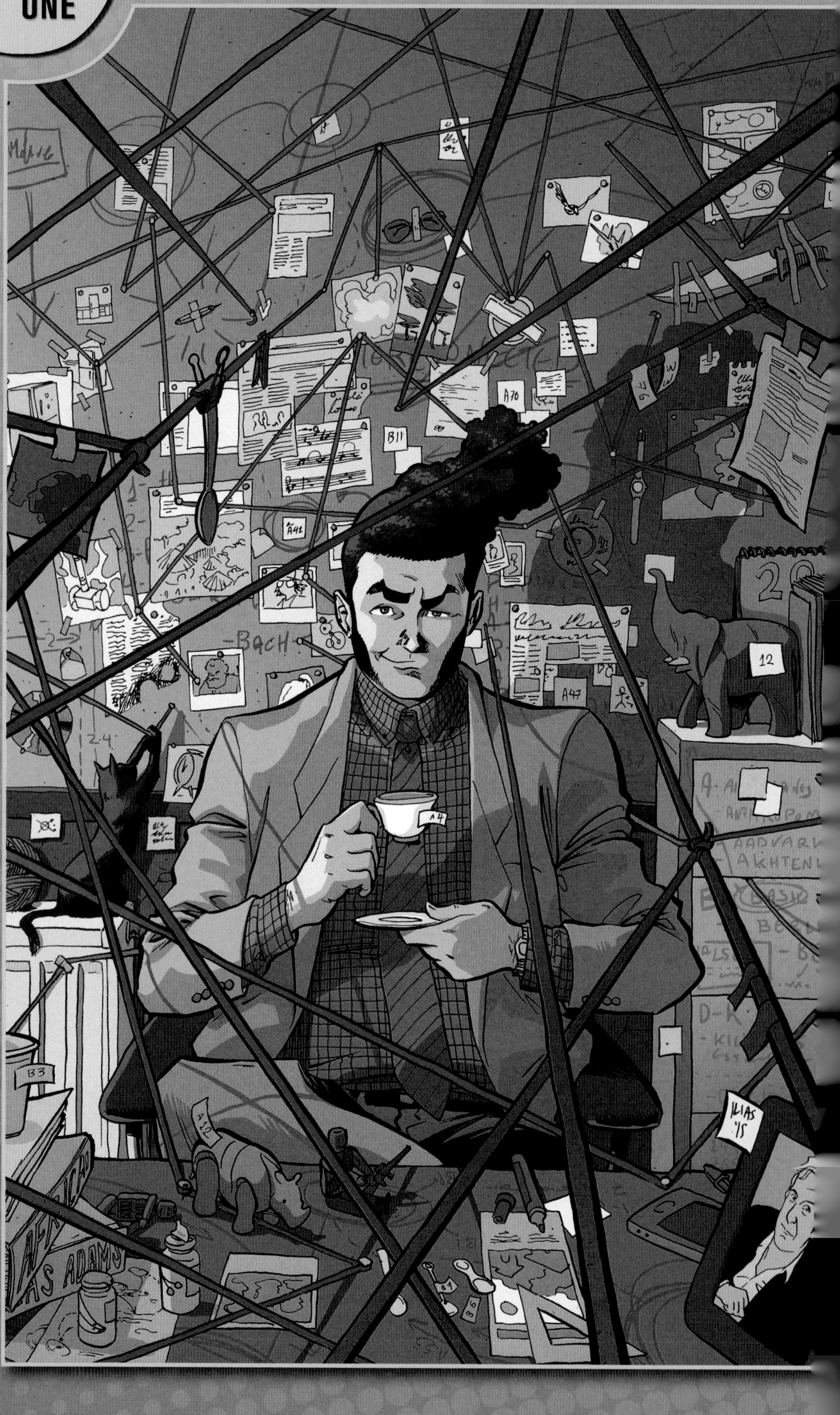
A70
B11
A41
12
A47
A4
B3
ILIAS '15

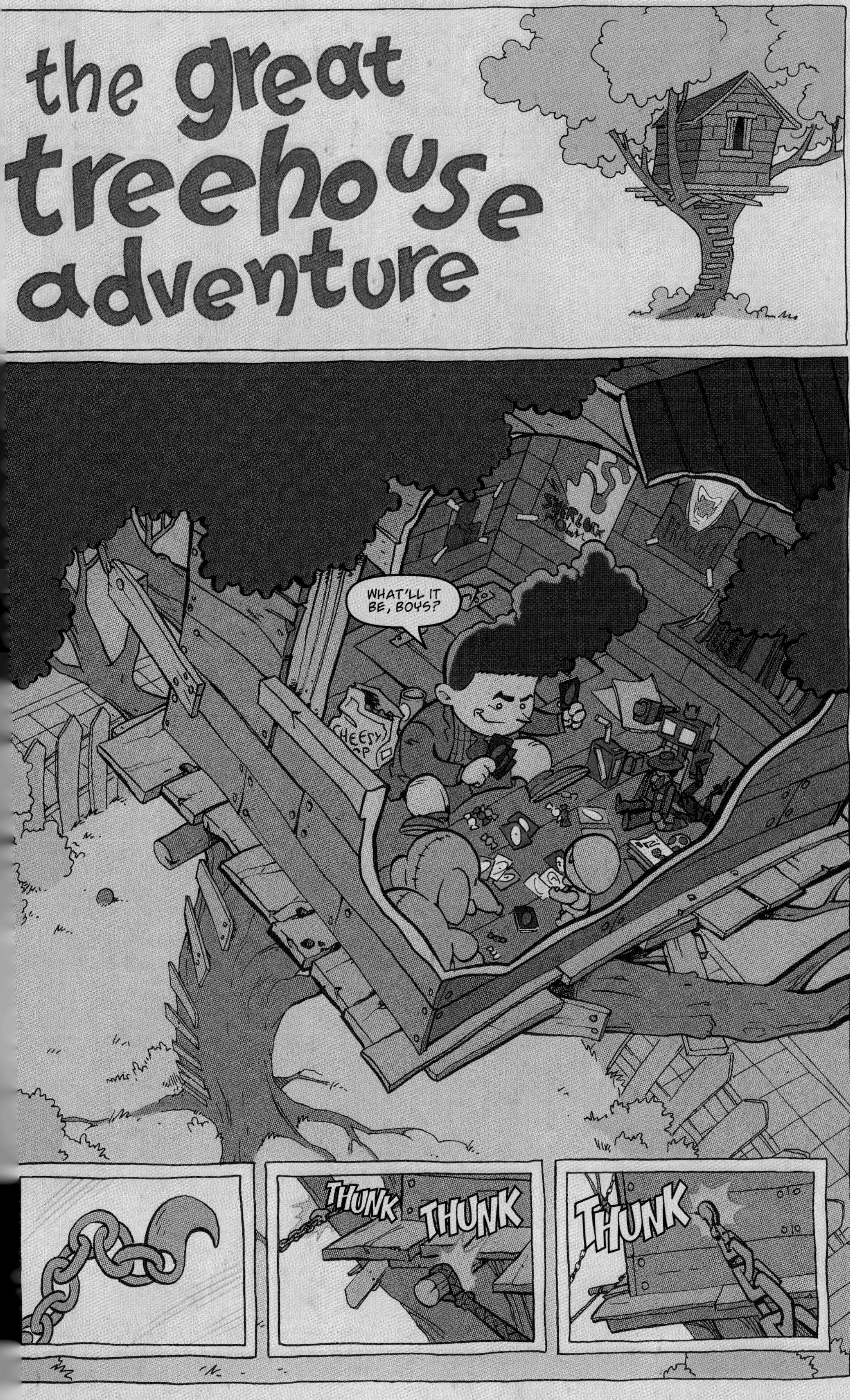
the great treehouse adventure
WHAT'LL IT BE, BOYS?
THUNK
THUNK
THUNK

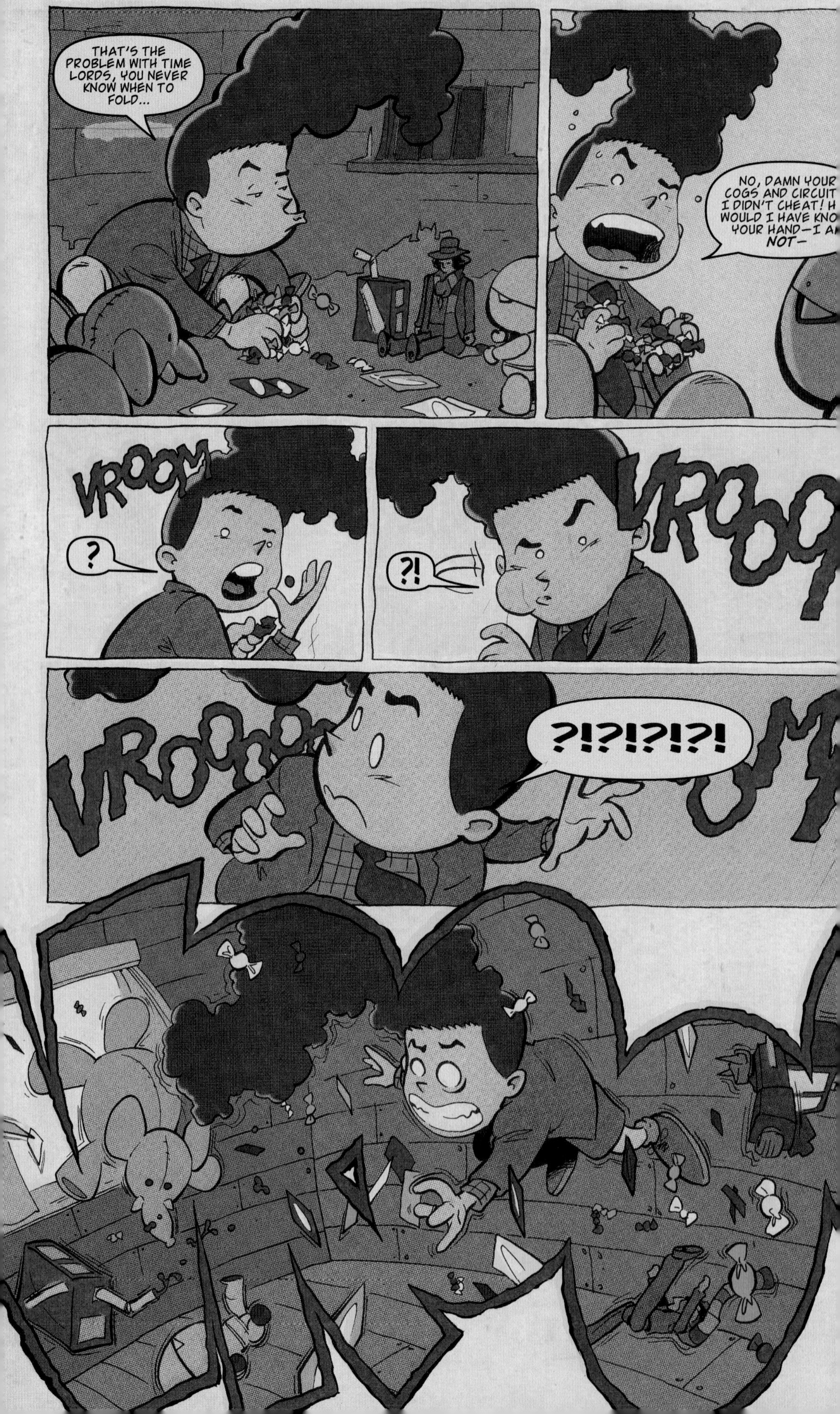
THAT'S THE PROBLEM WITH TIME LORDS, YOU NEVER KNOW WHEN TO FOLD...
NO, DAMN YOUR COGS AND CIRCUIT I DIDN'T CHEAT! H WOULD I HAVE KNO YOUR HAND—I A NOT—
VROOM
?
?!
VROOO
VROOOOOOOM
?!?!?!?!

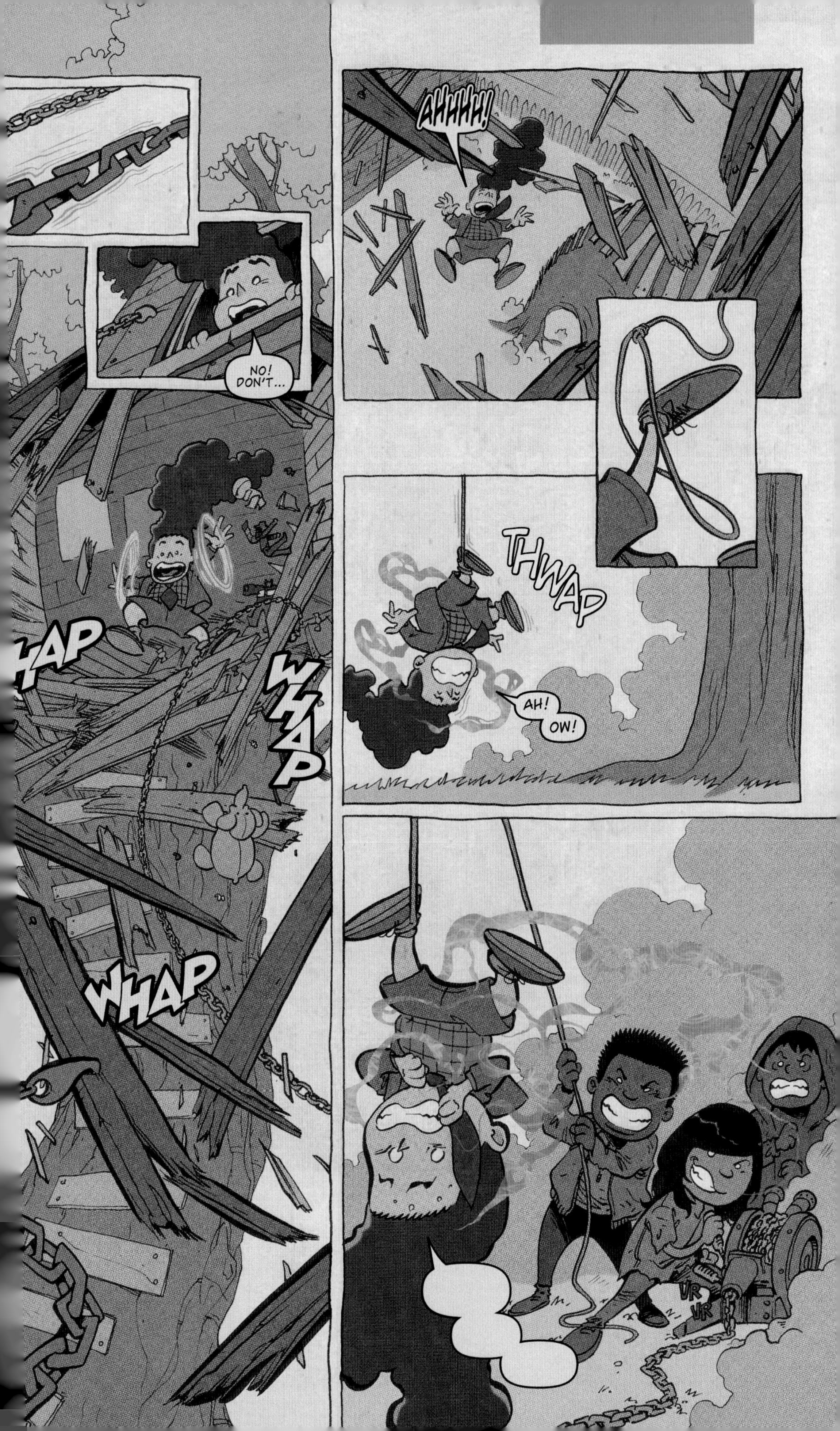
NO! DON'T...
HAP
WHAP
WHAP
AHHHH!
THWAP
AH!
OW!
VR
VR

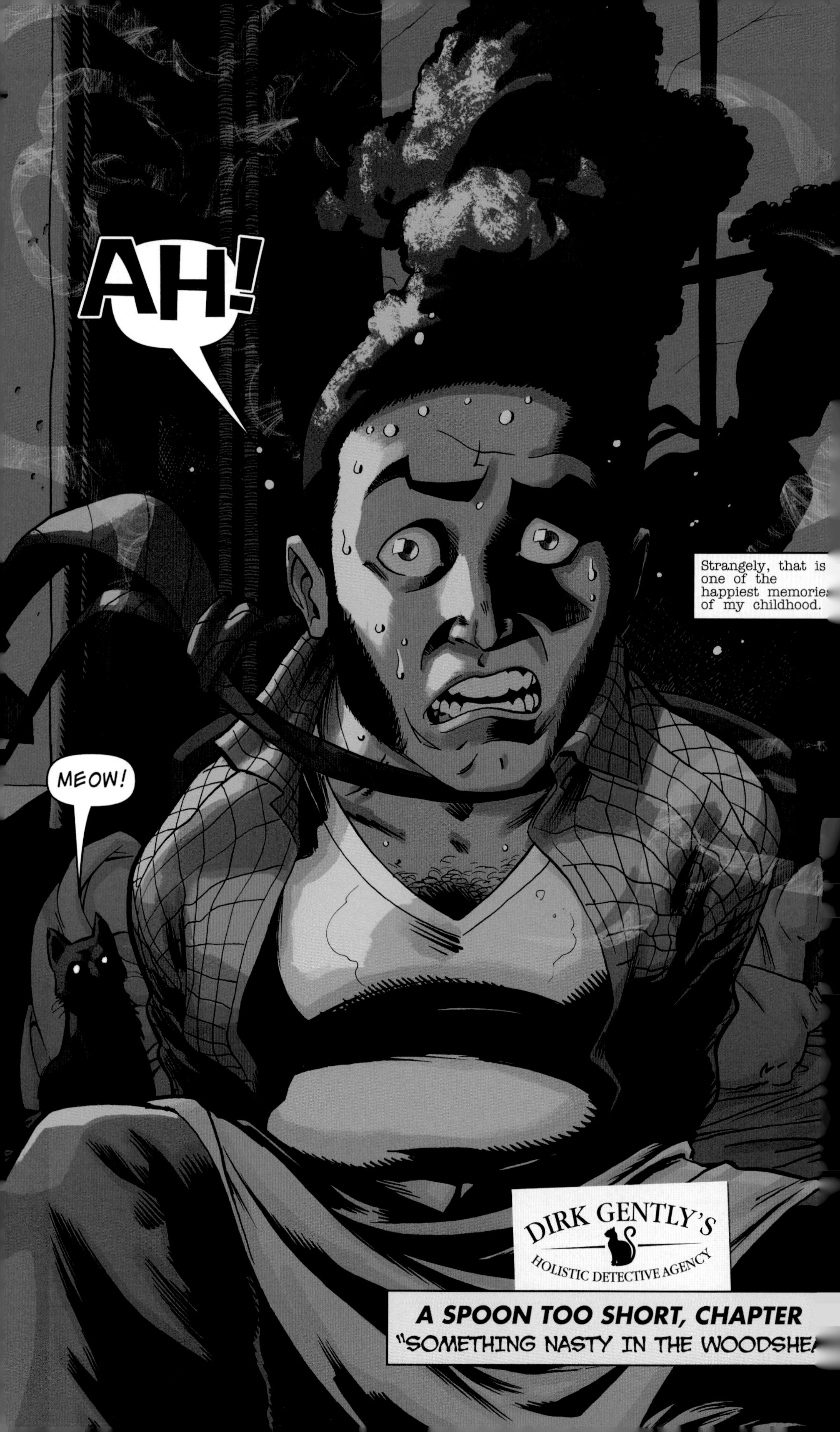
AH!
Strangely, that is one of the happiest memorie of my childhood.
MEOW!
DIRK GENTLY'S
HOLISTIC DETECTIVE AGENCY
A SPOON TOO SHORT, CHAPTER
"SOMETHING NASTY IN THE WOODSHE

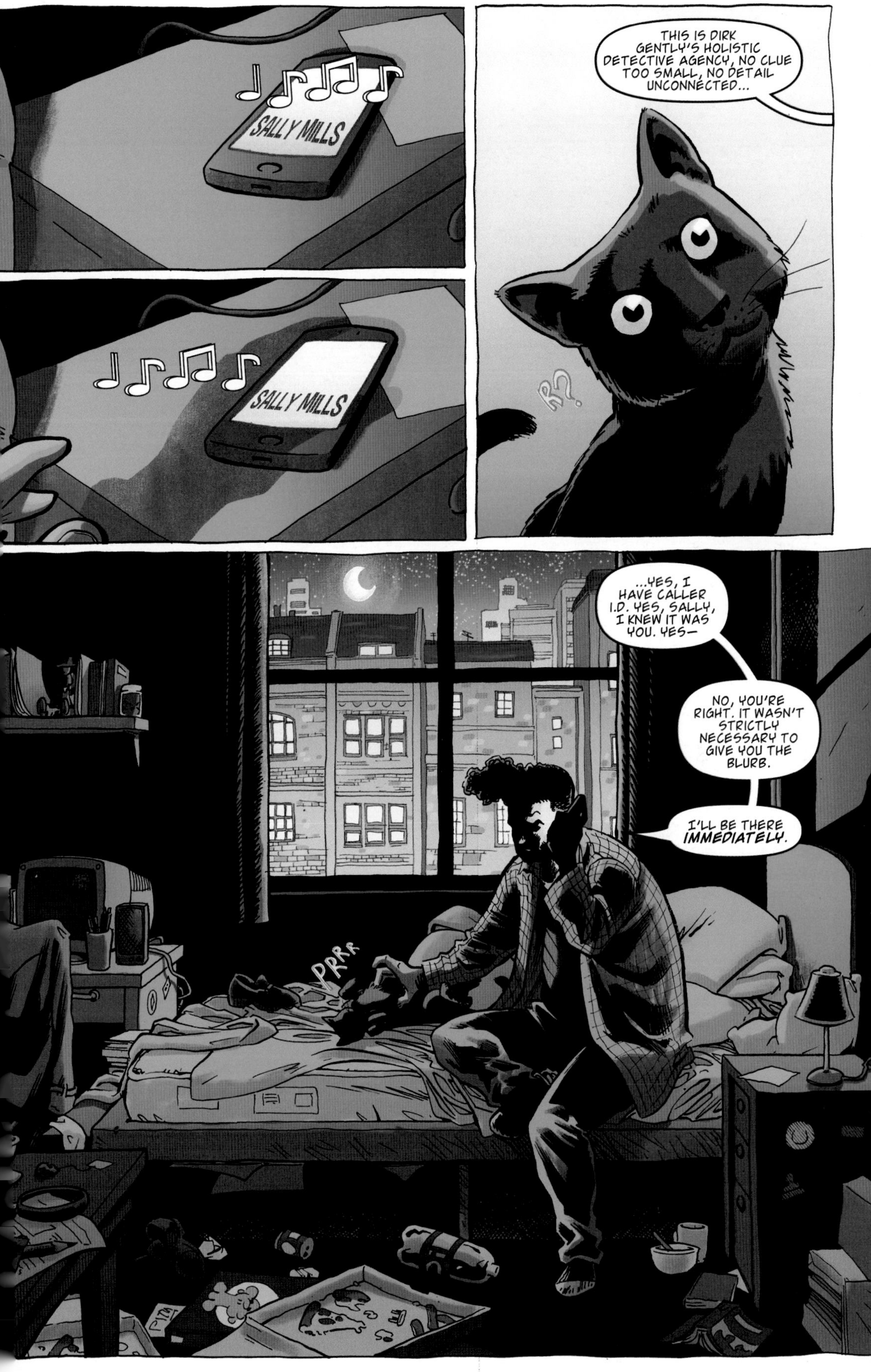
SALLY MILLS
SALLY MILLS
THIS IS DIRK GENTLY'S HOLISTIC DETECTIVE AGENCY, NO CLUE TOO SMALL, NO DETAIL UNCONNECTED...
...YES, I HAVE CALLER I.D. YES, SALLY, I KNEW IT WAS YOU. YES—
NO, YOU'RE RIGHT. IT WASN'T STRICTLY NECESSARY TO GIVE YOU THE BLURB.
I'LL BE THERE ***IMMEDIATELY***.
PRRR

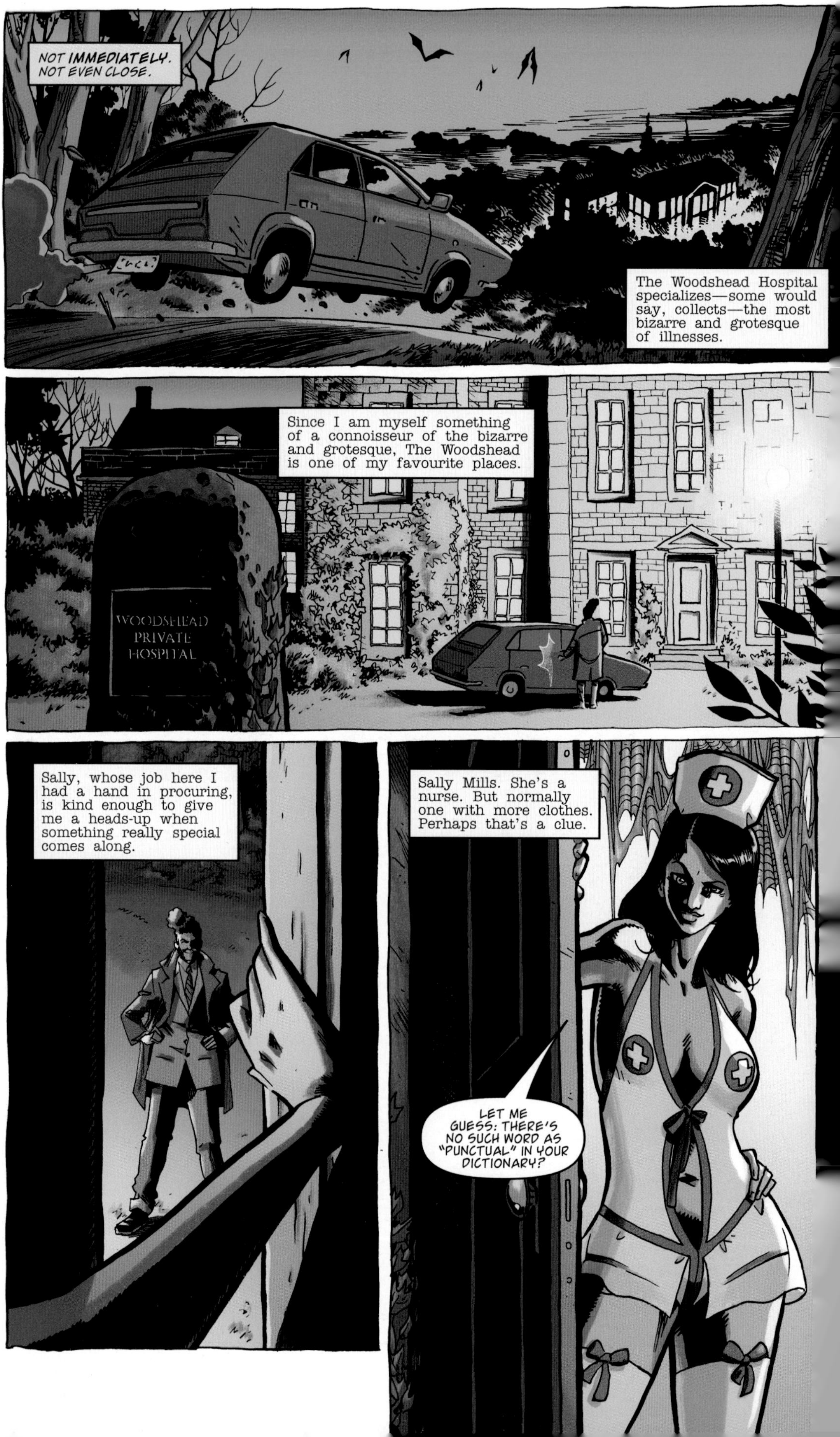
NOT IMMEDIATELY.
NOT EVEN CLOSE.
The Woodshead Hospital specializes—some would say, collects—the most bizarre and grotesque of illnesses.
Since I am myself something of a connoisseur of the bizarre and grotesque, The Woodshead is one of my favourite places.
WOODSHEAD PRIVATE HOSPITAL
Sally, whose job here I had a hand in procuring, is kind enough to give me a heads-up when something really special comes along.
Sally Mills. She's a nurse. But normally one with more clothes. Perhaps that's a clue.
LET ME GUESS: THERE'S NO SUCH WORD AS "PUNCTUAL" IN YOUR DICTIONARY?

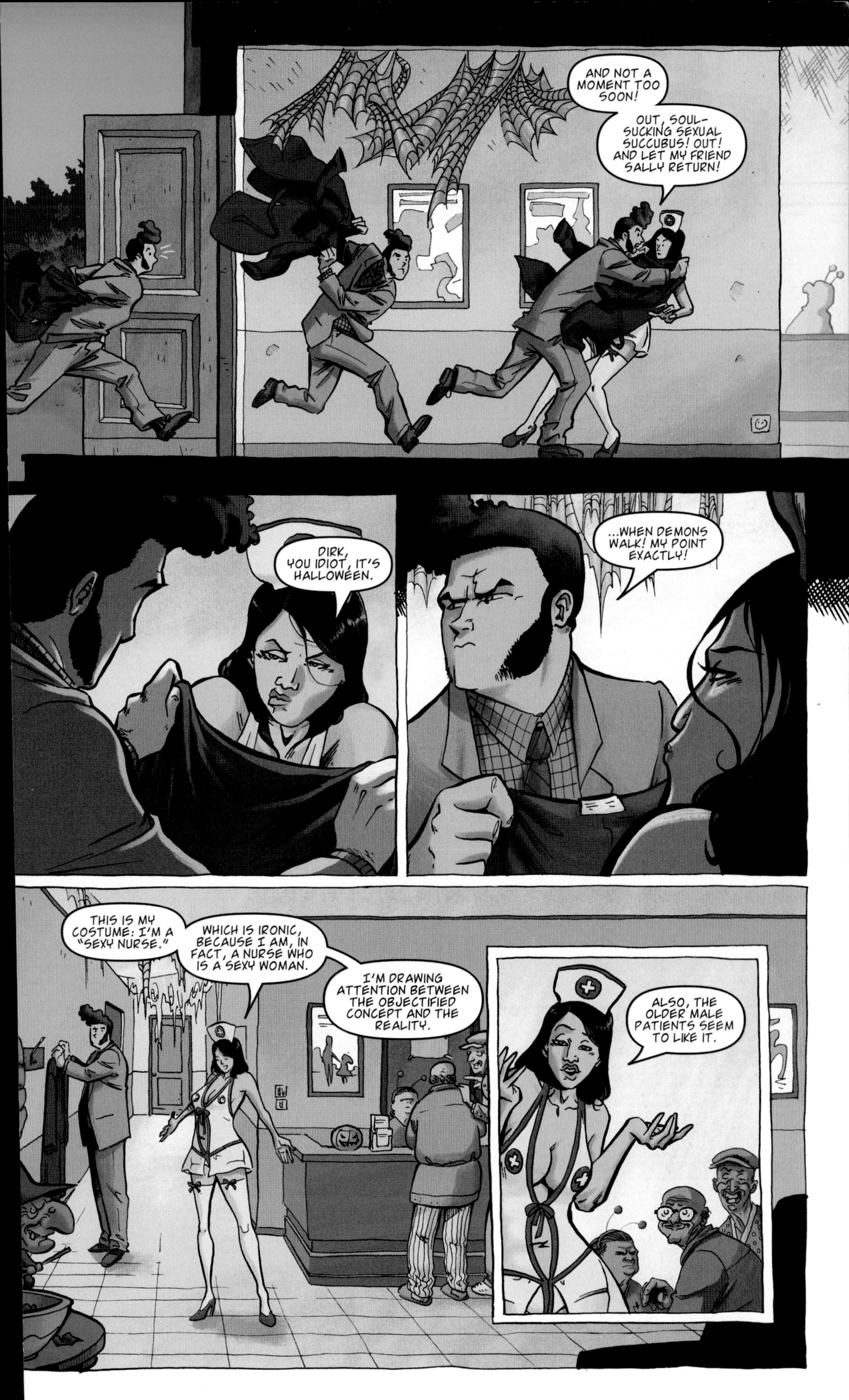
AND NOT A MOMENT TOO SOON!
OUT, SOUL-SUCKING SEXUAL SUCCUBUS! OUT! AND LET MY FRIEND SALLY RETURN!
DIRK, YOU IDIOT, IT'S HALLOWEEN.
...WHEN DEMONS WALK! MY POINT EXACTLY!
THIS IS MY COSTUME: I'M A "SEXY NURSE."
WHICH IS IRONIC, BECAUSE I AM, IN FACT, A NURSE WHO IS A SEXY WOMAN.
I'M DRAWING ATTENTION BETWEEN THE OBJECTIFIED CONCEPT AND THE REALITY.
ALSO, THE OLDER MALE PATIENTS SEEM TO LIKE IT.

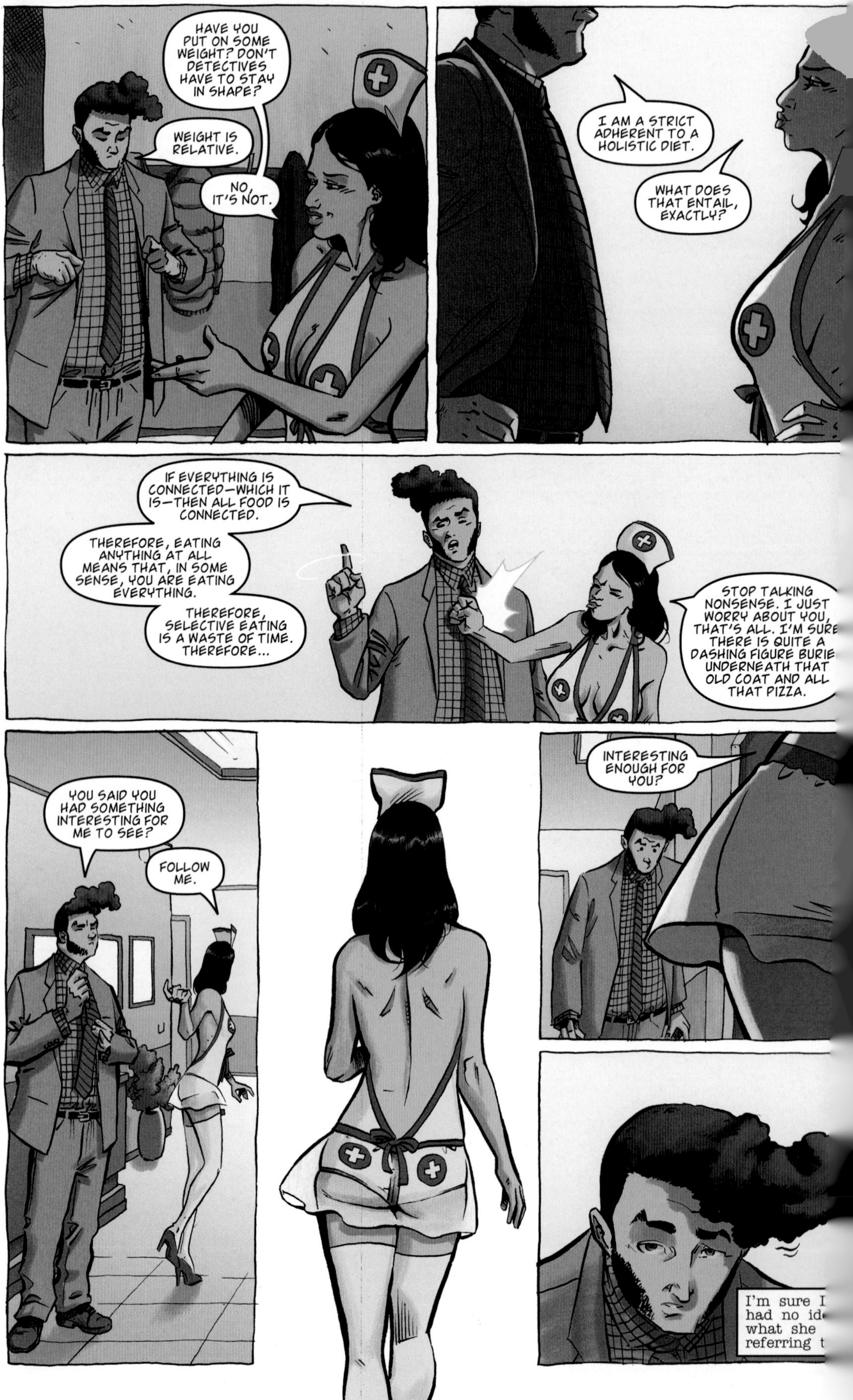
HAVE YOU PUT ON SOME WEIGHT? DON'T DETECTIVES HAVE TO STAY IN SHAPE?
WEIGHT IS RELATIVE.
NO, IT'S NOT.
I AM A STRICT ADHERENT TO A HOLISTIC DIET.
WHAT DOES THAT ENTAIL, EXACTLY?
IF EVERYTHING IS CONNECTED—WHICH IT IS—THEN ALL FOOD IS CONNECTED.
THEREFORE, EATING ANYTHING AT ALL MEANS THAT, IN SOME SENSE, YOU ARE EATING EVERYTHING.
THEREFORE, SELECTIVE EATING IS A WASTE OF TIME. THEREFORE...
STOP TALKING NONSENSE. I JUST WORRY ABOUT YOU, THAT'S ALL. I'M SURE THERE IS QUITE A DASHING FIGURE BURIE UNDERNEATH THAT OLD COAT AND ALL THAT PIZZA.
YOU SAID YOU HAD SOMETHING INTERESTING FOR ME TO SEE?
FOLLOW ME.
INTERESTING ENOUGH FOR YOU?
I'm sure I
had no id
what she
referring t

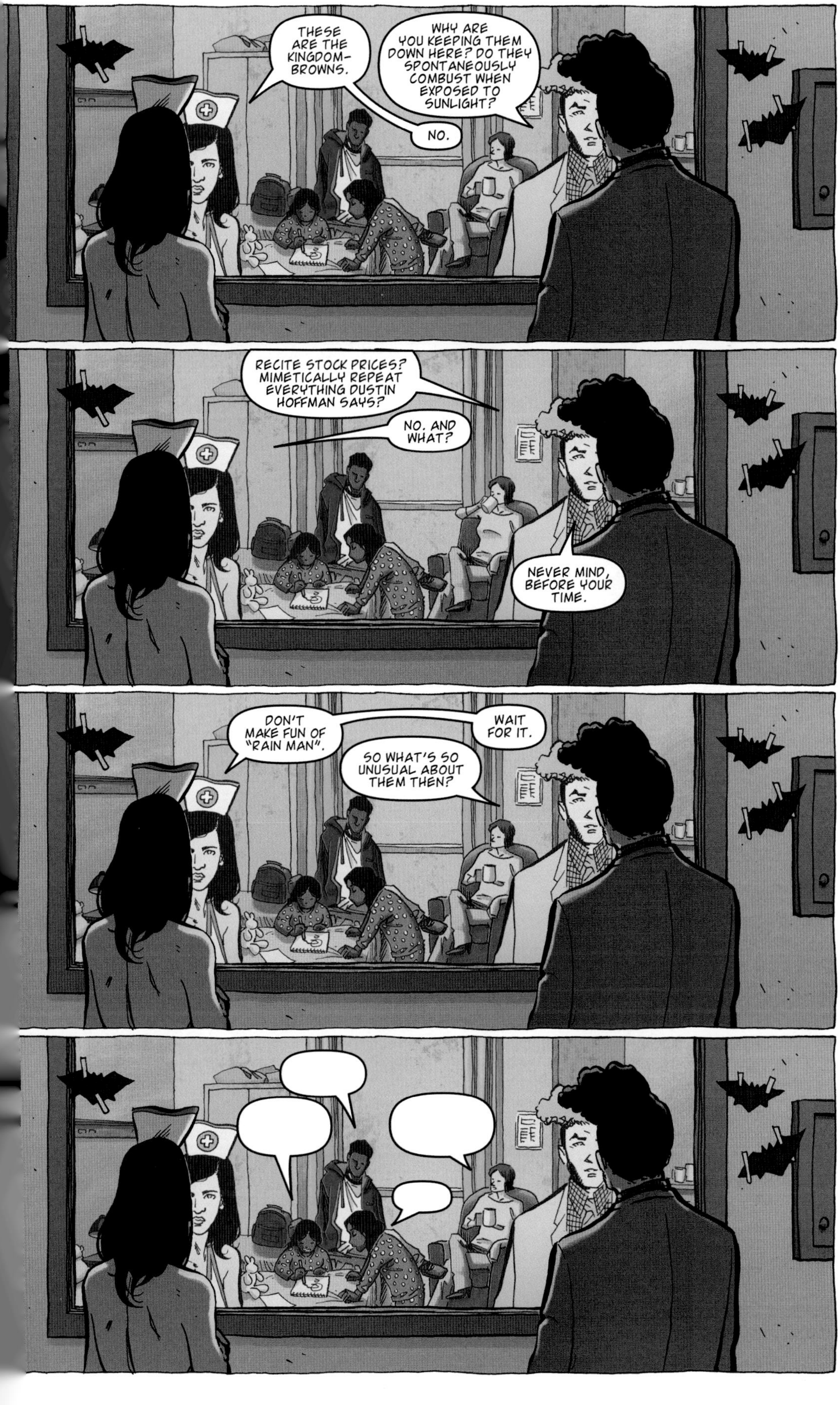
THESE ARE THE KINGDOM-BROWNS.
WHY ARE YOU KEEPING THEM DOWN HERE? DO THEY SPONTANEOUSLY COMBUST WHEN EXPOSED TO SUNLIGHT?
NO.
RECITE STOCK PRICES? MIMETICALLY REPEAT EVERYTHING DUSTIN HOFFMAN SAYS?
NO. AND WHAT?
NEVER MIND, BEFORE YOUR TIME.
DON'T MAKE FUN OF "RAIN MAN".
WAIT FOR IT.
SO WHAT'S SO UNUSUAL ABOUT THEM THEN?

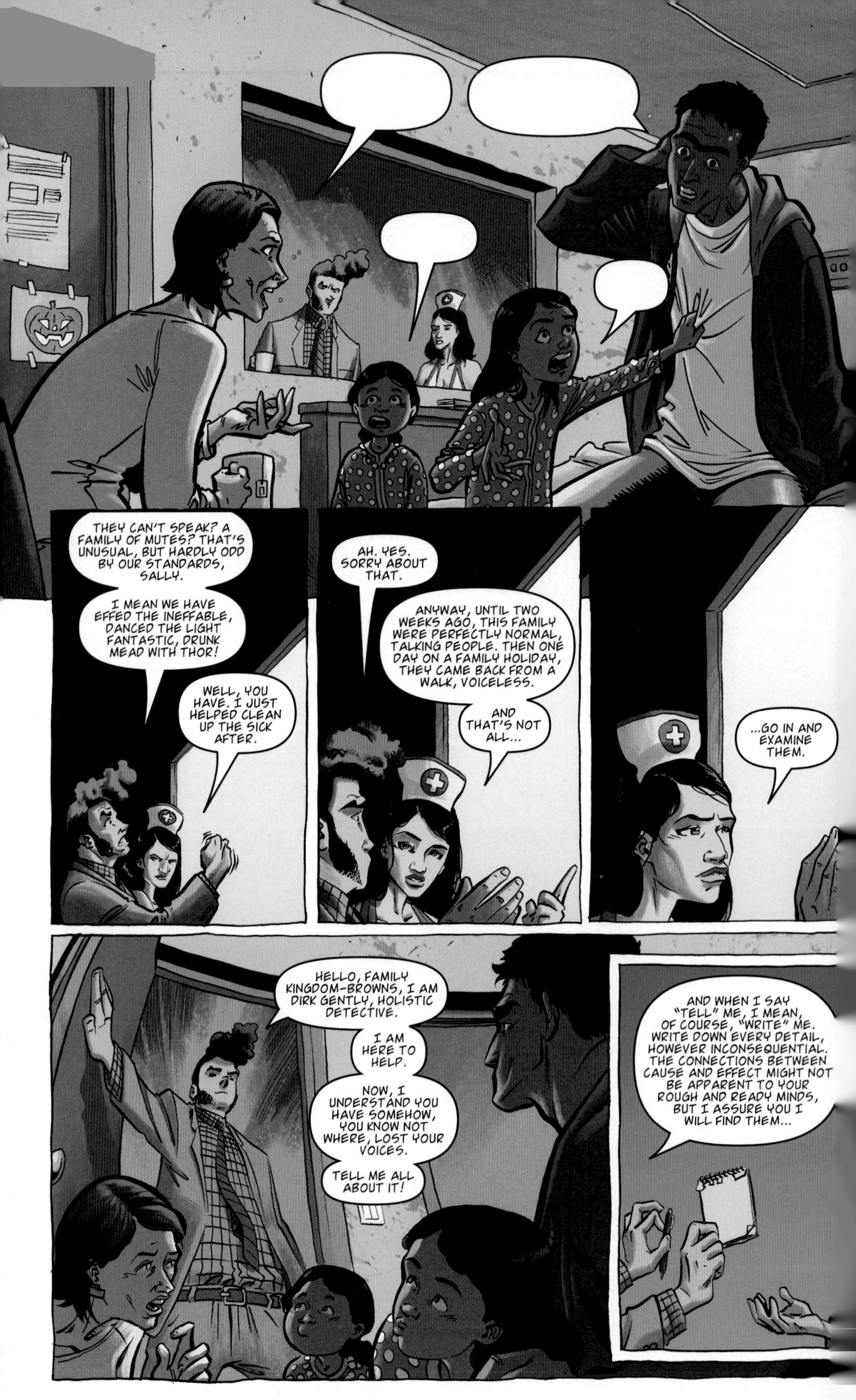
THEY CAN'T SPEAK? A FAMILY OF MUTES? THAT'S UNUSUAL, BUT HARDLY ODD BY OUR STANDARDS, SALLY.
I MEAN WE HAVE EFFED THE INEFFABLE, DANCED THE LIGHT FANTASTIC, DRUNK MEAD WITH THOR!
WELL, YOU HAVE. I JUST HELPED CLEAN UP THE SICK AFTER.
AH. YES. SORRY ABOUT THAT.
ANYWAY, UNTIL TWO WEEKS AGO, THIS FAMILY WERE PERFECTLY NORMAL, TALKING PEOPLE. THEN ONE DAY ON A FAMILY HOLIDAY, THEY CAME BACK FROM A WALK, VOICELESS.
AND THAT'S NOT ALL...
...GO IN AND EXAMINE THEM.
HELLO, FAMILY KINGDOM-BROWNS, I AM DIRK GENTLY, HOLISTIC DETECTIVE.
I AM HERE TO HELP.
NOW, I UNDERSTAND YOU HAVE SOMEHOW, YOU KNOW NOT WHERE, LOST YOUR VOICES.
TELL ME ALL ABOUT IT!
AND WHEN I SAY "TELL" ME, I MEAN, OF COURSE, "WRITE" ME. WRITE DOWN EVERY DETAIL, HOWEVER INCONSEQUENTIAL. THE CONNECTIONS BETWEEN CAUSE AND EFFECT MIGHT NOT BE APPARENT TO YOUR ROUGH AND READY MINDS, BUT I ASSURE YOU I WILL FIND THEM...

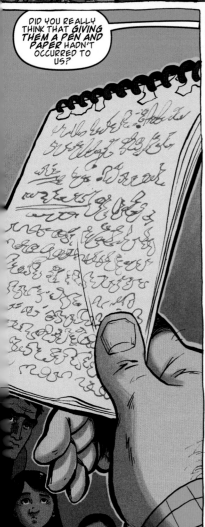

DID YOU REALLY THINK THAT *GIVING THEM A PEN AND PAPER* HADN'T OCCURRED TO US?

HMM. ARE THEY FOREIGN?

ONLY IF YOU COUNT HAMPSHIRE.

HYPOTHESIS: THEY ARE AN EMBEDDED SPY RING, CONCEALED UNDERCOVER IN DARKEST... HAMPSHIRE, CONDITIONED TO COMMUNICATE ONLY IN CYPHER.

ALTERNATIVE HYPOTHESIS: THEY ARE POSSESSED. THIS WRITING BEARS A STRONG RESEMBLANCE TO THE AUTOMATIC WRITING OF VICTORIAN MEDIUMS.

I hate it when Sally does eyebrows. I can't do eyebrows. Only Sally. And she's not even a Detective.

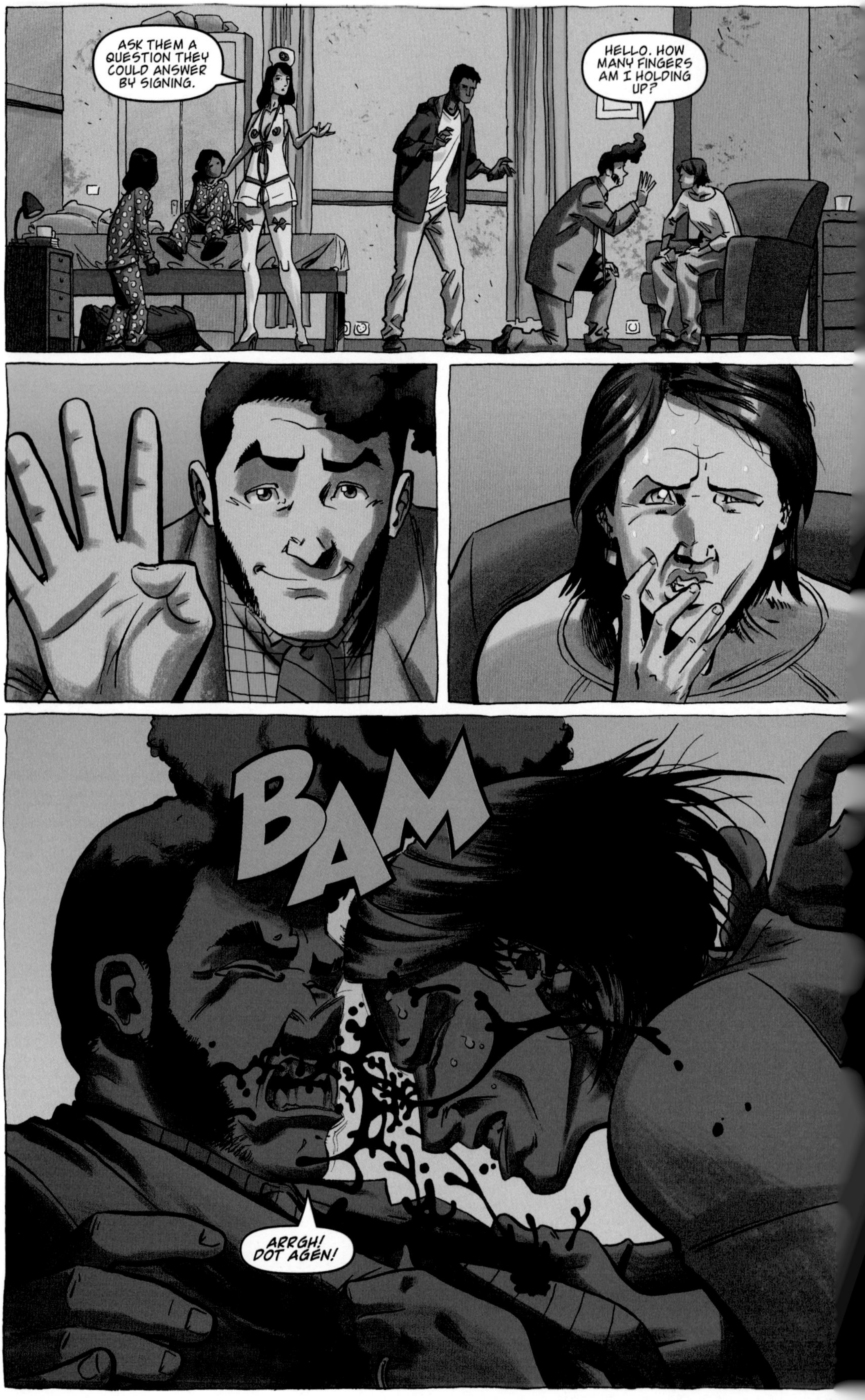
ASK THEM A QUESTION THEY COULD ANSWER BY SIGNING.
HELLO. HOW MANY FINGERS AM I HOLDING UP?
BAM
ARRGH! DOT AGEN!

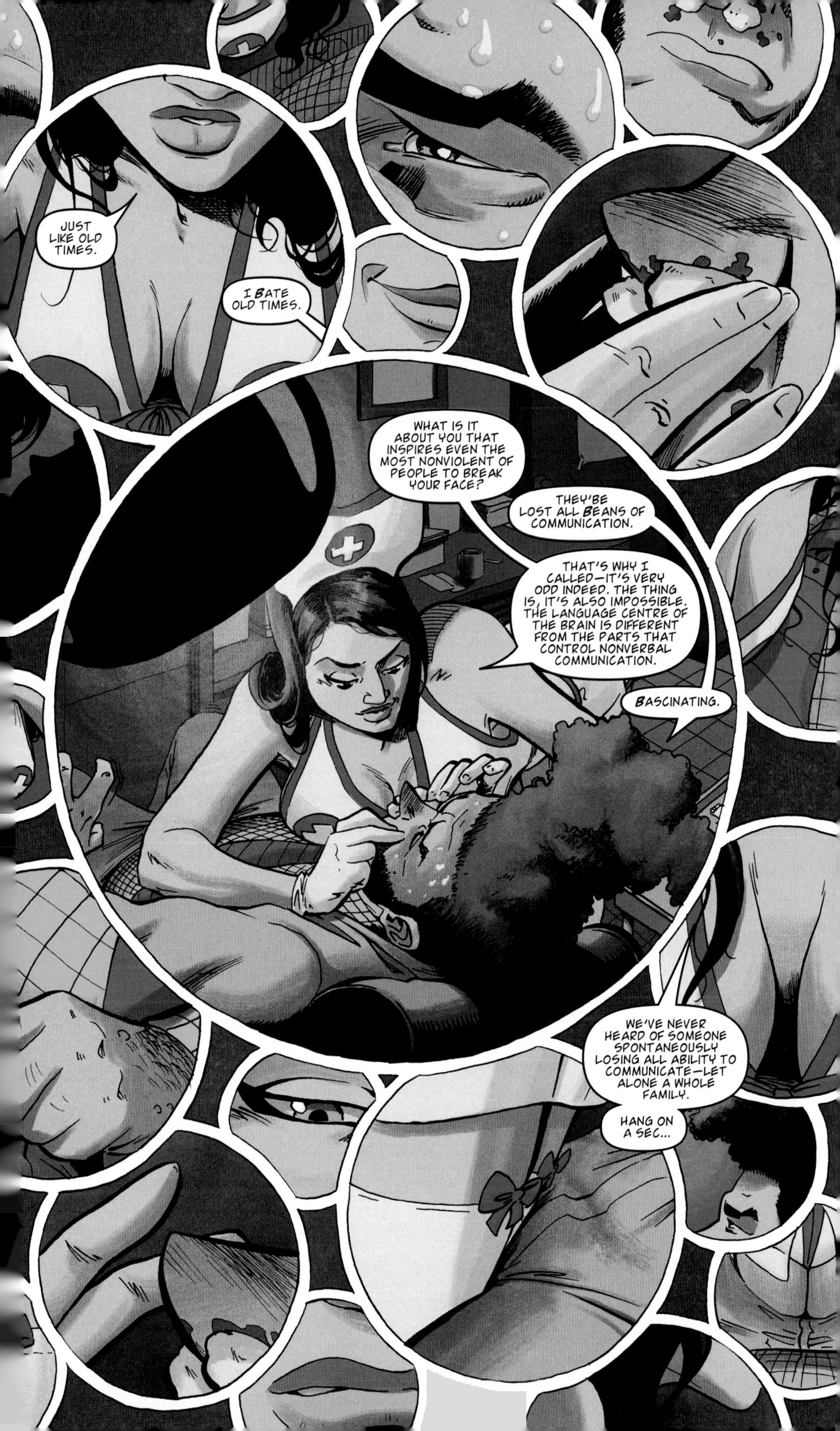
JUST LIKE OLD TIMES.
I BATE OLD TIMES.
WHAT IS IT ABOUT YOU THAT INSPIRES EVEN THE MOST NONVIOLENT OF PEOPLE TO BREAK YOUR FACE?
THEY'BE LOST ALL BEANS OF COMMUNICATION.
THAT'S WHY I CALLED—IT'S VERY ODD INDEED. THE THING IS, IT'S ALSO IMPOSSIBLE. THE LANGUAGE CENTRE OF THE BRAIN IS DIFFERENT FROM THE PARTS THAT CONTROL NONVERBAL COMMUNICATION.
BASCINATING.
WE'VE NEVER HEARD OF SOMEONE SPONTANEOUSLY LOSING ALL ABILITY TO COMMUNICATE—LET ALONE A WHOLE FAMILY.
HANG ON A SEC...

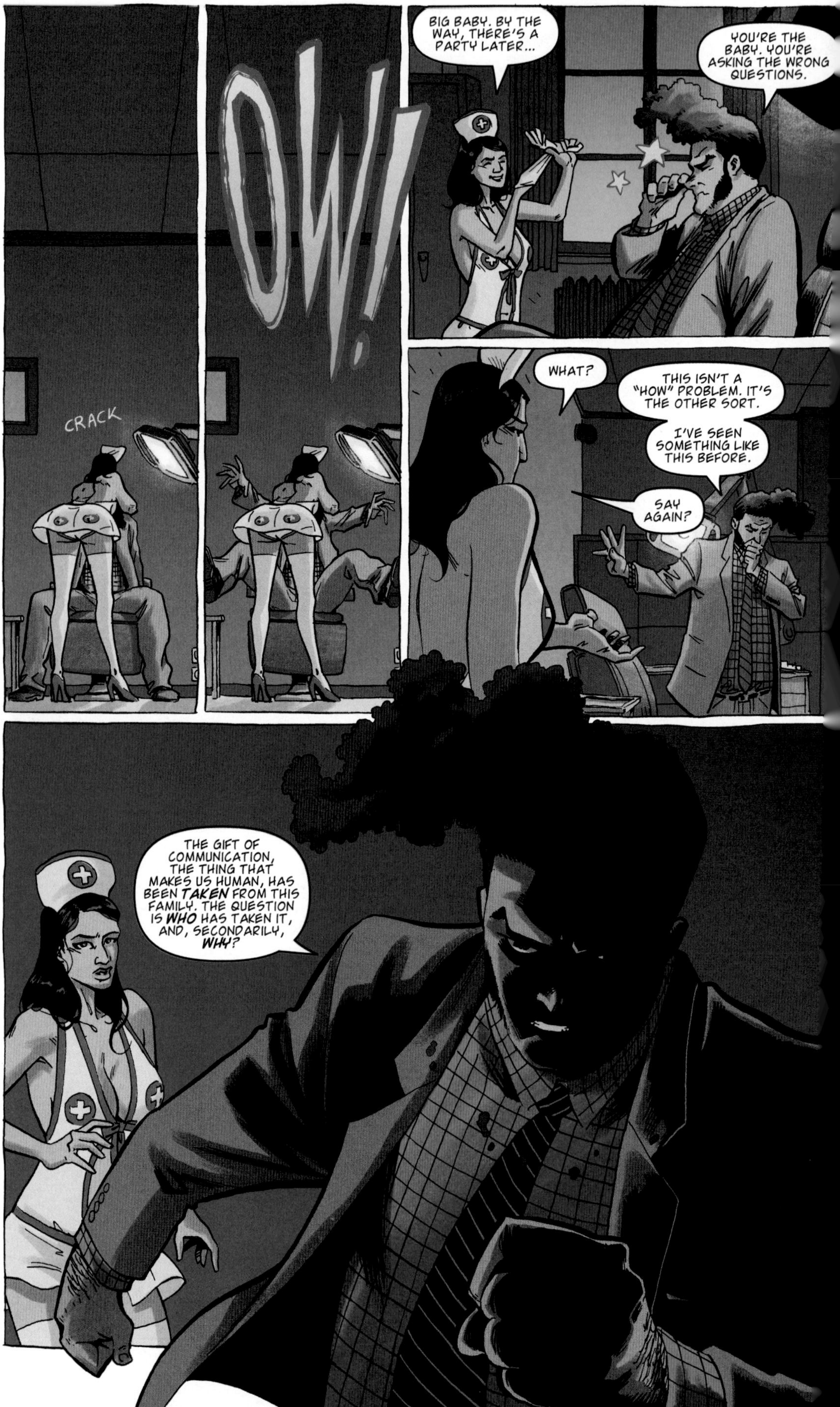
CRACK
OW!
BIG BABY. BY THE WAY, THERE'S A PARTY LATER...
YOU'RE THE BABY. YOU'RE ASKING THE WRONG QUESTIONS.
WHAT?
THIS ISN'T A "HOW" PROBLEM. IT'S THE OTHER SORT.
I'VE SEEN SOMETHING LIKE THIS BEFORE.
SAY AGAIN?
THE GIFT OF COMMUNICATION, THE THING THAT MAKES US HUMAN, HAS BEEN TAKEN FROM THIS FAMILY. THE QUESTION IS WHO HAS TAKEN IT, AND, SECONDARILY, WHY?

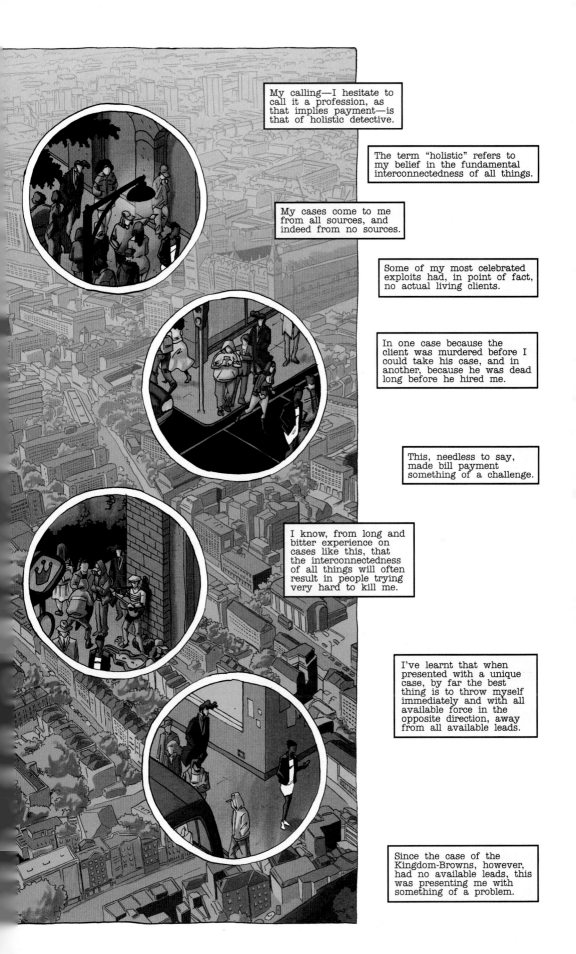

My calling—I hesitate to call it a profession, as that implies payment—is that of holistic detective.

The term "holistic" refers to my belief in the fundamental interconnectedness of all things.

My cases come to me from all sources, and indeed from no sources.

Some of my most celebrated exploits had, in point of fact, no actual living clients.

In one case because the client was murdered before I could take his case, and in another, because he was dead long before he hired me.

This, needless to say, made bill payment something of a challenge.

I know, from long and bitter experience on cases like this, that the interconnectedness of all things will often result in people trying very hard to kill me.

I've learnt that when presented with a unique case, by far the best thing is to throw myself immediately and with all available force in the opposite direction, away from all available leads.

Since the case of the Kingdom-Browns, however, had no available leads, this was presenting me with something of a problem.

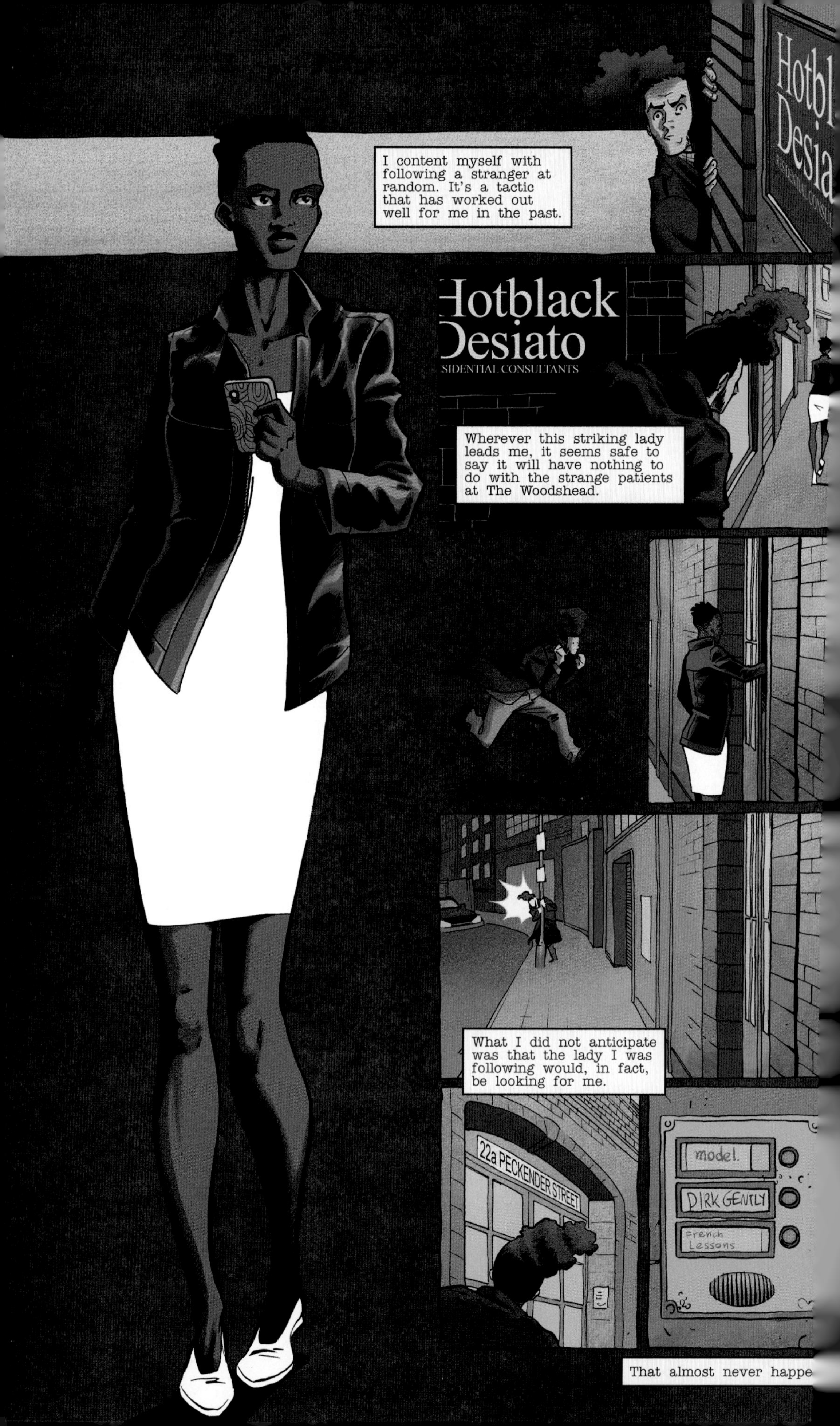
Hotbl
Desia
I content myself with following a stranger at random. It's a tactic that has worked out well for me in the past.
Hotblack
Desiato
SIDENTIAL CONSULTANTS
Wherever this striking lady leads me, it seems safe to say it will have nothing to do with the strange patients at The Woodshead.
What I did not anticipate was that the lady I was following would, in fact, be looking for me.
22a PECKENDER STREET
model.
DIRK GENTLY
French Lessons
That almost never happe

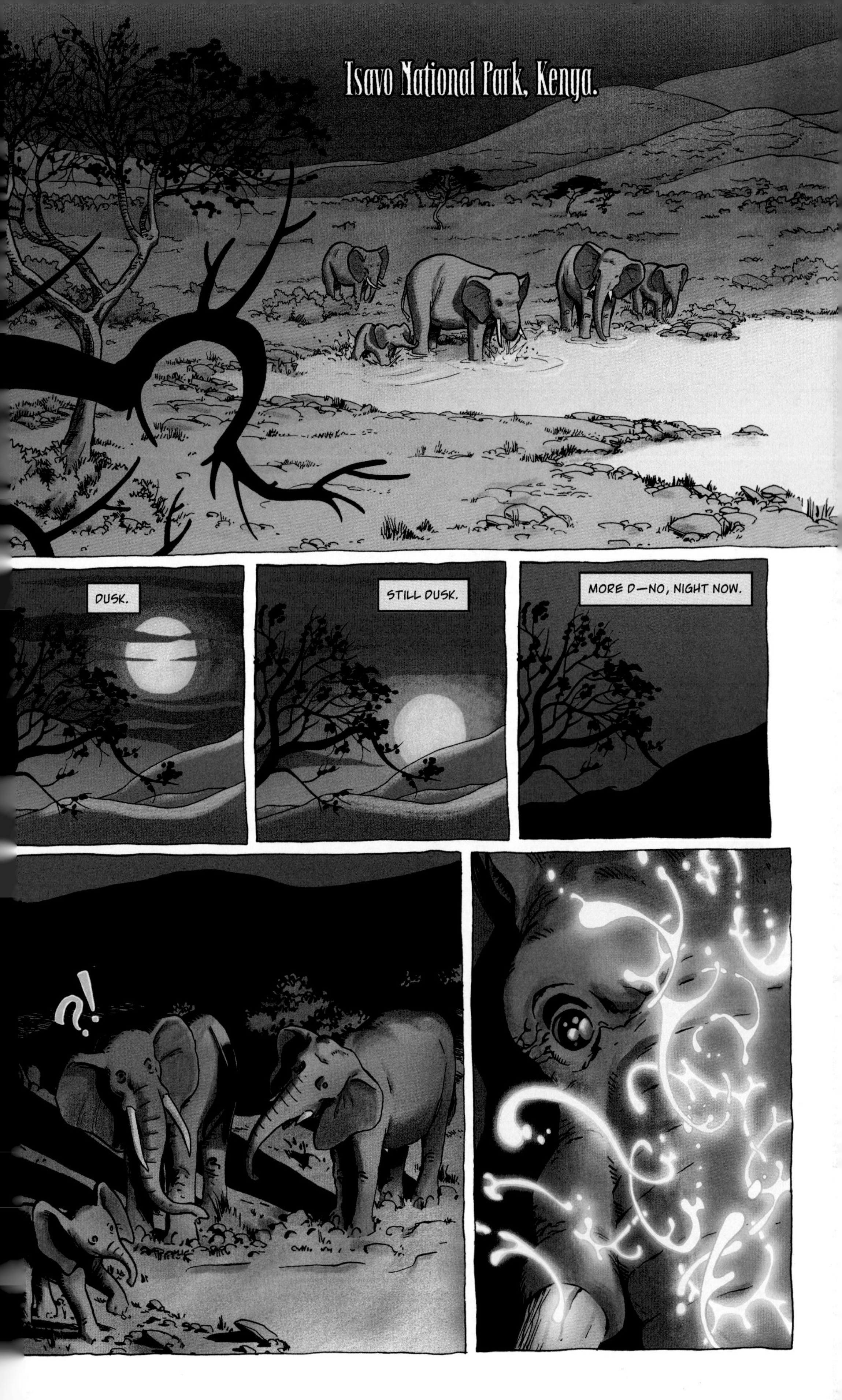
Tsavo National Park, Kenya.
DUSK.
STILL DUSK.
MORE D—NO, NIGHT NOW.
?!

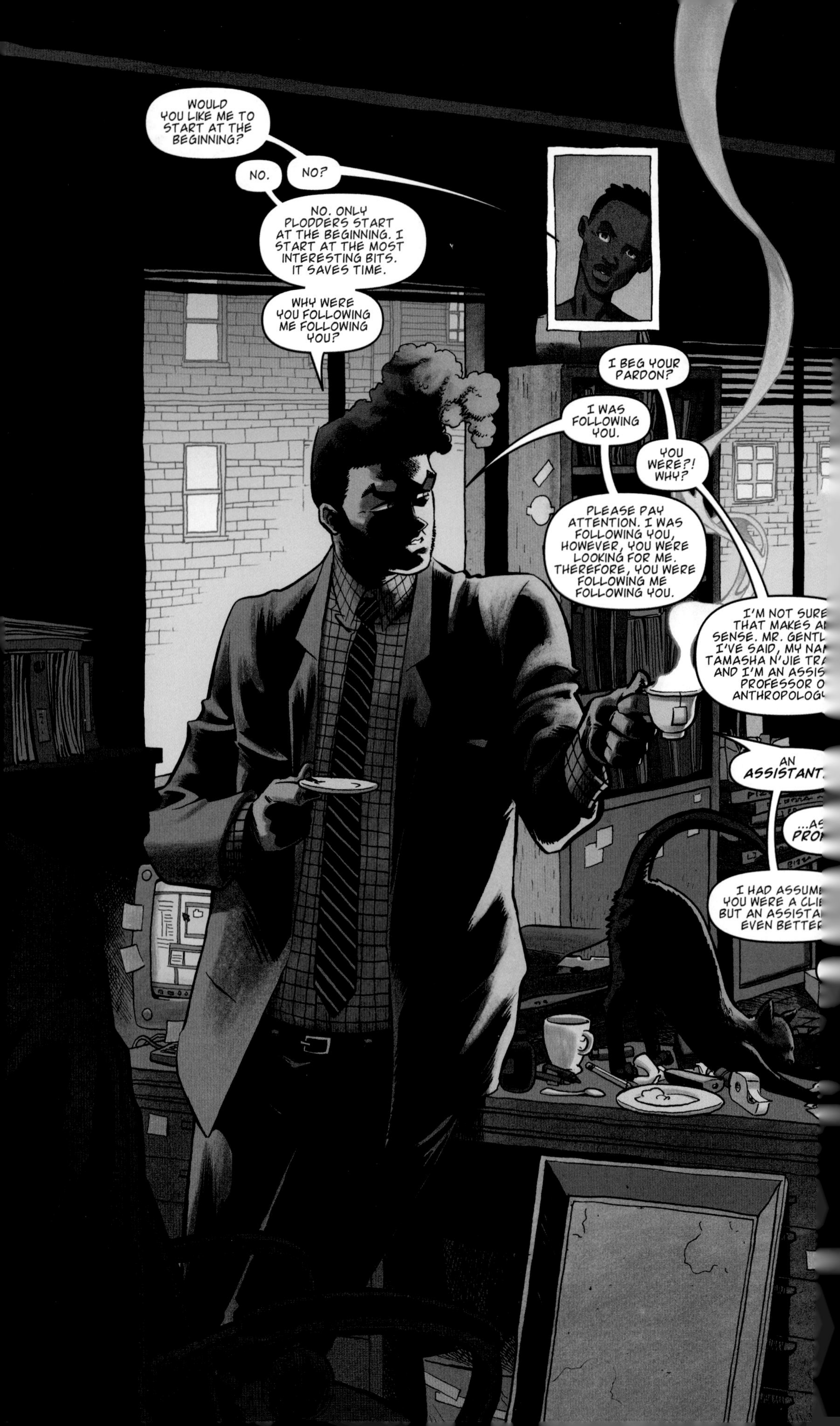
WOULD YOU LIKE ME TO START AT THE BEGINNING?
NO.
NO?
NO. ONLY PLODDERS START AT THE BEGINNING. I START AT THE MOST INTERESTING BITS. IT SAVES TIME.
WHY WERE YOU FOLLOWING ME FOLLOWING YOU?
I BEG YOUR PARDON?
I WAS FOLLOWING YOU.
YOU WERE?! WHY?
PLEASE PAY ATTENTION. I WAS FOLLOWING YOU, HOWEVER, YOU WERE LOOKING FOR ME. THEREFORE, YOU WERE FOLLOWING ME FOLLOWING YOU.
I'M NOT SURE THAT MAKES A SENSE. MR. GENTL I'VE SAID, MY NAM TAMASHA N'JIE TRA AND I'M AN ASSIS PROFESSOR O ANTHROPOLOG
AN ASSISTANT
...AS PRO
I HAD ASSUM YOU WERE A CLIE BUT AN ASSISTA EVEN BETTER

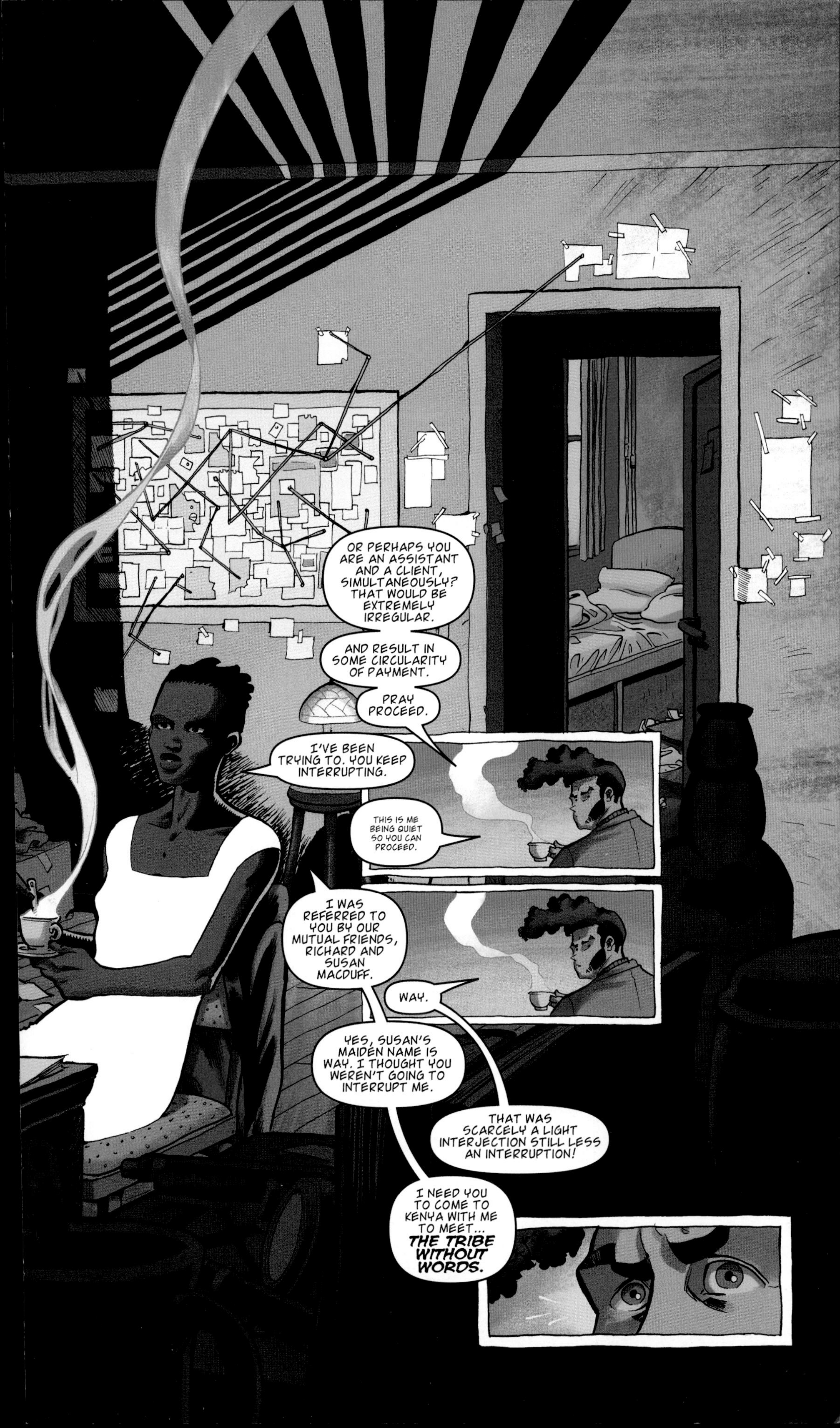

OR PERHAPS YOU ARE AN ASSISTANT AND A CLIENT, SIMULTANEOUSLY? THAT WOULD BE EXTREMELY IRREGULAR.
AND RESULT IN SOME CIRCULARITY OF PAYMENT.
PRAY PROCEED.
I'VE BEEN TRYING TO. YOU KEEP INTERRUPTING.
THIS IS ME BEING QUIET SO YOU CAN PROCEED.
I WAS REFERRED TO YOU BY OUR MUTUAL FRIENDS, RICHARD AND SUSAN MACDUFF.
WAY.
YES, SUSAN'S MAIDEN NAME IS WAY. I THOUGHT YOU WEREN'T GOING TO INTERRUPT ME.
THAT WAS SCARCELY A LIGHT INTERJECTION STILL LESS AN INTERRUPTION!
I NEED YOU TO COME TO KENYA WITH ME TO MEET... ***THE TRIBE WITHOUT WORDS.***

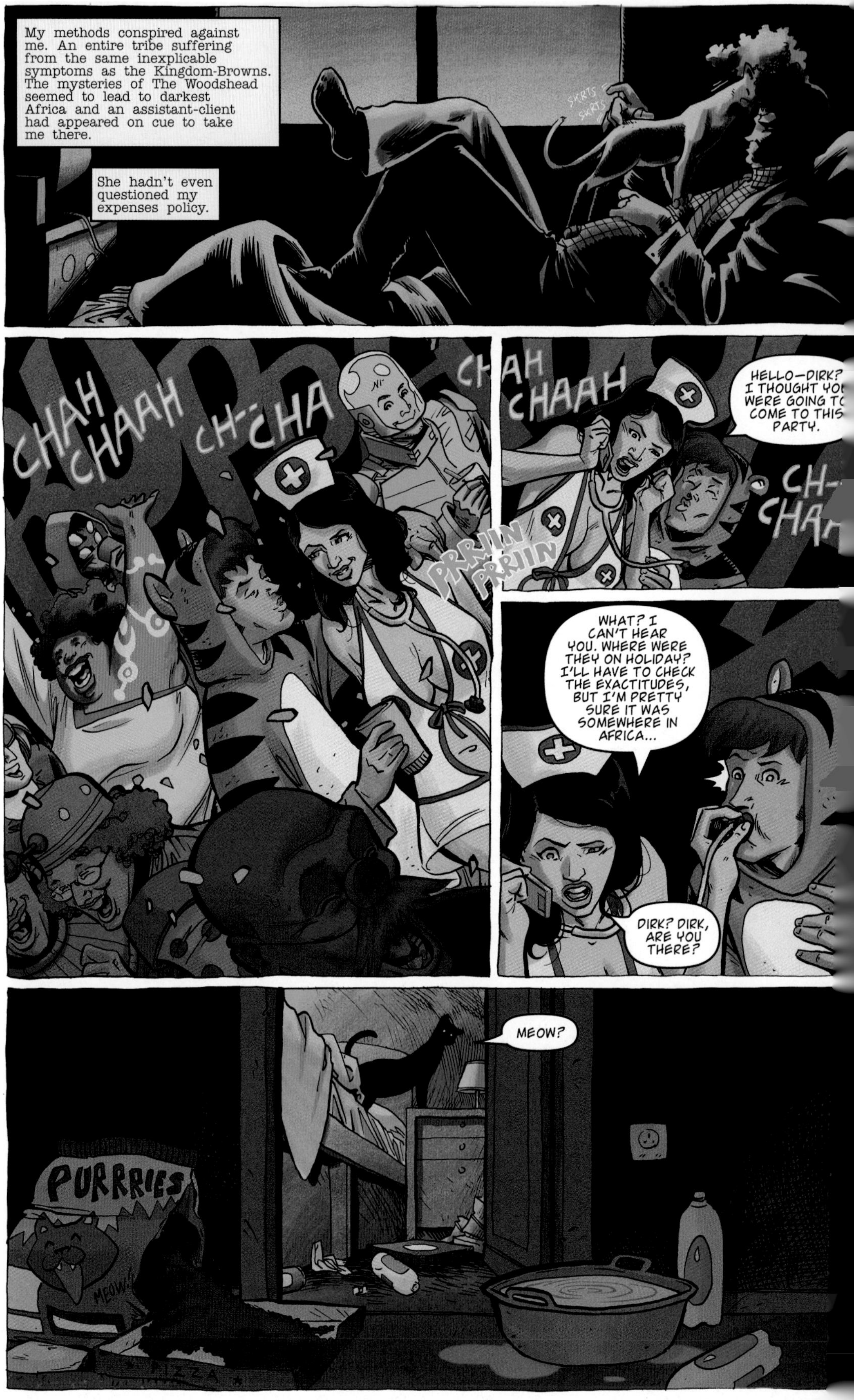
My methods conspired against me. An entire tribe suffering from the same inexplicable symptoms as the Kingdom-Browns. The mysteries of The Woodshead seemed to lead to darkest Africa and an assistant-client had appeared on cue to take me there.
She hadn't even questioned my expenses policy.
SKRTS SKRTS
CHAH CHAAH CH-CHA
PRRIIN PRRIIN
CHAH CHAAH
HELLO—DIRK? I THOUGHT YOU WERE GOING TO COME TO THIS PARTY.
CH-CHA
WHAT? I CAN'T HEAR YOU. WHERE WERE THEY ON HOLIDAY? I'LL HAVE TO CHECK THE EXACTITUDES, BUT I'M PRETTY SURE IT WAS SOMEWHERE IN AFRICA...
DIRK? DIRK, ARE YOU THERE?
MEOW?
PURRRIES
MEOW!
PIZZA

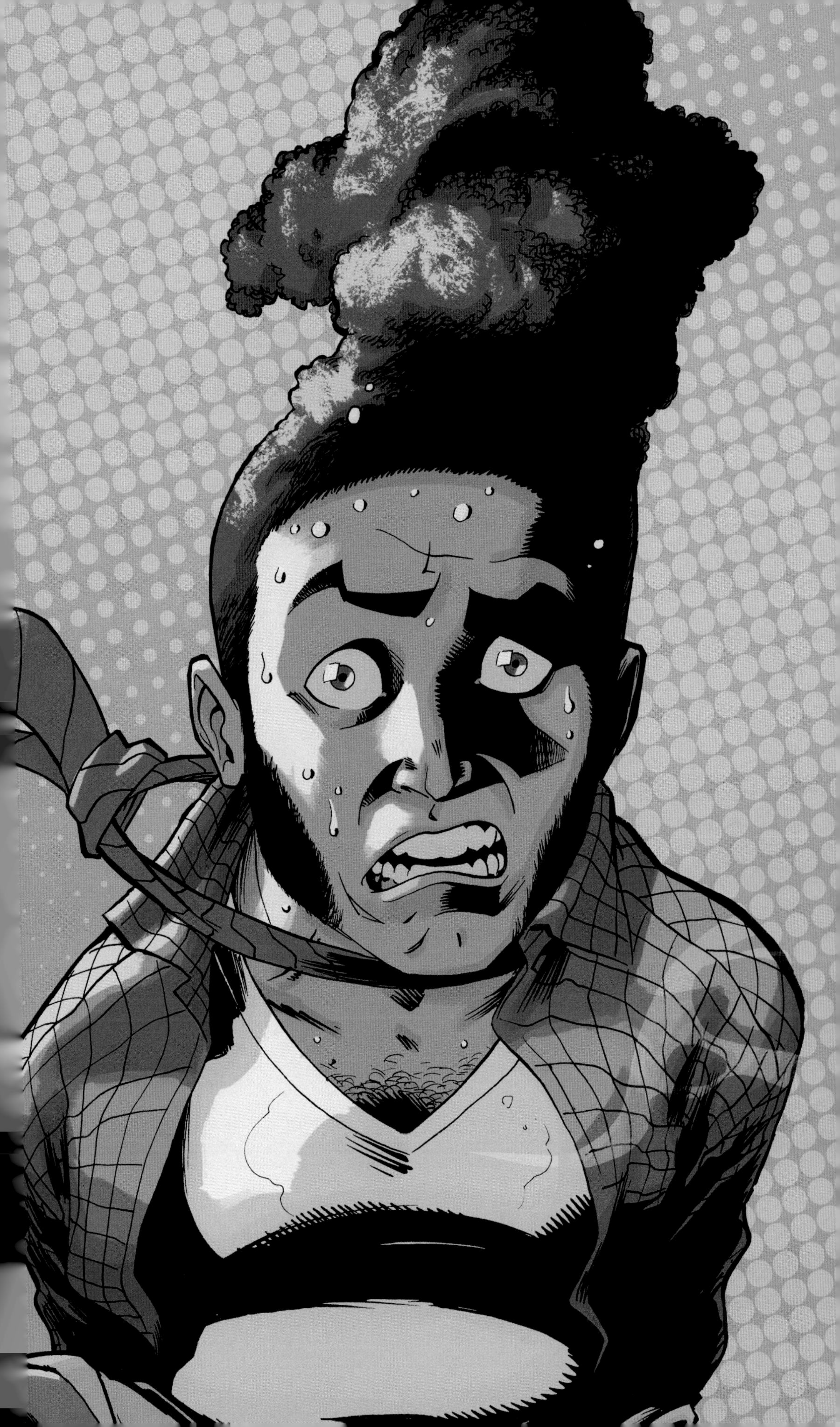

CHAPTER TWO

Cover Art by **ILIAS KYRIAZ**

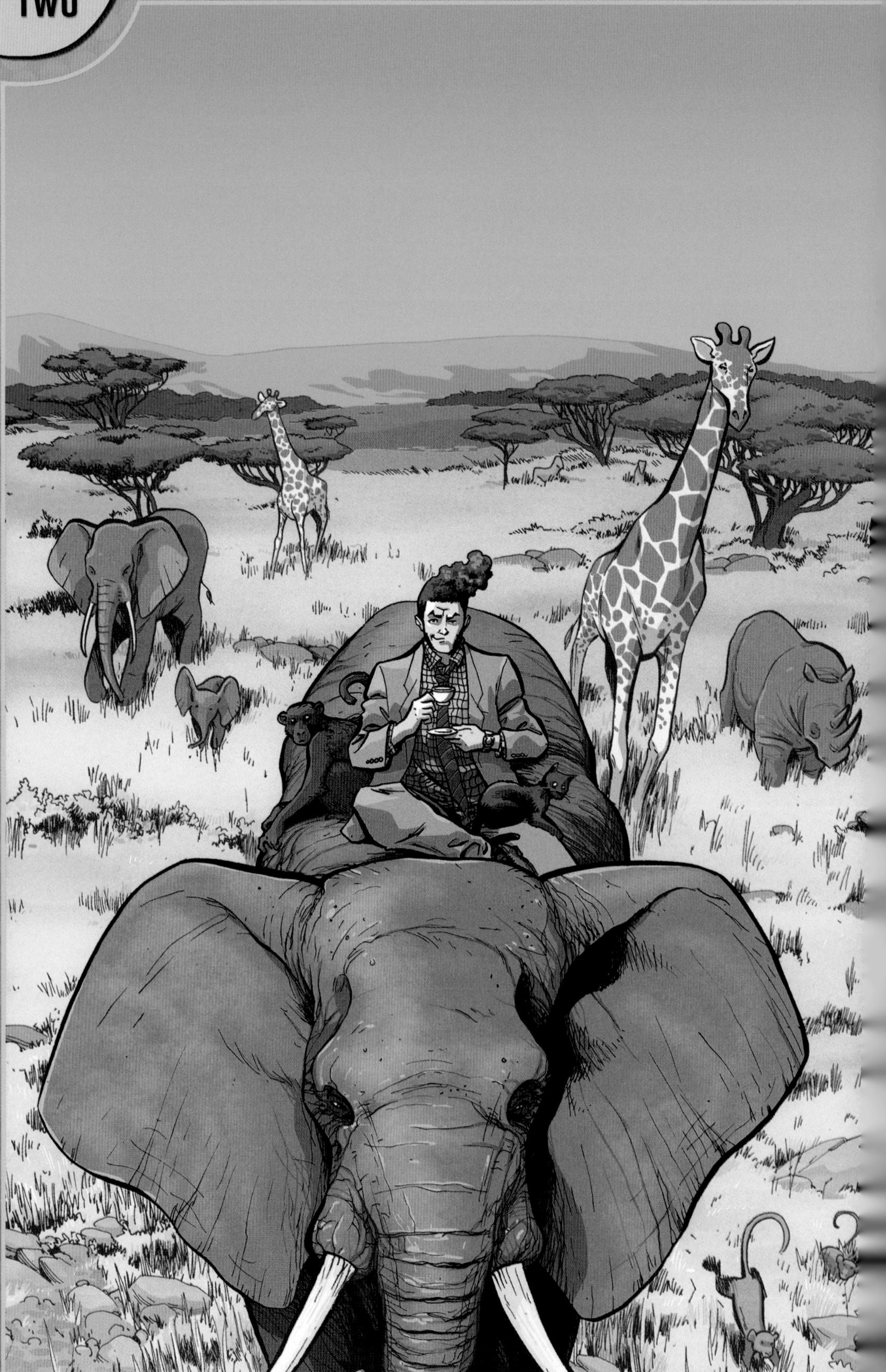

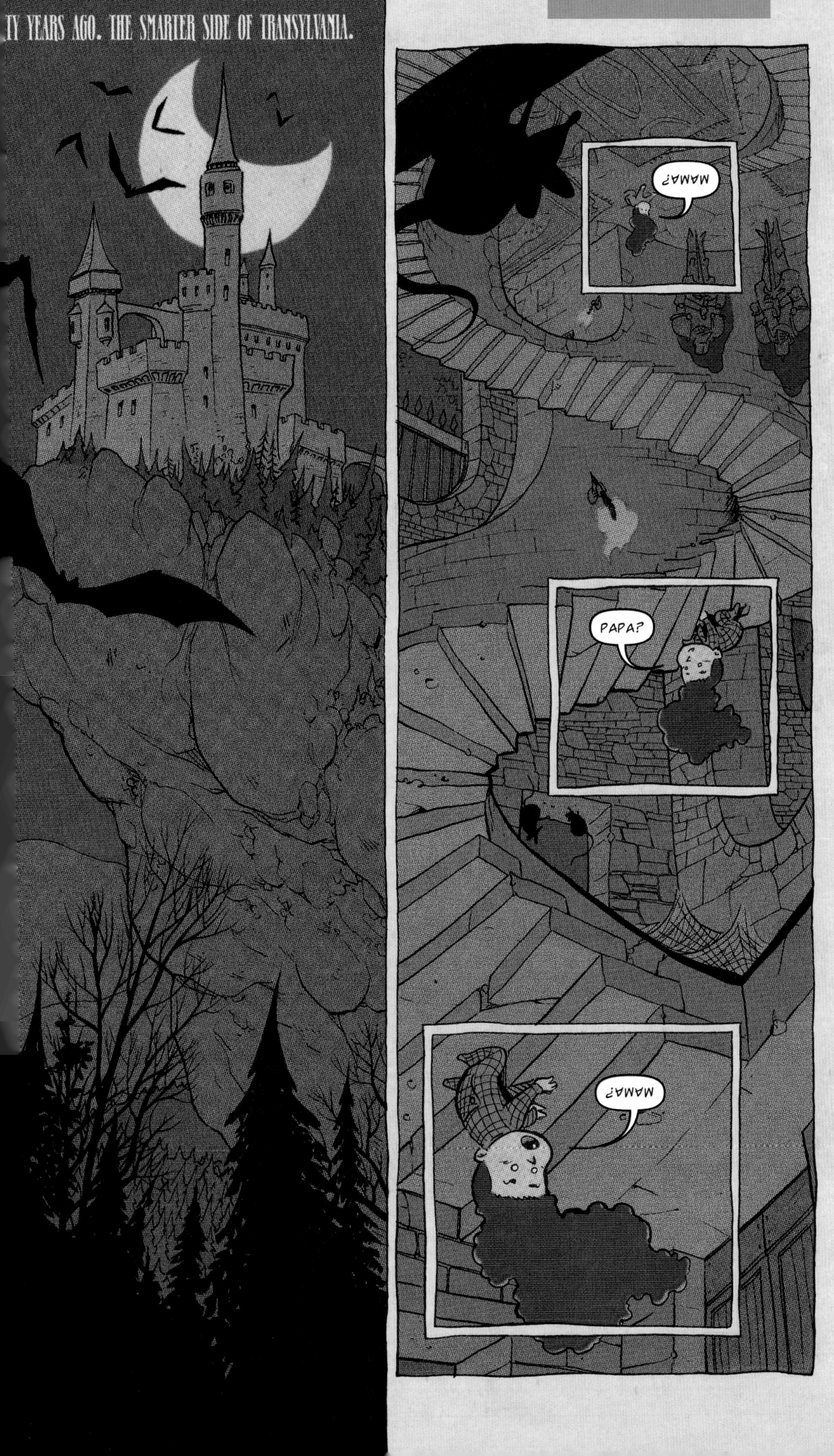
YEARS AGO. THE SMARTER SIDE OF TRANSYLVANIA.
MAMA?
PAPA?
MAMA?

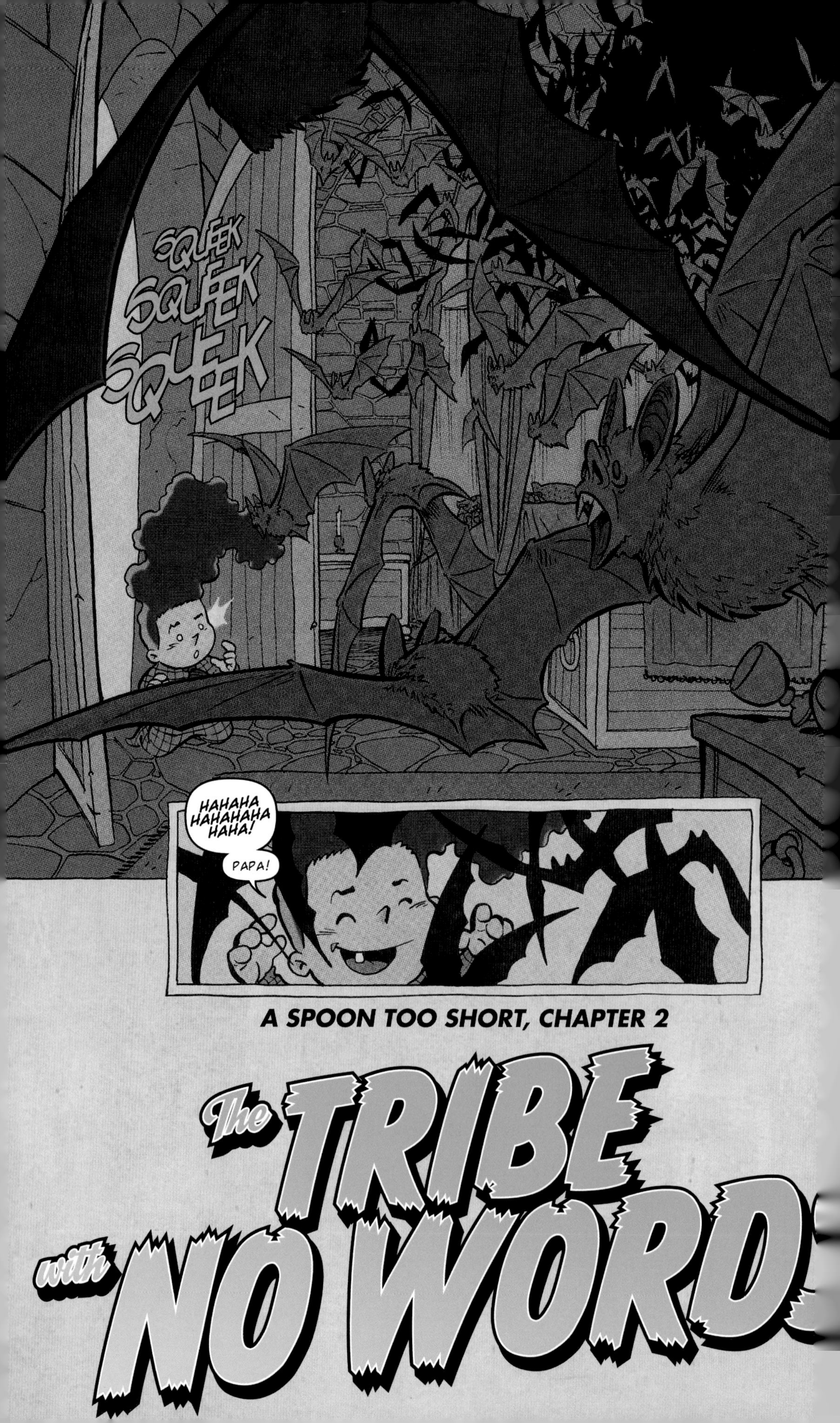
SQUEEK
SQUEEK
SQUEEK
HAHAHA HAHAHAHA HAHA!
PAPA!

A SPOON TOO SHORT, CHAPTER 2

The TRIBE with NO WORDS

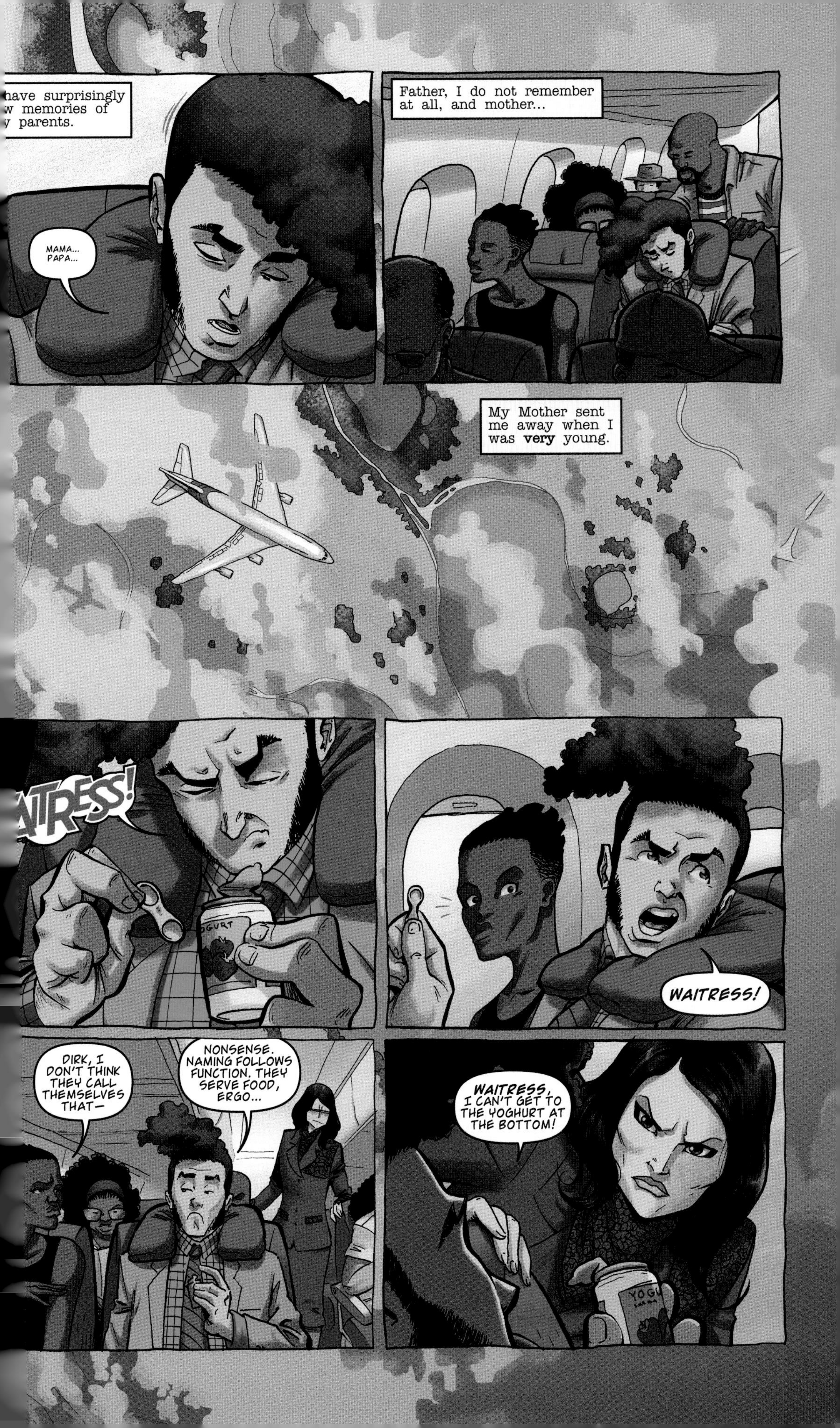
have surprisingly
w memories of
y parents.
MAMA...
PAPA...
Father, I do not remember at all, and mother...
My Mother sent me away when I was **very** young.
WAITRESS!
WAITRESS!
DIRK, I DON'T THINK THEY CALL THEMSELVES THAT—
NONSENSE. NAMING FOLLOWS FUNCTION. THEY SERVE FOOD, ERGO...
WAITRESS, I CAN'T GET TO THE YOGHURT AT THE BOTTOM!

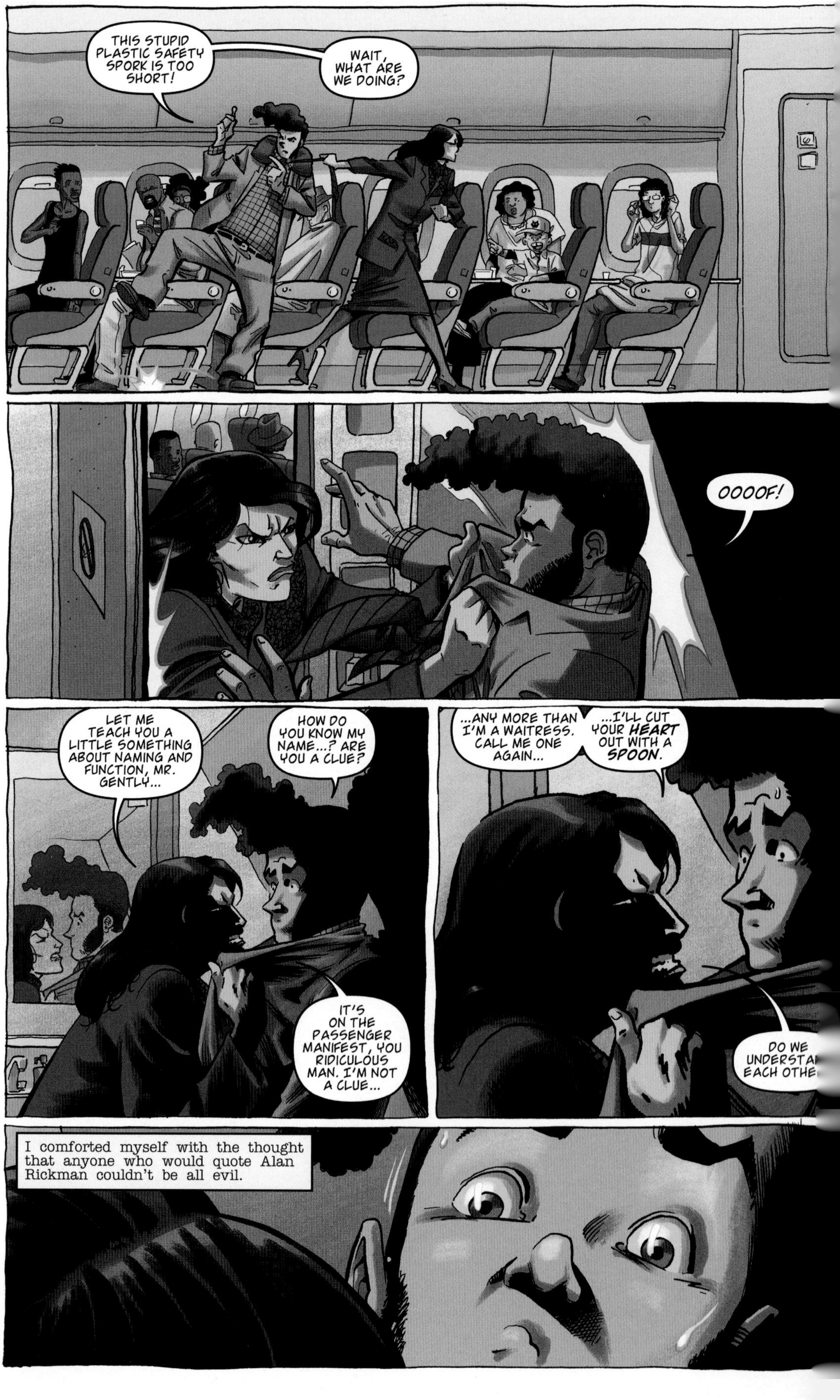
THIS STUPID PLASTIC SAFETY SPORK IS TOO SHORT!
WAIT, WHAT ARE WE DOING?
OOOOF!
LET ME TEACH YOU A LITTLE SOMETHING ABOUT NAMING AND FUNCTION, MR. GENTLY...
HOW DO YOU KNOW MY NAME...? ARE YOU A CLUE?
IT'S ON THE PASSENGER MANIFEST, YOU RIDICULOUS MAN. I'M NOT A CLUE...
...ANY MORE THAN I'M A WAITRESS. CALL ME ONE AGAIN...
...I'LL CUT YOUR ***HEART*** OUT WITH A ***SPOON***.
DO WE UNDERSTA
EACH OTHE
I comforted myself with the thought that anyone who would quote Alan Rickman couldn't be all evil.

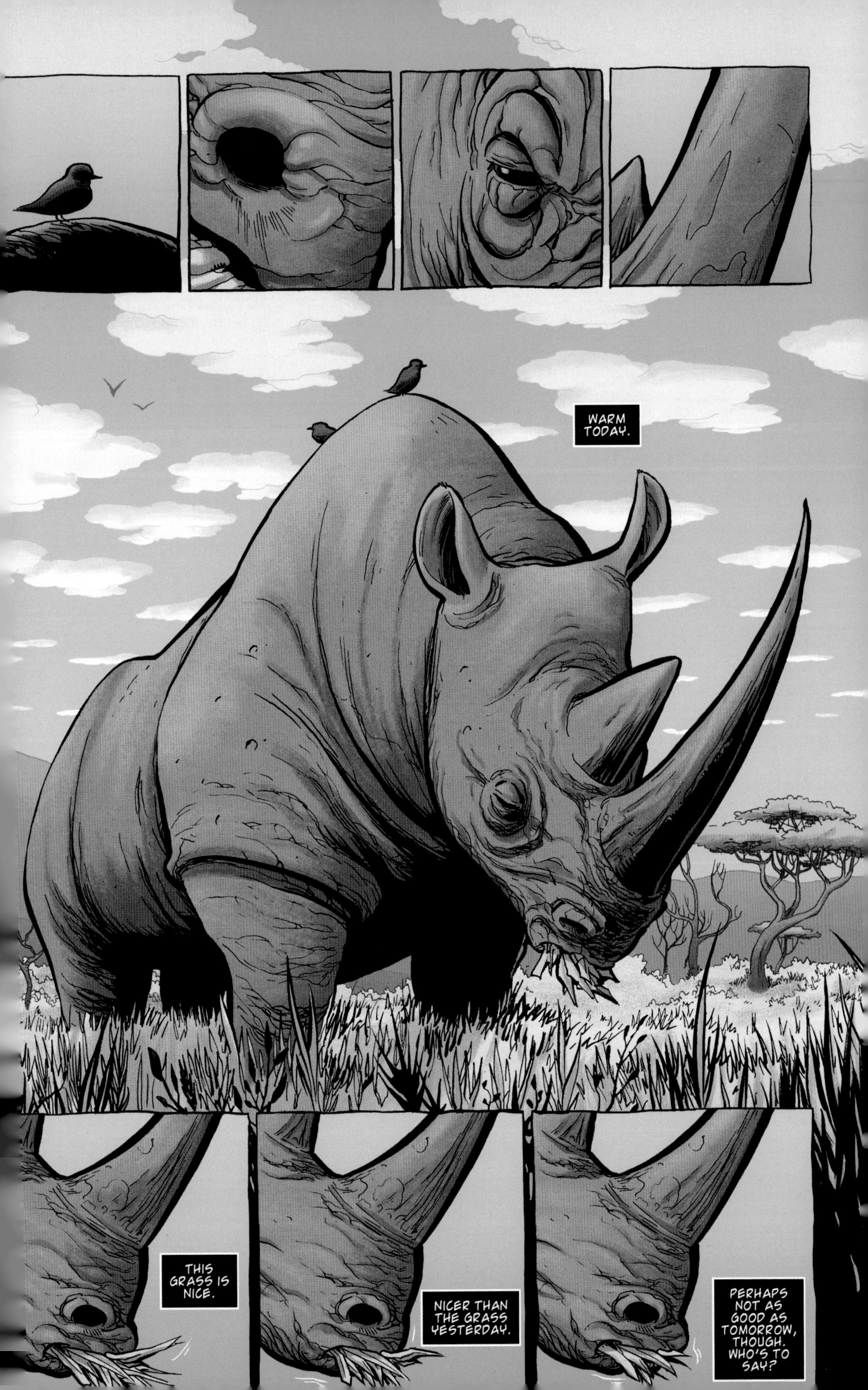
WARM TODAY.
THIS GRASS IS NICE.
NICER THAN THE GRASS YESTERDAY.
PERHAPS NOT AS GOOD AS TOMORROW, THOUGH. WHO'S TO SAY?

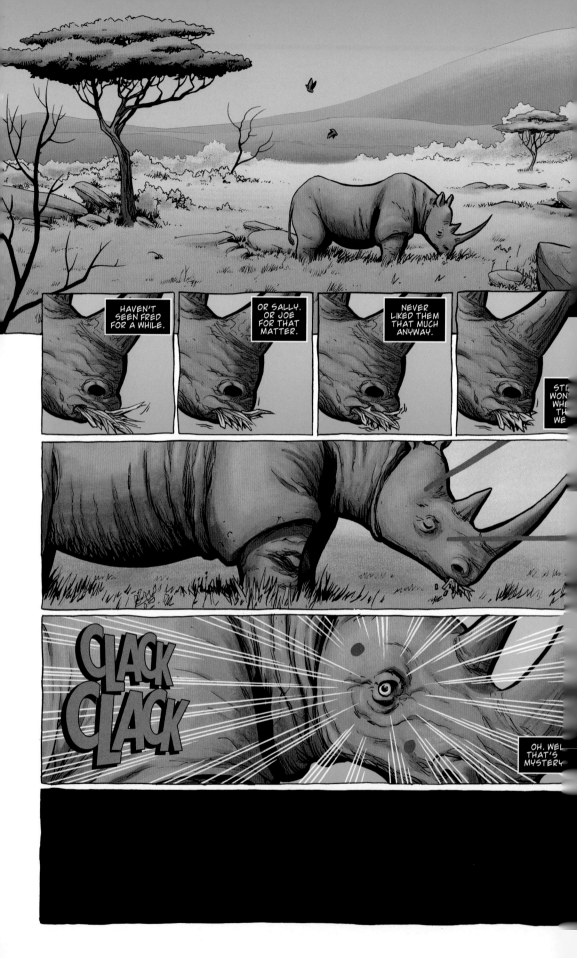

HAVEN'T SEEN FRED FOR A WHILE.

OR SALLY. OR JOE FOR THAT MATTER.

NEVER LIKED THEM THAT MUCH ANYWAY.

STI WON' WHE TH WE

CLACK CLACK

OH. WEL THAT'S MYSTERY

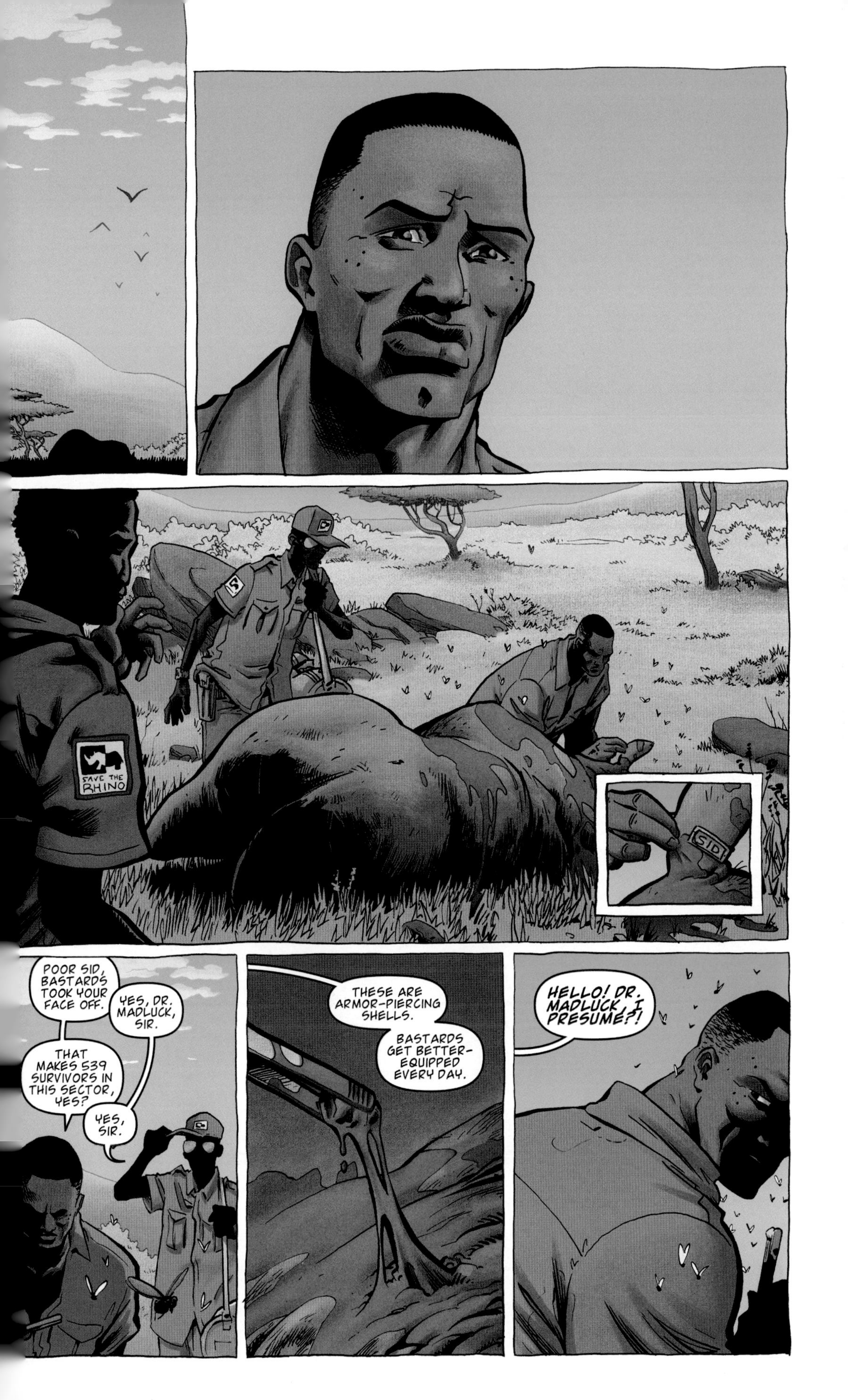
SAVE THE RHINO
SID
POOR SID, BASTARDS TOOK YOUR FACE OFF.
YES, DR. MADLUCK, SIR.
THAT MAKES 539 SURVIVORS IN THIS SECTOR, YES?
YES, SIR.
THESE ARE ARMOR-PIERCING SHELLS.
BASTARDS GET BETTER-EQUIPPED EVERY DAY.
HELLO! DR. MADLUCK, I PRESUME?!

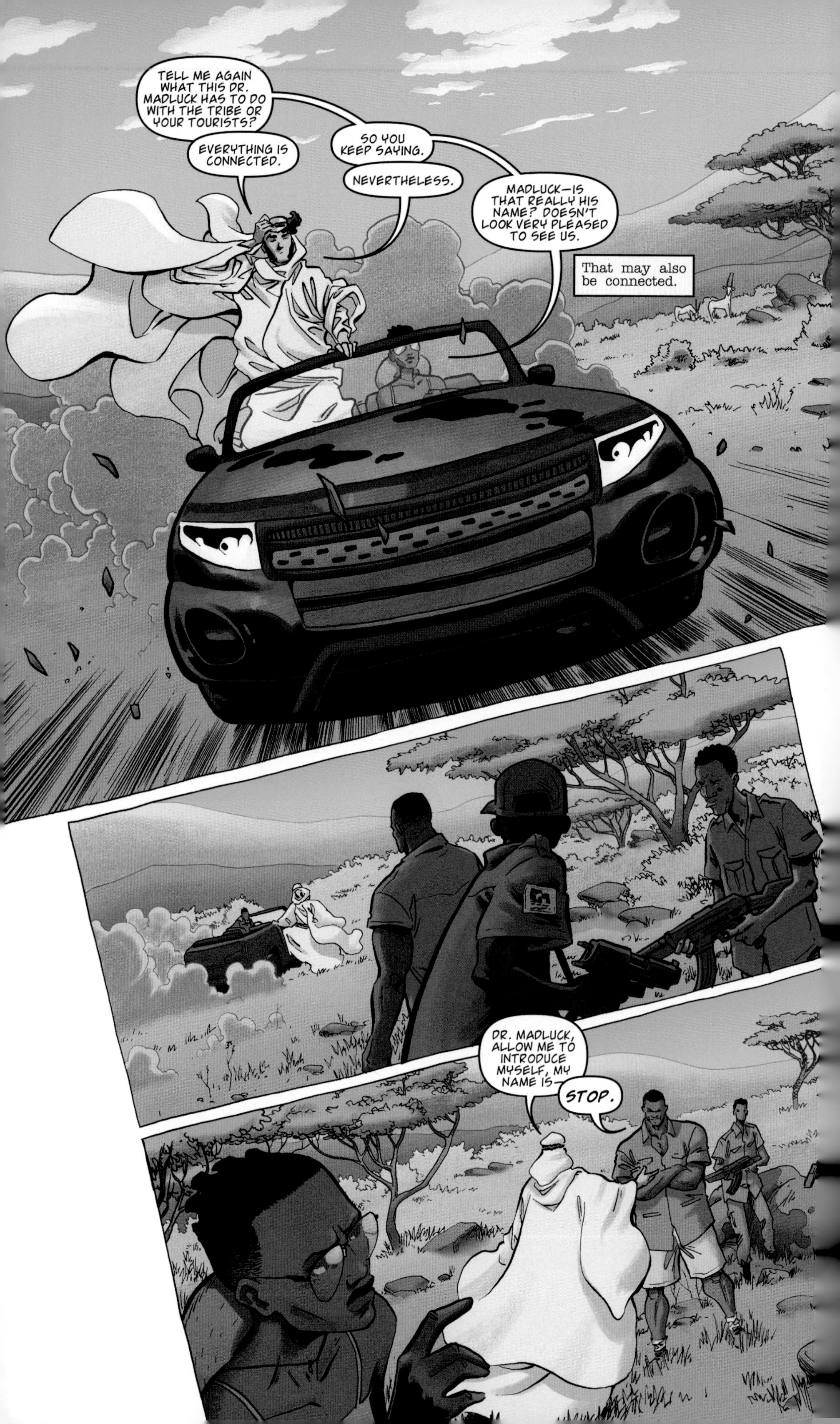
TELL ME AGAIN WHAT THIS DR. MADLUCK HAS TO DO WITH THE TRIBE OR YOUR TOURISTS?
EVERYTHING IS CONNECTED.
SO YOU KEEP SAYING.
NEVERTHELESS.
MADLUCK—IS THAT REALLY HIS NAME? DOESN'T LOOK VERY PLEASED TO SEE US.
That may also be connected.
DR. MADLUCK, ALLOW ME TO INTRODUCE MYSELF, MY NAME IS—
STOP.

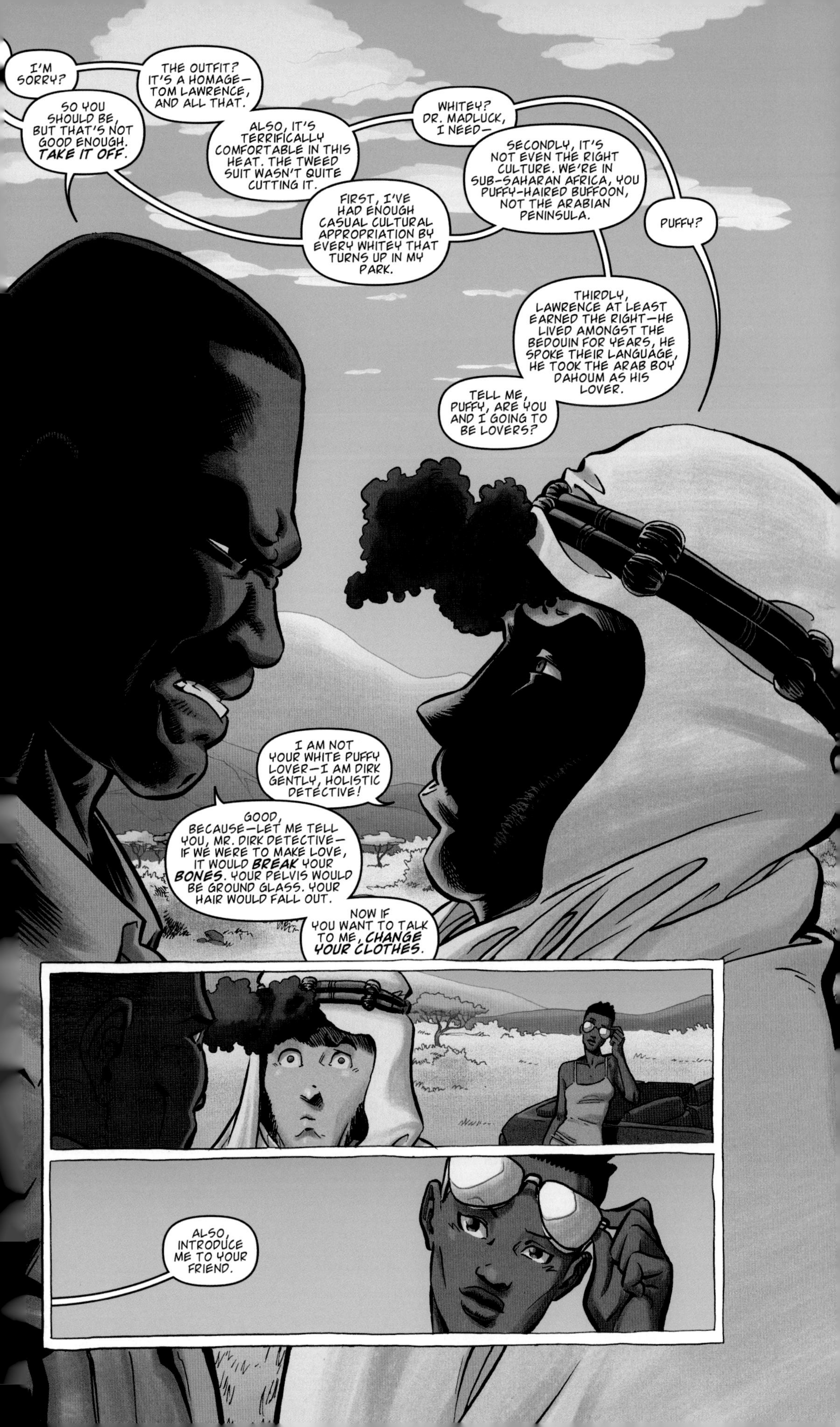
I'M SORRY?
THE OUTFIT? IT'S A HOMAGE—TOM LAWRENCE, AND ALL THAT.
SO YOU SHOULD BE, BUT THAT'S NOT GOOD ENOUGH. TAKE IT OFF.
ALSO, IT'S TERRIFICALLY COMFORTABLE IN THIS HEAT. THE TWEED SUIT WASN'T QUITE CUTTING IT.
WHITEY? DR. MADLUCK, I NEED—
FIRST, I'VE HAD ENOUGH CASUAL CULTURAL APPROPRIATION BY EVERY WHITEY THAT TURNS UP IN MY PARK.
SECONDLY, IT'S NOT EVEN THE RIGHT CULTURE. WE'RE IN SUB-SAHARAN AFRICA, YOU PUFFY-HAIRED BUFFOON, NOT THE ARABIAN PENINSULA.
PUFFY?
THIRDLY, LAWRENCE AT LEAST EARNED THE RIGHT—HE LIVED AMONGST THE BEDOUIN FOR YEARS, HE SPOKE THEIR LANGUAGE, HE TOOK THE ARAB BOY DAHOUM AS HIS LOVER.
TELL ME, PUFFY, ARE YOU AND I GOING TO BE LOVERS?
I AM NOT YOUR WHITE PUFFY LOVER—I AM DIRK GENTLY, HOLISTIC DETECTIVE!
GOOD, BECAUSE—LET ME TELL YOU, MR. DIRK DETECTIVE—IF WE WERE TO MAKE LOVE, IT WOULD BREAK YOUR BONES. YOUR PELVIS WOULD BE GROUND GLASS. YOUR HAIR WOULD FALL OUT.
NOW IF YOU WANT TO TALK TO ME, CHANGE YOUR CLOTHES.
ALSO, INTRODUCE ME TO YOUR FRIEND.

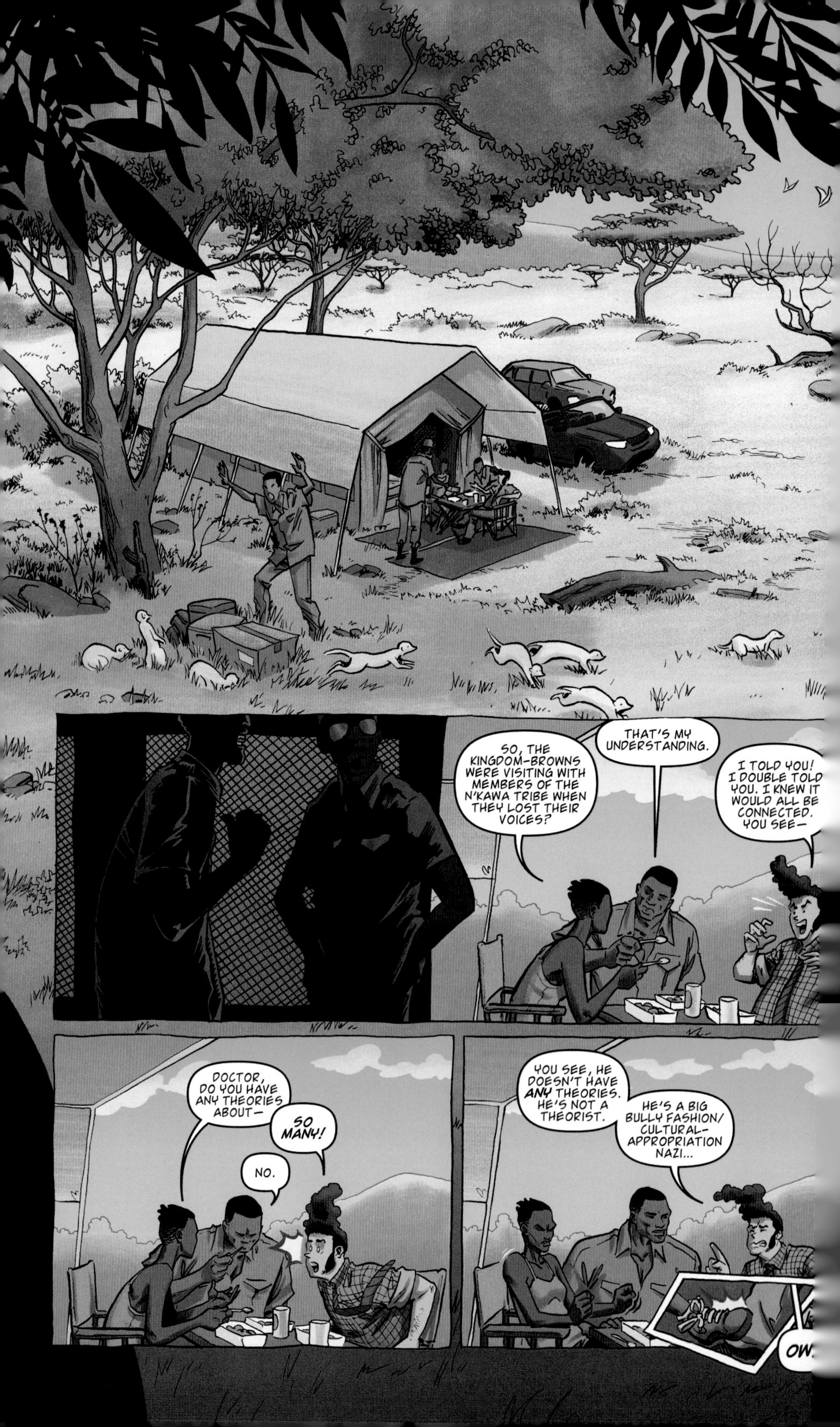
SO, THE KINGDOM-BROWNS WERE VISITING WITH MEMBERS OF THE N'KAWA TRIBE WHEN THEY LOST THEIR VOICES?
THAT'S MY UNDERSTANDING.
I TOLD YOU! I DOUBLE TOLD YOU. I KNEW IT WOULD ALL BE CONNECTED. YOU SEE—
DOCTOR, DO YOU HAVE ANY THEORIES ABOUT—
SO MANY!
NO.
YOU SEE, HE DOESN'T HAVE ANY THEORIES. HE'S NOT A THEORIST.
HE'S A BIG BULLY FASHION/ CULTURAL-APPROPRIATION NAZI...
OW

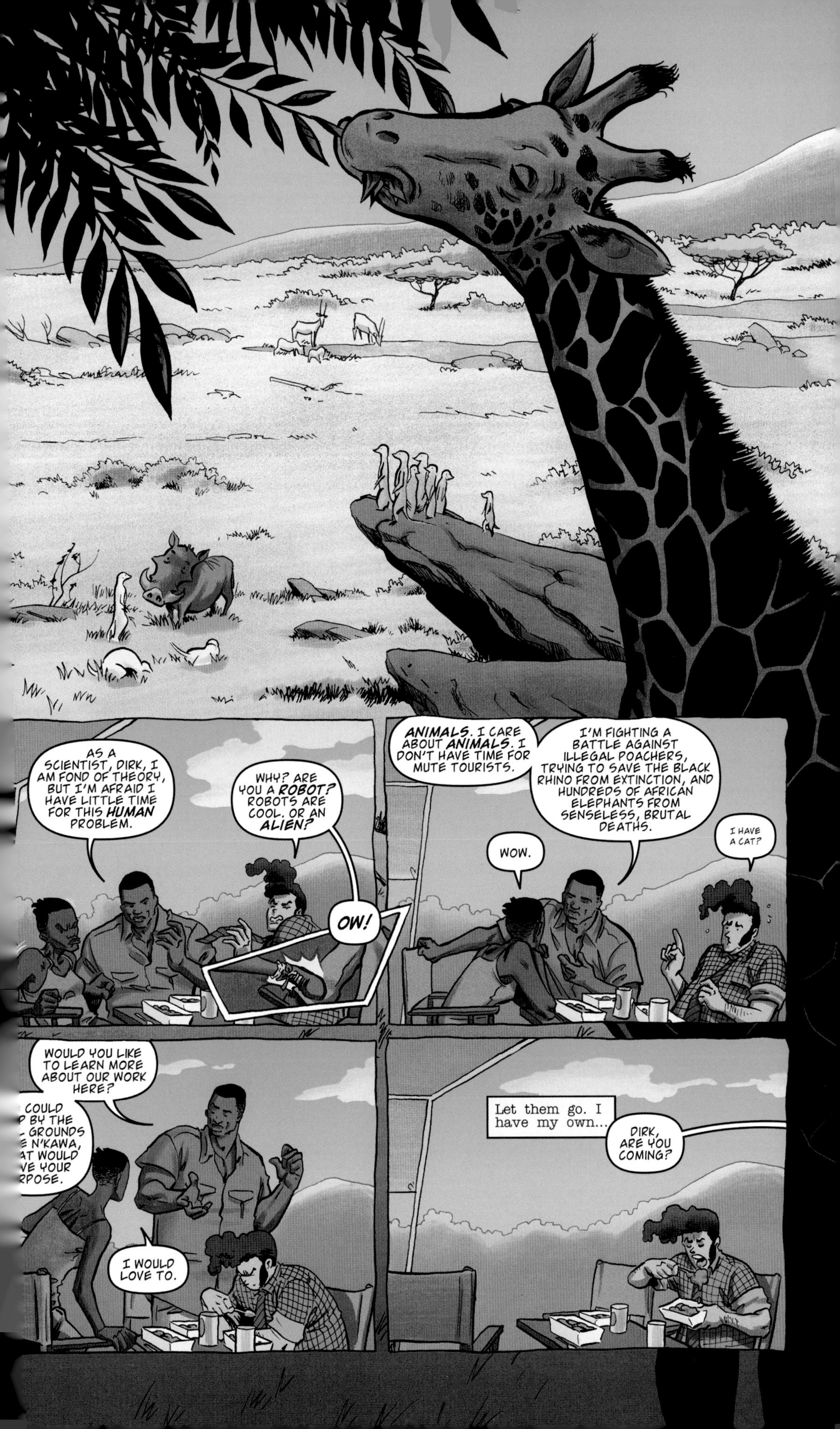
AS A SCIENTIST, DIRK, I AM FOND OF THEORY, BUT I'M AFRAID I HAVE LITTLE TIME FOR THIS HUMAN PROBLEM.
WHY? ARE YOU A ROBOT? ROBOTS ARE COOL. OR AN ALIEN?
OW!
ANIMALS. I CARE ABOUT ANIMALS. I DON'T HAVE TIME FOR MUTE TOURISTS.
I'M FIGHTING A BATTLE AGAINST ILLEGAL POACHERS, TRYING TO SAVE THE BLACK RHINO FROM EXTINCTION, AND HUNDREDS OF AFRICAN ELEPHANTS FROM SENSELESS, BRUTAL DEATHS.
WOW.
I HAVE A CAT?
WOULD YOU LIKE TO LEARN MORE ABOUT OUR WORK HERE?
E COULD P BY THE - GROUNDS E N'KAWA, AT WOULD VE YOUR RPOSE.
I WOULD LOVE TO.
Let them go. I have my own...
DIRK, ARE YOU COMING?

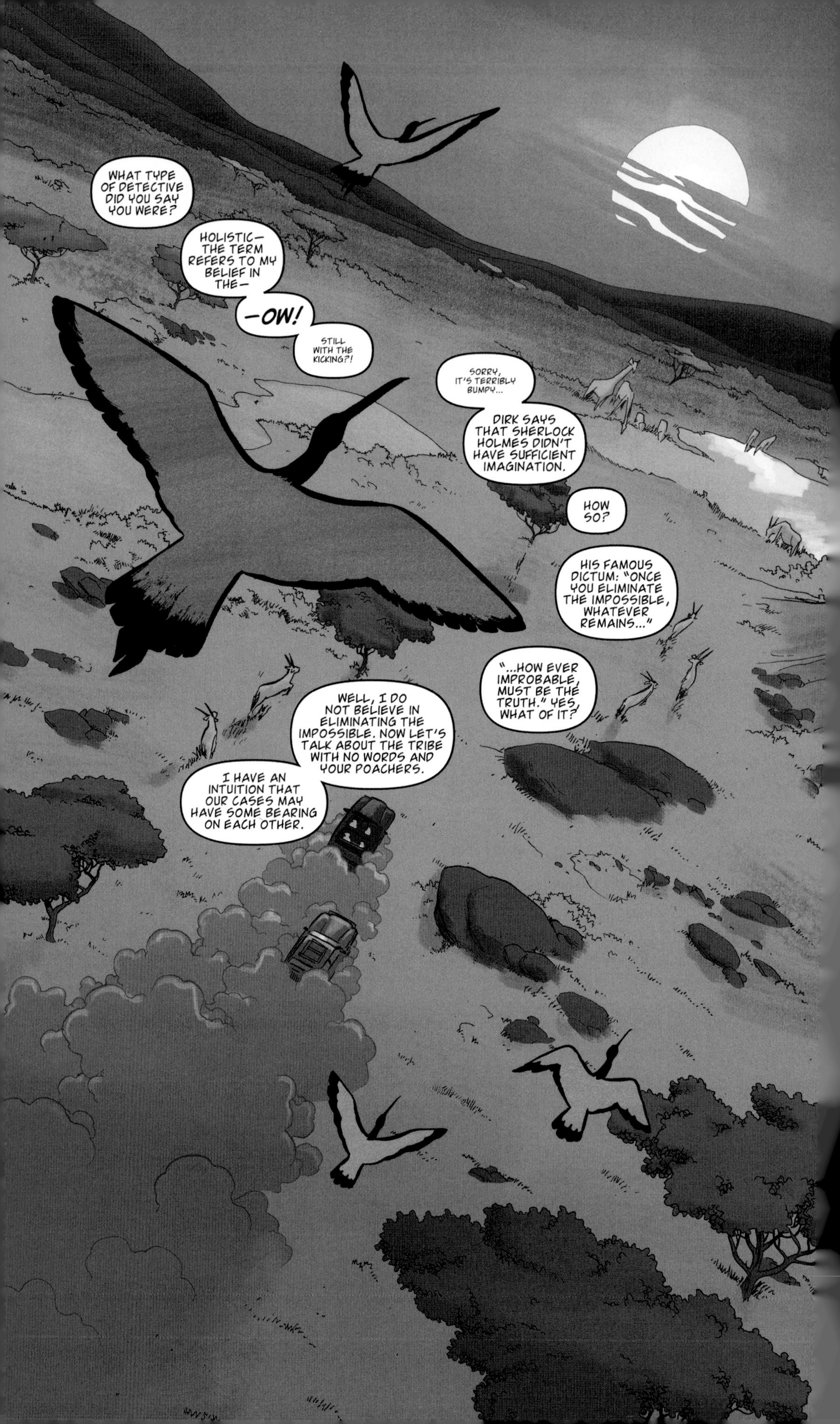
WHAT TYPE OF DETECTIVE DID YOU SAY YOU WERE?
HOLISTIC— THE TERM REFERS TO MY BELIEF IN THE—
—OW!
STILL WITH THE KICKING?!
SORRY, IT'S TERRIBLY BUMPY...
DIRK SAYS THAT SHERLOCK HOLMES DIDN'T HAVE SUFFICIENT IMAGINATION.
HOW SO?
HIS FAMOUS DICTUM: "ONCE YOU ELIMINATE THE IMPOSSIBLE, WHATEVER REMAINS..."
"...HOW EVER IMPROBABLE, MUST BE THE TRUTH." YES, WHAT OF IT?
WELL, I DO NOT BELIEVE IN ELIMINATING THE IMPOSSIBLE. NOW LET'S TALK ABOUT THE TRIBE WITH NO WORDS AND YOUR POACHERS.
I HAVE AN INTUITION THAT OUR CASES MAY HAVE SOME BEARING ON EACH OTHER.

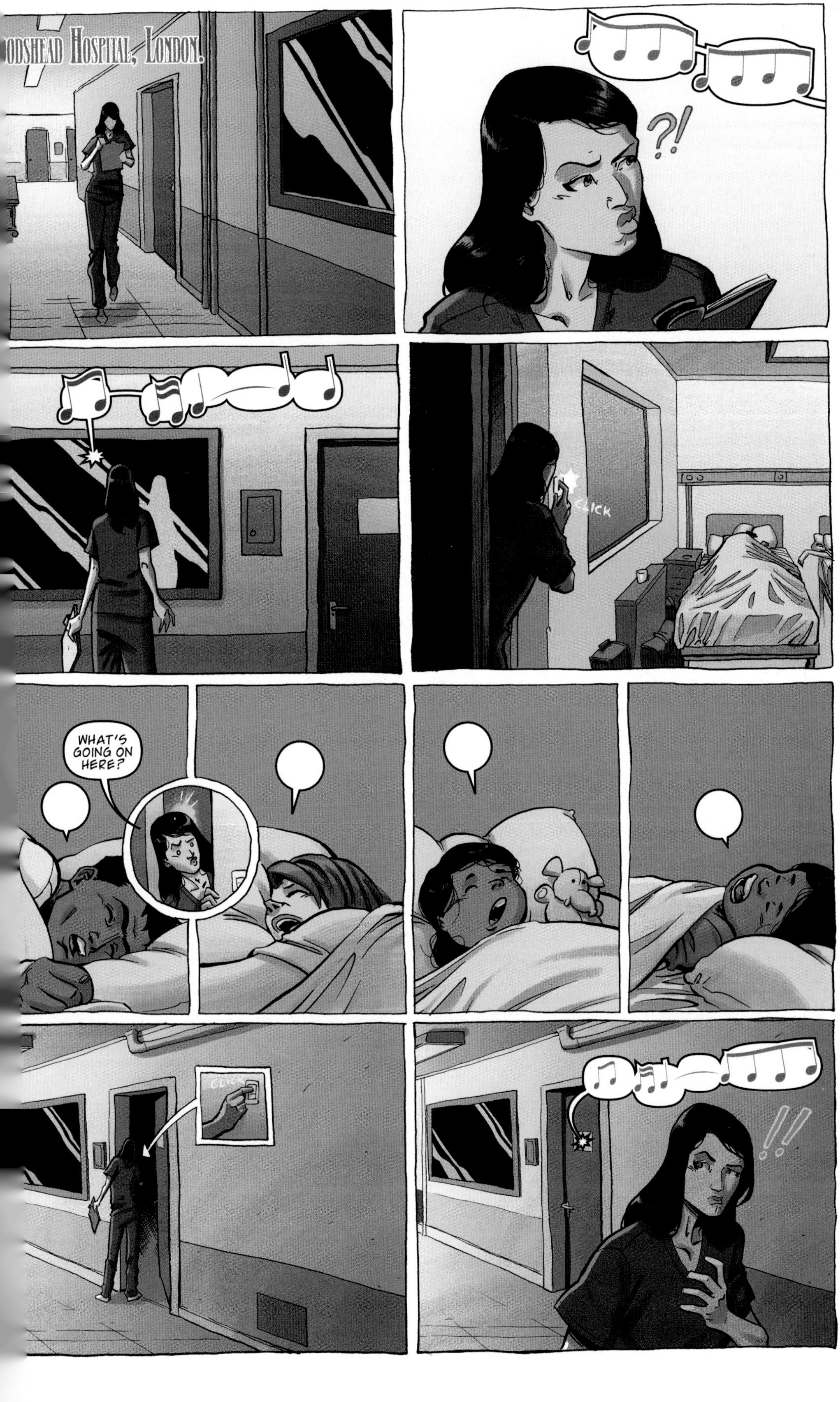
ODSHEAD HOSPITAL, LONDON.
?!
CLICK
WHAT'S GOING ON HERE?
CLICK
!!

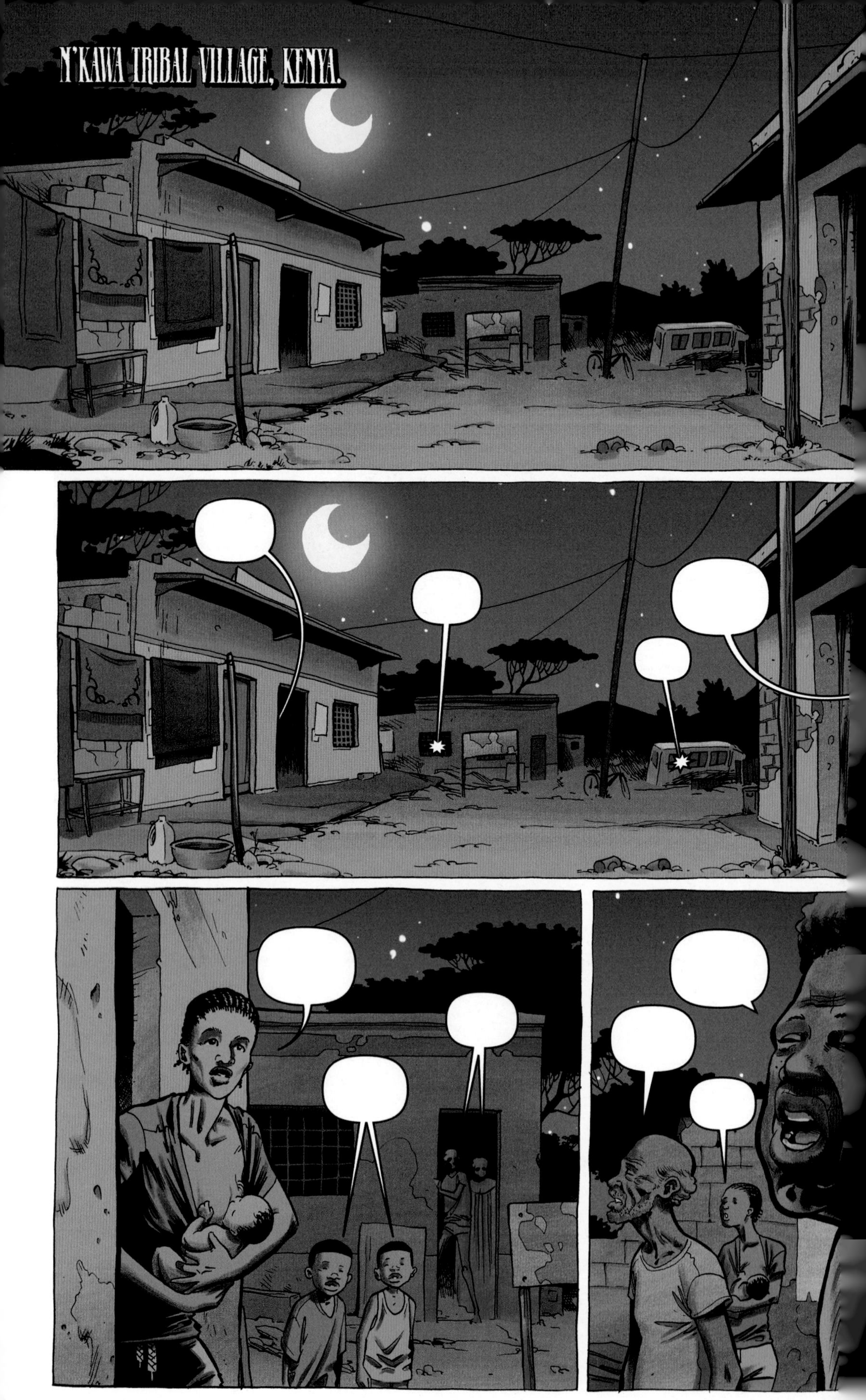
N'KAWA TRIBAL VILLAGE, KENYA.

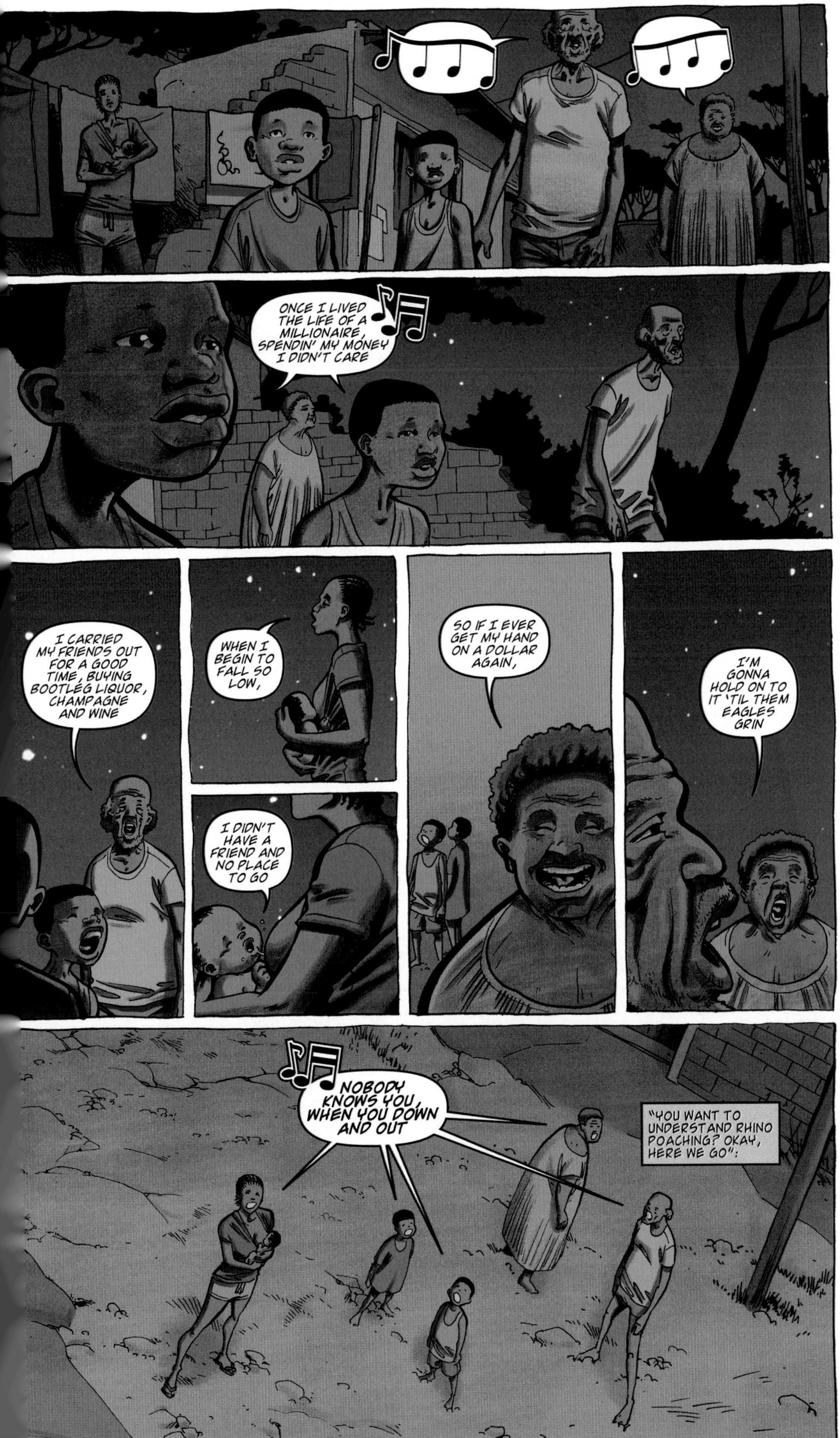
ONCE I LIVED THE LIFE OF A MILLIONAIRE, SPENDIN' MY MONEY I DIDN'T CARE
I CARRIED MY FRIENDS OUT FOR A GOOD TIME, BUYING BOOTLEG LIQUOR, CHAMPAGNE AND WINE
WHEN I BEGIN TO FALL SO LOW,
I DIDN'T HAVE A FRIEND AND NO PLACE TO GO
SO IF I EVER GET MY HAND ON A DOLLAR AGAIN,
I'M GONNA HOLD ON TO IT 'TIL THEM EAGLES GRIN
NOBODY KNOWS YOU, WHEN YOU DOWN AND OUT
"YOU WANT TO UNDERSTAND RHINO POACHING? OKAY, HERE WE GO":

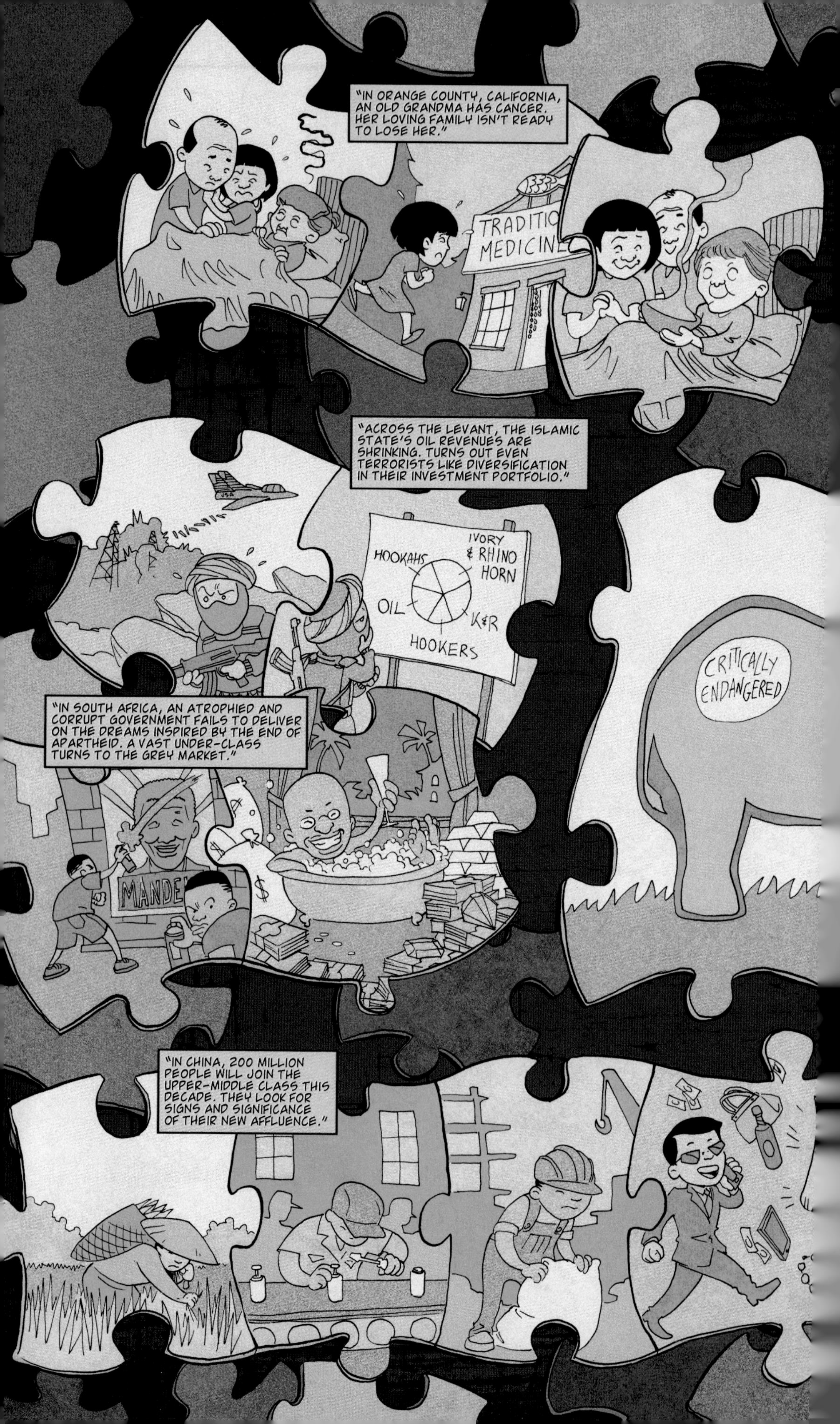
"IN ORANGE COUNTY, CALIFORNIA, AN OLD GRANDMA HAS CANCER. HER LOVING FAMILY ISN'T READY TO LOSE HER."
TRADITIO MEDICINE
"ACROSS THE LEVANT, THE ISLAMIC STATE'S OIL REVENUES ARE SHRINKING. TURNS OUT EVEN TERRORISTS LIKE DIVERSIFICATION IN THEIR INVESTMENT PORTFOLIO."
IVORY & RHINO HORN
HOOKAHS
OIL
K&R
HOOKERS
CRITICALLY ENDANGERED
"IN SOUTH AFRICA, AN ATROPHIED AND CORRUPT GOVERNMENT FAILS TO DELIVER ON THE DREAMS INSPIRED BY THE END OF APARTHEID. A VAST UNDER-CLASS TURNS TO THE GREY MARKET."
MANDE
"IN CHINA, 200 MILLION PEOPLE WILL JOIN THE UPPER-MIDDLE CLASS THIS DECADE. THEY LOOK FOR SIGNS AND SIGNIFICANCE OF THEIR NEW AFFLUENCE."

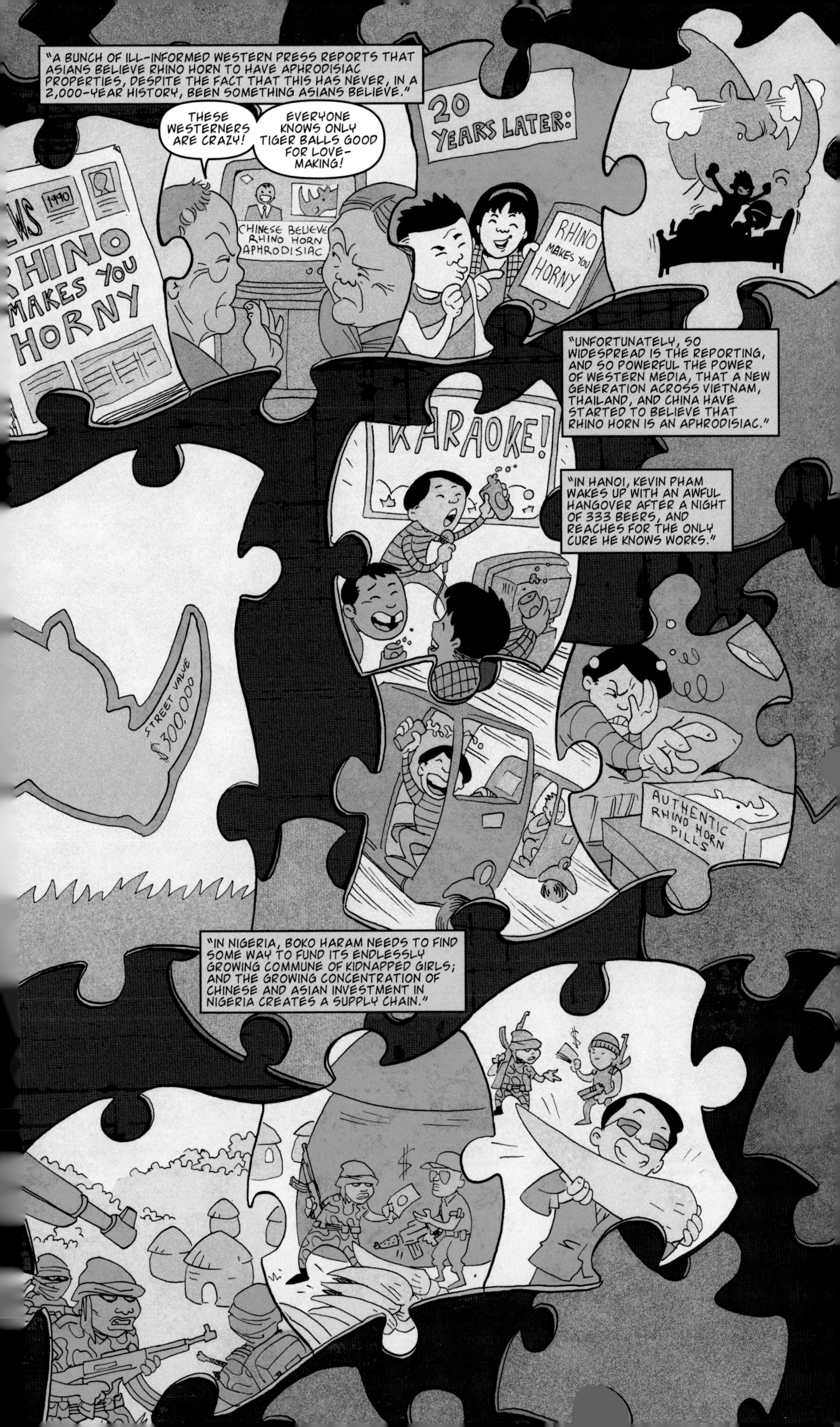
"A BUNCH OF ILL-INFORMED WESTERN PRESS REPORTS THAT ASIANS BELIEVE RHINO HORN TO HAVE APHRODISIAC PROPERTIES, DESPITE THE FACT THAT THIS HAS NEVER, IN A 2,000-YEAR HISTORY, BEEN SOMETHING ASIANS BELIEVE."
1990
RHINO MAKES YOU HORNY
THESE WESTERNERS ARE CRAZY!
EVERYONE KNOWS ONLY TIGER BALLS GOOD FOR LOVE-MAKING!
CHINESE BELIEVE RHINO HORN APHRODISIAC
20 YEARS LATER:
RHINO MAKES YOU HORNY
"UNFORTUNATELY, SO WIDESPREAD IS THE REPORTING, AND SO POWERFUL THE POWER OF WESTERN MEDIA, THAT A NEW GENERATION ACROSS VIETNAM, THAILAND, AND CHINA HAVE STARTED TO BELIEVE THAT RHINO HORN IS AN APHRODISIAC."
KARAOKE!
"IN HANOI, KEVIN PHAM WAKES UP WITH AN AWFUL HANGOVER AFTER A NIGHT OF 333 BEERS, AND REACHES FOR THE ONLY CURE HE KNOWS WORKS."
STREET VALUE $300,000
AUTHENTIC RHINO HORN PILLS
"IN NIGERIA, BOKO HARAM NEEDS TO FIND SOME WAY TO FUND ITS ENDLESSLY GROWING COMMUNE OF KIDNAPPED GIRLS; AND THE GROWING CONCENTRATION OF CHINESE AND ASIAN INVESTMENT IN NIGERIA CREATES A SUPPLY CHAIN."

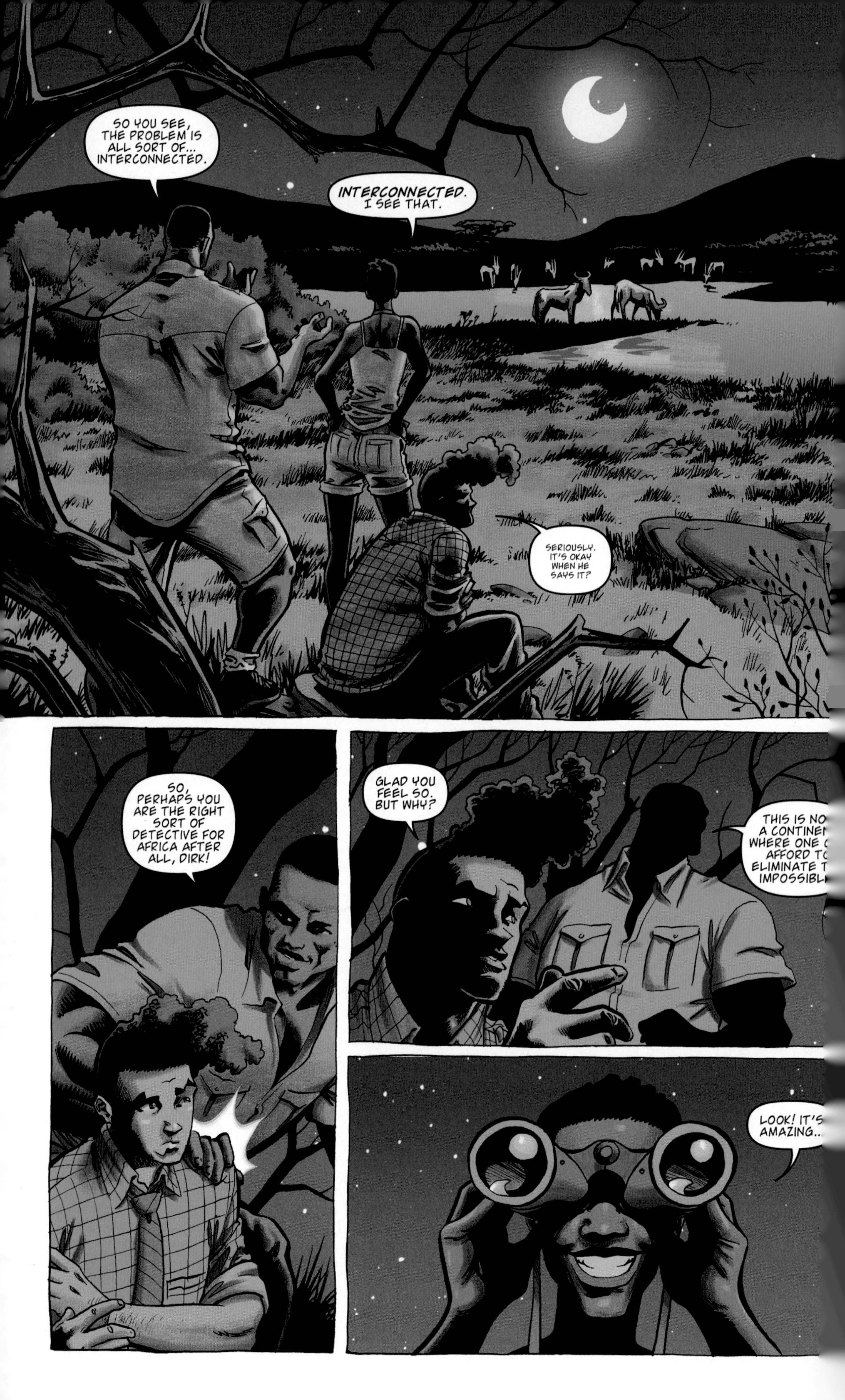
SO YOU SEE, THE PROBLEM IS ALL SORT OF... INTERCONNECTED.
INTERCONNECTED. I SEE THAT.
SERIOUSLY. IT'S OKAY WHEN HE SAYS IT?
SO, PERHAPS YOU ARE THE RIGHT SORT OF DETECTIVE FOR AFRICA AFTER ALL, DIRK!
GLAD YOU FEEL SO. BUT WHY?
THIS IS NO
A CONTINEN
WHERE ONE C
AFFORD TO
ELIMINATE T
IMPOSSIBL
LOOK! IT'S AMAZING...

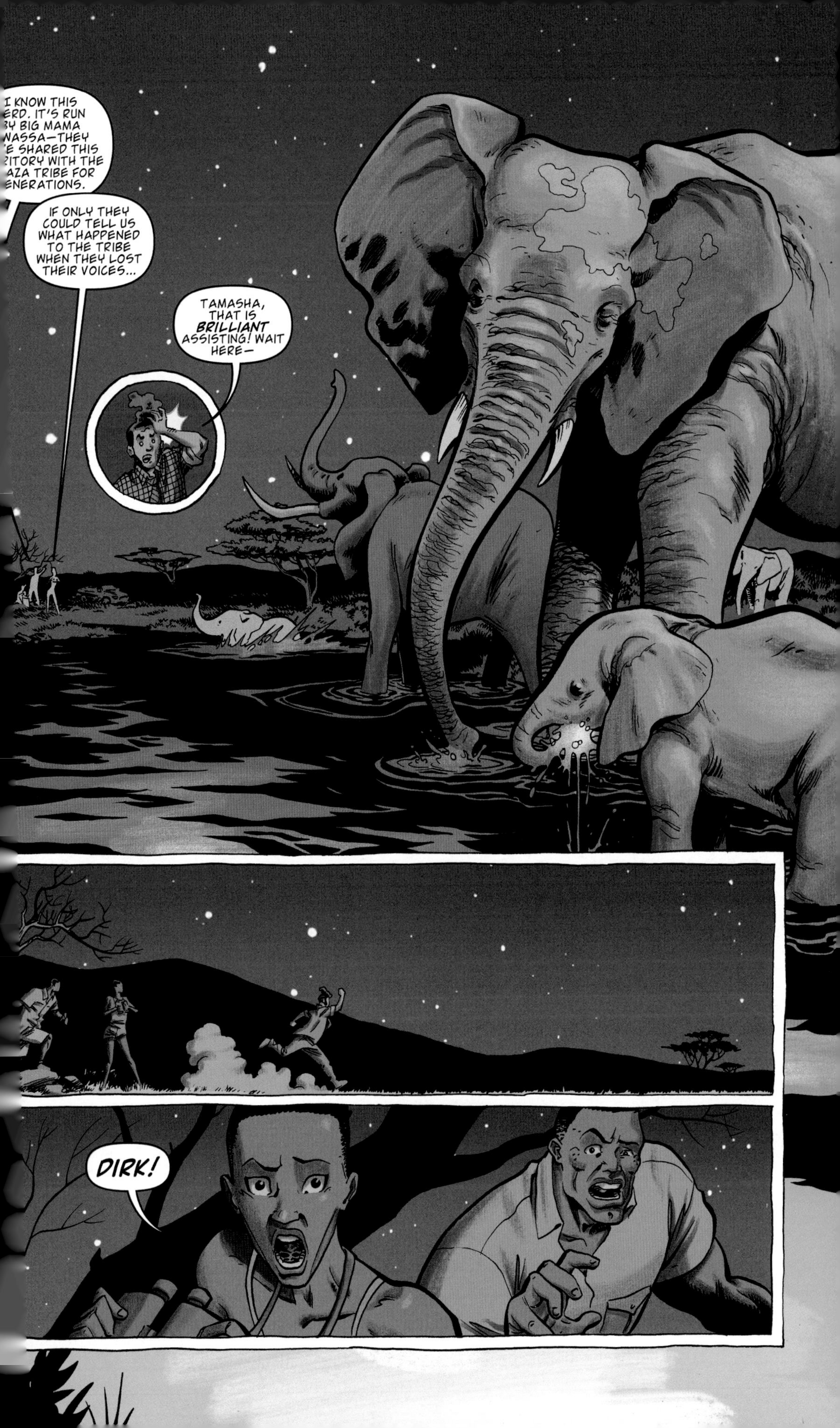
I KNOW THIS
ERD. IT'S RUN
BY BIG MAMA
NASSA—THEY
'E SHARED THIS
RITORY WITH THE
AZA TRIBE FOR
ENERATIONS.
IF ONLY THEY COULD TELL US WHAT HAPPENED TO THE TRIBE WHEN THEY LOST THEIR VOICES...
TAMASHA, THAT IS BRILLIANT ASSISTING! WAIT HERE—
DIRK!

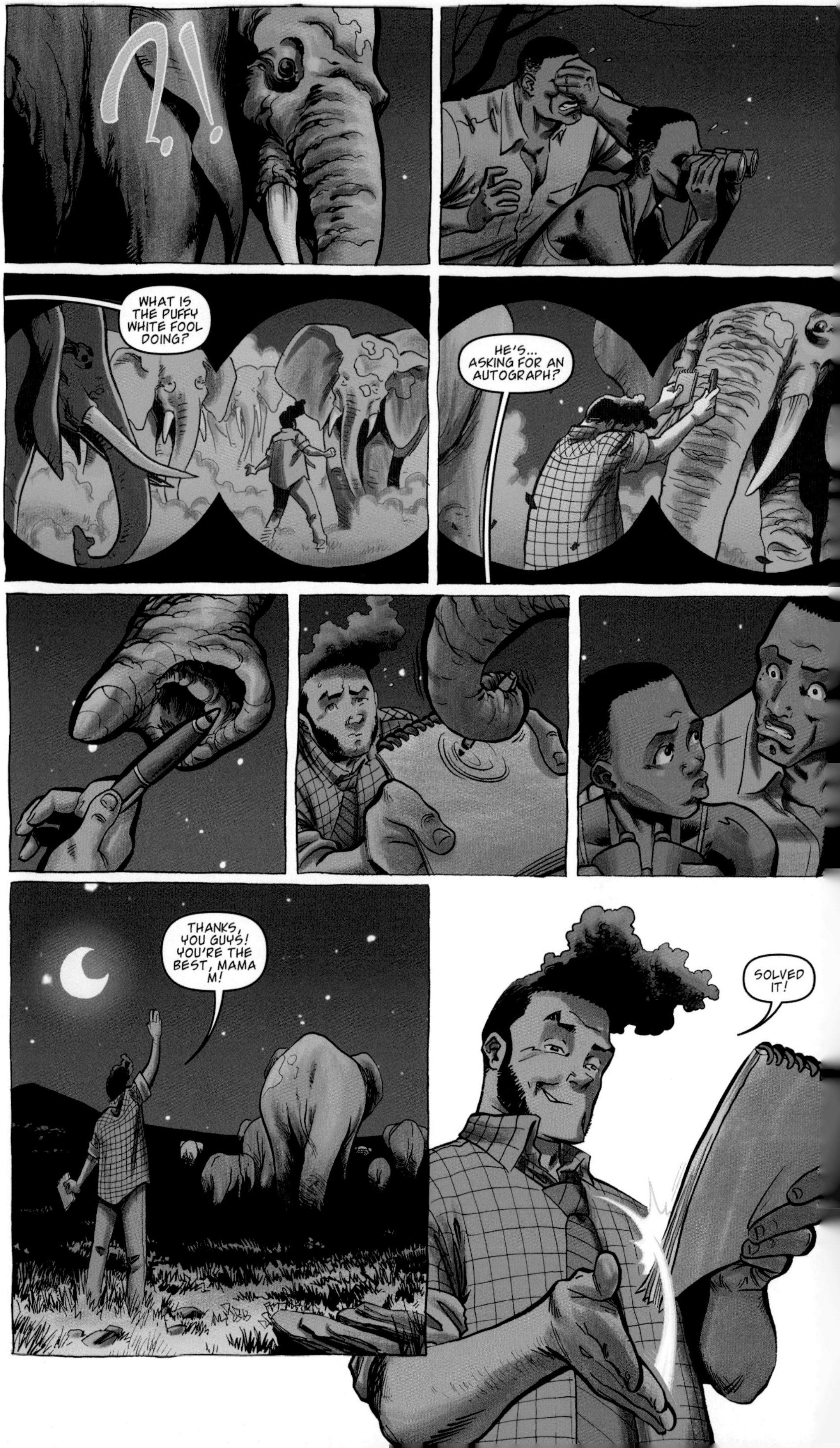
?!
WHAT IS THE PUFFY WHITE FOOL DOING?
HE'S... ASKING FOR AN AUTOGRAPH?
THANKS, YOU GUYS! YOU'RE THE BEST, MAMA M!
SOLVED IT!

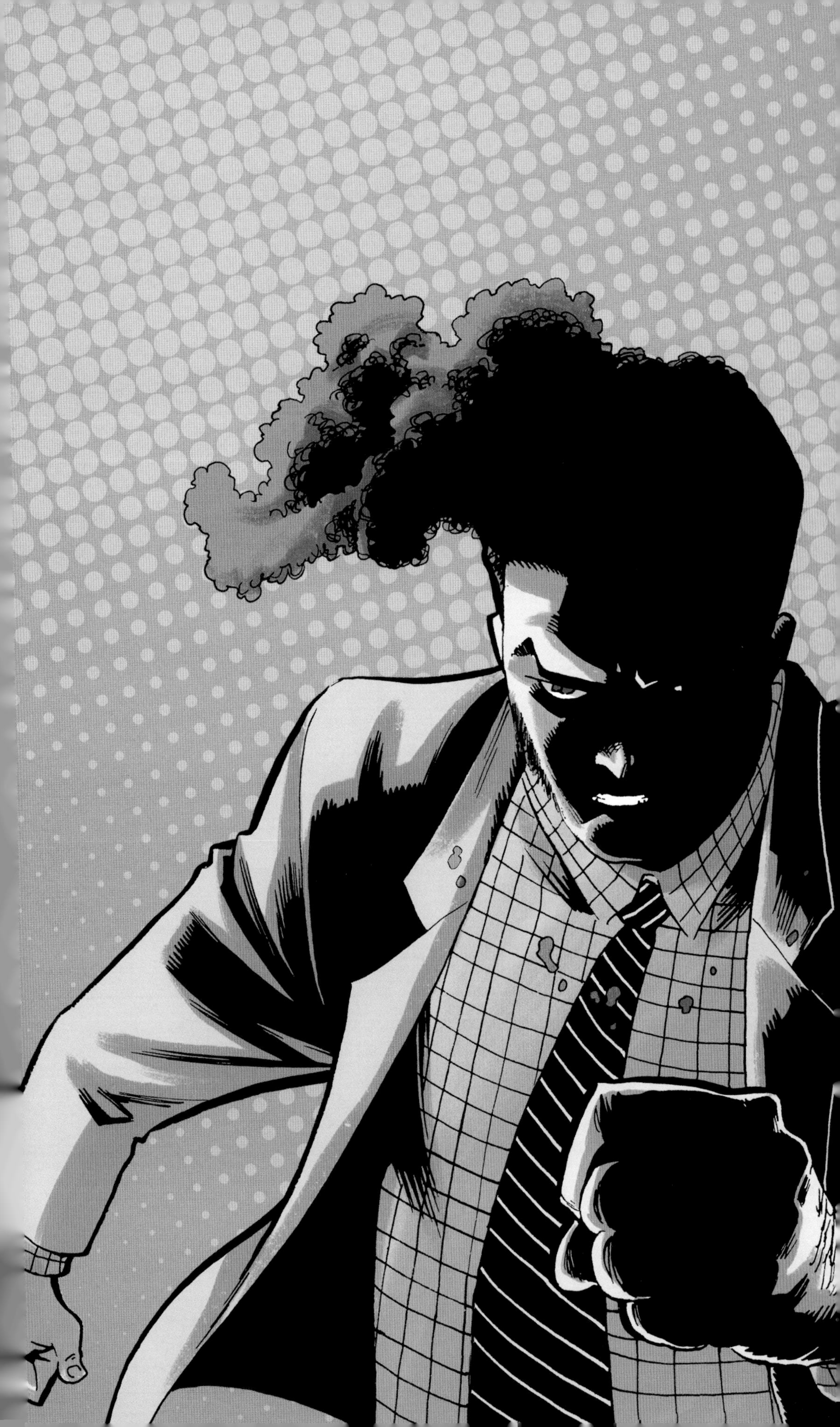

CHAPTER THREE

Cover Art by **ILIAS KYRIAZ**

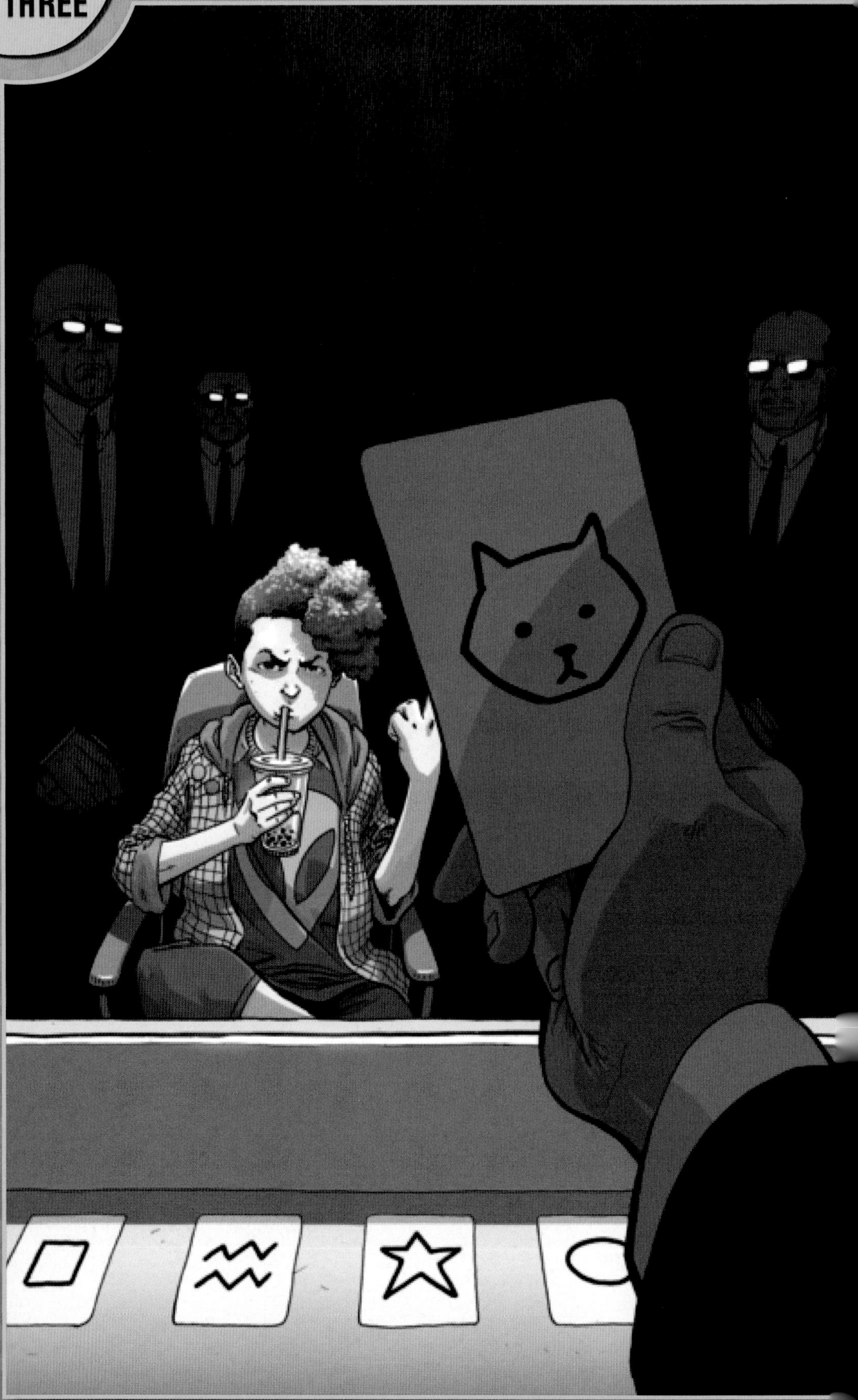

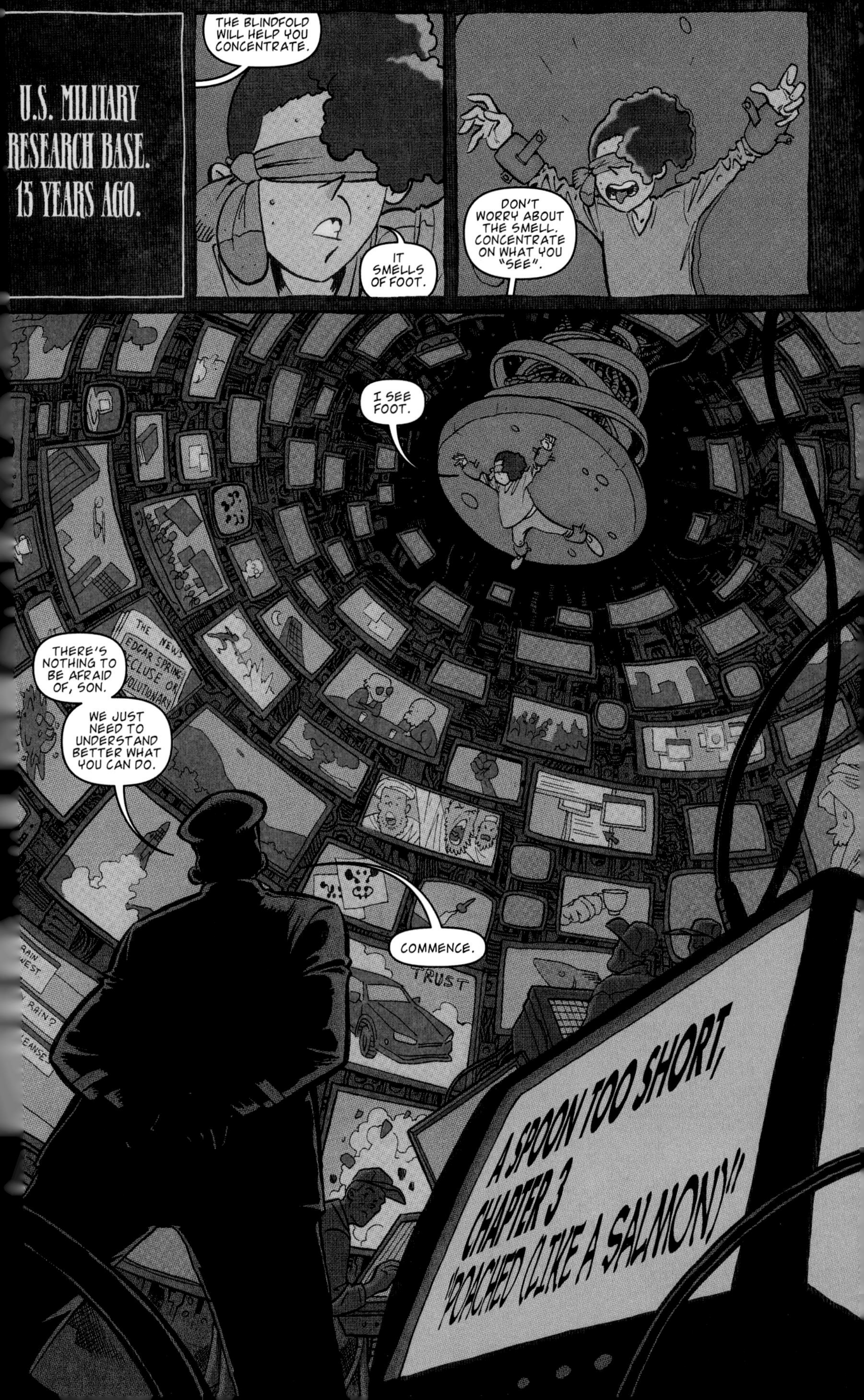
U.S. MILITARY RESEARCH BASE. 15 YEARS AGO.
THE BLINDFOLD WILL HELP YOU CONCENTRATE.
IT SMELLS OF FOOT.
DON'T WORRY ABOUT THE SMELL. CONCENTRATE ON WHAT YOU "SEE".
I SEE FOOT.
THERE'S NOTHING TO BE AFRAID OF, SON.
WE JUST NEED TO UNDERSTAND BETTER WHAT YOU CAN DO.
COMMENCE.
TRUST
A SPOON TOO SHORT, CHAPTER 3 "POACHED (LIKE A SALMON)"

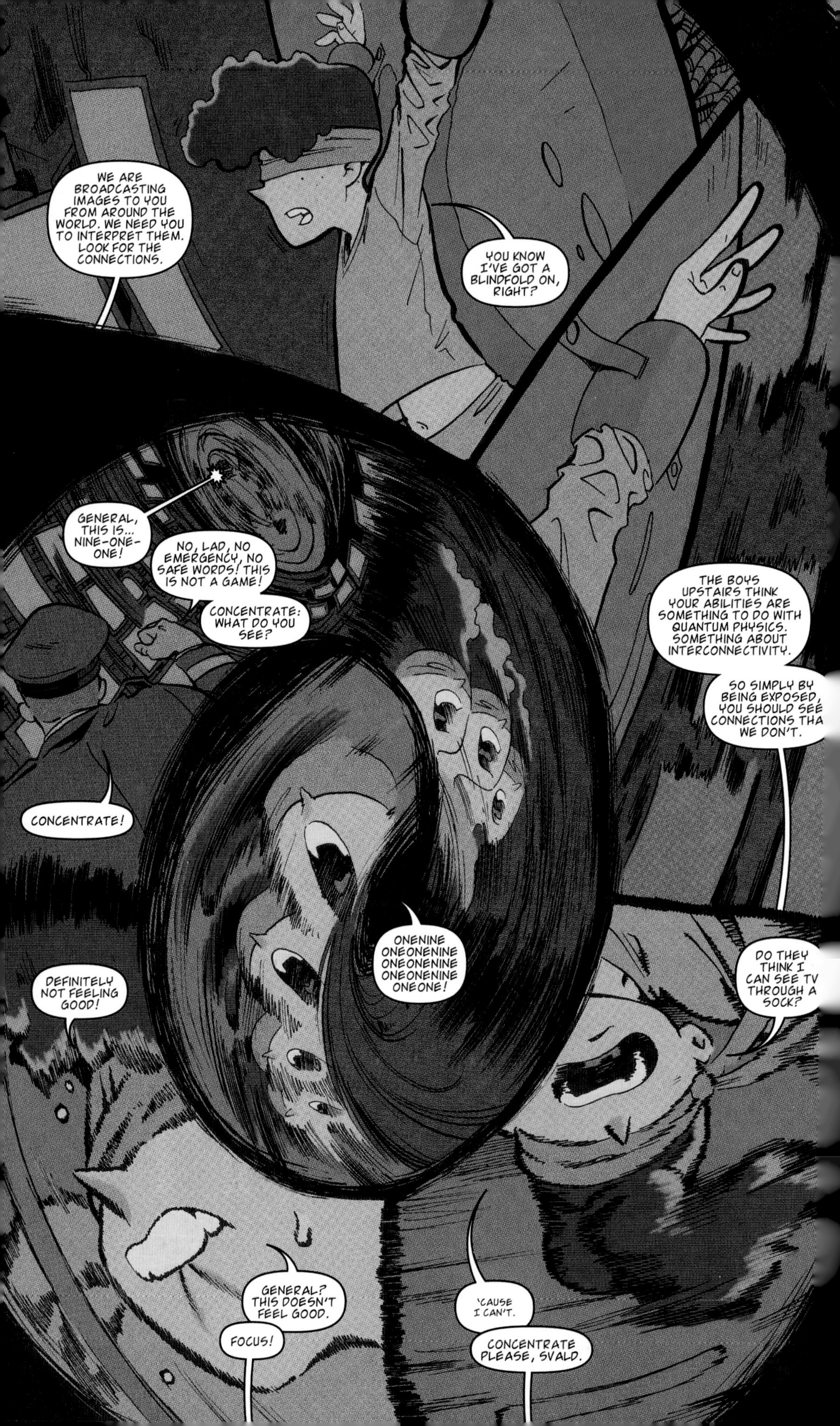
WE ARE BROADCASTING IMAGES TO YOU FROM AROUND THE WORLD. WE NEED YOU TO INTERPRET THEM. LOOK FOR THE CONNECTIONS.
YOU KNOW I'VE GOT A BLINDFOLD ON, RIGHT?
GENERAL, THIS IS... NINE-ONE-ONE!
NO, LAD, NO EMERGENCY, NO SAFE WORDS! THIS IS NOT A GAME!
CONCENTRATE: WHAT DO YOU SEE?
THE BOYS UPSTAIRS THINK YOUR ABILITIES ARE SOMETHING TO DO WITH QUANTUM PHYSICS. SOMETHING ABOUT INTERCONNECTIVITY.
SO SIMPLY BY BEING EXPOSED, YOU SHOULD SEE CONNECTIONS THA WE DON'T.
CONCENTRATE!
ONENINE ONEONENINE ONEONENINE ONEONENINE ONEONE!
DEFINITELY NOT FEELING GOOD!
DO THEY THINK I CAN SEE TV THROUGH A SOCK?
GENERAL? THIS DOESN'T FEEL GOOD.
FOCUS!
'CAUSE I CAN'T.
CONCENTRATE PLEASE, SVALD.

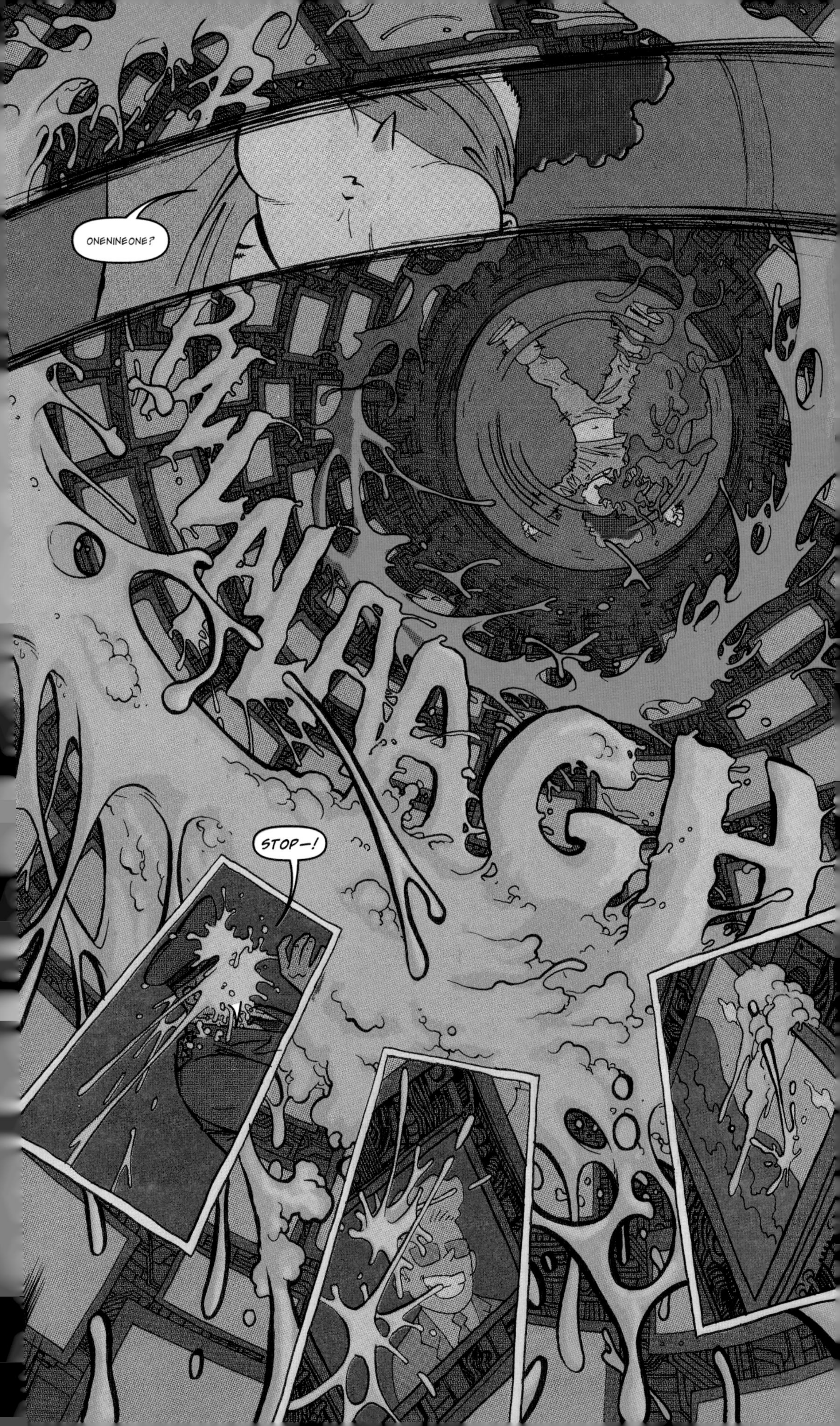
ONENINEONE?
STOP—!

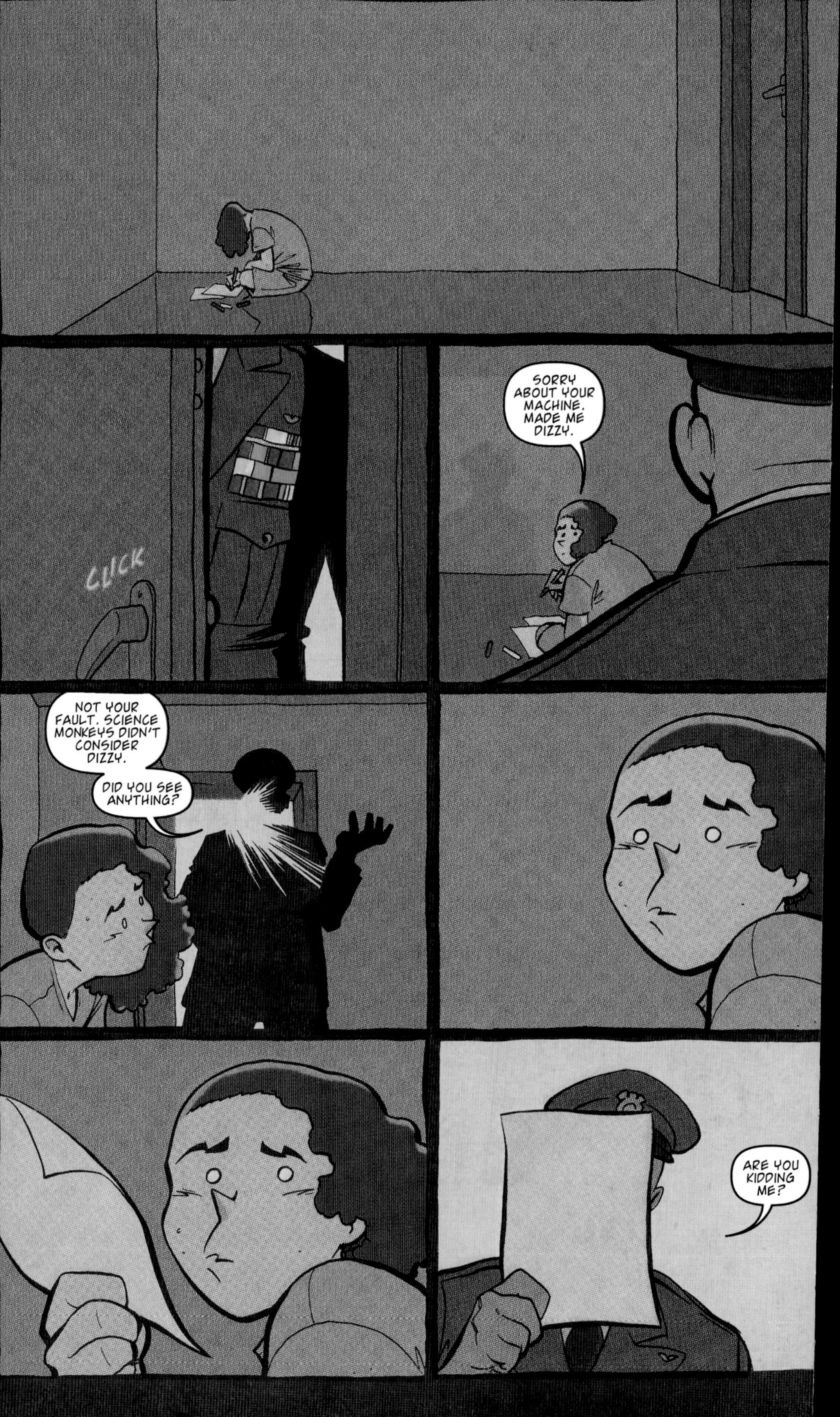
CLICK
SORRY ABOUT YOUR MACHINE. MADE ME DIZZY.
NOT YOUR FAULT. SCIENCE MONKEYS DIDN'T CONSIDER DIZZY.
DID YOU SEE ANYTHING?
ARE YOU KIDDING ME?

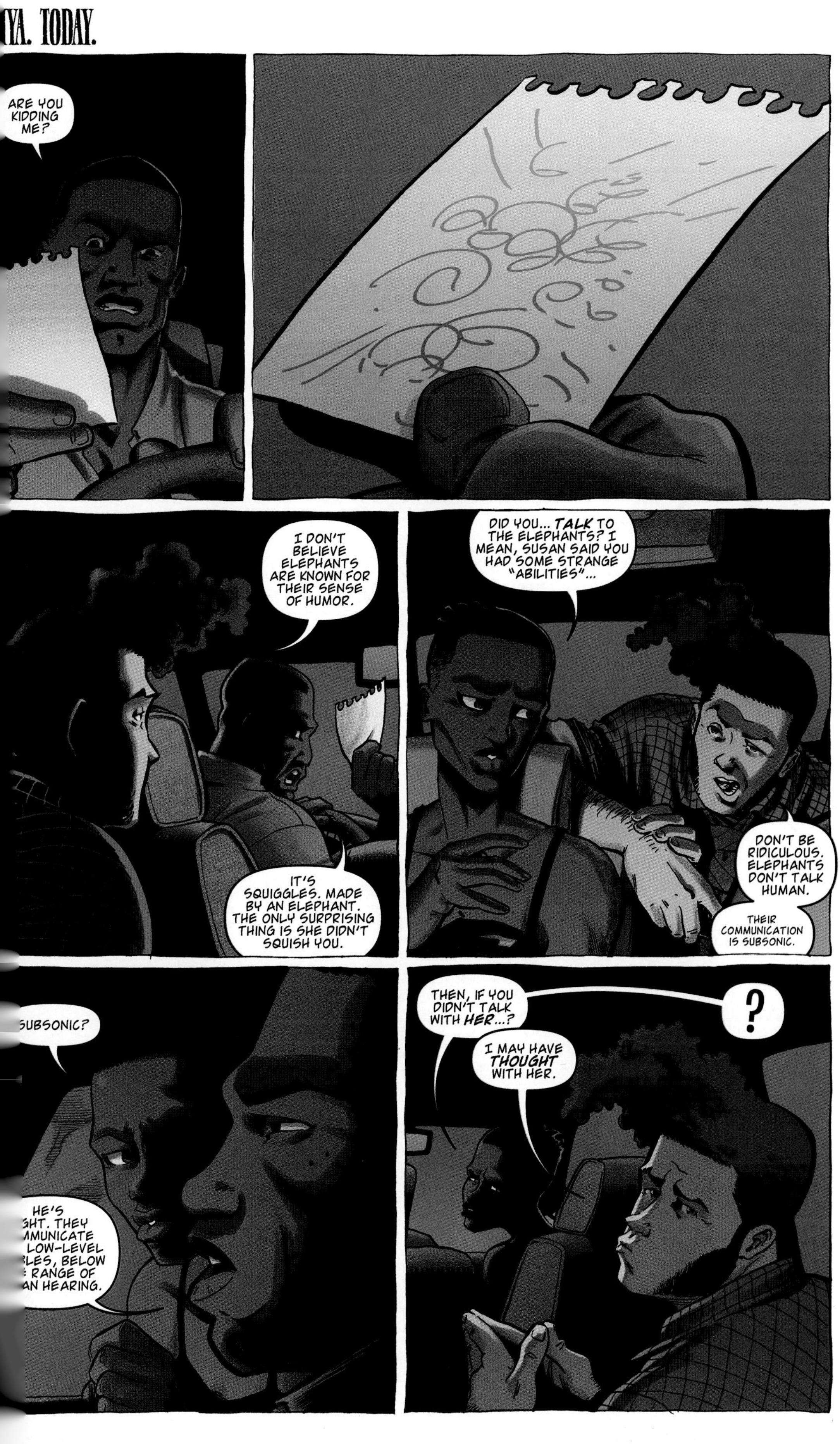
YA. TODAY.
ARE YOU KIDDING ME?
I DON'T BELIEVE ELEPHANTS ARE KNOWN FOR THEIR SENSE OF HUMOR.
IT'S SQUIGGLES. MADE BY AN ELEPHANT. THE ONLY SURPRISING THING IS SHE DIDN'T SQUISH YOU.
DID YOU... TALK TO THE ELEPHANTS? I MEAN, SUSAN SAID YOU HAD SOME STRANGE "ABILITIES"...
DON'T BE RIDICULOUS. ELEPHANTS DON'T TALK HUMAN.
THEIR COMMUNICATION IS SUBSONIC.
SUBSONIC?
HE'S GHT. THEY MMUNICATE LOW-LEVEL LES, BELOW RANGE OF AN HEARING.
THEN, IF YOU DIDN'T TALK WITH HER...?
?
I MAY HAVE THOUGHT WITH HER.

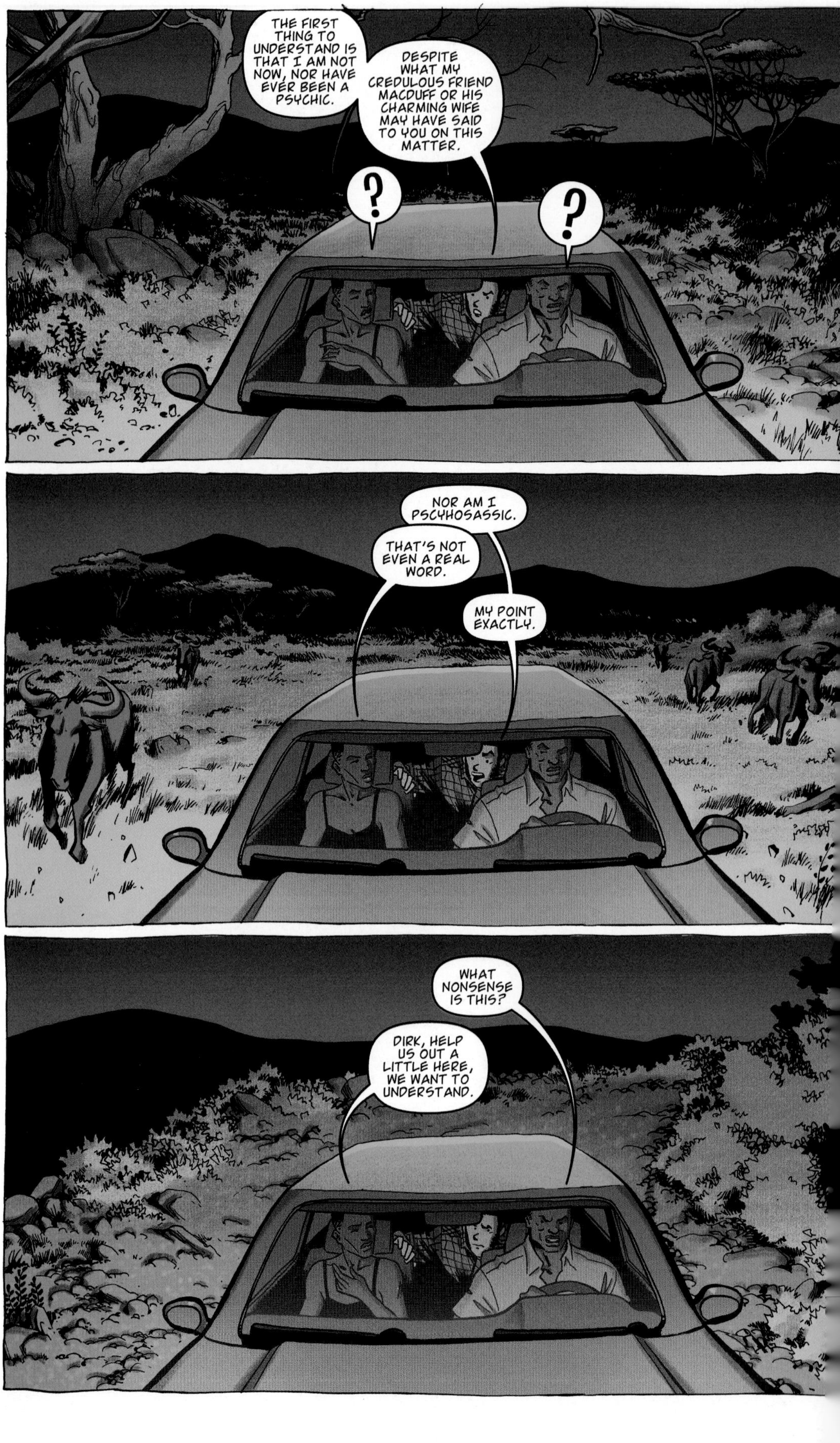
THE FIRST THING TO UNDERSTAND IS THAT I AM NOT NOW, NOR HAVE EVER BEEN A PSYCHIC.
DESPITE WHAT MY CREDULOUS FRIEND MACDUFF OR HIS CHARMING WIFE MAY HAVE SAID TO YOU ON THIS MATTER.
?
?
NOR AM I PSCYHOSASSIC.
THAT'S NOT EVEN A REAL WORD.
MY POINT EXACTLY.
WHAT NONSENSE IS THIS?
DIRK, HELP US OUT A LITTLE HERE, WE WANT TO UNDERSTAND.

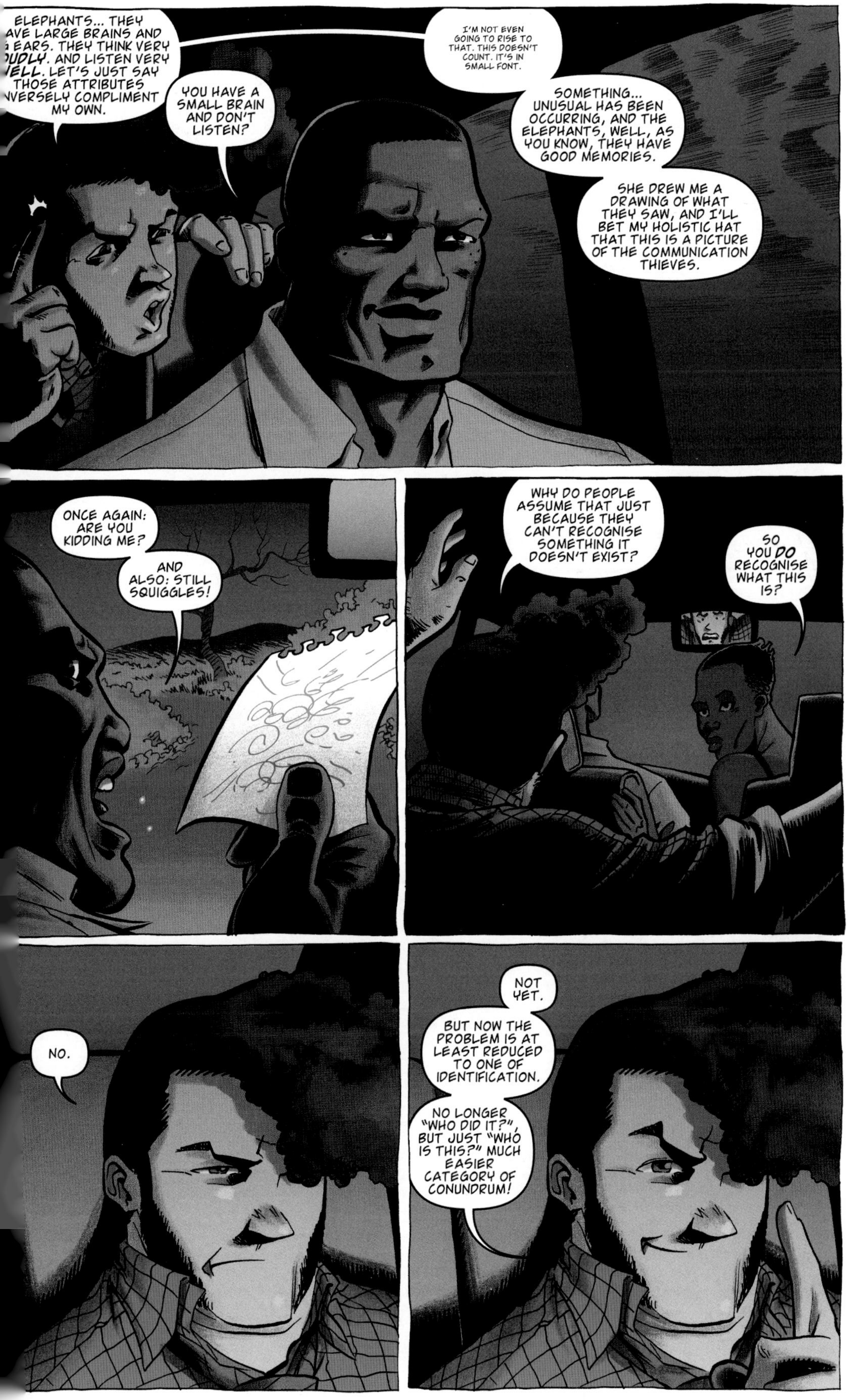
ELEPHANTS... THEY HAVE LARGE BRAINS AND BIG EARS. THEY THINK VERY LOUDLY. AND LISTEN VERY WELL. LET'S JUST SAY THOSE ATTRIBUTES INVERSELY COMPLIMENT MY OWN.
I'M NOT EVEN GOING TO RISE TO THAT. THIS DOESN'T COUNT. IT'S IN SMALL FONT.
YOU HAVE A SMALL BRAIN AND DON'T LISTEN?
SOMETHING... UNUSUAL HAS BEEN OCCURRING, AND THE ELEPHANTS, WELL, AS YOU KNOW, THEY HAVE GOOD MEMORIES.
SHE DREW ME A DRAWING OF WHAT THEY SAW, AND I'LL BET MY HOLISTIC HAT THAT THIS IS A PICTURE OF THE COMMUNICATION THIEVES.
ONCE AGAIN: ARE YOU KIDDING ME?
AND ALSO: STILL SQUIGGLES!
WHY DO PEOPLE ASSUME THAT JUST BECAUSE THEY CAN'T RECOGNISE SOMETHING IT DOESN'T EXIST?
SO YOU DO RECOGNISE WHAT THIS IS?
NO.
NOT YET.
BUT NOW THE PROBLEM IS AT LEAST REDUCED TO ONE OF IDENTIFICATION.
NO LONGER "WHO DID IT?", BUT JUST "WHO IS THIS?" MUCH EASIER CATEGORY OF CONUNDRUM!

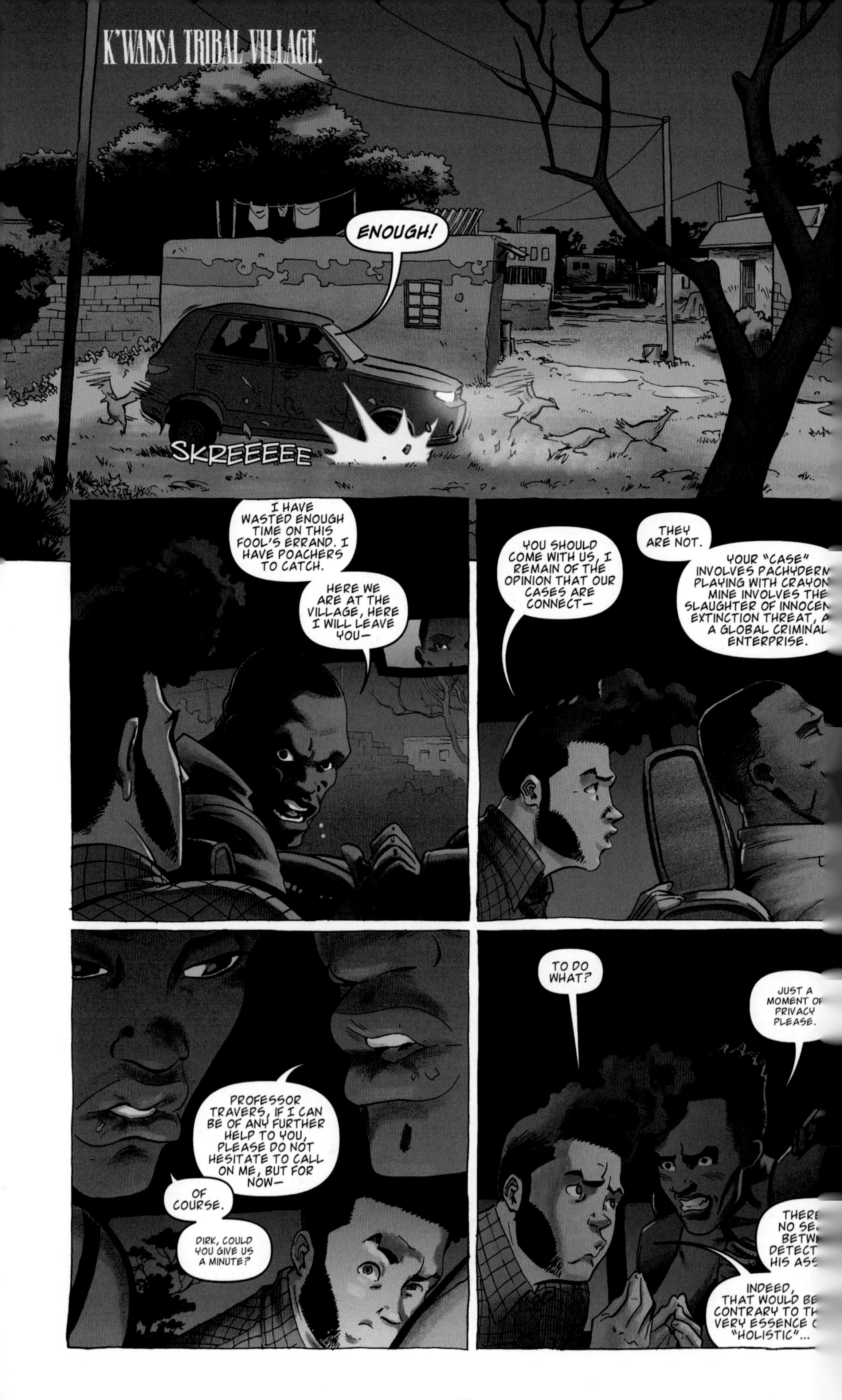
K'WANSA TRIBAL VILLAGE.
ENOUGH!
SKREEEEEE
I HAVE WASTED ENOUGH TIME ON THIS FOOL'S ERRAND. I HAVE POACHERS TO CATCH.
HERE WE ARE AT THE VILLAGE, HERE I WILL LEAVE YOU—
YOU SHOULD COME WITH US, I REMAIN OF THE OPINION THAT OUR CASES ARE CONNECT—
THEY ARE NOT.
YOUR "CASE" INVOLVES PACHYDERM PLAYING WITH CRAYON MINE INVOLVES THE SLAUGHTER OF INNOCEN EXTINCTION THREAT, A A GLOBAL CRIMINAL ENTERPRISE.
PROFESSOR TRAVERS, IF I CAN BE OF ANY FURTHER HELP TO YOU, PLEASE DO NOT HESITATE TO CALL ON ME, BUT FOR NOW—
OF COURSE.
DIRK, COULD YOU GIVE US A MINUTE?
TO DO WHAT?
JUST A MOMENT OF PRIVACY PLEASE.
THERE NO SE BETW DETECT HIS ASS
INDEED, THAT WOULD BE CONTRARY TO TH VERY ESSENCE "HOLISTIC"...

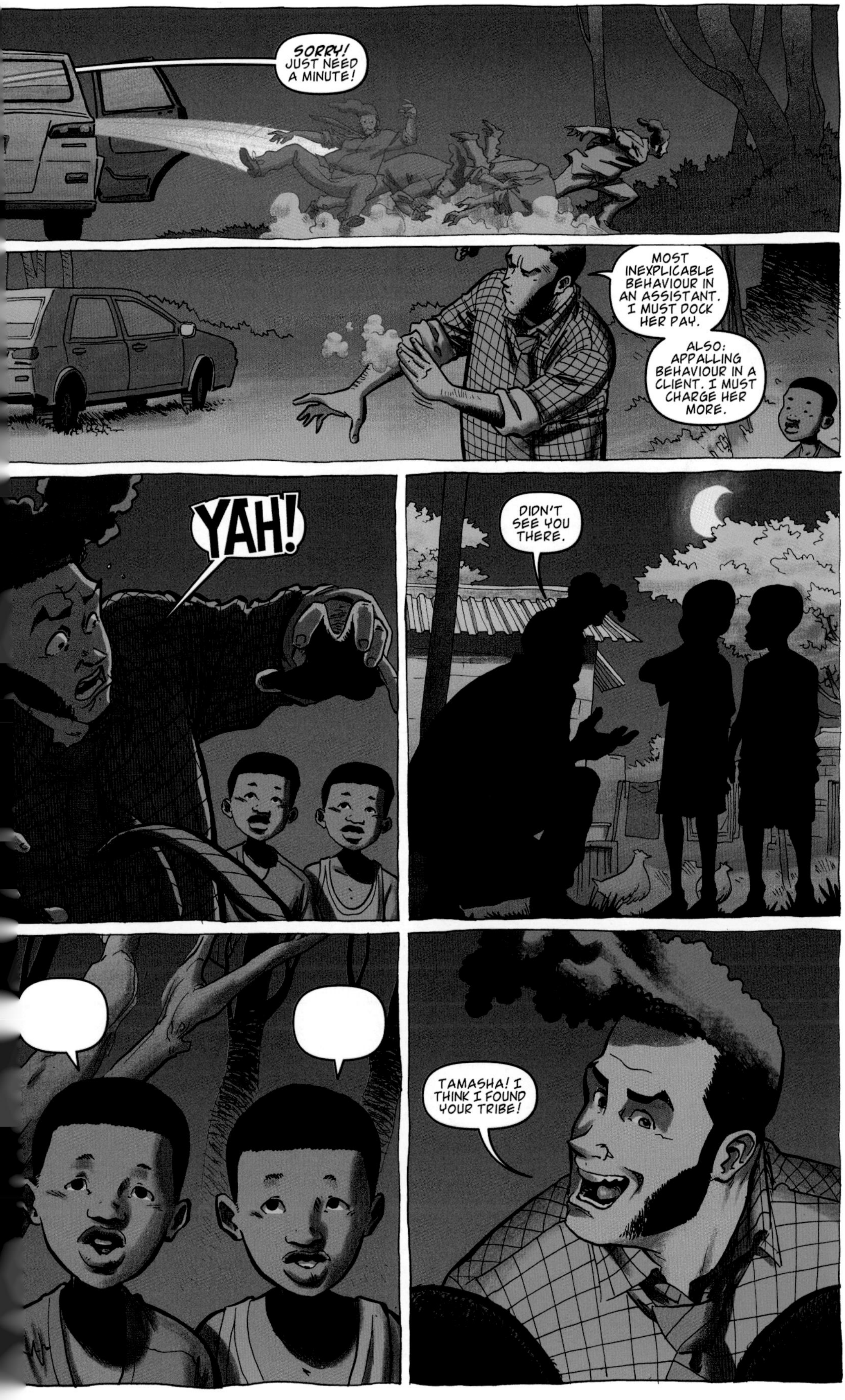
SORRY! JUST NEED A MINUTE!
MOST INEXPLICABLE BEHAVIOUR IN AN ASSISTANT. I MUST DOCK HER PAY.
ALSO: APPALLING BEHAVIOUR IN A CLIENT. I MUST CHARGE HER MORE.
YAH!
DIDN'T SEE YOU THERE.
TAMASHA! I THINK I FOUND YOUR TRIBE!

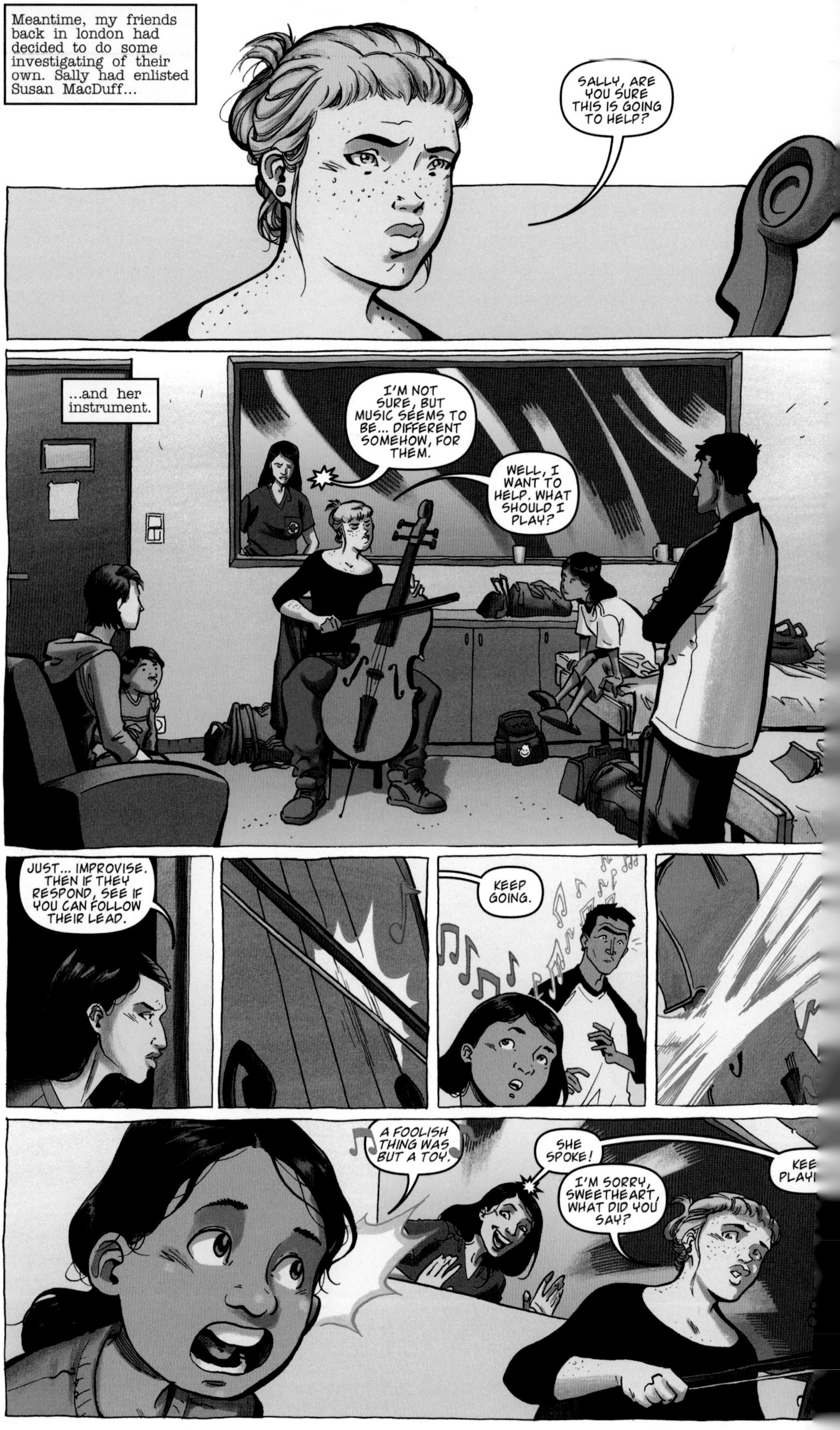

Meantime, my friends back in london had decided to do some investigating of their own. Sally had enlisted Susan MacDuff...
SALLY, ARE YOU SURE THIS IS GOING TO HELP?
...and her instrument.
I'M NOT SURE, BUT MUSIC SEEMS TO BE... DIFFERENT SOMEHOW, FOR THEM.
WELL, I WANT TO HELP. WHAT SHOULD I PLAY?
JUST... IMPROVISE. THEN IF THEY RESPOND, SEE IF YOU CAN FOLLOW THEIR LEAD.
KEEP GOING.
A FOOLISH THING WAS BUT A TOY.
SHE SPOKE!
I'M SORRY, SWEETHEART, WHAT DID YOU SAY?
KEE PLAYI

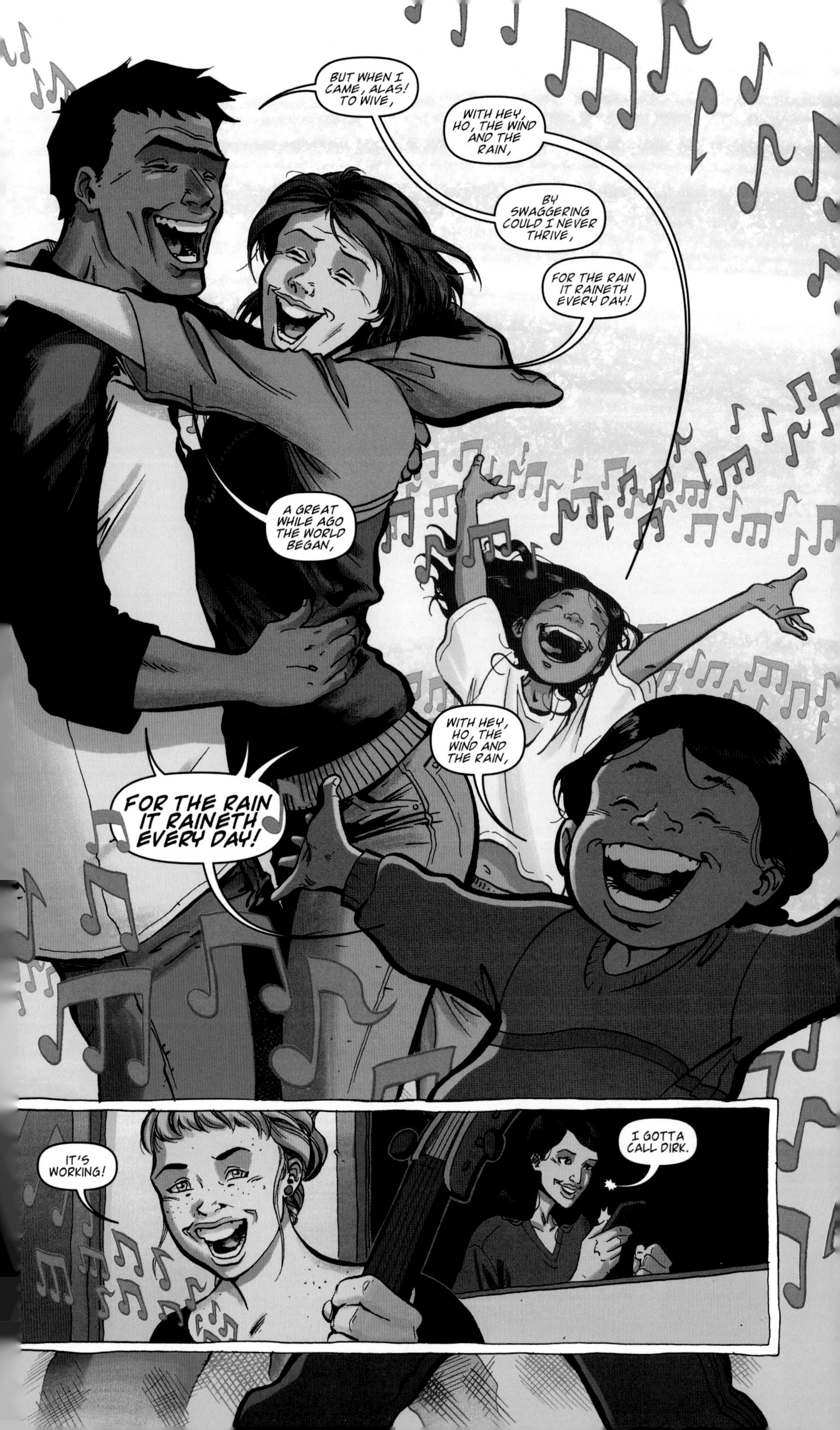
BUT WHEN I CAME, ALAS! TO WIVE,
WITH HEY, HO, THE WIND AND THE RAIN,
BY SWAGGERING COULD I NEVER THRIVE,
FOR THE RAIN IT RAINETH EVERY DAY!
A GREAT WHILE AGO THE WORLD BEGAN,
WITH HEY, HO, THE WIND AND THE RAIN,
FOR THE RAIN IT RAINETH EVERY DAY!
IT'S WORKING!
I GOTTA CALL DIRK.

Meantime, with the K'wansa, our own breakthrough had not yet broken... *uh*... through.

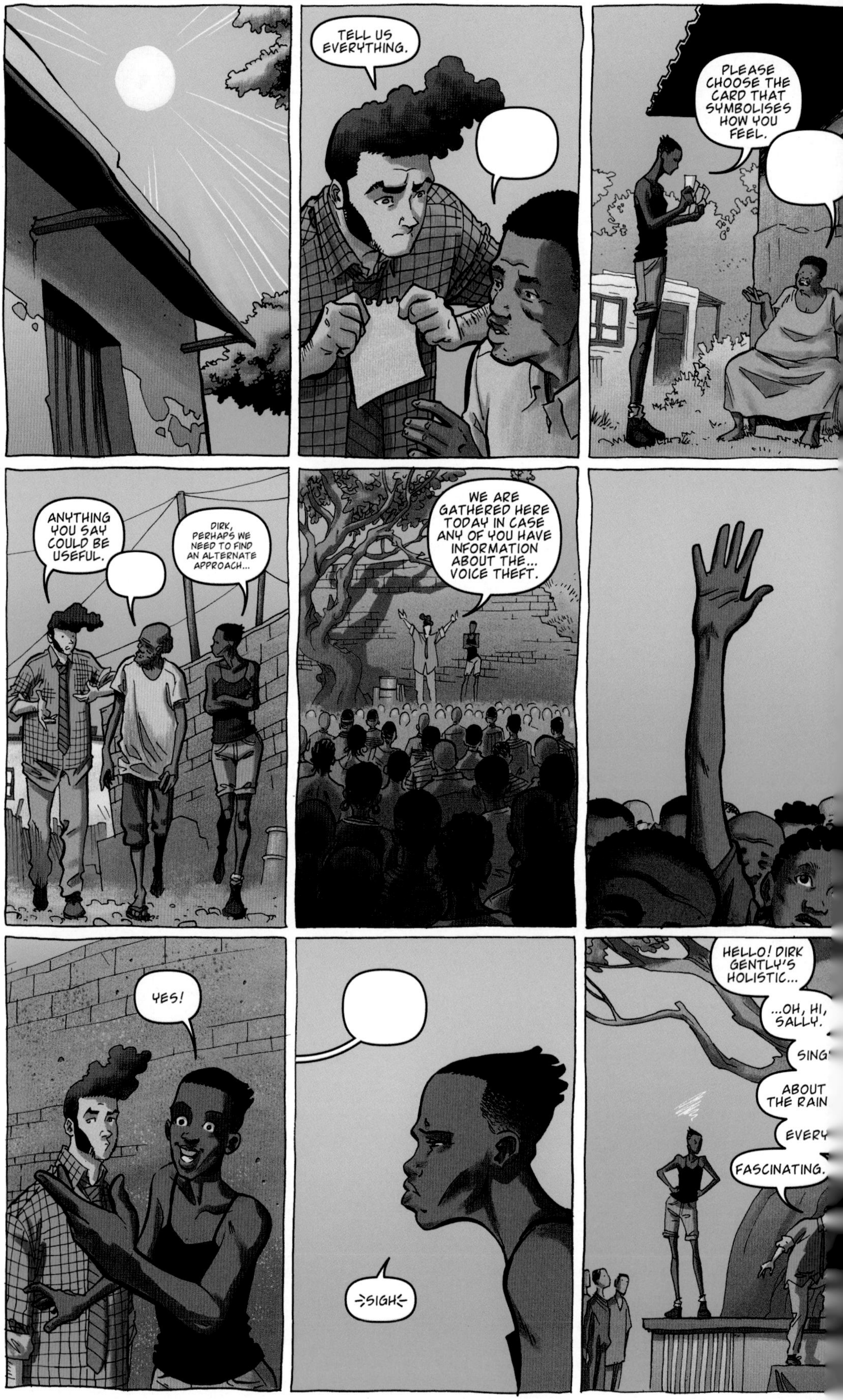
TELL US EVERYTHING.
PLEASE CHOOSE THE CARD THAT SYMBOLISES HOW YOU FEEL.
ANYTHING YOU SAY COULD BE USEFUL.
DIRK, PERHAPS WE NEED TO FIND AN ALTERNATE APPROACH...
WE ARE GATHERED HERE TODAY IN CASE ANY OF YOU HAVE INFORMATION ABOUT THE... VOICE THEFT.
YES!
SIGH
HELLO! DIRK GENTLY'S HOLISTIC...
...OH, HI, SALLY.
SING
ABOUT THE RAIN
EVERY
FASCINATING.

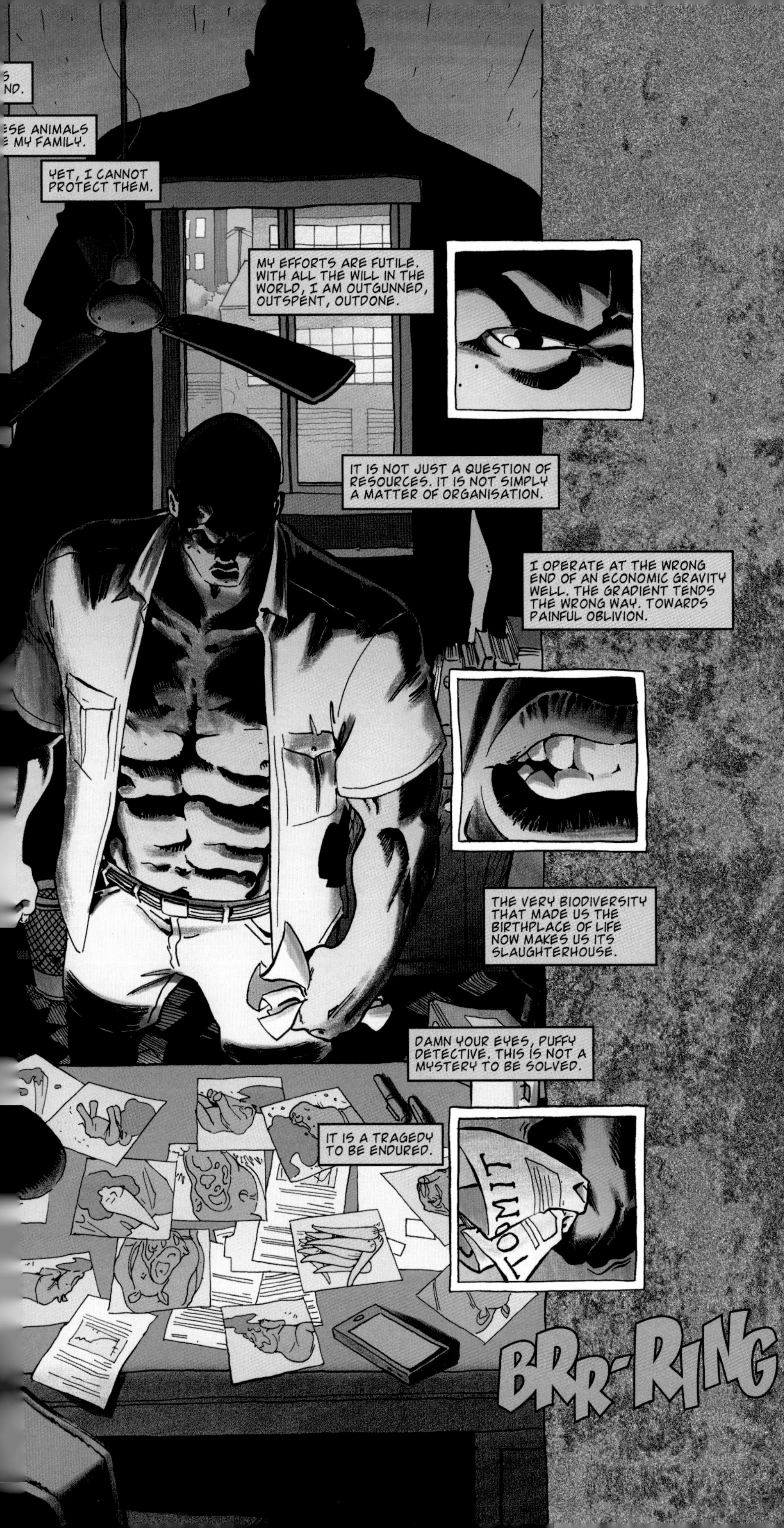

S
ND.
ESE ANIMALS
E MY FAMILY.
YET, I CANNOT PROTECT THEM.
MY EFFORTS ARE FUTILE. WITH ALL THE WILL IN THE WORLD, I AM OUTGUNNED, OUTSPENT, OUTDONE.
IT IS NOT JUST A QUESTION OF RESOURCES. IT IS NOT SIMPLY A MATTER OF ORGANISATION.
I OPERATE AT THE WRONG END OF AN ECONOMIC GRAVITY WELL. THE GRADIENT TENDS THE WRONG WAY. TOWARDS PAINFUL OBLIVION.
THE VERY BIODIVERSITY THAT MADE US THE BIRTHPLACE OF LIFE NOW MAKES US ITS SLAUGHTERHOUSE.
DAMN YOUR EYES, PUFFY DETECTIVE. THIS IS NOT A MYSTERY TO BE SOLVED.
IT IS A TRAGEDY TO BE ENDURED.
BRR-RING

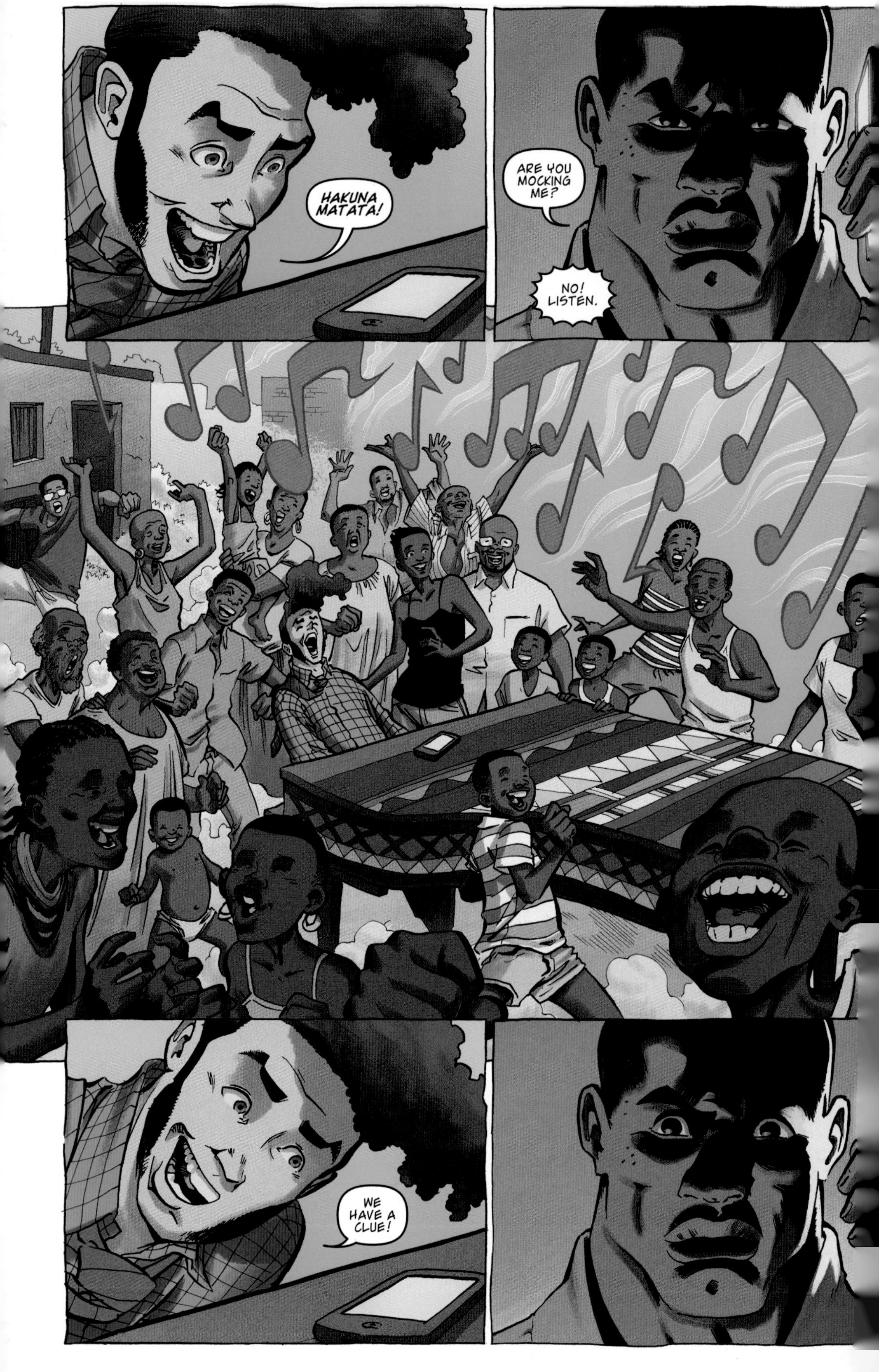
HAKUNA MATATA!
ARE YOU MOCKING ME?
NO! LISTEN.
WE HAVE A CLUE!

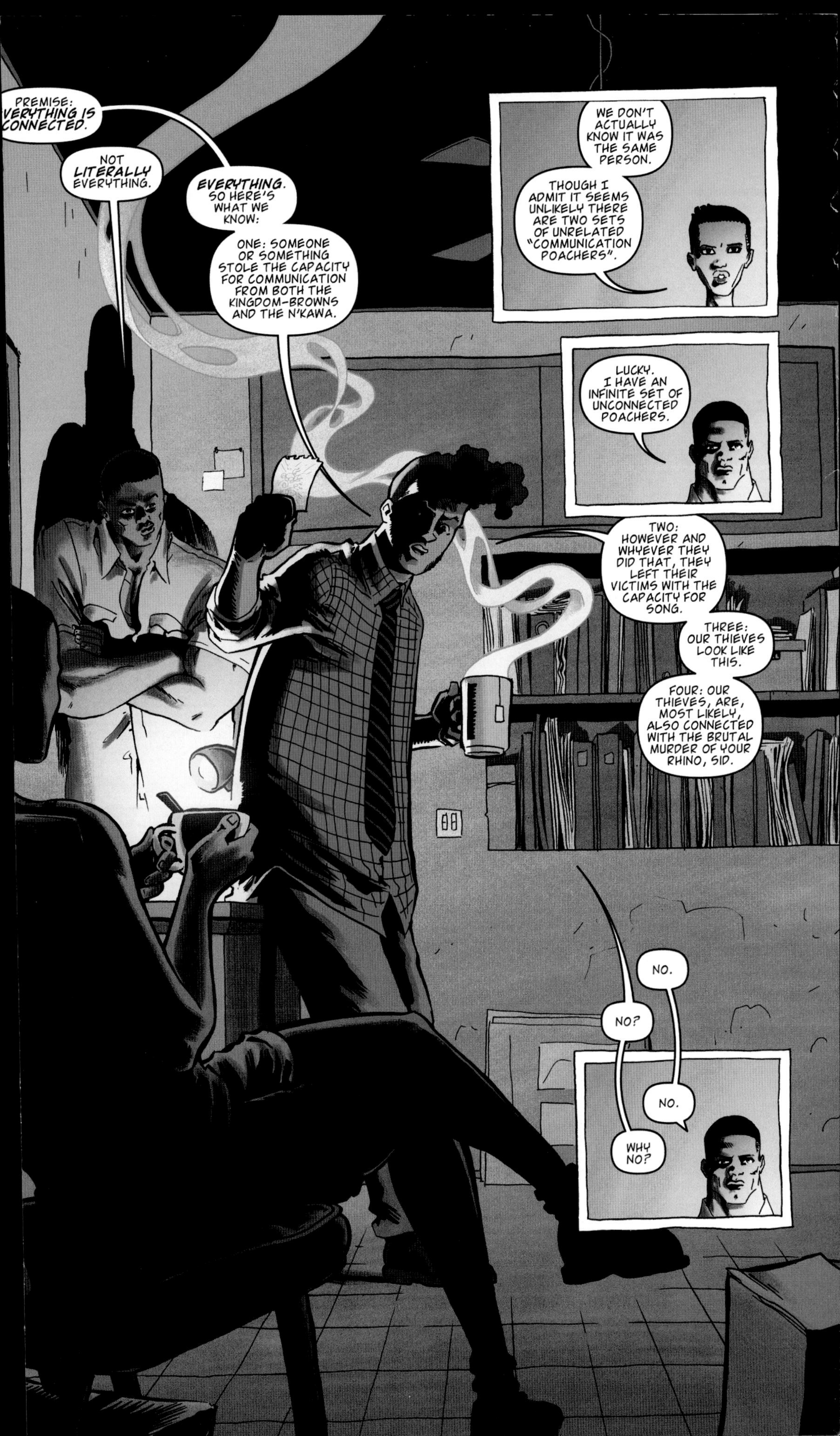
PREMISE: EVERYTHING IS CONNECTED.
NOT LITERALLY EVERYTHING.
EVERYTHING. SO HERE'S WHAT WE KNOW:
ONE: SOMEONE OR SOMETHING STOLE THE CAPACITY FOR COMMUNICATION FROM BOTH THE KINGDOM-BROWNS AND THE N'KAWA.
WE DON'T ACTUALLY KNOW IT WAS THE SAME PERSON.
THOUGH I ADMIT IT SEEMS UNLIKELY THERE ARE TWO SETS OF UNRELATED "COMMUNICATION POACHERS".
LUCKY. I HAVE AN INFINITE SET OF UNCONNECTED POACHERS.
TWO: HOWEVER AND WHYEVER THEY DID THAT, THEY LEFT THEIR VICTIMS WITH THE CAPACITY FOR SONG.
THREE: OUR THIEVES LOOK LIKE THIS.
FOUR: OUR THIEVES, ARE, MOST LIKELY, ALSO CONNECTED WITH THE BRUTAL MURDER OF YOUR RHINO, SID.
NO.
NO?
NO.
WHY NO?

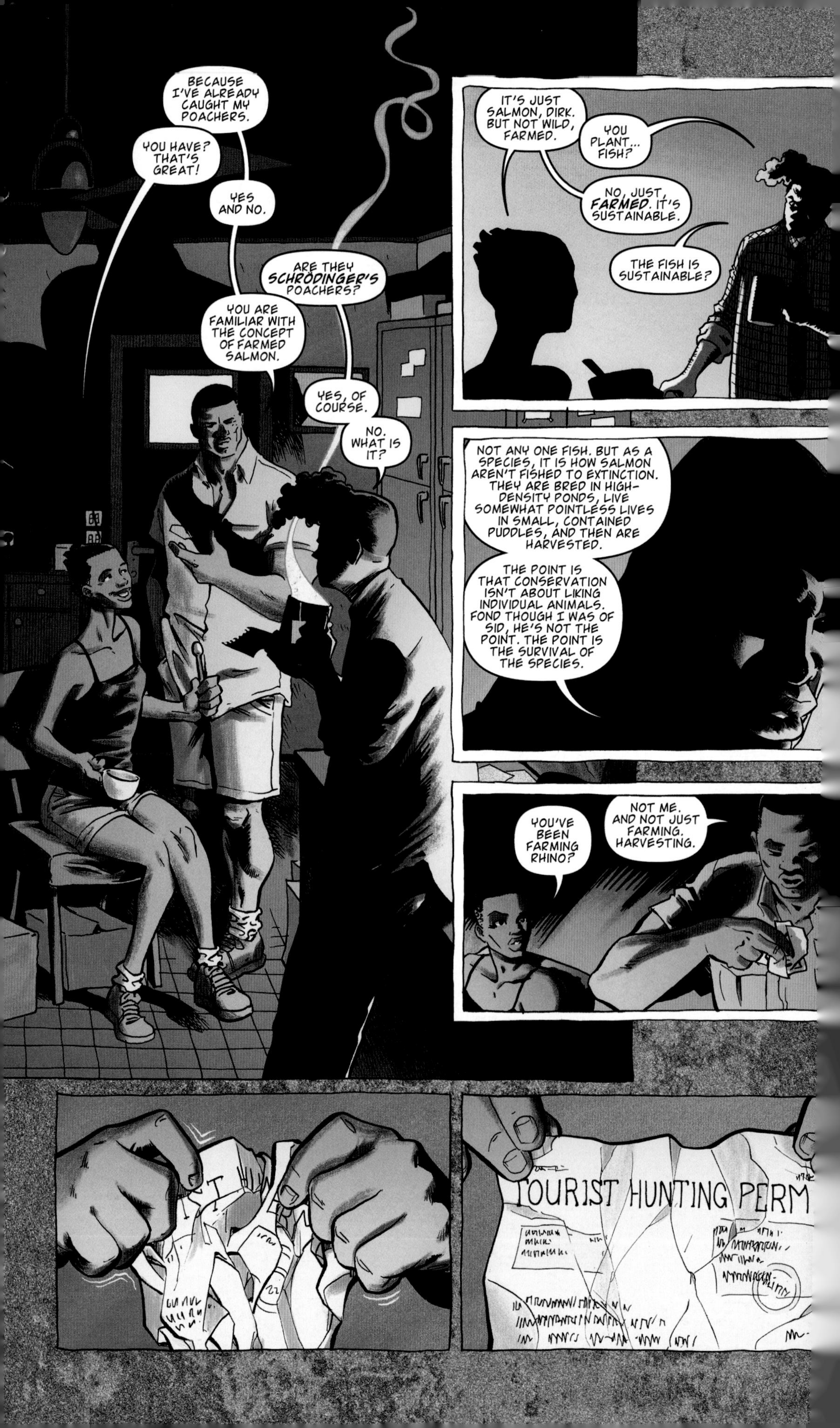
BECAUSE I'VE ALREADY CAUGHT MY POACHERS.
YOU HAVE? THAT'S GREAT!
YES AND NO.
YOU ARE FAMILIAR WITH THE CONCEPT OF FARMED SALMON.
ARE THEY SCHRÖDINGER'S POACHERS?
YES, OF COURSE.
NO. WHAT IS IT?
IT'S JUST SALMON, DIRK. BUT NOT WILD, FARMED.
YOU PLANT... FISH?
NO, JUST, FARMED. IT'S SUSTAINABLE.
THE FISH IS SUSTAINABLE?
NOT ANY ONE FISH. BUT AS A SPECIES, IT IS HOW SALMON AREN'T FISHED TO EXTINCTION. THEY ARE BRED IN HIGH-DENSITY PONDS, LIVE SOMEWHAT POINTLESS LIVES IN SMALL, CONTAINED PUDDLES, AND THEN ARE HARVESTED.
THE POINT IS THAT CONSERVATION ISN'T ABOUT LIKING INDIVIDUAL ANIMALS. FOND THOUGH I WAS OF SID, HE'S NOT THE POINT. THE POINT IS THE SURVIVAL OF THE SPECIES.
YOU'VE BEEN FARMING RHINO?
NOT ME. AND NOT JUST FARMING. HARVESTING.
TOURIST HUNTING PERM

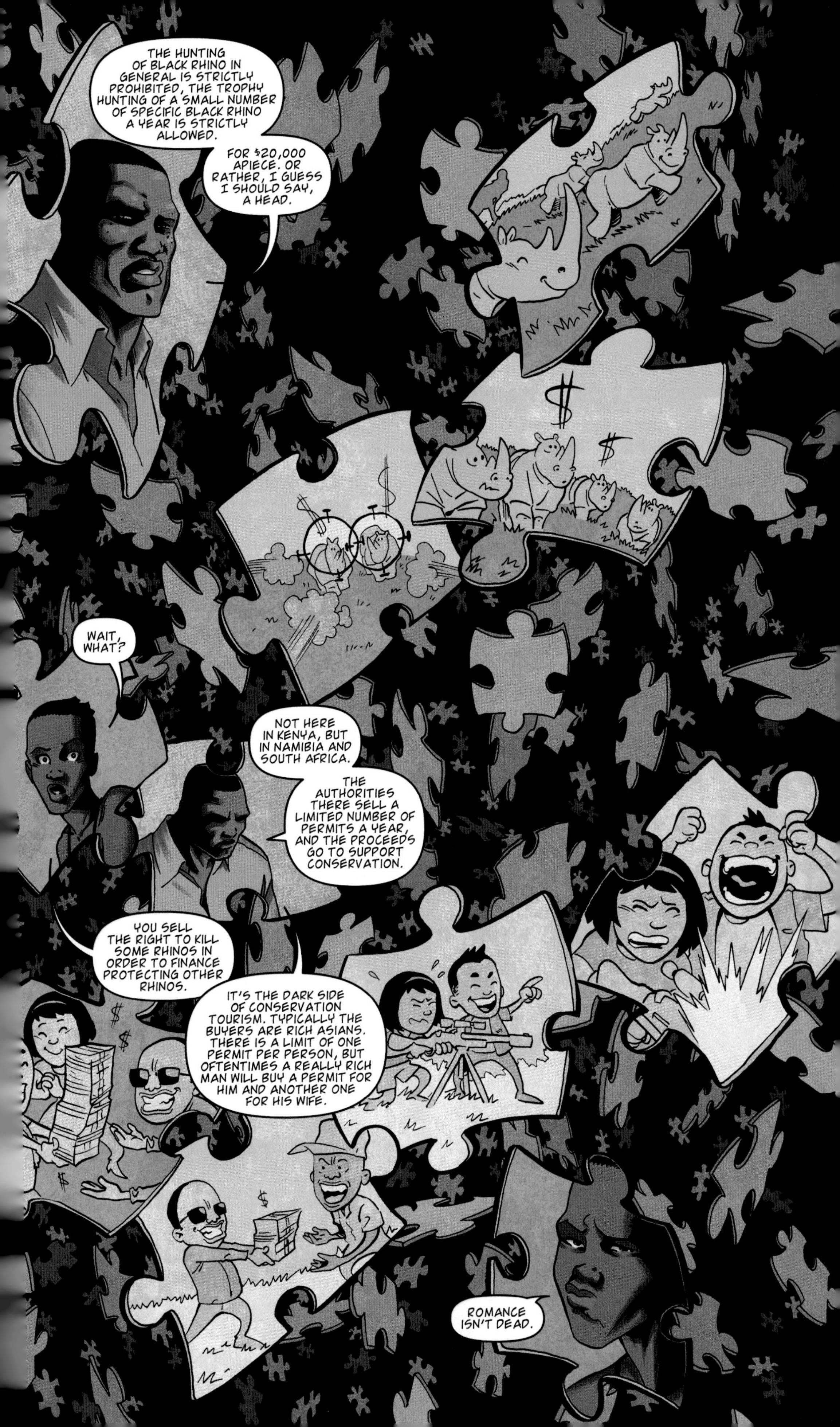
THE HUNTING OF BLACK RHINO IN GENERAL IS STRICTLY PROHIBITED, THE TROPHY HUNTING OF A SMALL NUMBER OF SPECIFIC BLACK RHINO A YEAR IS STRICTLY ALLOWED.
FOR $20,000 APIECE. OR RATHER, I GUESS I SHOULD SAY, A HEAD.
WAIT, WHAT?
NOT HERE IN KENYA, BUT IN NAMIBIA AND SOUTH AFRICA.
THE AUTHORITIES THERE SELL A LIMITED NUMBER OF PERMITS A YEAR, AND THE PROCEEDS GO TO SUPPORT CONSERVATION.
YOU SELL THE RIGHT TO KILL SOME RHINOS IN ORDER TO FINANCE PROTECTING OTHER RHINOS.
IT'S THE DARK SIDE OF CONSERVATION TOURISM. TYPICALLY THE BUYERS ARE RICH ASIANS. THERE IS A LIMIT OF ONE PERMIT PER PERSON, BUT OFTENTIMES A REALLY RICH MAN WILL BUY A PERMIT FOR HIM AND ANOTHER ONE FOR HIS WIFE.
ROMANCE ISN'T DEAD.

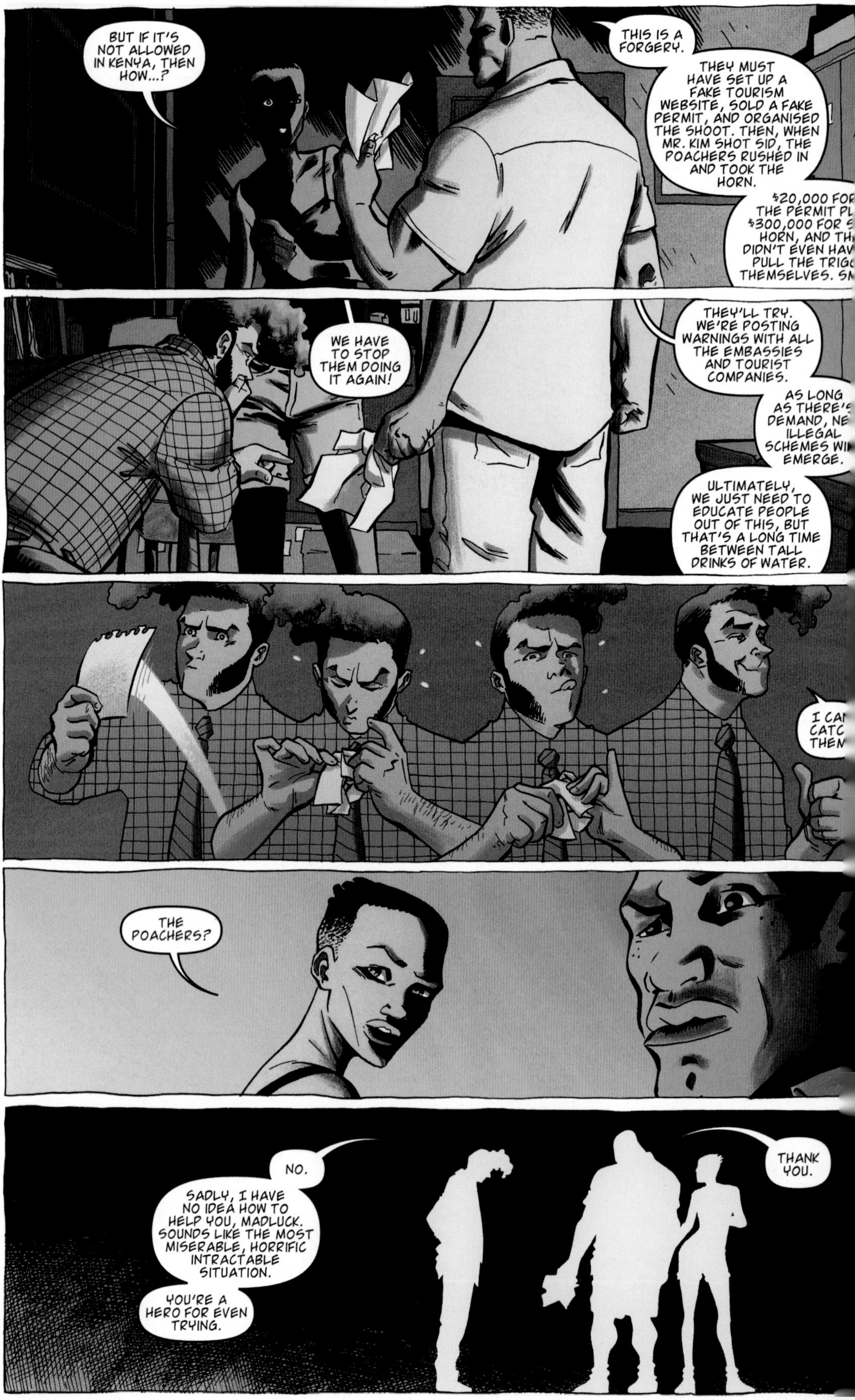

BUT IF IT'S NOT ALLOWED IN KENYA, THEN HOW...?
THIS IS A FORGERY.
THEY MUST HAVE SET UP A FAKE TOURISM WEBSITE, SOLD A FAKE PERMIT, AND ORGANISED THE SHOOT. THEN, WHEN MR. KIM SHOT SID, THE POACHERS RUSHED IN AND TOOK THE HORN.
$20,000 FOR THE PERMIT PL $300,000 FOR HORN, AND TH DIDN'T EVEN HAV PULL THE TRIG THEMSELVES.
WE HAVE TO STOP THEM DOING IT AGAIN!
THEY'LL TRY. WE'RE POSTING WARNINGS WITH ALL THE EMBASSIES AND TOURIST COMPANIES.
AS LONG AS THERE'S DEMAND, NE ILLEGAL SCHEMES WI EMERGE.
ULTIMATELY, WE JUST NEED TO EDUCATE PEOPLE OUT OF THIS, BUT THAT'S A LONG TIME BETWEEN TALL DRINKS OF WATER.
I CA CATC THEM
THE POACHERS?
NO.
SADLY, I HAVE NO IDEA HOW TO HELP YOU, MADLUCK. SOUNDS LIKE THE MOST MISERABLE, HORRIFIC INTRACTABLE SITUATION.
YOU'RE A HERO FOR EVEN TRYING.
THANK YOU.

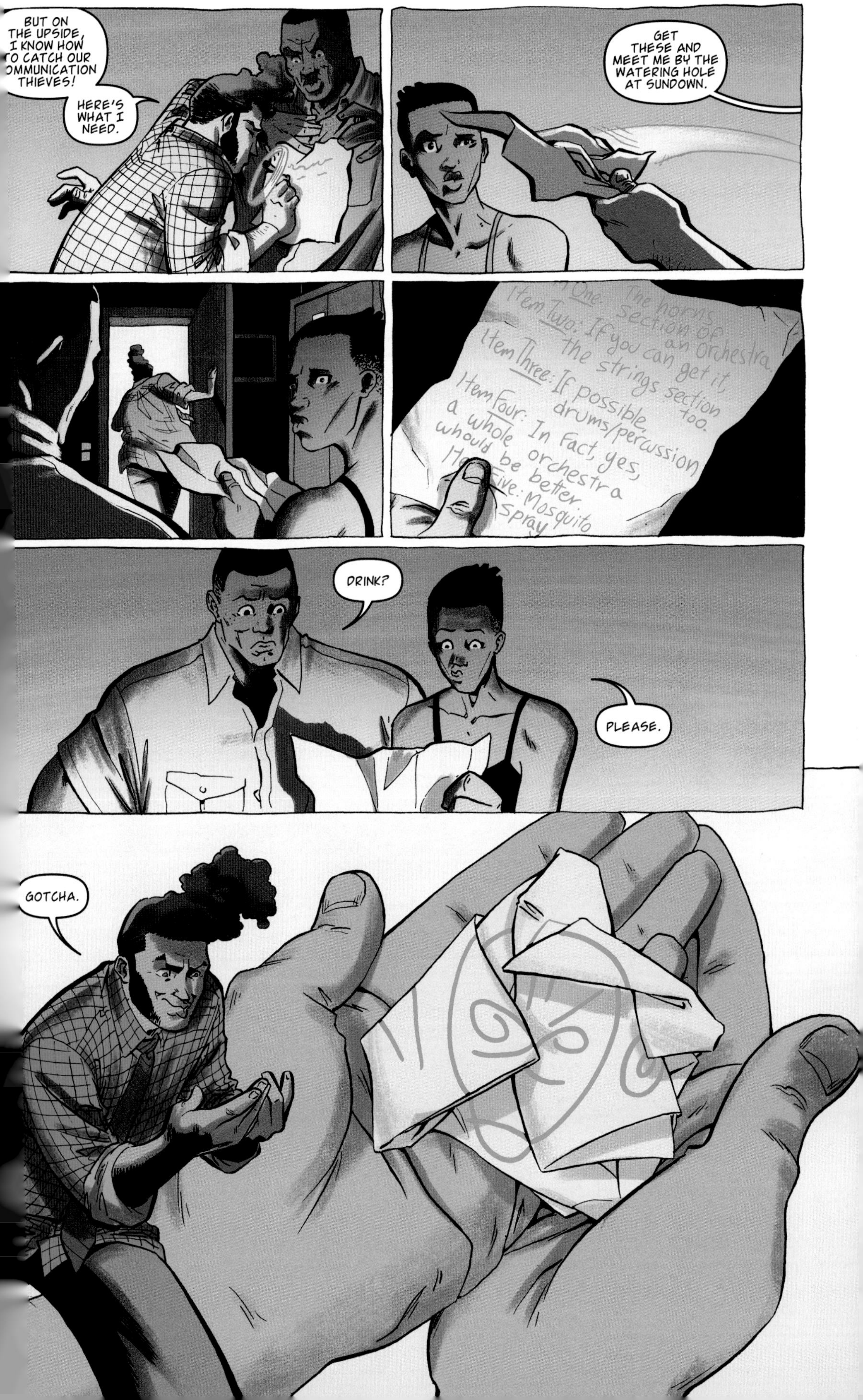
BUT ON THE UPSIDE, I KNOW HOW O CATCH OUR OMMUNICATION THIEVES!
HERE'S WHAT I NEED.
GET THESE AND MEET ME BY THE WATERING HOLE AT SUNDOWN.
One: The horns section of an Orchestra.
Item Two: If you can get it, the strings section too.
Item Three: If possible, drums/percussion.
Item Four: In Fact, yes, a whole orchestra whould be better.
Ite Five: Mosquito spray
DRINK?
PLEASE.
GOTCHA.

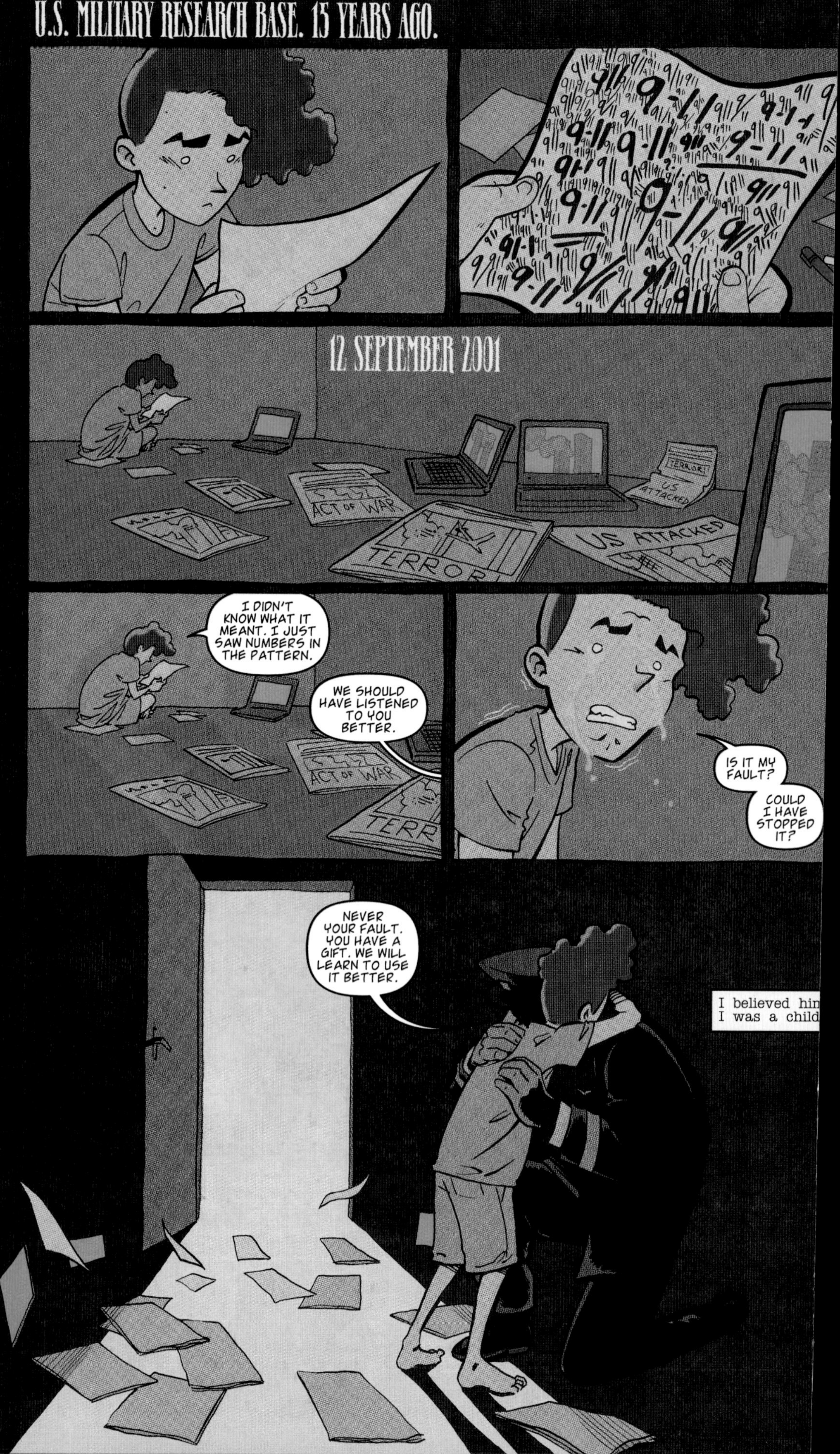
U.S. MILITARY RESEARCH BASE. 15 YEARS AGO.
12 SEPTEMBER 2001
ACT OF WAR
TERROR
US ATTACKED
I DIDN'T KNOW WHAT IT MEANT. I JUST SAW NUMBERS IN THE PATTERN.
WE SHOULD HAVE LISTENED TO YOU BETTER.
IS IT MY FAULT?
COULD I HAVE STOPPED IT?
NEVER YOUR FAULT. YOU HAVE A GIFT. WE WILL LEARN TO USE IT BETTER.
I believed hin
I was a child

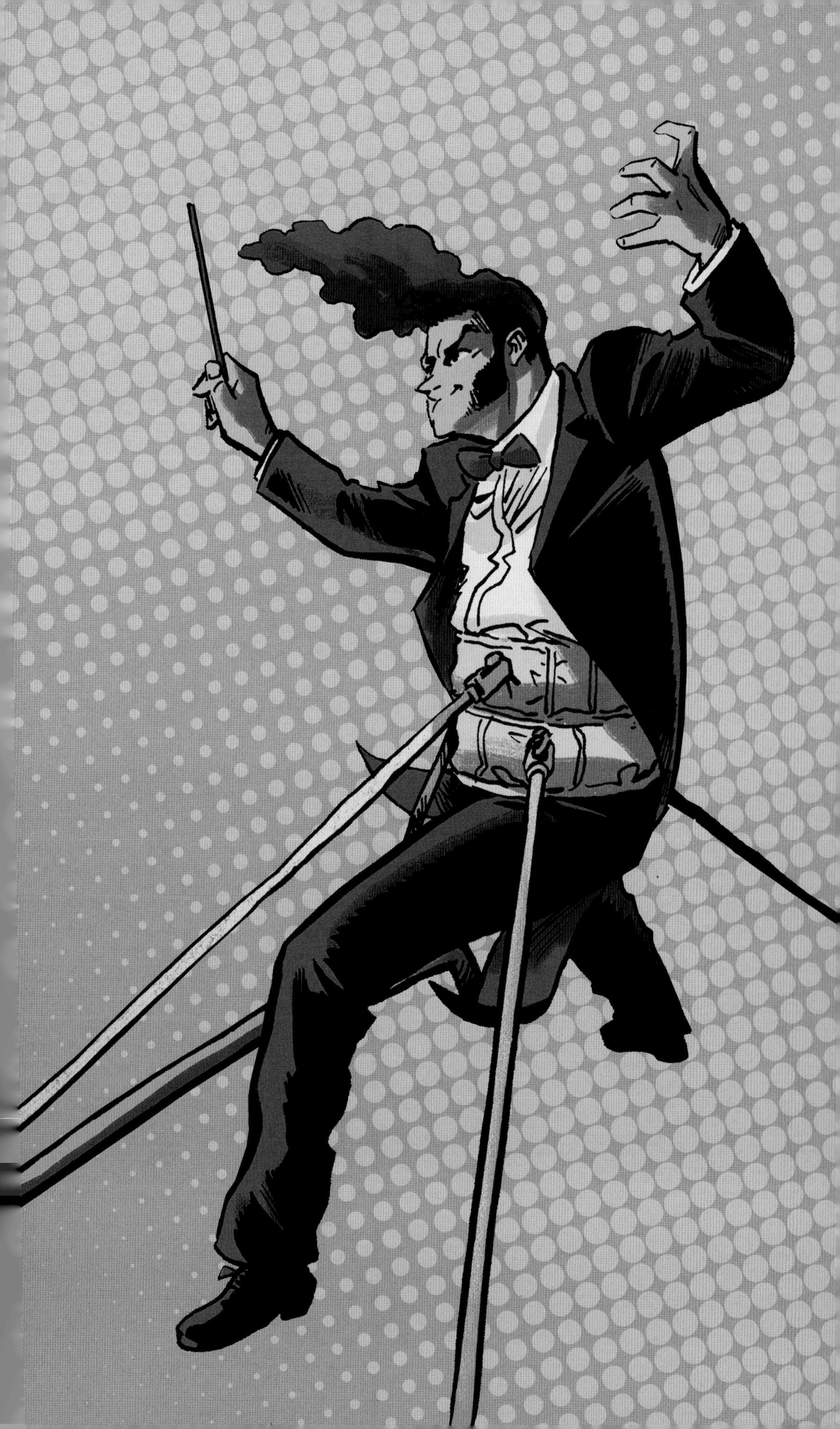

CHAPTER
FOUR

Cover Art by ILIAS KYRIAZ

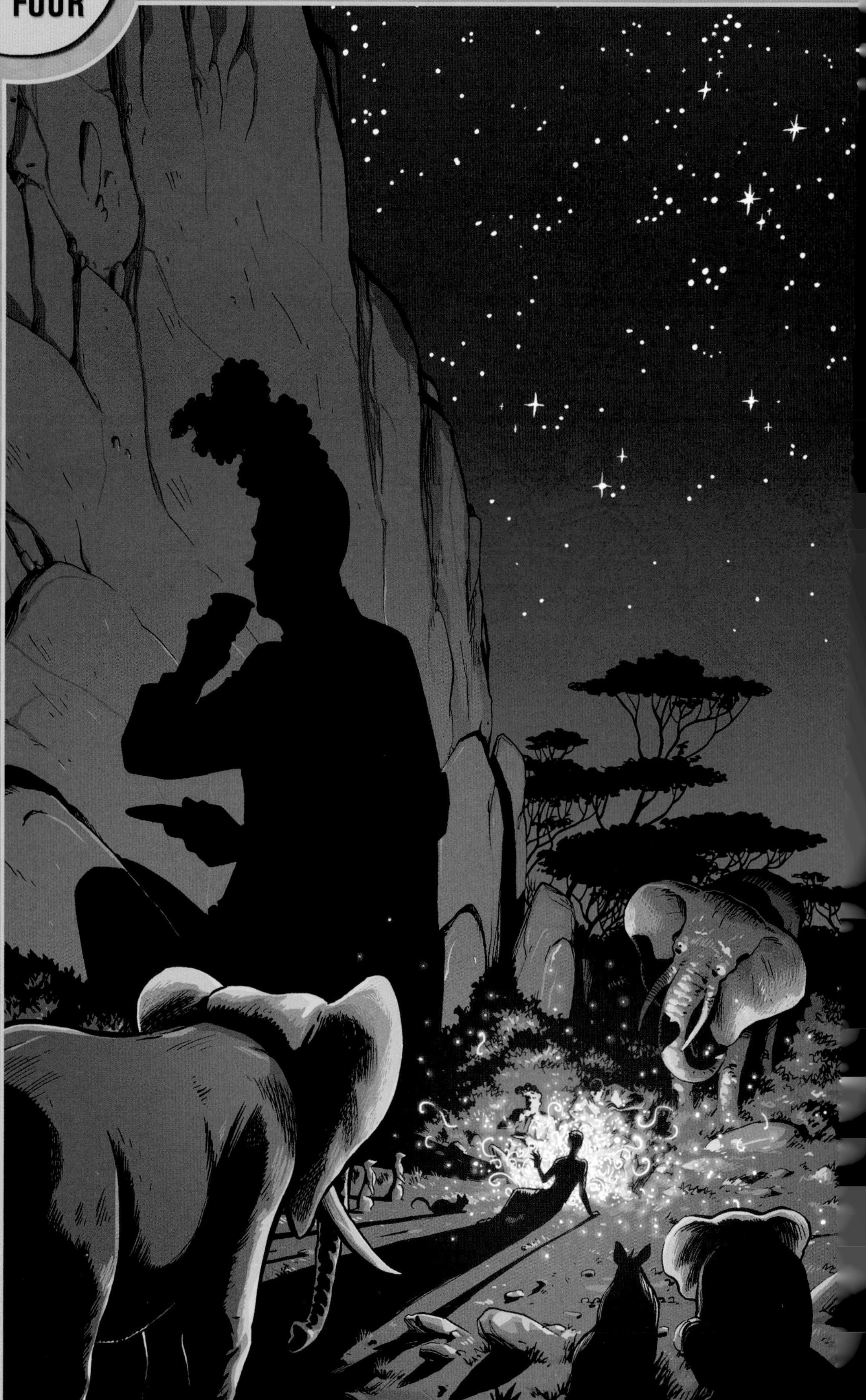

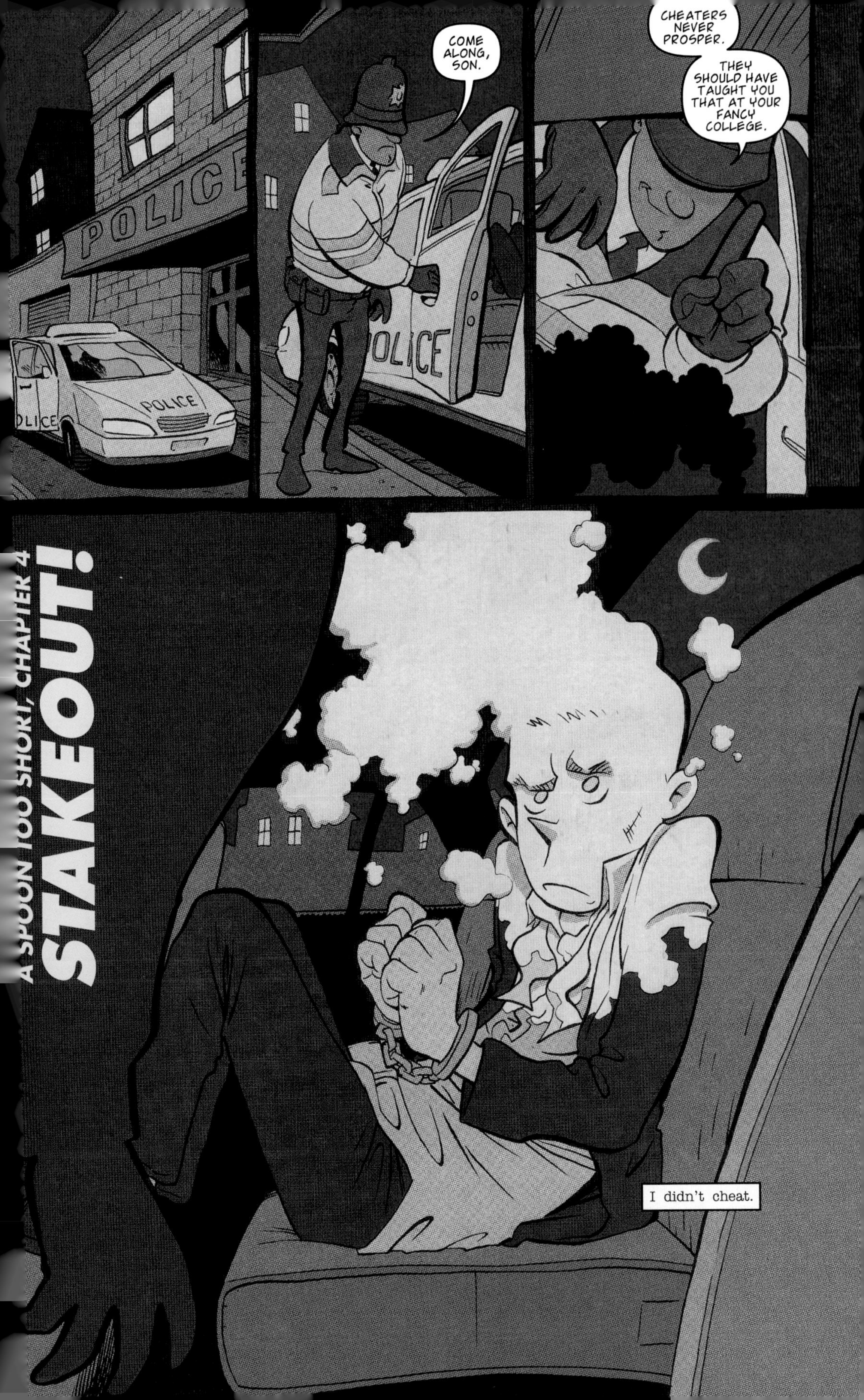
COME ALONG, SON.
CHEATERS NEVER PROSPER.
THEY SHOULD HAVE TAUGHT YOU THAT AT YOUR FANCY COLLEGE.
A SPOON TOO SHORT, CHAPTER 4
STAKEOUT!
I didn't cheat.

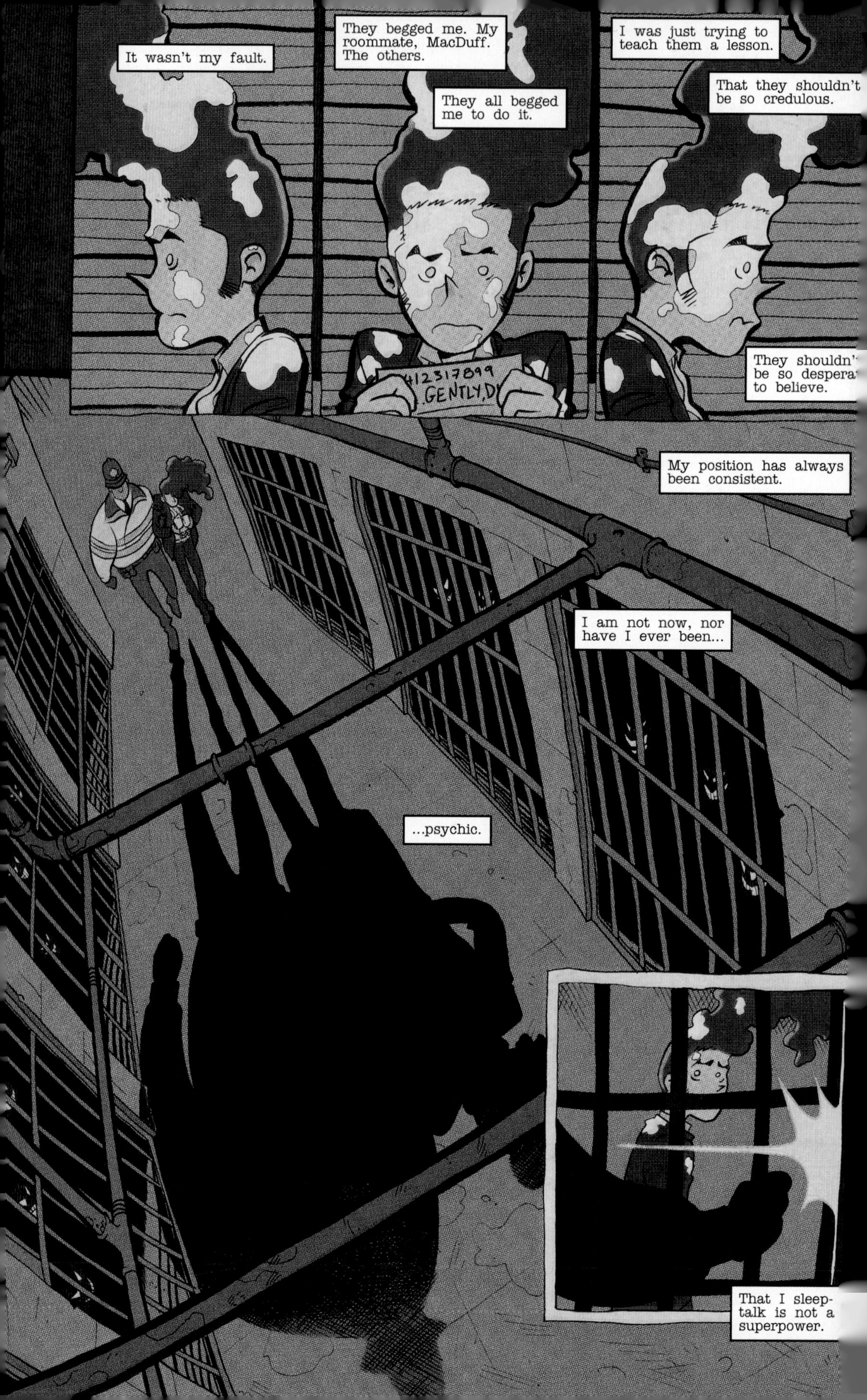
It wasn't my fault.
They begged me. My roommate, MacDuff. The others.
They all begged me to do it.
412317899
GENTLY, D
I was just trying to teach them a lesson.
That they shouldn't be so credulous.
They shouldn't be so despera to believe.
My position has always been consistent.
I am not now, nor have I ever been...
...psychic.
That I sleep-talk is not a superpower.

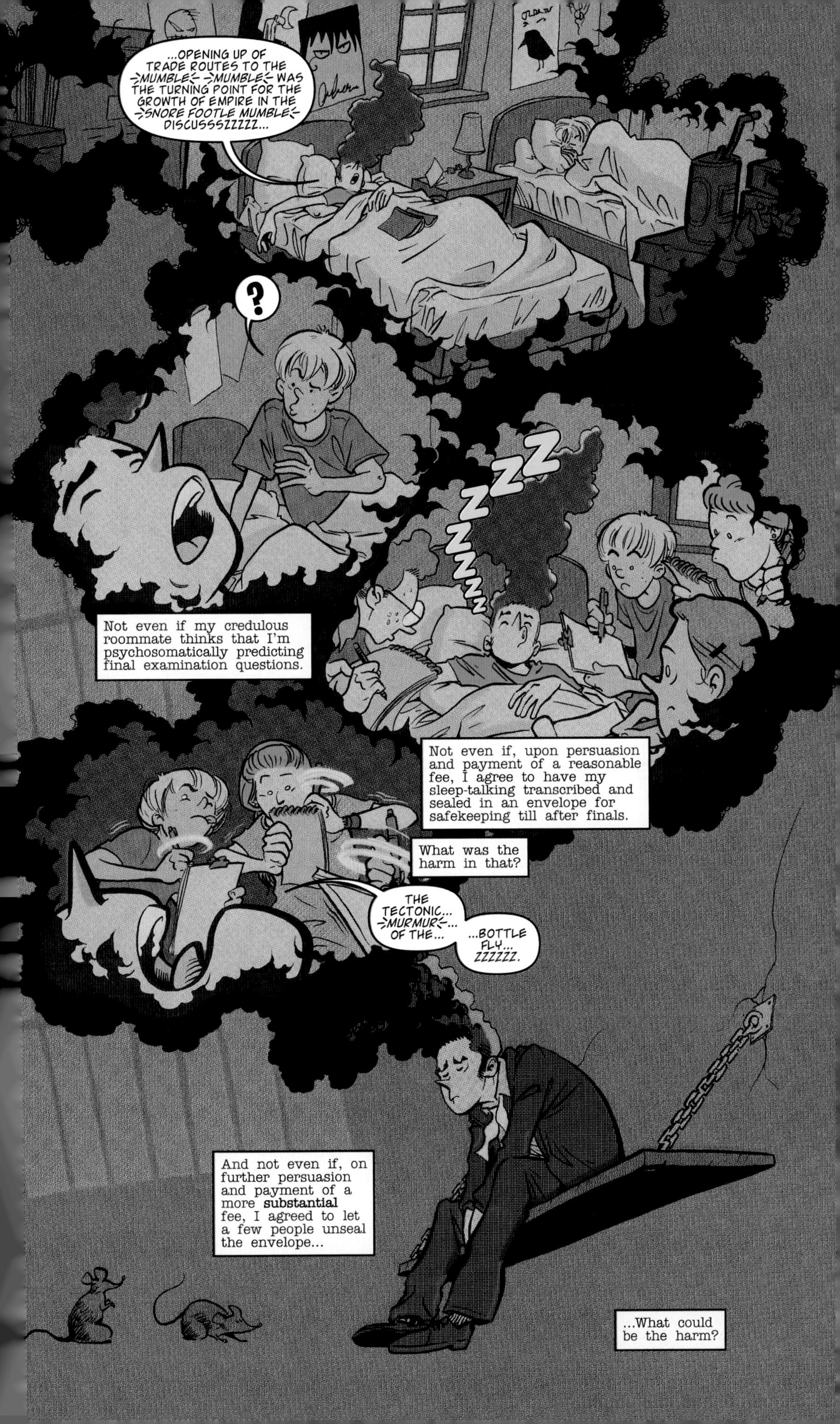
...OPENING UP OF TRADE ROUTES TO THE MUMBLE MUMBLE WAS THE TURNING POINT FOR THE GROWTH OF EMPIRE IN THE SNORE FOOTLE MUMBLE DISCUSSSZZZZZ...
?
ZZZZZZZ
Not even if my credulous roommate thinks that I'm psychosomatically predicting final examination questions.
Not even if, upon persuasion and payment of a reasonable fee, I agree to have my sleep-talking transcribed and sealed in an envelope for safekeeping till after finals.
What was the harm in that?
THE TECTONIC... MURMUR... OF THE...
...BOTTLE FLY... ZZZZZZ.
And not even if, on further persuasion and payment of a more **substantial** fee, I agreed to let a few people unseal the envelope...
...What could be the harm?

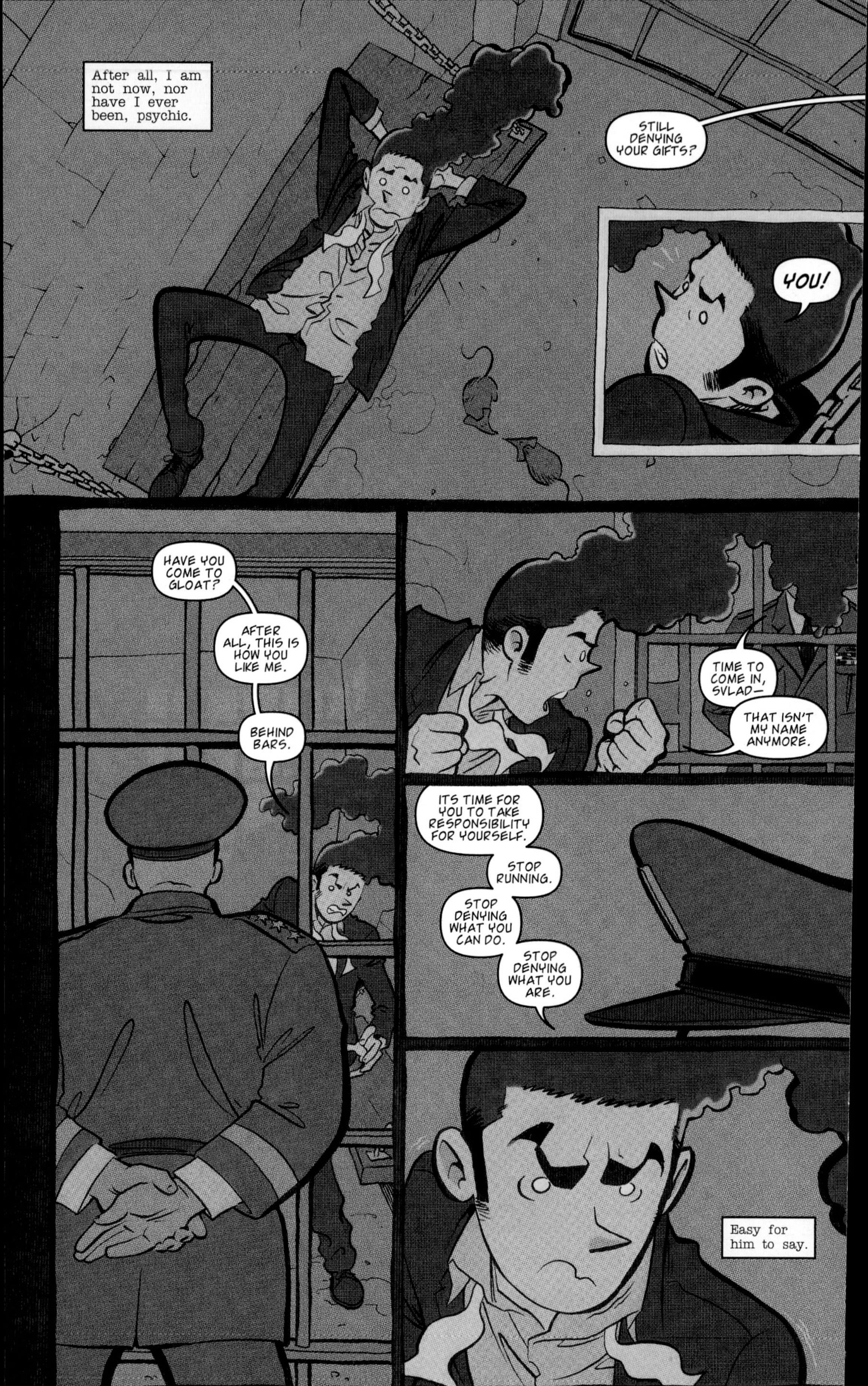
After all, I am not now, nor have I ever been, psychic.
STILL DENYING YOUR GIFTS?
YOU!
HAVE YOU COME TO GLOAT?
AFTER ALL, THIS IS HOW YOU LIKE ME.
BEHIND BARS.
TIME TO COME IN, SVLAD—
THAT ISN'T MY NAME ANYMORE.
ITS TIME FOR YOU TO TAKE RESPONSIBILITY FOR YOURSELF.
STOP RUNNING.
STOP DENYING WHAT YOU CAN DO.
STOP DENYING WHAT YOU ARE.
Easy for him to say.

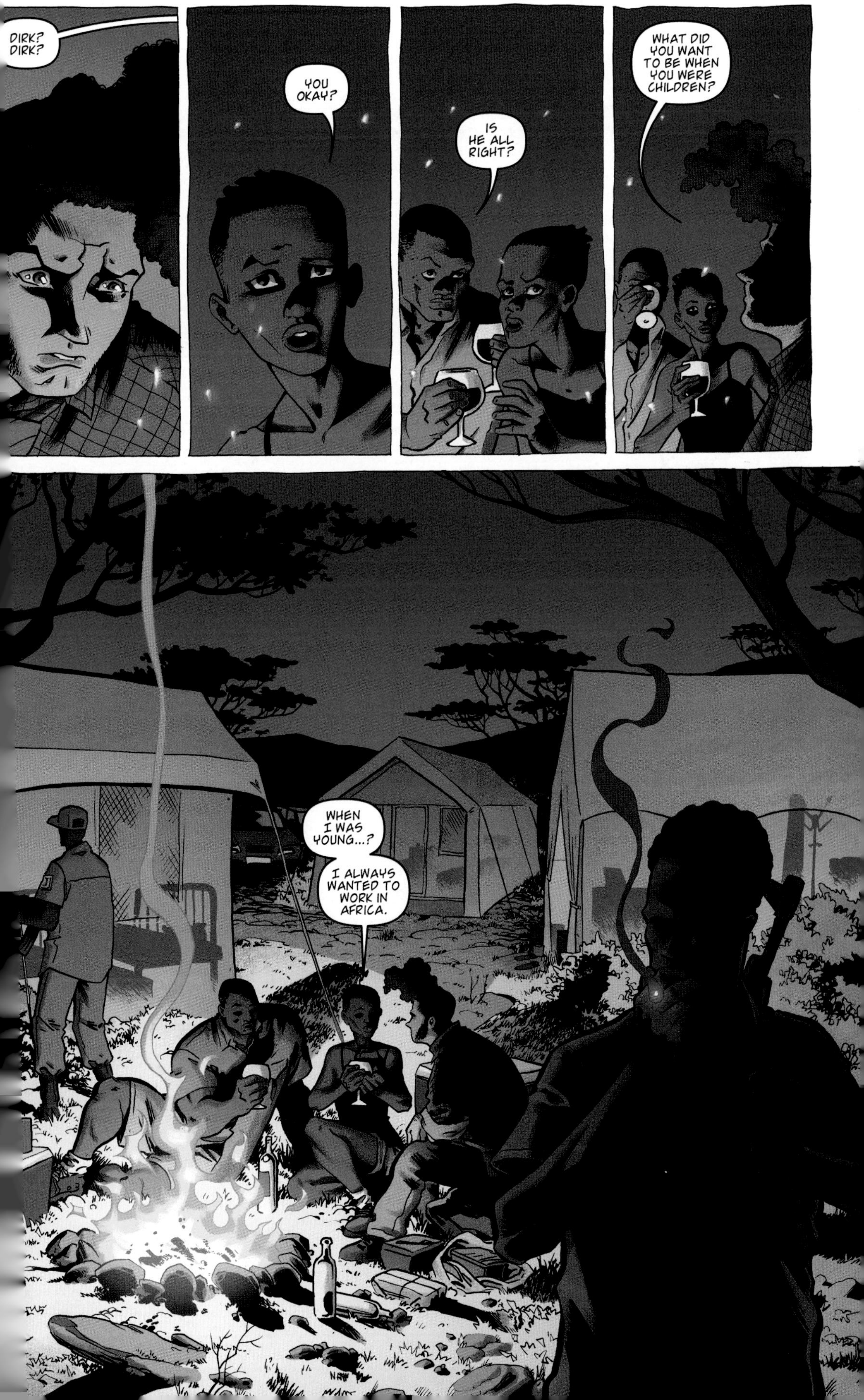
DIRK? DIRK?
YOU OKAY?
IS HE ALL RIGHT?
WHAT DID YOU WANT TO BE WHEN YOU WERE CHILDREN?
WHEN I WAS YOUNG...?
I ALWAYS WANTED TO WORK IN AFRICA.

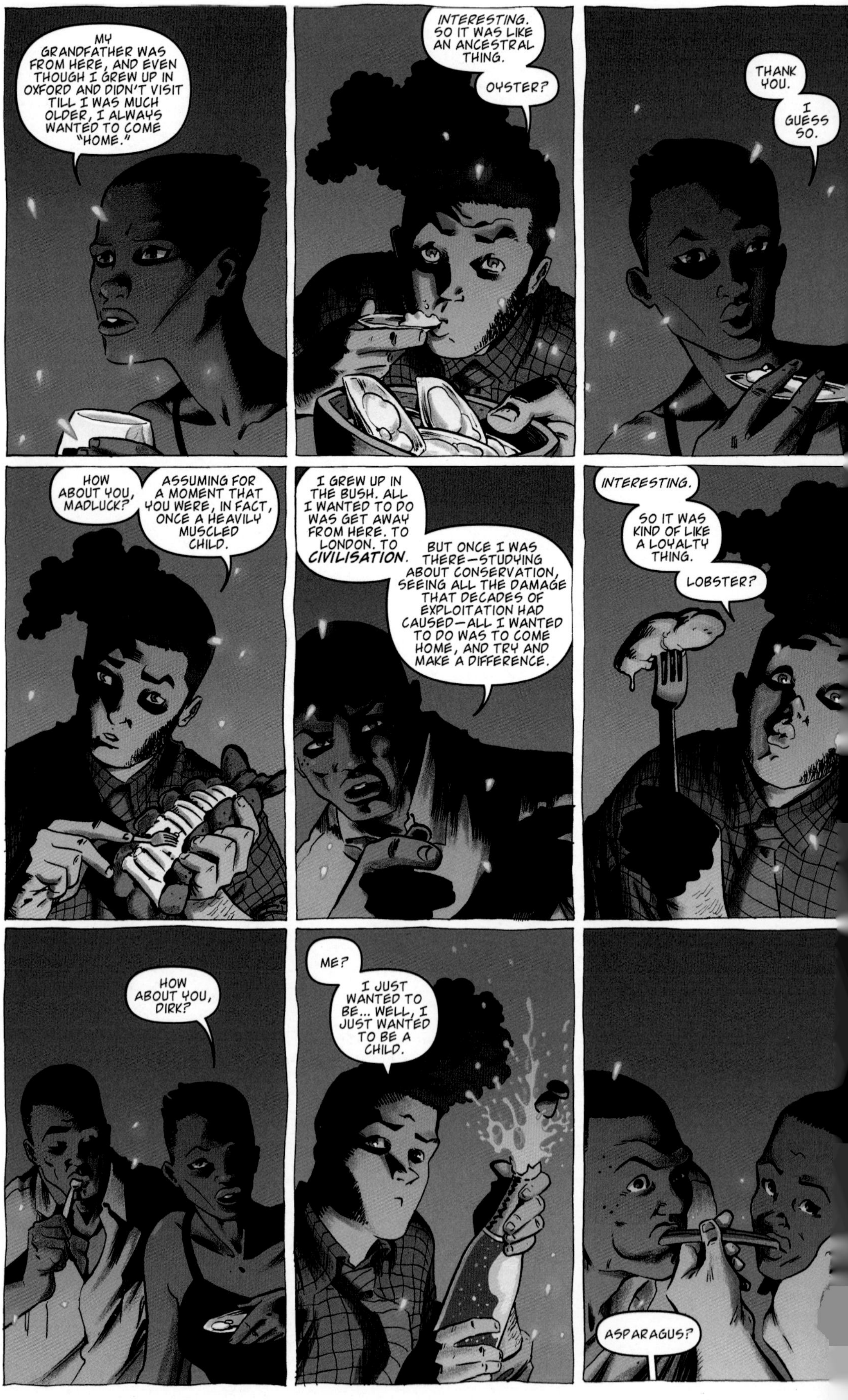
MY GRANDFATHER WAS FROM HERE, AND EVEN THOUGH I GREW UP IN OXFORD AND DIDN'T VISIT TILL I WAS MUCH OLDER, I ALWAYS WANTED TO COME "HOME."
INTERESTING. SO IT WAS LIKE AN ANCESTRAL THING.
OYSTER?
THANK YOU.
I GUESS SO.
HOW ABOUT YOU, MADLUCK?
ASSUMING FOR A MOMENT THAT YOU WERE, IN FACT, ONCE A HEAVILY MUSCLED CHILD.
I GREW UP IN THE BUSH. ALL I WANTED TO DO WAS GET AWAY FROM HERE. TO LONDON. TO CIVILISATION.
BUT ONCE I WAS THERE—STUDYING ABOUT CONSERVATION, SEEING ALL THE DAMAGE THAT DECADES OF EXPLOITATION HAD CAUSED—ALL I WANTED TO DO WAS TO COME HOME, AND TRY AND MAKE A DIFFERENCE.
INTERESTING.
SO IT WAS KIND OF LIKE A LOYALTY THING.
LOBSTER?
HOW ABOUT YOU, DIRK?
ME?
I JUST WANTED TO BE... WELL, I JUST WANTED TO BE A CHILD.
ASPARAGUS?

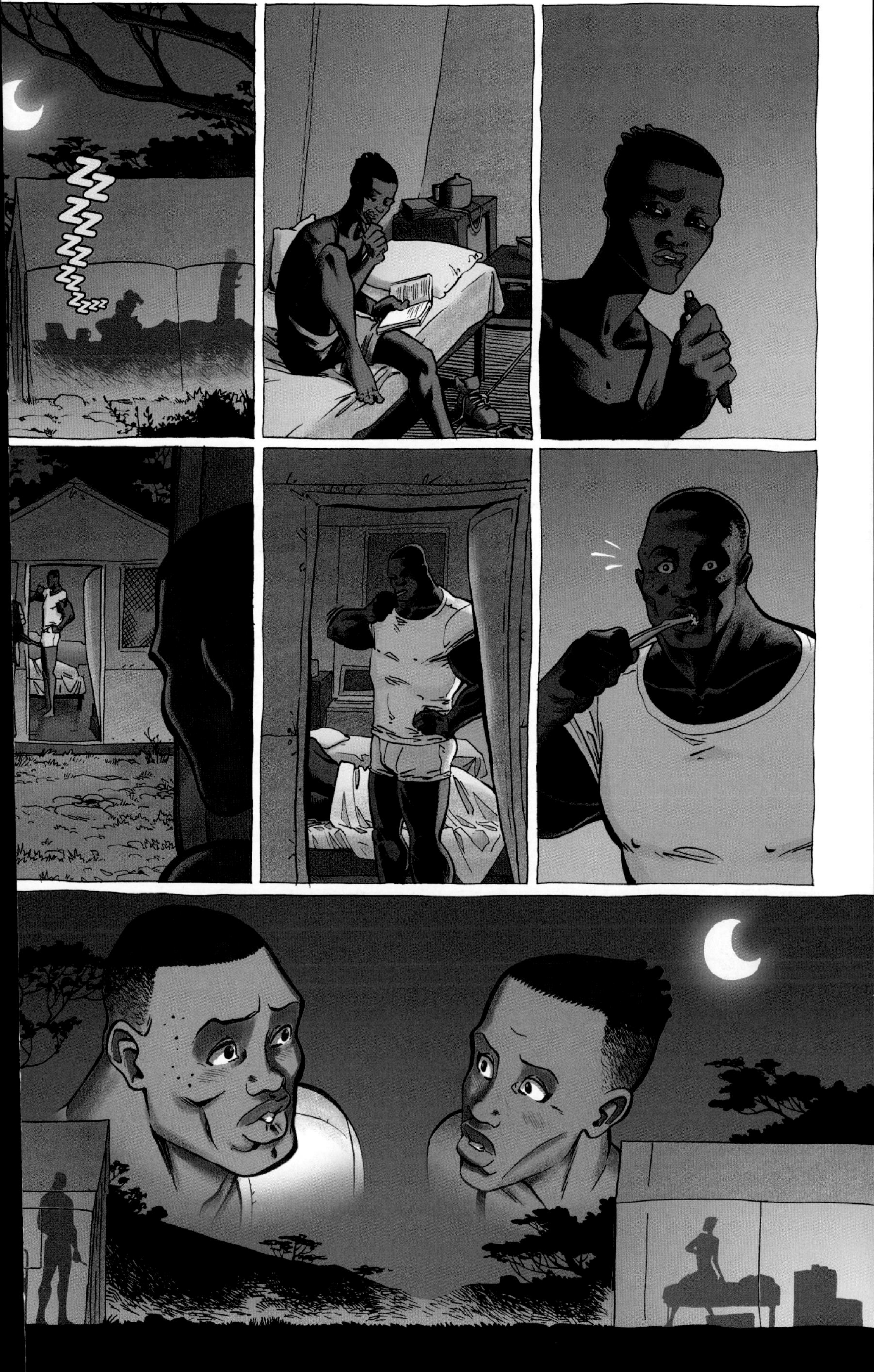

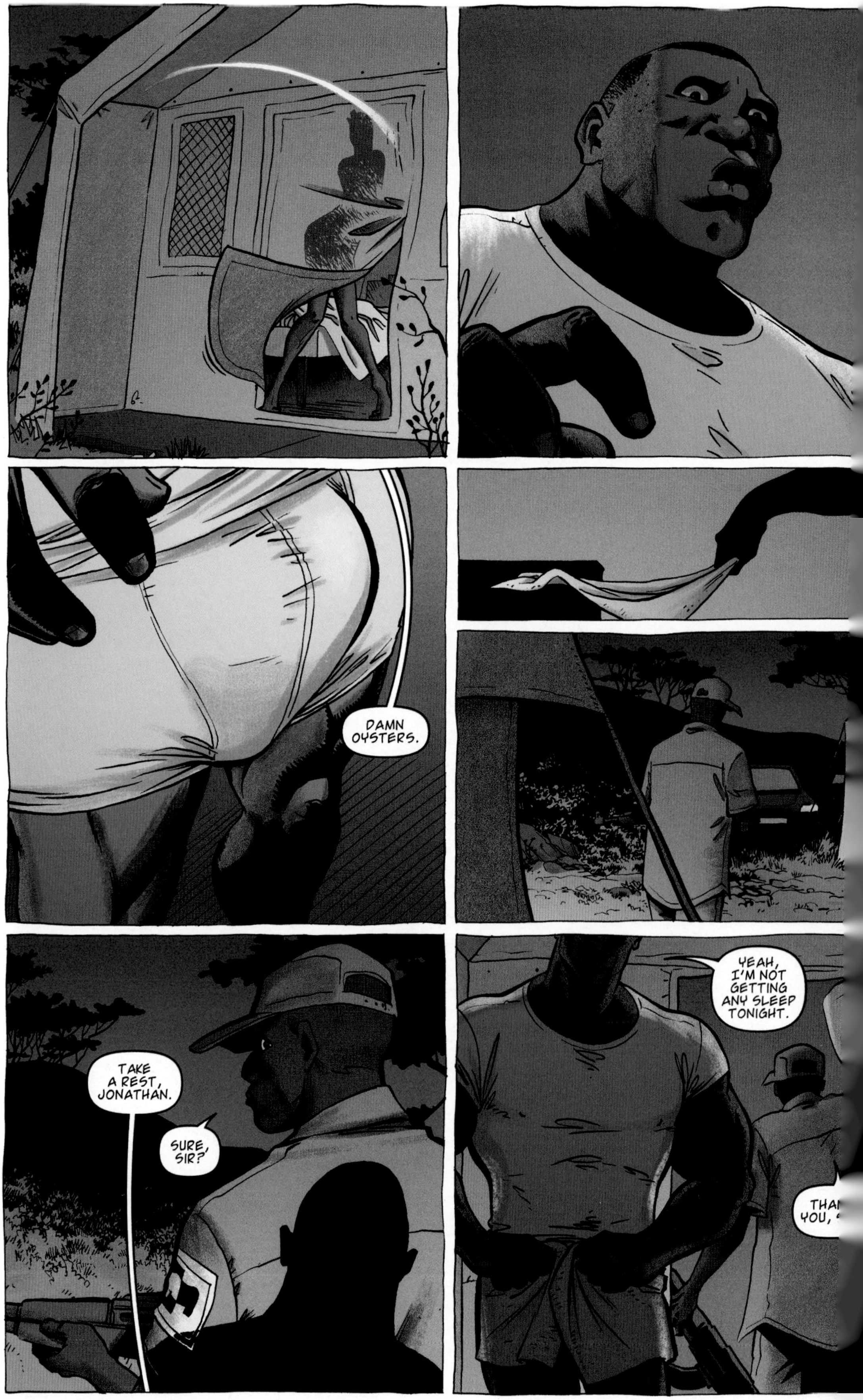
DAMN OYSTERS.
TAKE A REST, JONATHAN.
SURE, SIR?'
YEAH, I'M NOT GETTING ANY SLEEP TONIGHT.
THA YOU,

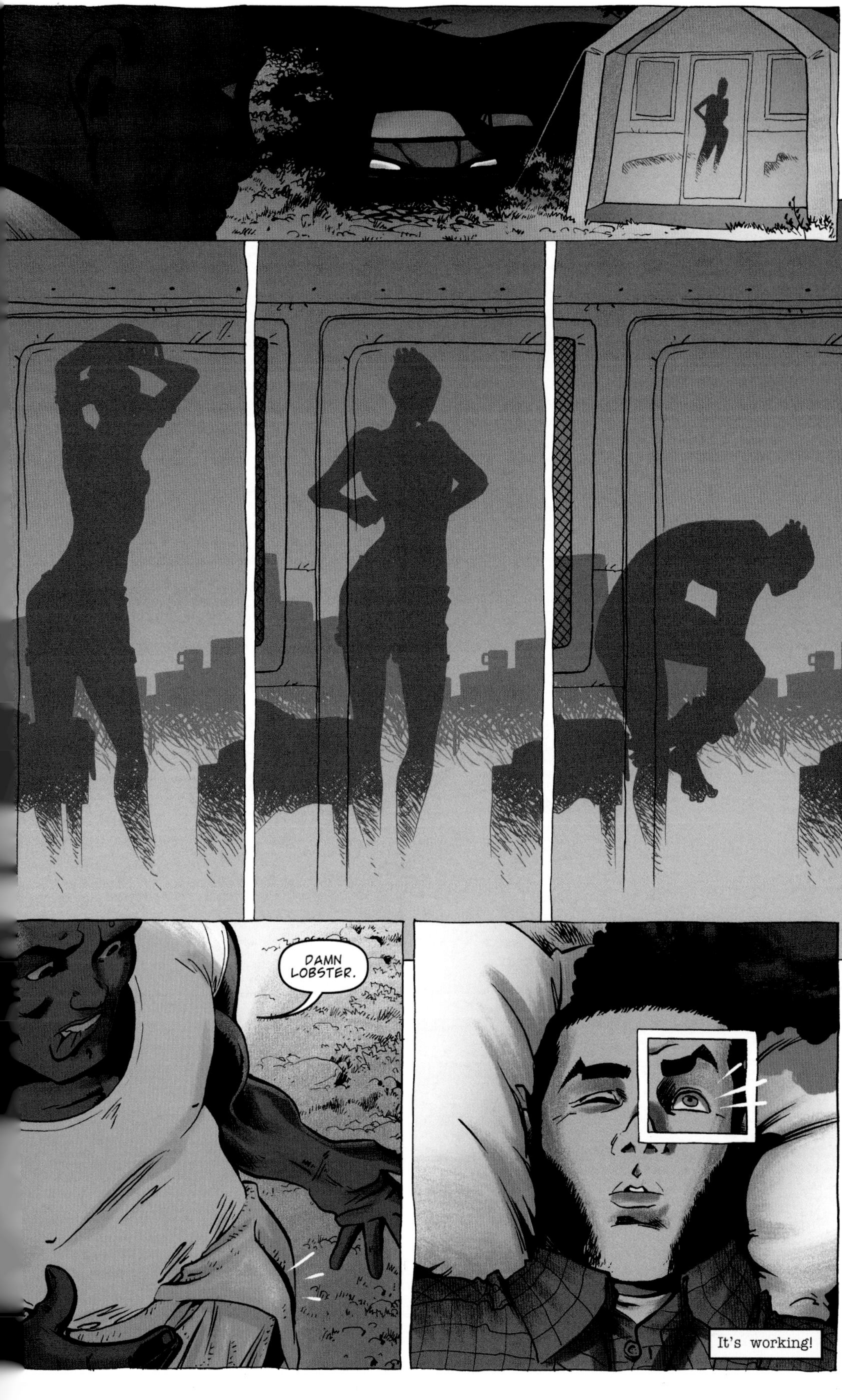
DAMN LOBSTER.
It's working!

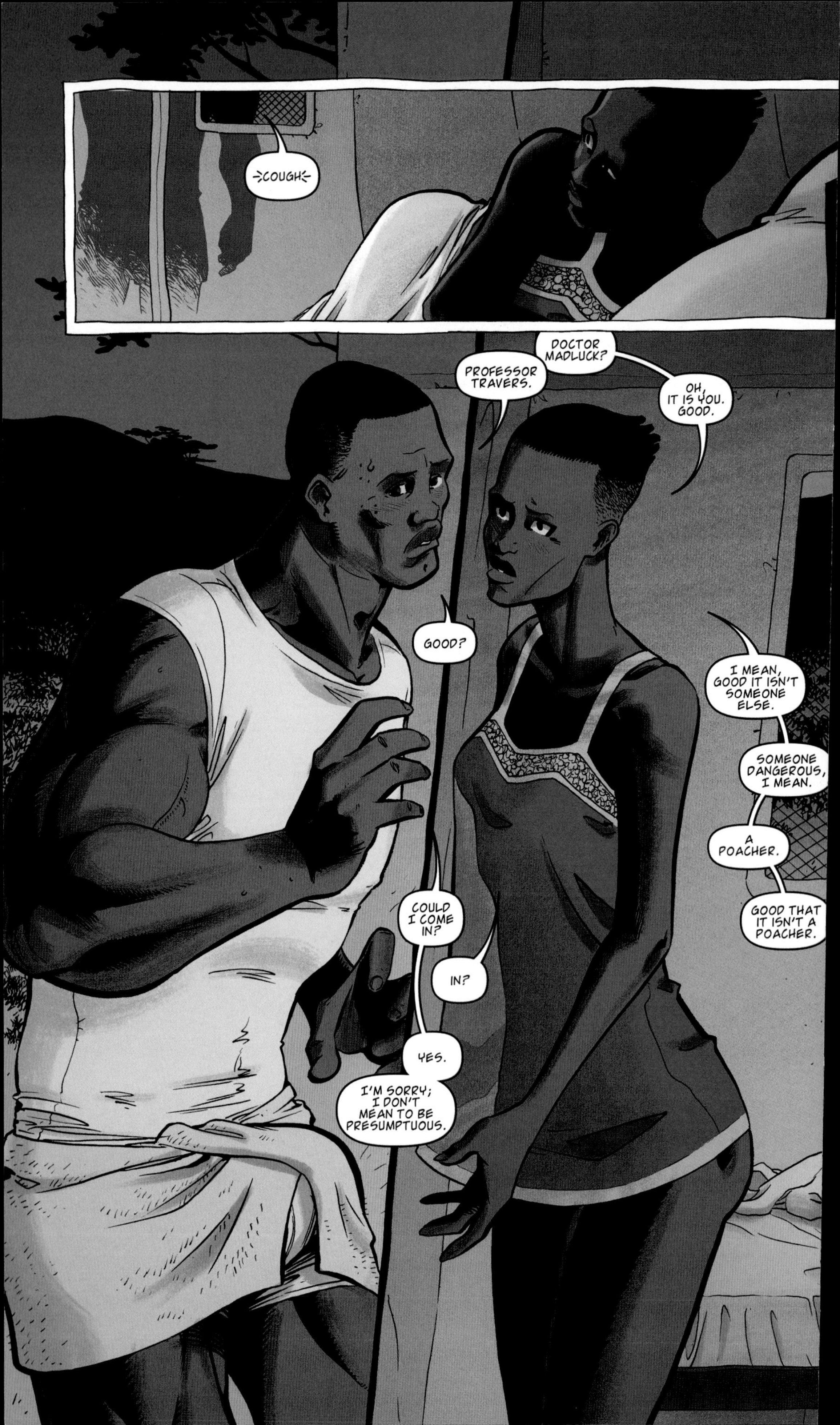
COUGH
DOCTOR MADLUCK?
PROFESSOR TRAVERS.
OH, IT IS YOU. GOOD.
GOOD?
I MEAN, GOOD IT ISN'T SOMEONE ELSE.
SOMEONE DANGEROUS, I MEAN.
A POACHER.
GOOD THAT IT ISN'T A POACHER.
COULD I COME IN?
IN?
YES.
I'M SORRY; I DON'T MEAN TO BE PRESUMPTUOUS.

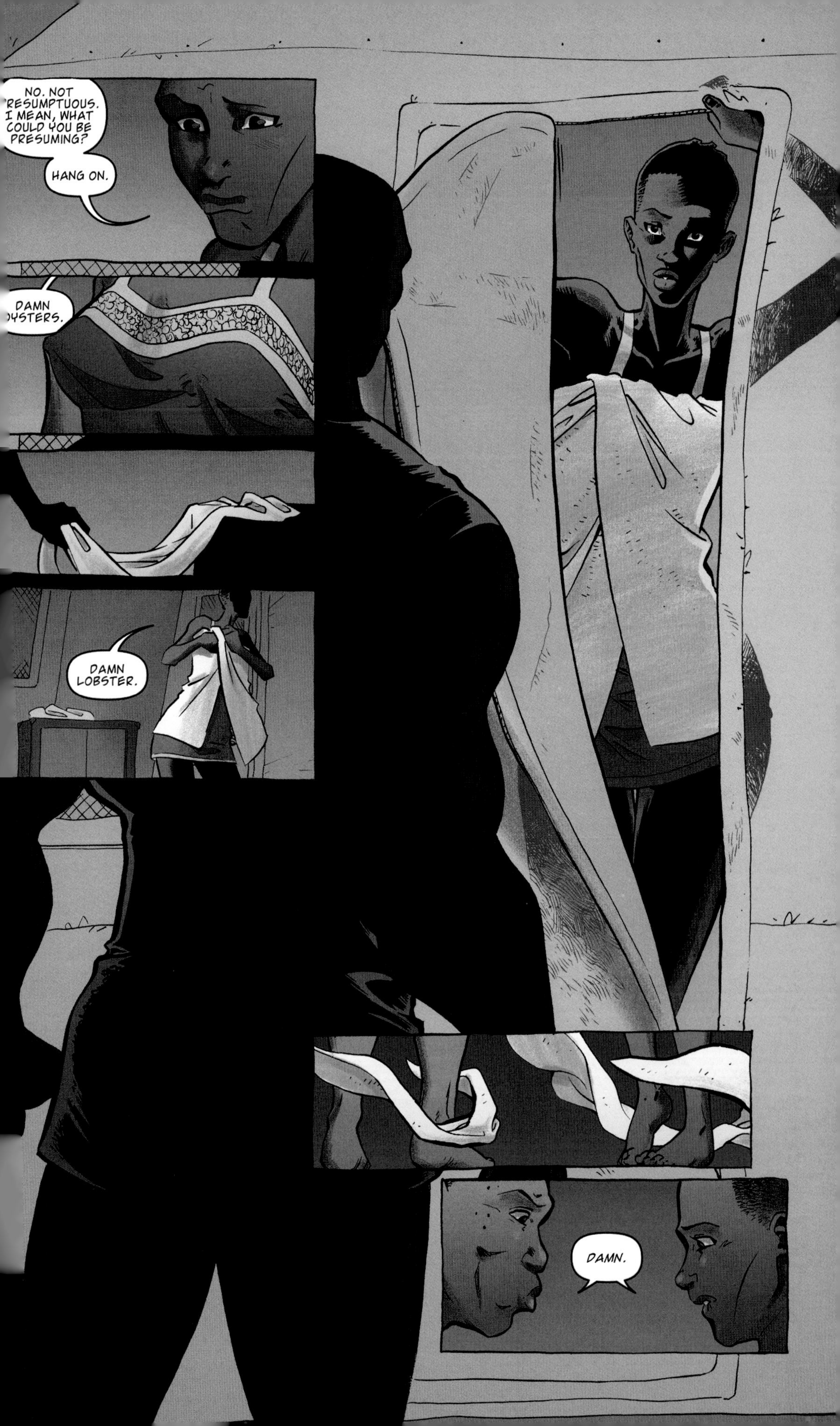
NO. NOT PRESUMPTUOUS. I MEAN, WHAT COULD YOU BE PRESUMING?
HANG ON.
DAMN OYSTERS.
DAMN LOBSTER.
DAMN.

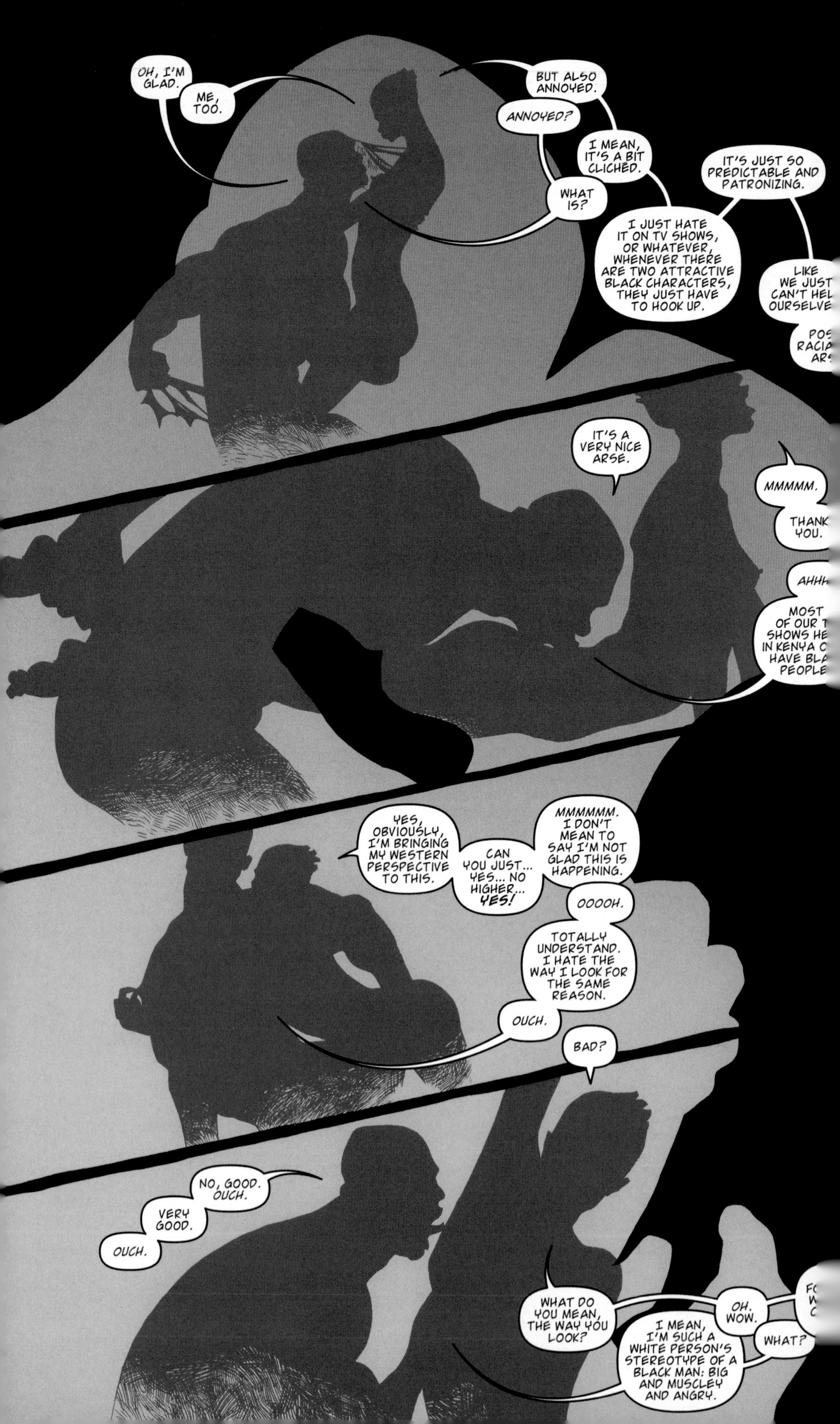
OH, I'M GLAD.
ME, TOO.
BUT ALSO ANNOYED.
ANNOYED?
I MEAN, IT'S A BIT CLICHED.
WHAT IS?
I JUST HATE IT ON TV SHOWS, OR WHATEVER, WHENEVER THERE ARE TWO ATTRACTIVE BLACK CHARACTERS, THEY JUST HAVE TO HOOK UP.
IT'S JUST SO PREDICTABLE AND PATRONIZING.
LIKE WE JUST CAN'T HEL OURSELVE
POS RACIA ARS
IT'S A VERY NICE ARSE.
MMMMM.
THANK YOU.
AHHH
MOST OF OUR T SHOWS HE IN KENYA C HAVE BLA PEOPLE
YES, OBVIOUSLY, I'M BRINGING MY WESTERN PERSPECTIVE TO THIS.
MMMMMM. I DON'T MEAN TO SAY I'M NOT GLAD THIS IS HAPPENING.
CAN YOU JUST... YES... NO HIGHER... YES!
OOOOH.
TOTALLY UNDERSTAND. I HATE THE WAY I LOOK FOR THE SAME REASON.
OUCH.
BAD?
NO, GOOD. OUCH.
VERY GOOD.
OUCH.
WHAT DO YOU MEAN, THE WAY YOU LOOK?
OH. WOW.
I MEAN, I'M SUCH A WHITE PERSON'S STEREOTYPE OF A BLACK MAN: BIG AND MUSCLEY AND ANGRY.
WHAT?

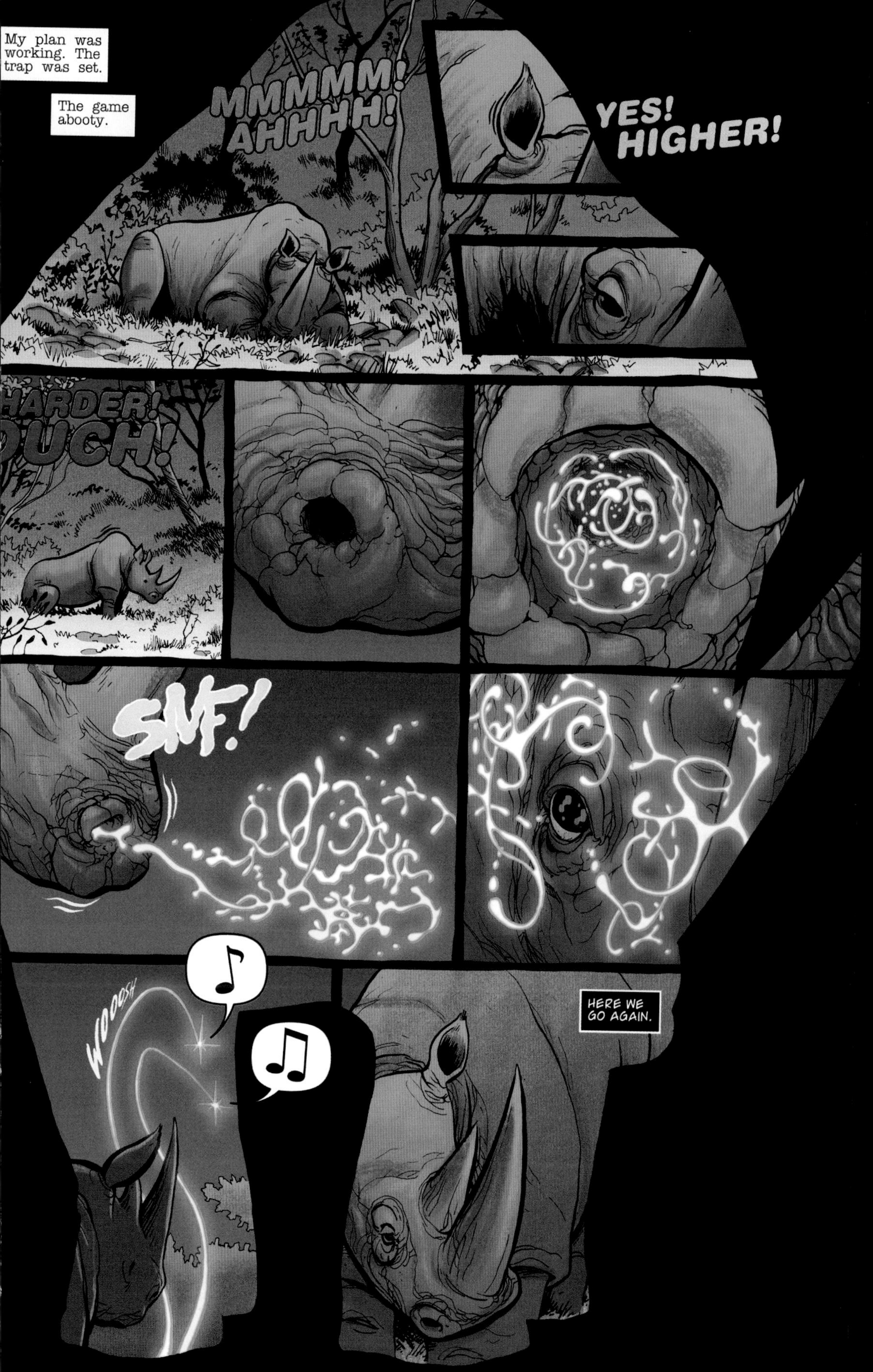
My plan was working. The trap was set.
The game abooty.
MMMMMM! AHHHH!
YES! HIGHER!
HARDER! OUCH!
SNF!
WOOOSH
♪
♫
HERE WE GO AGAIN.

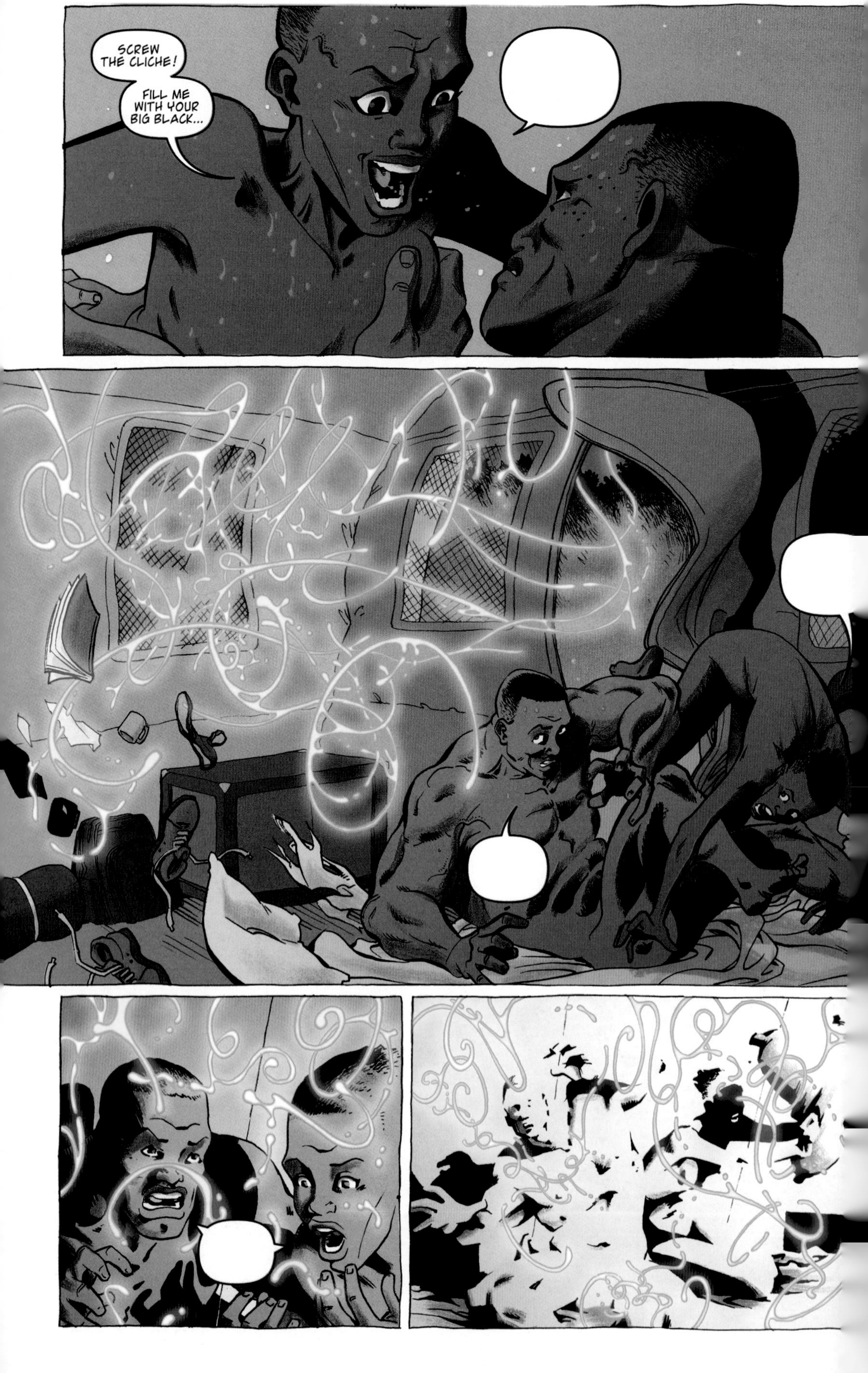
SCREW THE CLICHE!
FILL ME WITH YOUR BIG BLACK...

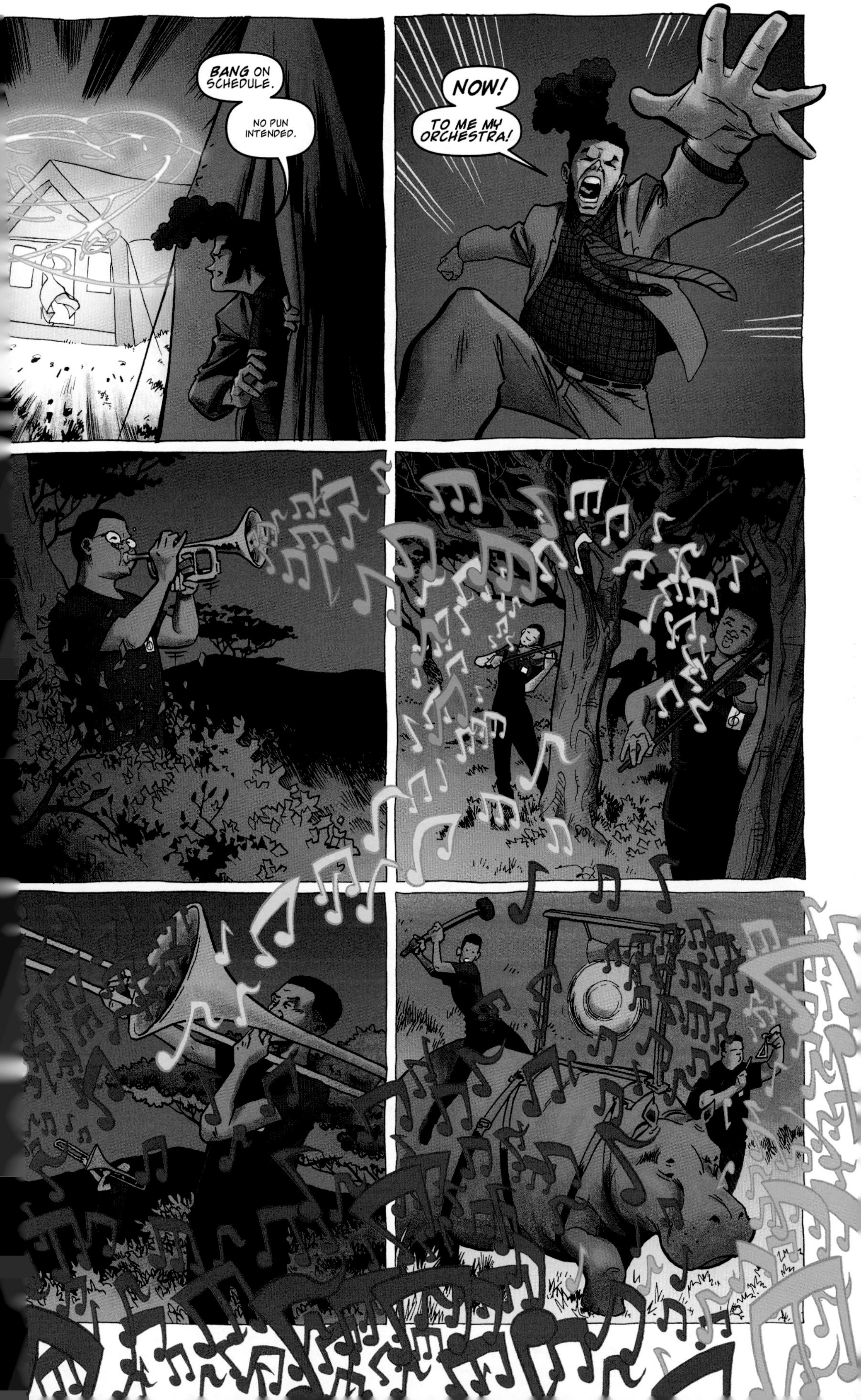
BANG ON SCHEDULE.
NO PUN INTENDED.
NOW!
TO ME MY ORCHESTRA!

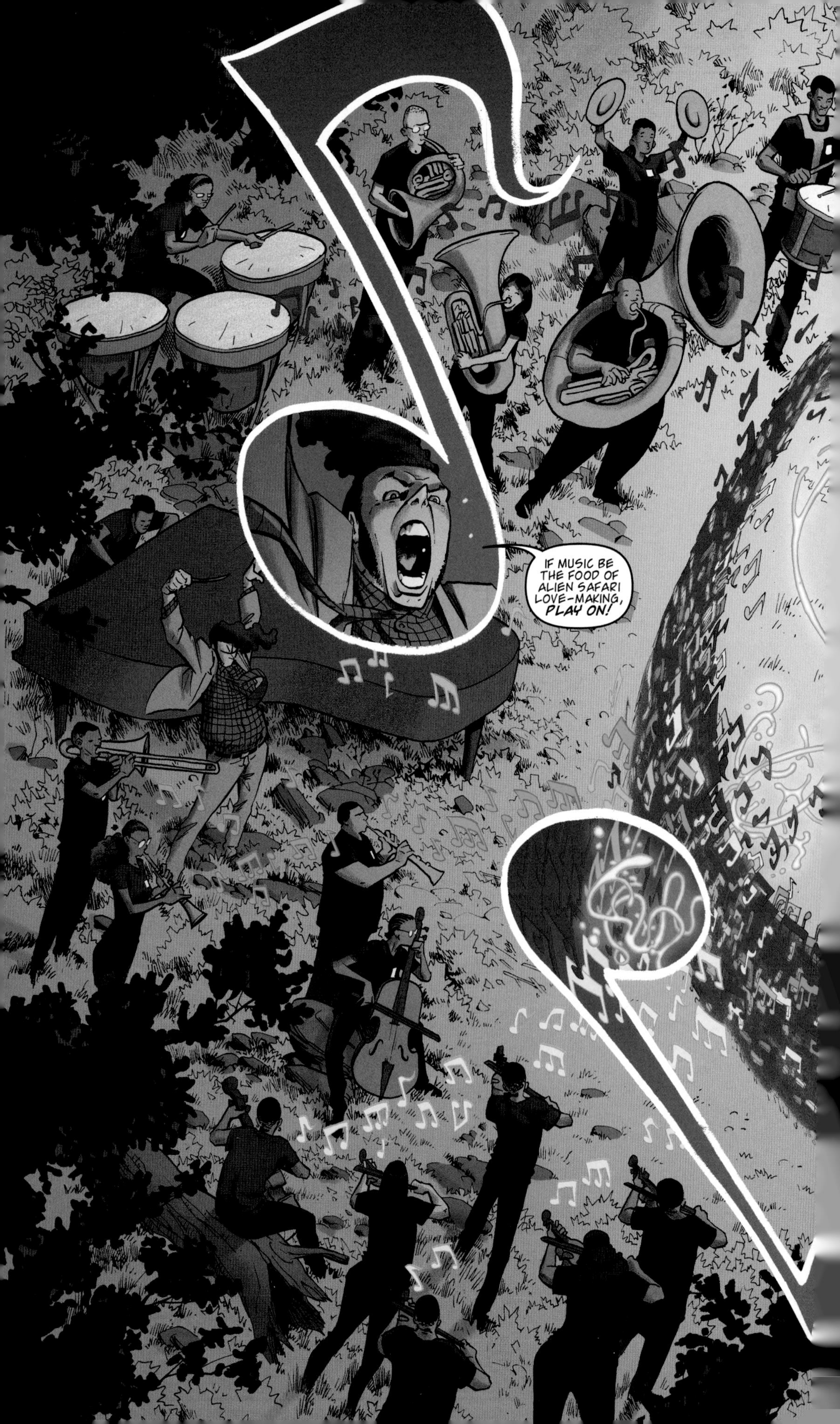
IF MUSIC BE THE FOOD OF ALIEN SAFARI LOVE-MAKING, PLAY ON!

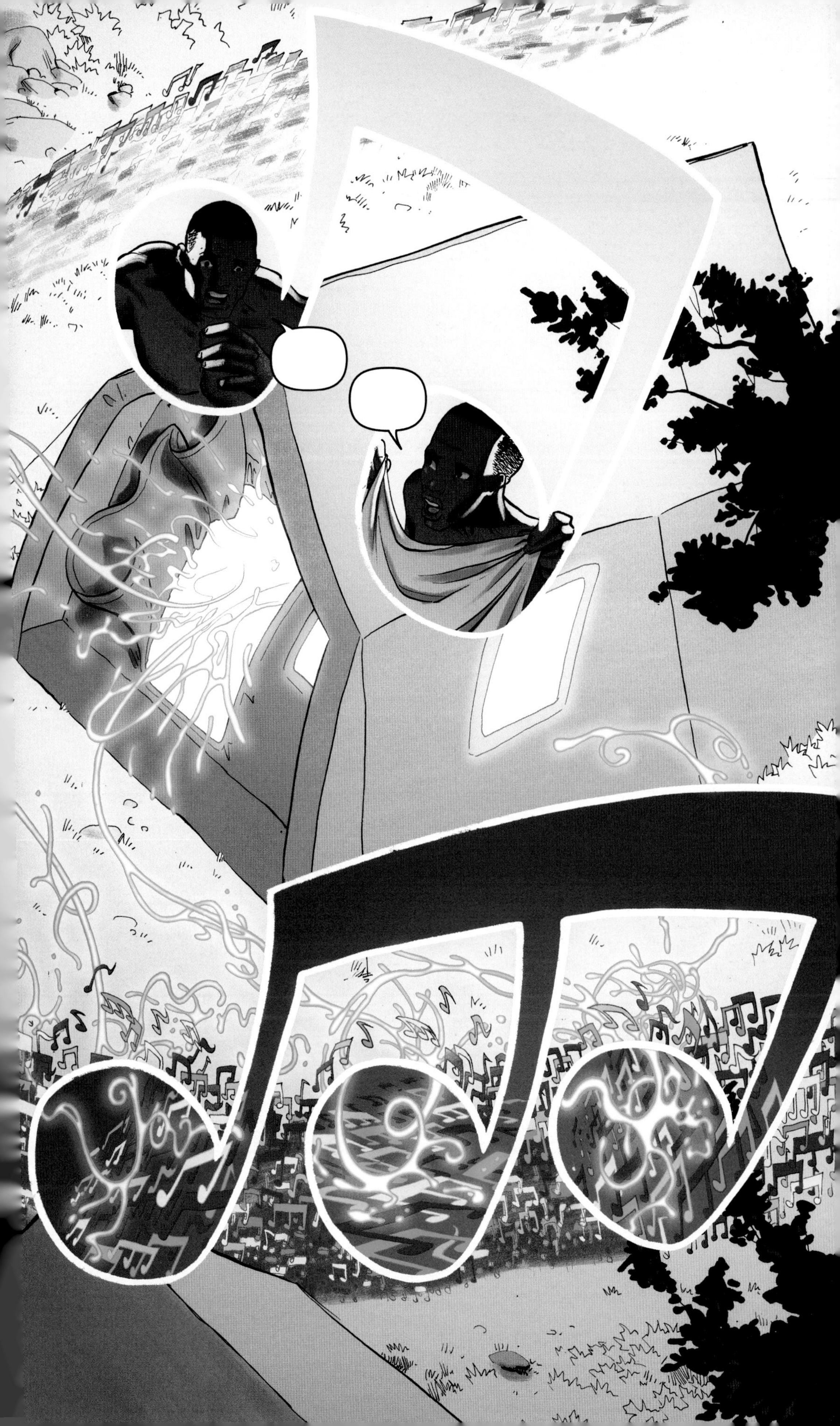

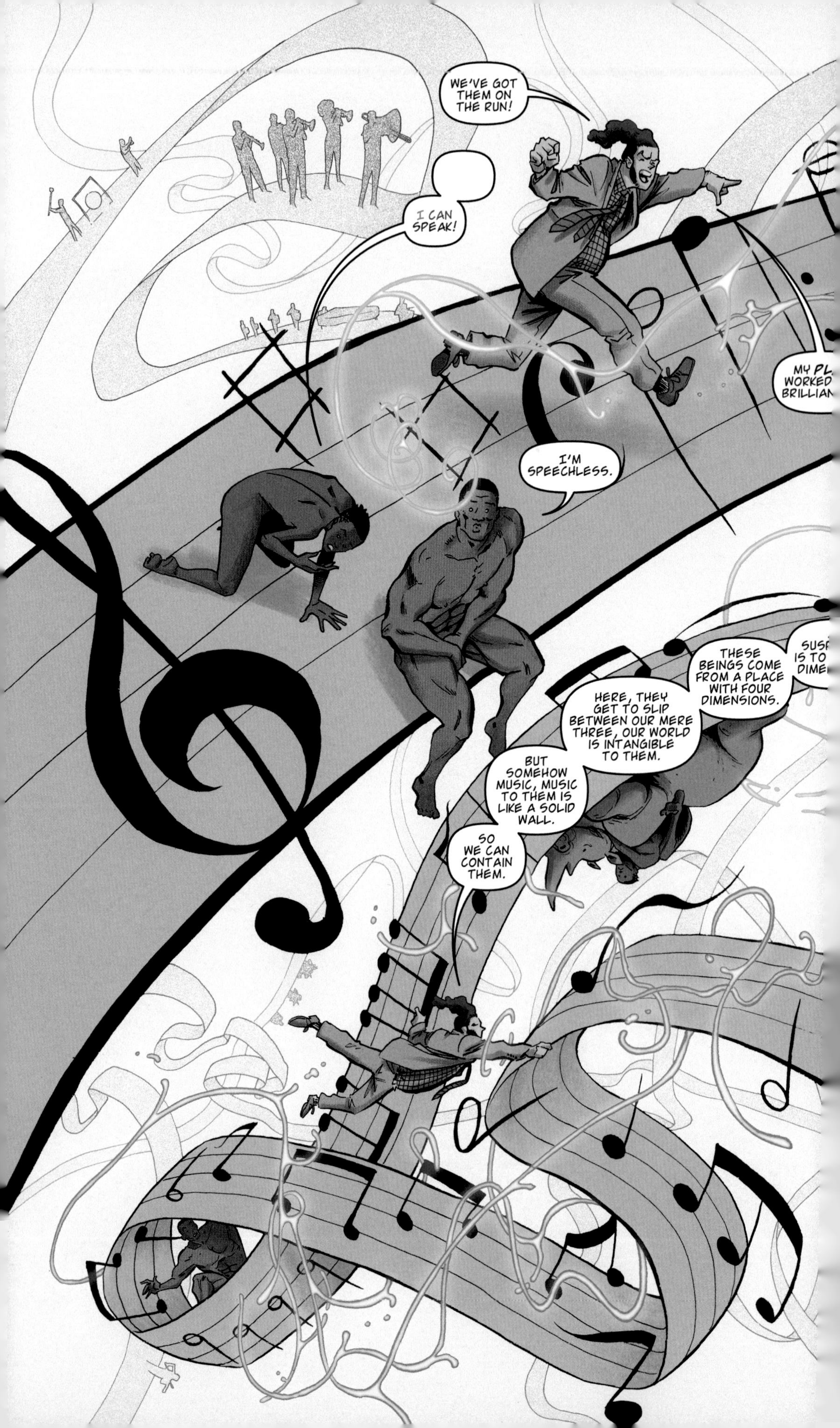
WE'VE GOT THEM ON THE RUN!
I CAN SPEAK!
I'M SPEECHLESS.
THESE BEINGS COME FROM A PLACE WITH FOUR DIMENSIONS.
HERE, THEY GET TO SLIP BETWEEN OUR MERE THREE, OUR WORLD IS INTANGIBLE TO THEM.
BUT SOMEHOW MUSIC, MUSIC TO THEM IS LIKE A SOLID WALL.
SO WE CAN CONTAIN THEM.

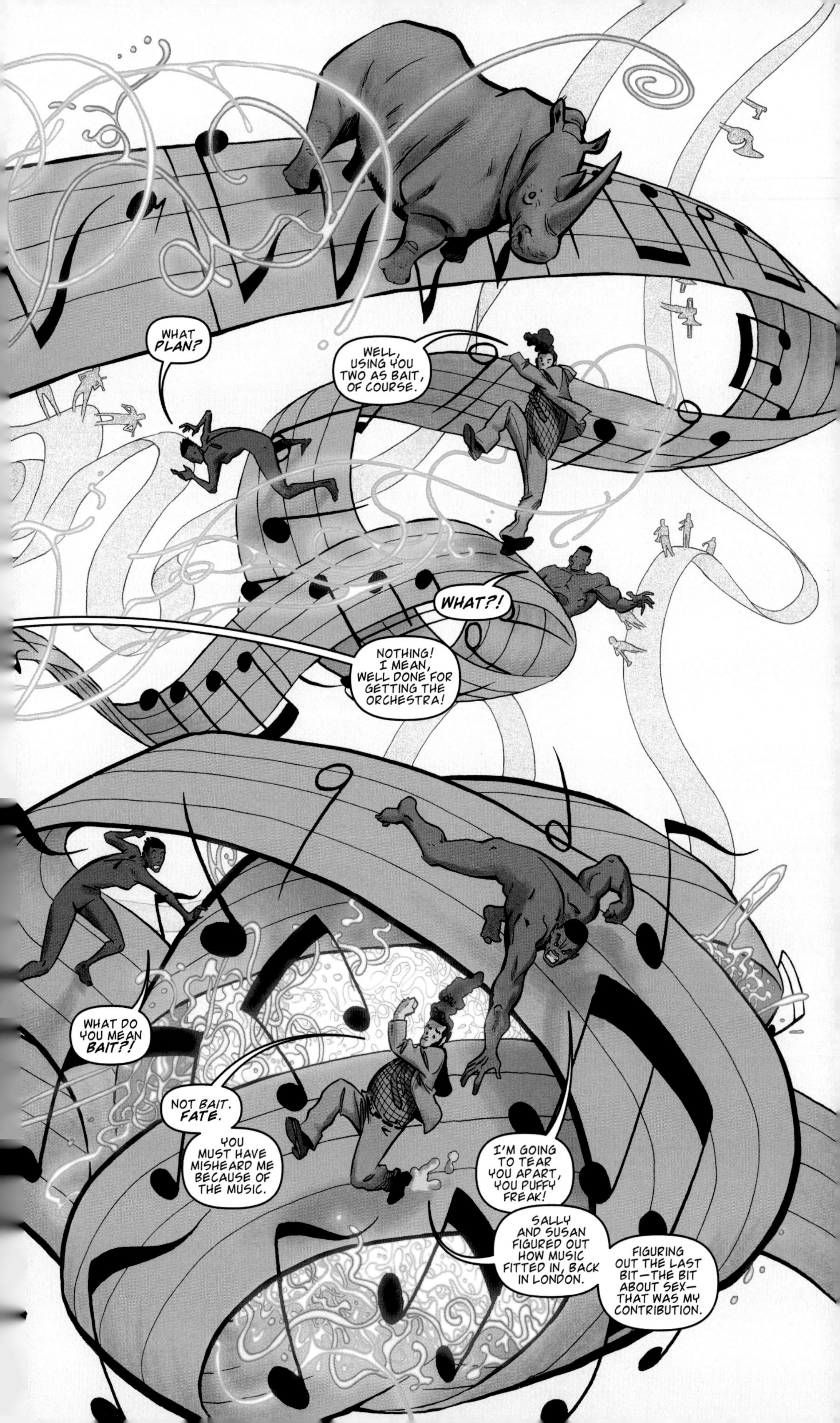

WHAT PLAN?
WELL, USING YOU TWO AS BAIT, OF COURSE.
WHAT?!
NOTHING! I MEAN, WELL DONE FOR GETTING THE ORCHESTRA!
WHAT DO YOU MEAN BAIT?!
NOT BAIT. FATE.
YOU MUST HAVE MISHEARD ME BECAUSE OF THE MUSIC.
I'M GOING TO TEAR YOU APART, YOU PUFFY FREAK!
SALLY AND SUSAN FIGURED OUT HOW MUSIC FITTED IN, BACK IN LONDON.
FIGURING OUT THE LAST BIT—THE BIT ABOUT SEX—THAT WAS MY CONTRIBUTION.

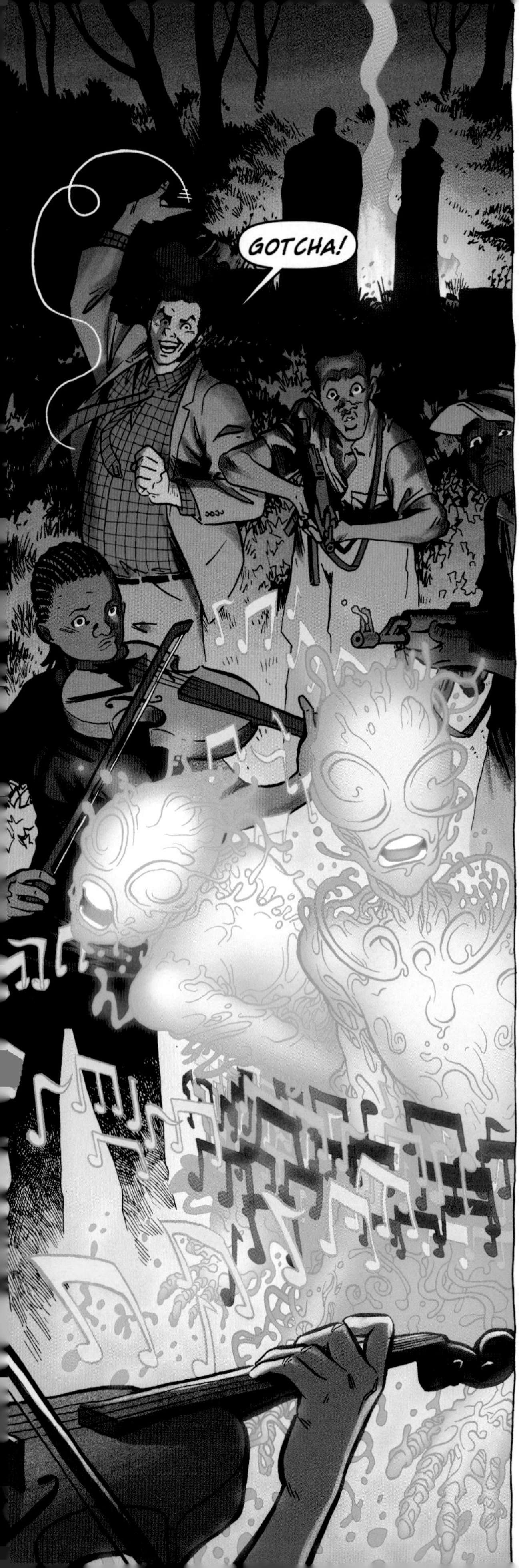
GOTCHA!

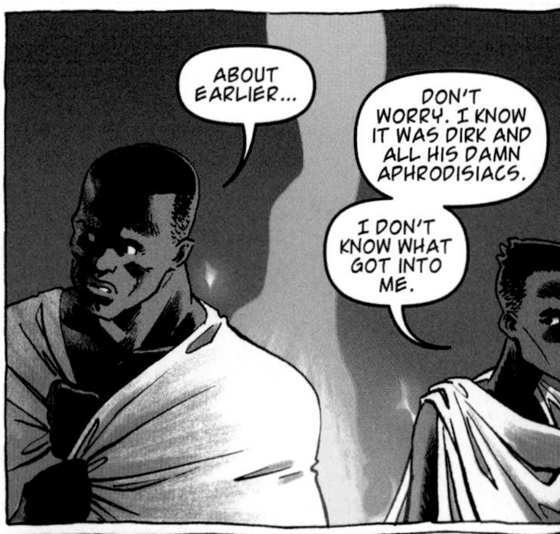
ABOUT EARLIER...
DON'T WORRY. I KNOW IT WAS DIRK AND ALL HIS DAMN APHRODISIACS.
I DON'T KNOW WHAT GOT INTO ME.

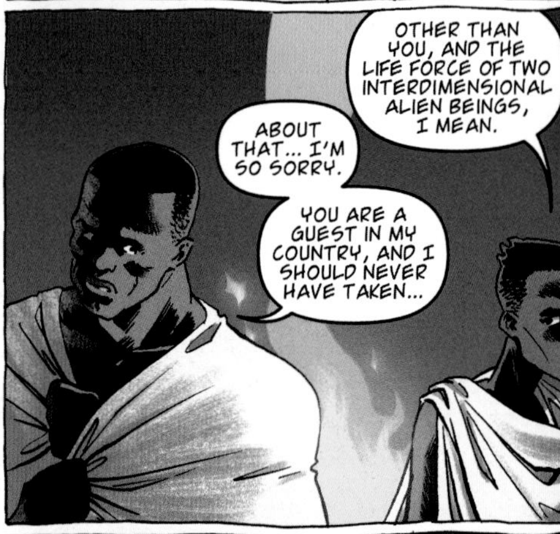
OTHER THAN YOU, AND THE LIFE FORCE OF TWO INTERDIMENSIONAL ALIEN BEINGS, I MEAN.
ABOUT THAT... I'M SO SORRY.
YOU ARE A GUEST IN MY COUNTRY, AND I SHOULD NEVER HAVE TAKEN...

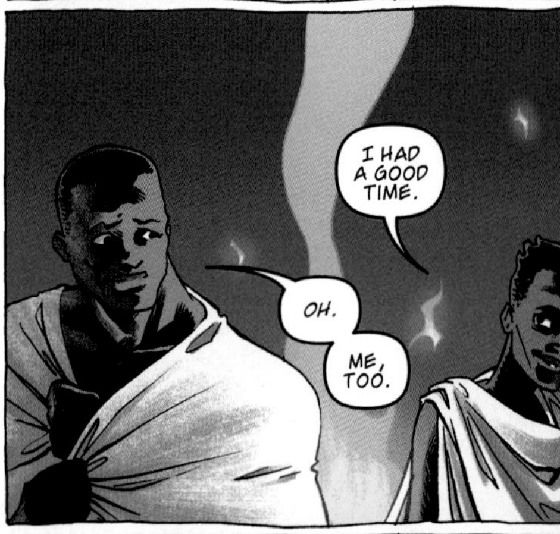
I HAD A GOOD TIME.
OH.
ME, TOO.

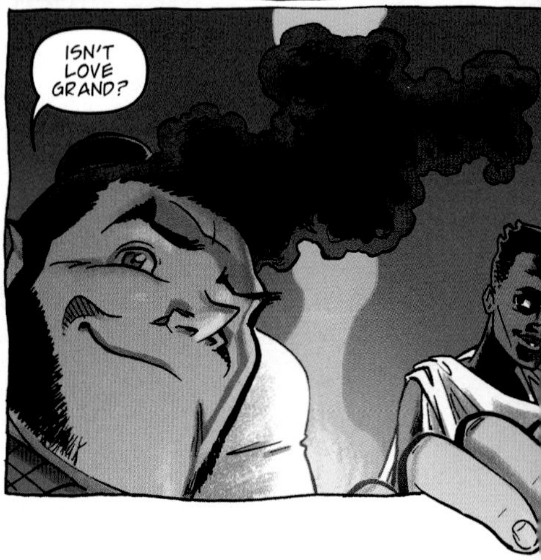
ISN'T LOVE GRAND?

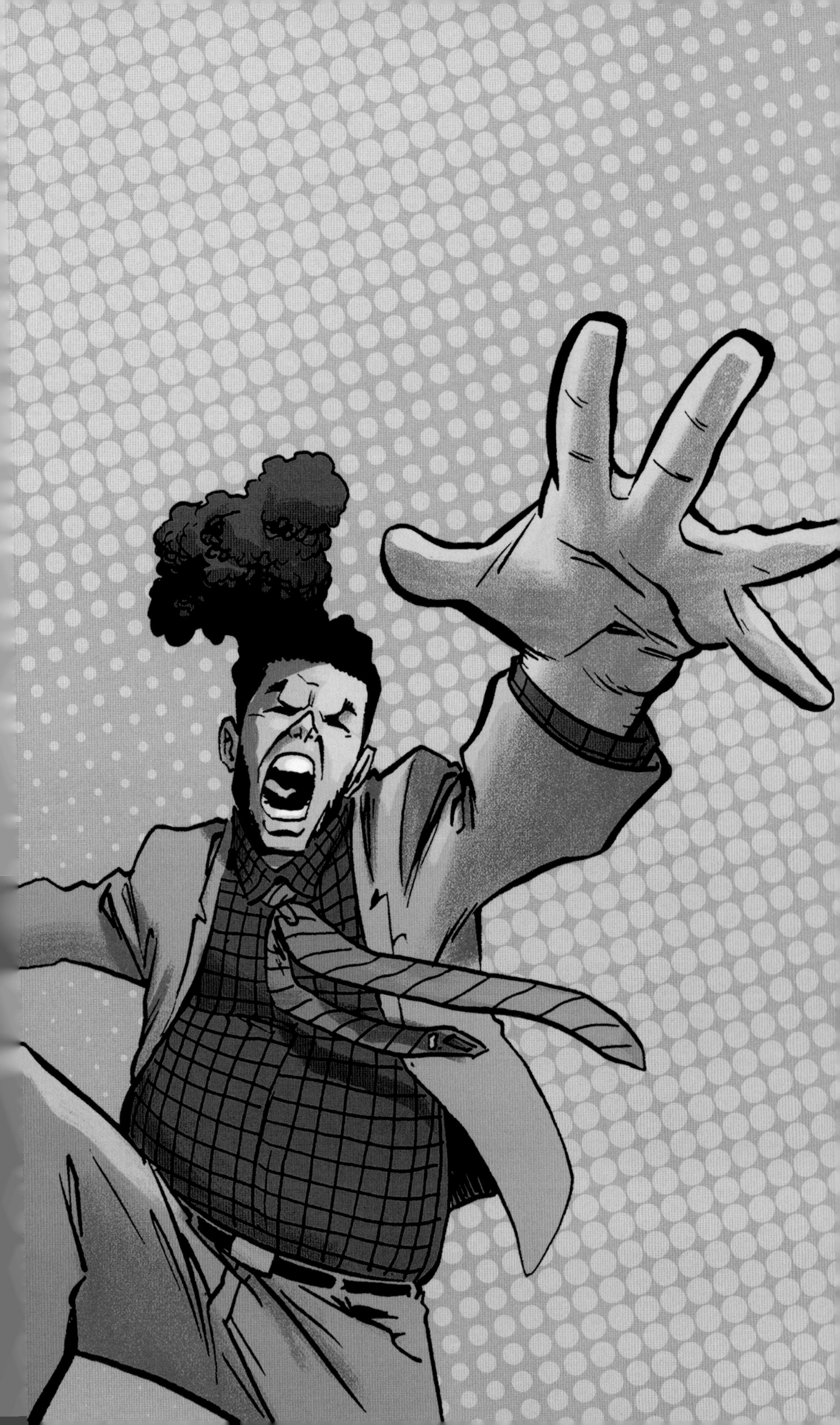

CHAPTER FIVE

Cover Art by **ILIAS KYRIAZ**

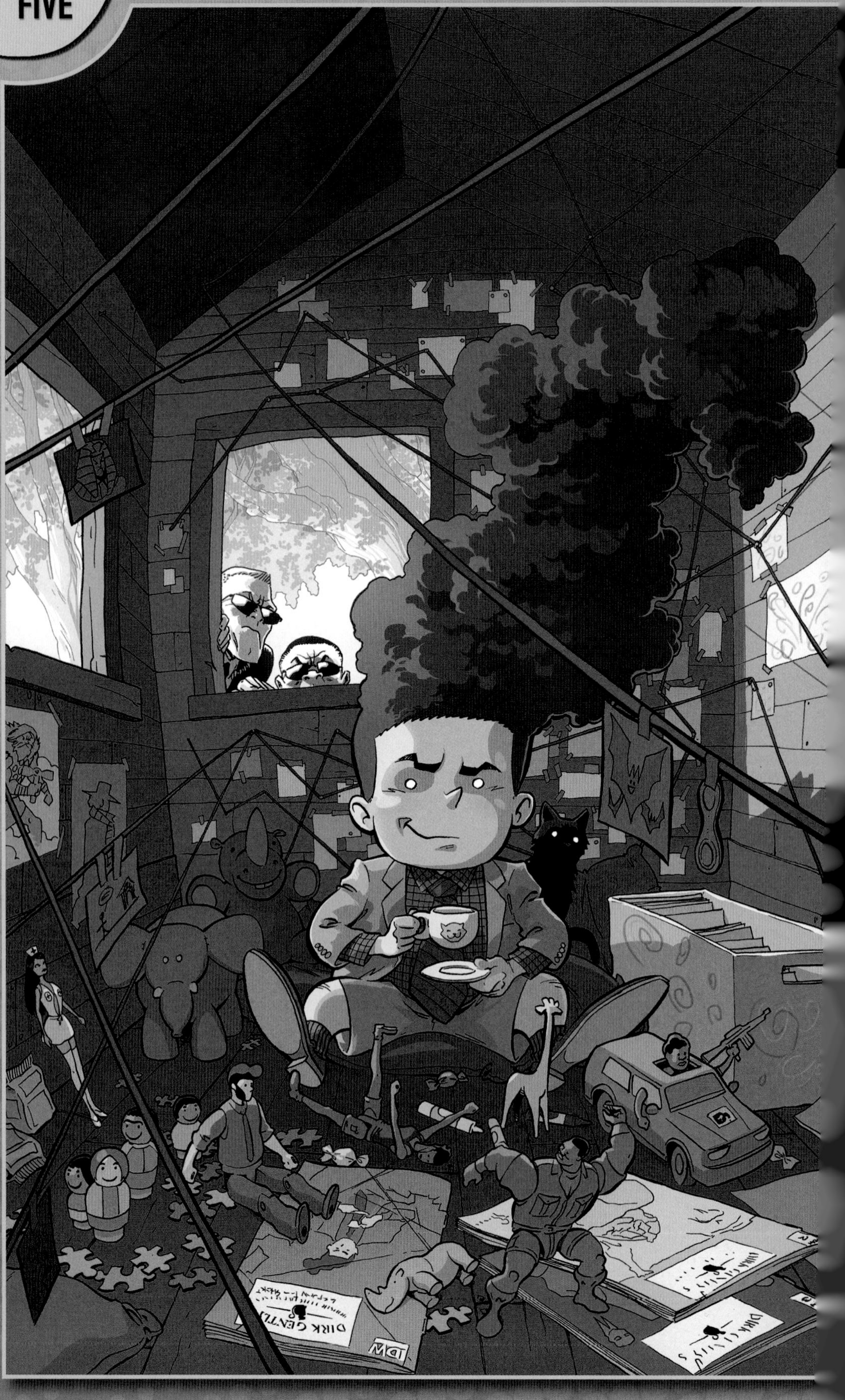

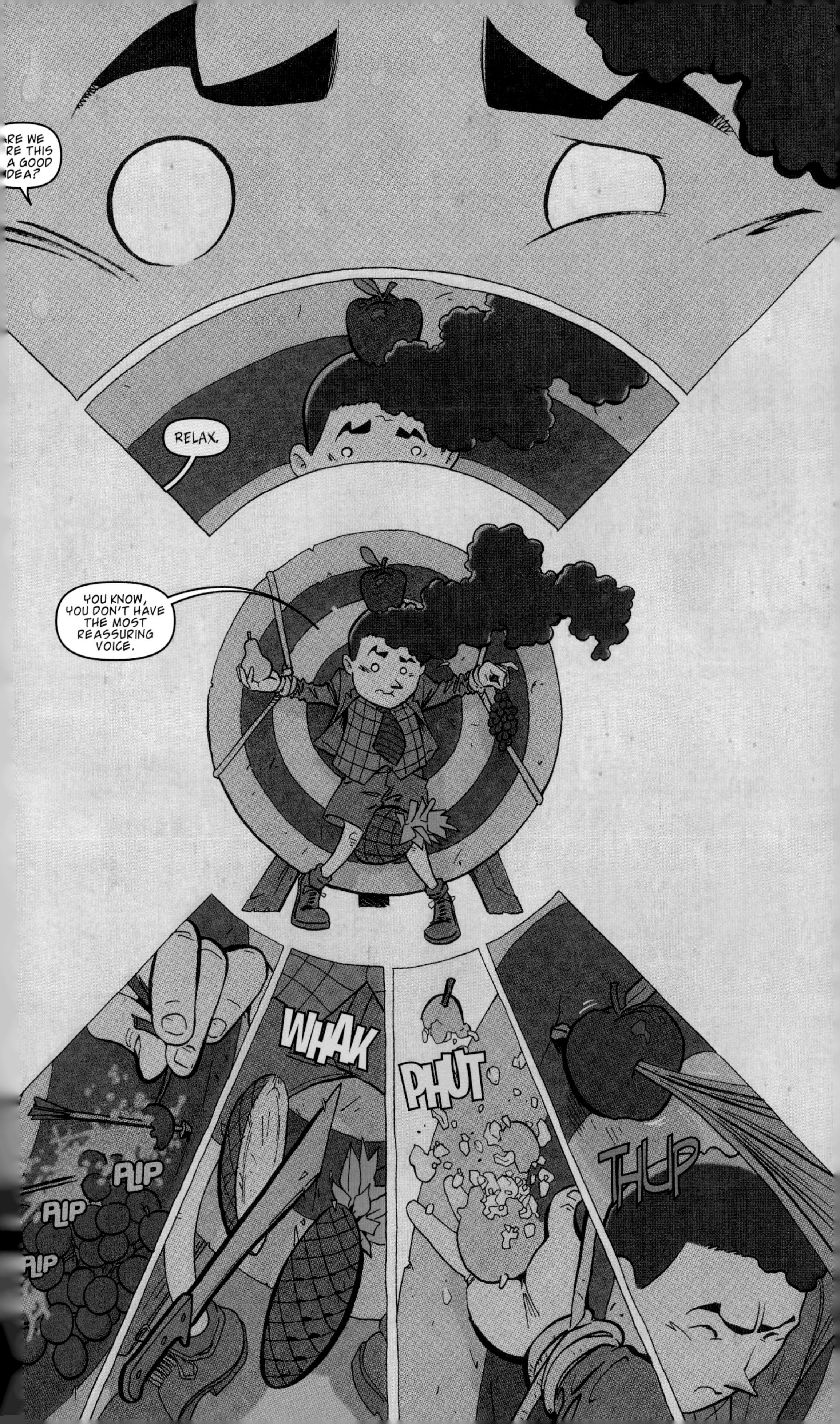

RE WE
RE THIS
A GOOD
DEA?
RELAX.
YOU KNOW, YOU DON'T HAVE THE MOST REASSURING VOICE.
WHAK
PHUT
THUP
PLIP
PLIP
PLIP

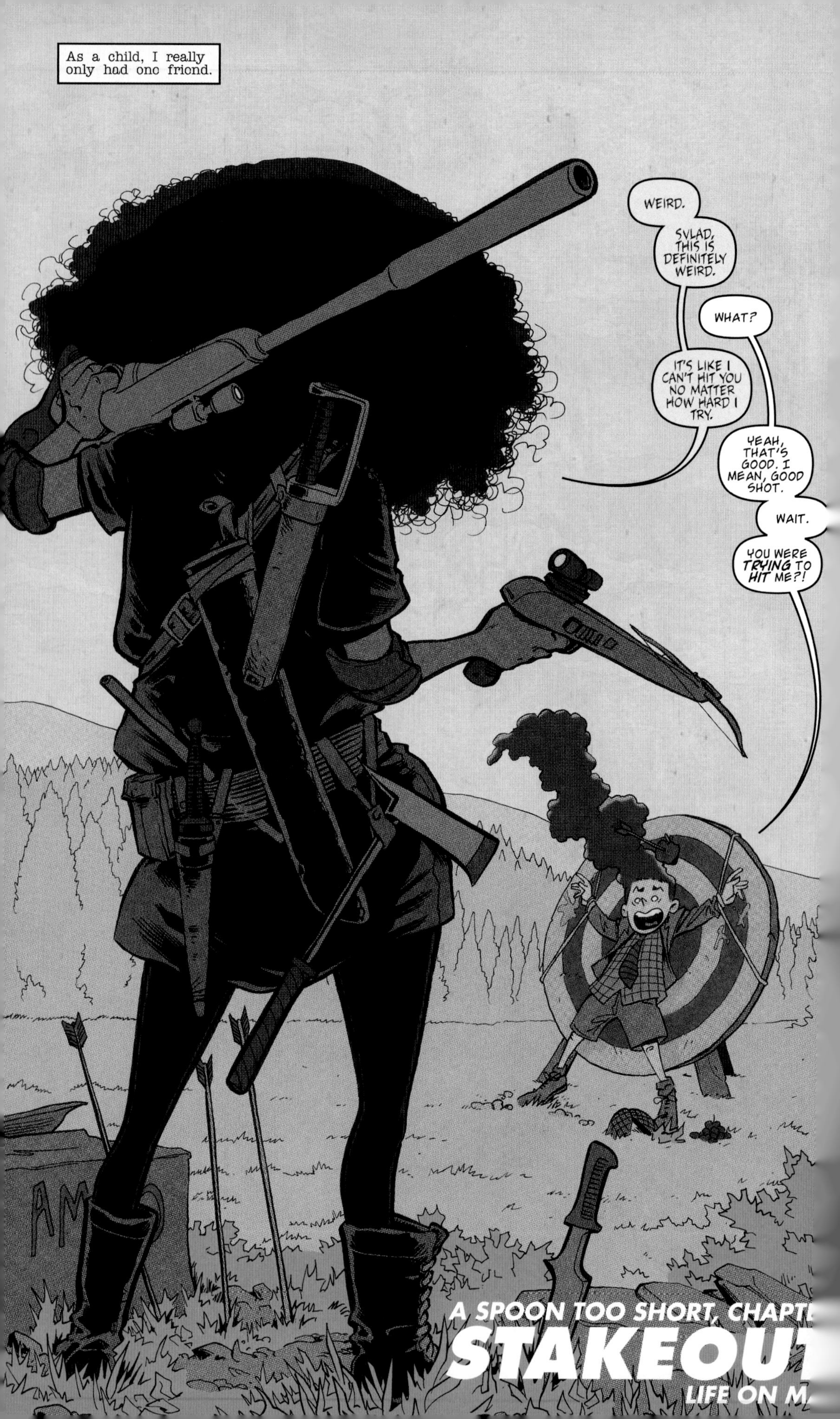
As a child, I really only had one friend.
WEIRD.
SVLAD, THIS IS DEFINITELY WEIRD.
WHAT?
IT'S LIKE I CAN'T HIT YOU NO MATTER HOW HARD I TRY.
YEAH, THAT'S GOOD. I MEAN, GOOD SHOT.
WAIT.
YOU WERE *TRYING* TO *HIT* ME?!
A SPOON TOO SHORT, CHAPT
STAKEOUT
LIFE ON M

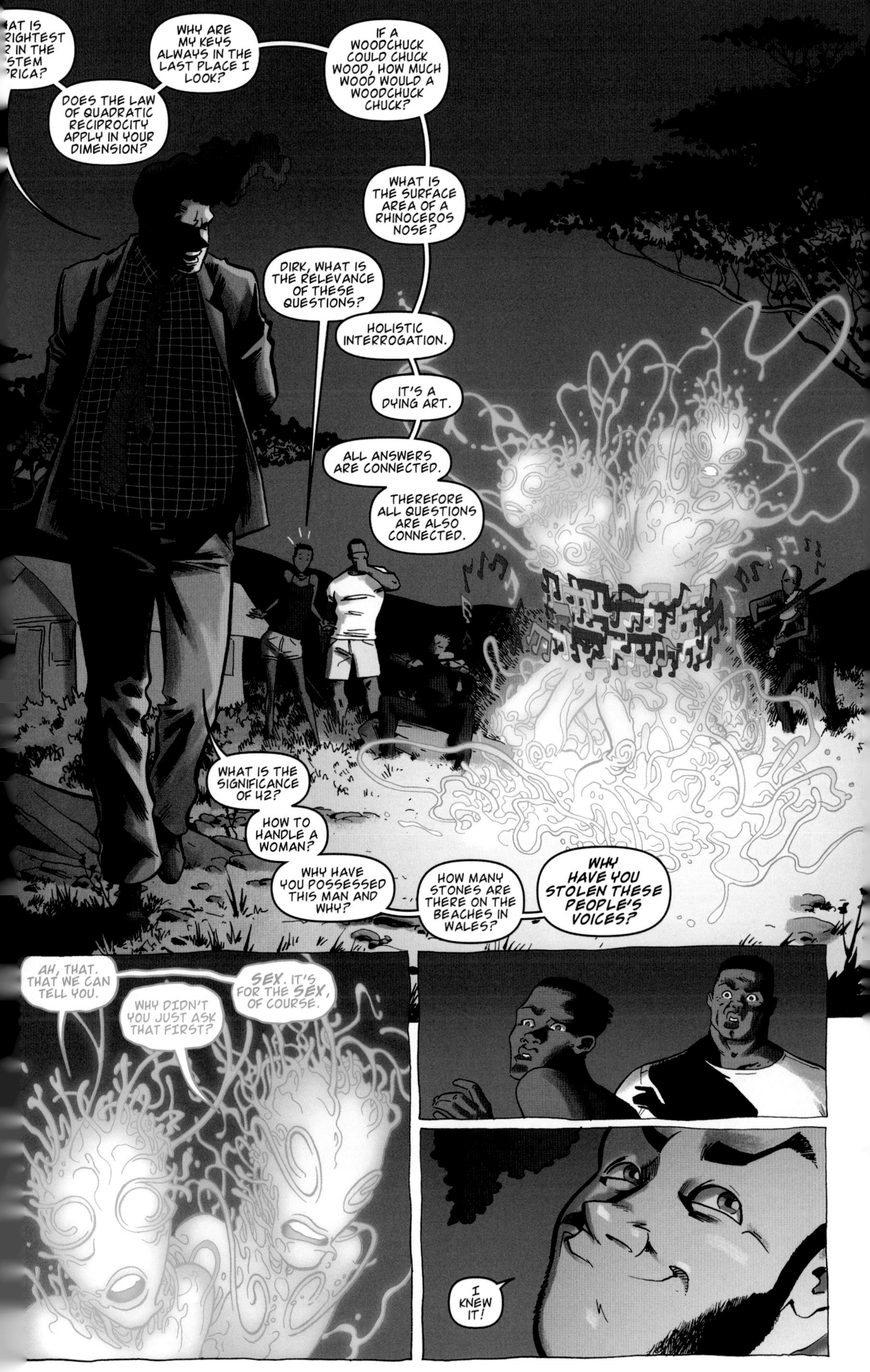

DOES THE LAW OF QUADRATIC RECIPROCITY APPLY IN YOUR DIMENSION?
WHY ARE MY KEYS ALWAYS IN THE LAST PLACE I LOOK?
IF A WOODCHUCK COULD CHUCK WOOD, HOW MUCH WOOD WOULD A WOODCHUCK CHUCK?
WHAT IS THE SURFACE AREA OF A RHINOCEROS NOSE?
DIRK, WHAT IS THE RELEVANCE OF THESE QUESTIONS?
HOLISTIC INTERROGATION.
IT'S A DYING ART.
ALL ANSWERS ARE CONNECTED.
THEREFORE ALL QUESTIONS ARE ALSO CONNECTED.
WHAT IS THE SIGNIFICANCE OF 42?
HOW TO HANDLE A WOMAN?
WHY HAVE YOU POSSESSED THIS MAN AND WHY?
HOW MANY STONES ARE THERE ON THE BEACHES IN WALES?
WHY HAVE YOU STOLEN THESE PEOPLE'S VOICES?
AH, THAT. THAT WE CAN TELL YOU.
WHY DIDN'T YOU JUST ASK THAT FIRST?
SEX. IT'S FOR THE SEX, OF COURSE.
I KNEW IT!

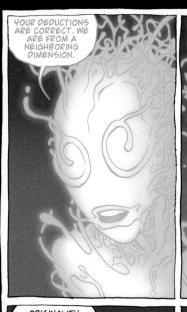

YOUR DEDUCTIONS ARE CORRECT. WE ARE FROM A NEIGHBORING DIMENSION.

WITH FOUR DIMENSIONS.

WE CALL IT THE FOURTH DIMENSION.

ORIGINALITY NOT YOUR STRONG SUIT, THEN?

WE ARE CONNOISSEURS OF PLEASURE.

OF MUSIC. AND LOVEMAKING.

YOU TWO ARE DELECTABLE.

WHEN WE FOUND A PATH INTO YOUR DIMENSION...

WE WERE IMMEDIATELY DRAWN BY THE CARNAL OPPORTUNITIES OFFERED BY YOUR DELIGHTFUL RACE.

SO WARM. SO SQUIRMY. SO FULL OF SOUNDS AND SQUEALS.

ABOUT THAT...

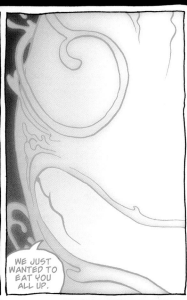

WE JUST WANTED TO EAT YOU ALL UP.

SUCK THE MARROW FROM YOUR BONES.

BUT NOT IN A CANNIBAL-LY TYPE OF WAY.

NO. JUST AS A KIND OF... ORAL STIMULANT...

YOU SUCKED OUT OUR VOICES, OUR ABILITY TO COMMUNICATE...

...AS AN APHRODISIAC?

YES! SOLVED IT!

FOR REALS THIS TIME.

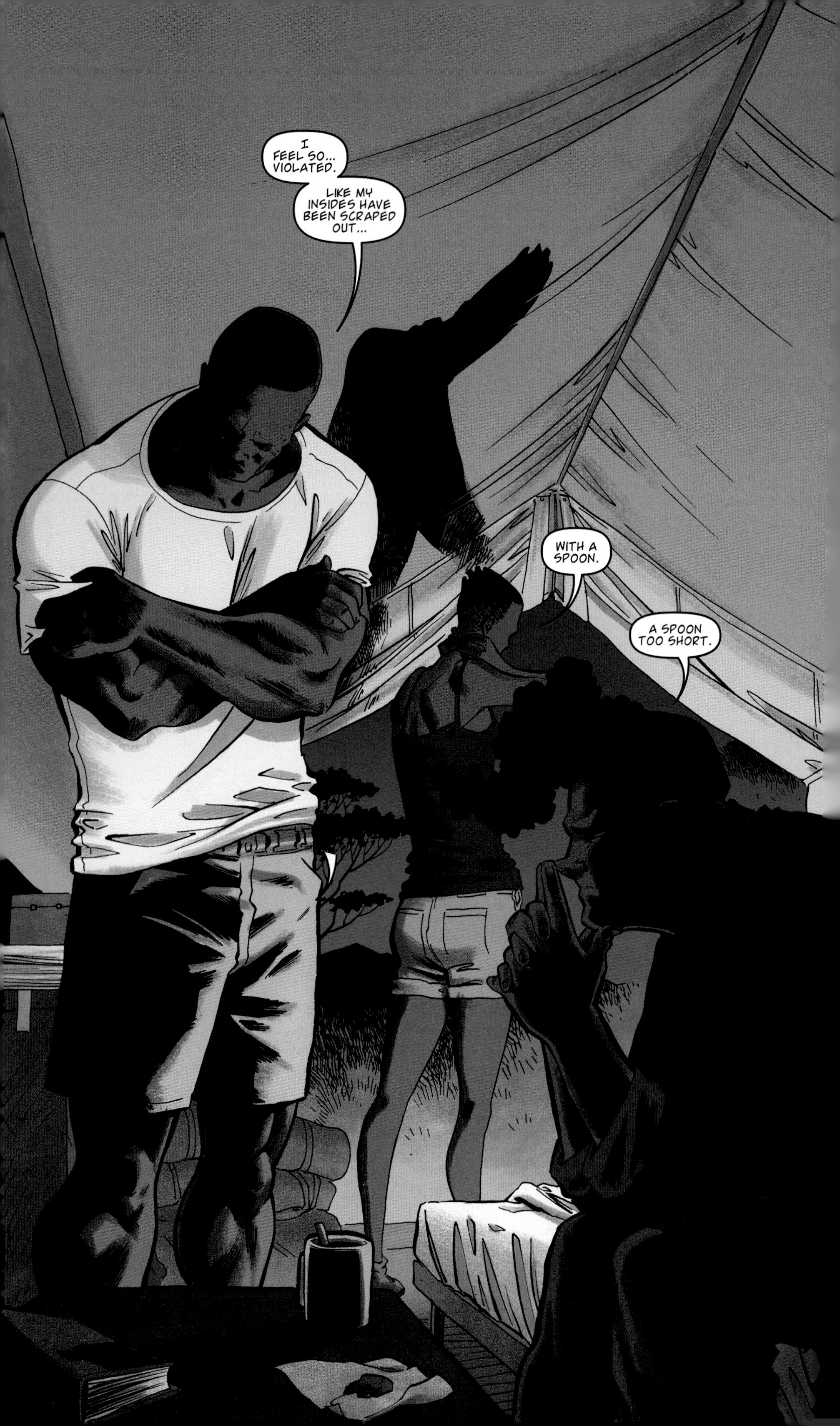
I FEEL SO... VIOLATED.
LIKE MY INSIDES HAVE BEEN SCRAPED OUT...
WITH A SPOON.
A SPOON TOO SHORT.

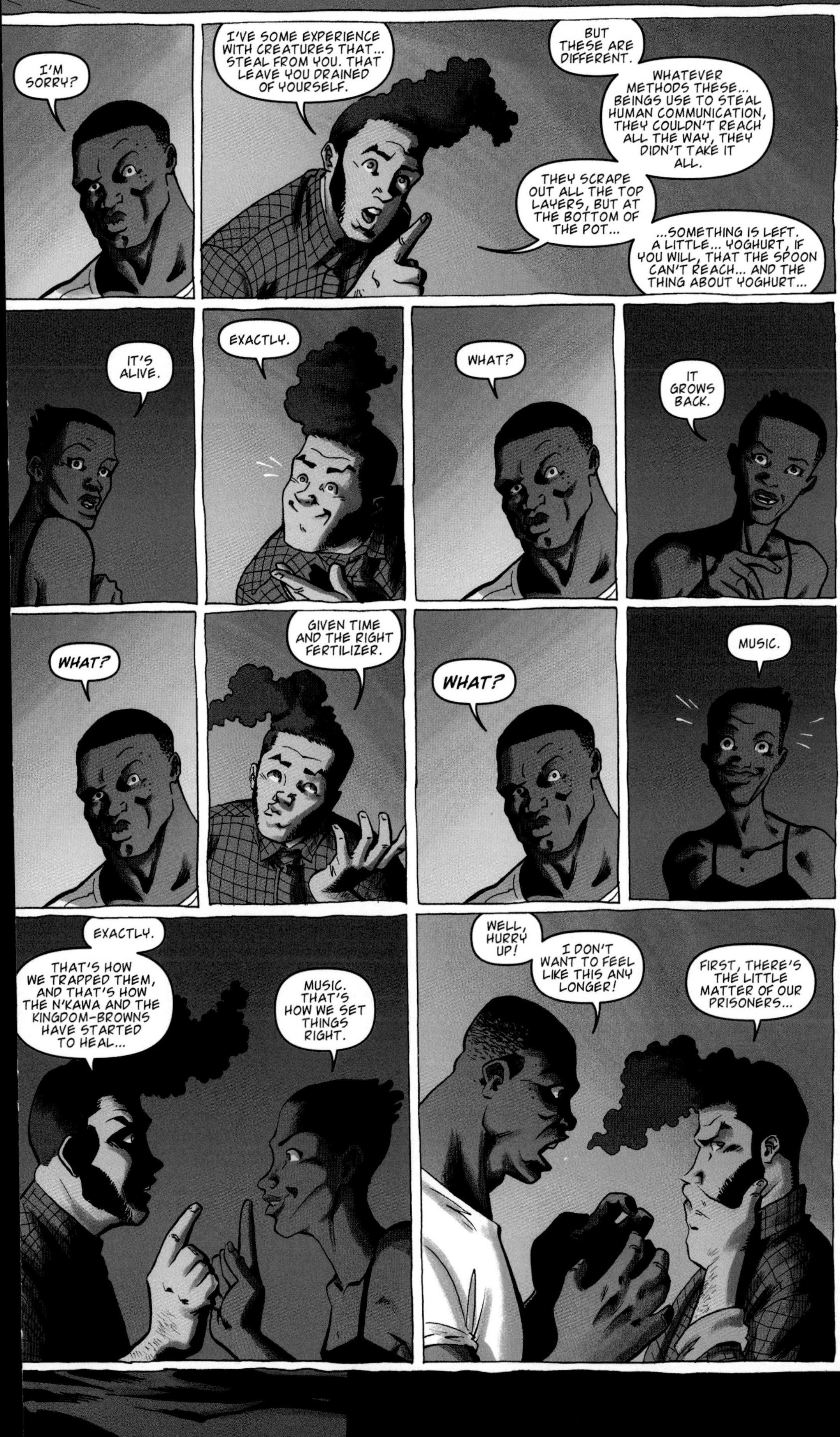
I'M SORRY?
I'VE SOME EXPERIENCE WITH CREATURES THAT... STEAL FROM YOU. THAT LEAVE YOU DRAINED OF YOURSELF.
BUT THESE ARE DIFFERENT.
WHATEVER METHODS THESE... BEINGS USE TO STEAL HUMAN COMMUNICATION, THEY COULDN'T REACH ALL THE WAY, THEY DIDN'T TAKE IT ALL.
THEY SCRAPE OUT ALL THE TOP LAYERS, BUT AT THE BOTTOM OF THE POT...
...SOMETHING IS LEFT. A LITTLE... YOGHURT, IF YOU WILL, THAT THE SPOON CAN'T REACH... AND THE THING ABOUT YOGHURT...
IT'S ALIVE.
EXACTLY.
WHAT?
IT GROWS BACK.
WHAT?
GIVEN TIME AND THE RIGHT FERTILIZER.
WHAT?
MUSIC.
EXACTLY.
THAT'S HOW WE TRAPPED THEM, AND THAT'S HOW THE N'KAWA AND THE KINGDOM-BROWNS HAVE STARTED TO HEAL...
MUSIC. THAT'S HOW WE SET THINGS RIGHT.
WELL, HURRY UP!
I DON'T WANT TO FEEL LIKE THIS ANY LONGER!
FIRST, THERE'S THE LITTLE MATTER OF OUR PRISONERS...

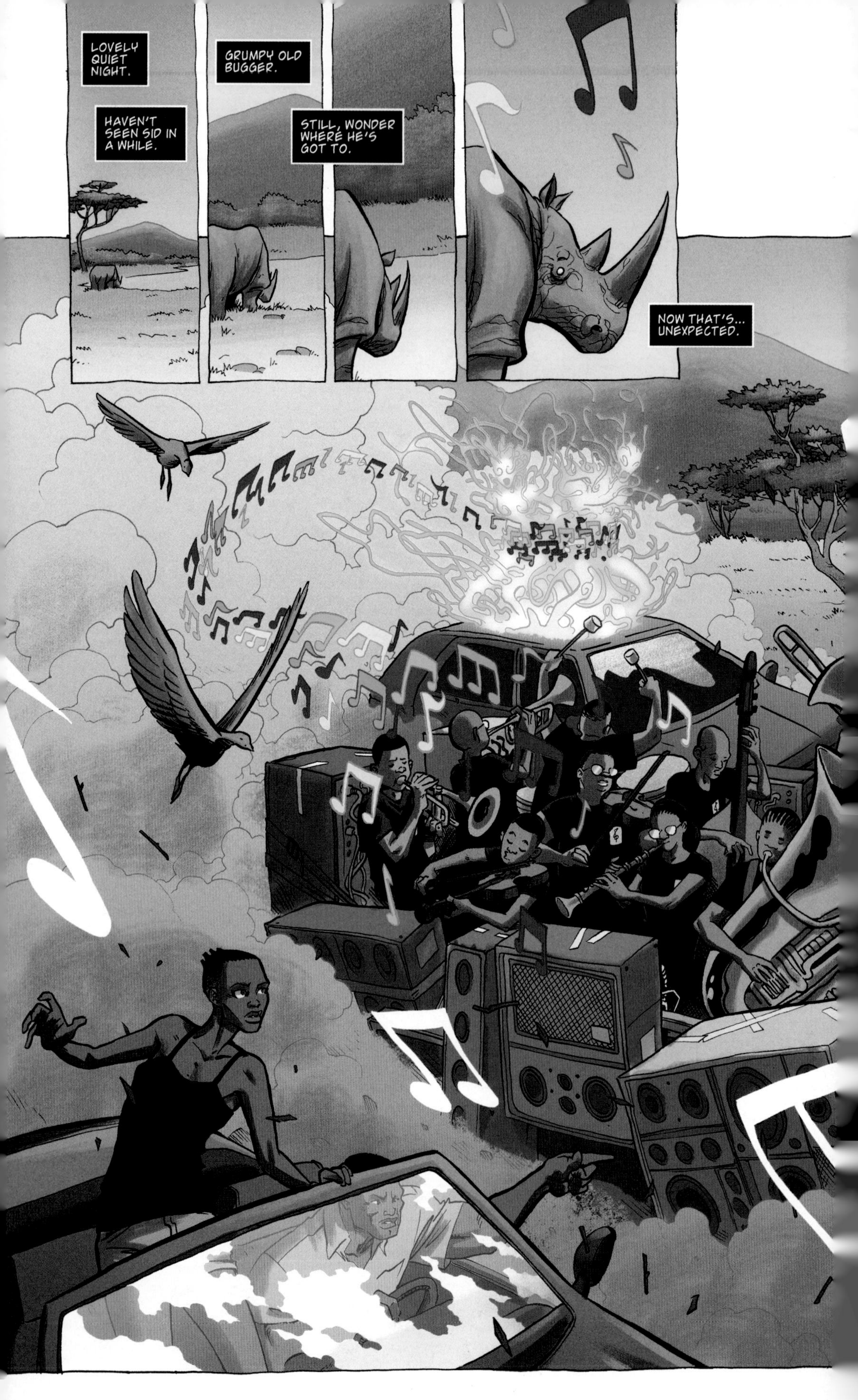

LOVELY QUIET NIGHT.
HAVEN'T SEEN SID IN A WHILE.
GRUMPY OLD BUGGER.
STILL, WONDER WHERE HE'S GOT TO.
NOW THAT'S... UNEXPECTED.

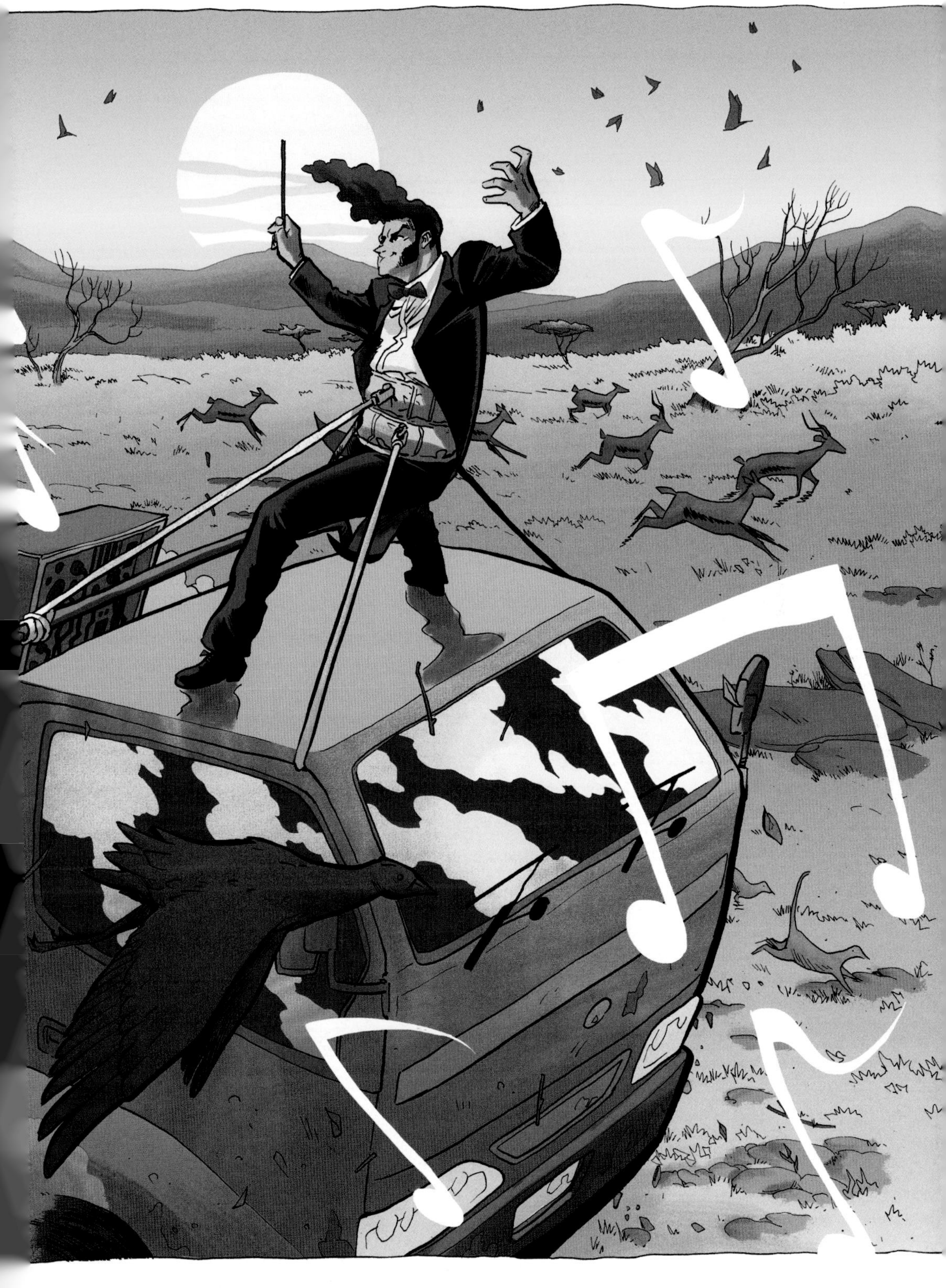

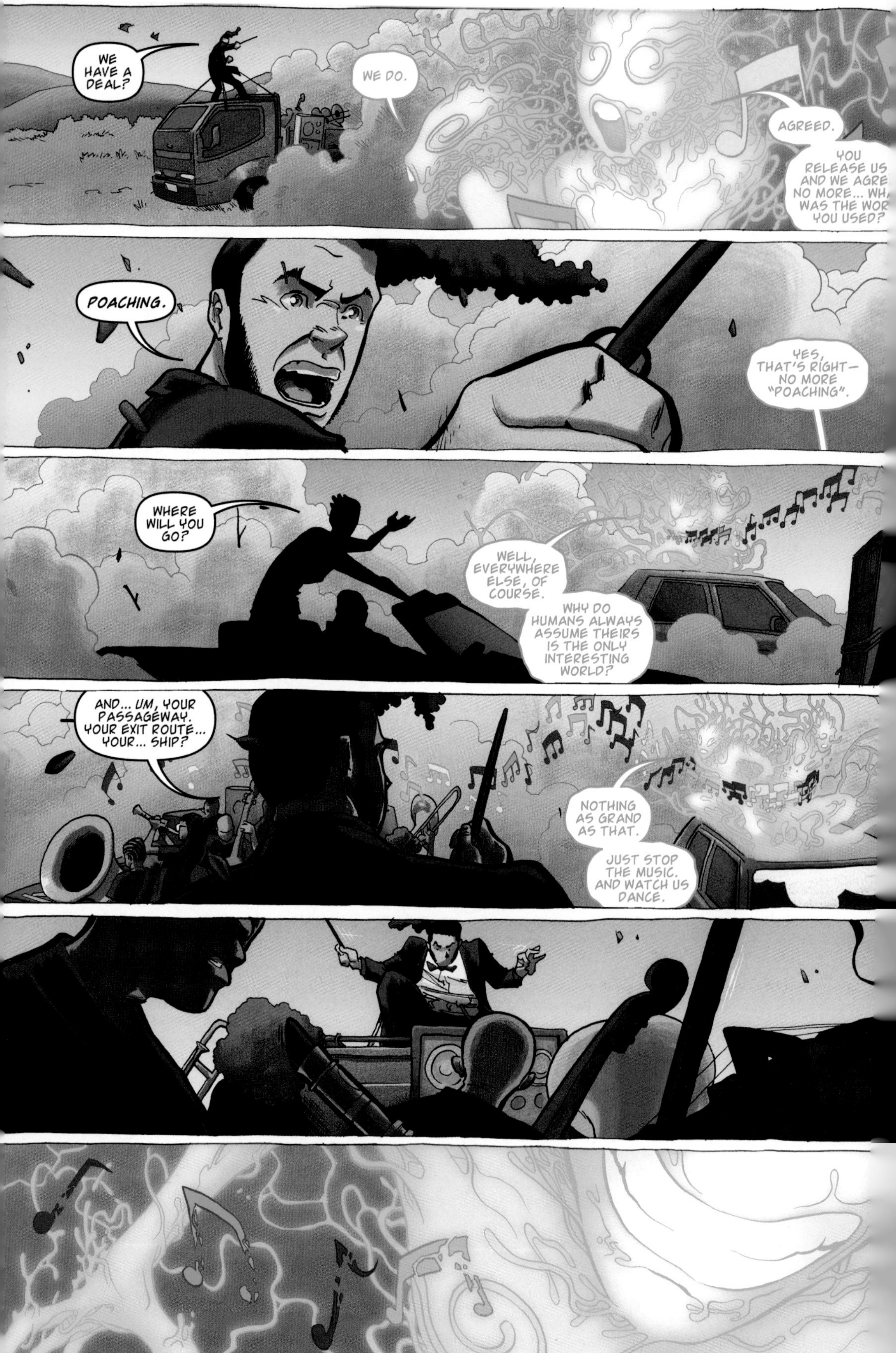

WE HAVE A DEAL?
WE DO.
AGREED.
YOU RELEASE US AND WE AGRE NO MORE... WH WAS THE WOR YOU USED?
POACHING.
YES, THAT'S RIGHT— NO MORE "POACHING".
WHERE WILL YOU GO?
WELL, EVERYWHERE ELSE, OF COURSE.
WHY DO HUMANS ALWAYS ASSUME THEIRS IS THE ONLY INTERESTING WORLD?
AND... UM, YOUR PASSAGEWAY. YOUR EXIT ROUTE... YOUR... SHIP?
NOTHING AS GRAND AS THAT.
JUST STOP THE MUSIC. AND WATCH US DANCE.

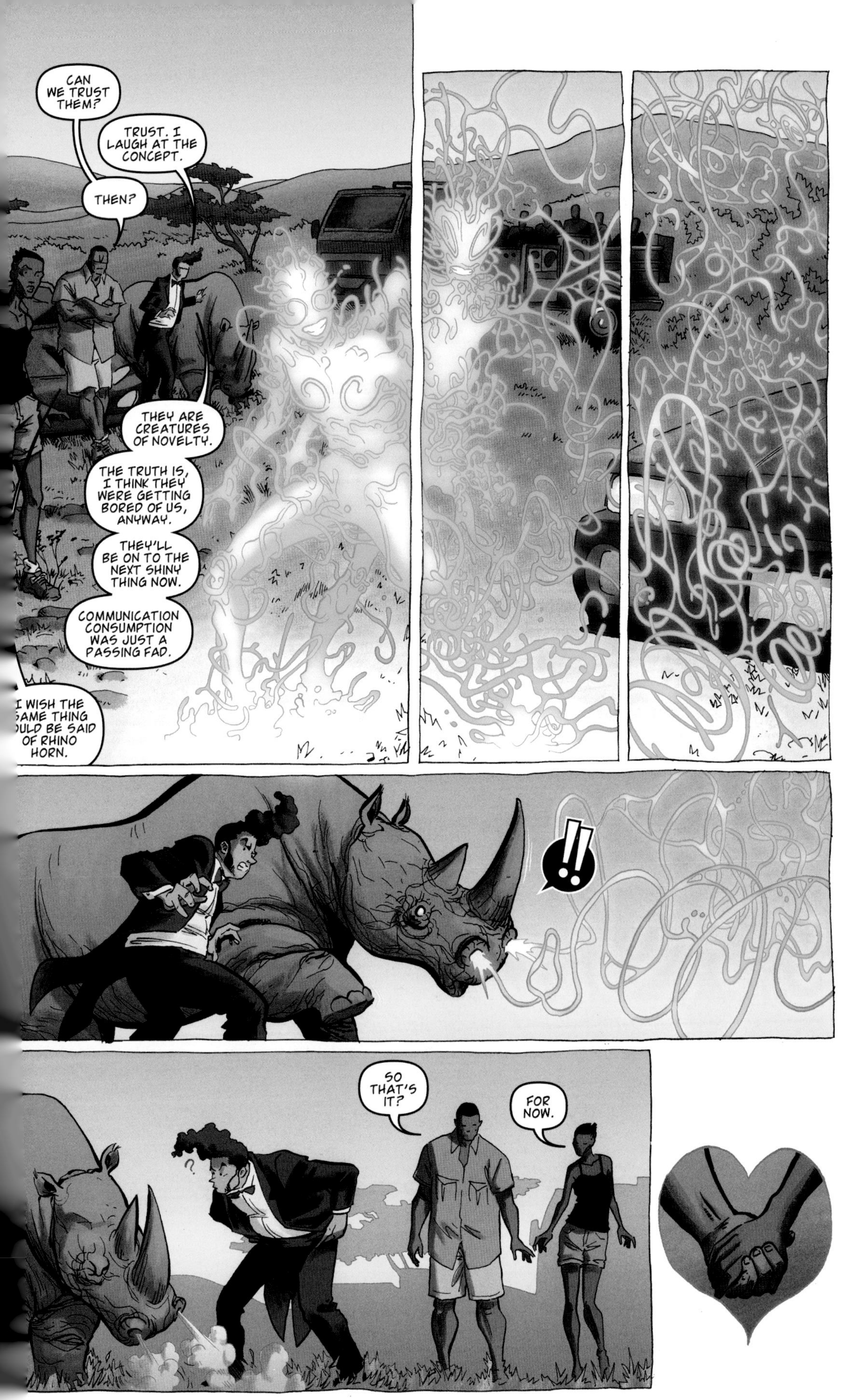
CAN WE TRUST THEM?
TRUST. I LAUGH AT THE CONCEPT.
THEN?
THEY ARE CREATURES OF NOVELTY.
THE TRUTH IS, I THINK THEY WERE GETTING BORED OF US, ANYWAY.
THEY'LL BE ON TO THE NEXT SHINY THING NOW.
COMMUNICATION CONSUMPTION WAS JUST A PASSING FAD.
I WISH THE SAME THING OULD BE SAID OF RHINO HORN.
!!
SO THAT'S IT?
FOR NOW.
?

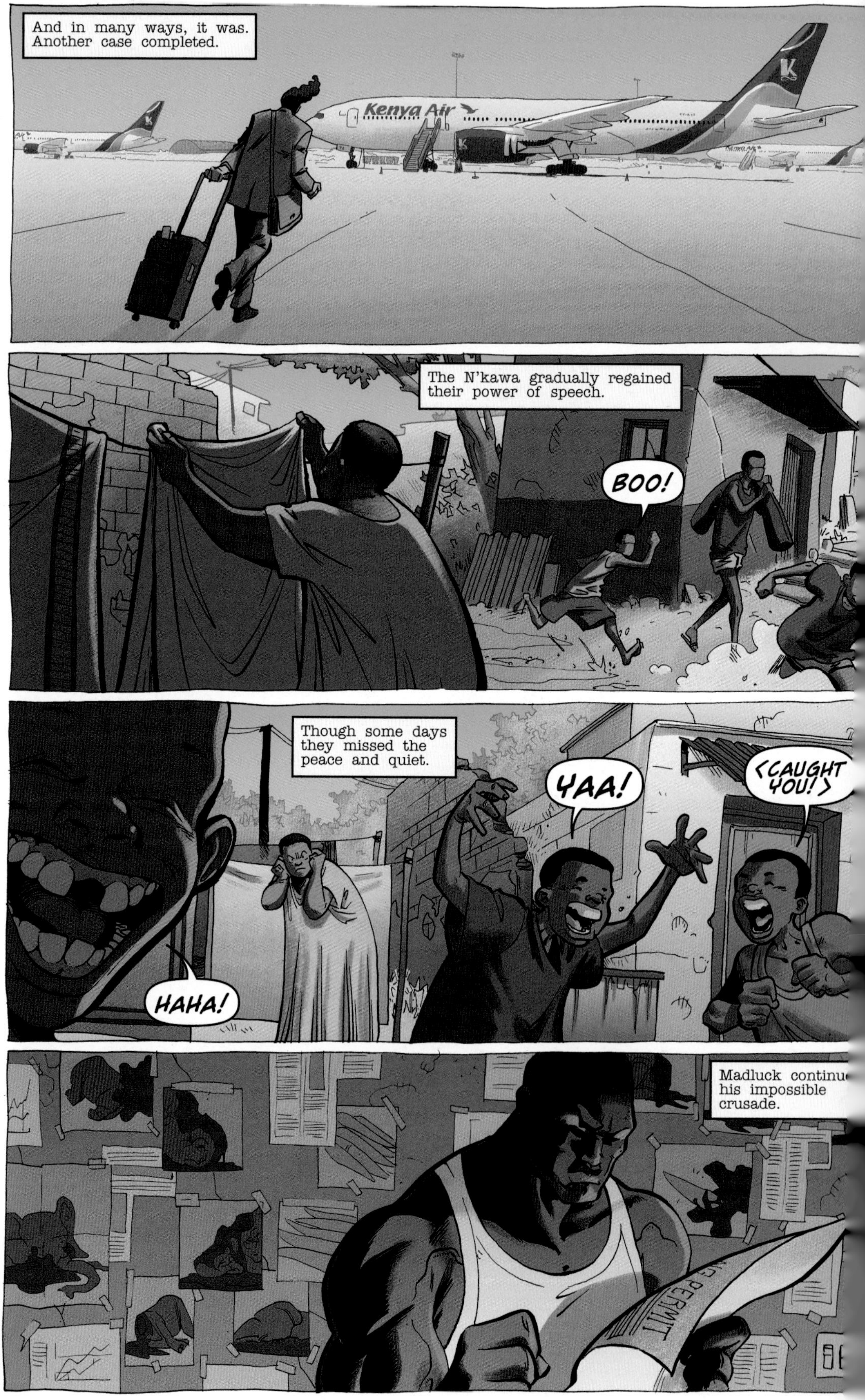
And in many ways, it was. Another case completed.
Kenya Air
The N'kawa gradually regained their power of speech.
BOO!
Though some days they missed the peace and quiet.
HAHA!
YAA!
<CAUGHT YOU!>
Madluck continu his impossible crusade.

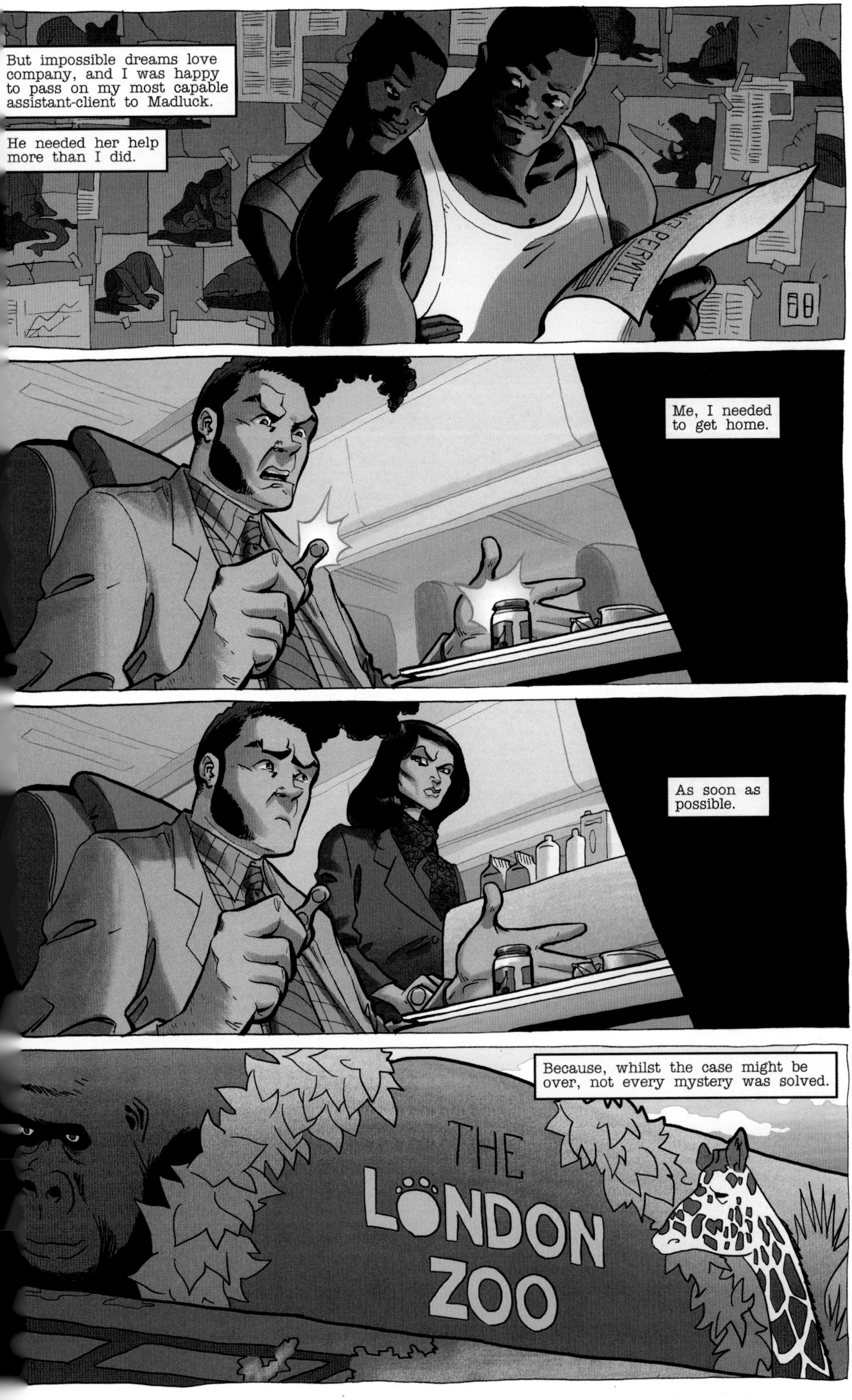
But impossible dreams love company, and I was happy to pass on my most capable assistant-client to Madluck.
He needed her help more than I did.
Me, I needed to get home.
As soon as possible.
Because, whilst the case might be over, not every mystery was solved.
THE LÖNDON ZOO

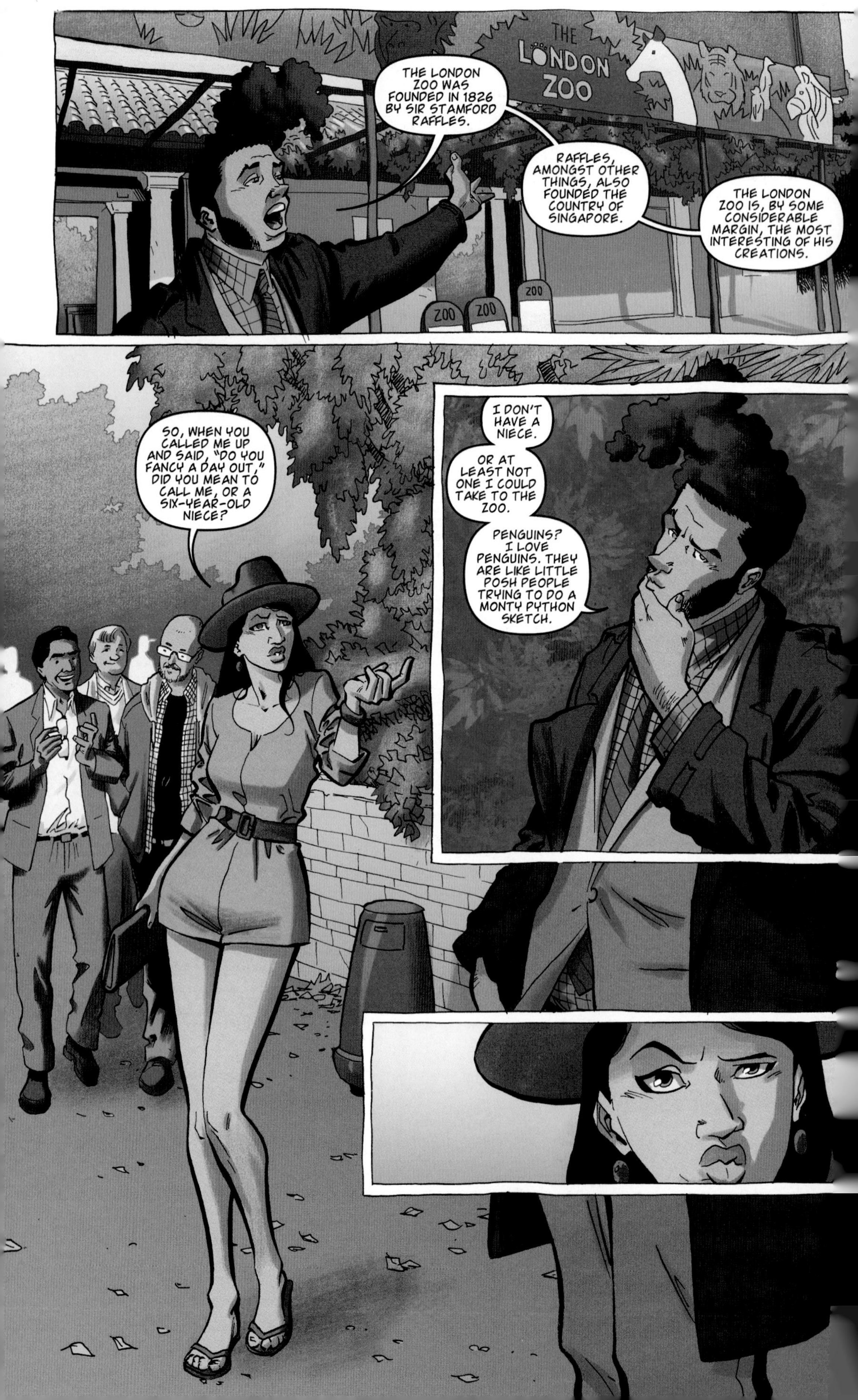
THE LONDON ZOO
ZOO
ZOO
ZOO
ZOO
THE LONDON ZOO WAS FOUNDED IN 1826 BY SIR STAMFORD RAFFLES.
RAFFLES, AMONGST OTHER THINGS, ALSO FOUNDED THE COUNTRY OF SINGAPORE.
THE LONDON ZOO IS, BY SOME CONSIDERABLE MARGIN, THE MOST INTERESTING OF HIS CREATIONS.
SO, WHEN YOU CALLED ME UP AND SAID, "DO YOU FANCY A DAY OUT," DID YOU MEAN TO CALL ME, OR A SIX-YEAR-OLD NIECE?
I DON'T HAVE A NIECE.
OR AT LEAST NOT ONE I COULD TAKE TO THE ZOO.
PENGUINS? I LOVE PENGUINS. THEY ARE LIKE LITTLE POSH PEOPLE TRYING TO DO A MONTY PYTHON SKETCH.

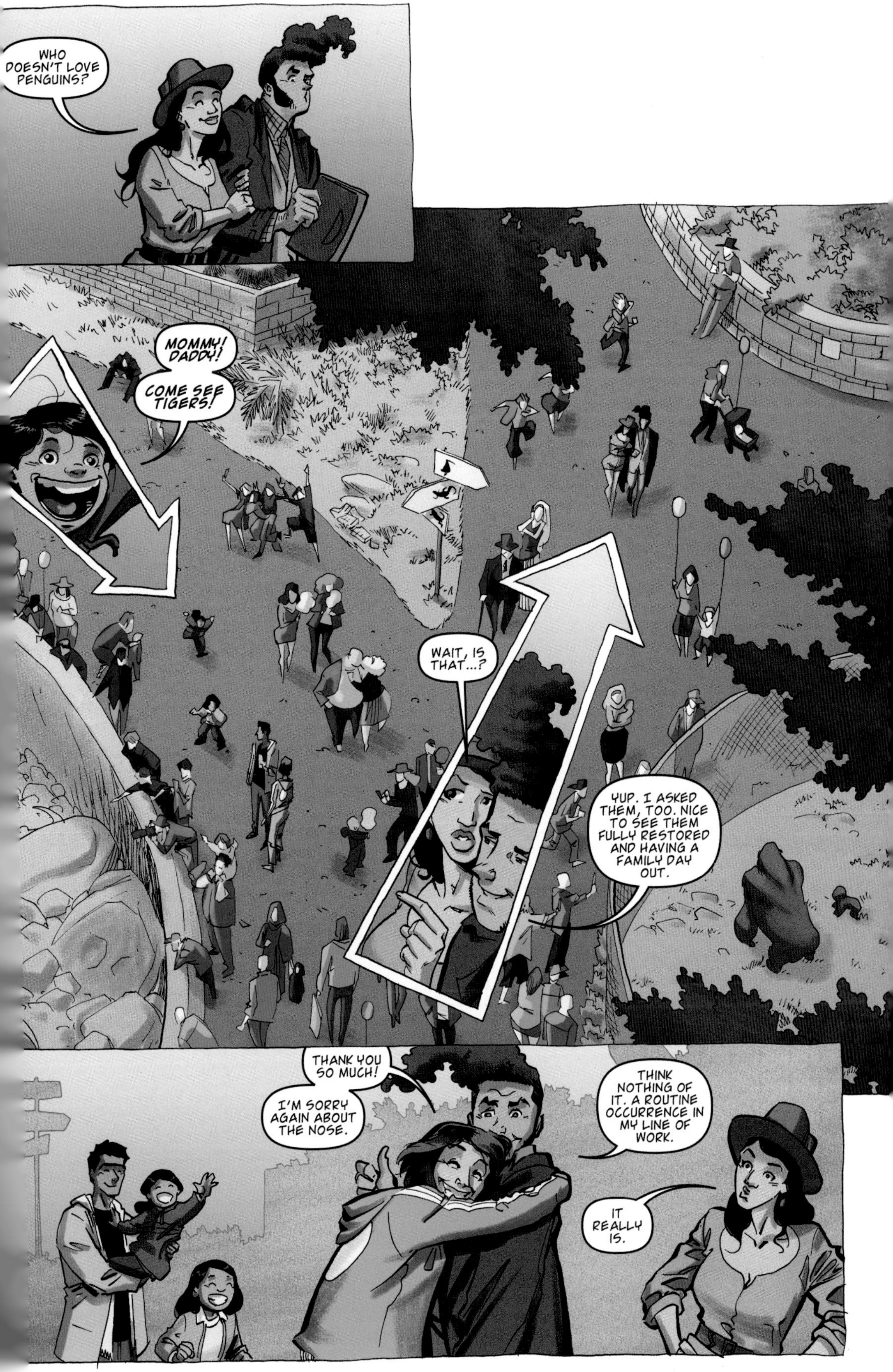
WHO DOESN'T LOVE PENGUINS?
MOMMY! DADDY!
COME SEE TIGERS!
WAIT, IS THAT...?
YUP. I ASKED THEM, TOO. NICE TO SEE THEM FULLY RESTORED AND HAVING A FAMILY DAY OUT.
THANK YOU SO MUCH!
I'M SORRY AGAIN ABOUT THE NOSE.
THINK NOTHING OF IT. A ROUTINE OCCURRENCE IN MY LINE OF WORK.
IT REALLY IS.

SOUNDS LIKE THE CASE ENDED SUCCESSFULLY FOR EVERYONE.

ALMOST EVERYONE.

SID STILL ATE IT.

MADLUCK IS STILL IN A GUNFIGHT WIELDING A PAPERCLIP.

AND... I STILL DON'T FULLY UNDERSTAND HOW THE COMMUNICATION POACHERS GOT INTO OUR DIMENSION.

YOU'VE HELPED A LOT OF PEOPLE, DIRK.

WHY NOT JUST TAKE THIS MOMENT?

I NEED...

I NEED KNOW WHA SO SPEC ABOUT THE LINING O RHINOCER NOSE.

WA WHA

DIRK GENTLY!

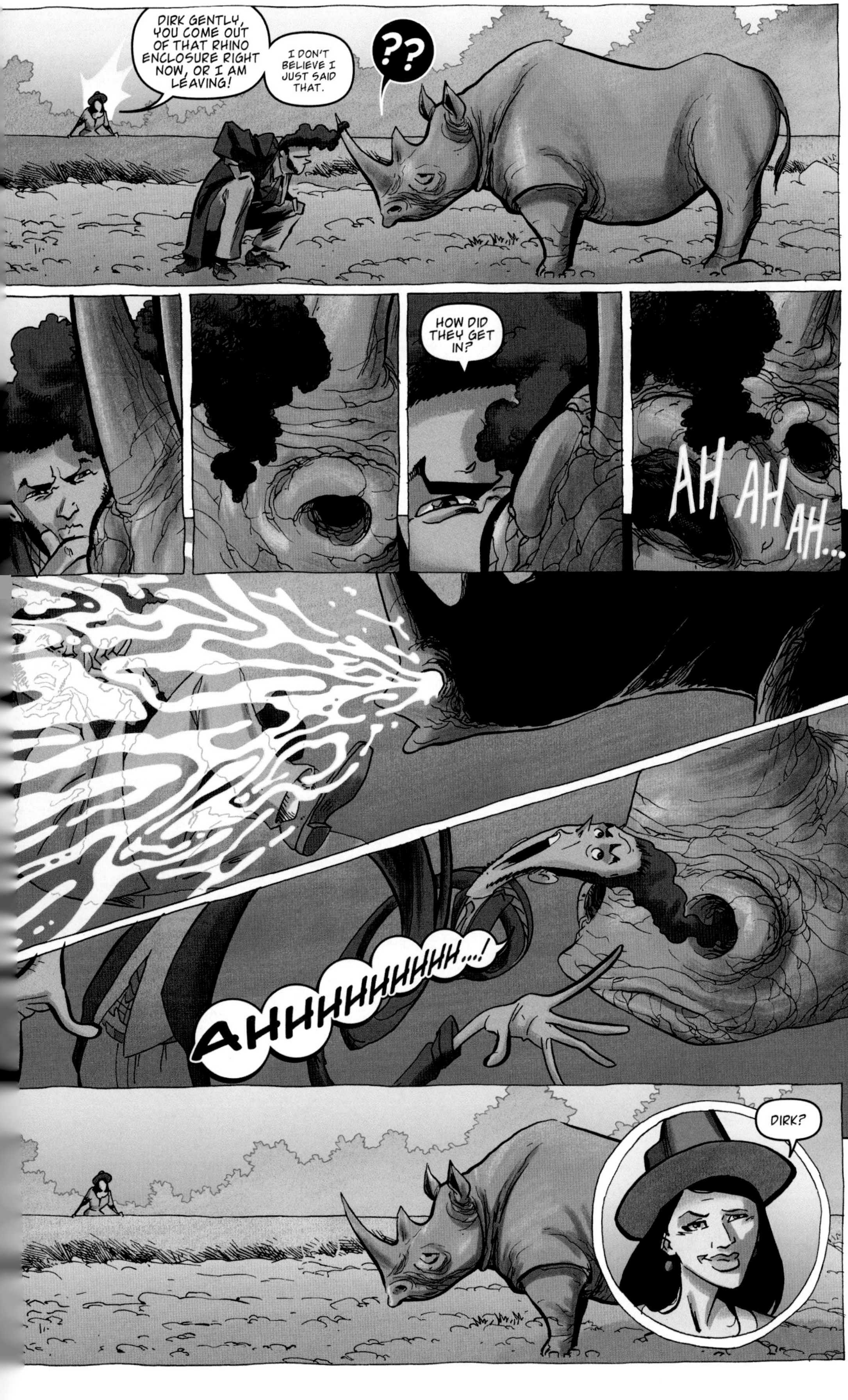
DIRK GENTLY, YOU COME OUT OF THAT RHINO ENCLOSURE RIGHT NOW, OR I AM LEAVING!
I DON'T BELIEVE I JUST SAID THAT.
??
HOW DID THEY GET IN?
AH AH AH...
AHHHHHHHHHH...!
DIRK?

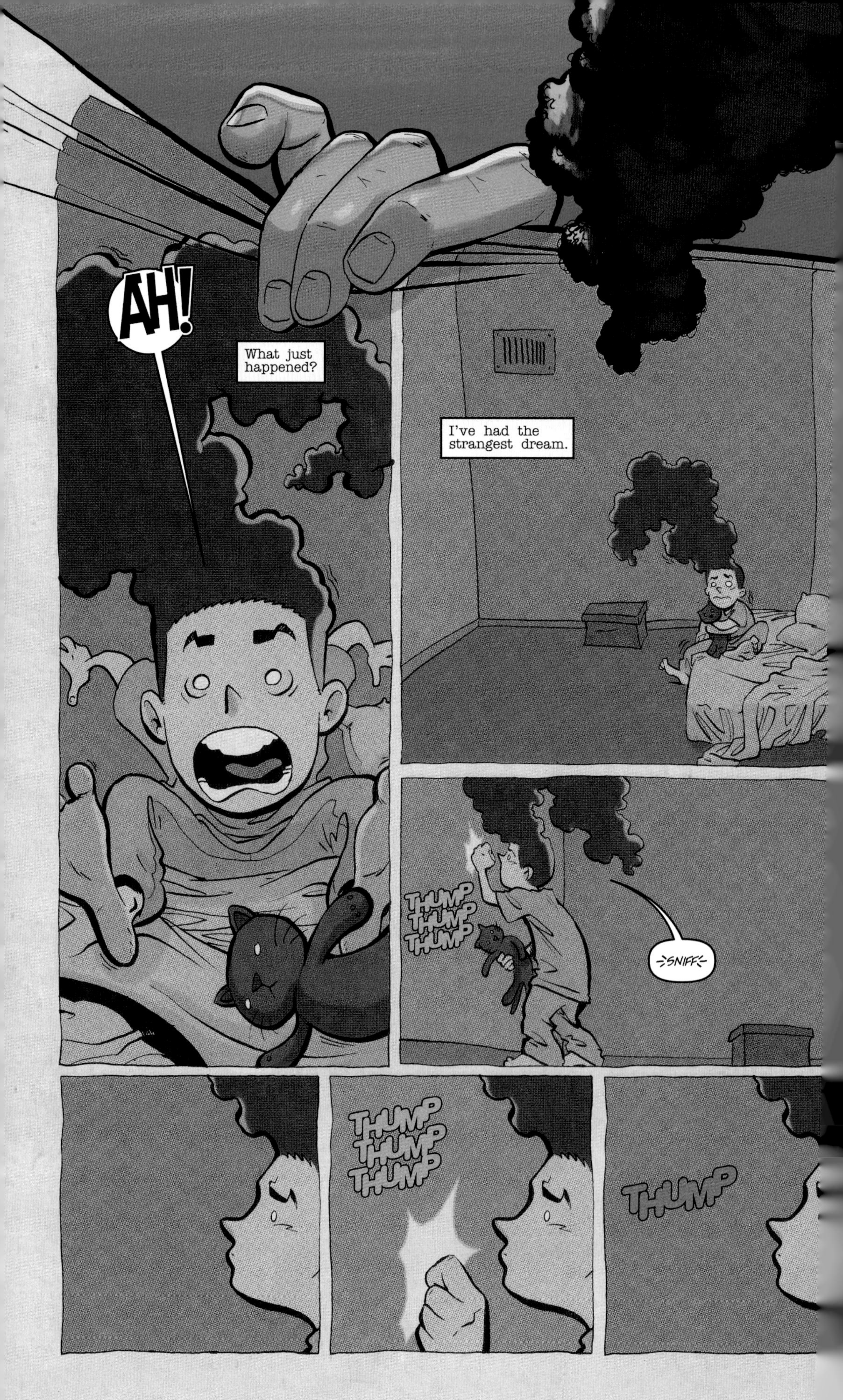
AH!
What just happened?
I've had the strangest dream.
THUMP THUMP THUMP
SNIFF
THUMP THUMP THUMP
THUMP

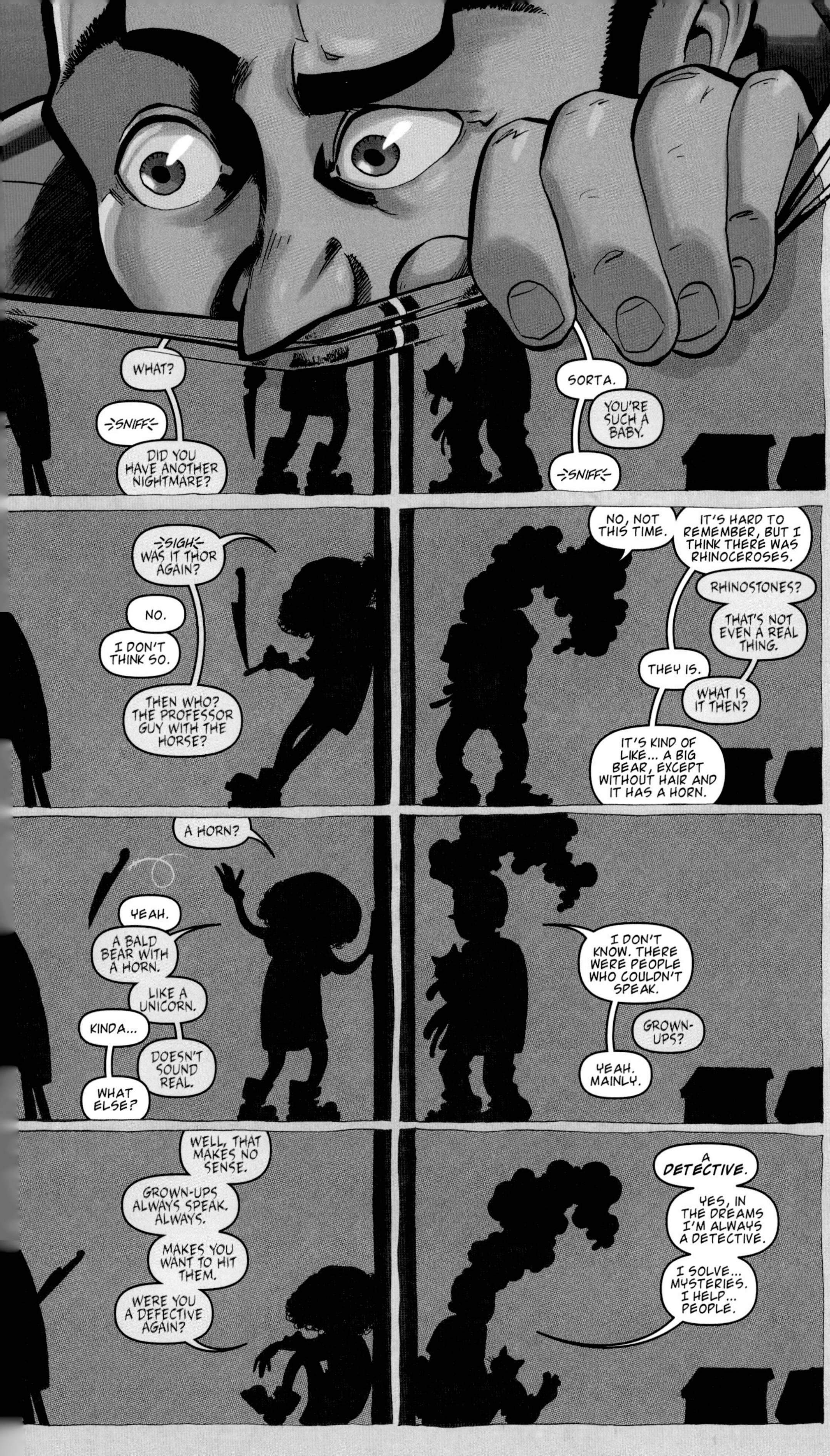
WHAT?
-SNIFF-
DID YOU HAVE ANOTHER NIGHTMARE?
SORTA.
YOU'RE SUCH A BABY.
-SNIFF-
-SIGH- WAS IT THOR AGAIN?
NO.
I DON'T THINK SO.
THEN WHO? THE PROFESSOR GUY WITH THE HORSE?
NO, NOT THIS TIME.
IT'S HARD TO REMEMBER, BUT I THINK THERE WAS RHINOCEROSES.
RHINOSTONES?
THAT'S NOT EVEN A REAL THING.
THEY IS.
WHAT IS IT THEN?
IT'S KIND OF LIKE... A BIG BEAR, EXCEPT WITHOUT HAIR AND IT HAS A HORN.
A HORN?
YEAH.
A BALD BEAR WITH A HORN.
LIKE A UNICORN.
KINDA...
DOESN'T SOUND REAL.
WHAT ELSE?
I DON'T KNOW. THERE WERE PEOPLE WHO COULDN'T SPEAK.
GROWN-UPS?
YEAH. MAINLY.
WELL, THAT MAKES NO SENSE.
GROWN-UPS ALWAYS SPEAK. ALWAYS.
MAKES YOU WANT TO HIT THEM.
WERE YOU A DEFECTIVE AGAIN?
A DETECTIVE.
YES, IN THE DREAMS I'M ALWAYS A DETECTIVE.
I SOLVE... MYSTERIES. I HELP... PEOPLE.

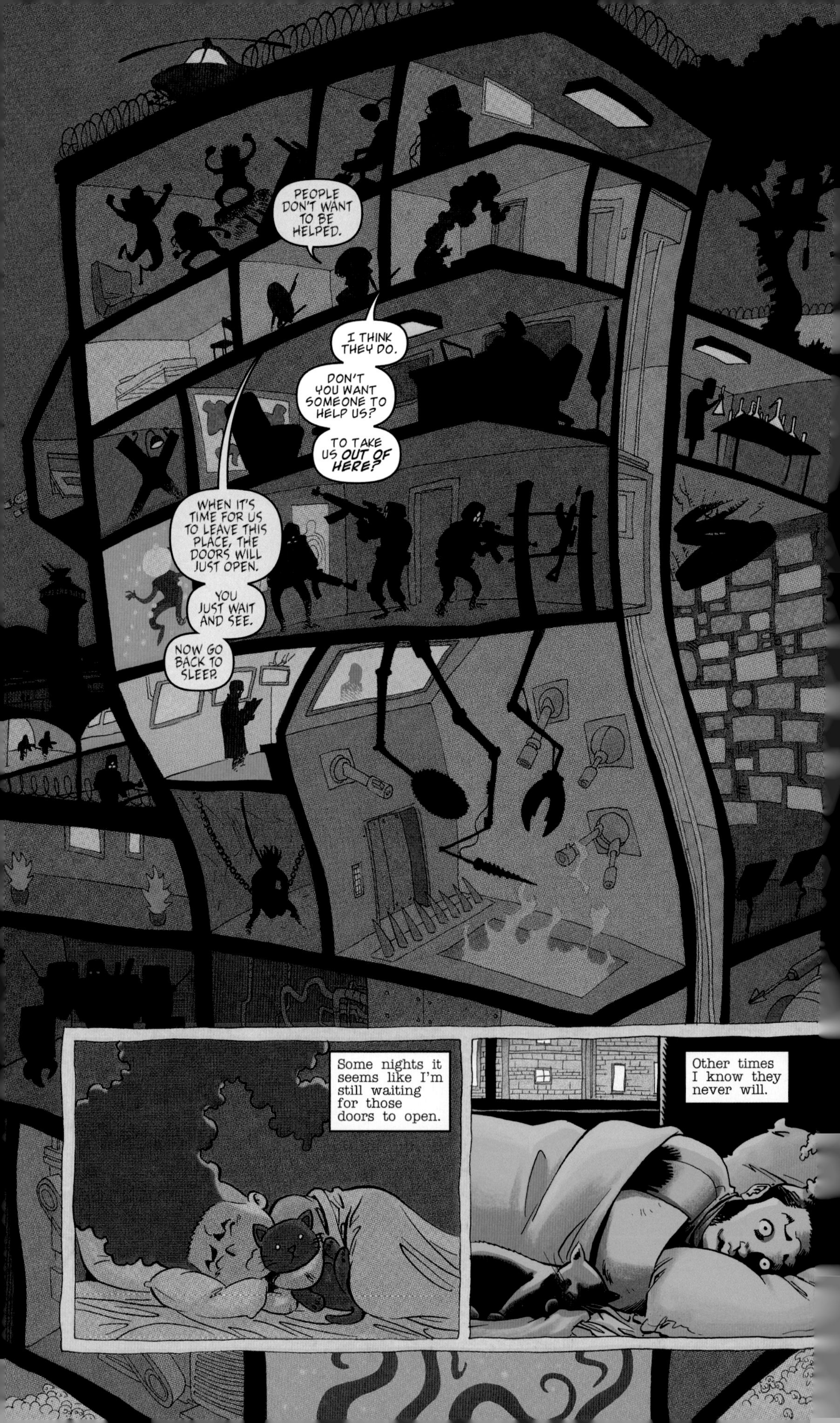
PEOPLE DON'T WANT TO BE HELPED.
I THINK THEY DO.
DON'T YOU WANT SOMEONE TO HELP US?
TO TAKE US OUT OF HERE?
WHEN IT'S TIME FOR US TO LEAVE THIS PLACE, THE DOORS WILL JUST OPEN.
YOU JUST WAIT AND SEE.
NOW GO BACK TO SLEEP.
Some nights it seems like I'm still waiting for those doors to open.
Other times I know they never will.

Dirk Gently's
HOLISTIC DETECTIVE AGENCY

The Interconnectedness of All Kings

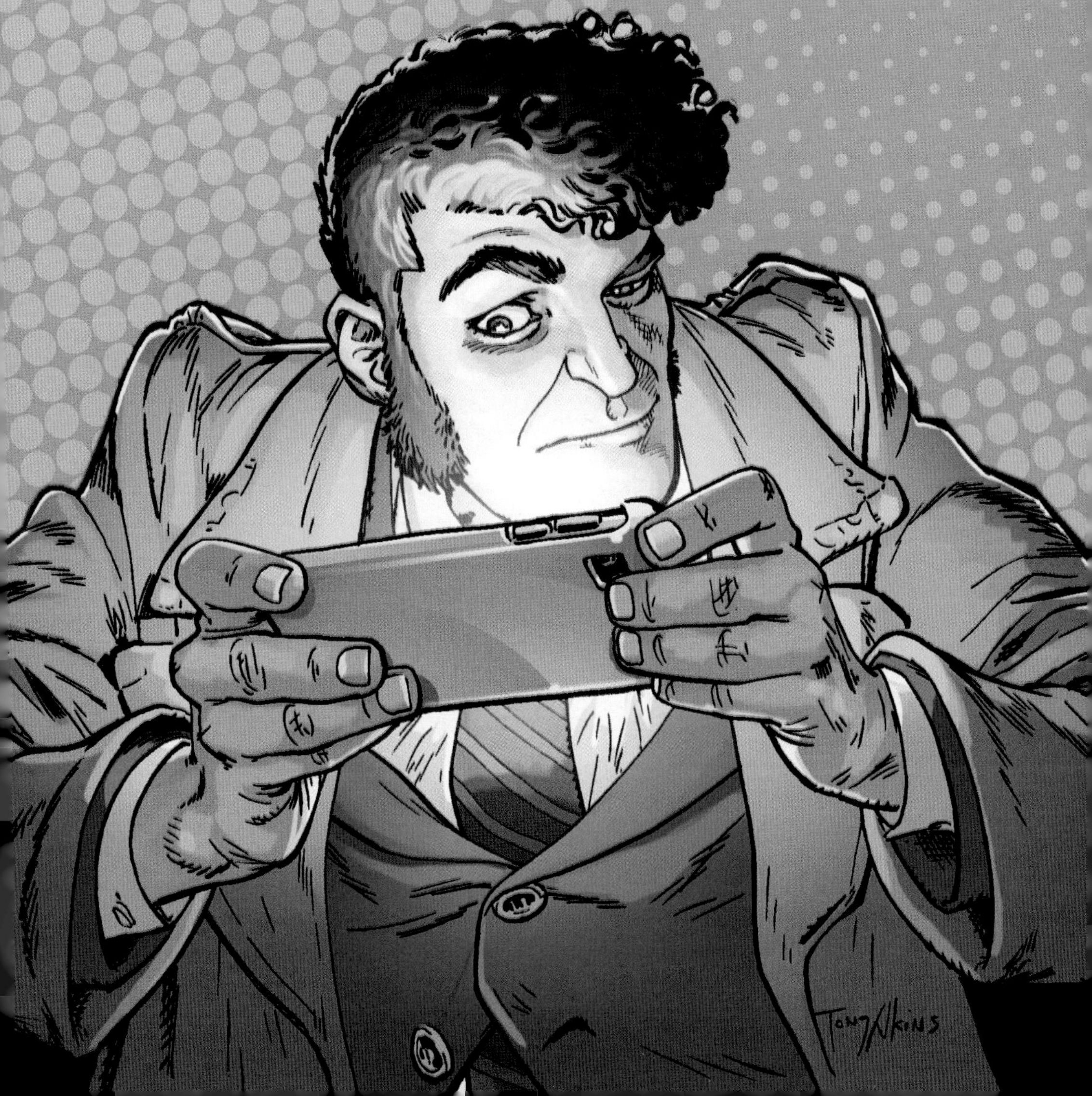

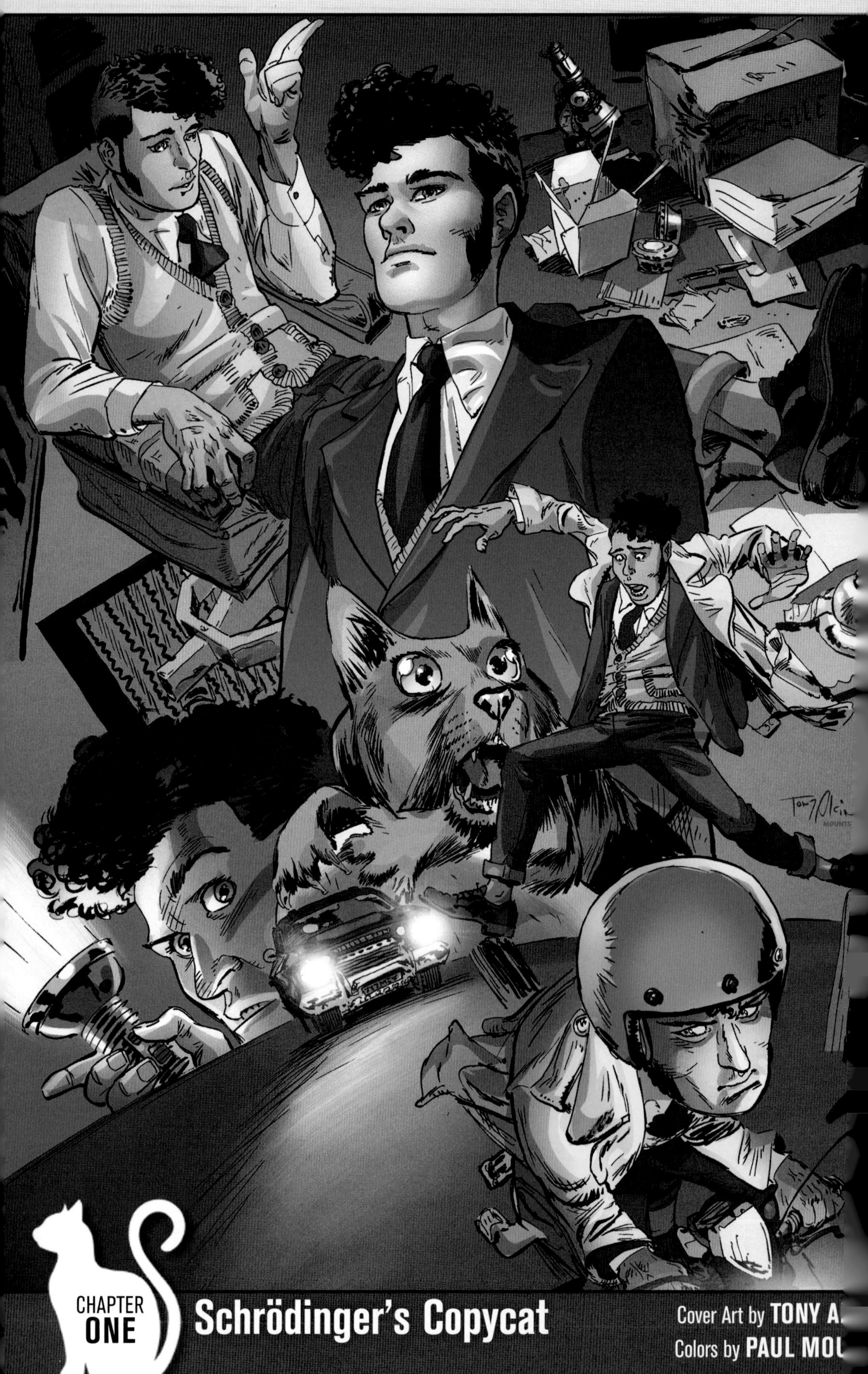

CHAPTER ONE

Schrödinger's Copycat

Cover Art by **TONY A**

Colors by **PAUL MOU**

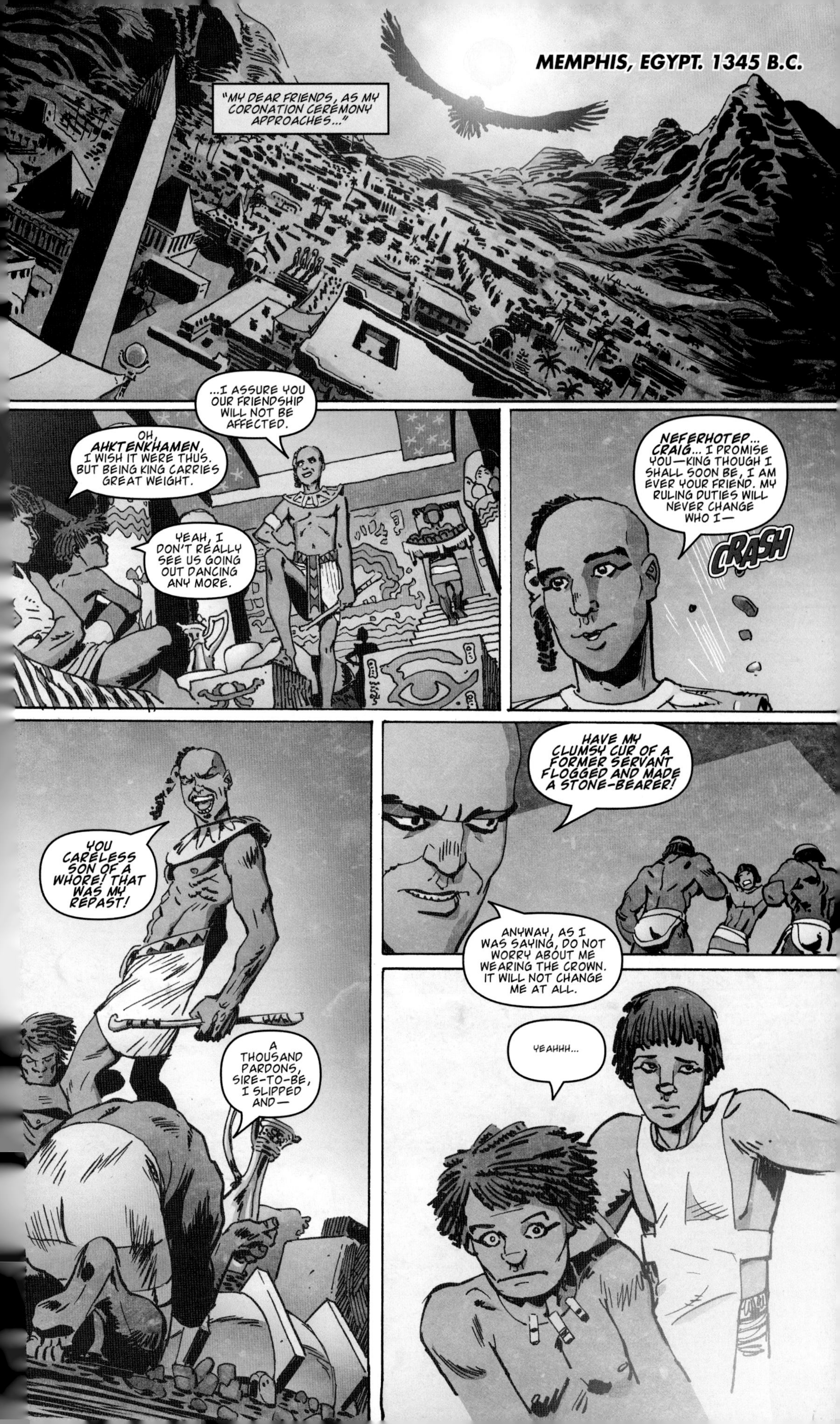
MEMPHIS, EGYPT. 1345 B.C.
"MY DEAR FRIENDS, AS MY CORONATION CEREMONY APPROACHES..."
...I ASSURE YOU OUR FRIENDSHIP WILL NOT BE AFFECTED.
OH, AHKTENKHAMEN, I WISH IT WERE THUS. BUT BEING KING CARRIES GREAT WEIGHT.
YEAH, I DON'T REALLY SEE US GOING OUT DANCING ANY MORE.
NEFERHOTEP... CRAIG... I PROMISE YOU—KING THOUGH I SHALL SOON BE, I AM EVER YOUR FRIEND. MY RULING DUTIES WILL NEVER CHANGE WHO I—
CRASH
YOU CARELESS SON OF A WHORE! THAT WAS MY REPAST!
A THOUSAND PARDONS, SIRE-TO-BE, I SLIPPED AND—
HAVE MY CLUMSY CUR OF A FORMER SERVANT FLOGGED AND MADE A STONE-BEARER!
ANYWAY, AS I WAS SAYING, DO NOT WORRY ABOUT ME WEARING THE CROWN. IT WILL NOT CHANGE ME AT ALL.
YEAHHH...

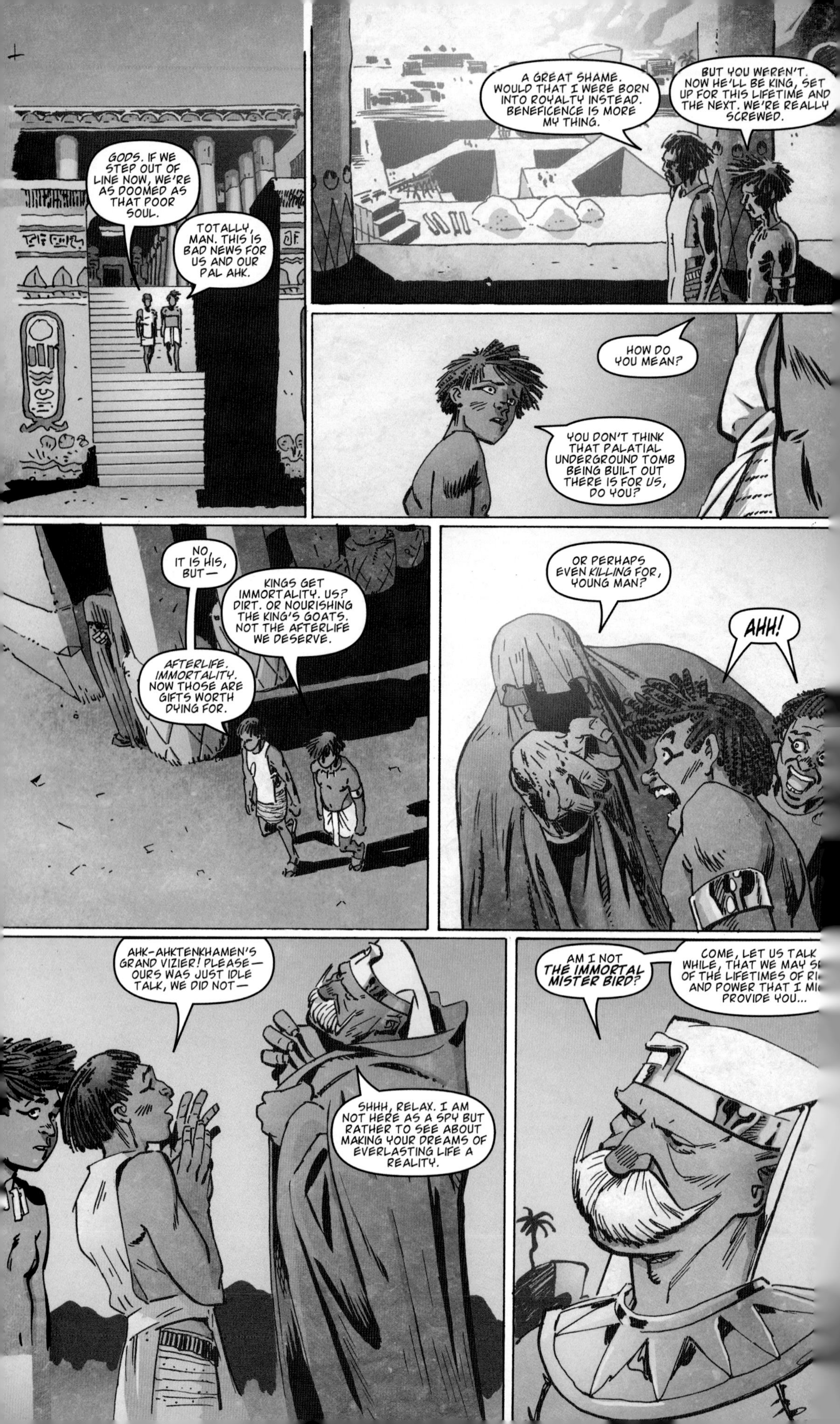
GODS. IF WE STEP OUT OF LINE NOW, WE'RE AS DOOMED AS THAT POOR SOUL.
TOTALLY, MAN. THIS IS BAD NEWS FOR US AND OUR PAL AHK.
A GREAT SHAME. WOULD THAT I WERE BORN INTO ROYALTY INSTEAD. BENEFICENCE IS MORE MY THING.
BUT YOU WEREN'T. NOW HE'LL BE KING, SET UP FOR THIS LIFETIME AND THE NEXT. WE'RE REALLY SCREWED.
HOW DO YOU MEAN?
YOU DON'T THINK THAT PALATIAL UNDERGROUND TOMB BEING BUILT OUT THERE IS FOR US, DO YOU?
NO, IT IS HIS, BUT—
KINGS GET IMMORTALITY. US? DIRT. OR NOURISHING THE KING'S GOATS. NOT THE AFTERLIFE WE DESERVE.
AFTERLIFE. IMMORTALITY. NOW THOSE ARE GIFTS WORTH DYING FOR.
OR PERHAPS EVEN KILLING FOR, YOUNG MAN?
AHH!
AHK-AHKTENKHAMEN'S GRAND VIZIER! PLEASE— OURS WAS JUST IDLE TALK, WE DID NOT—
SHHH, RELAX. I AM NOT HERE AS A SPY BUT RATHER TO SEE ABOUT MAKING YOUR DREAMS OF EVERLASTING LIFE A REALITY.
AM I NOT THE IMMORTAL MISTER BIRD?

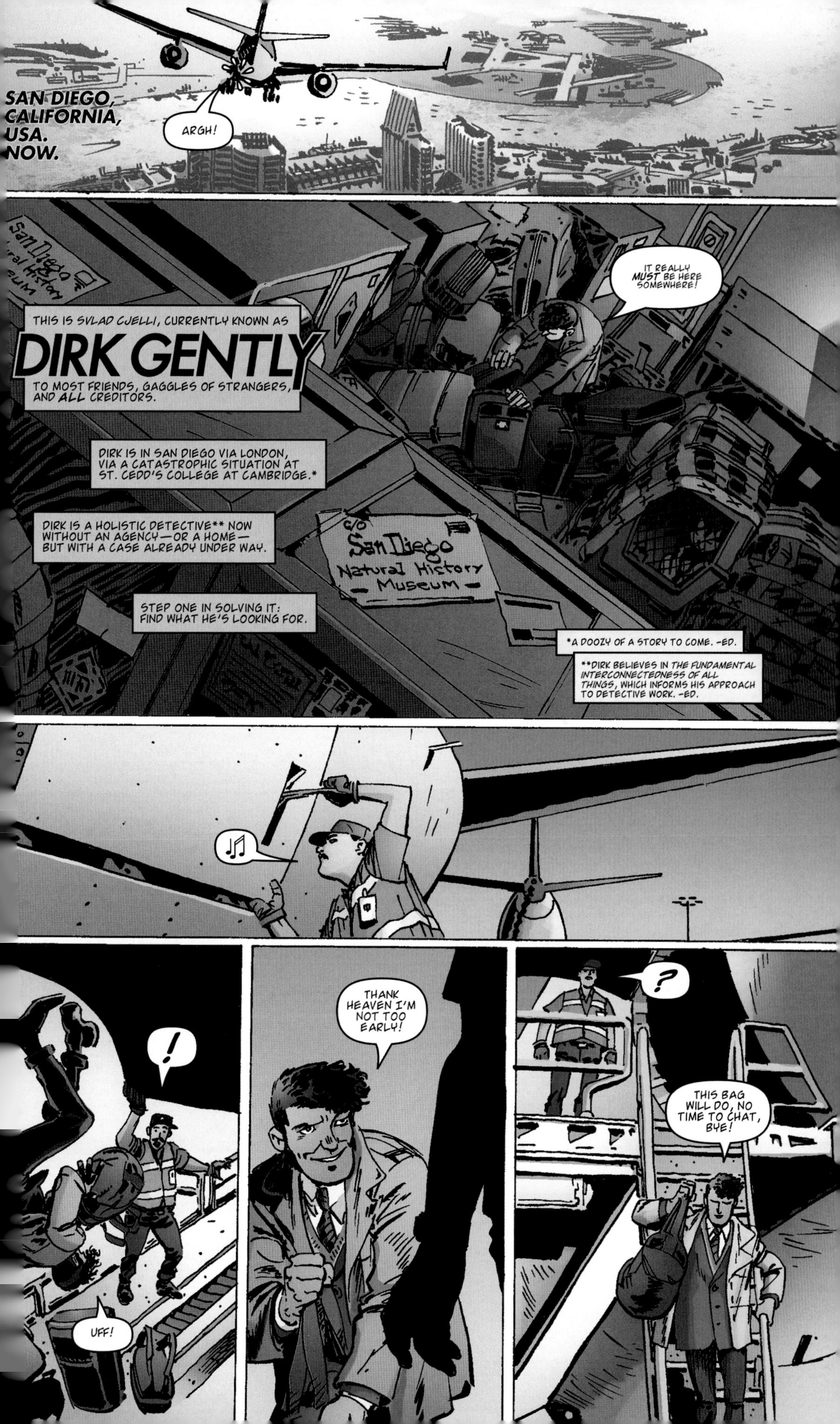
SAN DIEGO, CALIFORNIA, USA. NOW.
ARGH!
San Diego Natural History Museum
IT REALLY MUST BE HERE SOMEWHERE!
THIS IS SVLAD CJELLI, CURRENTLY KNOWN AS
DIRK GENTLY
TO MOST FRIENDS, GAGGLES OF STRANGERS, AND ALL CREDITORS.
DIRK IS IN SAN DIEGO VIA LONDON, VIA A CATASTROPHIC SITUATION AT ST. CEDD'S COLLEGE AT CAMBRIDGE.*
DIRK IS A HOLISTIC DETECTIVE** NOW WITHOUT AN AGENCY—OR A HOME—BUT WITH A CASE ALREADY UNDER WAY.
c/o San Diego Natural History Museum
STEP ONE IN SOLVING IT: FIND WHAT HE'S LOOKING FOR.
*A DOOZY OF A STORY TO COME. -ED.
**DIRK BELIEVES IN THE FUNDAMENTAL INTERCONNECTEDNESS OF ALL THINGS, WHICH INFORMS HIS APPROACH TO DETECTIVE WORK. -ED.
♫
!
UFF!
THANK HEAVEN I'M NOT TOO EARLY!
?
THIS BAG WILL DO, NO TIME TO CHAT, BYE!

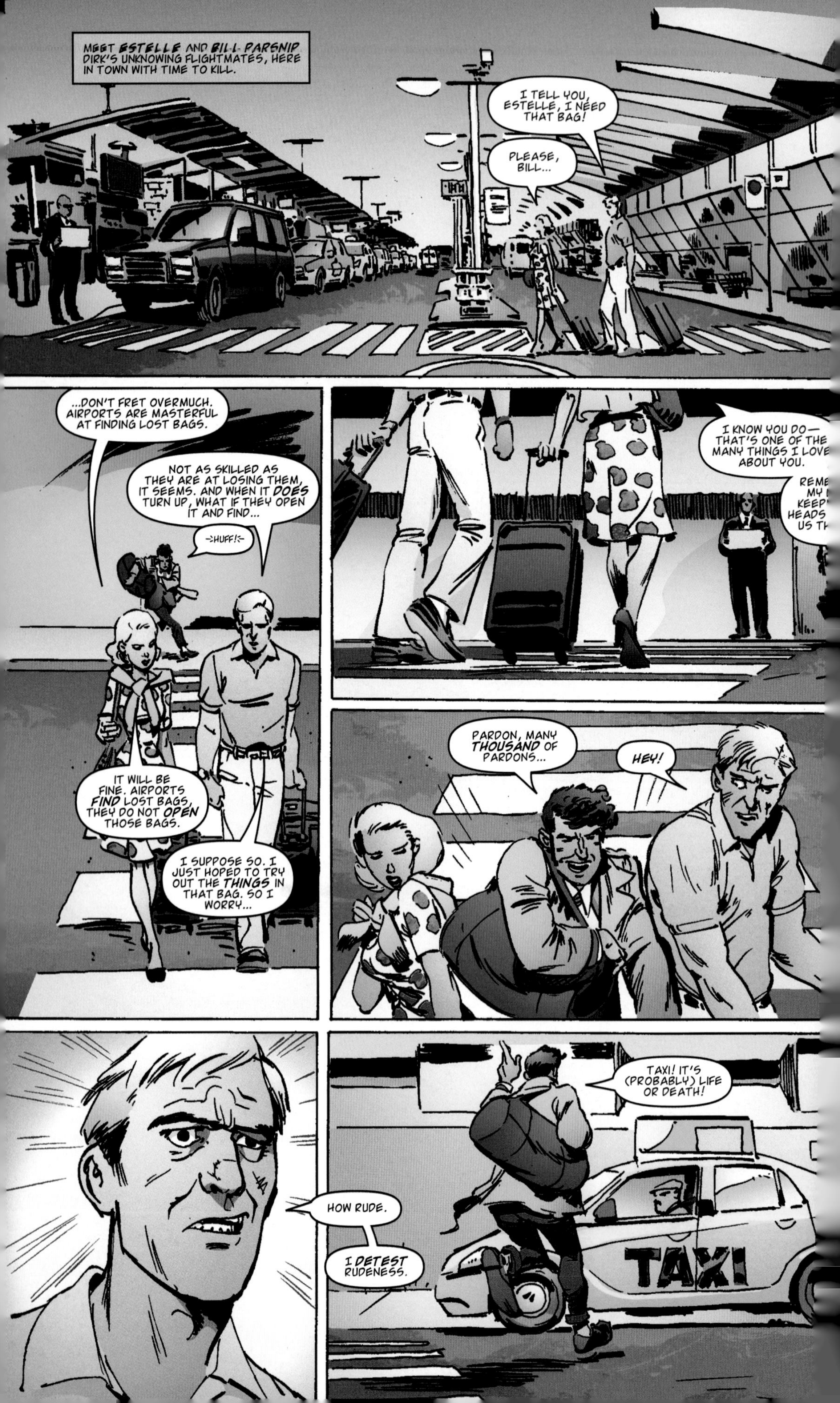
MEET ESTELLE AND BILL PARSNIP DIRK'S UNKNOWING FLIGHTMATES, HERE IN TOWN WITH TIME TO KILL.
I TELL YOU, ESTELLE, I NEED THAT BAG!
PLEASE, BILL...
...DON'T FRET OVERMUCH. AIRPORTS ARE MASTERFUL AT FINDING LOST BAGS.
NOT AS SKILLED AS THEY ARE AT LOSING THEM, IT SEEMS. AND WHEN IT DOES TURN UP, WHAT IF THEY OPEN IT AND FIND...
HUFF!
IT WILL BE FINE. AIRPORTS FIND LOST BAGS, THEY DO NOT OPEN THOSE BAGS.
I SUPPOSE SO. I JUST HOPED TO TRY OUT THE THINGS IN THAT BAG. SO I WORRY...
I KNOW YOU DO— THAT'S ONE OF THE MANY THINGS I LOVE ABOUT YOU.
PARDON, MANY THOUSAND OF PARDONS...
HEY!
HOW RUDE.
I DETEST RUDENESS.
TAXI! IT'S (PROBABLY) LIFE OR DEATH!
TAXI

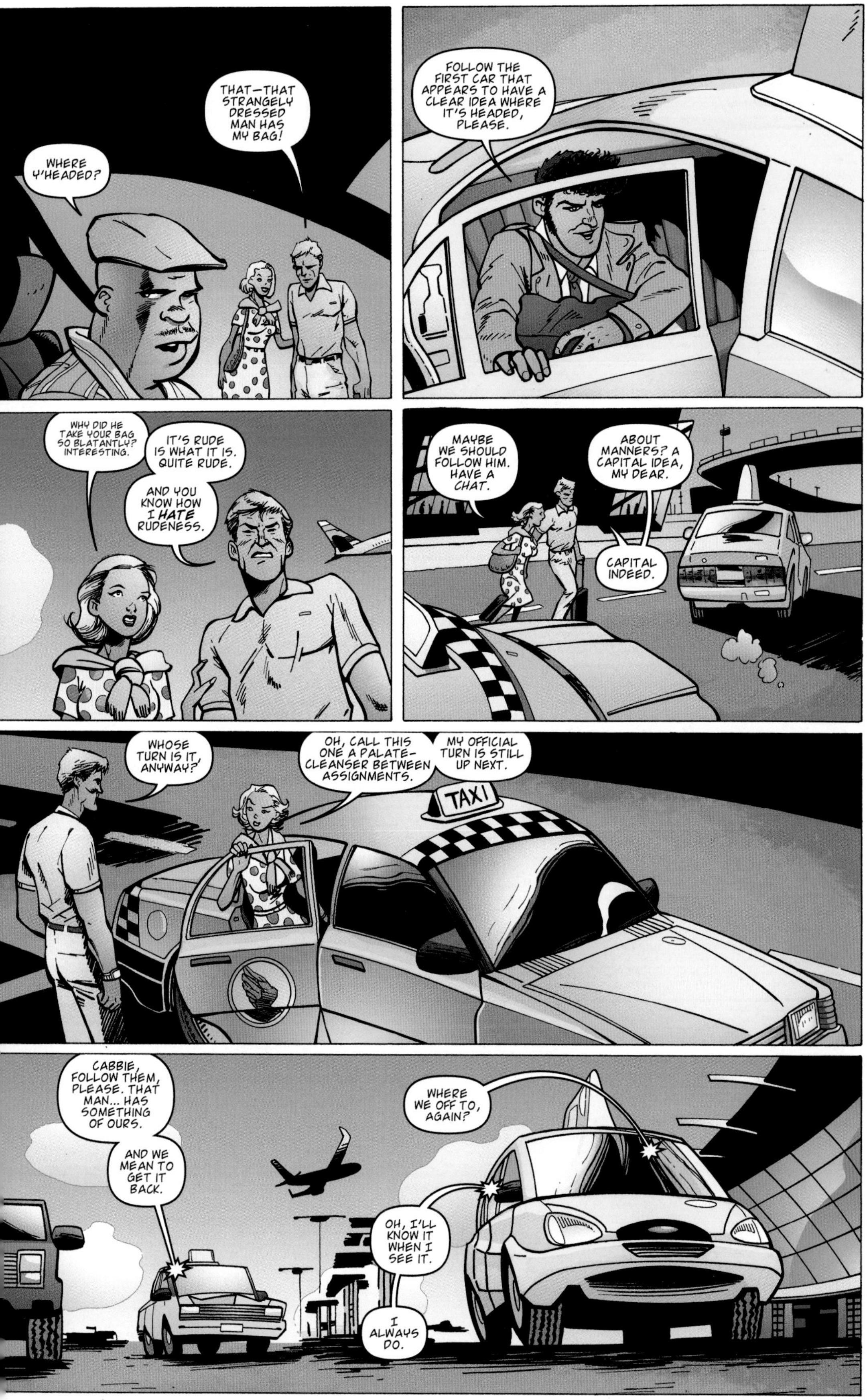
THAT—THAT STRANGELY DRESSED MAN HAS MY BAG!
WHERE Y'HEADED?
FOLLOW THE FIRST CAR THAT APPEARS TO HAVE A CLEAR IDEA WHERE IT'S HEADED, PLEASE.
WHY DID HE TAKE YOUR BAG SO BLATANTLY? INTERESTING.
IT'S RUDE IS WHAT IT IS. QUITE RUDE.
AND YOU KNOW HOW I HATE RUDENESS.
MAYBE WE SHOULD FOLLOW HIM. HAVE A CHAT.
ABOUT MANNERS? A CAPITAL IDEA, MY DEAR.
CAPITAL INDEED.
WHOSE TURN IS IT, ANYWAY?
OH, CALL THIS ONE A PALATE-CLEANSER BETWEEN ASSIGNMENTS.
MY OFFICIAL TURN IS STILL UP NEXT.
TAXI
CABBIE, FOLLOW THEM, PLEASE. THAT MAN... HAS SOMETHING OF OURS.
AND WE MEAN TO GET IT BACK.
WHERE WE OFF TO, AGAIN?
OH, I'LL KNOW IT WHEN I SEE IT.
I ALWAYS DO.

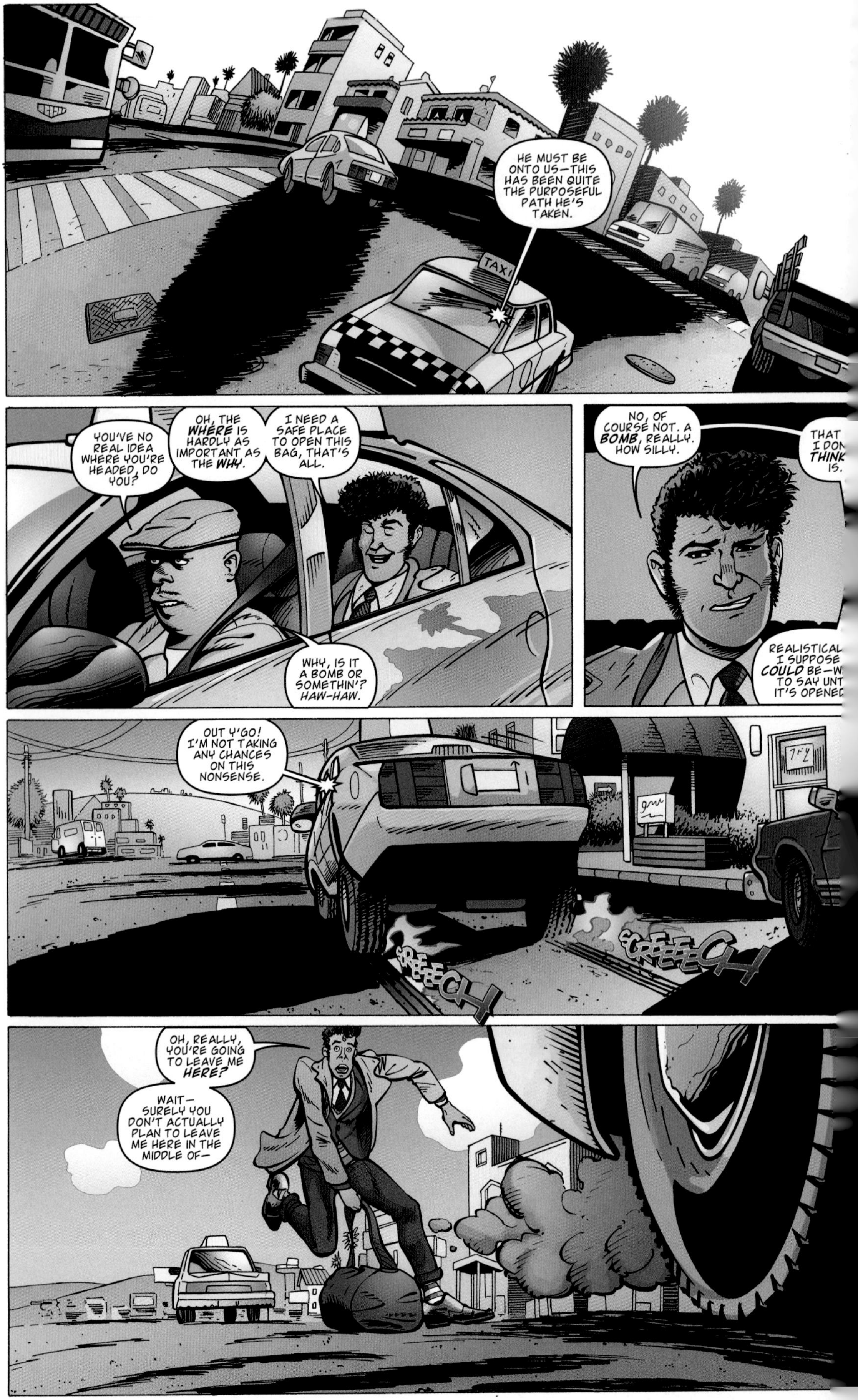
HE MUST BE ONTO US—THIS HAS BEEN QUITE THE PURPOSEFUL PATH HE'S TAKEN.
TAXI
YOU'VE NO REAL IDEA WHERE YOU'RE HEADED, DO YOU?
OH, THE **WHERE** IS HARDLY AS IMPORTANT AS THE **WHY**.
I NEED A SAFE PLACE TO OPEN THIS BAG, THAT'S ALL.
WHY, IS IT A BOMB OR SOMETHIN'? *HAW-HAW.*
NO, OF COURSE NOT. A **BOMB**, REALLY. HOW SILLY.
THAT I DON **THINK** IS.
REALISTICAL I SUPPOSE **COULD** BE—W TO SAY UNT IT'S OPENED
OUT Y'GO! I'M NOT TAKING ANY CHANCES ON THIS NONSENSE.
SCREEECH
SCREEECH
OH, REALLY, YOU'RE GOING TO LEAVE ME **HERE?**
WAIT— SURELY YOU DON'T ACTUALLY PLAN TO LEAVE ME HERE IN THE MIDDLE OF—

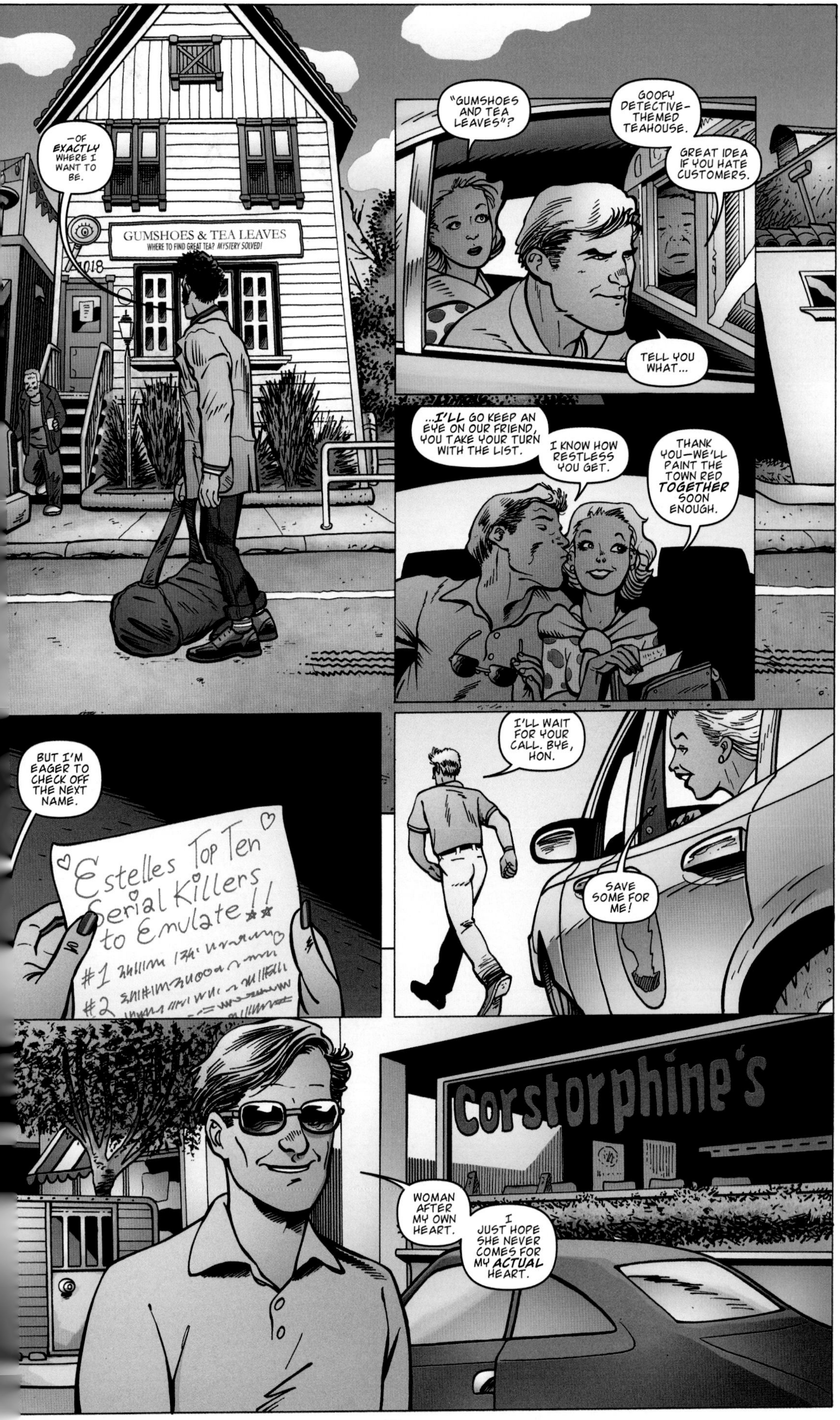
GUMSHOES & TEA LEAVES
WHERE TO FIND GREAT TEA? MYSTERY SOLVED!
—OF *EXACTLY* WHERE I WANT TO BE.
"GUMSHOES AND TEA LEAVES"?
GOOFY DETECTIVE-THEMED TEAHOUSE.
GREAT IDEA IF YOU HATE CUSTOMERS.
TELL YOU WHAT...
...*I'LL* GO KEEP AN EYE ON OUR FRIEND, YOU TAKE YOUR TURN WITH THE LIST.
I KNOW HOW RESTLESS YOU GET.
THANK YOU—WE'LL PAINT THE TOWN RED *TOGETHER* SOON ENOUGH.
BUT I'M EAGER TO CHECK OFF THE NEXT NAME.
Estelles Top Ten Serial Killers to Emulate!!
#1
#2
I'LL WAIT FOR YOUR CALL. BYE, HON.
SAVE SOME FOR ME!
Corstorphine's
WOMAN AFTER MY OWN HEART.
I JUST HOPE SHE NEVER COMES FOR MY *ACTUAL* HEART.

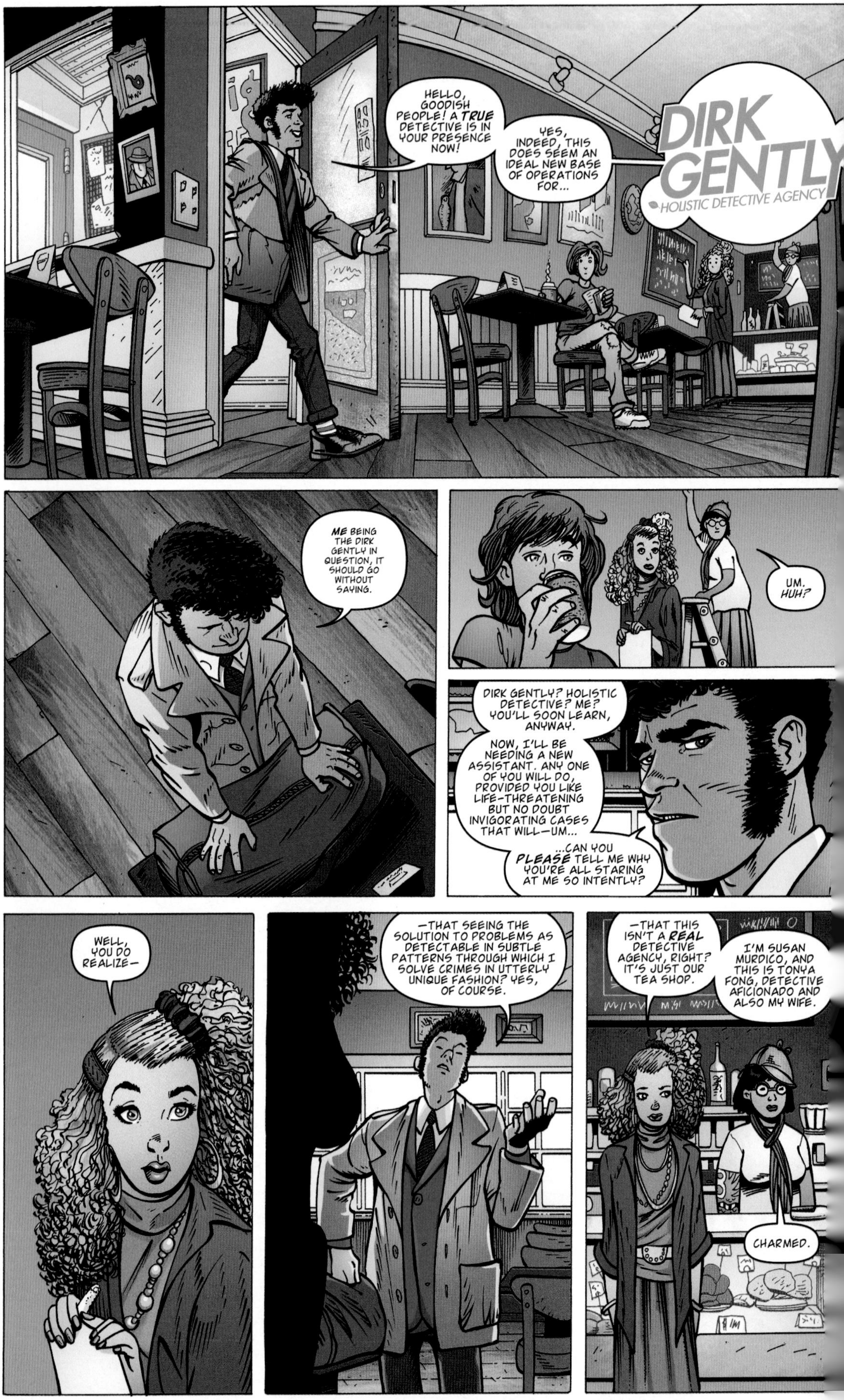
HELLO, GOODISH PEOPLE! A TRUE DETECTIVE IS IN YOUR PRESENCE NOW!
YES, INDEED, THIS DOES SEEM AN IDEAL NEW BASE OF OPERATIONS FOR...
DIRK GENTLY
HOLISTIC DETECTIVE AGENCY
ME BEING THE DIRK GENTLY IN QUESTION, IT SHOULD GO WITHOUT SAYING.
UM. HUH?
DIRK GENTLY? HOLISTIC DETECTIVE? ME? YOU'LL SOON LEARN, ANYWAY.
NOW, I'LL BE NEEDING A NEW ASSISTANT. ANY ONE OF YOU WILL DO, PROVIDED YOU LIKE LIFE-THREATENING BUT NO DOUBT INVIGORATING CASES THAT WILL—UM...
...CAN YOU PLEASE TELL ME WHY YOU'RE ALL STARING AT ME SO INTENTLY?
WELL, YOU DO REALIZE—
—THAT SEEING THE SOLUTION TO PROBLEMS AS DETECTABLE IN SUBTLE PATTERNS THROUGH WHICH I SOLVE CRIMES IN UTTERLY UNIQUE FASHION? YES, OF COURSE.
—THAT THIS ISN'T A REAL DETECTIVE AGENCY, RIGHT? IT'S JUST OUR TEA SHOP.
I'M SUSAN MURDICO, AND THIS IS TONYA FONG, DETECTIVE AFICIONADO AND ALSO MY WIFE.
CHARMED.

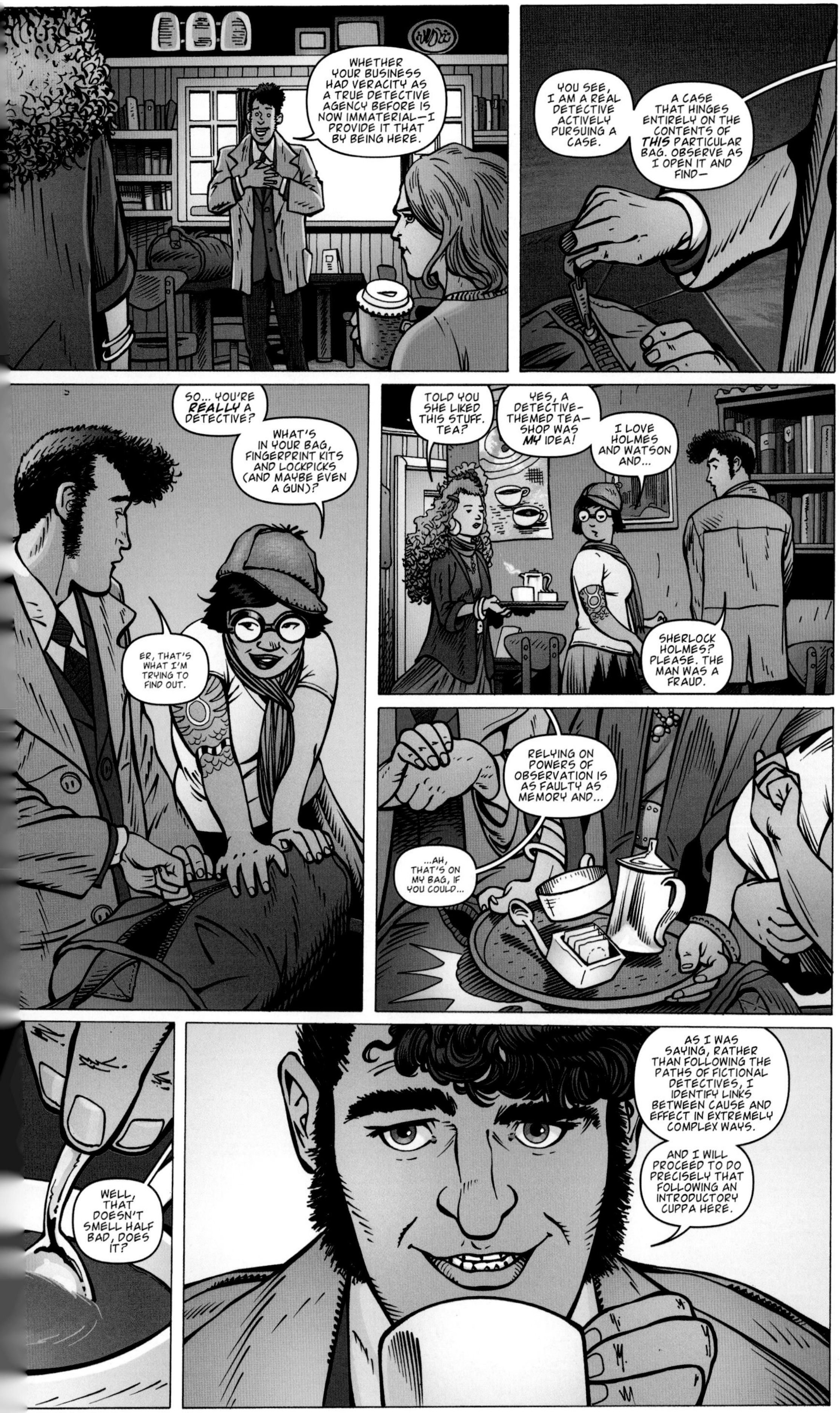
WHETHER YOUR BUSINESS HAD VERACITY AS A TRUE DETECTIVE AGENCY BEFORE IS NOW IMMATERIAL—I PROVIDE IT THAT BY BEING HERE.
YOU SEE, I AM A REAL DETECTIVE ACTIVELY PURSUING A CASE.
A CASE THAT HINGES ENTIRELY ON THE CONTENTS OF THIS PARTICULAR BAG. OBSERVE AS I OPEN IT AND FIND—
SO... YOU'RE REALLY A DETECTIVE?
WHAT'S IN YOUR BAG, FINGERPRINT KITS AND LOCKPICKS (AND MAYBE EVEN A GUN)?
ER, THAT'S WHAT I'M TRYING TO FIND OUT.
TOLD YOU SHE LIKED THIS STUFF. TEA?
YES, A DETECTIVE-THEMED TEA-SHOP WAS MY IDEA!
I LOVE HOLMES AND WATSON AND...
SHERLOCK HOLMES? PLEASE. THE MAN WAS A FRAUD.
RELYING ON POWERS OF OBSERVATION IS AS FAULTY AS MEMORY AND...
...AH, THAT'S ON MY BAG, IF YOU COULD...
WELL, THAT DOESN'T SMELL HALF BAD, DOES IT?
AS I WAS SAYING, RATHER THAN FOLLOWING THE PATHS OF FICTIONAL DETECTIVES, I IDENTIFY LINKS BETWEEN CAUSE AND EFFECT IN EXTREMELY COMPLEX WAYS.
AND I WILL PROCEED TO DO PRECISELY THAT FOLLOWING AN INTRODUCTORY CUPPA HERE.

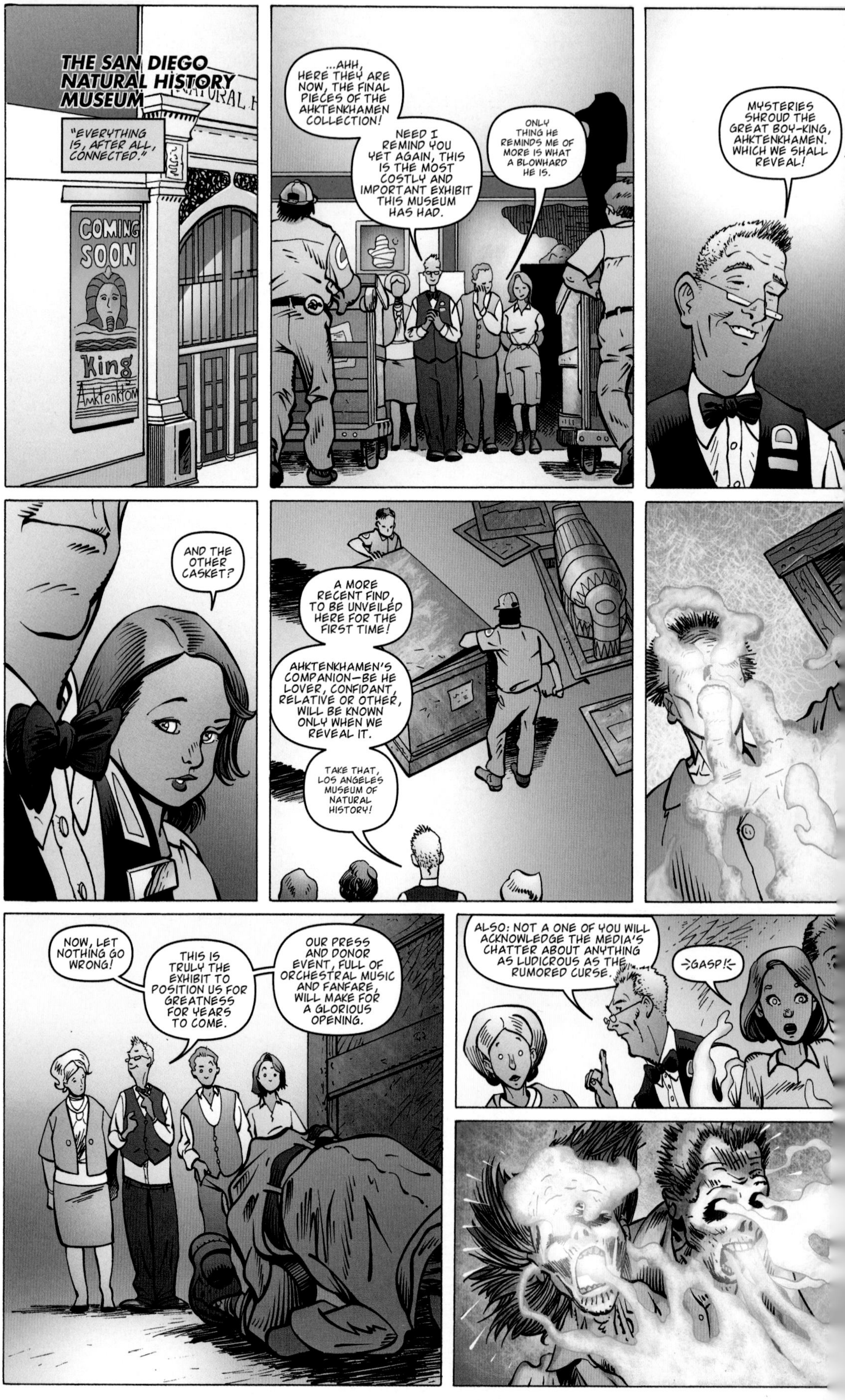
THE SAN DIEGO NATURAL HISTORY MUSEUM
"EVERYTHING IS, AFTER ALL, CONNECTED."
COMING SOON
King
...AHH, HERE THEY ARE NOW, THE FINAL PIECES OF THE AHKTENKHAMEN COLLECTION!
NEED I REMIND YOU YET AGAIN, THIS IS THE MOST COSTLY AND IMPORTANT EXHIBIT THIS MUSEUM HAS HAD.
ONLY THING HE REMINDS ME OF MORE IS WHAT A BLOWHARD HE IS.
MYSTERIES SHROUD THE GREAT BOY-KING, AHKTENKHAMEN. WHICH WE SHALL REVEAL!
AND THE OTHER CASKET?
A MORE RECENT FIND, TO BE UNVEILED HERE FOR THE FIRST TIME!
AHKTENKHAMEN'S COMPANION—BE HE LOVER, CONFIDANT, RELATIVE OR OTHER, WILL BE KNOWN ONLY WHEN WE REVEAL IT.
TAKE THAT, LOS ANGELES MUSEUM OF NATURAL HISTORY!
NOW, LET NOTHING GO WRONG!
THIS IS TRULY THE EXHIBIT TO POSITION US FOR GREATNESS FOR YEARS TO COME.
OUR PRESS AND DONOR EVENT, FULL OF ORCHESTRAL MUSIC AND FANFARE, WILL MAKE FOR A GLORIOUS OPENING.
ALSO: NOT A ONE OF YOU WILL ACKNOWLEDGE THE MEDIA'S CHATTER ABOUT ANYTHING AS LUDICROUS AS THE RUMORED CURSE.
GASP!

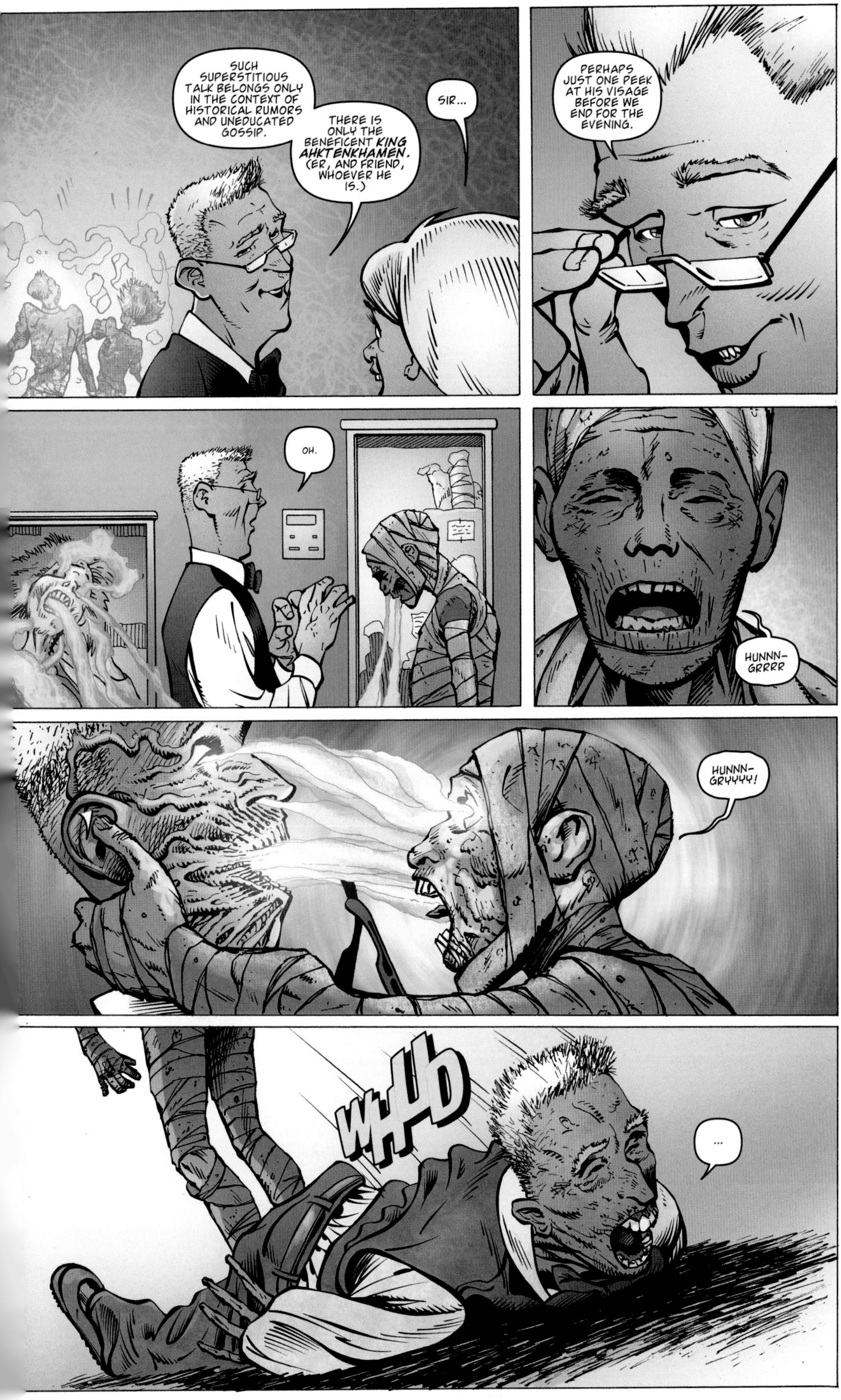
SUCH SUPERSTITIOUS TALK BELONGS ONLY IN THE CONTEXT OF HISTORICAL RUMORS AND UNEDUCATED GOSSIP.
THERE IS ONLY THE BENEFICENT **KING AHKTENKHAMEN.** (ER, AND FRIEND, WHOEVER HE IS.)
SIR...
PERHAPS JUST ONE PEEK AT HIS VISAGE BEFORE WE END FOR THE EVENING.
OH.
HUNNN-GRRRR
HUNNN-GRYYYY!
WHUD
...

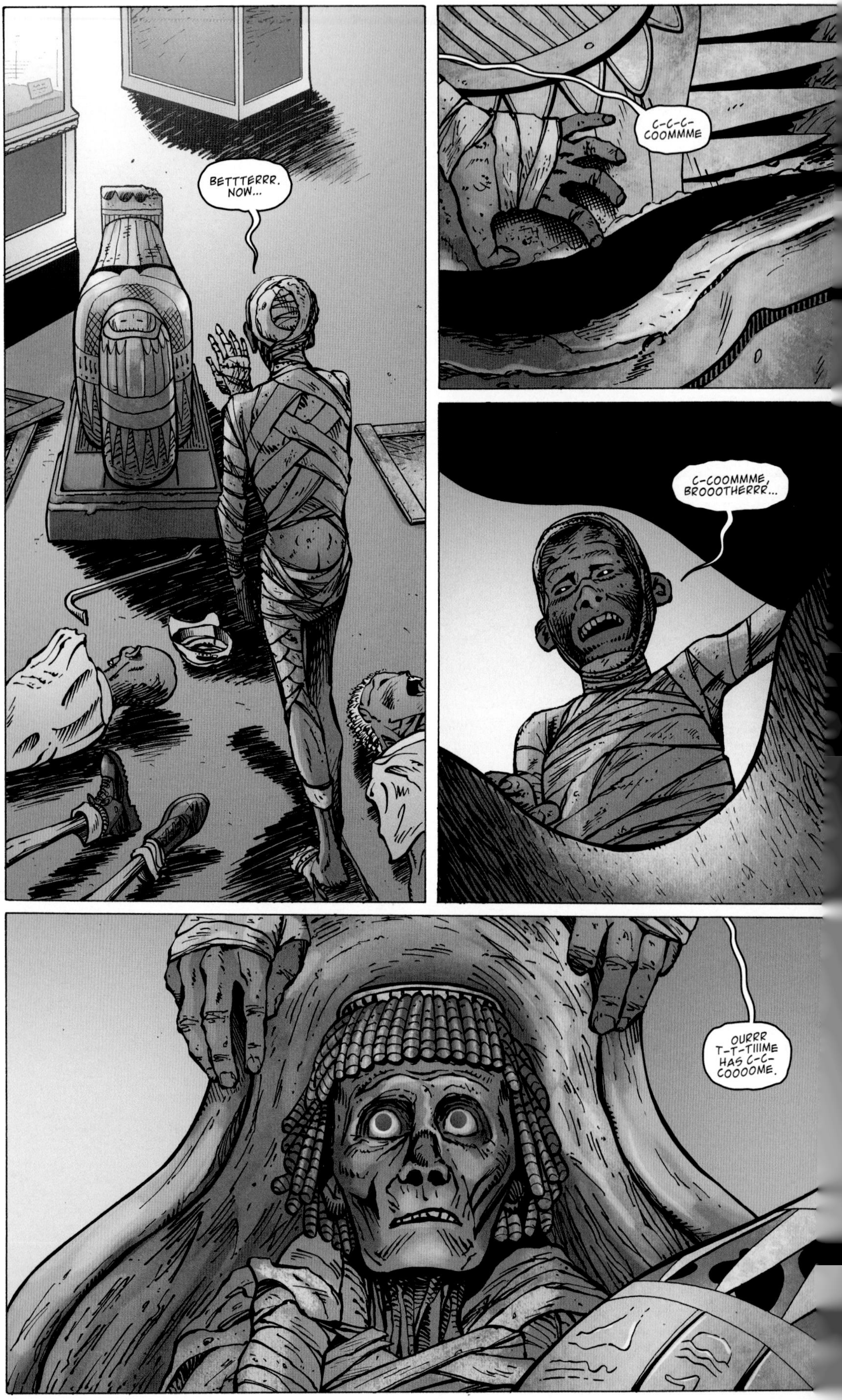
BETTTERRR. NOW...
C-C-C-COOMMME
C-COOMMME, BROOOTHERRR...
OURRR T-T-TIIIME HAS C-C-COOOOME.

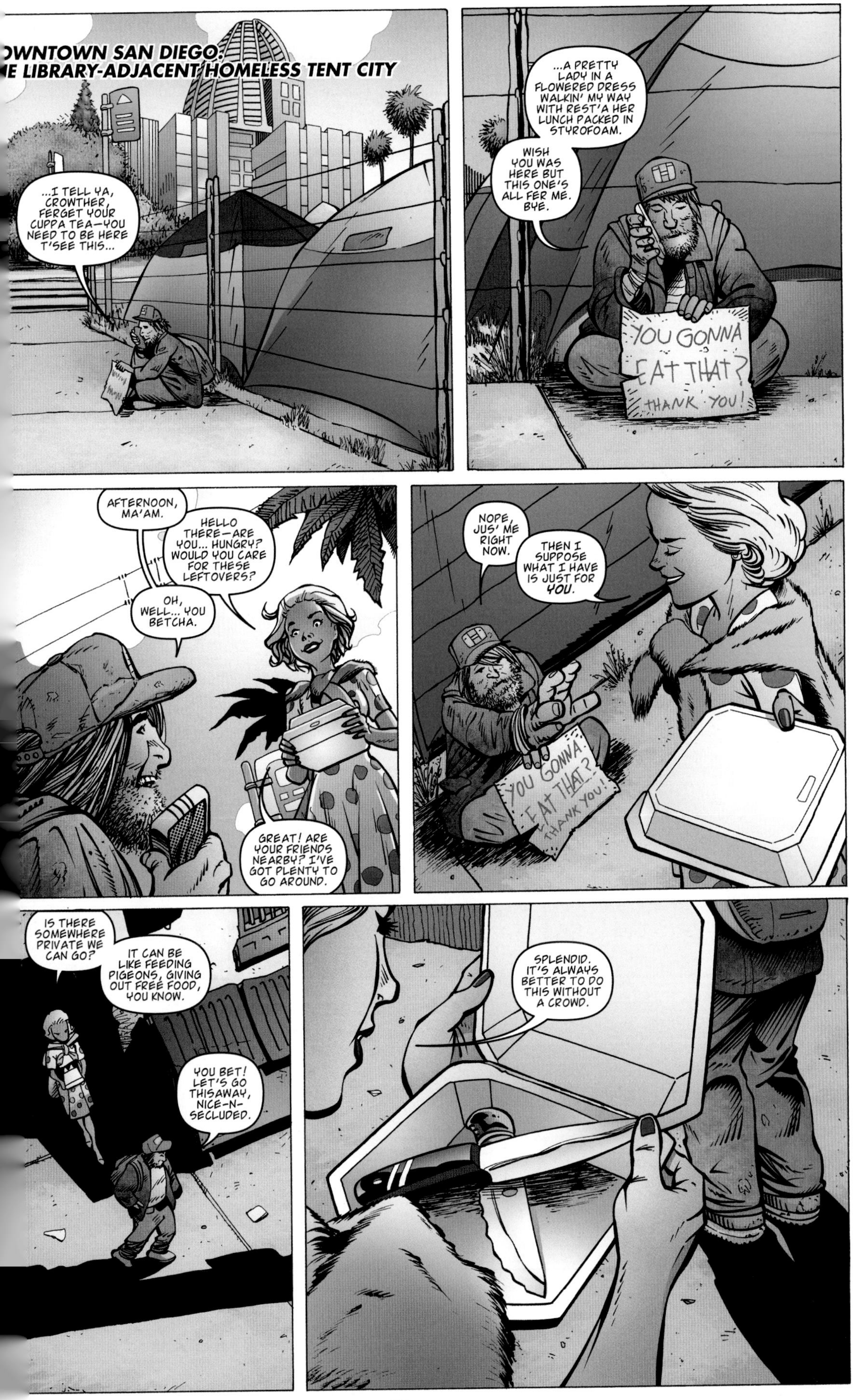

OWNTOWN SAN DIEGO:
E LIBRARY-ADJACENT HOMELESS TENT CITY
...I TELL YA, CROWTHER, FERGET YOUR CUPPA TEA—YOU NEED TO BE HERE T'SEE THIS...
...A PRETTY LADY IN A FLOWERED DRESS WALKIN' MY WAY WITH REST'A HER LUNCH PACKED IN STYROFOAM.
WISH YOU WAS HERE BUT THIS ONE'S ALL FER ME. BYE.
YOU GONNA EAT THAT? THANK YOU!
AFTERNOON, MA'AM.
HELLO THERE—ARE YOU... HUNGRY? WOULD YOU CARE FOR THESE LEFTOVERS?
OH, WELL... YOU BETCHA.
GREAT! ARE YOUR FRIENDS NEARBY? I'VE GOT PLENTY TO GO AROUND.
NOPE, JUS' ME RIGHT NOW.
THEN I SUPPOSE WHAT I HAVE IS JUST FOR *YOU*.
YOU GONNA EAT THAT? THANK YOU!
IS THERE SOMEWHERE PRIVATE WE CAN GO?
IT CAN BE LIKE FEEDING PIGEONS, GIVING OUT FREE FOOD, YOU KNOW.
YOU BET! LET'S GO THISAWAY, NICE-N-SECLUDED.
SPLENDID. IT'S ALWAYS BETTER TO DO THIS WITHOUT A CROWD.

A SHORT TIME LATER.

NOT QUITE THE TURNOUT I'D HOPED FOR, BUT I'M ABLE TO SCRATCH ONE MORE NAME, ANYWAY.

YOUR BAGGAGE-THIEF STILL INSIDE?

GREAT. I'LL MAKE MY WAY BACK THERE AND WE CAN FIND A PROPER NAME ON THE LIST TO SUIT HIM.

GUMSHOES & TEA LEAVES
WHERE TO FIND GREAT TEA? MYSTERY SOLVED!

1018

I'M SURE THERE ARE NUMEROUS CANDIDATES—NEARLY EVERYONE HAS WANTED TO KILL AN ENGLISHMAN AT ONE TIME OR ANOTHER.

1018

GUMSHOES & TEA LEAVES
WHERE TO FIND GREAT TEA? MYSTERY SOLVED!

SO, TELL US ABOUT THIS CASE OF YOURS.

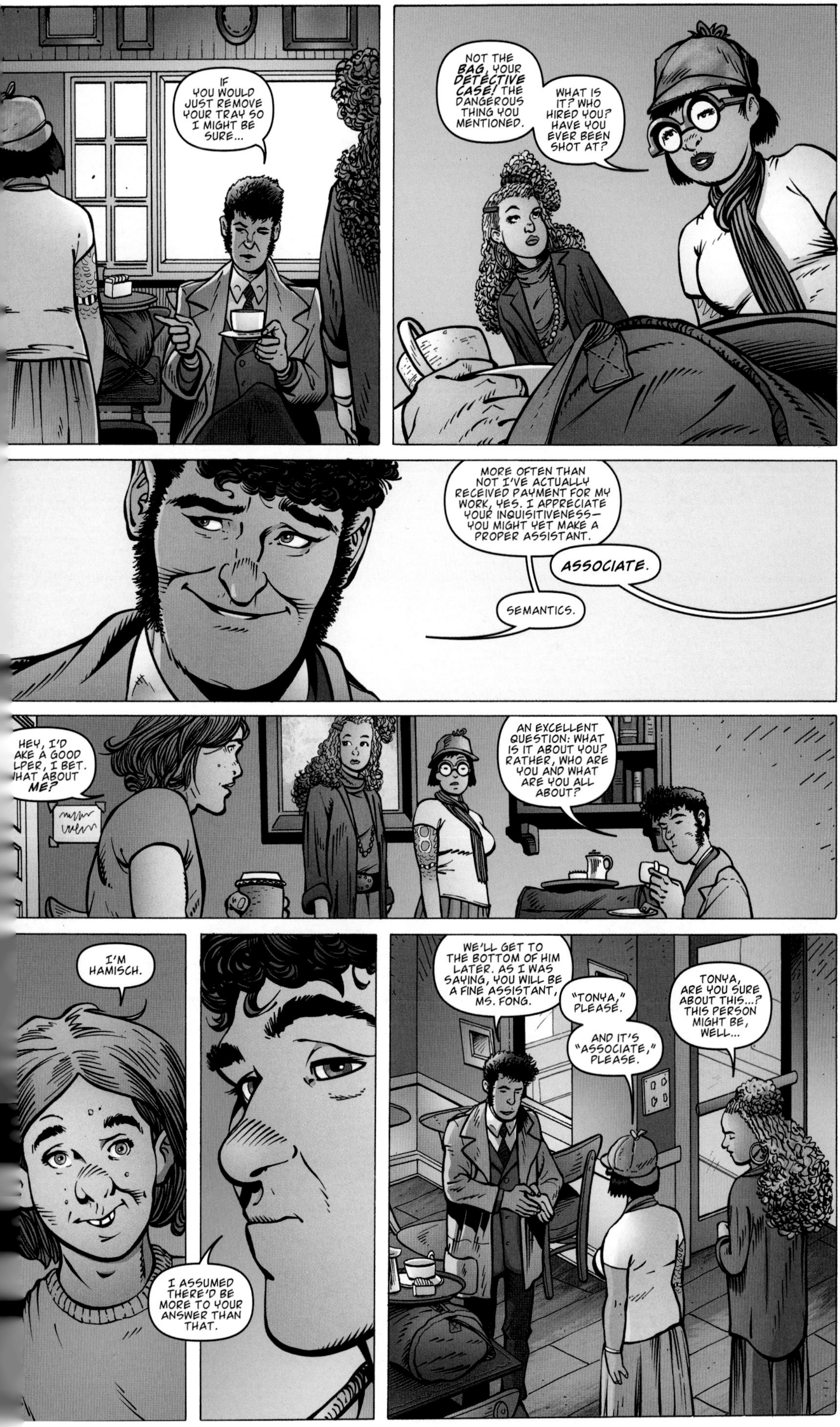
IF YOU WOULD JUST REMOVE YOUR TRAY SO I MIGHT BE SURE...
NOT THE BAG, YOUR DETECTIVE CASE! THE DANGEROUS THING YOU MENTIONED.
WHAT IS IT? WHO HIRED YOU? HAVE YOU EVER BEEN SHOT AT?
MORE OFTEN THAN NOT I'VE ACTUALLY RECEIVED PAYMENT FOR MY WORK, YES. I APPRECIATE YOUR INQUISITIVENESS— YOU MIGHT YET MAKE A PROPER ASSISTANT.
ASSOCIATE.
SEMANTICS.
HEY, I'D AKE A GOOD LPER, I BET. HAT ABOUT ME?
AN EXCELLENT QUESTION: WHAT IS IT ABOUT YOU? RATHER, WHO ARE YOU AND WHAT ARE YOU ALL ABOUT?
I'M HAMISCH.
I ASSUMED THERE'D BE MORE TO YOUR ANSWER THAN THAT.
WE'LL GET TO THE BOTTOM OF HIM LATER. AS I WAS SAYING, YOU WILL BE A FINE ASSISTANT, MS. FONG.
"TONYA," PLEASE.
AND IT'S "ASSOCIATE," PLEASE.
TONYA, ARE YOU SURE ABOUT THIS...? THIS PERSON MIGHT BE, WELL...

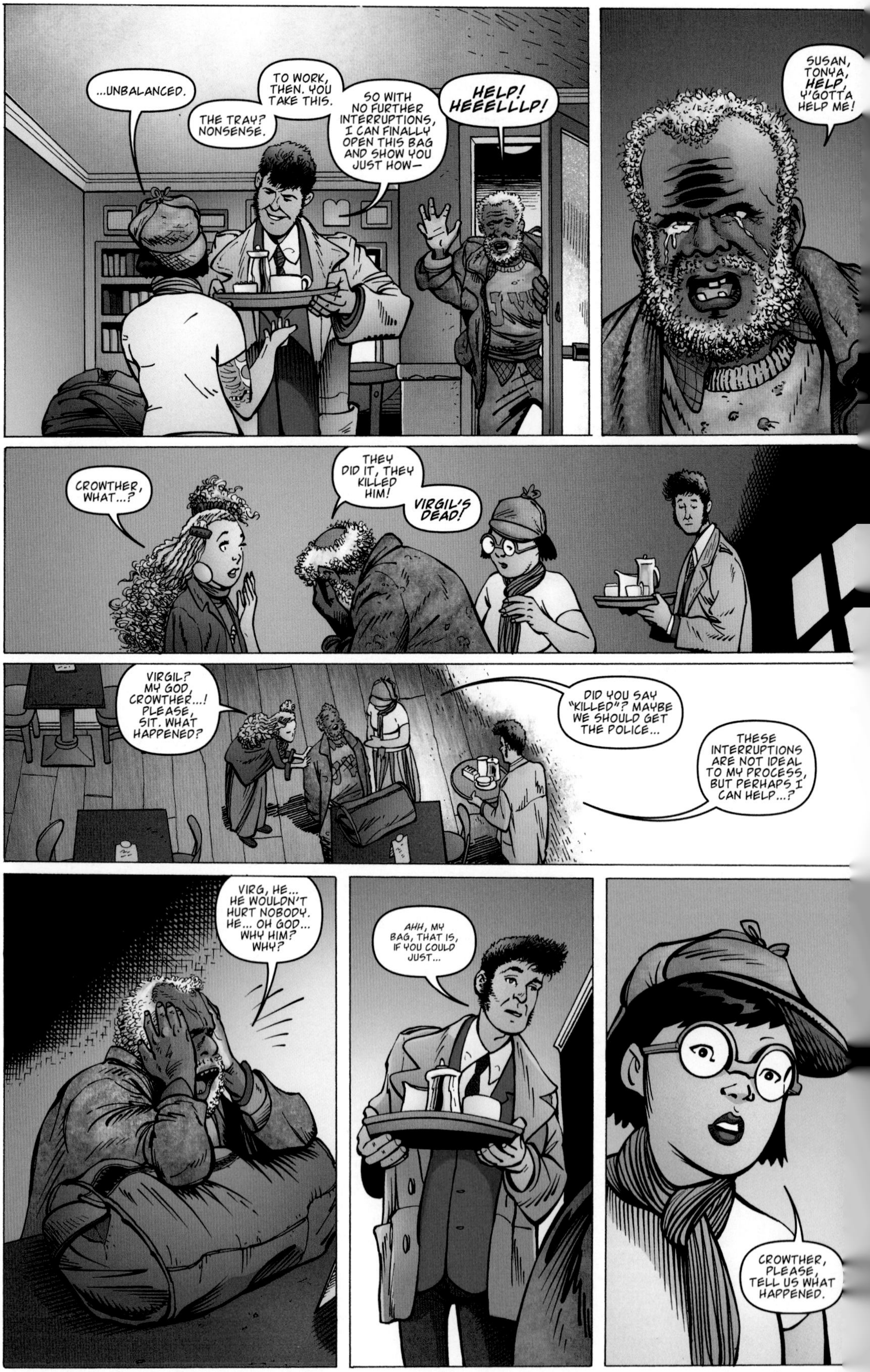
...UNBALANCED.
THE TRAY? NONSENSE.
TO WORK, THEN. YOU TAKE THIS.
SO WITH NO FURTHER INTERRUPTIONS, I CAN FINALLY OPEN THIS BAG AND SHOW YOU JUST HOW—
HELP! HEEELLLP!
SUSAN, TONYA, HELP, Y'GOTTA HELP ME!
CROWTHER, WHAT...?
THEY DID IT, THEY KILLED HIM!
VIRGIL'S DEAD!
VIRGIL? MY GOD, CROWTHER...! PLEASE, SIT. WHAT HAPPENED?
DID YOU SAY "KILLED"? MAYBE WE SHOULD GET THE POLICE...
THESE INTERRUPTIONS ARE NOT IDEAL TO MY PROCESS, BUT PERHAPS I CAN HELP...?
VIRG, HE... HE WOULDN'T HURT NOBODY. HE... OH GOD... WHY HIM? WHY?
AHH, MY BAG, THAT IS, IF YOU COULD JUST...
CROWTHER, PLEASE, TELL US WHAT HAPPENED.

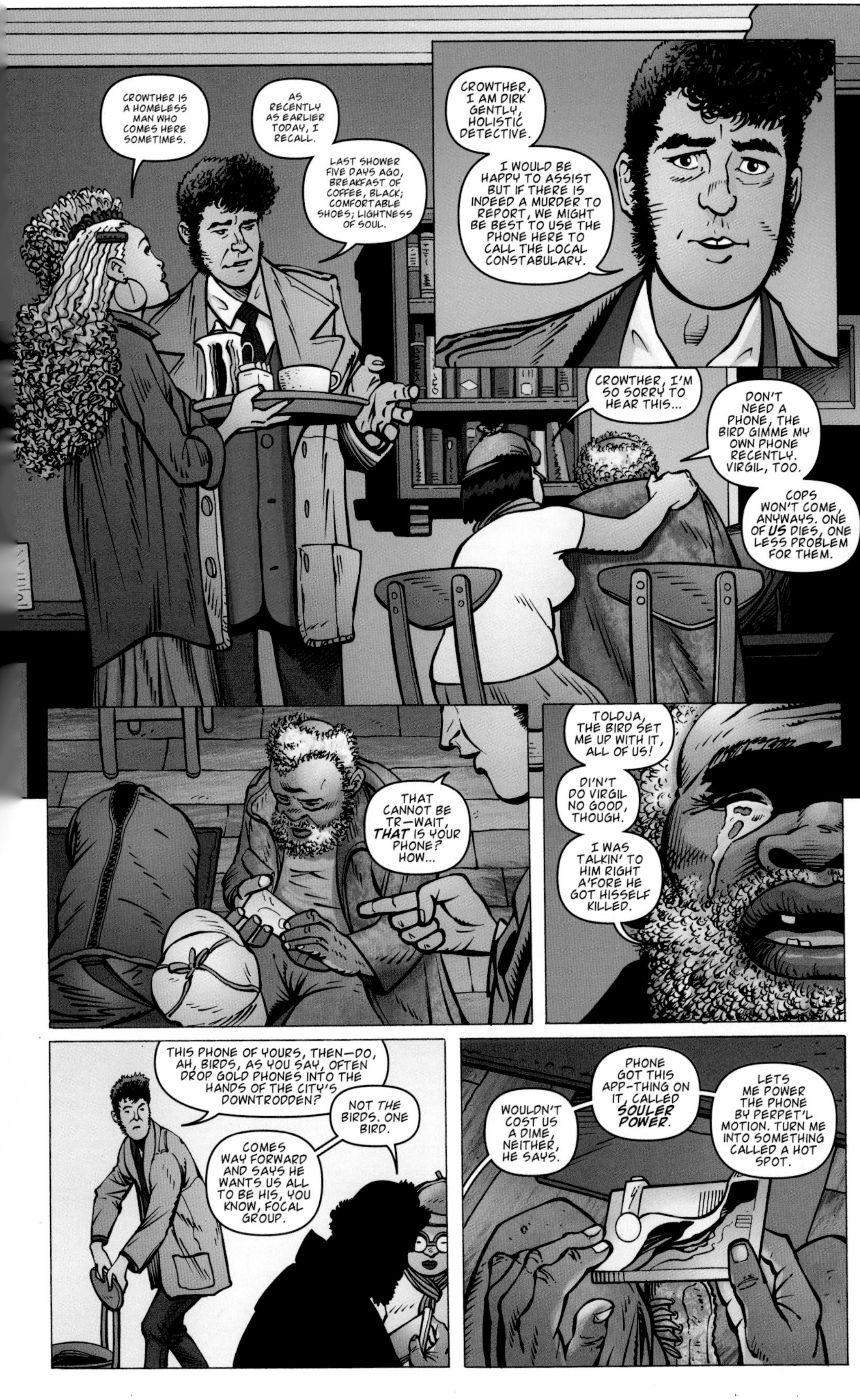
CROWTHER IS A HOMELESS MAN WHO COMES HERE SOMETIMES.
AS RECENTLY AS EARLIER TODAY, I RECALL.
LAST SHOWER FIVE DAYS AGO, BREAKFAST OF COFFEE, BLACK; COMFORTABLE SHOES; LIGHTNESS OF SOUL.
CROWTHER, I AM DIRK GENTLY, HOLISTIC DETECTIVE.
I WOULD BE HAPPY TO ASSIST BUT IF THERE IS INDEED A MURDER TO REPORT, WE MIGHT BE BEST TO USE THE PHONE HERE TO CALL THE LOCAL CONSTABULARY.
CROWTHER, I'M SO SORRY TO HEAR THIS...
DON'T NEED A PHONE, THE BIRD GIMME MY OWN PHONE RECENTLY. VIRGIL, TOO.
COPS WON'T COME, ANYWAYS. ONE OF *US* DIES, ONE LESS PROBLEM FOR THEM.
THAT CANNOT BE TR—WAIT, *THAT* IS YOUR PHONE? HOW...
TOLDJA, THE BIRD SET ME UP WITH IT, ALL OF US!
DI'N'T DO VIRGIL NO GOOD, THOUGH.
I WAS TALKIN' TO HIM RIGHT A'FORE HE GOT HISSELF KILLED.
THIS PHONE OF YOURS, THEN—DO, AH, BIRDS, AS YOU SAY, OFTEN DROP GOLD PHONES INTO THE HANDS OF THE CITY'S DOWNTRODDEN?
NOT *THE* BIRDS. ONE BIRD.
COMES WAY FORWARD AND SAYS HE WANTS US ALL TO BE HIS, YOU KNOW, FOCAL GROUP.
WOULDN'T COST US A DIME, NEITHER, HE SAYS.
PHONE GOT THIS APP-THING ON IT, CALLED ***SOULER POWER***.
LETS ME POWER THE PHONE BY PERPET'L MOTION. TURN ME INTO SOMETHING CALLED A HOT SPOT.

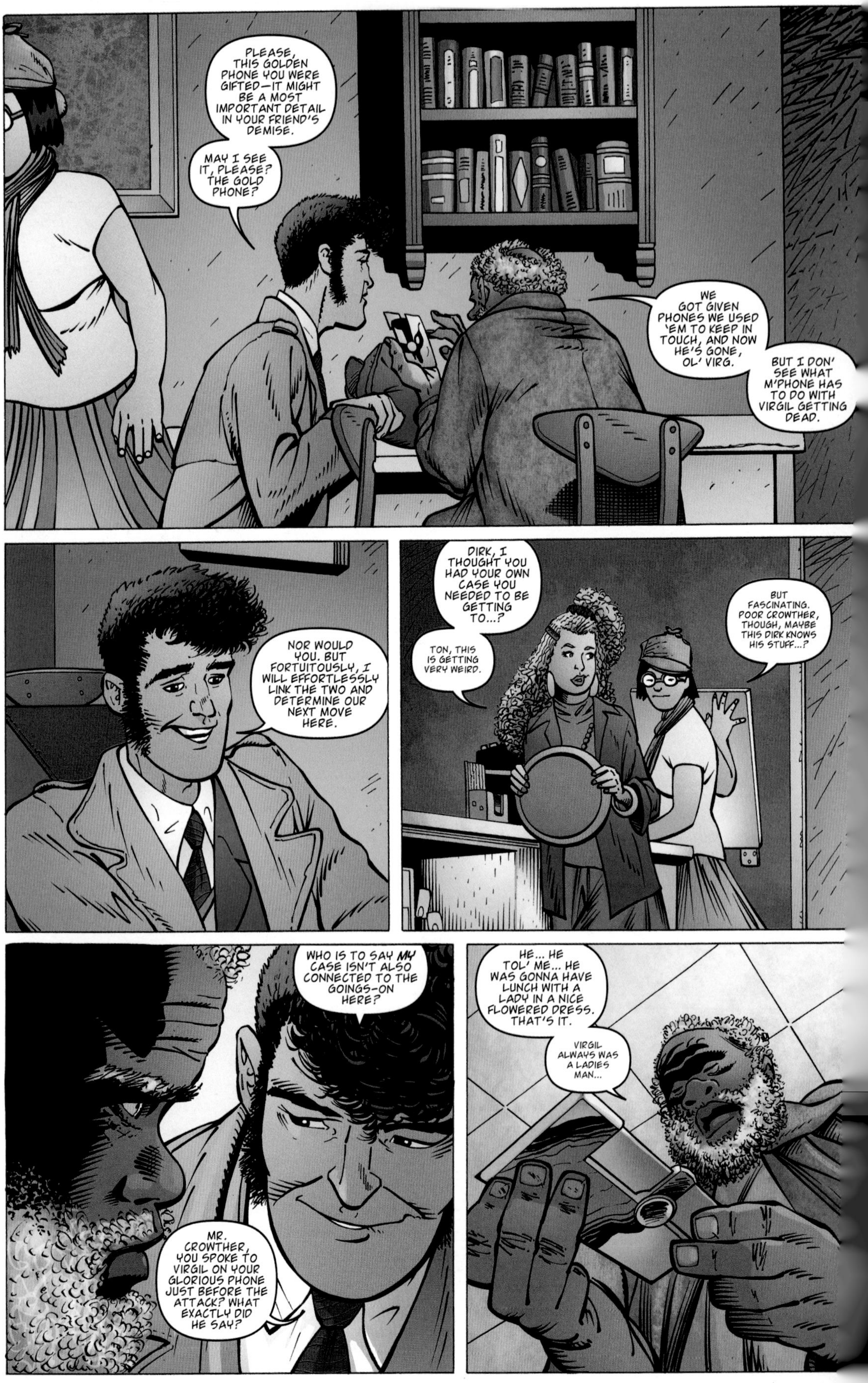
PLEASE, THIS GOLDEN PHONE YOU WERE GIFTED—IT MIGHT BE A MOST IMPORTANT DETAIL IN YOUR FRIEND'S DEMISE.
MAY I SEE IT, PLEASE? THE GOLD PHONE?
WE GOT GIVEN PHONES WE USED 'EM TO KEEP IN TOUCH, AND NOW HE'S GONE, OL' VIRG.
BUT I DON' SEE WHAT M'PHONE HAS TO DO WITH VIRGIL GETTING DEAD.
NOR WOULD YOU. BUT FORTUITOUSLY, I WILL EFFORTLESSLY LINK THE TWO AND DETERMINE OUR NEXT MOVE HERE.
DIRK, I THOUGHT YOU HAD YOUR OWN CASE YOU NEEDED TO BE GETTING TO...?
TON, THIS IS GETTING VERY WEIRD.
BUT FASCINATING. POOR CROWTHER, THOUGH, MAYBE THIS DIRK KNOWS HIS STUFF...?
WHO IS TO SAY MY CASE ISN'T ALSO CONNECTED TO THE GOINGS-ON HERE?
MR. CROWTHER, YOU SPOKE TO VIRGIL ON YOUR GLORIOUS PHONE JUST BEFORE THE ATTACK? WHAT EXACTLY DID HE SAY?
HE... HE TOL' ME... HE WAS GONNA HAVE LUNCH WITH A LADY IN A NICE FLOWERED DRESS. THAT'S IT.
VIRGIL ALWAYS WAS A LADIES MAN...

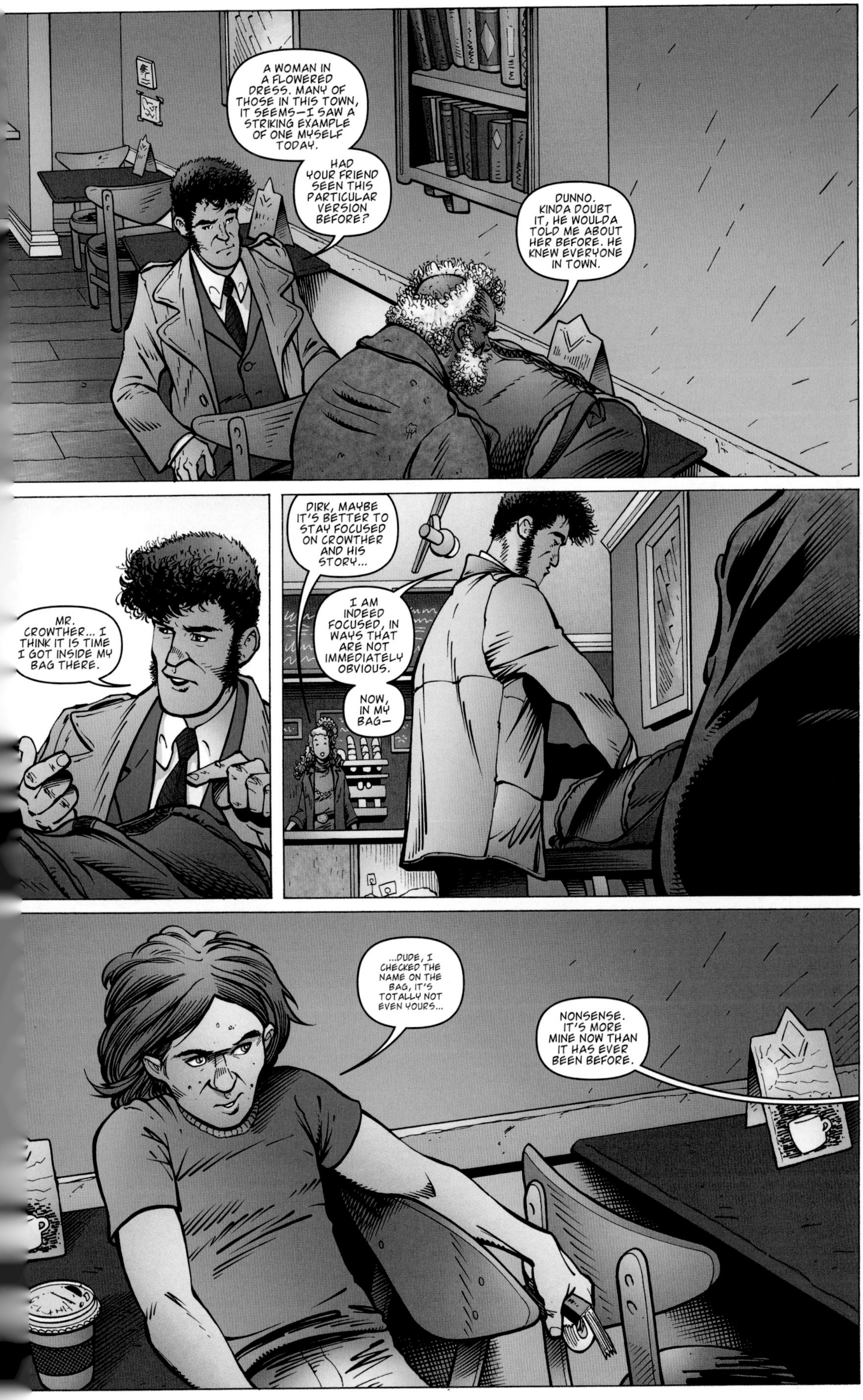
A WOMAN IN A FLOWERED DRESS. MANY OF THOSE IN THIS TOWN, IT SEEMS—I SAW A STRIKING EXAMPLE OF ONE MYSELF TODAY.
HAD YOUR FRIEND SEEN THIS PARTICULAR VERSION BEFORE?
DUNNO. KINDA DOUBT IT, HE WOULDA TOLD ME ABOUT HER BEFORE. HE KNEW EVERYONE IN TOWN.
MR. CROWTHER... I THINK IT IS TIME I GOT INSIDE MY BAG THERE.
DIRK, MAYBE IT'S BETTER TO STAY FOCUSED ON CROWTHER AND HIS STORY...
I AM INDEED FOCUSED, IN WAYS THAT ARE NOT IMMEDIATELY OBVIOUS.
NOW, IN MY BAG—
...DUDE, I CHECKED THE NAME ON THE BAG, IT'S TOTALLY NOT EVEN YOURS...
NONSENSE. IT'S MORE MINE NOW THAN IT HAS EVER BEEN BEFORE.

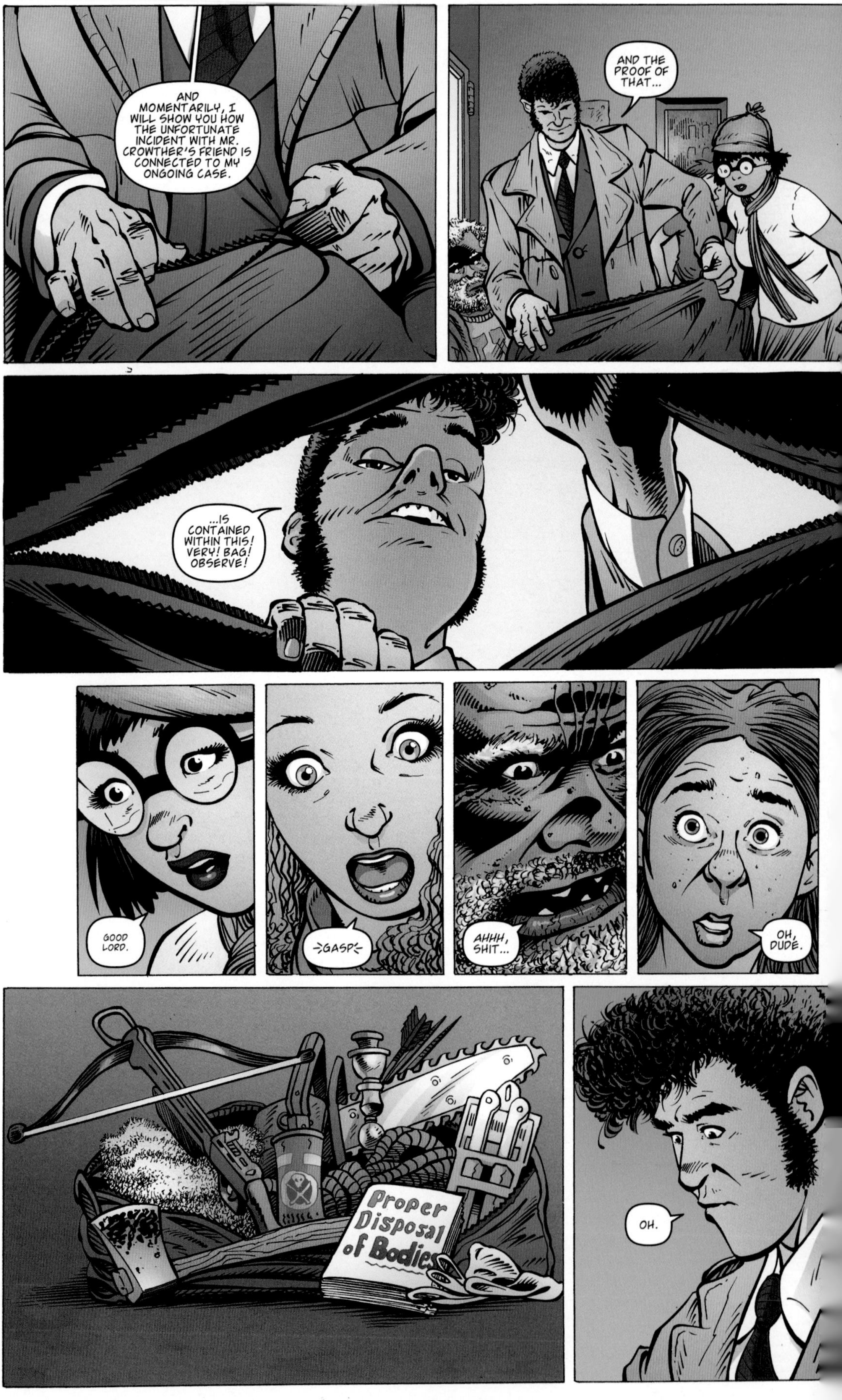
AND MOMENTARILY, I WILL SHOW YOU HOW THE UNFORTUNATE INCIDENT WITH MR. CROWTHER'S FRIEND IS CONNECTED TO MY ONGOING CASE.
AND THE PROOF OF THAT...
...IS CONTAINED WITHIN THIS! VERY! BAG! OBSERVE!
GOOD LORD.
GASP
AHHH, SHIT...
OH, DUDE.
Proper Disposal of Bodies
OH.

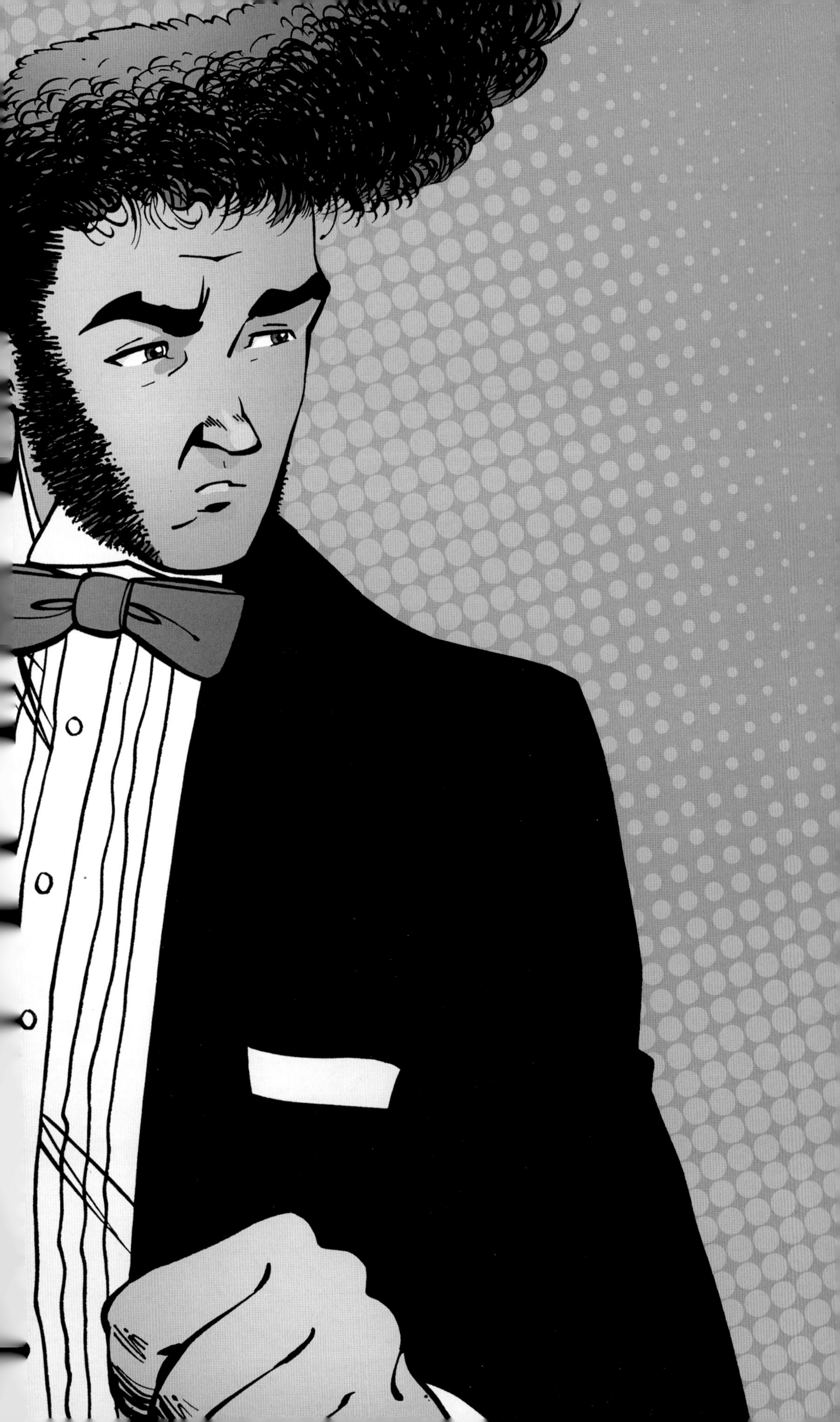

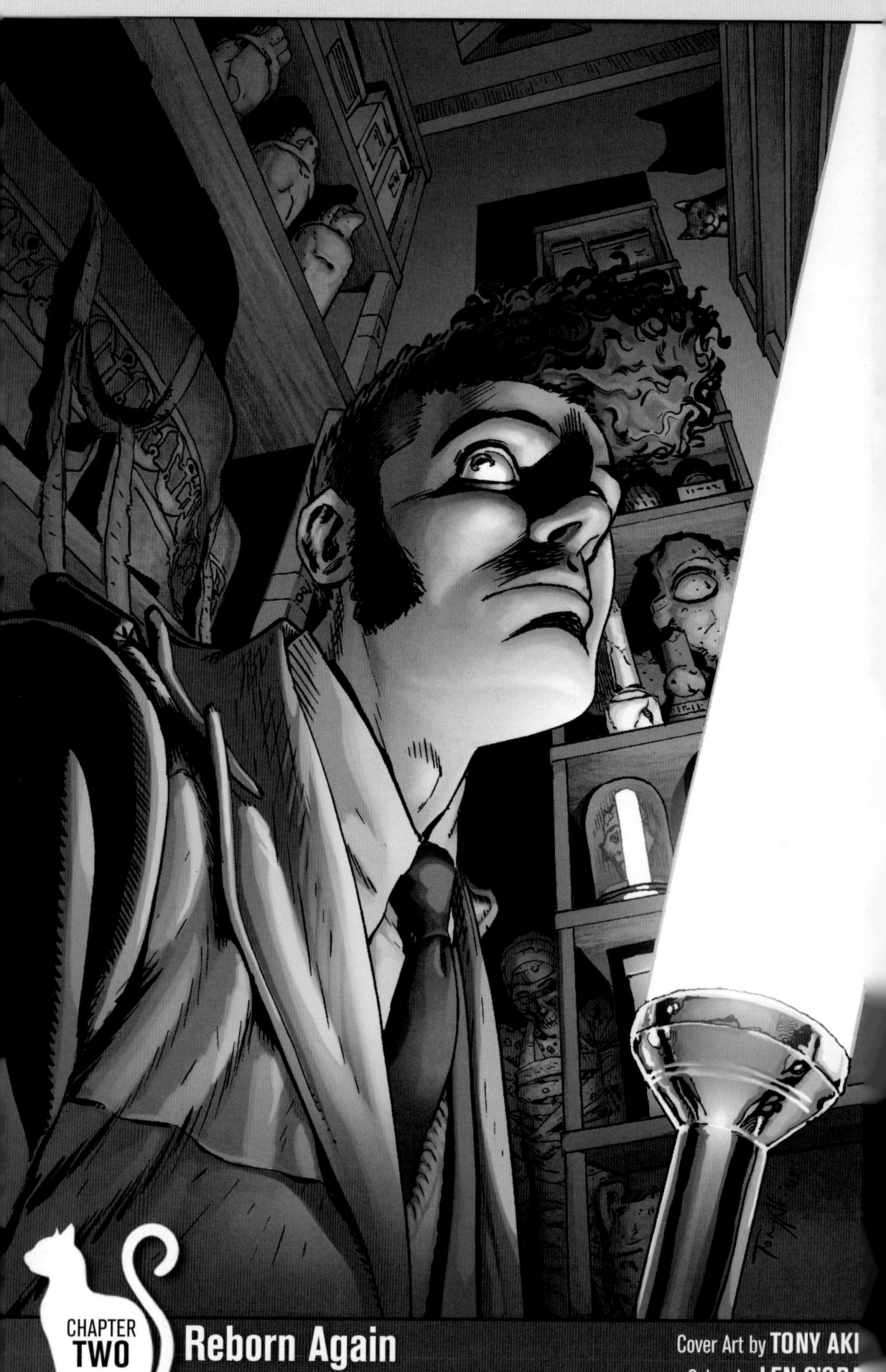

CHAPTER TWO

Reborn Again

Cover Art by **TONY AKI**
Colors by **LEN O'GRA**

BALBOA PARK.

"...EXTERIORS FOR THE MANSION IN CITIZEN KANE SHOT HERE IN YOUR VERY OWN BALBOA PARK..."

HMM, I DON'T KNOW IF THAT'S TRUE.

DIRK, I DON'T UNDERSTAND WHY WE'RE *HERE* WHEN YOU HAVE A CASE...

OH, IT'S QUITE TRUE, TONYA...

...AND IN FACT, SOME OF THE ZOO ANIMALS FEATURED IN THAT MOVIE ARE *STILL ALIVE* AND LOCATED ON THE PREMISES HERE!

NOW I *KNOW* THAT CAN'T BE RIGHT...

WE ARE HERE, TONYA, AS PART OF MY PROCESS.

ONE MUST UNDERSTAND THE HISTORY OF A PLACE IN ORDER TO DRAW PROPER CONCLUSIONS ABOUT ITS PRESENT.

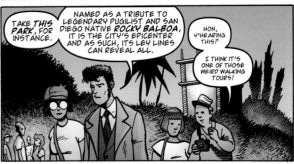

TAKE *THIS* PARK, FOR INSTANCE.

NAMED AS A TRIBUTE TO LEGENDARY PUGILIST AND SAN DIEGO NATIVE *ROCKY BALBOA*, IT IS THE CITY'S EPICENTER AND AS SUCH, ITS LEY LINES CAN REVEAL ALL.

HON, Y'HEARING THIS?

I THINK IT'S ONE OF THOSE WEIRD WALKING TOURS!

UH, DIRK, I GREW UP HERE.

THESE FACTS SOUND WRONG TO ME.

ALSO, YOU SEEM TO BE ATTRACTING A CROWD.

THE ANSWERS ANYONE SEEKS ABOUT A TOWN CAN BE FOUND WITHIN ITS MANY STREET MEATS OR ITS MUSEUMS, BOTH OF WHICH ABOUND IN THIS PARK.

SERIOUSLY, A *LOT* OF PEOPLE ARE FOLLOWING US NOW.

SO MAYBE LOWER YOUR VOICE—

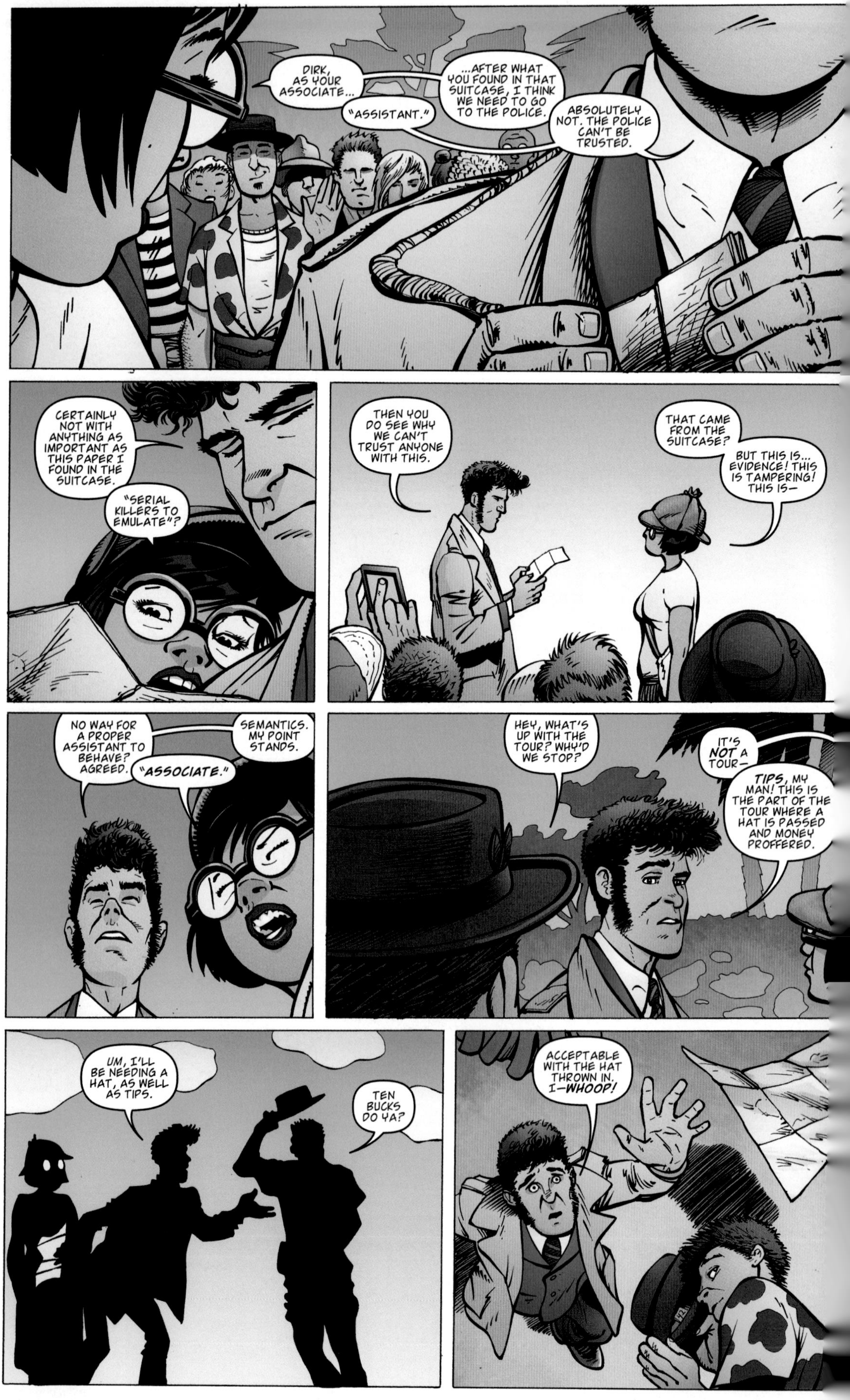
DIRK, AS YOUR ASSOCIATE...
"ASSISTANT."
...AFTER WHAT YOU FOUND IN THAT SUITCASE, I THINK WE NEED TO GO TO THE POLICE.
ABSOLUTELY NOT. THE POLICE CAN'T BE TRUSTED.
CERTAINLY NOT WITH ANYTHING AS IMPORTANT AS THIS PAPER I FOUND IN THE SUITCASE.
"SERIAL KILLERS TO EMULATE"?
THEN YOU DO SEE WHY WE CAN'T TRUST ANYONE WITH THIS.
THAT CAME FROM THE SUITCASE?
BUT THIS IS... EVIDENCE! THIS IS TAMPERING! THIS IS—
NO WAY FOR A PROPER ASSISTANT TO BEHAVE? AGREED.
"ASSOCIATE."
SEMANTICS. MY POINT STANDS.
HEY, WHAT'S UP WITH THE TOUR? WHY'D WE STOP?
IT'S NOT A TOUR—
TIPS, MY MAN! THIS IS THE PART OF THE TOUR WHERE A HAT IS PASSED AND MONEY PROFFERED.
UM, I'LL BE NEEDING A HAT, AS WELL AS TIPS.
TEN BUCKS DO YA?
ACCEPTABLE WITH THE HAT THROWN IN. I—WHOOP!

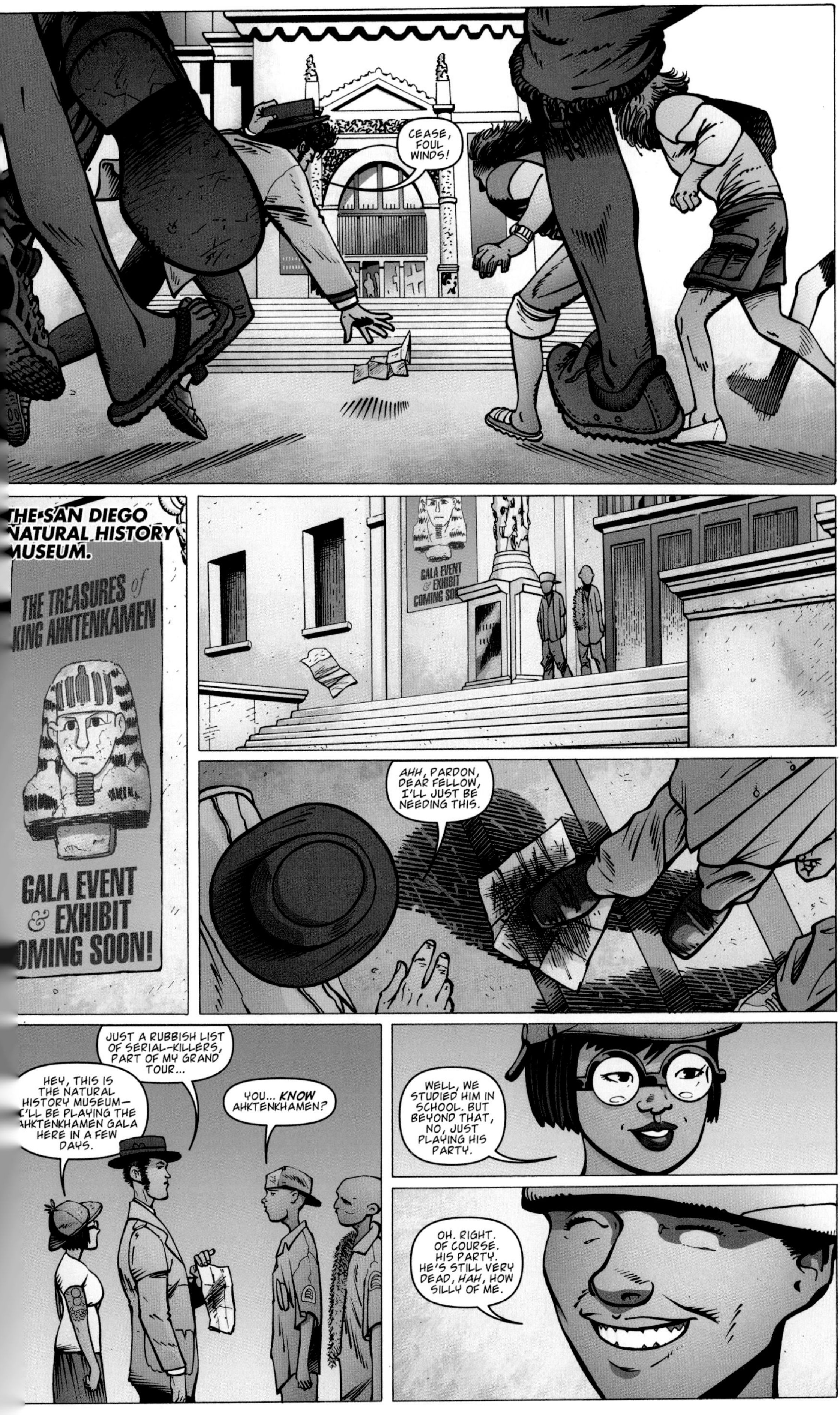
CEASE, FOUL WINDS!
THE SAN DIEGO NATURAL HISTORY MUSEUM.
THE TREASURES of KING AHKTENKAMEN
GALA EVENT & EXHIBIT COMING SOON!
GALA EVENT & EXHIBIT COMING SOO
AHH, PARDON, DEAR FELLOW, I'LL JUST BE NEEDING THIS.
HEY, THIS IS THE NATURAL HISTORY MUSEUM— I'LL BE PLAYING THE AHKTENKHAMEN GALA HERE IN A FEW DAYS.
JUST A RUBBISH LIST OF SERIAL-KILLERS, PART OF MY GRAND TOUR...
YOU... KNOW AHKTENKHAMEN?
WELL, WE STUDIED HIM IN SCHOOL. BUT BEYOND THAT, NO, JUST PLAYING HIS PARTY.
OH. RIGHT. OF COURSE. HIS PARTY. HE'S STILL VERY DEAD, HAH, HOW SILLY OF ME.

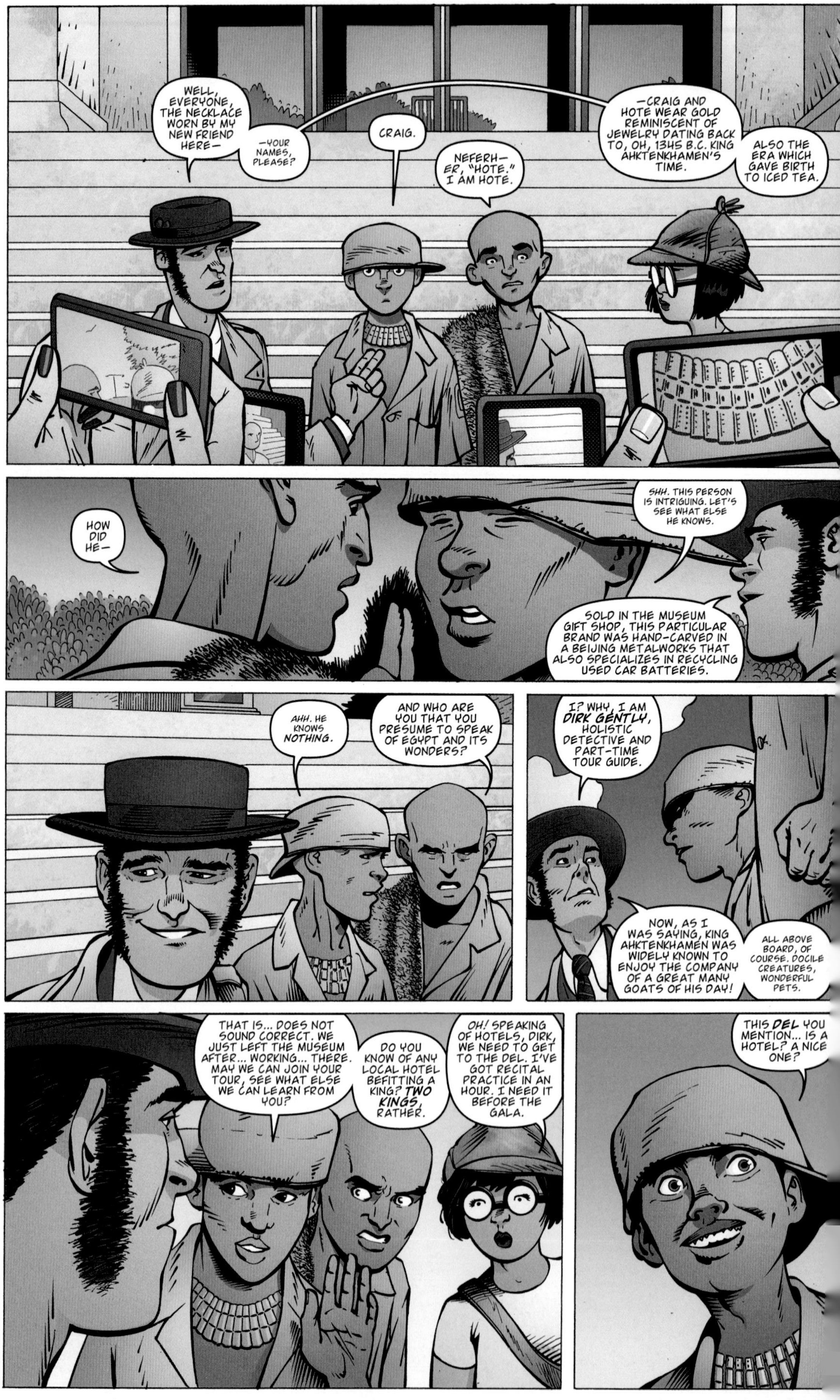
WELL, EVERYONE, THE NECKLACE WORN BY MY NEW FRIEND HERE—
—YOUR NAMES, PLEASE?
CRAIG.
NEFERH— ER, "HOTE." I AM HOTE.
—CRAIG AND HOTE WEAR GOLD REMINISCENT OF JEWELRY DATING BACK TO, OH, 1345 B.C. KING AHKTENKHAMEN'S TIME.
ALSO THE ERA WHICH GAVE BIRTH TO ICED TEA.
HOW DID HE—
SHH. THIS PERSON IS INTRIGUING. LET'S SEE WHAT ELSE HE KNOWS.
SOLD IN THE MUSEUM GIFT SHOP, THIS PARTICULAR BRAND WAS HAND-CARVED IN A BEIJING METALWORKS THAT ALSO SPECIALIZES IN RECYCLING USED CAR BATTERIES.
AHH. HE KNOWS NOTHING.
AND WHO ARE YOU THAT YOU PRESUME TO SPEAK OF EGYPT AND ITS WONDERS?
I? WHY, I AM DIRK GENTLY, HOLISTIC DETECTIVE AND PART-TIME TOUR GUIDE.
NOW, AS I WAS SAYING, KING AHKTENKHAMEN WAS WIDELY KNOWN TO ENJOY THE COMPANY OF A GREAT MANY GOATS OF HIS DAY!
ALL ABOVE BOARD, OF COURSE. DOCILE CREATURES, WONDERFUL PETS.
THAT IS... DOES NOT SOUND CORRECT. WE JUST LEFT THE MUSEUM AFTER... WORKING... THERE. MAY WE CAN JOIN YOUR TOUR, SEE WHAT ELSE WE CAN LEARN FROM YOU?
DO YOU KNOW OF ANY LOCAL HOTEL BEFITTING A KING? TWO KINGS, RATHER.
OH! SPEAKING OF HOTELS, DIRK, WE NEED TO GET TO THE DEL. I'VE GOT RECITAL PRACTICE IN AN HOUR. I NEED IT BEFORE THE GALA.
THIS DEL YOU MENTION... IS A HOTEL? A NICE ONE?

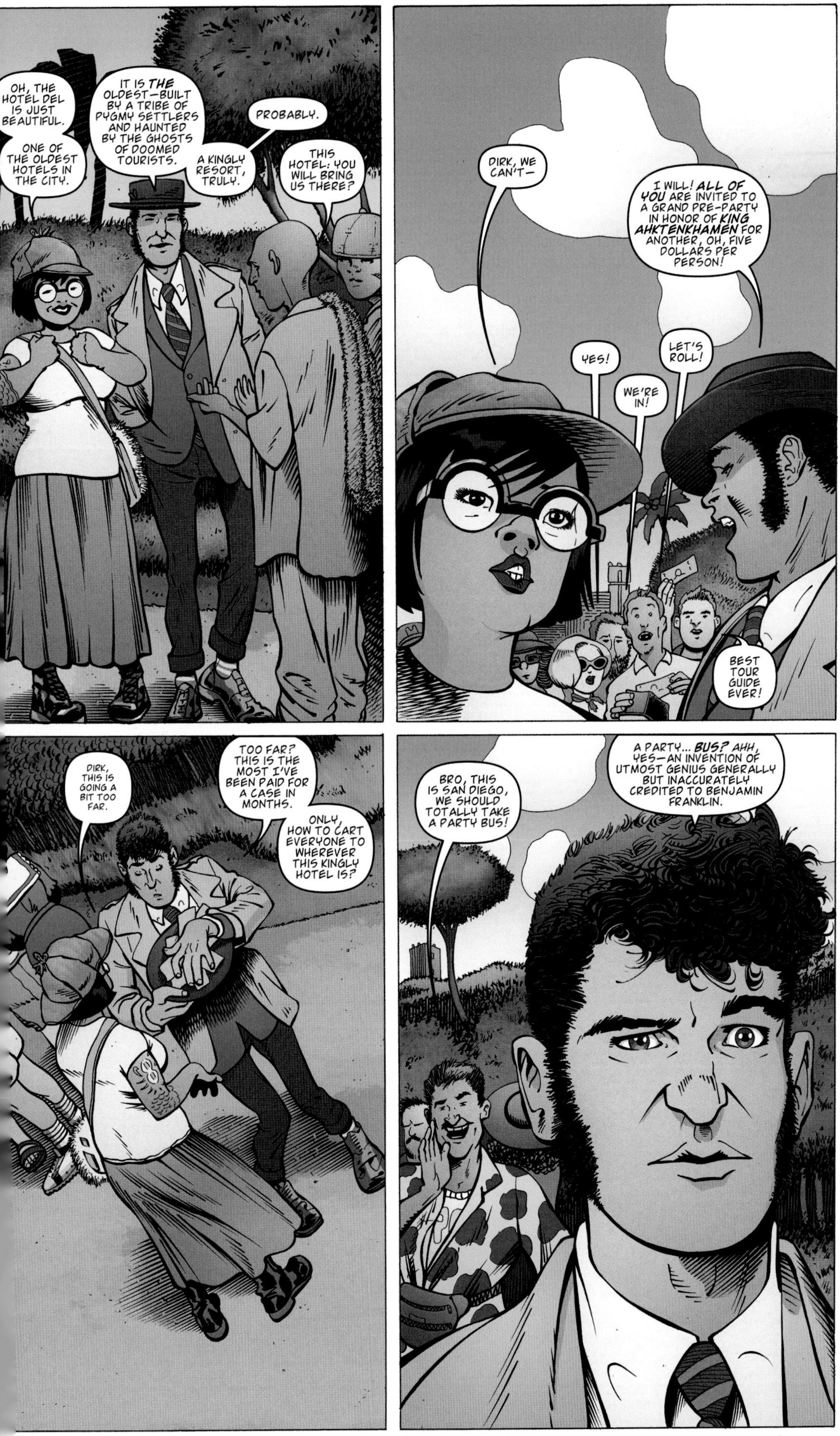
OH, THE HOTEL DEL IS JUST BEAUTIFUL.
ONE OF THE OLDEST HOTELS IN THE CITY.
IT IS *THE* OLDEST—BUILT BY A TRIBE OF PYGMY SETTLERS AND HAUNTED BY THE GHOSTS OF DOOMED TOURISTS.
PROBABLY.
A KINGLY RESORT, TRULY.
THIS HOTEL: YOU WILL BRING US THERE?
DIRK, WE CAN'T—
I WILL! ***ALL OF YOU*** ARE INVITED TO A GRAND PRE-PARTY IN HONOR OF ***KING AHKTENKHAMEN*** FOR ANOTHER, OH, FIVE DOLLARS PER PERSON!
YES!
WE'RE IN!
LET'S ROLL!
BEST TOUR GUIDE EVER!
DIRK, THIS IS GOING A BIT TOO FAR.
TOO FAR? THIS IS THE MOST I'VE BEEN PAID FOR A CASE IN MONTHS.
ONLY, HOW TO CART EVERYONE TO WHEREVER THIS KINGLY HOTEL IS?
BRO, THIS IS SAN DIEGO, WE SHOULD TOTALLY TAKE A PARTY BUS!
A PARTY... ***BUS?*** AHH, YES—AN INVENTION OF UTMOST GENIUS GENERALLY BUT INACCURATELY CREDITED TO BENJAMIN FRANKLIN.

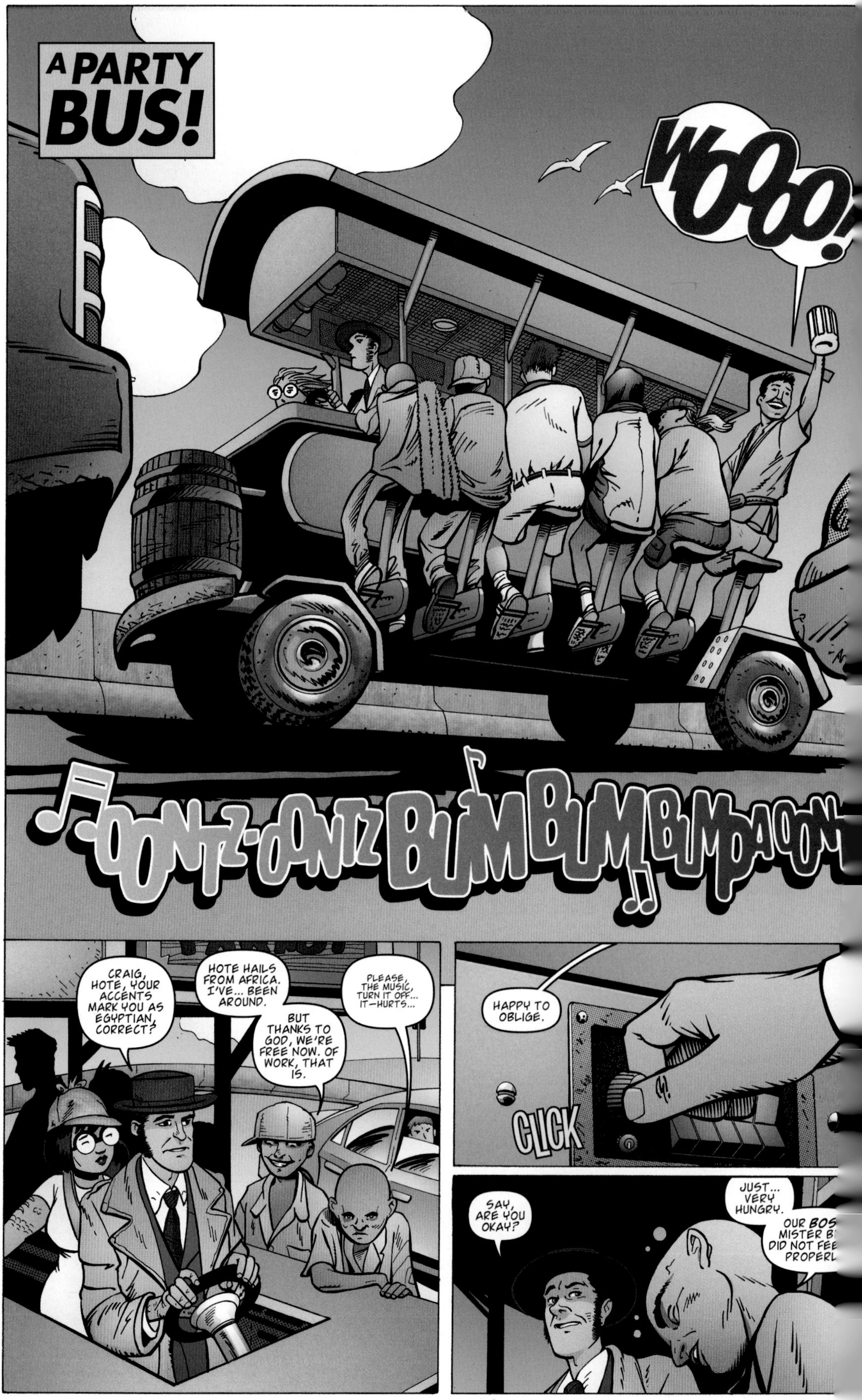
A PARTY BUS!
WOOOO!
OONTZ-OONTZ BUM BUM BUMPA
CRAIG, HOTE, YOUR ACCENTS MARK YOU AS EGYPTIAN, CORRECT?
HOTE HAILS FROM AFRICA. I'VE... BEEN AROUND.
BUT THANKS TO GOD, WE'RE FREE NOW. OF WORK, THAT IS.
PLEASE, THE MUSIC, TURN IT OFF... IT—HURTS...
HAPPY TO OBLIGE.
CLICK
SAY, ARE YOU OKAY?
JUST... VERY HUNGRY.
OUR BOS MISTER B DID NOT FEE PROPERL

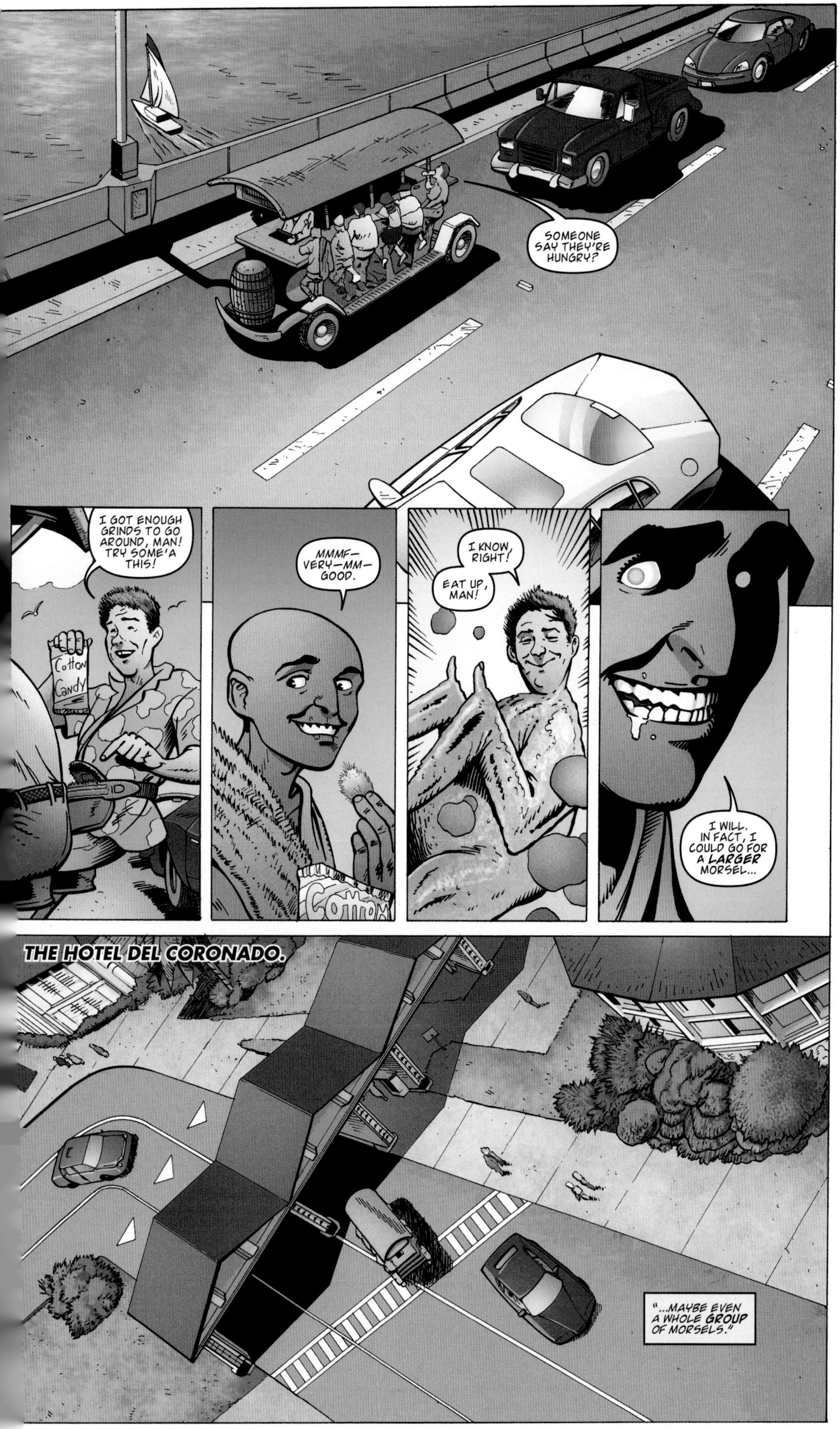
SOMEONE SAY THEY'RE HUNGRY?
I GOT ENOUGH GRINDS TO GO AROUND, MAN! TRY SOME'A THIS!
Cotton Candy
MMMF—VERY—MM—GOOD.
I KNOW, RIGHT!
EAT UP, MAN!
I WILL. IN FACT, I COULD GO FOR A LARGER MORSEL...
THE HOTEL DEL CORONADO.
"...MAYBE EVEN A WHOLE GROUP OF MORSELS."

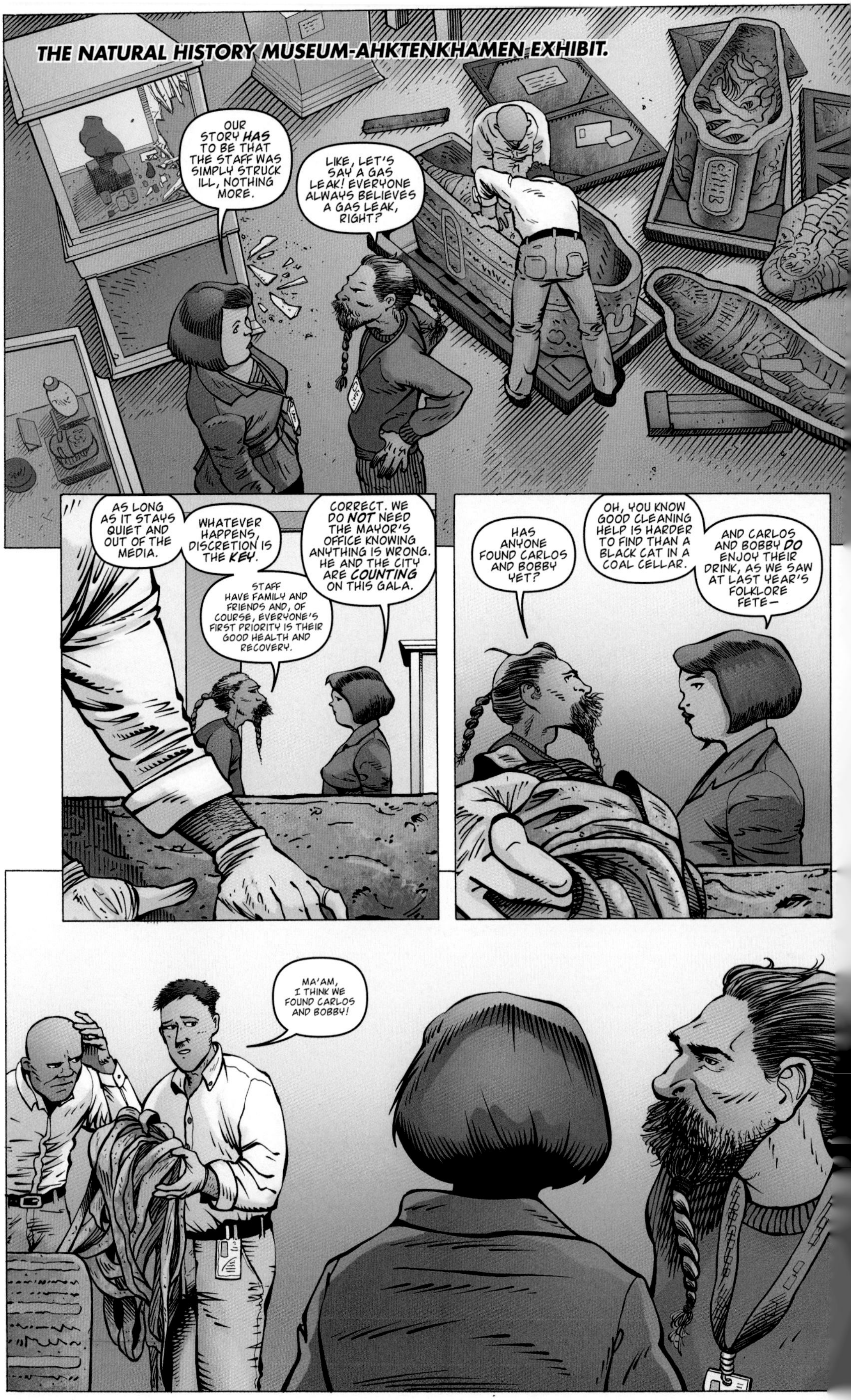
THE NATURAL HISTORY MUSEUM-AHKTENKHAMEN EXHIBIT.
OUR STORY HAS TO BE THAT THE STAFF WAS SIMPLY STRUCK ILL, NOTHING MORE.
LIKE, LET'S SAY A GAS LEAK! EVERYONE ALWAYS BELIEVES A GAS LEAK, RIGHT?
AS LONG AS IT STAYS QUIET AND OUT OF THE MEDIA.
WHATEVER HAPPENS, DISCRETION IS THE KEY.
STAFF HAVE FAMILY AND FRIENDS AND, OF COURSE, EVERYONE'S FIRST PRIORITY IS THEIR GOOD HEALTH AND RECOVERY.
CORRECT. WE DO NOT NEED THE MAYOR'S OFFICE KNOWING ANYTHING IS WRONG. HE AND THE CITY ARE COUNTING ON THIS GALA.
HAS ANYONE FOUND CARLOS AND BOBBY YET?
OH, YOU KNOW GOOD CLEANING HELP IS HARDER TO FIND THAN A BLACK CAT IN A COAL CELLAR.
AND CARLOS AND BOBBY DO ENJOY THEIR DRINK, AS WE SAW AT LAST YEAR'S FOLKLORE FETE—
MA'AM, I THINK WE FOUND CARLOS AND BOBBY!

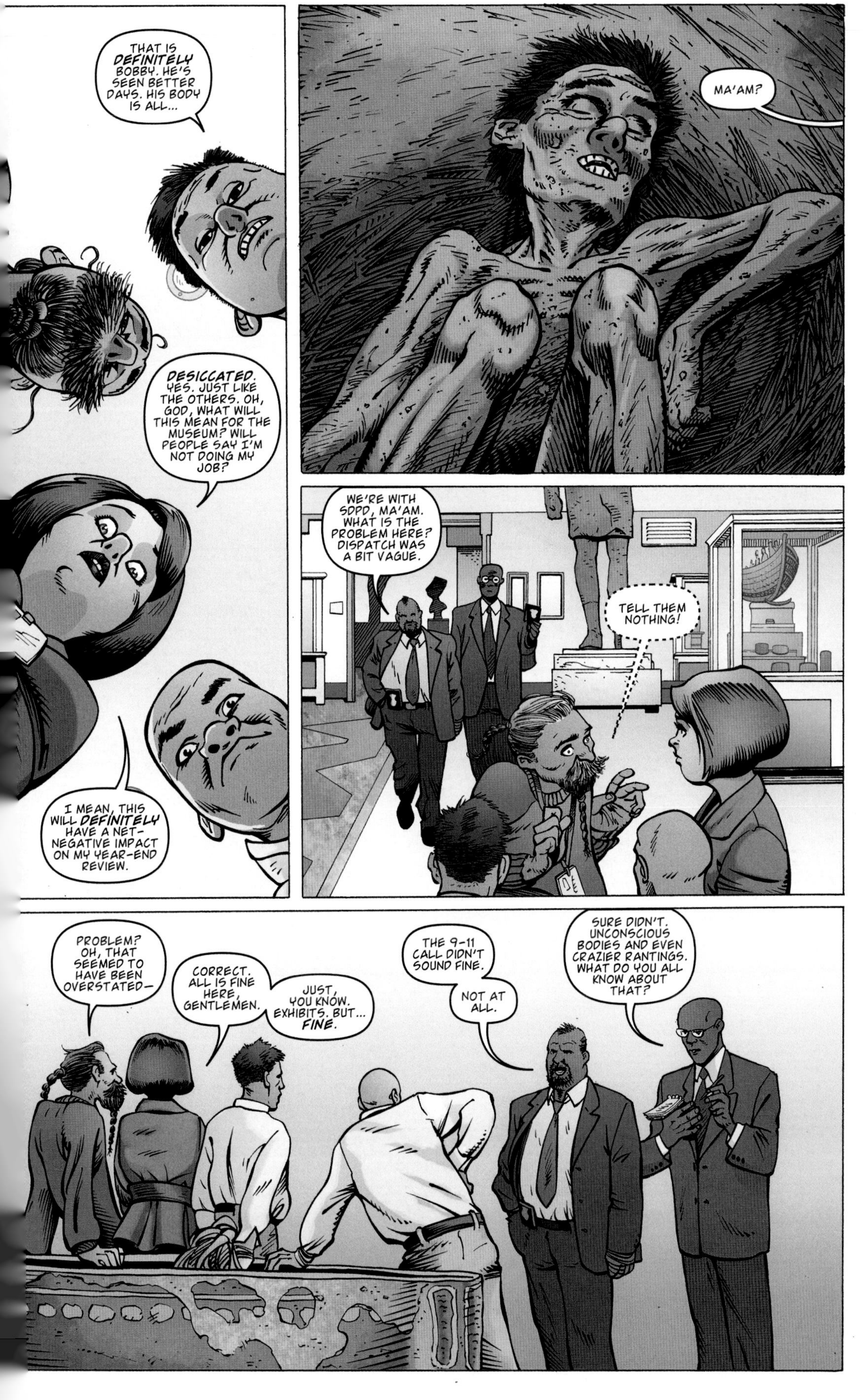
THAT IS DEFINITELY BOBBY. HE'S SEEN BETTER DAYS. HIS BODY IS ALL...
MA'AM?
DESICCATED. YES. JUST LIKE THE OTHERS. OH, GOD, WHAT WILL THIS MEAN FOR THE MUSEUM? WILL PEOPLE SAY I'M NOT DOING MY JOB?
I MEAN, THIS WILL DEFINITELY HAVE A NET-NEGATIVE IMPACT ON MY YEAR-END REVIEW.
WE'RE WITH SDPD, MA'AM. WHAT IS THE PROBLEM HERE? DISPATCH WAS A BIT VAGUE.
TELL THEM NOTHING!
PROBLEM? OH, THAT SEEMED TO HAVE BEEN OVERSTATED—
CORRECT. ALL IS FINE HERE, GENTLEMEN.
JUST, YOU KNOW. EXHIBITS. BUT... FINE.
THE 9-11 CALL DIDN'T SOUND FINE.
NOT AT ALL.
SURE DIDN'T. UNCONSCIOUS BODIES AND EVEN CRAZIER RANTINGS. WHAT DO YOU ALL KNOW ABOUT THAT?

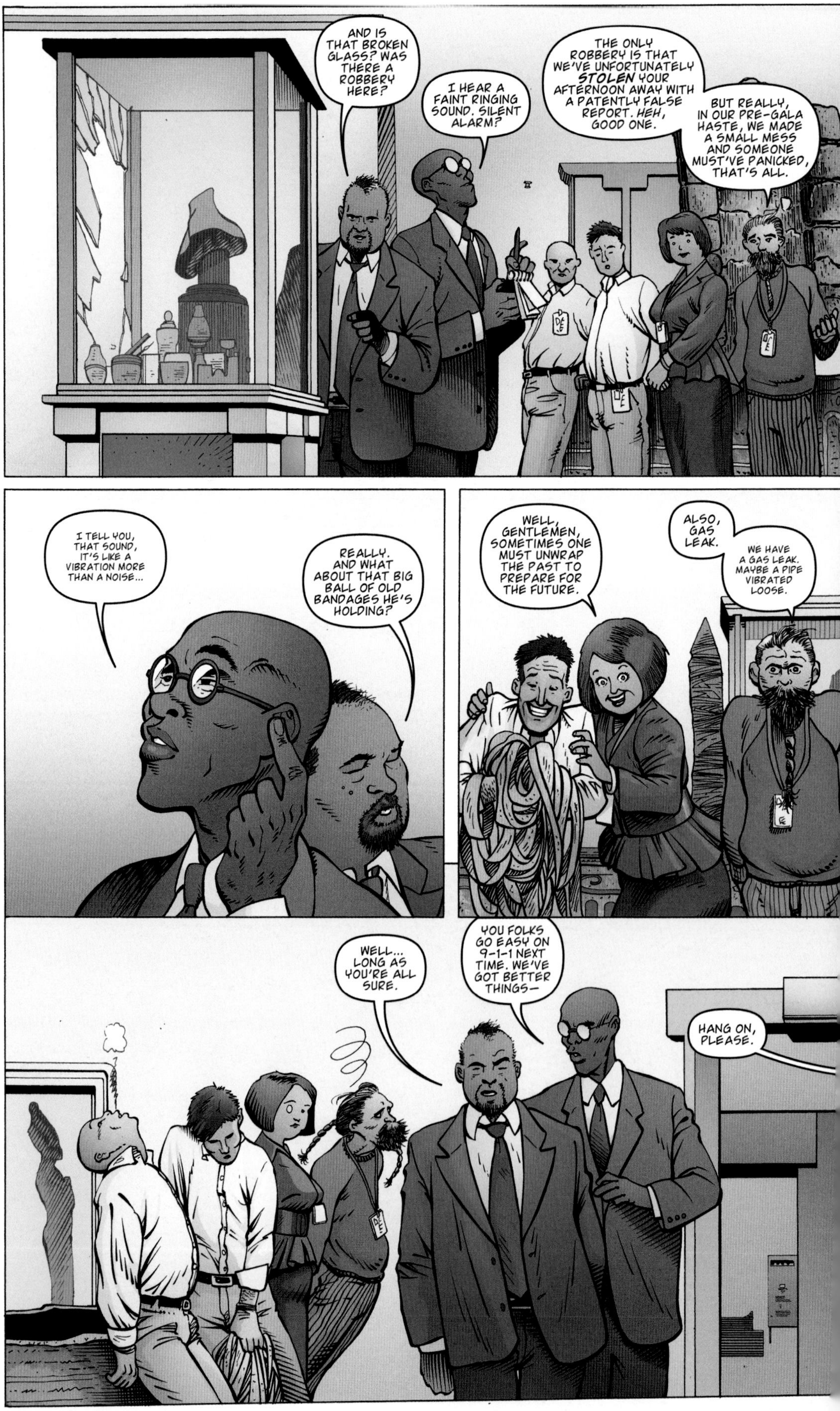

AND IS THAT BROKEN GLASS? WAS THERE A ROBBERY HERE?
I HEAR A FAINT RINGING SOUND. SILENT ALARM?
THE ONLY ROBBERY IS THAT WE'VE UNFORTUNATELY STOLEN YOUR AFTERNOON AWAY WITH A PATENTLY FALSE REPORT. HEH, GOOD ONE.
BUT REALLY, IN OUR PRE-GALA HASTE, WE MADE A SMALL MESS AND SOMEONE MUST'VE PANICKED, THAT'S ALL.
I TELL YOU, THAT SOUND, IT'S LIKE A VIBRATION MORE THAN A NOISE...
REALLY. AND WHAT ABOUT THAT BIG BALL OF OLD BANDAGES HE'S HOLDING?
WELL, GENTLEMEN, SOMETIMES ONE MUST UNWRAP THE PAST TO PREPARE FOR THE FUTURE.
ALSO, GAS LEAK.
WE HAVE A GAS LEAK. MAYBE A PIPE VIBRATED LOOSE.
WELL... LONG AS YOU'RE ALL SURE.
YOU FOLKS GO EASY ON 9-1-1 NEXT TIME. WE'VE GOT BETTER THINGS—
HANG ON, PLEASE.

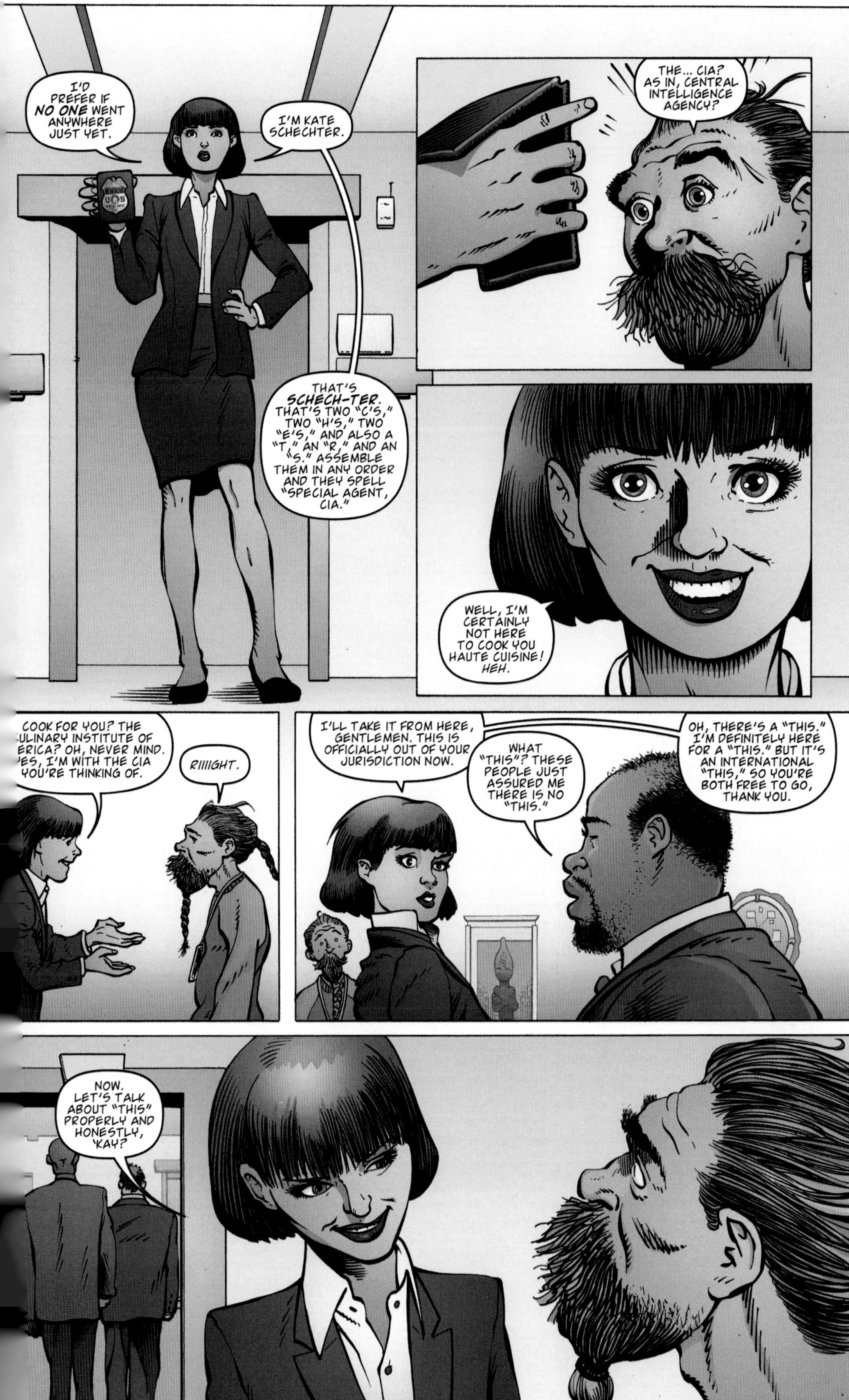

I'D PREFER IF NO ONE WENT ANYWHERE JUST YET.
I'M KATE SCHECHTER.
THAT'S SCHECH-TER. THAT'S TWO "C'S," TWO "H'S," TWO "E'S," AND ALSO A "T," AN "R," AND AN "S." ASSEMBLE THEM IN ANY ORDER AND THEY SPELL "SPECIAL AGENT, CIA."
THE... CIA? AS IN, CENTRAL INTELLIGENCE AGENCY?
WELL, I'M CERTAINLY NOT HERE TO COOK YOU HAUTE CUISINE! HEH.
COOK FOR YOU? THE ULINARY INSTITUTE OF ERICA? OH, NEVER MIND. ES, I'M WITH THE CIA YOU'RE THINKING OF.
RIIIIGHT.
I'LL TAKE IT FROM HERE, GENTLEMEN. THIS IS OFFICIALLY OUT OF YOUR JURISDICTION NOW.
WHAT "THIS"? THESE PEOPLE JUST ASSURED ME THERE IS NO "THIS."
OH, THERE'S A "THIS." I'M DEFINITELY HERE FOR A "THIS." BUT IT'S AN INTERNATIONAL "THIS," SO YOU'RE BOTH FREE TO GO, THANK YOU.
NOW. LET'S TALK ABOUT "THIS" PROPERLY AND HONESTLY, 'KAY?

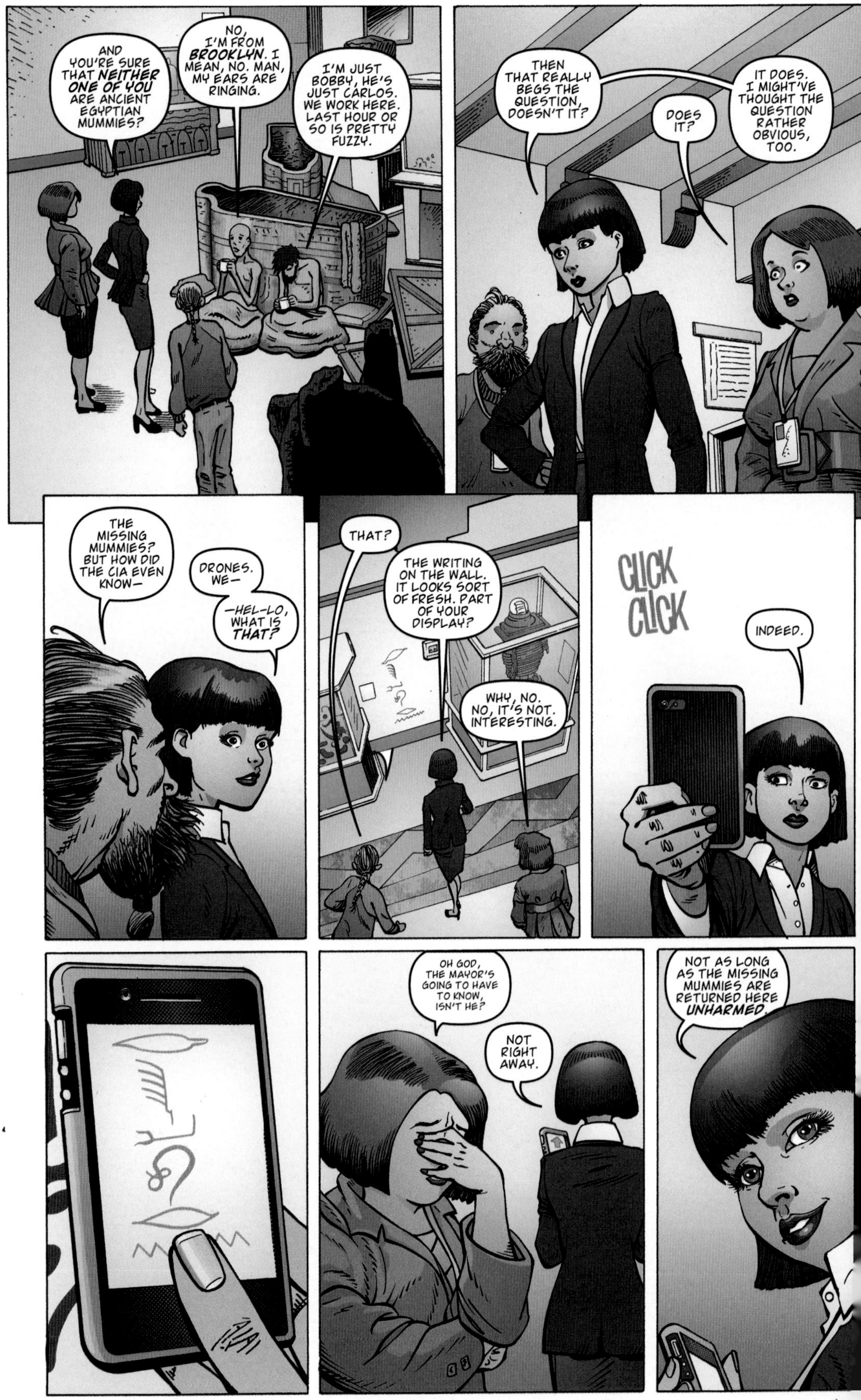
AND YOU'RE SURE THAT NEITHER ONE OF YOU ARE ANCIENT EGYPTIAN MUMMIES?
NO, I'M FROM BROOKLYN. I MEAN, NO. MAN, MY EARS ARE RINGING.
I'M JUST BOBBY, HE'S JUST CARLOS. WE WORK HERE. LAST HOUR OR SO IS PRETTY FUZZY.
THEN THAT REALLY BEGS THE QUESTION, DOESN'T IT?
DOES IT?
IT DOES. I MIGHT'VE THOUGHT THE QUESTION RATHER OBVIOUS, TOO.
THE MISSING MUMMIES? BUT HOW DID THE CIA EVEN KNOW—
DRONES. WE—
—HEL-LO, WHAT IS THAT?
THAT?
THE WRITING ON THE WALL. IT LOOKS SORT OF FRESH. PART OF YOUR DISPLAY?
WHY, NO. NO, IT'S NOT. INTERESTING.
CLICK CLICK
INDEED.
OH GOD, THE MAYOR'S GOING TO HAVE TO KNOW, ISN'T HE?
NOT RIGHT AWAY.
NOT AS LONG AS THE MISSING MUMMIES ARE RETURNED HERE UNHARMED.

EVERYBODY INSIDE, PLEASE, THE TOUR CONTINUES...

THIS IS A PLACE WHERE WE COULD REALLY HAVE SOME FUN.

I'M HUNGRY ENOUGH TO ABSORB THE LIFEFORCE OF EVERONE HERE.

DIRK? WE WOULD LIKE A PALATIAL ROOM. PERHAPS A PARTY UPSTAIRS?

A PRINCELY IDEA!

ONLY, THERE IS THE MATTER OF FUNDING SUCH A FETE...

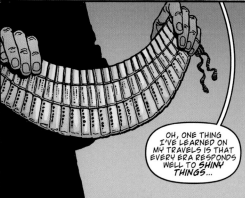

OH, ONE THING I'VE LEARNED ON MY TRAVELS IS THAT EVERY ERA RESPONDS WELL TO SHINY THINGS...

FINALLY, THEY'RE LEAVING.

I'M GOING TO HEAD IN AND GET MY BAG BACK.

I TOLD YOU, PATIENCE ALWAYS BEARS OUT.

I'LL FOLLOW THE GROUP, HOPEFULLY TO THE GAUDILY DRESSED BAGGAGE-THIEF—

AND THEN SETTLE ALL THEIR HASH FOR THEM.

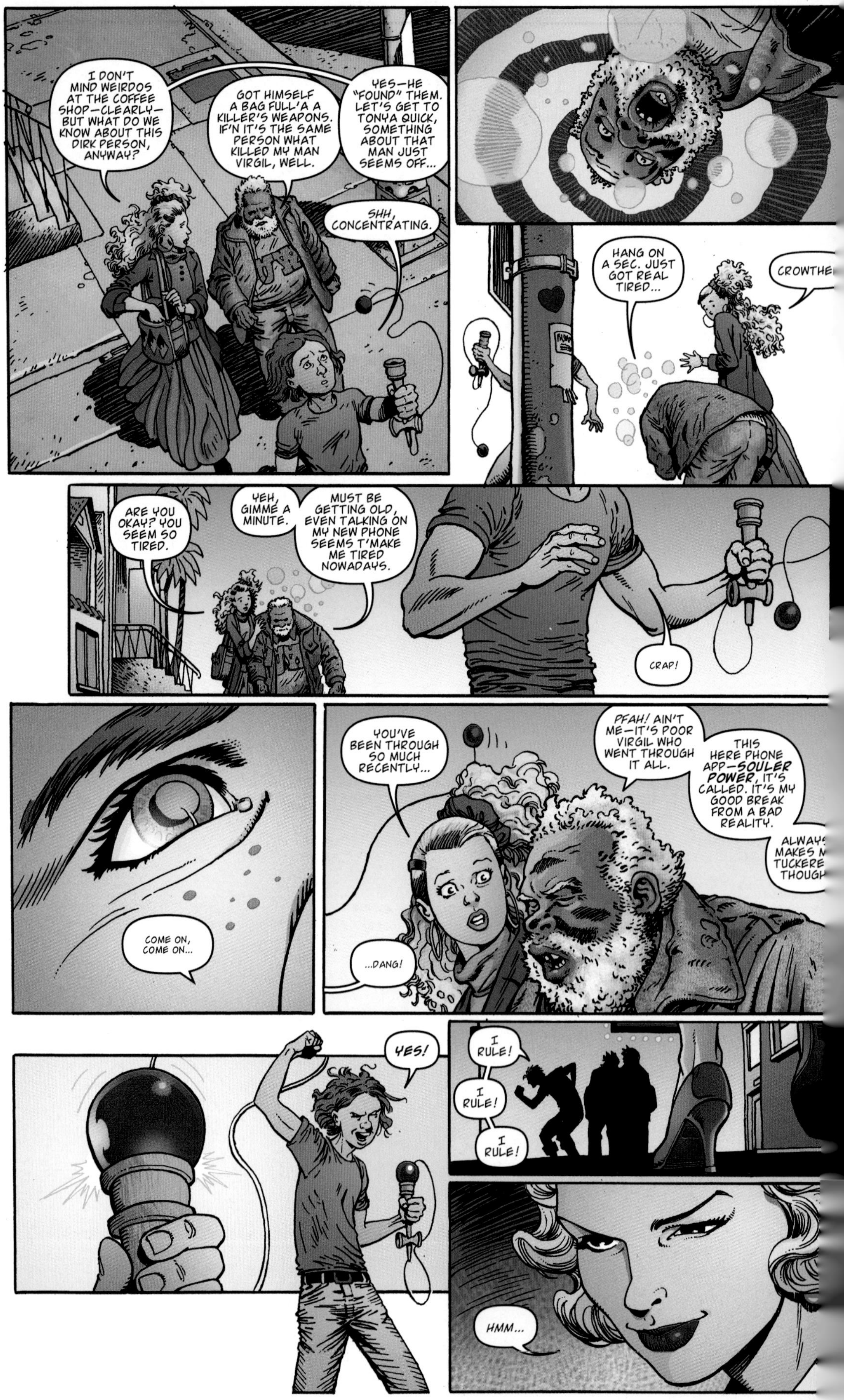
I DON'T MIND WEIRDOS AT THE COFFEE SHOP—CLEARLY—BUT WHAT DO WE KNOW ABOUT THIS DIRK PERSON, ANYWAY?
GOT HIMSELF A BAG FULL'A A KILLER'S WEAPONS. IF'N IT'S THE SAME PERSON WHAT KILLED MY MAN VIRGIL, WELL.
YES—HE "FOUND" THEM. LET'S GET TO TONYA QUICK, SOMETHING ABOUT THAT MAN JUST SEEMS OFF...
SHH, CONCENTRATING.
HANG ON A SEC. JUST GOT REAL TIRED...
CROWTHE
ARE YOU OKAY? YOU SEEM SO TIRED.
YEH, GIMME A MINUTE.
MUST BE GETTING OLD, EVEN TALKING ON MY NEW PHONE SEEMS T'MAKE ME TIRED NOWADAYS.
CRAP!
COME ON, COME ON...
YOU'VE BEEN THROUGH SO MUCH RECENTLY...
...DANG!
PFAH! AIN'T ME—IT'S POOR VIRGIL WHO WENT THROUGH IT ALL.
THIS HERE PHONE APP—SOULER POWER, IT'S CALLED. IT'S MY GOOD BREAK FROM A BAD REALITY.
ALWAYS MAKES M TUCKERE THOUGH
YES!
I RULE!
I RULE!
I RULE!
HMM...

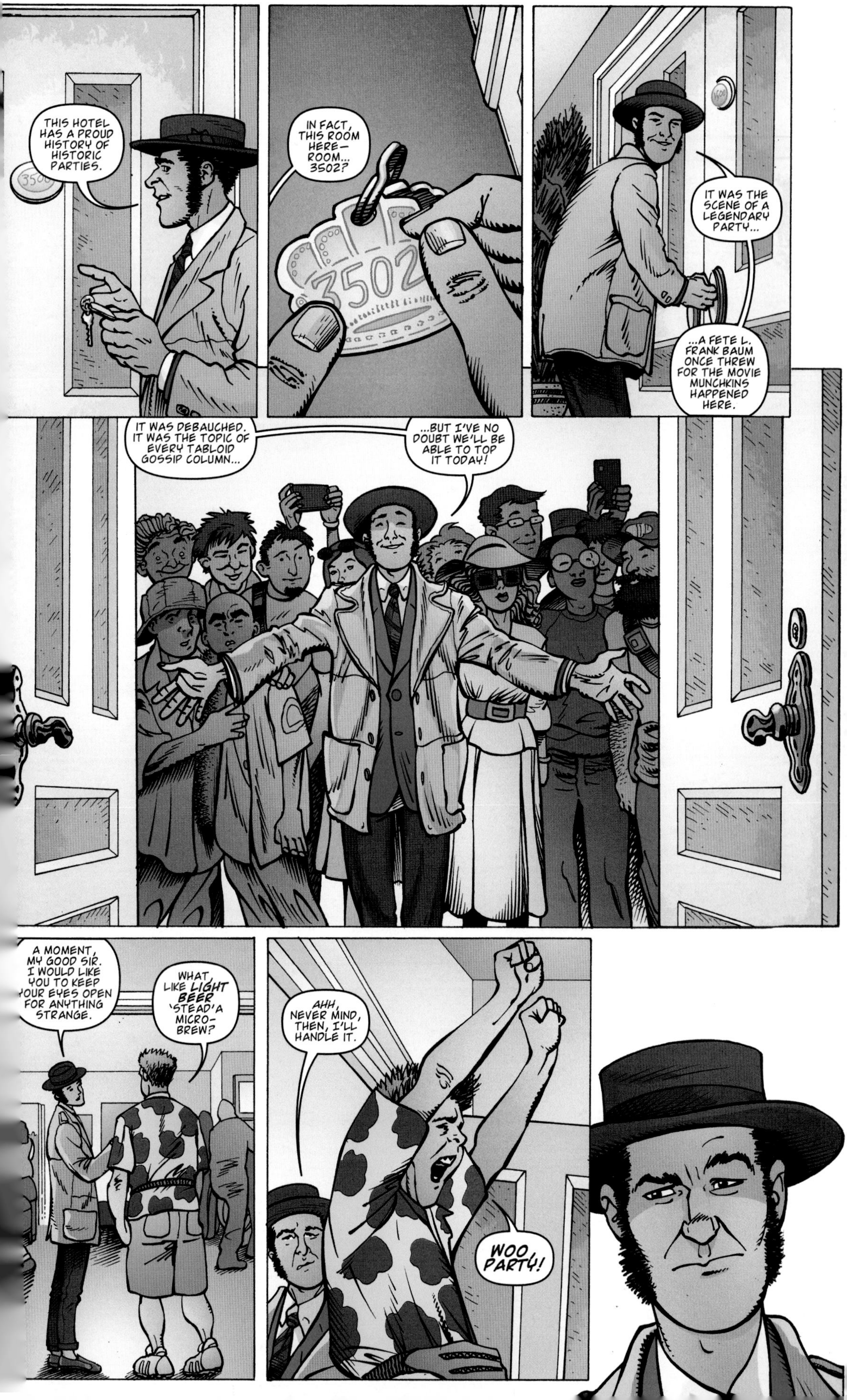
THIS HOTEL HAS A PROUD HISTORY OF HISTORIC PARTIES.
IN FACT, THIS ROOM HERE— ROOM... 3502?
IT WAS THE SCENE OF A LEGENDARY PARTY...
...A FETE L. FRANK BAUM ONCE THREW FOR THE MOVIE MUNCHKINS HAPPENED HERE.
IT WAS DEBAUCHED. IT WAS THE TOPIC OF EVERY TABLOID GOSSIP COLUMN...
...BUT I'VE NO DOUBT WE'LL BE ABLE TO TOP IT TODAY!
A MOMENT, MY GOOD SIR. I WOULD LIKE YOU TO KEEP YOUR EYES OPEN FOR ANYTHING STRANGE.
WHAT, LIKE LIGHT BEER 'STEAD'A MICRO-BREW?
AHH, NEVER MIND, THEN, I'LL HANDLE IT.
WOO PARTY!

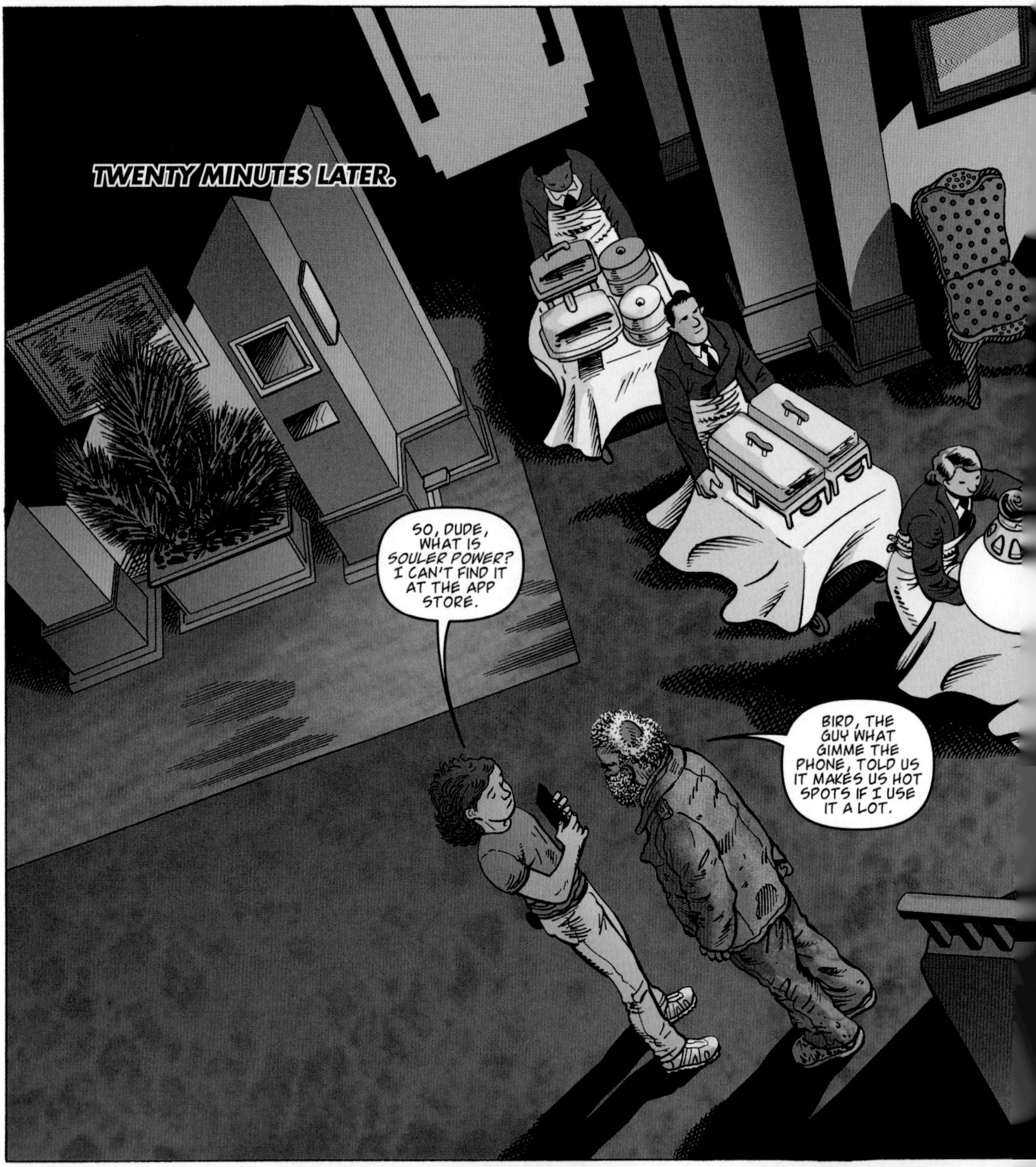
TWENTY MINUTES LATER.
SO, DUDE, WHAT IS SOULER POWER? I CAN'T FIND IT AT THE APP STORE.
BIRD, THE GUY WHAT GIMME THE PHONE, TOLD US IT MAKES US HOT SPOTS IF I USE IT A LOT.

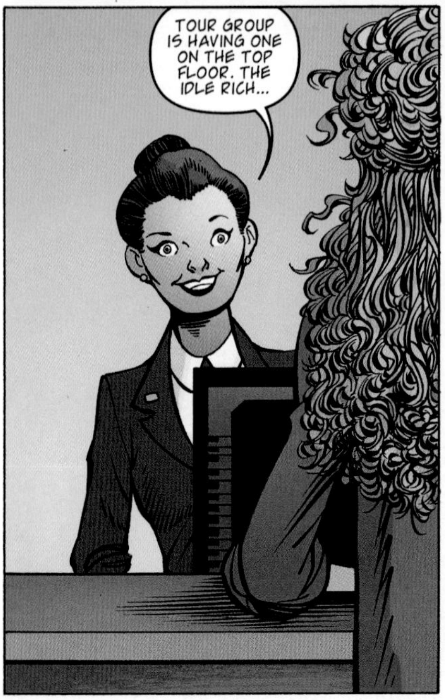
TOUR GROUP IS HAVING ONE ON THE TOP FLOOR. THE IDLE RICH...

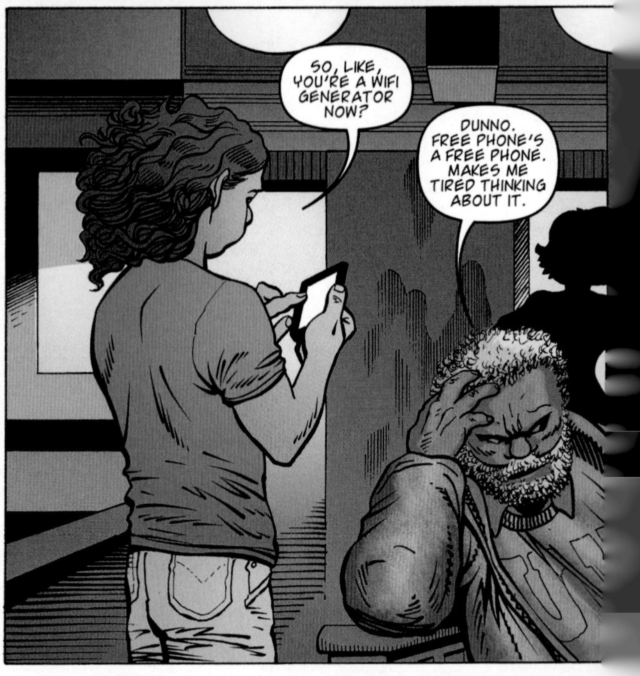
SO, LIKE, YOU'RE A WIFI GENERATOR NOW?
DUNNO. FREE PHONE'S A FREE PHONE. MAKES ME TIRED THINKING ABOUT IT.

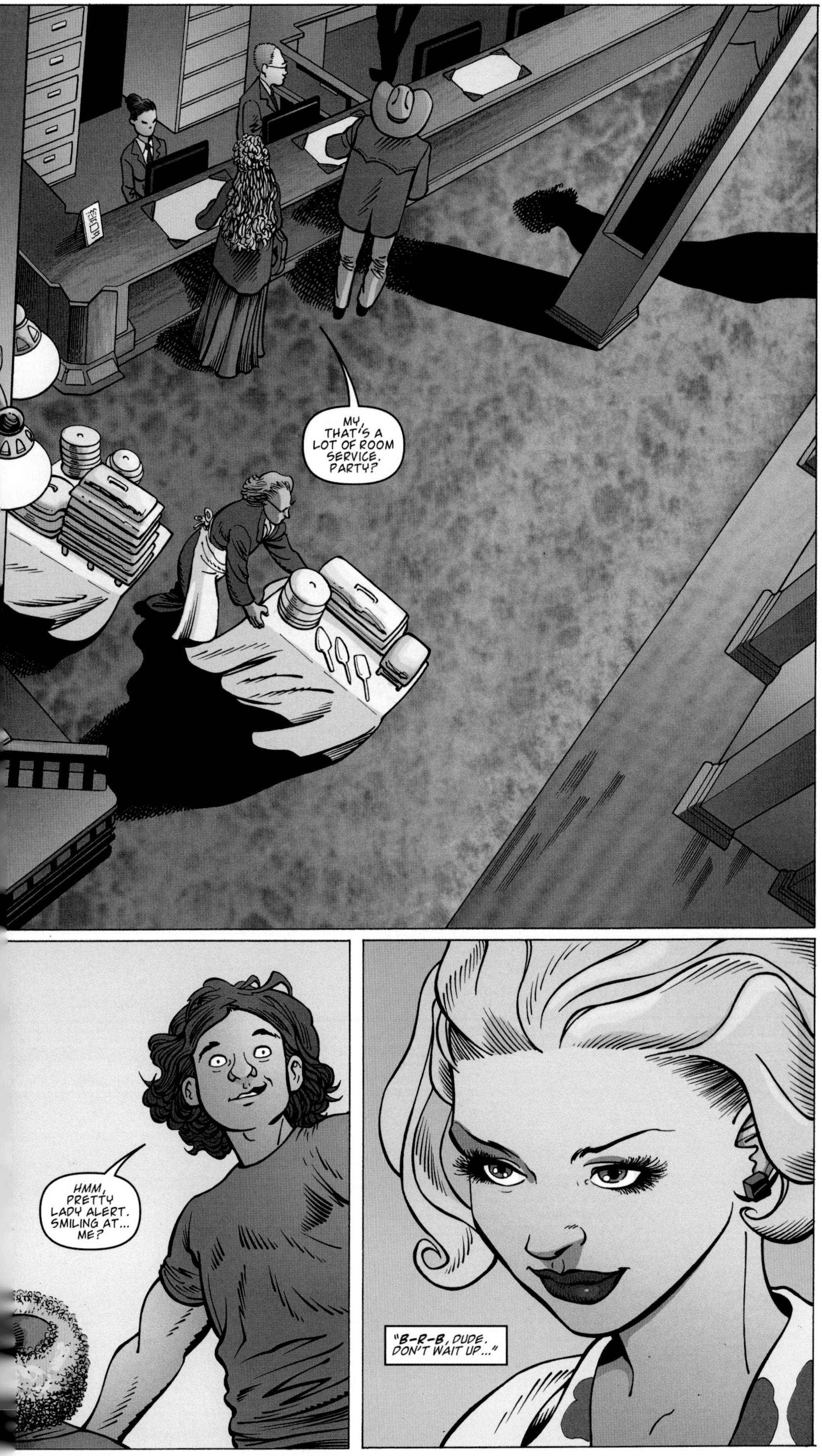
MY, THAT'S A LOT OF ROOM SERVICE. PARTY?
HMM, PRETTY LADY ALERT. SMILING AT... ME?
"B-R-B, DUDE. DON'T WAIT UP..."

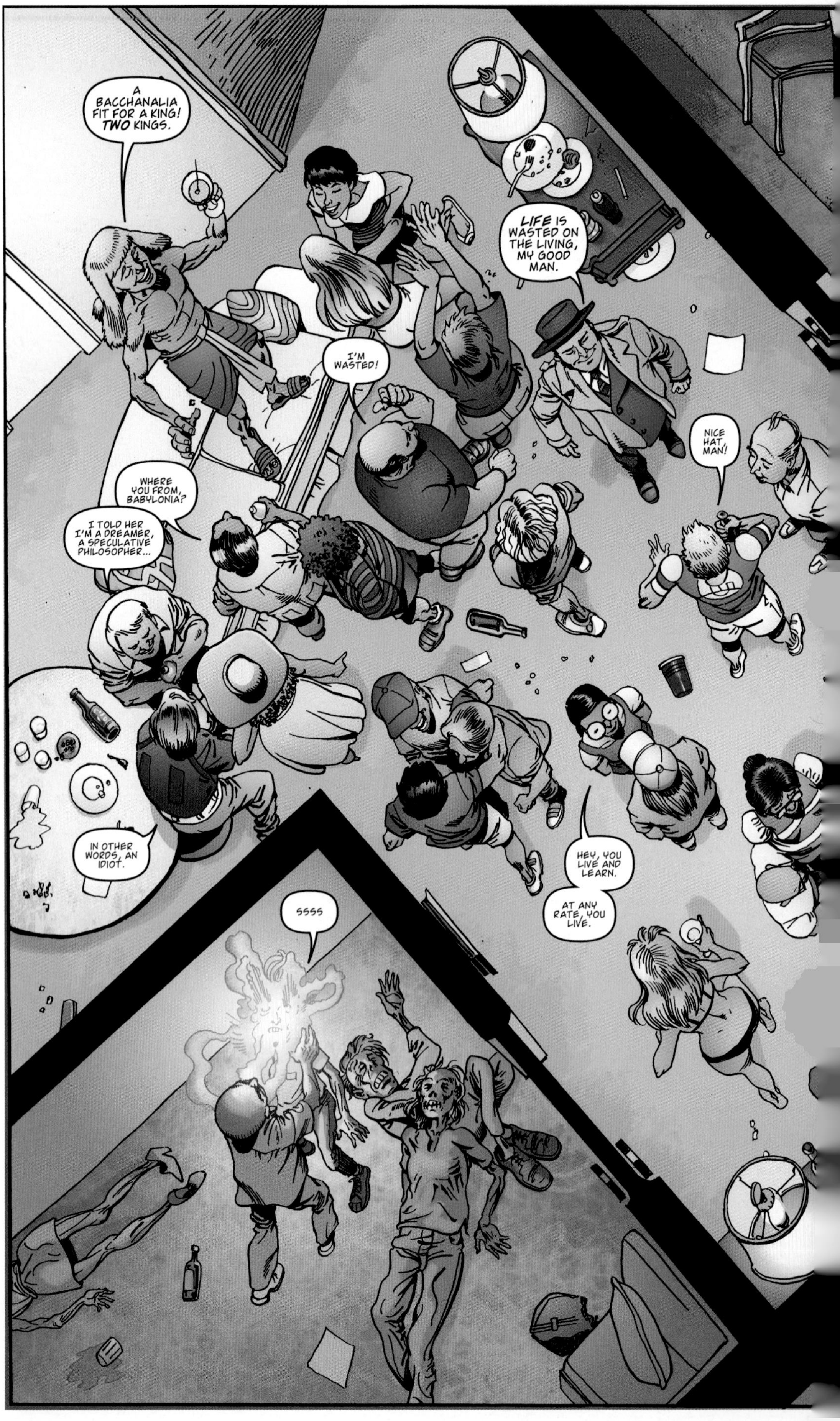
A BACCHANALIA FIT FOR A KING! TWO KINGS.
LIFE IS WASTED ON THE LIVING, MY GOOD MAN.
I'M WASTED!
NICE HAT, MAN!
WHERE YOU FROM, BABYLONIA?
I TOLD HER I'M A DREAMER, A SPECULATIVE PHILOSOPHER...
IN OTHER WORDS, AN IDIOT.
HEY, YOU LIVE AND LEARN.
AT ANY RATE, YOU LIVE.
SSSS

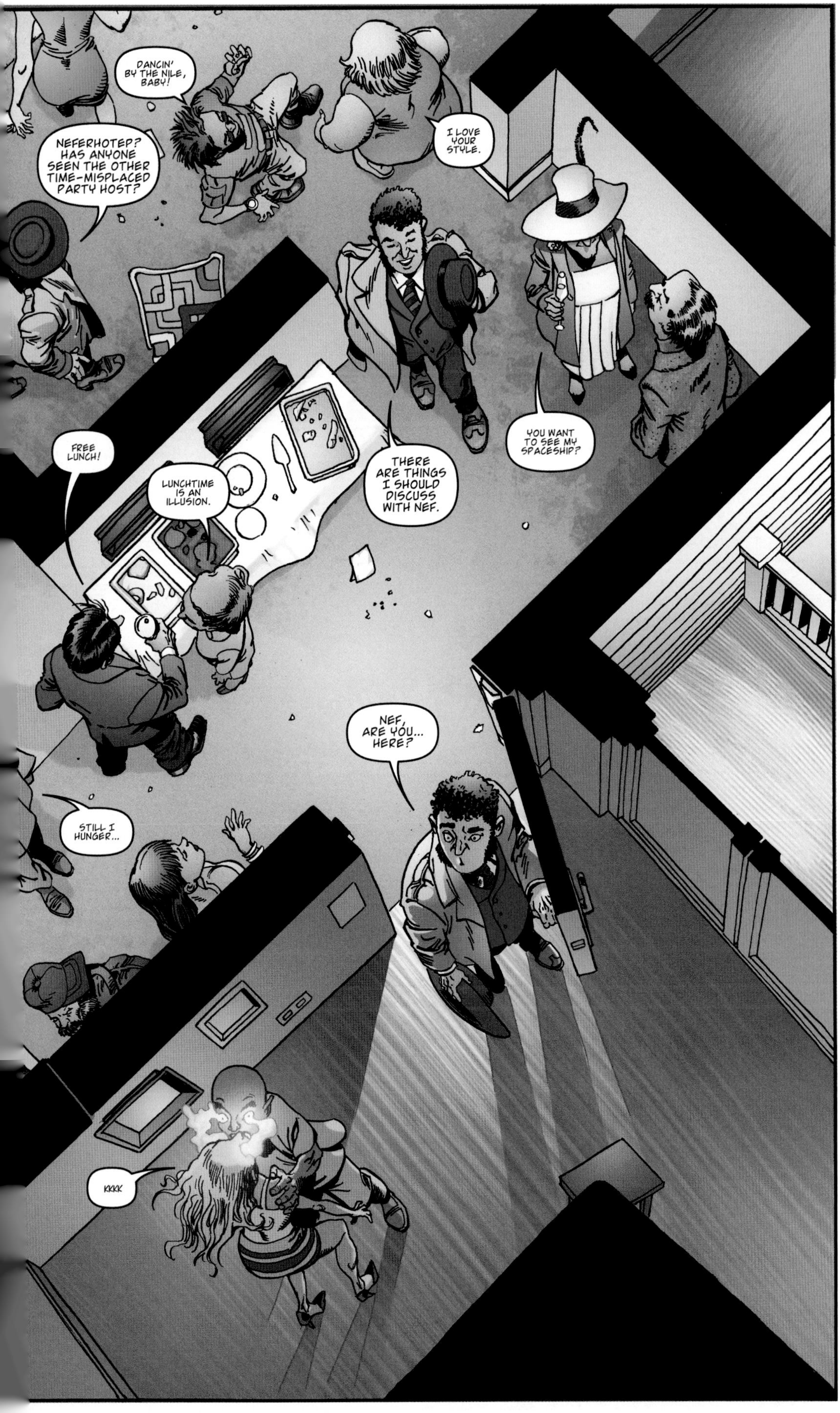
DANCIN' BY THE NILE, BABY!
I LOVE YOUR STYLE.
NEFERHOTEP? HAS ANYONE SEEN THE OTHER TIME-MISPLACED PARTY HOST?
YOU WANT TO SEE MY SPACESHIP?
THERE ARE THINGS I SHOULD DISCUSS WITH NEF.
FREE LUNCH!
LUNCHTIME IS AN ILLUSION.
NEF, ARE YOU... HERE?
STILL I HUNGER...
KKKK

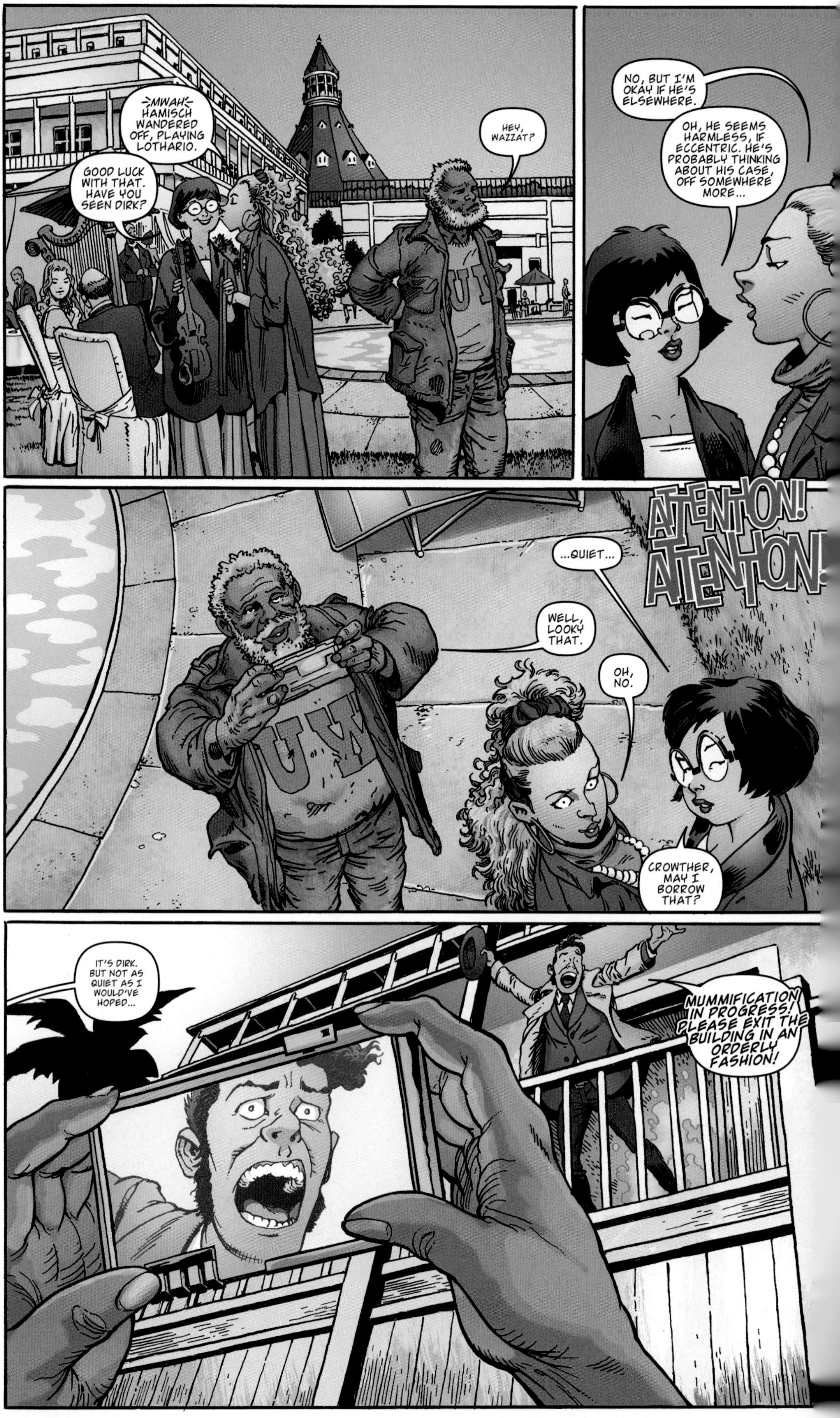
-MWAH- HAMISCH WANDERED OFF, PLAYING LOTHARIO.
GOOD LUCK WITH THAT. HAVE YOU SEEN DIRK?
HEY, WAZZAT?
NO, BUT I'M OKAY IF HE'S ELSEWHERE.
OH, HE SEEMS HARMLESS, IF ECCENTRIC. HE'S PROBABLY THINKING ABOUT HIS CASE, OFF SOMEWHERE MORE...
ATTENTION! ATTENTION!
...QUIET...
WELL, LOOKY THAT.
OH, NO.
CROWTHER, MAY I BORROW THAT?
IT'S DIRK. BUT NOT AS QUIET AS I WOULD'VE HOPED...
MUMMIFICATION IN PROGRESS! PLEASE EXIT THE BUILDING IN AN ORDERLY FASHION!

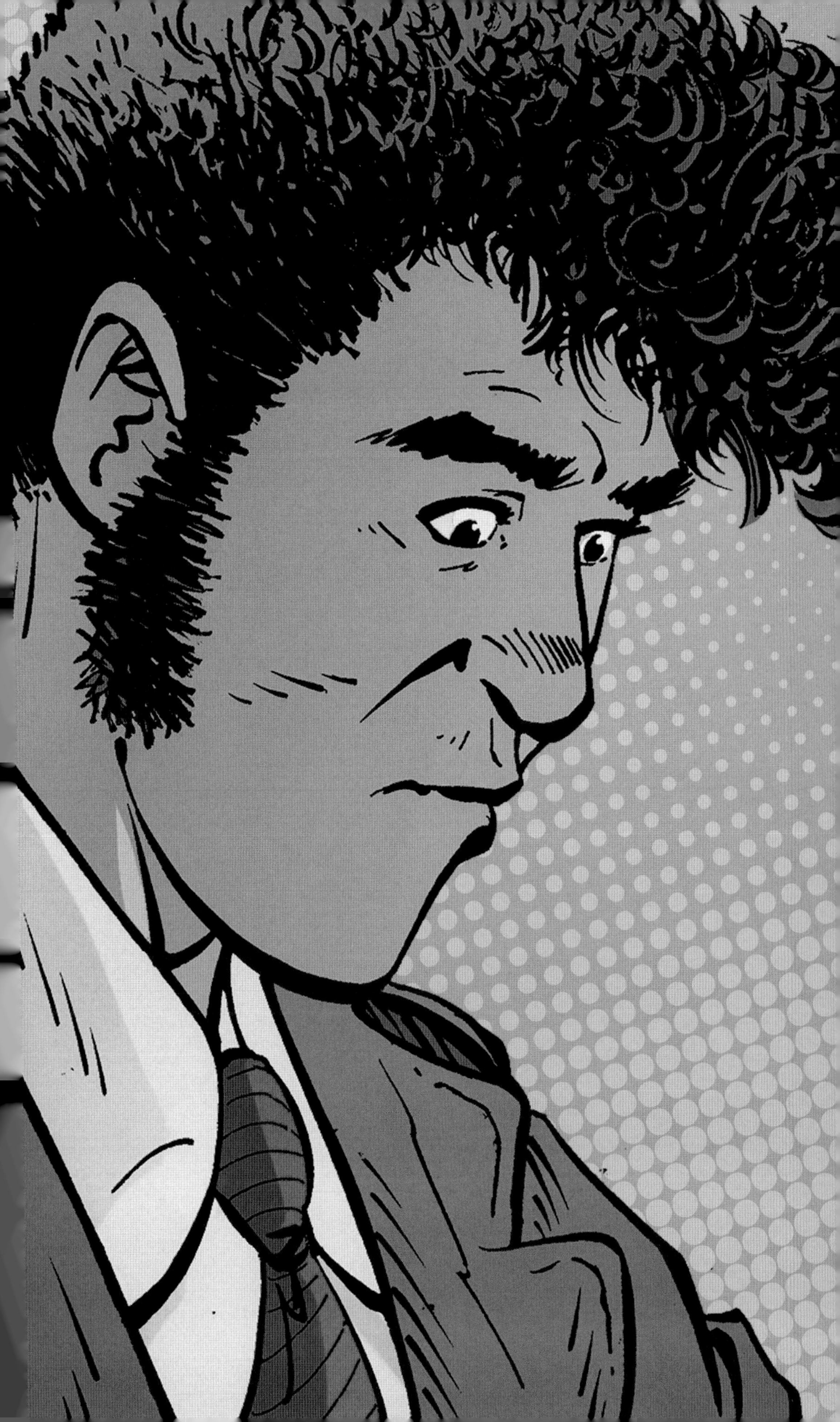

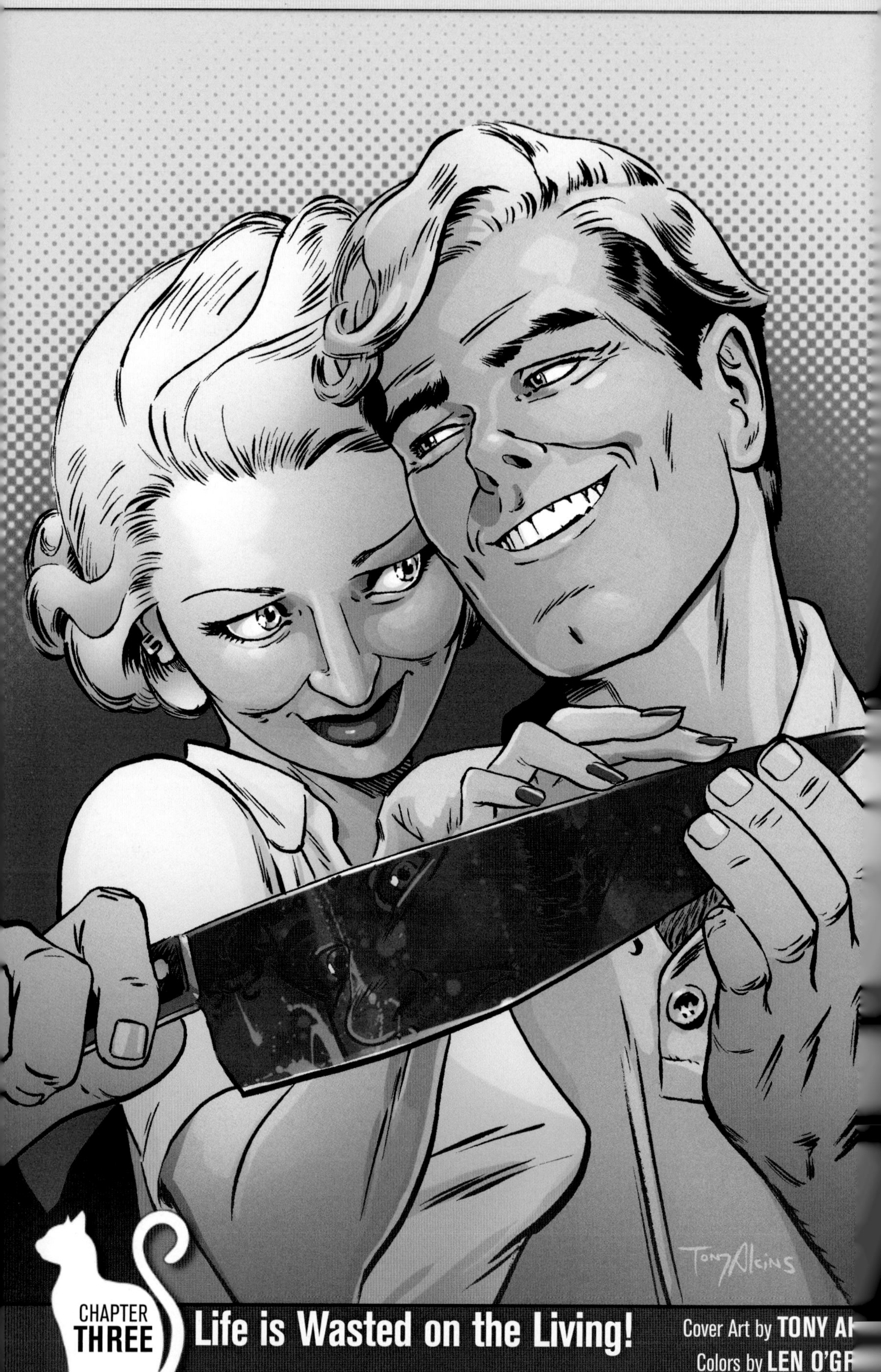

CHAPTER THREE

Life is Wasted on the Living!

Cover Art by TONY A
Colors by LEN O'GR

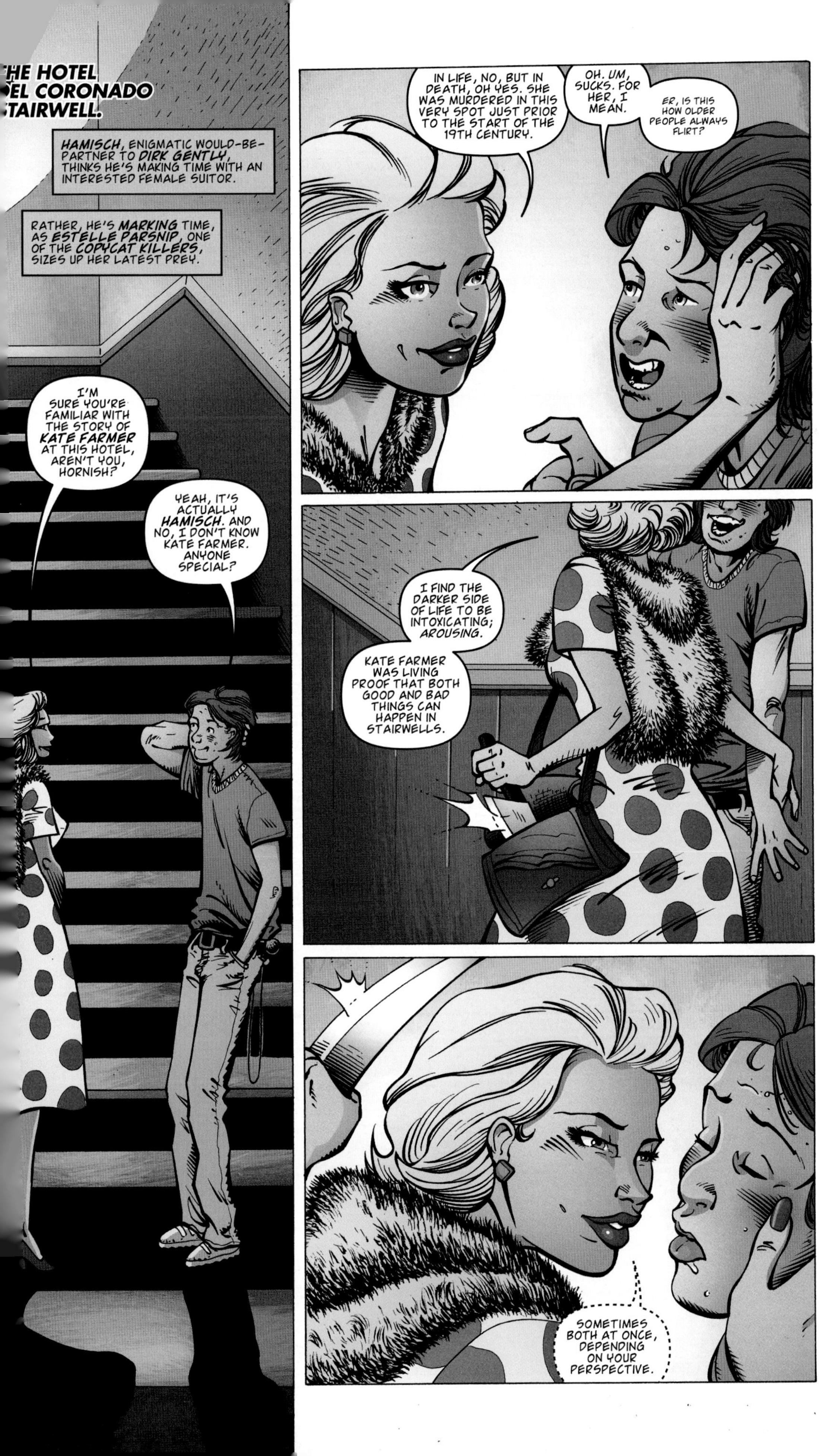

THE HOTEL DEL CORONADO STAIRWELL.
HAMISCH, ENIGMATIC WOULD-BE-PARTNER TO DIRK GENTLY, THINKS HE'S MAKING TIME WITH AN INTERESTED FEMALE SUITOR.
RATHER, HE'S MARKING TIME, AS ESTELLE PARSNIP, ONE OF THE COPYCAT KILLERS, SIZES UP HER LATEST PREY.
I'M SURE YOU'RE FAMILIAR WITH THE STORY OF KATE FARMER AT THIS HOTEL, AREN'T YOU, HORNISH?
YEAH, IT'S ACTUALLY HAMISCH. AND NO, I DON'T KNOW KATE FARMER. ANYONE SPECIAL?
IN LIFE, NO, BUT IN DEATH, OH YES. SHE WAS MURDERED IN THIS VERY SPOT JUST PRIOR TO THE START OF THE 19TH CENTURY.
OH. UM, SUCKS. FOR HER, I MEAN.
ER, IS THIS HOW OLDER PEOPLE ALWAYS FLIRT?
I FIND THE DARKER SIDE OF LIFE TO BE INTOXICATING; AROUSING.
KATE FARMER WAS LIVING PROOF THAT BOTH GOOD AND BAD THINGS CAN HAPPEN IN STAIRWELLS.
SOMETIMES BOTH AT ONCE, DEPENDING ON YOUR PERSPECTIVE.

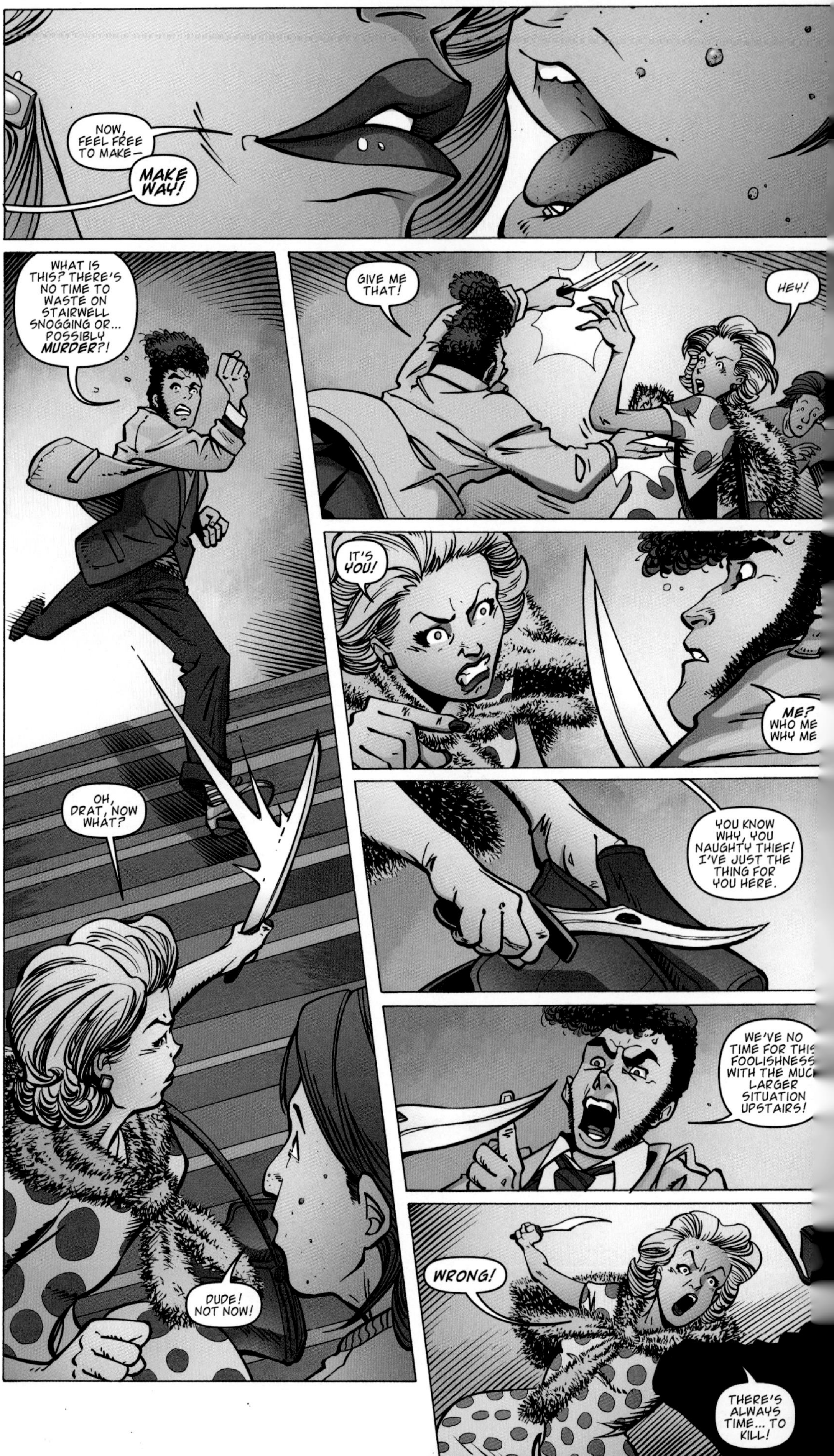
NOW, FEEL FREE TO MAKE—
MAKE WAY!
WHAT IS THIS? THERE'S NO TIME TO WASTE ON STAIRWELL SNOGGING OR... POSSIBLY MURDER?!
OH, DRAT, NOW WHAT?
DUDE! NOT NOW!
GIVE ME THAT!
HEY!
IT'S YOU!
ME? WHO ME WHY ME
YOU KNOW WHY, YOU NAUGHTY THIEF! I'VE JUST THE THING FOR YOU HERE.
WE'VE NO TIME FOR THIS FOOLISHNESS WITH THE MUCH LARGER SITUATION UPSTAIRS!
WRONG!
THERE'S ALWAYS TIME... TO KILL!

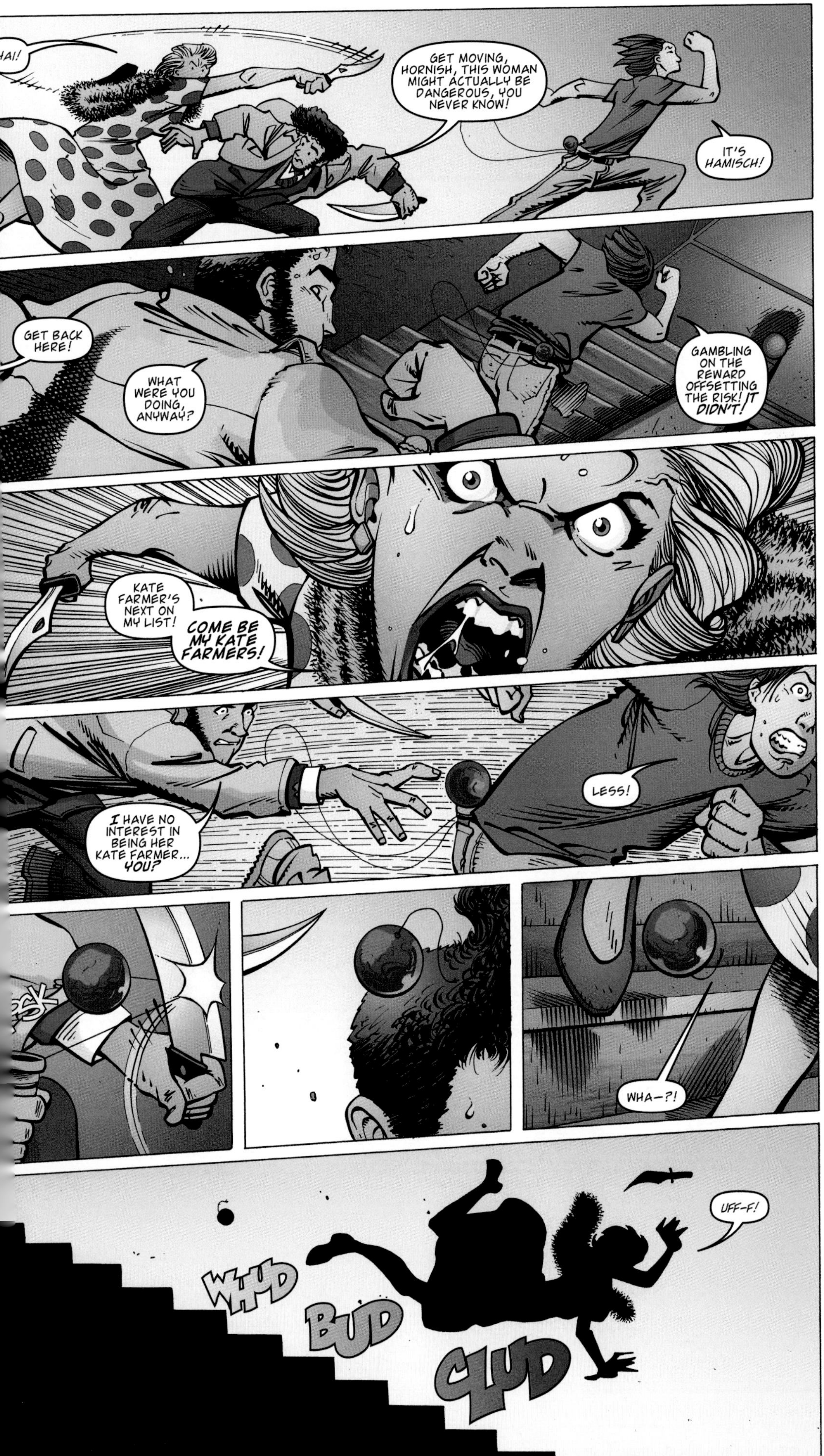
HAI!
GET MOVING, HORNISH, THIS WOMAN MIGHT ACTUALLY BE DANGEROUS, YOU NEVER KNOW!
IT'S HAMISCH!
GET BACK HERE!
WHAT WERE YOU DOING, ANYWAY?
GAMBLING ON THE REWARD OFFSETTING THE RISK! IT DIDN'T!
KATE FARMER'S NEXT ON MY LIST!
COME BE MY KATE FARMERS!
I HAVE NO INTEREST IN BEING HER KATE FARMER... YOU?
LESS!
WHA-?!
UFF-F!
WHUD
BUD
CLUD

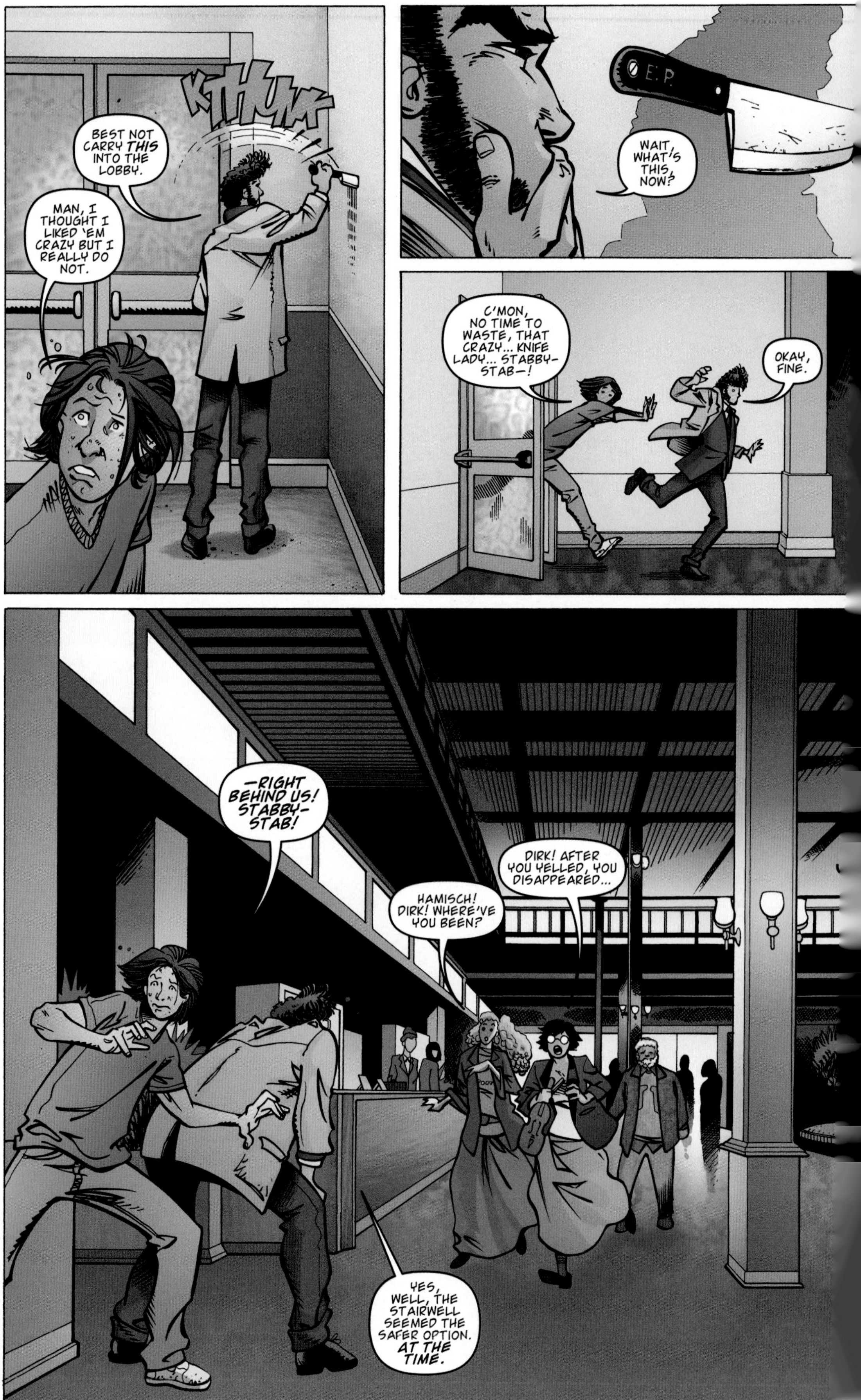
KTHUNK
BEST NOT CARRY THIS INTO THE LOBBY.
MAN, I THOUGHT I LIKED 'EM CRAZY BUT I REALLY DO NOT.
E.P.
WAIT, WHAT'S THIS, NOW?
C'MON, NO TIME TO WASTE, THAT CRAZY... KNIFE LADY... STABBY-STAB—!
OKAY, FINE.
—RIGHT BEHIND US! STABBY-STAB!
HAMISCH! DIRK! WHERE'VE YOU BEEN?
DIRK! AFTER YOU YELLED, YOU DISAPPEARED...
YES, WELL, THE STAIRWELL SEEMED THE SAFER OPTION. AT THE TIME.

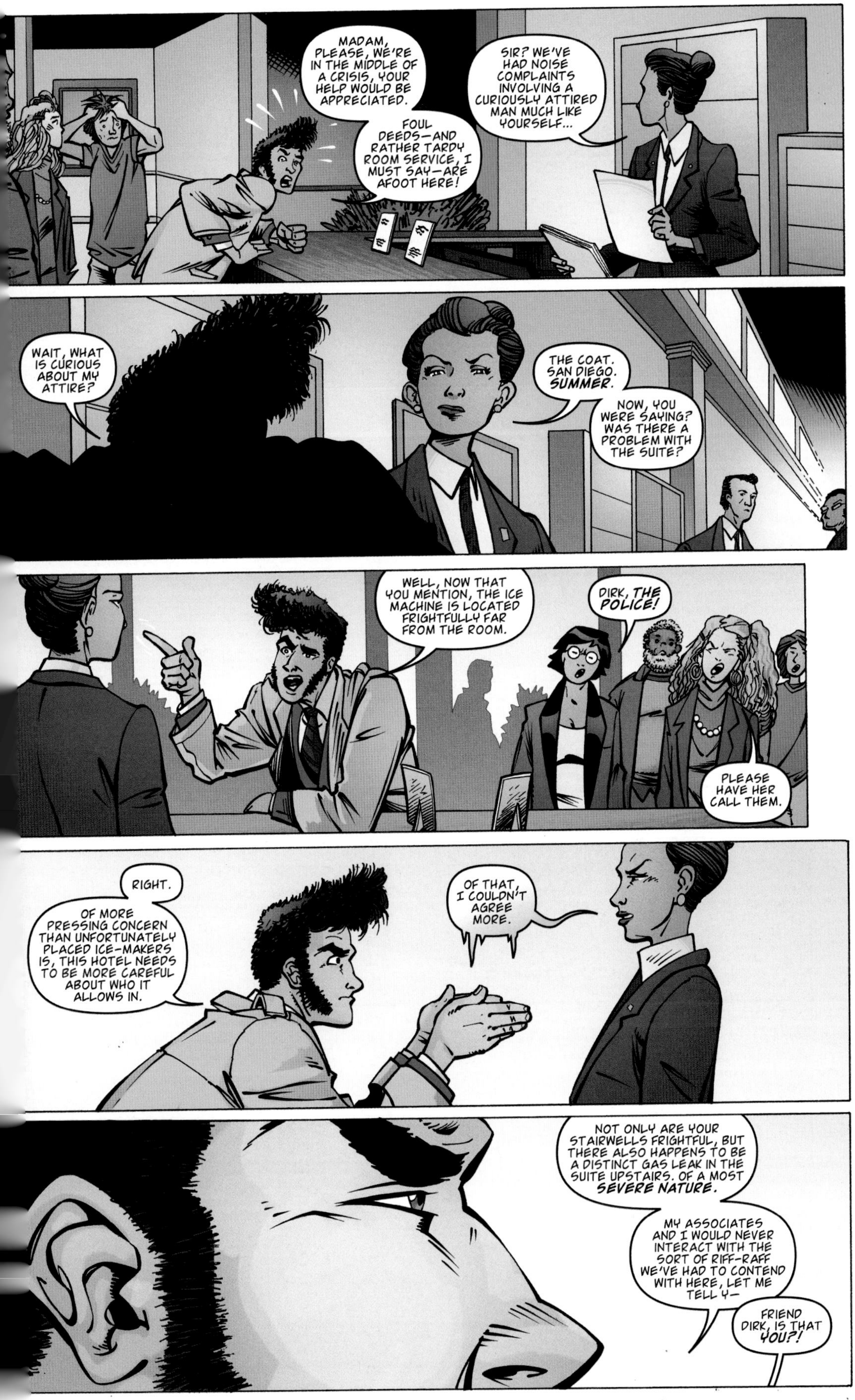
MADAM, PLEASE, WE'RE IN THE MIDDLE OF A CRISIS, YOUR HELP WOULD BE APPRECIATED.
FOUL DEEDS—AND RATHER TARDY ROOM SERVICE, I MUST SAY—ARE AFOOT HERE!
SIR? WE'VE HAD NOISE COMPLAINTS INVOLVING A CURIOUSLY ATTIRED MAN MUCH LIKE YOURSELF...
WAIT, WHAT IS CURIOUS ABOUT MY ATTIRE?
THE COAT. SAN DIEGO. SUMMER.
NOW, YOU WERE SAYING? WAS THERE A PROBLEM WITH THE SUITE?
WELL, NOW THAT YOU MENTION, THE ICE MACHINE IS LOCATED FRIGHTFULLY FAR FROM THE ROOM.
DIRK, THE POLICE!
PLEASE HAVE HER CALL THEM.
RIGHT.
OF MORE PRESSING CONCERN THAN UNFORTUNATELY PLACED ICE-MAKERS IS, THIS HOTEL NEEDS TO BE MORE CAREFUL ABOUT WHO IT ALLOWS IN.
OF THAT, I COULDN'T AGREE MORE.
NOT ONLY ARE YOUR STAIRWELLS FRIGHTFUL, BUT THERE ALSO HAPPENS TO BE A DISTINCT GAS LEAK IN THE SUITE UPSTAIRS. OF A MOST SEVERE NATURE.
MY ASSOCIATES AND I WOULD NEVER INTERACT WITH THE SORT OF RIFF-RAFF WE'VE HAD TO CONTEND WITH HERE, LET ME TELL Y—
FRIEND DIRK, IS THAT YOU?!

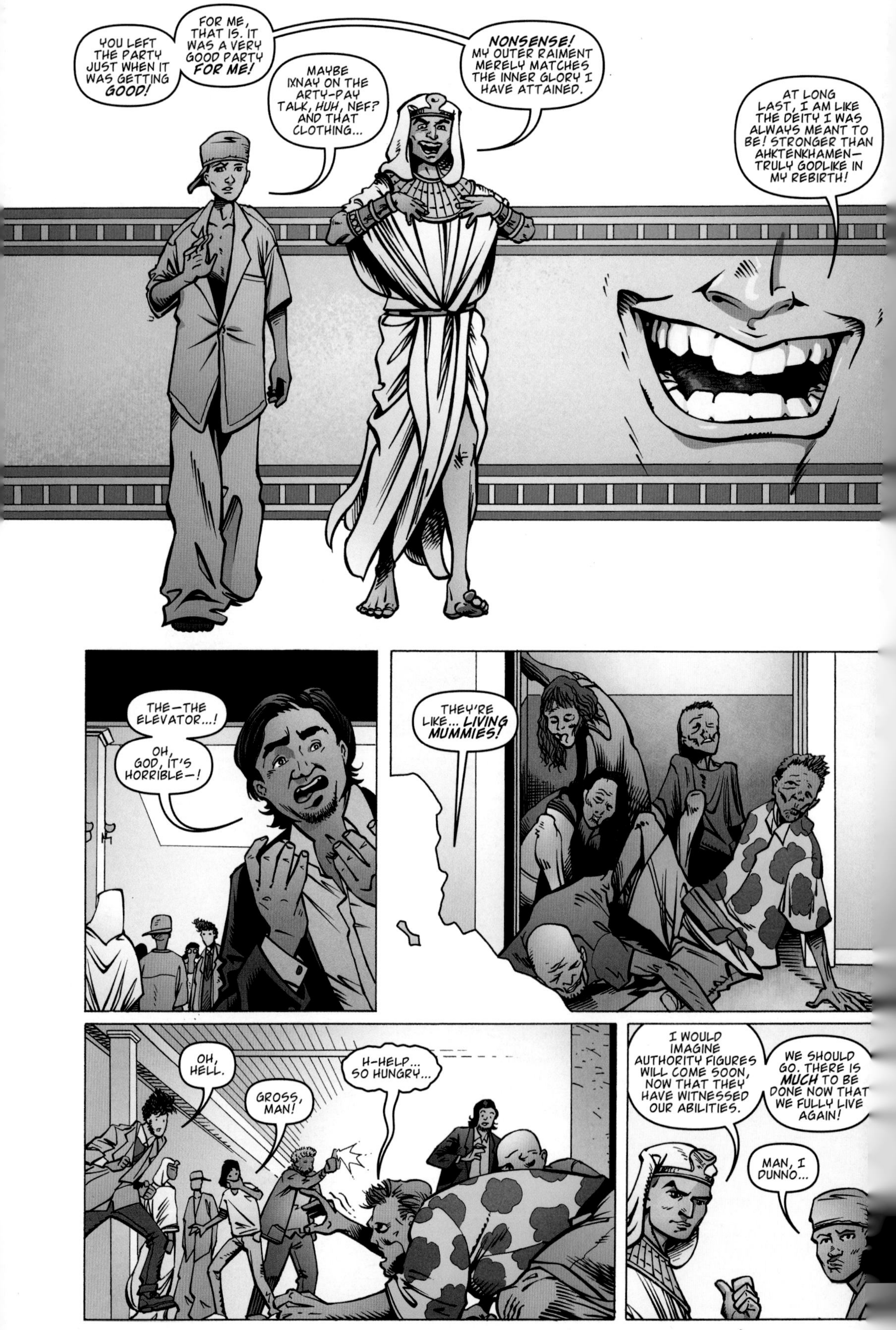
YOU LEFT THE PARTY JUST WHEN IT WAS GETTING GOOD!
FOR ME, THAT IS. IT WAS A VERY GOOD PARTY FOR ME!
MAYBE IXNAY ON THE ARTY-PAY TALK, HUH, NEF? AND THAT CLOTHING...
NONSENSE! MY OUTER RAIMENT MERELY MATCHES THE INNER GLORY I HAVE ATTAINED.
AT LONG LAST, I AM LIKE THE DEITY I WAS ALWAYS MEANT TO BE! STRONGER THAN AHKTENKHAMEN—TRULY GODLIKE IN MY REBIRTH!
THE—THE ELEVATOR...!
OH, GOD, IT'S HORRIBLE—!
THEY'RE LIKE... LIVING MUMMIES!
OH, HELL.
GROSS, MAN!
H-HELP... SO HUNGRY...
I WOULD IMAGINE AUTHORITY FIGURES WILL COME SOON, NOW THAT THEY HAVE WITNESSED OUR ABILITIES.
WE SHOULD GO. THERE IS MUCH TO BE DONE NOW THAT WE FULLY LIVE AGAIN!
MAN, I DUNNO...

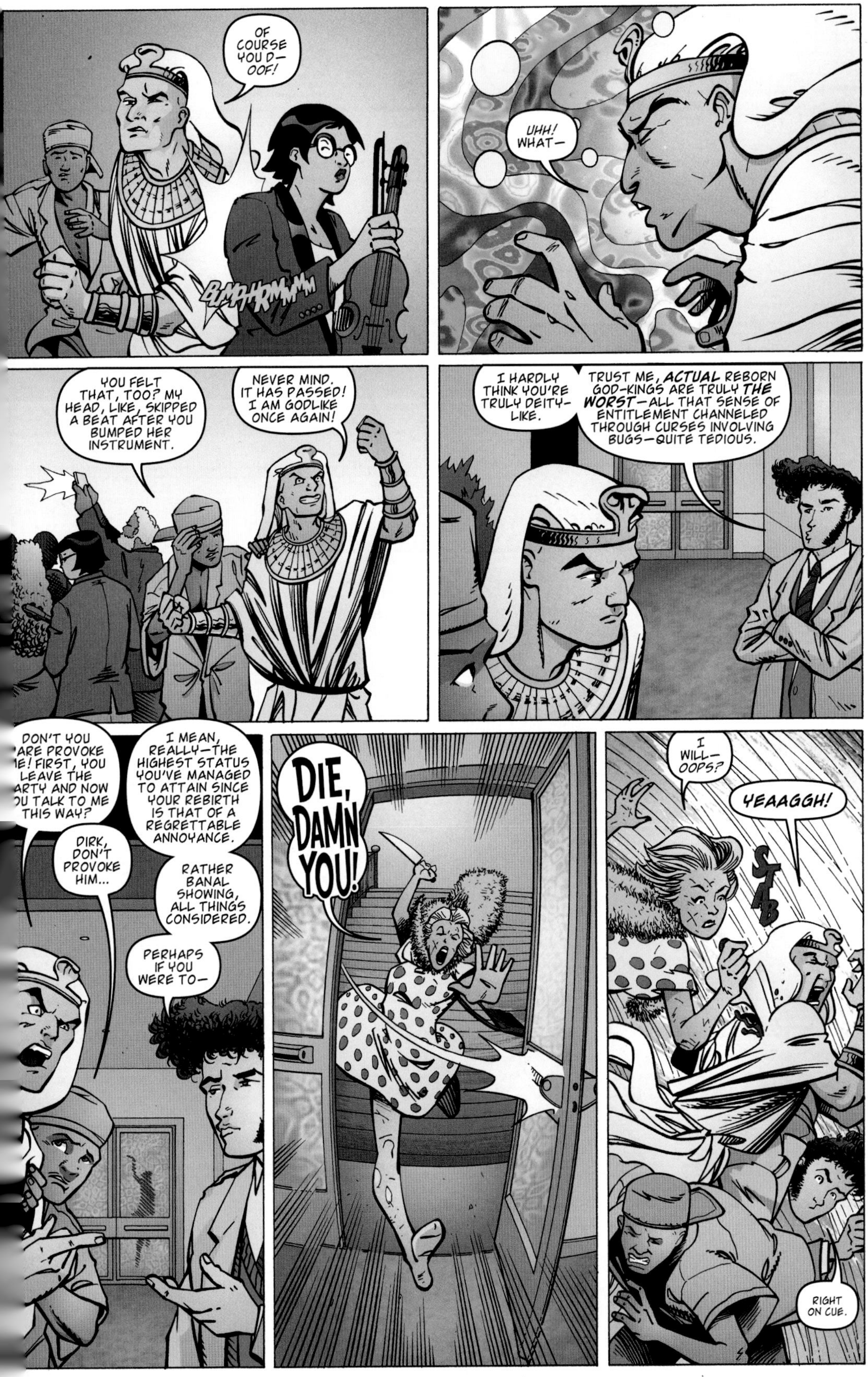
OF COURSE YOU D— OOF!
BMPHRMMMM
UHH! WHAT—
YOU FELT THAT, TOO? MY HEAD, LIKE, SKIPPED A BEAT AFTER YOU BUMPED HER INSTRUMENT.
NEVER MIND. IT HAS PASSED! I AM GODLIKE ONCE AGAIN!
I HARDLY THINK YOU'RE TRULY DEITY-LIKE.
TRUST ME, ACTUAL REBORN GOD-KINGS ARE TRULY THE WORST—ALL THAT SENSE OF ENTITLEMENT CHANNELED THROUGH CURSES INVOLVING BUGS—QUITE TEDIOUS.
DON'T YOU ARE PROVOKE E! FIRST, YOU LEAVE THE ARTY AND NOW OU TALK TO ME THIS WAY?
I MEAN, REALLY—THE HIGHEST STATUS YOU'VE MANAGED TO ATTAIN SINCE YOUR REBIRTH IS THAT OF A REGRETTABLE ANNOYANCE.
DIRK, DON'T PROVOKE HIM...
RATHER BANAL SHOWING, ALL THINGS CONSIDERED.
PERHAPS IF YOU WERE TO—
DIE, DAMN YOU!
I WILL— OOPS?
YEAAGGH!
RIGHT ON CUE.

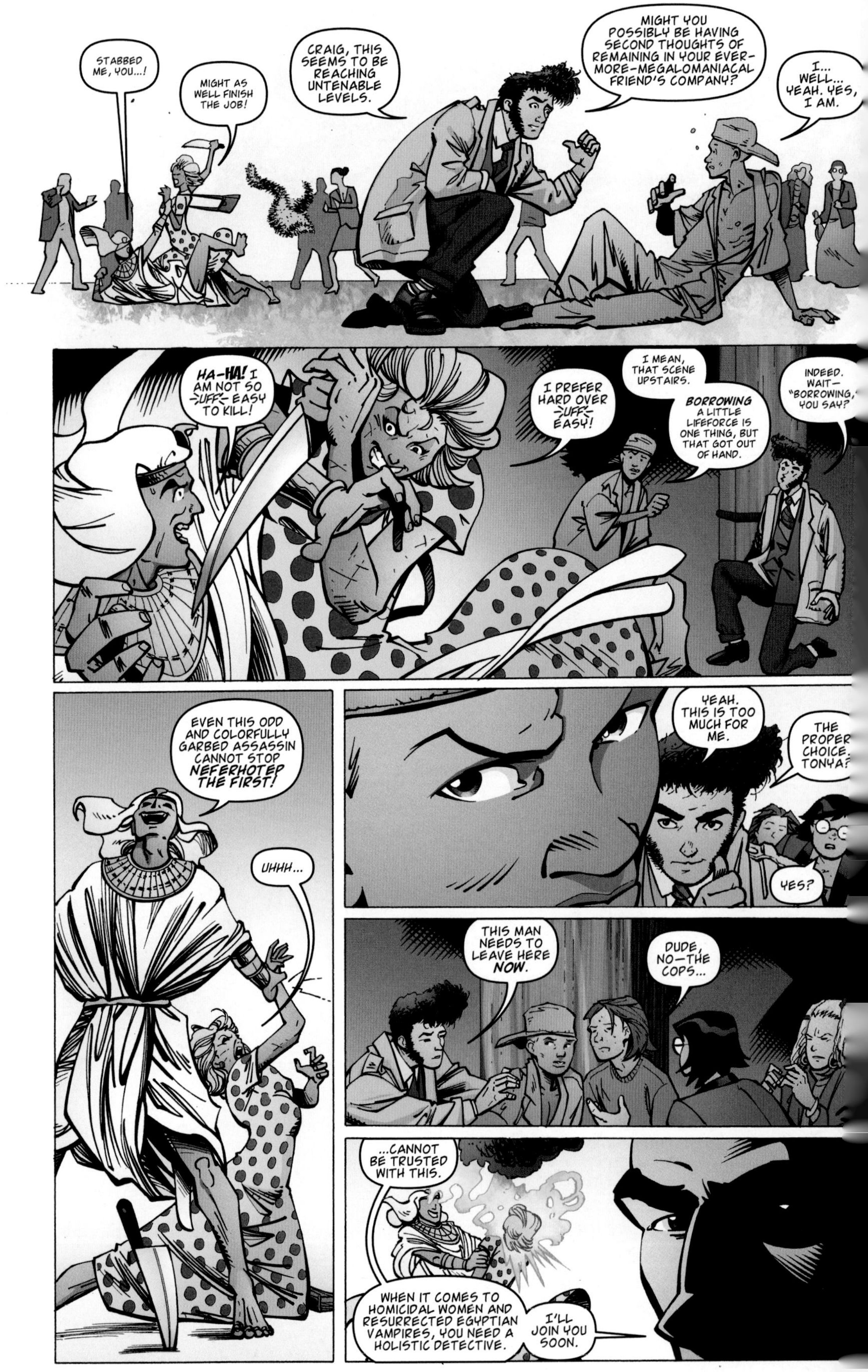
STABBED ME, YOU...!
MIGHT AS WELL FINISH THE JOB!
CRAIG, THIS SEEMS TO BE REACHING UNTENABLE LEVELS.
MIGHT YOU POSSIBLY BE HAVING SECOND THOUGHTS OF REMAINING IN YOUR EVER-MORE-MEGALOMANIACAL FRIEND'S COMPANY?
I... WELL... YEAH. YES, I AM.
HA-HA! I AM NOT SO -UFF- EASY TO KILL!
I PREFER HARD OVER -UFF- EASY!
I MEAN, THAT SCENE UPSTAIRS.
BORROWING A LITTLE LIFEFORCE IS ONE THING, BUT THAT GOT OUT OF HAND.
INDEED. WAIT— "BORROWING," YOU SAY?
EVEN THIS ODD AND COLORFULLY GARBED ASSASSIN CANNOT STOP NEFERHOTEP THE FIRST!
UHHH...
YEAH. THIS IS TOO MUCH FOR ME.
THE PROPER CHOICE. TONYA?
YES?
THIS MAN NEEDS TO LEAVE HERE NOW.
DUDE, NO—THE COPS...
...CANNOT BE TRUSTED WITH THIS.
WHEN IT COMES TO HOMICIDAL WOMEN AND RESURRECTED EGYPTIAN VAMPIRES, YOU NEED A HOLISTIC DETECTIVE.
I'LL JOIN YOU SOON.

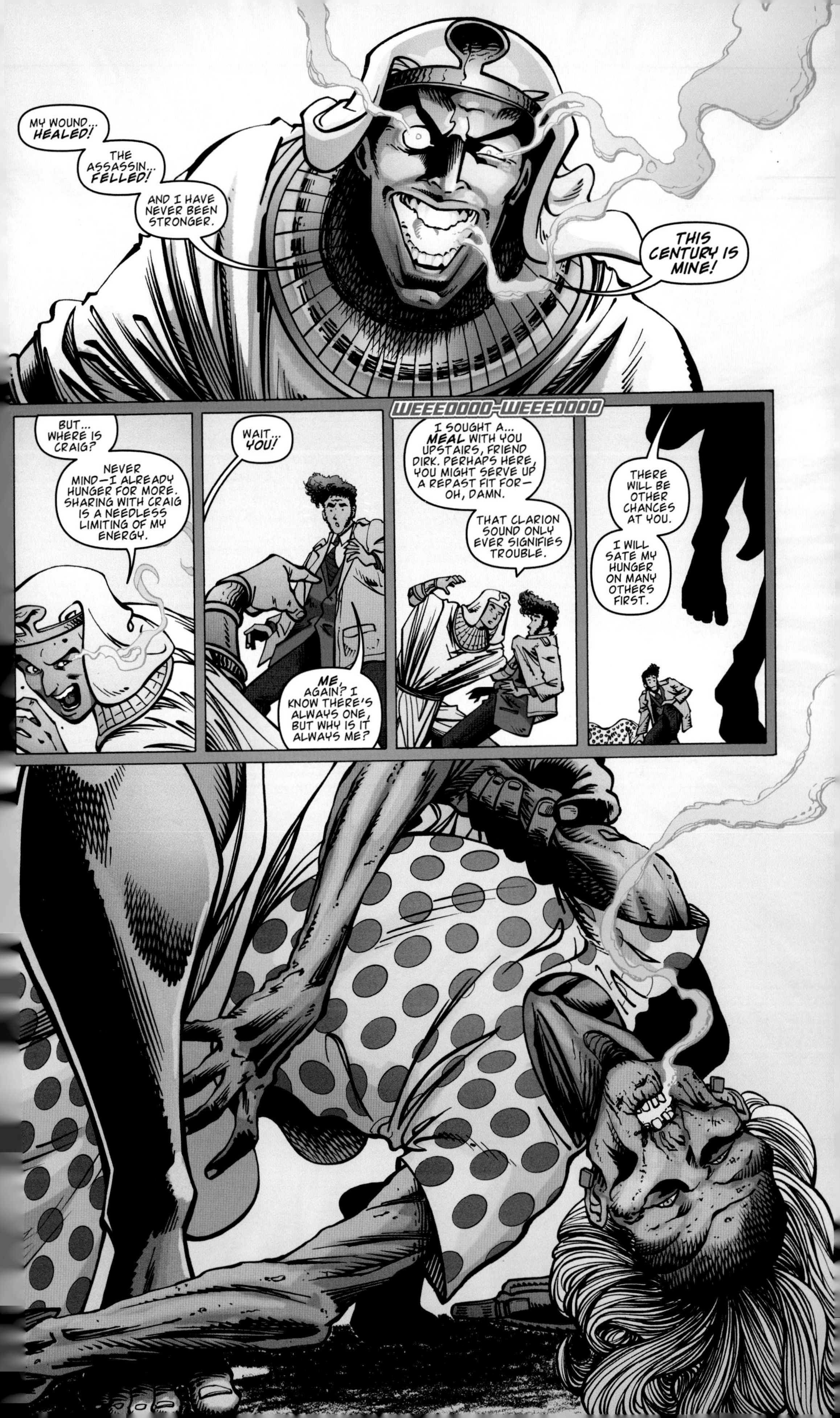
MY WOUND... HEALED!
THE ASSASSIN... FELLED!
AND I HAVE NEVER BEEN STRONGER.
THIS CENTURY IS MINE!
WEEEOOOO-WEEEOOOO
BUT... WHERE IS CRAIG?
NEVER MIND—I ALREADY HUNGER FOR MORE. SHARING WITH CRAIG IS A NEEDLESS LIMITING OF MY ENERGY.
WAIT... YOU!
ME, AGAIN? I KNOW THERE'S ALWAYS ONE, BUT WHY IS IT ALWAYS ME?
I SOUGHT A... MEAL WITH YOU UPSTAIRS, FRIEND DIRK. PERHAPS HERE, YOU MIGHT SERVE UP A REPAST FIT FOR—OH, DAMN.
THAT CLARION SOUND ONLY EVER SIGNIFIES TROUBLE.
THERE WILL BE OTHER CHANCES AT YOU.
I WILL SATE MY HUNGER ON MANY OTHERS FIRST.

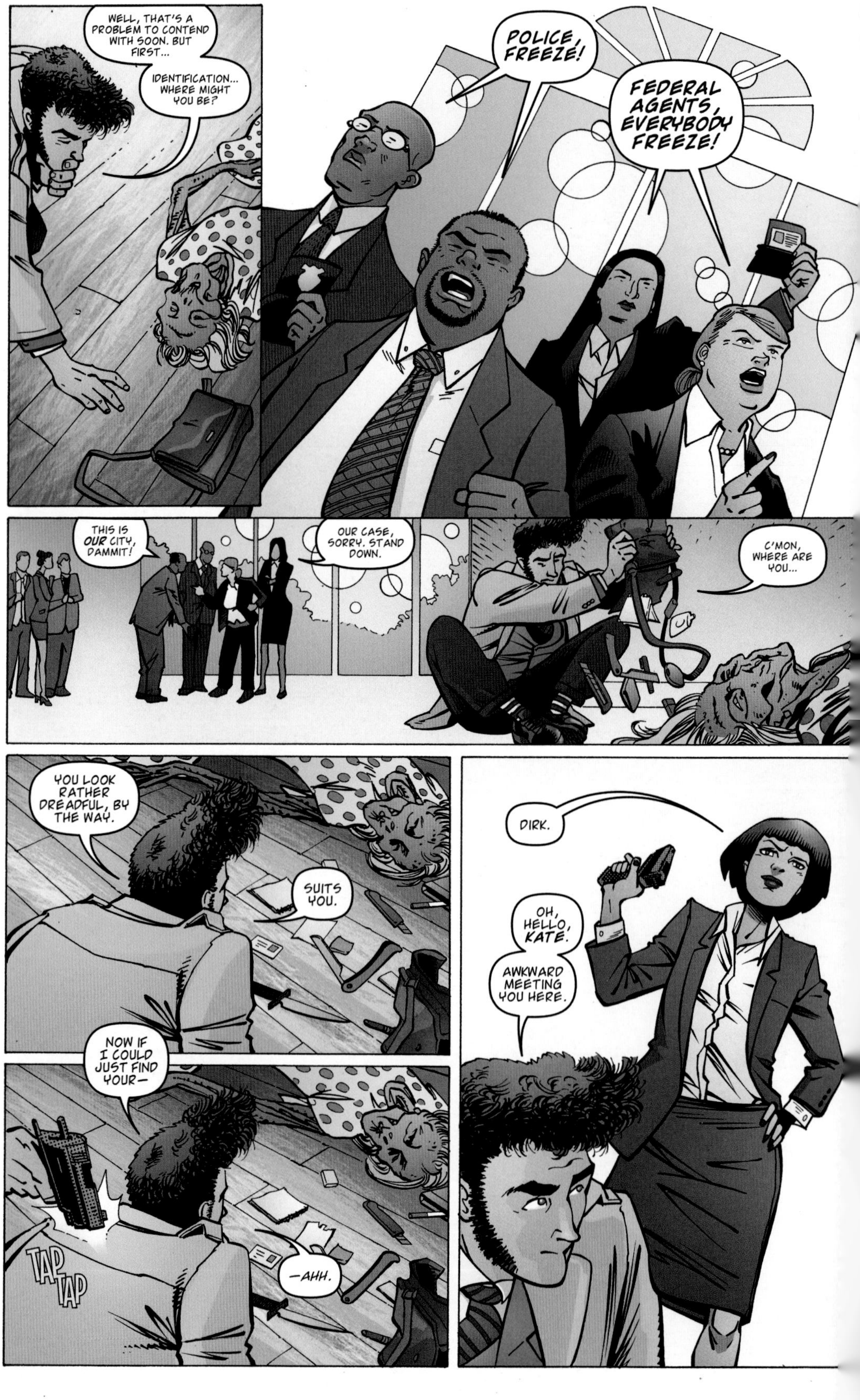
WELL, THAT'S A PROBLEM TO CONTEND WITH SOON. BUT FIRST...
IDENTIFICATION... WHERE MIGHT YOU BE?
POLICE, FREEZE!
FEDERAL AGENTS, EVERYBODY FREEZE!
THIS IS OUR CITY, DAMMIT!
OUR CASE, SORRY. STAND DOWN.
C'MON, WHERE ARE YOU...
YOU LOOK RATHER DREADFUL, BY THE WAY.
SUITS YOU.
NOW IF I COULD JUST FIND YOUR—
TAP TAP
—AHH.
DIRK.
OH, HELLO, KATE.
AWKWARD MEETING YOU HERE.

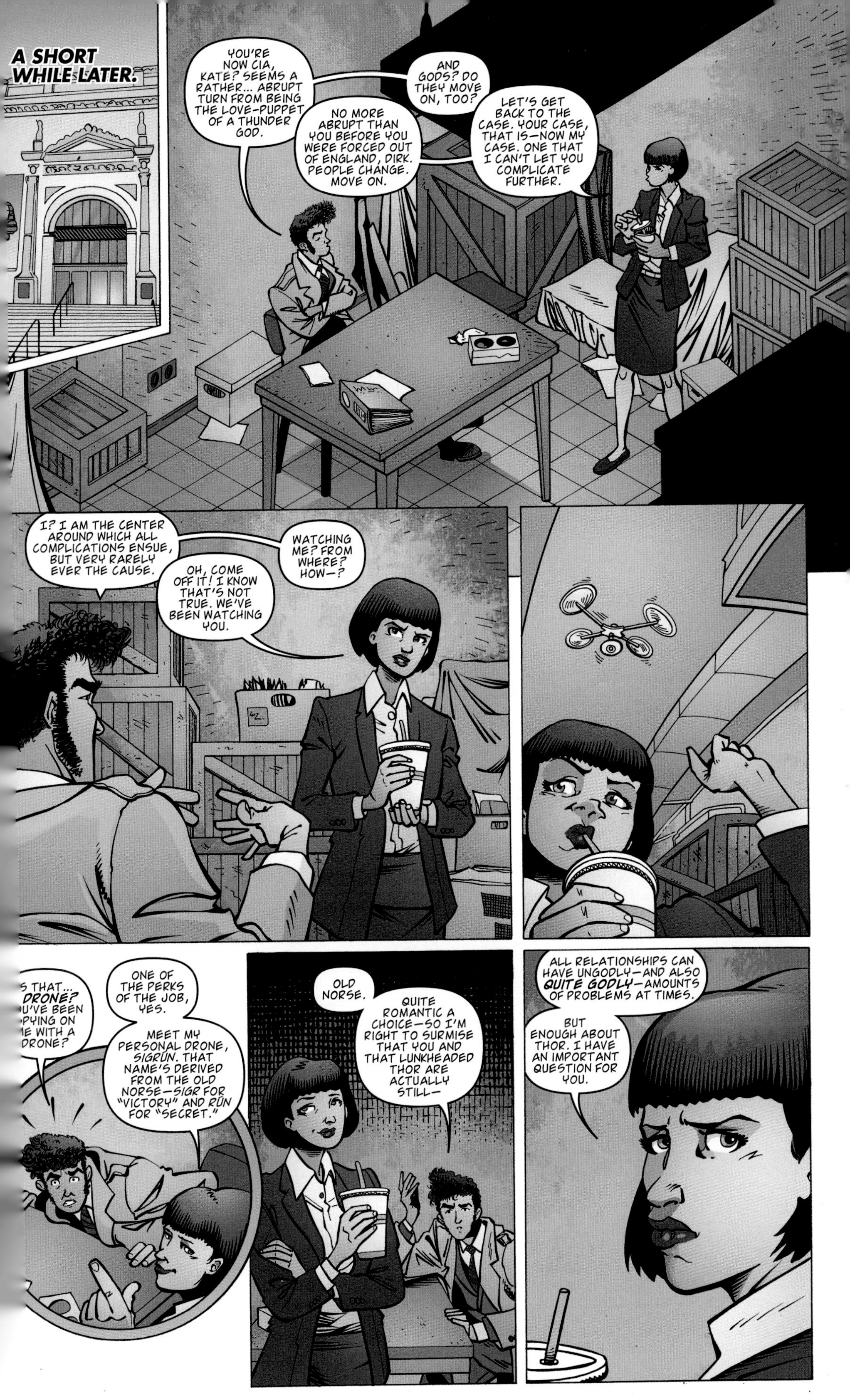
A SHORT WHILE LATER.
YOU'RE NOW CIA, KATE? SEEMS A RATHER... ABRUPT TURN FROM BEING THE LOVE-PUPPET OF A THUNDER GOD.
NO MORE ABRUPT THAN YOU BEFORE YOU WERE FORCED OUT OF ENGLAND, DIRK. PEOPLE CHANGE. MOVE ON.
AND GODS? DO THEY MOVE ON, TOO?
LET'S GET BACK TO THE CASE. YOUR CASE, THAT IS—NOW MY CASE. ONE THAT I CAN'T LET YOU COMPLICATE FURTHER.
I? I AM THE CENTER AROUND WHICH ALL COMPLICATIONS ENSUE, BUT VERY RARELY EVER THE CAUSE.
OH, COME OFF IT! I KNOW THAT'S NOT TRUE. WE'VE BEEN WATCHING YOU.
WATCHING ME? FROM WHERE? HOW—?
S THAT... DRONE? OU'VE BEEN PYING ON E WITH A DRONE?
ONE OF THE PERKS OF THE JOB, YES.
MEET MY PERSONAL DRONE, SIGRÚN. THAT NAME'S DERIVED FROM THE OLD NORSE—SIGR FOR "VICTORY" AND RÚN FOR "SECRET."
OLD NORSE.
QUITE ROMANTIC A CHOICE—SO I'M RIGHT TO SURMISE THAT YOU AND THAT LUNKHEADED THOR ARE ACTUALLY STILL—
ALL RELATIONSHIPS CAN HAVE UNGODLY—AND ALSO QUITE GODLY—AMOUNTS OF PROBLEMS AT TIMES.
BUT ENOUGH ABOUT THOR. I HAVE AN IMPORTANT QUESTION FOR YOU.

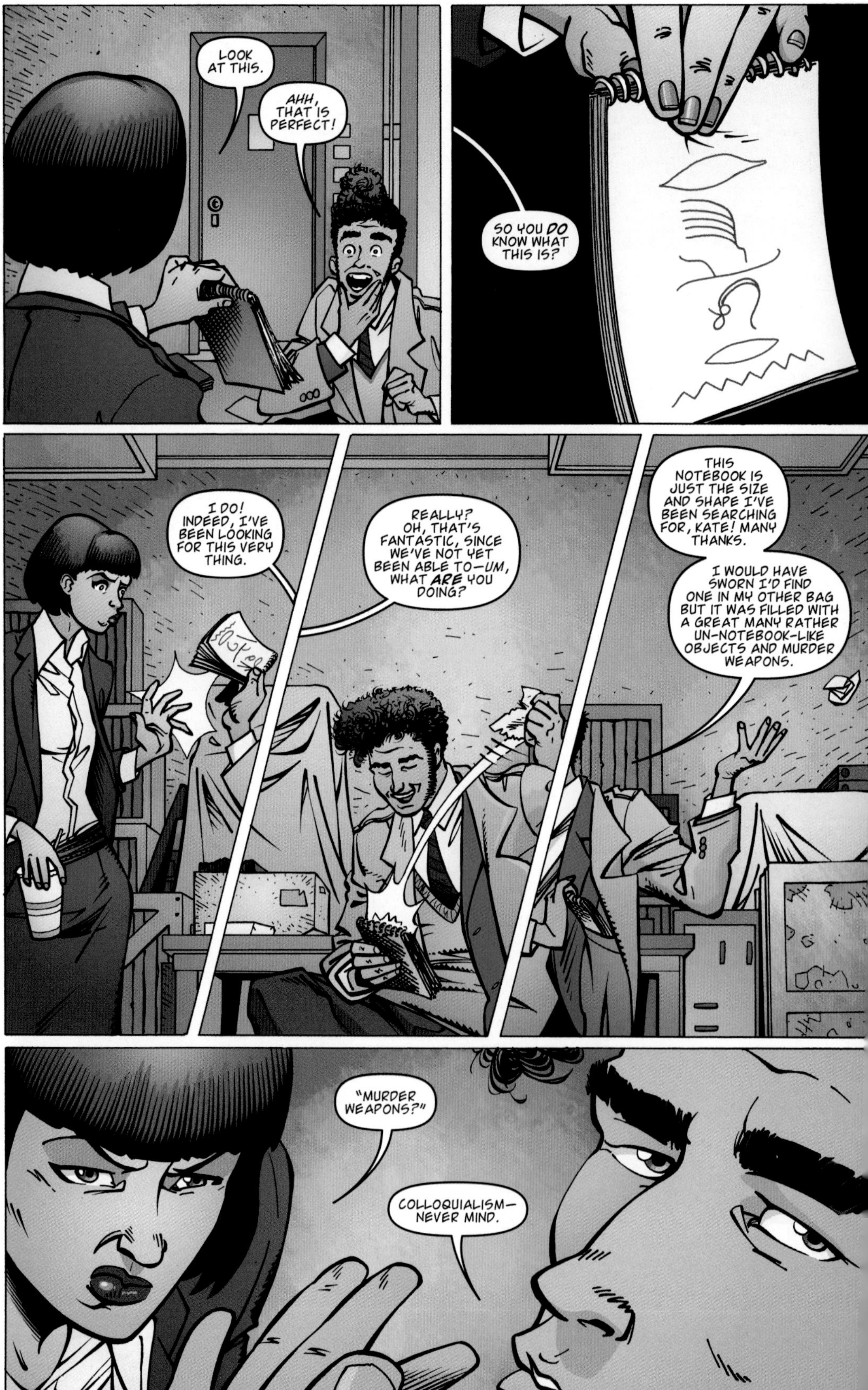
LOOK AT THIS.
AHH, THAT IS PERFECT!
SO YOU DO KNOW WHAT THIS IS?
I DO! INDEED, I'VE BEEN LOOKING FOR THIS VERY THING.
REALLY? OH, THAT'S FANTASTIC, SINCE WE'VE NOT YET BEEN ABLE TO—UM, WHAT ARE YOU DOING?
THIS NOTEBOOK IS JUST THE SIZE AND SHAPE I'VE BEEN SEARCHING FOR, KATE! MANY THANKS.
I WOULD HAVE SWORN I'D FIND ONE IN MY OTHER BAG BUT IT WAS FILLED WITH A GREAT MANY RATHER UN-NOTEBOOK-LIKE OBJECTS AND MURDER WEAPONS.
"MURDER WEAPONS?"
COLLOQUIALISM— NEVER MIND.

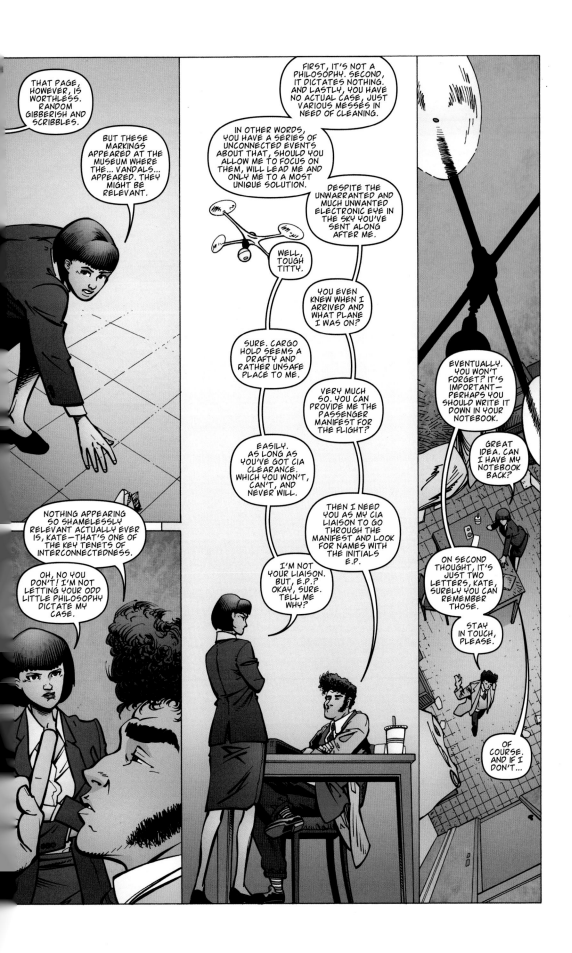

THAT PAGE, HOWEVER, IS WORTHLESS. RANDOM GIBBERISH AND SCRIBBLES.

BUT THESE MARKINGS APPEARED AT THE MUSEUM WHERE THE... VANDALS... APPEARED. THEY MIGHT BE RELEVANT.

FIRST, IT'S NOT A PHILOSOPHY. SECOND, IT DICTATES NOTHING. AND LASTLY, YOU HAVE NO ACTUAL CASE, JUST VARIOUS MESSES IN NEED OF CLEANING.

IN OTHER WORDS, YOU HAVE A SERIES OF UNCONNECTED EVENTS ABOUT THAT, SHOULD YOU ALLOW ME TO FOCUS ON THEM, WILL LEAD ME AND ONLY ME TO A MOST UNIQUE SOLUTION.

DESPITE THE UNWARRANTED AND MUCH UNWANTED ELECTRONIC EYE IN THE SKY YOU'VE SENT ALONG AFTER ME.

WELL, TOUGH TITTY.

YOU EVEN KNEW WHEN I ARRIVED AND WHAT PLANE I WAS ON?

SURE. CARGO HOLD SEEMS A DRAFTY AND RATHER UNSAFE PLACE TO ME.

VERY MUCH SO. YOU CAN PROVIDE ME THE PASSENGER MANIFEST FOR THE FLIGHT?

EASILY. AS LONG AS YOU'VE GOT CIA CLEARANCE. WHICH YOU WON'T, CAN'T, AND NEVER WILL.

NOTHING APPEARING SO SHAMELESSLY RELEVANT ACTUALLY EVER IS, KATE—THAT'S ONE OF THE KEY TENETS OF INTERCONNECTEDNESS.

OH, NO YOU DON'T! I'M NOT LETTING YOUR ODD LITTLE PHILOSOPHY DICTATE MY CASE.

THEN I NEED YOU AS MY CIA LIAISON TO GO THROUGH THE MANIFEST AND LOOK FOR NAMES WITH THE INITIALS E.P.

I'M NOT YOUR LIAISON. BUT, E.P.? OKAY, SURE. TELL ME WHY?

EVENTUALLY. YOU WON'T FORGET? IT'S IMPORTANT— PERHAPS YOU SHOULD WRITE IT DOWN IN YOUR NOTEBOOK.

GREAT IDEA. CAN I HAVE MY NOTEBOOK BACK?

ON SECOND THOUGHT, IT'S JUST TWO LETTERS, KATE, SURELY YOU CAN REMEMBER THOSE.

STAY IN TOUCH, PLEASE.

OF COURSE. AND IF I DON'T...

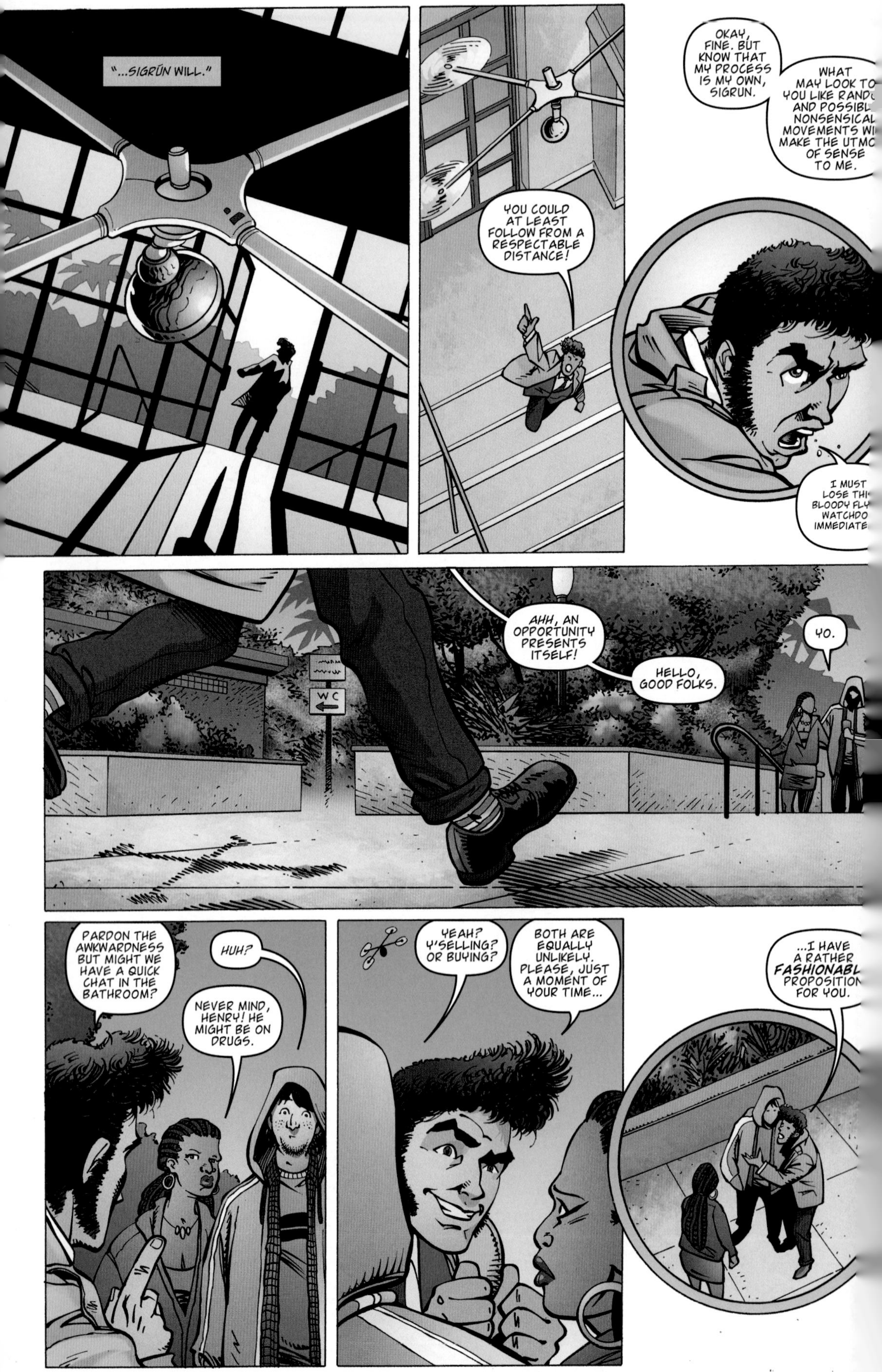
"...SIGRÚN WILL."
YOU COULD AT LEAST FOLLOW FROM A RESPECTABLE DISTANCE!
OKAY, FINE. BUT KNOW THAT MY PROCESS IS MY OWN, SIGRÚN.
WHAT MAY LOOK TO YOU LIKE RAND AND POSSIBL NONSENSICAL MOVEMENTS WI MAKE THE UTMO OF SENSE TO ME.
I MUST LOSE THI BLOODY FLY WATCHDO IMMEDIATE
W C
AHH, AN OPPORTUNITY PRESENTS ITSELF!
HELLO, GOOD FOLKS.
YO.
PARDON THE AWKWARDNESS BUT MIGHT WE HAVE A QUICK CHAT IN THE BATHROOM?
HUH?
NEVER MIND, HENRY! HE MIGHT BE ON DRUGS.
YEAH? Y'SELLING? OR BUYING?
BOTH ARE EQUALLY UNLIKELY. PLEASE, JUST A MOMENT OF YOUR TIME...
...I HAVE A RATHER FASHIONABL PROPOSITION FOR YOU.

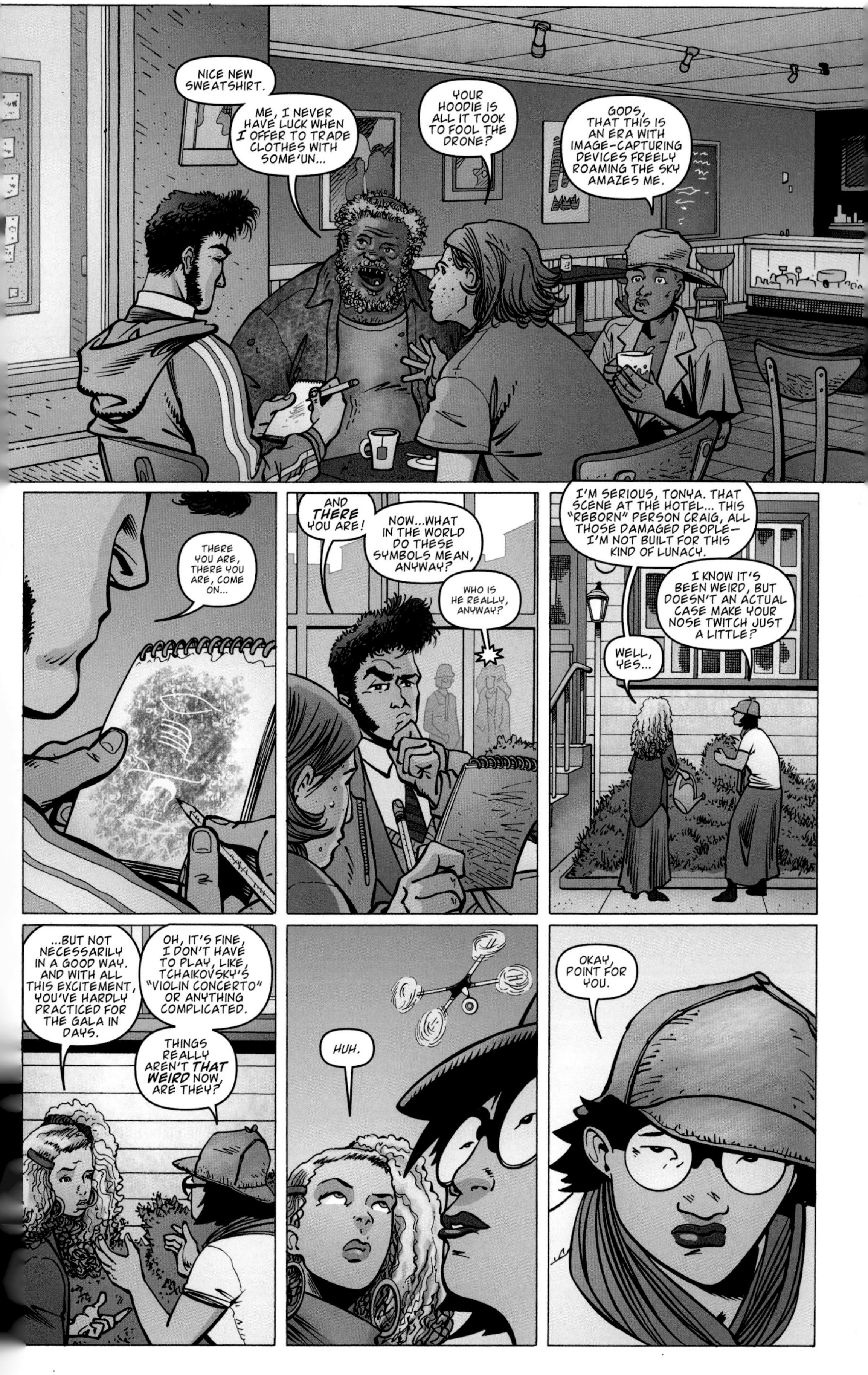
NICE NEW SWEATSHIRT.
ME, I NEVER HAVE LUCK WHEN I OFFER TO TRADE CLOTHES WITH SOME'UN...
YOUR HOODIE IS ALL IT TOOK TO FOOL THE DRONE?
GODS, THAT THIS IS AN ERA WITH IMAGE-CAPTURING DEVICES FREELY ROAMING THE SKY AMAZES ME.
THERE YOU ARE, THERE YOU ARE, COME ON...
AND THERE YOU ARE!
NOW...WHAT IN THE WORLD DO THESE SYMBOLS MEAN, ANYWAY?
WHO IS HE REALLY, ANYWAY?
I'M SERIOUS, TONYA. THAT SCENE AT THE HOTEL... THIS "REBORN" PERSON CRAIG, ALL THOSE DAMAGED PEOPLE— I'M NOT BUILT FOR THIS KIND OF LUNACY.
I KNOW IT'S BEEN WEIRD, BUT DOESN'T AN ACTUAL CASE MAKE YOUR NOSE TWITCH JUST A LITTLE?
WELL, YES...
...BUT NOT NECESSARILY IN A GOOD WAY. AND WITH ALL THIS EXCITEMENT, YOU'VE HARDLY PRACTICED FOR THE GALA IN DAYS.
OH, IT'S FINE, I DON'T HAVE TO PLAY, LIKE, TCHAIKOVSKY'S "VIOLIN CONCERTO" OR ANYTHING COMPLICATED.
THINGS REALLY AREN'T THAT WEIRD NOW, ARE THEY?
HUH.
OKAY, POINT FOR YOU.

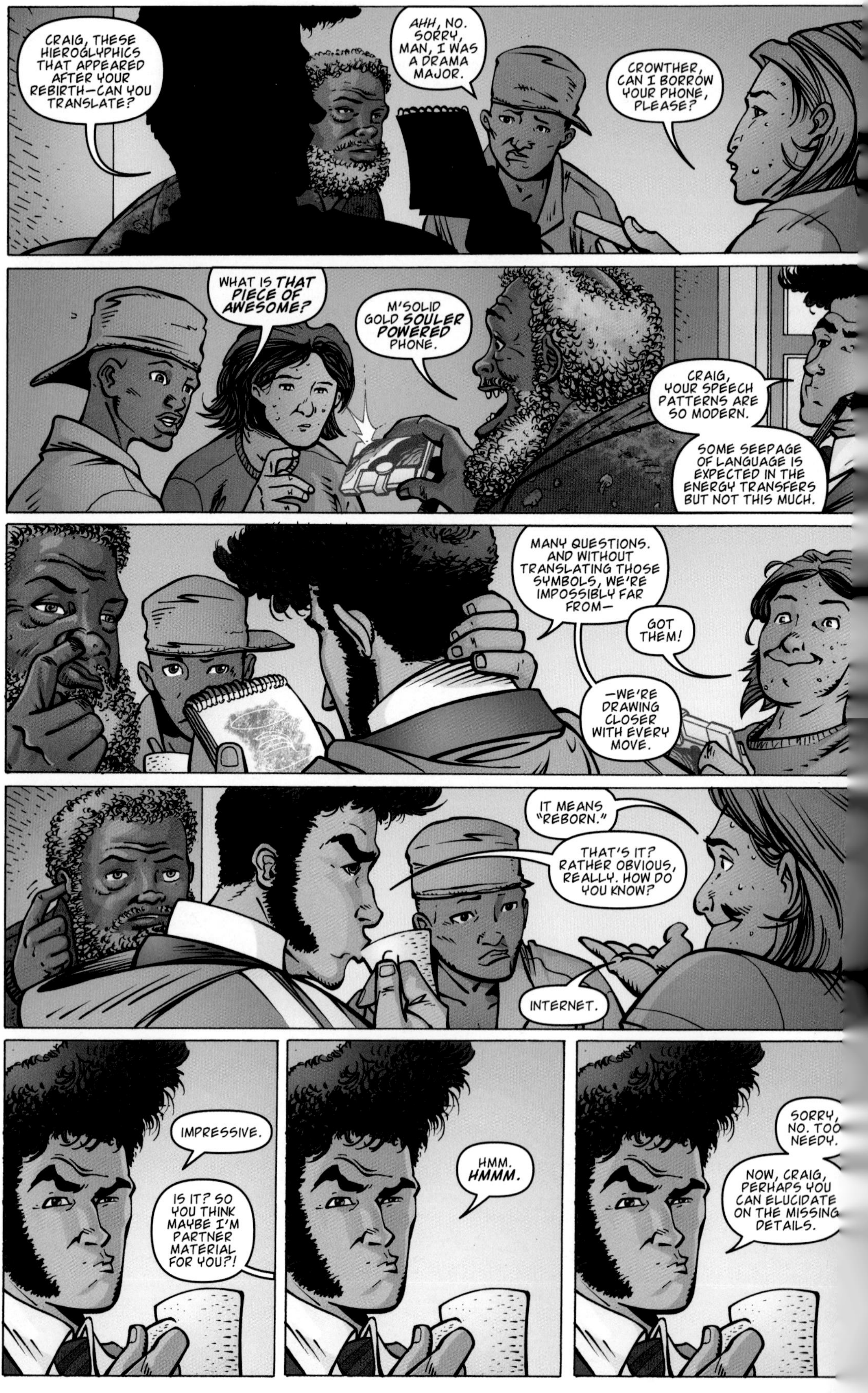
CRAIG, THESE HIEROGLYPHICS THAT APPEARED AFTER YOUR REBIRTH—CAN YOU TRANSLATE?
AHH, NO. SORRY, MAN, I WAS A DRAMA MAJOR.
CROWTHER, CAN I BORROW YOUR PHONE, PLEASE?
WHAT IS THAT PIECE OF AWESOME?
M'SOLID GOLD SOULER POWERED PHONE.
CRAIG, YOUR SPEECH PATTERNS ARE SO MODERN.
SOME SEEPAGE OF LANGUAGE IS EXPECTED IN THE ENERGY TRANSFERS BUT NOT THIS MUCH.
MANY QUESTIONS. AND WITHOUT TRANSLATING THOSE SYMBOLS, WE'RE IMPOSSIBLY FAR FROM—
GOT THEM!
—WE'RE DRAWING CLOSER WITH EVERY MOVE.
IT MEANS "REBORN."
THAT'S IT? RATHER OBVIOUS, REALLY. HOW DO YOU KNOW?
INTERNET.
IMPRESSIVE.
IS IT? SO YOU THINK MAYBE I'M PARTNER MATERIAL FOR YOU?!
HMM. HMMM.
SORRY, NO. TOO NEEDY.
NOW, CRAIG, PERHAPS YOU CAN ELUCIDATE ON THE MISSING DETAILS.

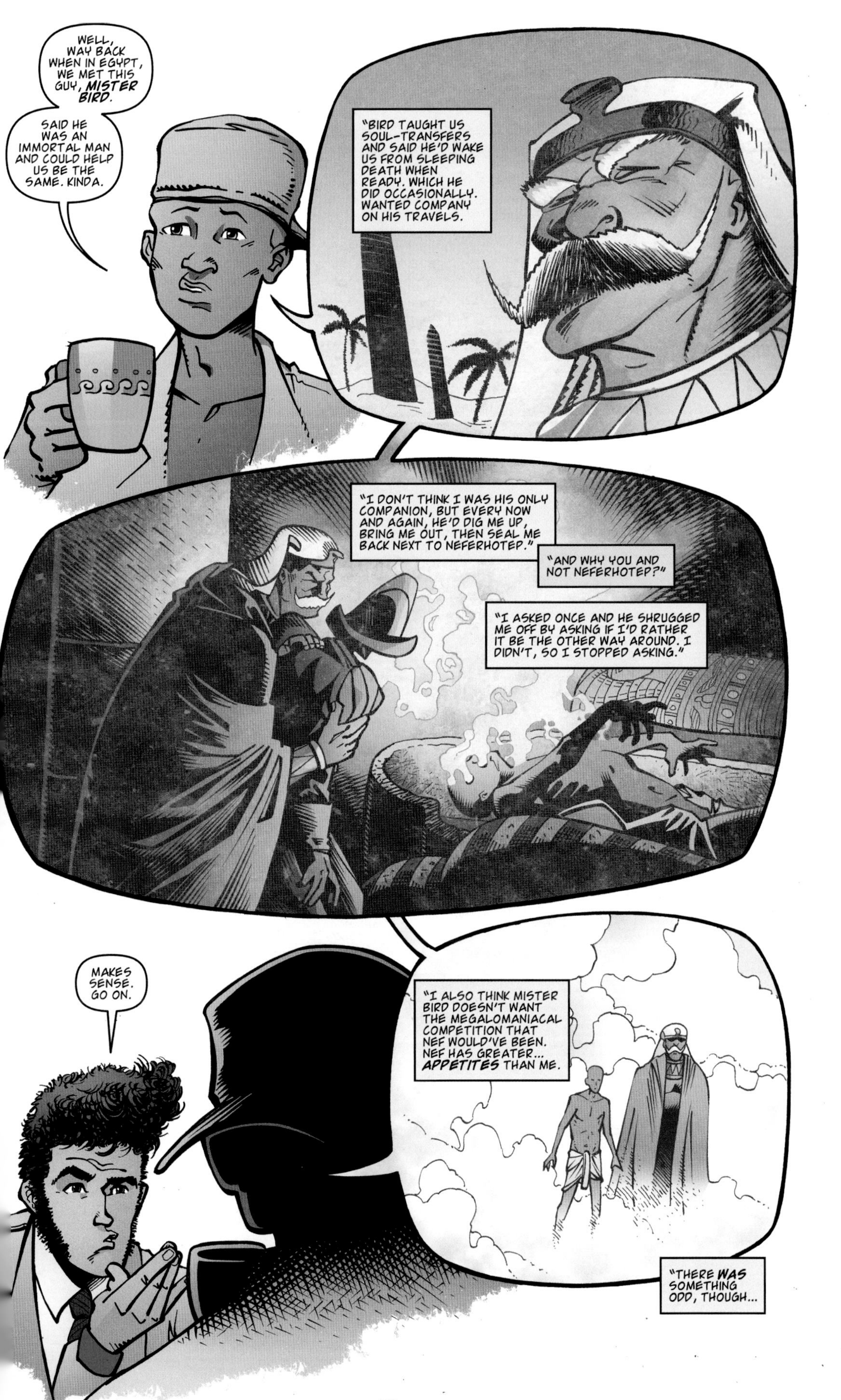
WELL, WAY BACK WHEN IN EGYPT, WE MET THIS GUY, *MISTER BIRD*.
SAID HE WAS AN IMMORTAL MAN AND COULD HELP US BE THE SAME. KINDA.
"BIRD TAUGHT US SOUL-TRANSFERS AND SAID HE'D WAKE US FROM SLEEPING DEATH WHEN READY. WHICH HE DID OCCASIONALLY. WANTED COMPANY ON HIS TRAVELS.
"I DON'T THINK I WAS HIS ONLY COMPANION, BUT EVERY NOW AND AGAIN, HE'D DIG ME UP, BRING ME OUT, THEN SEAL ME BACK NEXT TO NEFERHOTEP."
"AND WHY YOU AND NOT NEFERHOTEP?"
"I ASKED ONCE AND HE SHRUGGED ME OFF BY ASKING IF I'D RATHER IT BE THE OTHER WAY AROUND. I DIDN'T, SO I STOPPED ASKING."
MAKES SENSE. GO ON.
"I ALSO THINK MISTER BIRD DOESN'T WANT THE MEGALOMANIACAL COMPETITION THAT NEF WOULD'VE BEEN. NEF HAS GREATER... *APPETITES* THAN ME.
"THERE *WAS* SOMETHING ODD, THOUGH...

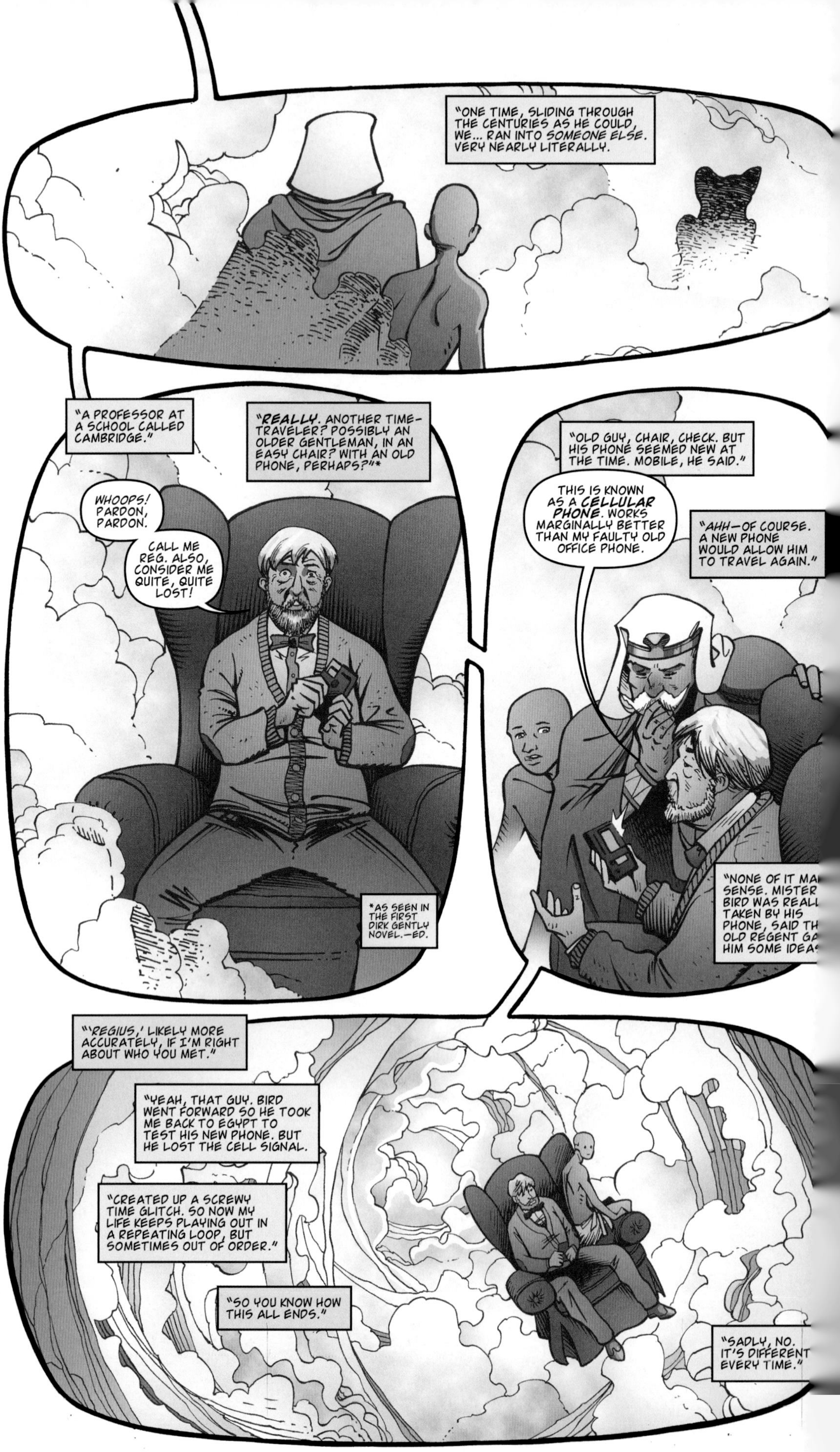
"ONE TIME, SLIDING THROUGH THE CENTURIES AS HE COULD, WE... RAN INTO SOMEONE ELSE. VERY NEARLY LITERALLY.
"A PROFESSOR AT A SCHOOL CALLED CAMBRIDGE."
"REALLY. ANOTHER TIME-TRAVELER? POSSIBLY AN OLDER GENTLEMAN, IN AN EASY CHAIR? WITH AN OLD PHONE, PERHAPS?"*
WHOOPS! PARDON, PARDON.
CALL ME REG. ALSO, CONSIDER ME QUITE, QUITE LOST!
*AS SEEN IN THE FIRST DIRK GENTLY NOVEL.—ED.
"OLD GUY, CHAIR, CHECK. BUT HIS PHONE SEEMED NEW AT THE TIME. MOBILE, HE SAID."
THIS IS KNOWN AS A CELLULAR PHONE. WORKS MARGINALLY BETTER THAN MY FAULTY OLD OFFICE PHONE.
"AHH—OF COURSE. A NEW PHONE WOULD ALLOW HIM TO TRAVEL AGAIN."
"NONE OF IT MA SENSE. MISTER BIRD WAS REALL TAKEN BY HIS PHONE, SAID TH OLD REGENT GA HIM SOME IDEAS
"'REGIUS,' LIKELY MORE ACCURATELY, IF I'M RIGHT ABOUT WHO YOU MET."
"YEAH, THAT GUY. BIRD WENT FORWARD SO HE TOOK ME BACK TO EGYPT TO TEST HIS NEW PHONE. BUT HE LOST THE CELL SIGNAL.
"CREATED UP A SCREWY TIME GLITCH. SO NOW MY LIFE KEEPS PLAYING OUT IN A REPEATING LOOP, BUT SOMETIMES OUT OF ORDER."
"SO YOU KNOW HOW THIS ALL ENDS."
"SADLY, NO. IT'S DIFFERENT EVERY TIME."

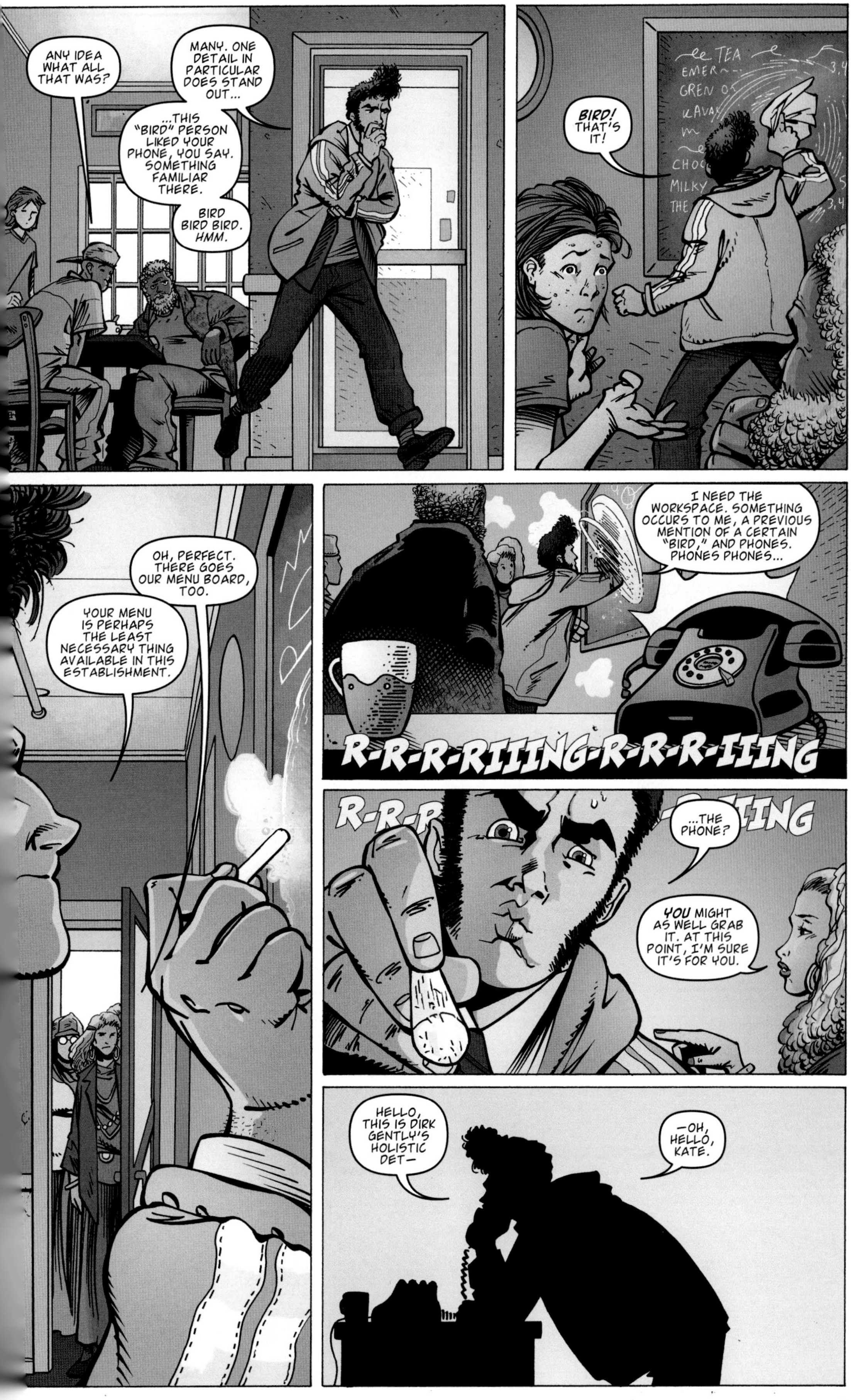
ANY IDEA WHAT ALL THAT WAS?
MANY. ONE DETAIL IN PARTICULAR DOES STAND OUT...
...THIS "BIRD" PERSON LIKED YOUR PHONE, YOU SAY. SOMETHING FAMILIAR THERE.
BIRD BIRD BIRD. HMM.
BIRD! THAT'S IT!
OH, PERFECT. THERE GOES OUR MENU BOARD, TOO.
YOUR MENU IS PERHAPS THE LEAST NECESSARY THING AVAILABLE IN THIS ESTABLISHMENT.
I NEED THE WORKSPACE. SOMETHING OCCURS TO ME, A PREVIOUS MENTION OF A CERTAIN "BIRD," AND PHONES. PHONES PHONES...
R-R-R-RIIING-R-R-R-IIING
...THE PHONE?
YOU MIGHT AS WELL GRAB IT. AT THIS POINT, I'M SURE IT'S FOR YOU.
HELLO, THIS IS DIRK GENTLY'S HOLISTIC DET—
—OH, HELLO, KATE.

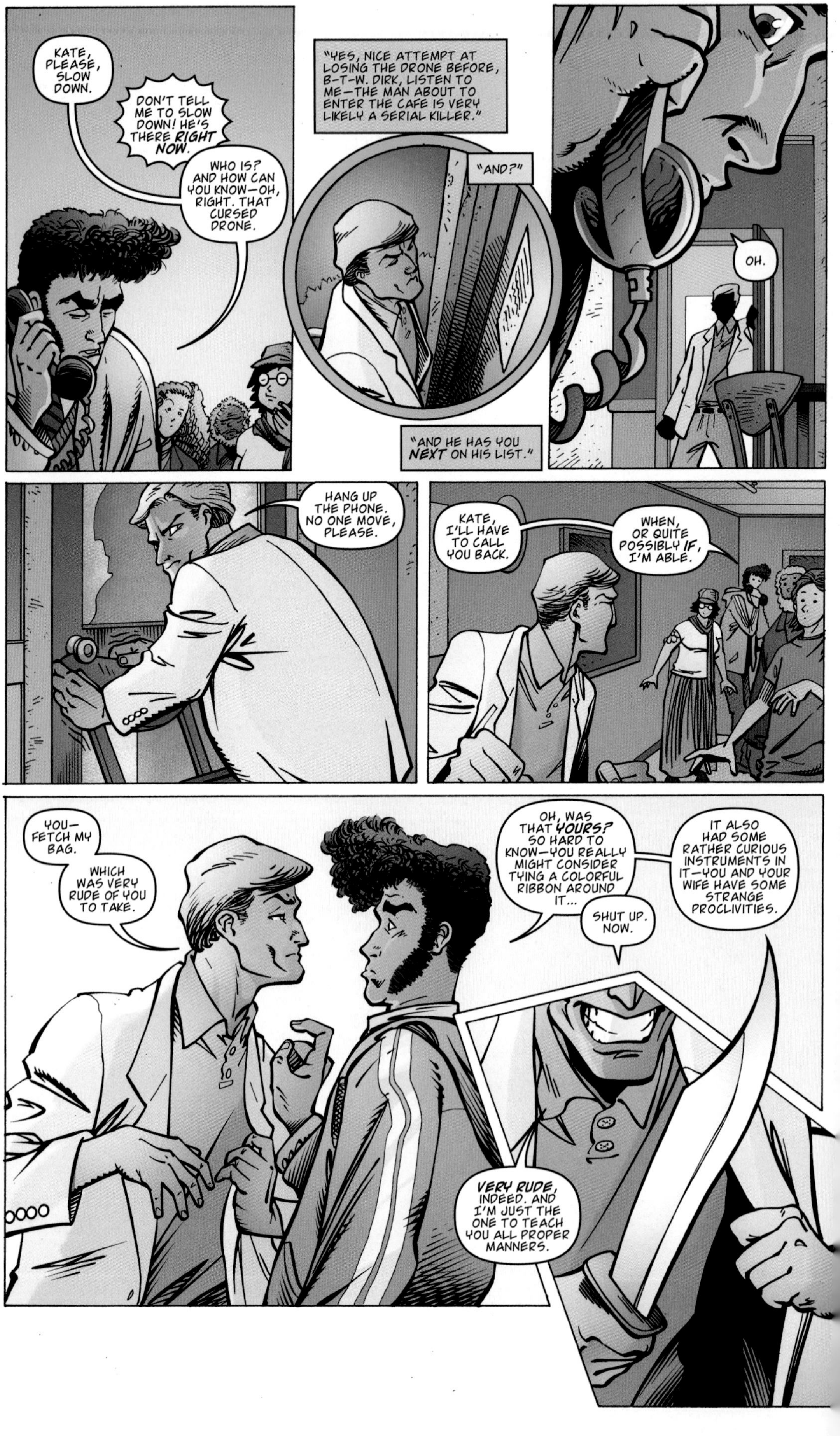
KATE, PLEASE, SLOW DOWN.
DON'T TELL ME TO SLOW DOWN! HE'S THERE RIGHT NOW.
WHO IS? AND HOW CAN YOU KNOW—OH, RIGHT. THAT CURSED DRONE.
"YES, NICE ATTEMPT AT LOSING THE DRONE BEFORE, B-T-W. DIRK, LISTEN TO ME—THE MAN ABOUT TO ENTER THE CAFE IS VERY LIKELY A SERIAL KILLER."
"AND?"
"AND HE HAS YOU NEXT ON HIS LIST."
OH.
HANG UP THE PHONE. NO ONE MOVE, PLEASE.
KATE, I'LL HAVE TO CALL YOU BACK.
WHEN, OR QUITE POSSIBLY IF, I'M ABLE.
YOU—FETCH MY BAG.
WHICH WAS VERY RUDE OF YOU TO TAKE.
OH, WAS THAT YOURS? SO HARD TO KNOW—YOU REALLY MIGHT CONSIDER TYING A COLORFUL RIBBON AROUND IT...
IT ALSO HAD SOME RATHER CURIOUS INSTRUMENTS IN IT—YOU AND YOUR WIFE HAVE SOME STRANGE PROCLIVITIES.
SHUT UP. NOW.
VERY RUDE, INDEED. AND I'M JUST THE ONE TO TEACH YOU ALL PROPER MANNERS.

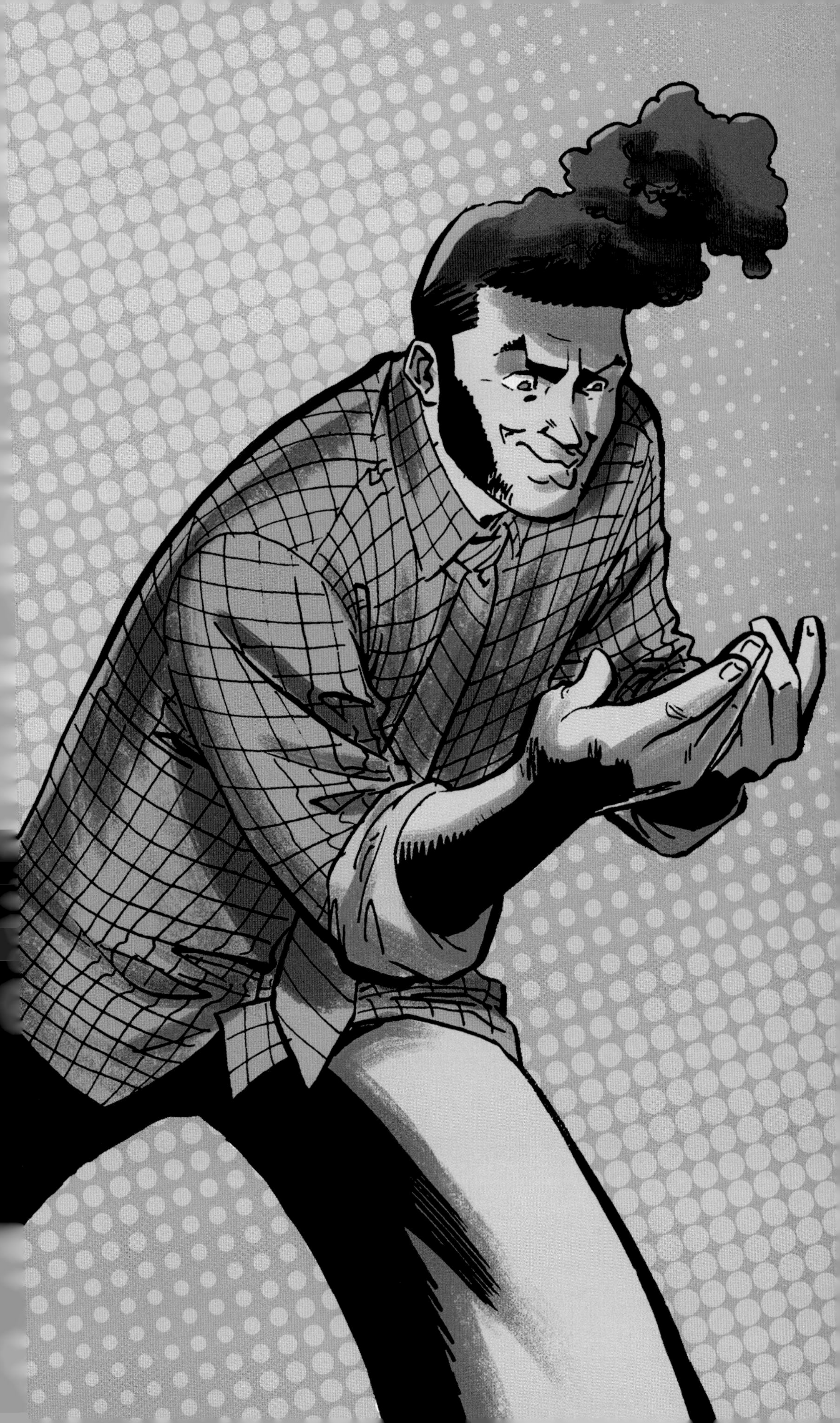

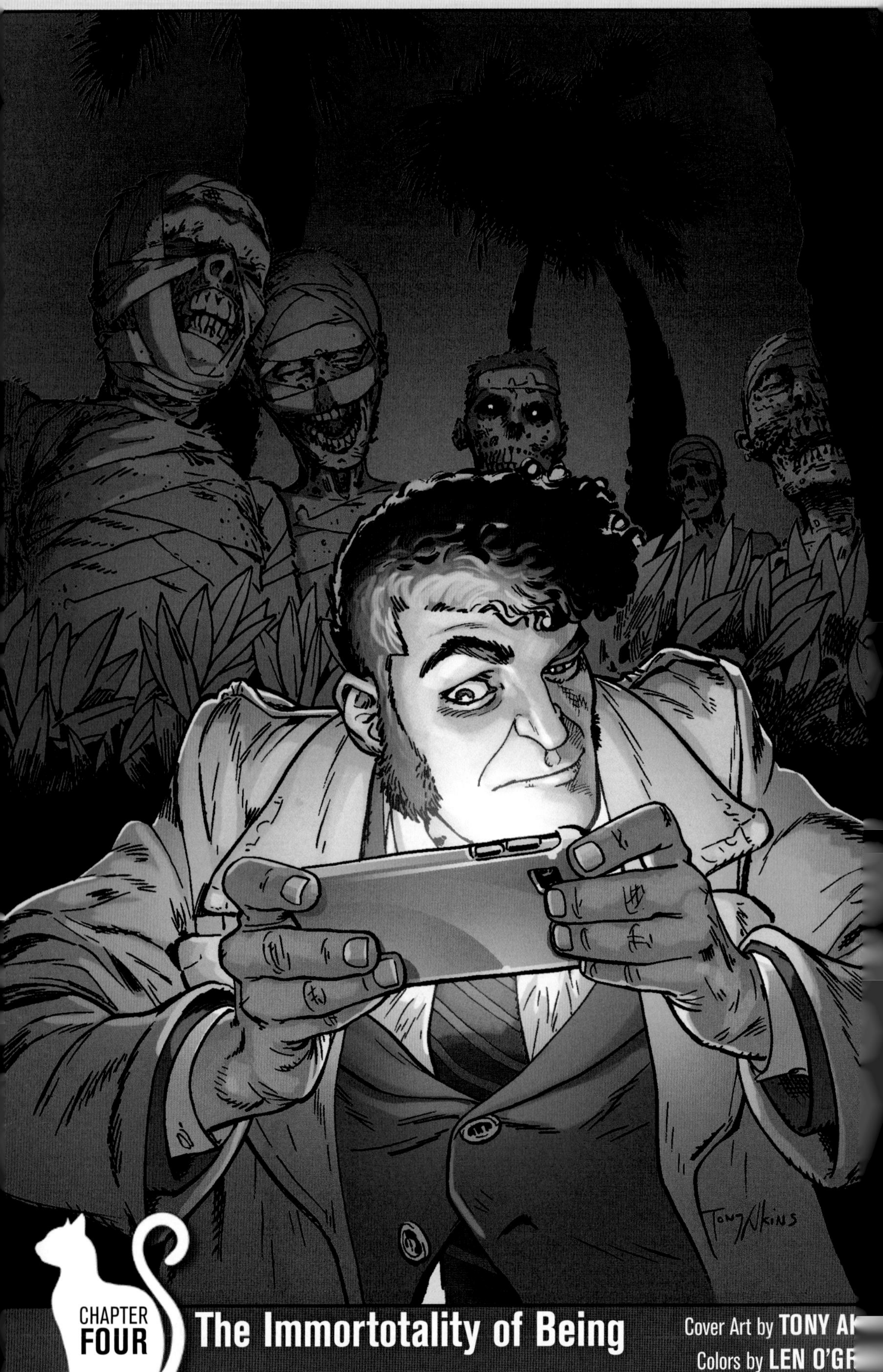

CHAPTER FOUR

The Immortotality of Being

Cover Art by **TONY A**
Colors by **LEN O'GR**

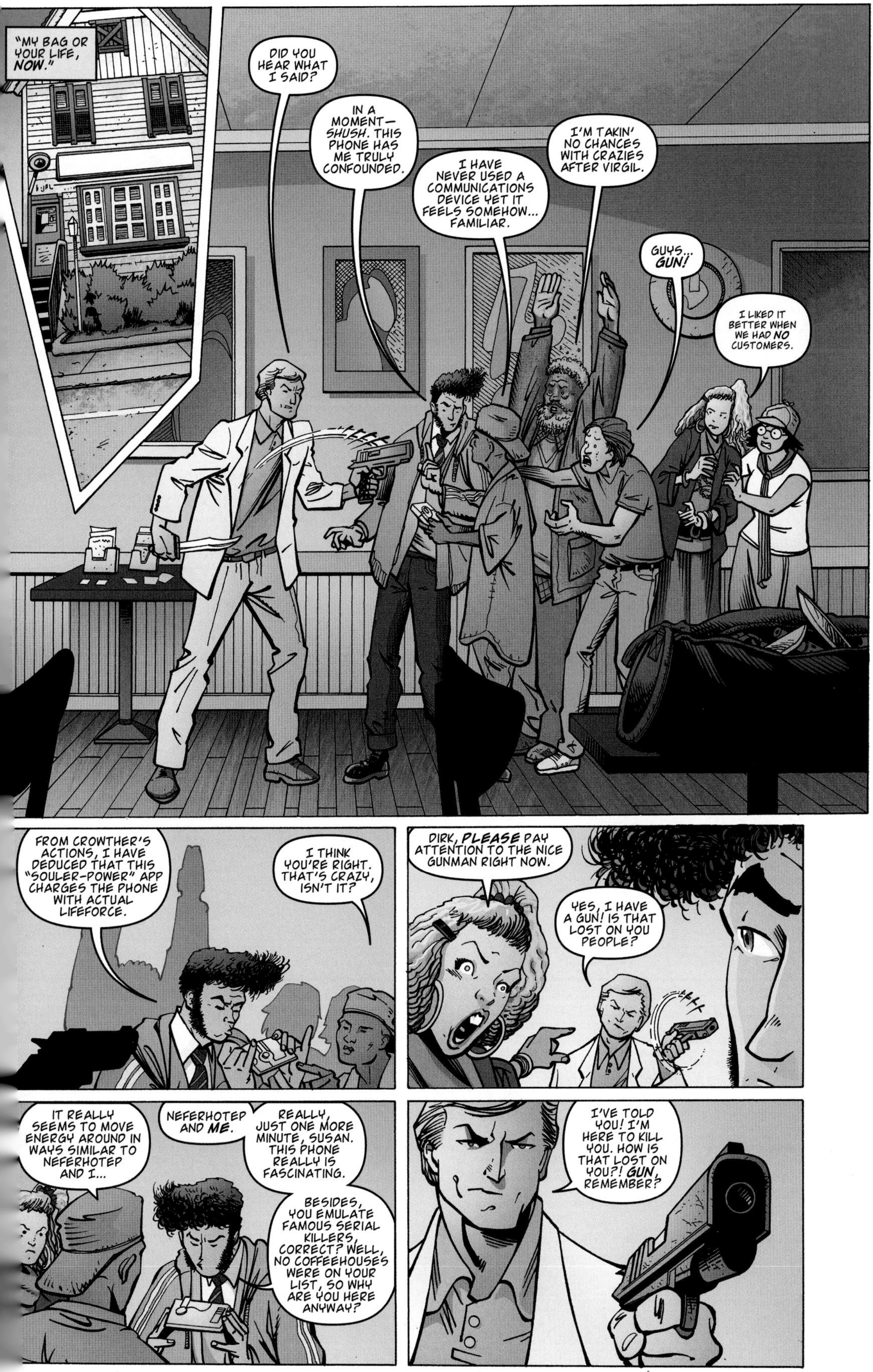
"MY BAG OR YOUR LIFE, NOW."
DID YOU HEAR WHAT I SAID?
IN A MOMENT— SHUSH. THIS PHONE HAS ME TRULY CONFOUNDED.
I HAVE NEVER USED A COMMUNICATIONS DEVICE YET IT FEELS SOMEHOW... FAMILIAR.
I'M TAKIN' NO CHANCES WITH CRAZIES AFTER VIRGIL.
GUYS... GUN!
I LIKED IT BETTER WHEN WE HAD NO CUSTOMERS.
FROM CROWTHER'S ACTIONS, I HAVE DEDUCED THAT THIS "SOULER-POWER" APP CHARGES THE PHONE WITH ACTUAL LIFEFORCE.
I THINK YOU'RE RIGHT. THAT'S CRAZY, ISN'T IT?
DIRK, PLEASE PAY ATTENTION TO THE NICE GUNMAN RIGHT NOW.
YES, I HAVE A GUN! IS THAT LOST ON YOU PEOPLE?
IT REALLY SEEMS TO MOVE ENERGY AROUND IN WAYS SIMILAR TO NEFERHOTEP AND I...
NEFERHOTEP AND ME.
REALLY, JUST ONE MORE MINUTE, SUSAN. THIS PHONE REALLY IS FASCINATING.
BESIDES, YOU EMULATE FAMOUS SERIAL KILLERS, CORRECT? WELL, NO COFFEEHOUSES WERE ON YOUR LIST, SO WHY ARE YOU HERE ANYWAY?
I'VE TOLD YOU! I'M HERE TO KILL YOU. HOW IS THAT LOST ON YOU?! GUN, REMEMBER?

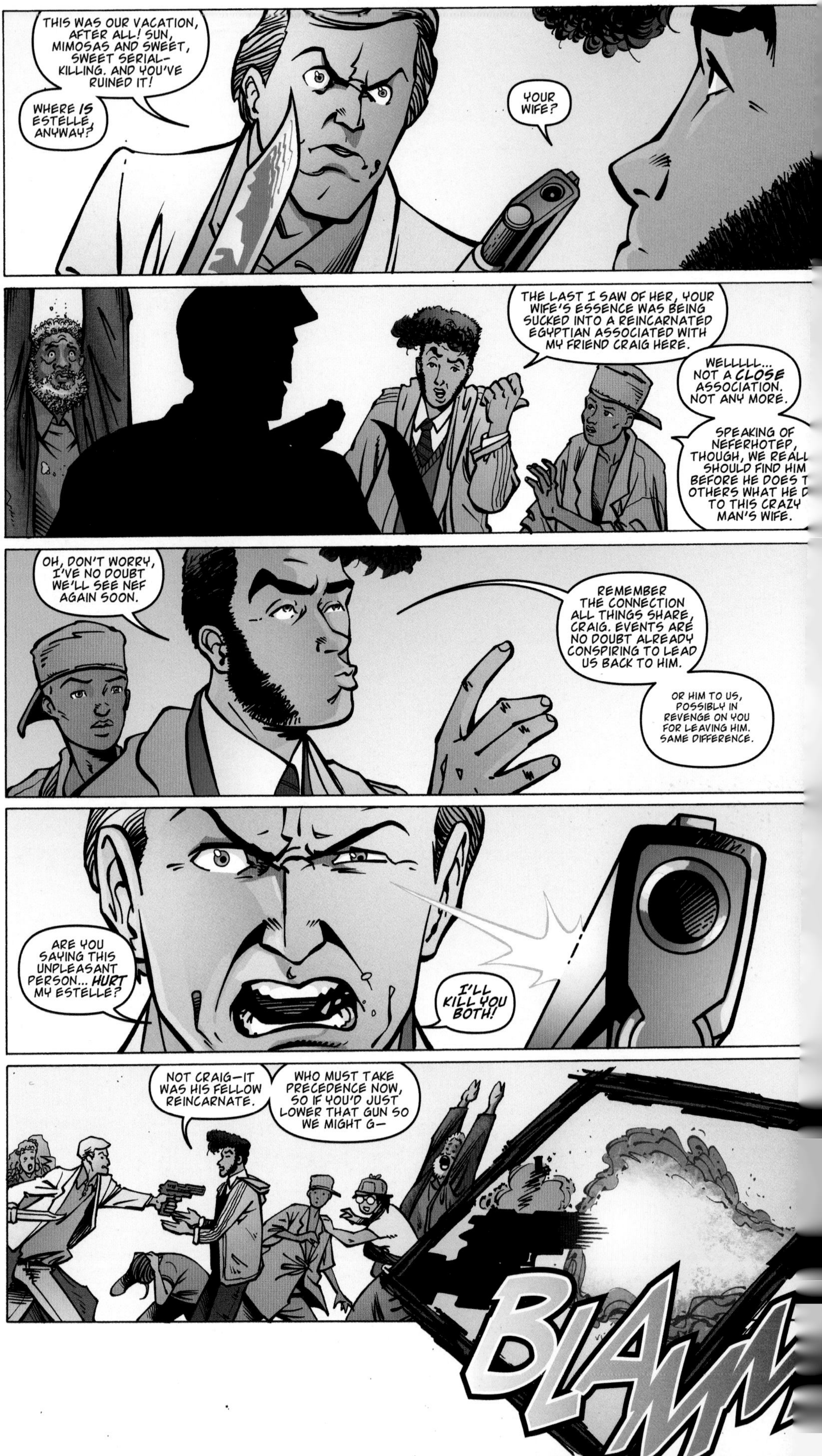
THIS WAS OUR VACATION, AFTER ALL! SUN, MIMOSAS AND SWEET, SWEET SERIAL-KILLING. AND YOU'VE RUINED IT!
WHERE IS ESTELLE, ANYWAY?
YOUR WIFE?
THE LAST I SAW OF HER, YOUR WIFE'S ESSENCE WAS BEING SUCKED INTO A REINCARNATED EGYPTIAN ASSOCIATED WITH MY FRIEND CRAIG HERE.
WELLLLL... NOT A CLOSE ASSOCIATION. NOT ANY MORE.
SPEAKING OF NEFERHOTEP, THOUGH, WE REALL SHOULD FIND HIM BEFORE HE DOES T OTHERS WHAT HE D TO THIS CRAZY MAN'S WIFE.
OH, DON'T WORRY, I'VE NO DOUBT WE'LL SEE NEF AGAIN SOON.
REMEMBER THE CONNECTION ALL THINGS SHARE, CRAIG. EVENTS ARE NO DOUBT ALREADY CONSPIRING TO LEAD US BACK TO HIM.
OR HIM TO US, POSSIBLY IN REVENGE ON YOU FOR LEAVING HIM. SAME DIFFERENCE.
ARE YOU SAYING THIS UNPLEASANT PERSON... HURT MY ESTELLE?
I'LL KILL YOU BOTH!
NOT CRAIG—IT WAS HIS FELLOW REINCARNATE.
WHO MUST TAKE PRECEDENCE NOW, SO IF YOU'D JUST LOWER THAT GUN SO WE MIGHT G—
BLAM

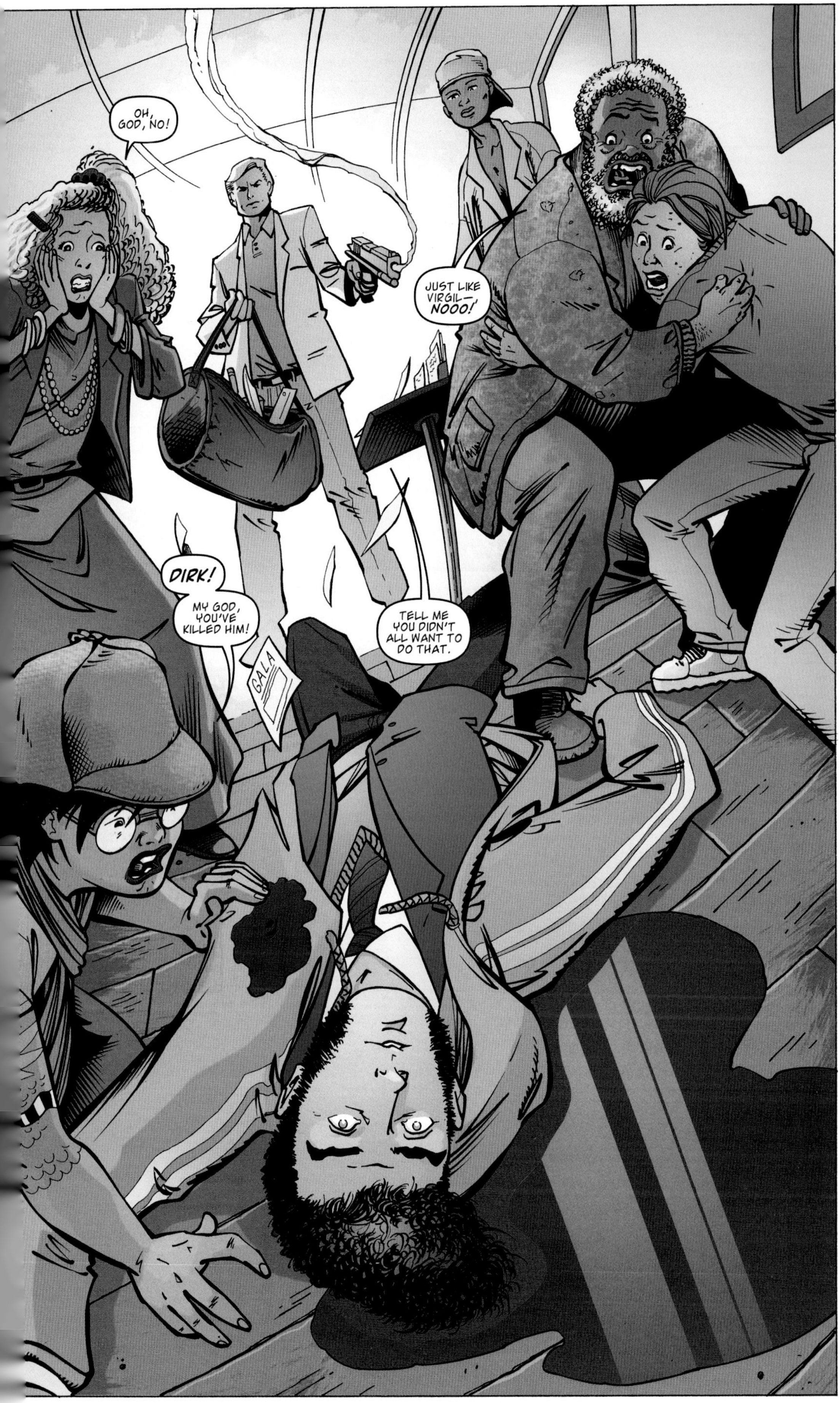
OH, GOD, NO!
JUST LIKE VIRGIL— NOOO!
DIRK!
MY GOD, YOU'VE KILLED HIM!
TELL ME YOU DIDN'T ALL WANT TO DO THAT.
GALA

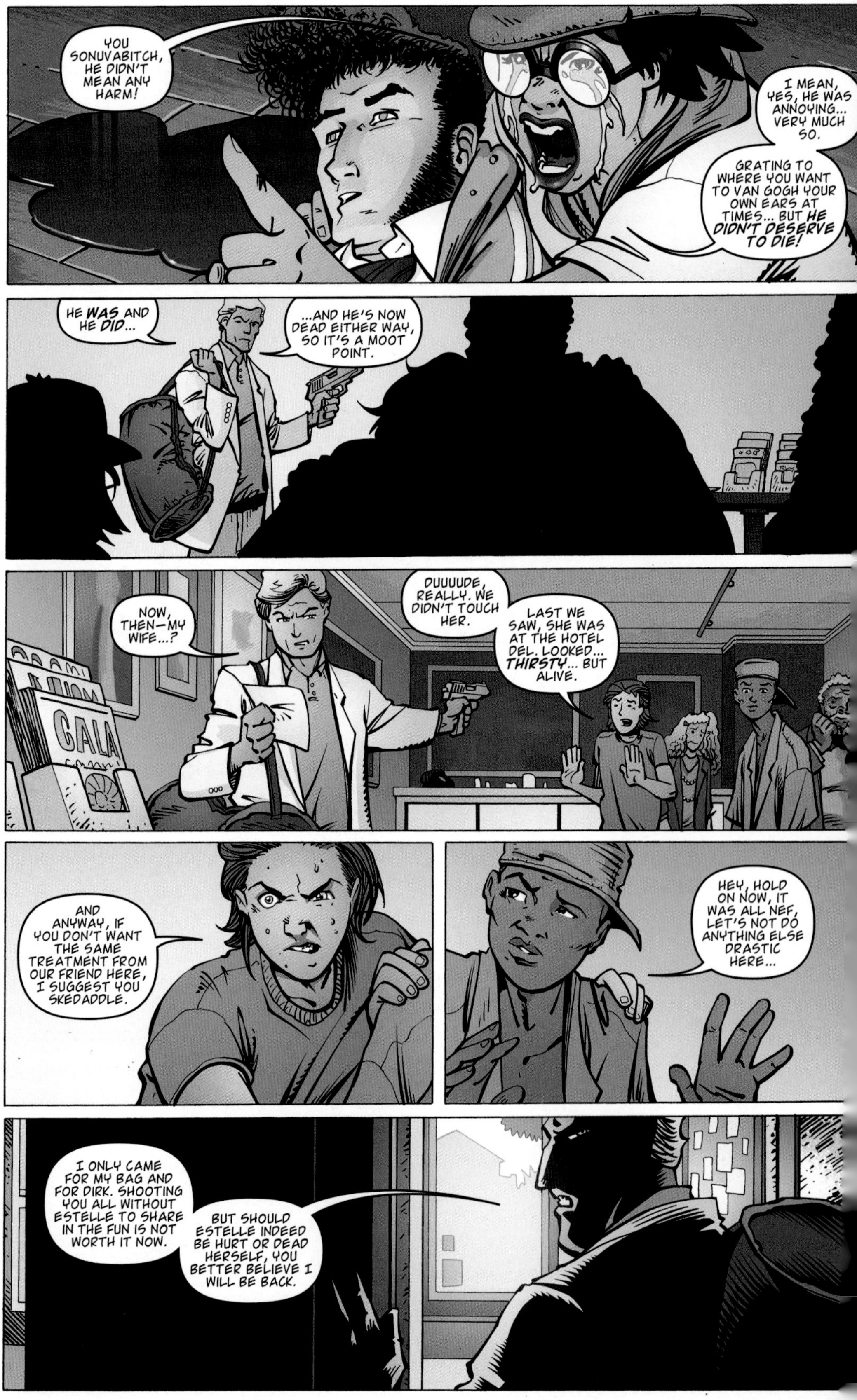
YOU SONUVABITCH, HE DIDN'T MEAN ANY HARM!
I MEAN, YES, HE WAS ANNOYING... VERY MUCH SO.
GRATING TO WHERE YOU WANT TO VAN GOGH YOUR OWN EARS AT TIMES... BUT HE DIDN'T DESERVE TO DIE!
HE WAS AND HE DID...
...AND HE'S NOW DEAD EITHER WAY, SO IT'S A MOOT POINT.
NOW, THEN—MY WIFE...?
DUUUUDE, REALLY. WE DIDN'T TOUCH HER.
LAST WE SAW, SHE WAS AT THE HOTEL DEL. LOOKED... THIRSTY... BUT ALIVE.
AND ANYWAY, IF YOU DON'T WANT THE SAME TREATMENT FROM OUR FRIEND HERE, I SUGGEST YOU SKEDADDLE.
HEY, HOLD ON NOW, IT WAS ALL NEF, LET'S NOT DO ANYTHING ELSE DRASTIC HERE...
I ONLY CAME FOR MY BAG AND FOR DIRK. SHOOTING YOU ALL WITHOUT ESTELLE TO SHARE IN THE FUN IS NOT WORTH IT NOW.
BUT SHOULD ESTELLE INDEED BE HURT OR DEAD HERSELF, YOU BETTER BELIEVE I WILL BE BACK.

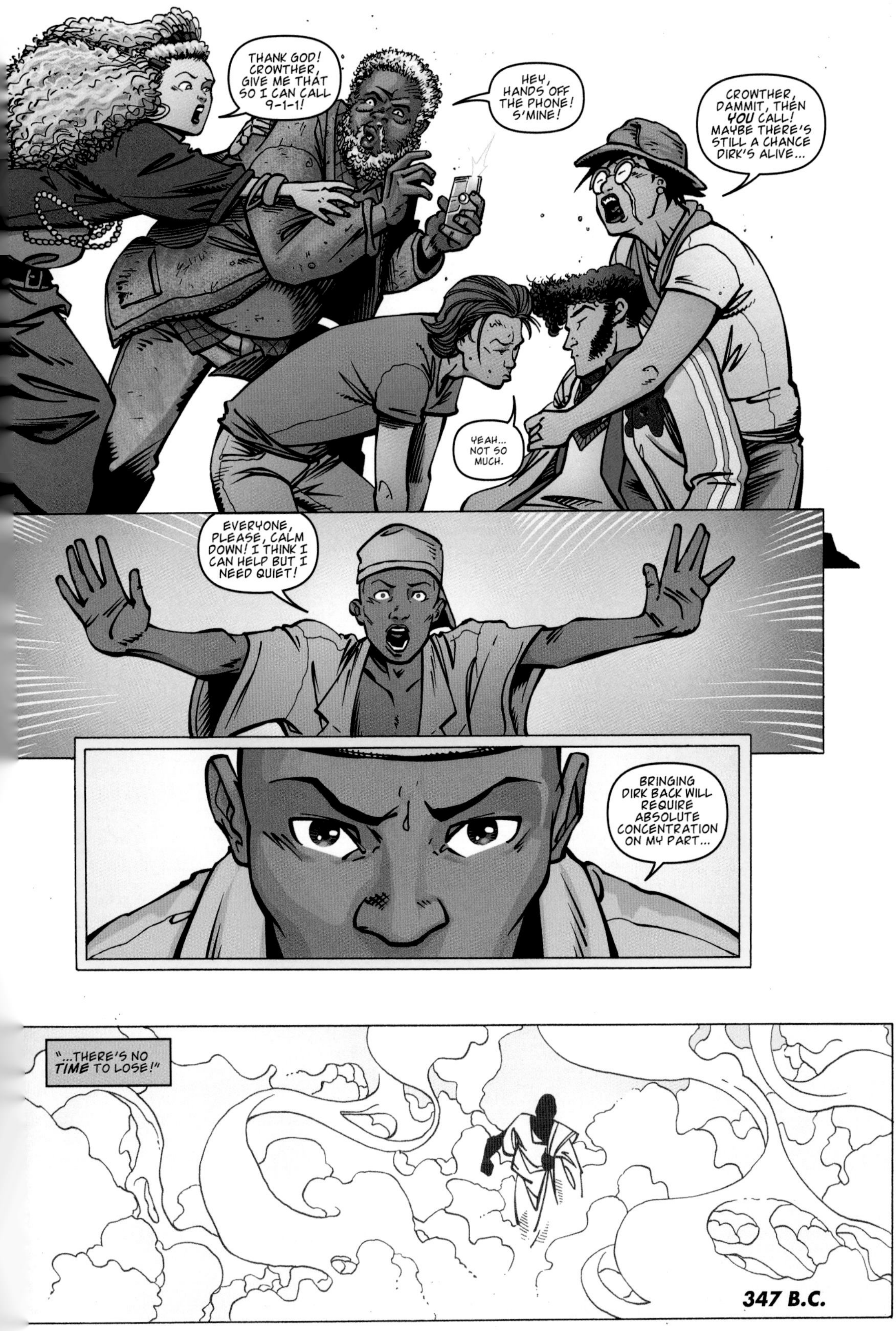
THANK GOD! CROWTHER, GIVE ME THAT SO I CAN CALL 9-1-1!
HEY, HANDS OFF THE PHONE! S'MINE!
CROWTHER, DAMMIT, THEN YOU CALL! MAYBE THERE'S STILL A CHANCE DIRK'S ALIVE...
YEAH... NOT SO MUCH.
EVERYONE, PLEASE, CALM DOWN! I THINK I CAN HELP BUT I NEED QUIET!
BRINGING DIRK BACK WILL REQUIRE ABSOLUTE CONCENTRATION ON MY PART...
"...THERE'S NO TIME TO LOSE!"
347 B.C.

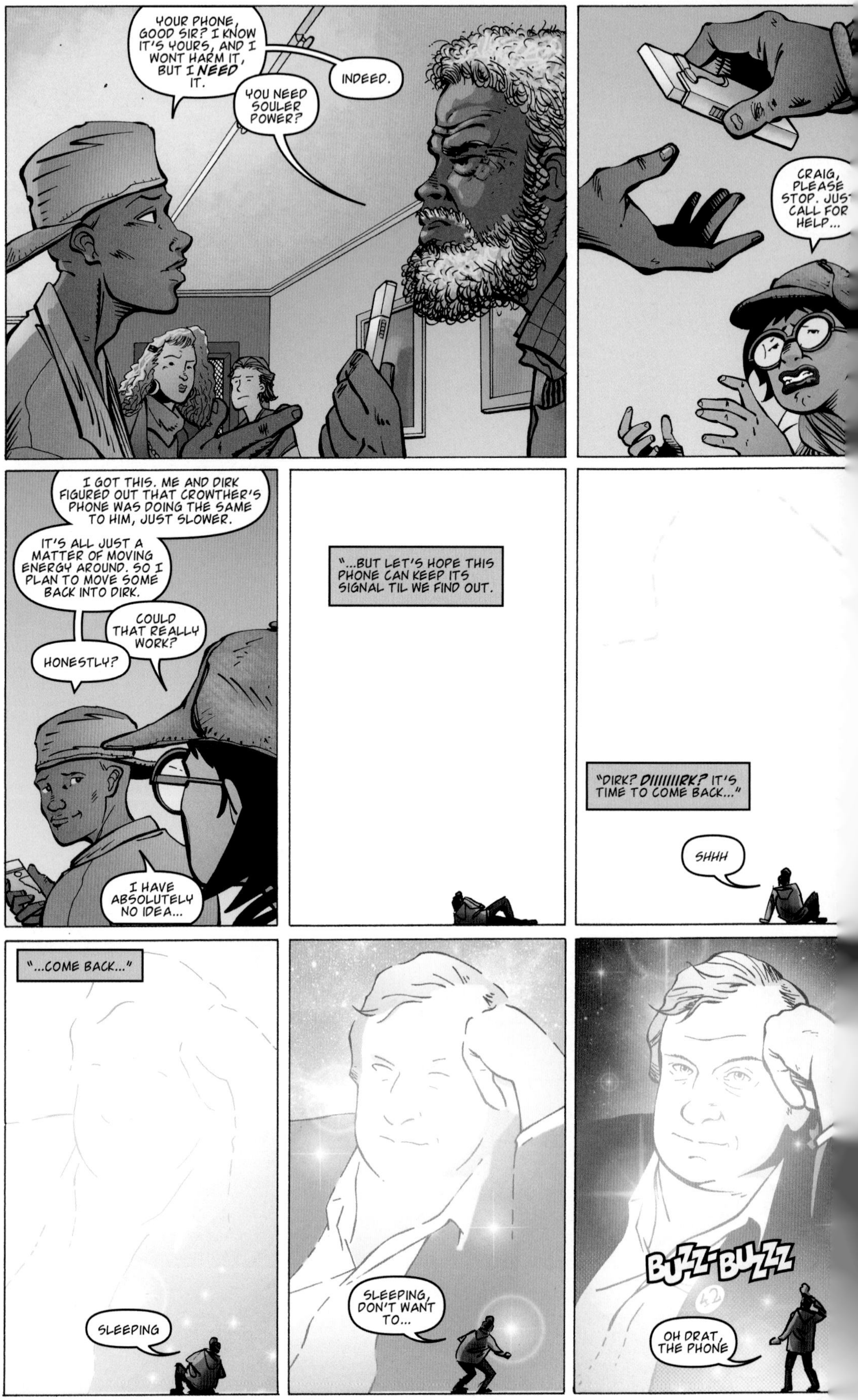
YOUR PHONE, GOOD SIR? I KNOW IT'S YOURS, AND I WONT HARM IT, BUT I NEED IT.
INDEED.
YOU NEED SOULER POWER?
CRAIG, PLEASE STOP. JUST CALL FOR HELP...
I GOT THIS. ME AND DIRK FIGURED OUT THAT CROWTHER'S PHONE WAS DOING THE SAME TO HIM, JUST SLOWER.
IT'S ALL JUST A MATTER OF MOVING ENERGY AROUND. SO I PLAN TO MOVE SOME BACK INTO DIRK.
COULD THAT REALLY WORK?
HONESTLY?
I HAVE ABSOLUTELY NO IDEA...
"...BUT LET'S HOPE THIS PHONE CAN KEEP ITS SIGNAL TIL WE FIND OUT.
"DIRK? DIIIIIIIRK? IT'S TIME TO COME BACK..."
SHHH
"...COME BACK..."
SLEEPING
SLEEPING, DON'T WANT TO...
BUZZ-BUZZZ
OH DRAT, THE PHONE

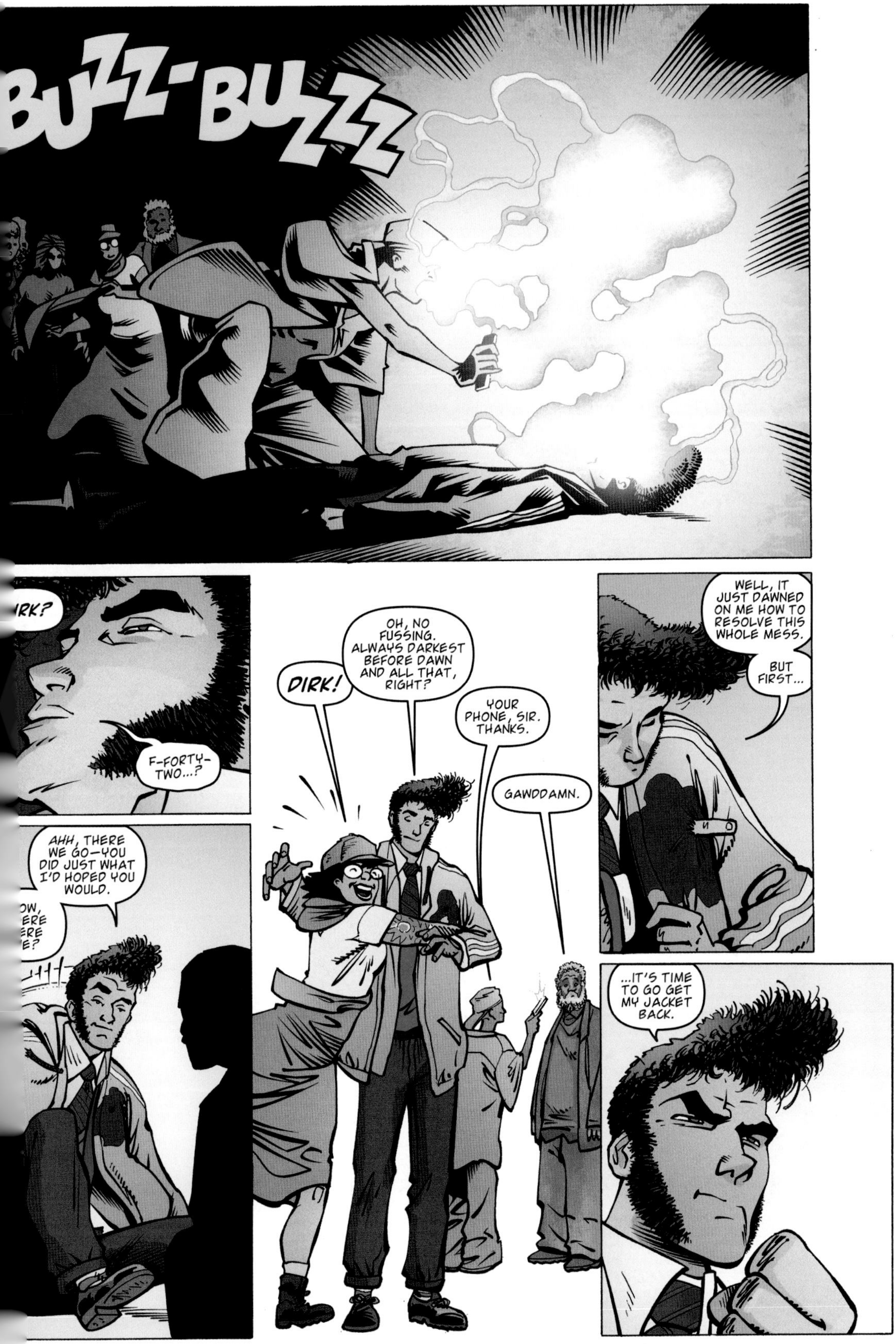
BUZZ-BUZZZ
RK?
F-FORTY-TWO...?
AHH, THERE WE GO—YOU DID JUST WHAT I'D HOPED YOU WOULD.
DIRK!
OH, NO FUSSING. ALWAYS DARKEST BEFORE DAWN AND ALL THAT, RIGHT?
YOUR PHONE, SIR. THANKS.
GAWDDAMN.
WELL, IT JUST DAWNED ON ME HOW TO RESOLVE THIS WHOLE MESS.
BUT FIRST...
...IT'S TIME TO GO GET MY JACKET BACK.

"I JUST HOPE THERE ARE NO MORE UNWELCOME BULLETS OR OTHER SUCH SURPRISES HEADED MY WAY."

200

SOON ENOUGH.

AHH, MUCH BETTER. NARY A BULLET HOLE TO BE FOUND IN THIS ONE.

DIRK, AFTER ALL THAT... I DON'T KNOW HOW MUCH MORE OF THIS I CAN REALLY BEAR. REINCARNATION, *SERIAL KILLERS* SOUL-POWERED PHONES...

OMELETS REMAIN UNMADE WITHOUT BROKEN EGGS, TONYA.

BUT I TAKE YOUR POINT.

I'D PREFER TO NOT ACTUALLY *BECOME* THAT BROKEN EGG AGAIN.

WHICH IS WHY IT'S TIME GET BACK TO T MUSEUM, WHE KATE WILL NEED MEET US. COM ALONG.

BUT HOW WILL YOUR AUTHORITATIVE FRIEND KNOW TO MEET US THERE...?

OH, ONE THING ABOUT KATE...

...SHE ALWAYS HAS HER WAYS.

KATE MEET AT MUSEUM 20 MIN

190

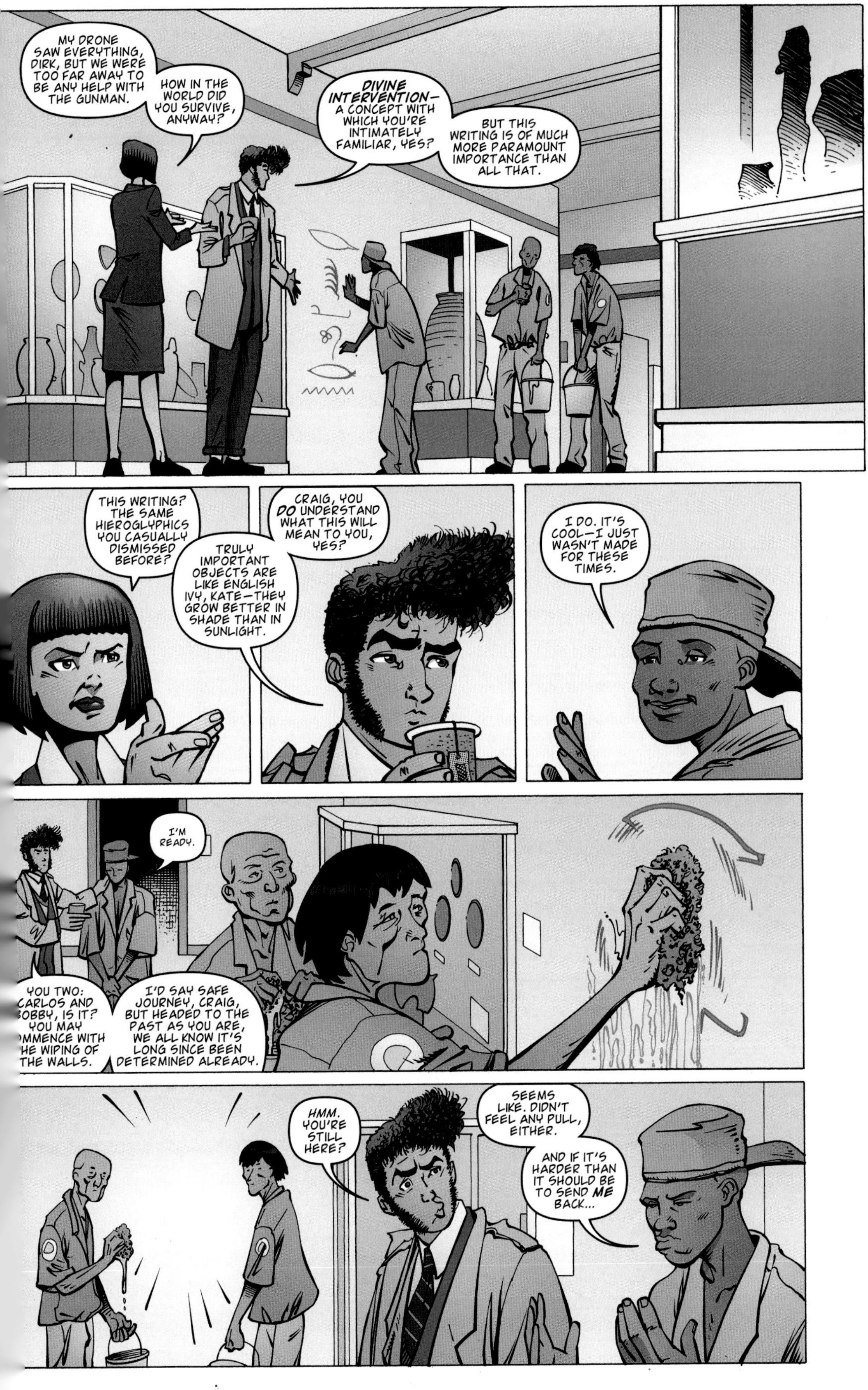

MY DRONE SAW EVERYTHING, DIRK, BUT WE WERE TOO FAR AWAY TO BE ANY HELP WITH THE GUNMAN.
HOW IN THE WORLD DID YOU SURVIVE, ANYWAY?
DIVINE INTERVENTION— A CONCEPT WITH WHICH YOU'RE INTIMATELY FAMILIAR, YES?
BUT THIS WRITING IS OF MUCH MORE PARAMOUNT IMPORTANCE THAN ALL THAT.
THIS WRITING? THE SAME HIEROGLYPHICS YOU CASUALLY DISMISSED BEFORE?
TRULY IMPORTANT OBJECTS ARE LIKE ENGLISH IVY, KATE—THEY GROW BETTER IN SHADE THAN IN SUNLIGHT.
CRAIG, YOU DO UNDERSTAND WHAT THIS WILL MEAN TO YOU, YES?
I DO. IT'S COOL—I JUST WASN'T MADE FOR THESE TIMES.
I'M READY.
YOU TWO: CARLOS AND BOBBY, IS IT? YOU MAY COMMENCE WITH THE WIPING OF THE WALLS.
I'D SAY SAFE JOURNEY, CRAIG, BUT HEADED TO THE PAST AS YOU ARE, WE ALL KNOW IT'S LONG SINCE BEEN DETERMINED ALREADY.
HMM. YOU'RE STILL HERE?
SEEMS LIKE. DIDN'T FEEL ANY PULL, EITHER.
AND IF IT'S HARDER THAN IT SHOULD BE TO SEND ME BACK...

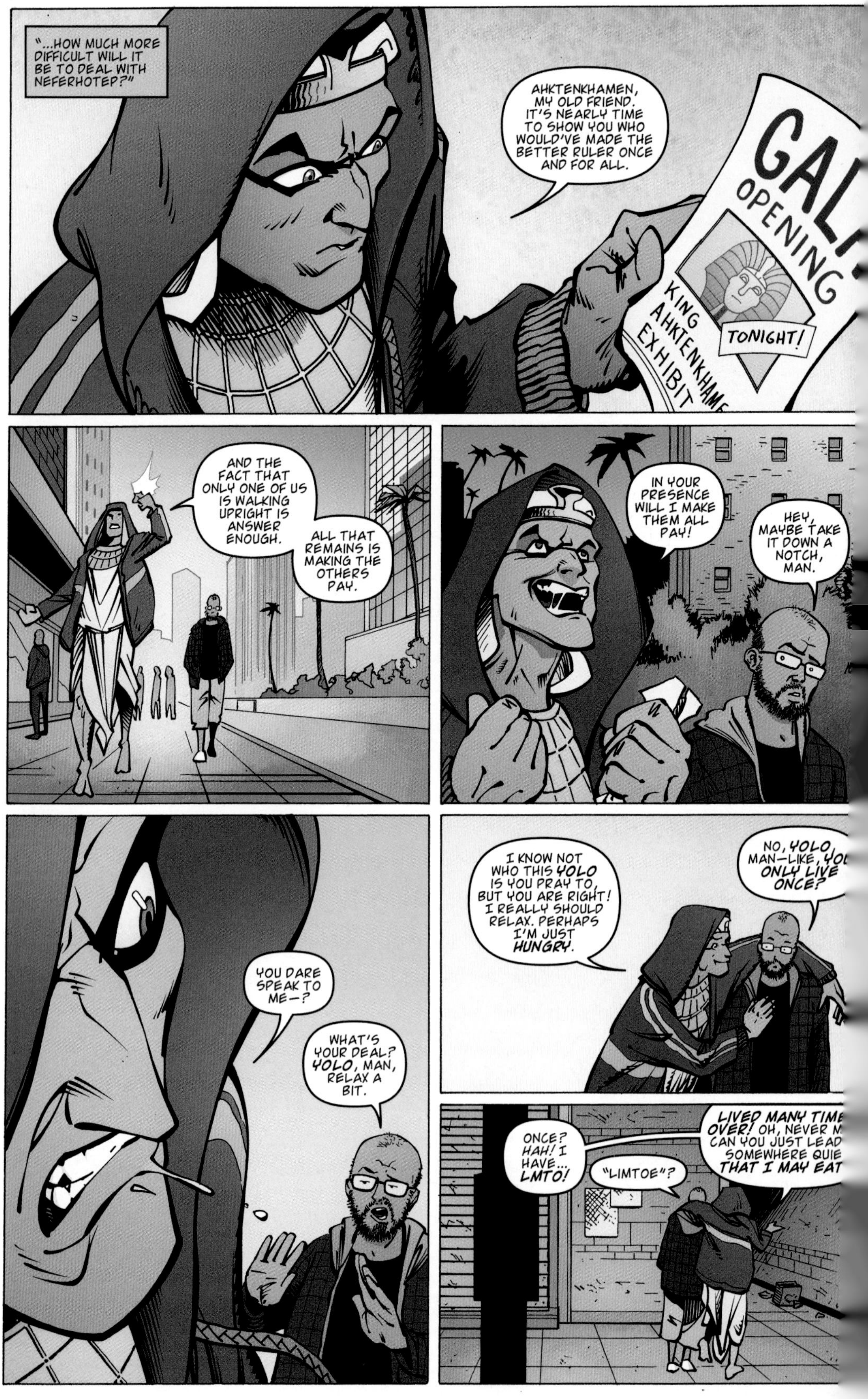
"...HOW MUCH MORE DIFFICULT WILL IT BE TO DEAL WITH NEFERHOTEP?"
AHKTENKHAMEN, MY OLD FRIEND. IT'S NEARLY TIME TO SHOW YOU WHO WOULD'VE MADE THE BETTER RULER ONCE AND FOR ALL.
GAL
OPENING
KING AHKTENKHAME
EXHIBIT
TONIGHT!
AND THE FACT THAT ONLY ONE OF US IS WALKING UPRIGHT IS ANSWER ENOUGH.
ALL THAT REMAINS IS MAKING THE OTHERS PAY.
IN YOUR PRESENCE WILL I MAKE THEM ALL PAY!
HEY, MAYBE TAKE IT DOWN A NOTCH, MAN.
YOU DARE SPEAK TO ME—?
WHAT'S YOUR DEAL? YOLO, MAN, RELAX A BIT.
I KNOW NOT WHO THIS YOLO IS YOU PRAY TO, BUT YOU ARE RIGHT! I REALLY SHOULD RELAX. PERHAPS I'M JUST HUNGRY.
NO, YOLO, MAN—LIKE, YOU ONLY LIVE ONCE?
ONCE? HAH! I HAVE... LMTO!
"LIMTOE"?
LIVED MANY TIME OVER! OH, NEVER M CAN YOU JUST LEAD SOMEWHERE QUIE THAT I MAY EAT

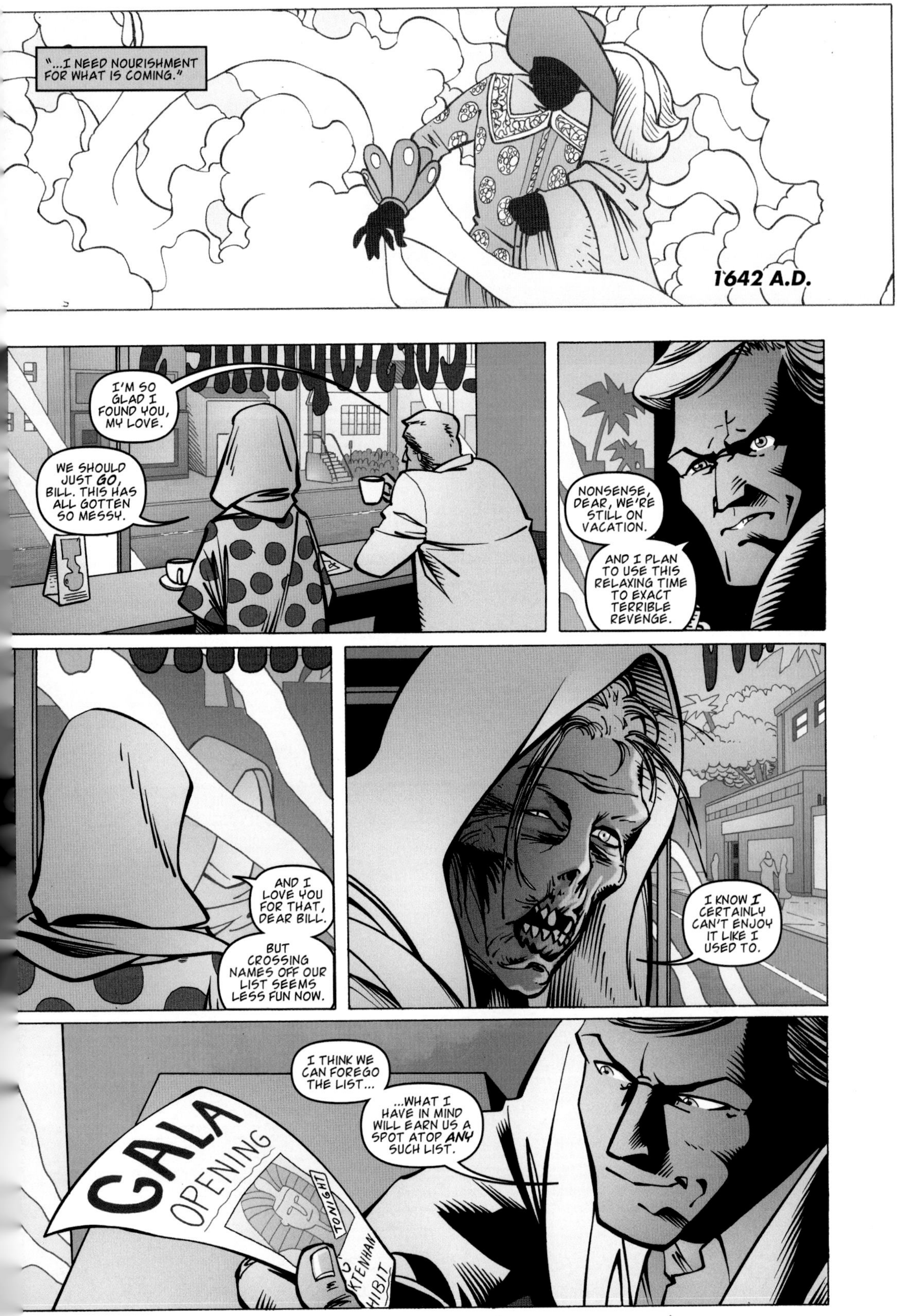
"...I NEED NOURISHMENT FOR WHAT IS COMING."
1642 A.D.
I'M SO GLAD I FOUND YOU, MY LOVE.
WE SHOULD JUST GO, BILL. THIS HAS ALL GOTTEN SO MESSY.
NONSENSE, DEAR, WE'RE STILL ON VACATION.
AND I PLAN TO USE THIS RELAXING TIME TO EXACT TERRIBLE REVENGE.
AND I LOVE YOU FOR THAT, DEAR BILL.
BUT CROSSING NAMES OFF OUR LIST SEEMS LESS FUN NOW.
I KNOW I CERTAINLY CAN'T ENJOY IT LIKE I USED TO.
I THINK WE CAN FOREGO THE LIST...
...WHAT I HAVE IN MIND WILL EARN US A SPOT ATOP ANY SUCH LIST.
GALA OPENING
TONIGHT

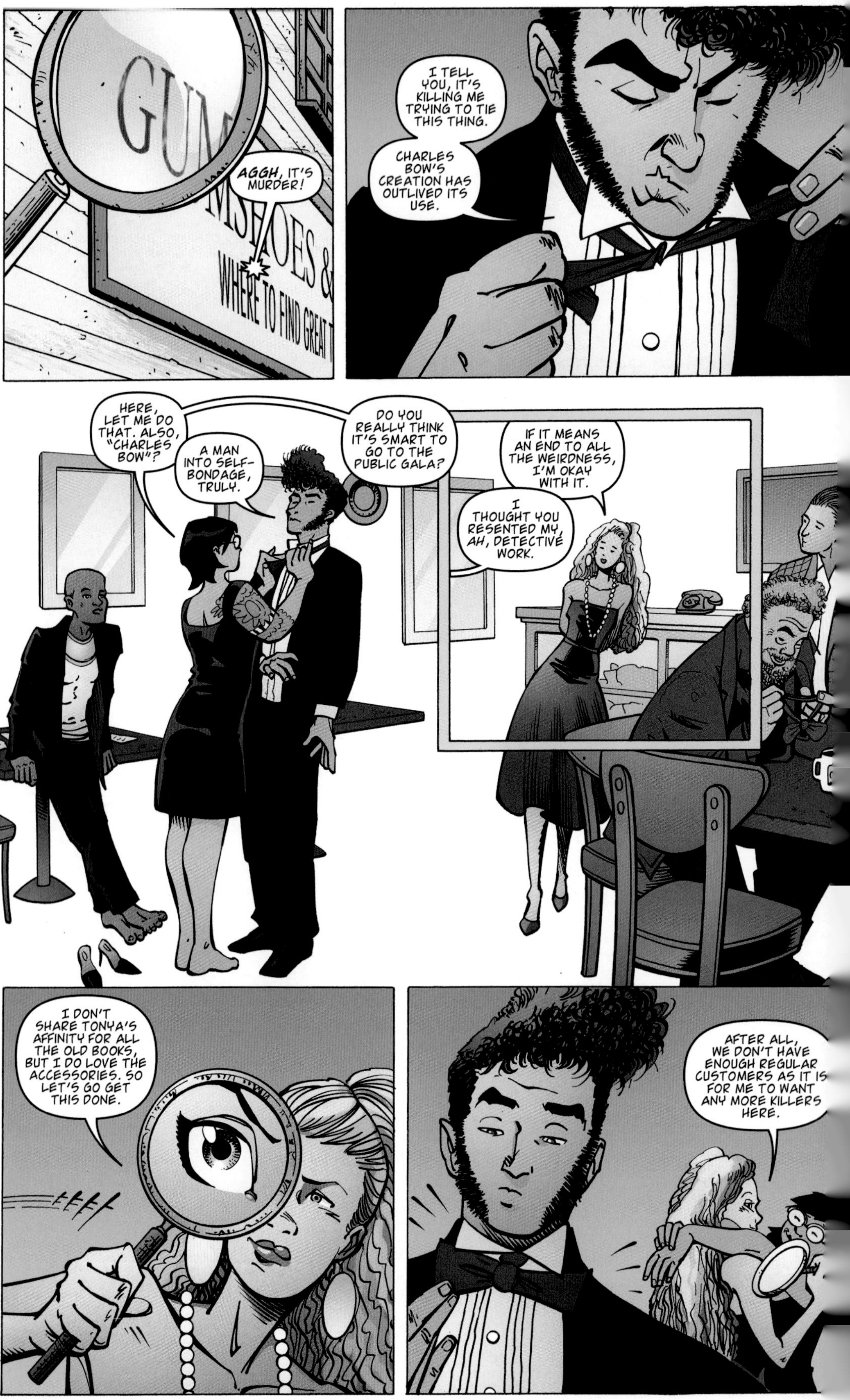
GUM
MSHOES &
WHERE TO FIND GREAT
AGGH, IT'S MURDER!
I TELL YOU, IT'S KILLING ME TRYING TO TIE THIS THING.
CHARLES BOW'S CREATION HAS OUTLIVED ITS USE.
HERE, LET ME DO THAT. ALSO, "CHARLES BOW"?
A MAN INTO SELF-BONDAGE, TRULY.
DO YOU REALLY THINK IT'S SMART TO GO TO THE PUBLIC GALA?
IF IT MEANS AN END TO ALL THE WEIRDNESS, I'M OKAY WITH IT.
I THOUGHT YOU RESENTED MY, AH, DETECTIVE WORK.
I DON'T SHARE TONYA'S AFFINITY FOR ALL THE OLD BOOKS, BUT I DO LOVE THE ACCESSORIES. SO LET'S GO GET THIS DONE.
AFTER ALL, WE DON'T HAVE ENOUGH REGULAR CUSTOMERS AS IT IS FOR ME TO WANT ANY MORE KILLERS HERE.

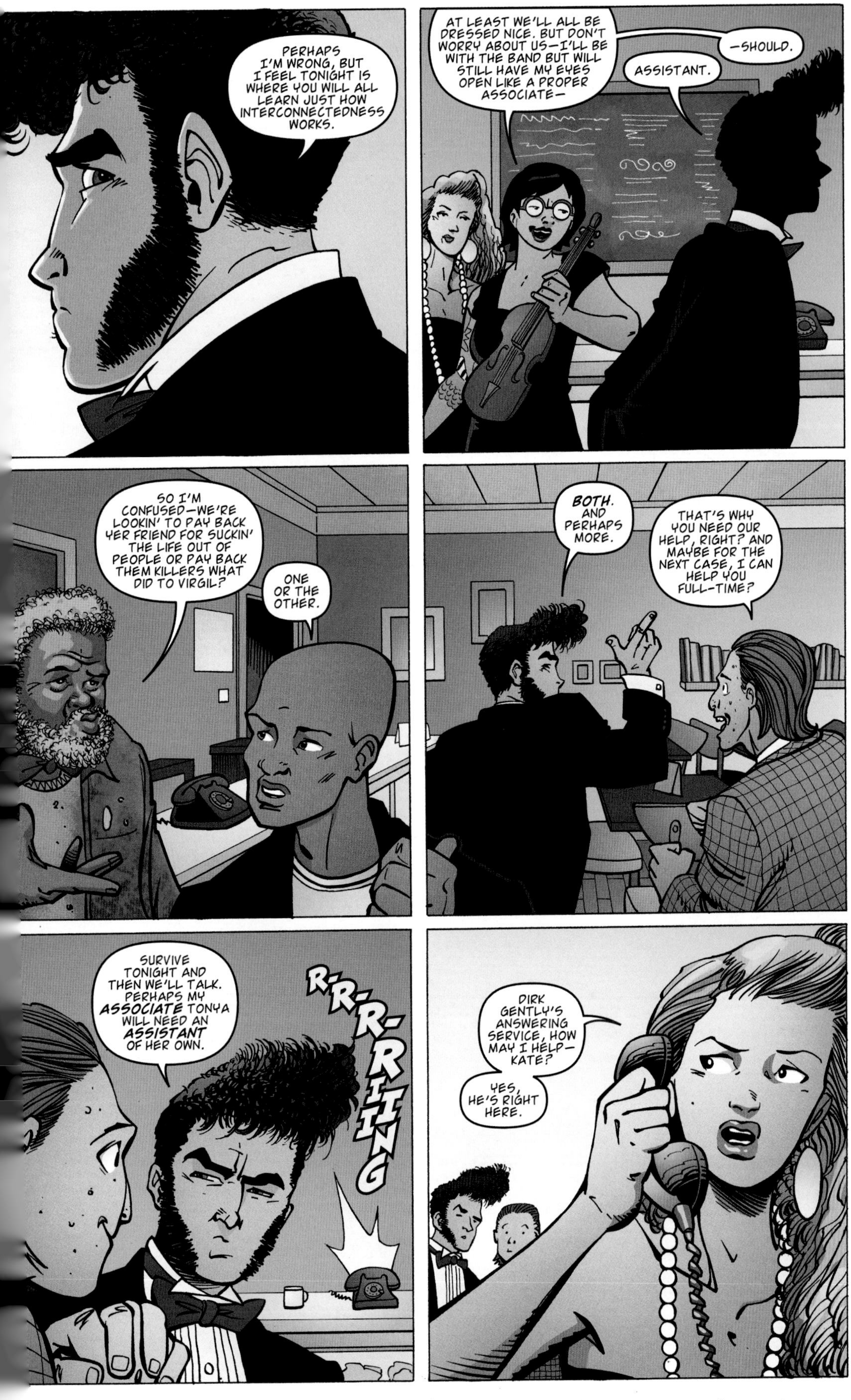

PERHAPS I'M WRONG, BUT I FEEL TONIGHT IS WHERE YOU WILL ALL LEARN JUST HOW INTERCONNECTEDNESS WORKS.
AT LEAST WE'LL ALL BE DRESSED NICE. BUT DON'T WORRY ABOUT US—I'LL BE WITH THE BAND BUT WILL STILL HAVE MY EYES OPEN LIKE A PROPER ASSOCIATE—
ASSISTANT.
—SHOULD.
SO I'M CONFUSED—WE'RE LOOKIN' TO PAY BACK YER FRIEND FOR SUCKIN' THE LIFE OUT OF PEOPLE OR PAY BACK THEM KILLERS WHAT DID TO VIRGIL?
ONE OR THE OTHER.
BOTH. AND PERHAPS MORE.
THAT'S WHY YOU NEED OUR HELP, RIGHT? AND MAYBE FOR THE NEXT CASE, I CAN HELP YOU FULL-TIME?
SURVIVE TONIGHT AND THEN WE'LL TALK. PERHAPS MY ASSOCIATE TONYA WILL NEED AN ASSISTANT OF HER OWN.
R-R-R-RIIING
DIRK GENTLY'S ANSWERING SERVICE, HOW MAY I HELP— KATE?
YES, HE'S RIGHT HERE.

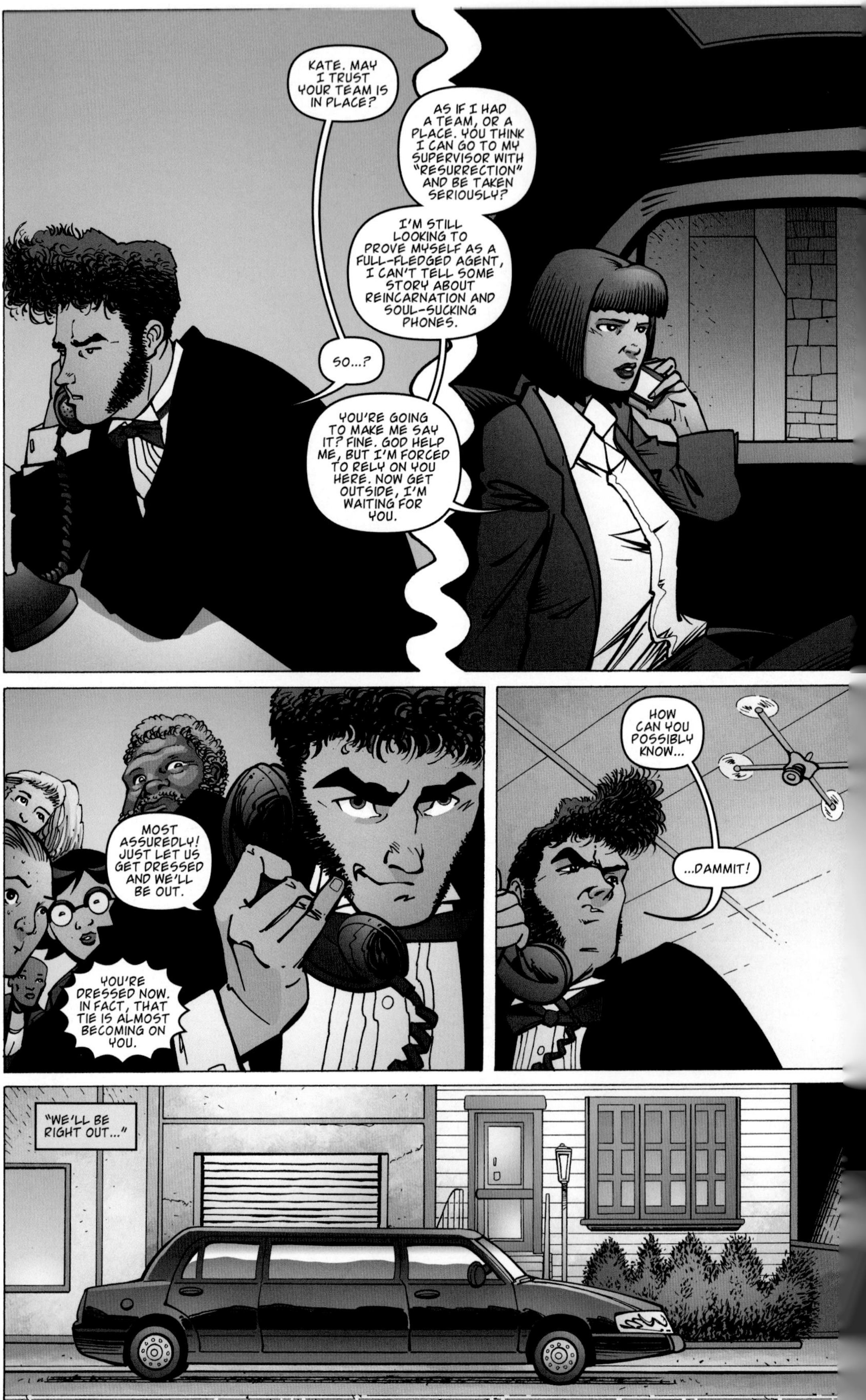
KATE. MAY I TRUST YOUR TEAM IS IN PLACE?
AS IF I HAD A TEAM, OR A PLACE. YOU THINK I CAN GO TO MY SUPERVISOR WITH "RESURRECTION" AND BE TAKEN SERIOUSLY?
I'M STILL LOOKING TO PROVE MYSELF AS A FULL-FLEDGED AGENT, I CAN'T TELL SOME STORY ABOUT REINCARNATION AND SOUL-SUCKING PHONES.
SO...?
YOU'RE GOING TO MAKE ME SAY IT? FINE. GOD HELP ME, BUT I'M FORCED TO RELY ON YOU HERE. NOW GET OUTSIDE, I'M WAITING FOR YOU.
MOST ASSUREDLY! JUST LET US GET DRESSED AND WE'LL BE OUT.
YOU'RE DRESSED NOW. IN FACT, THAT TIE IS ALMOST BECOMING ON YOU.
HOW CAN YOU POSSIBLY KNOW...
...DAMMIT!
"WE'LL BE RIGHT OUT..."

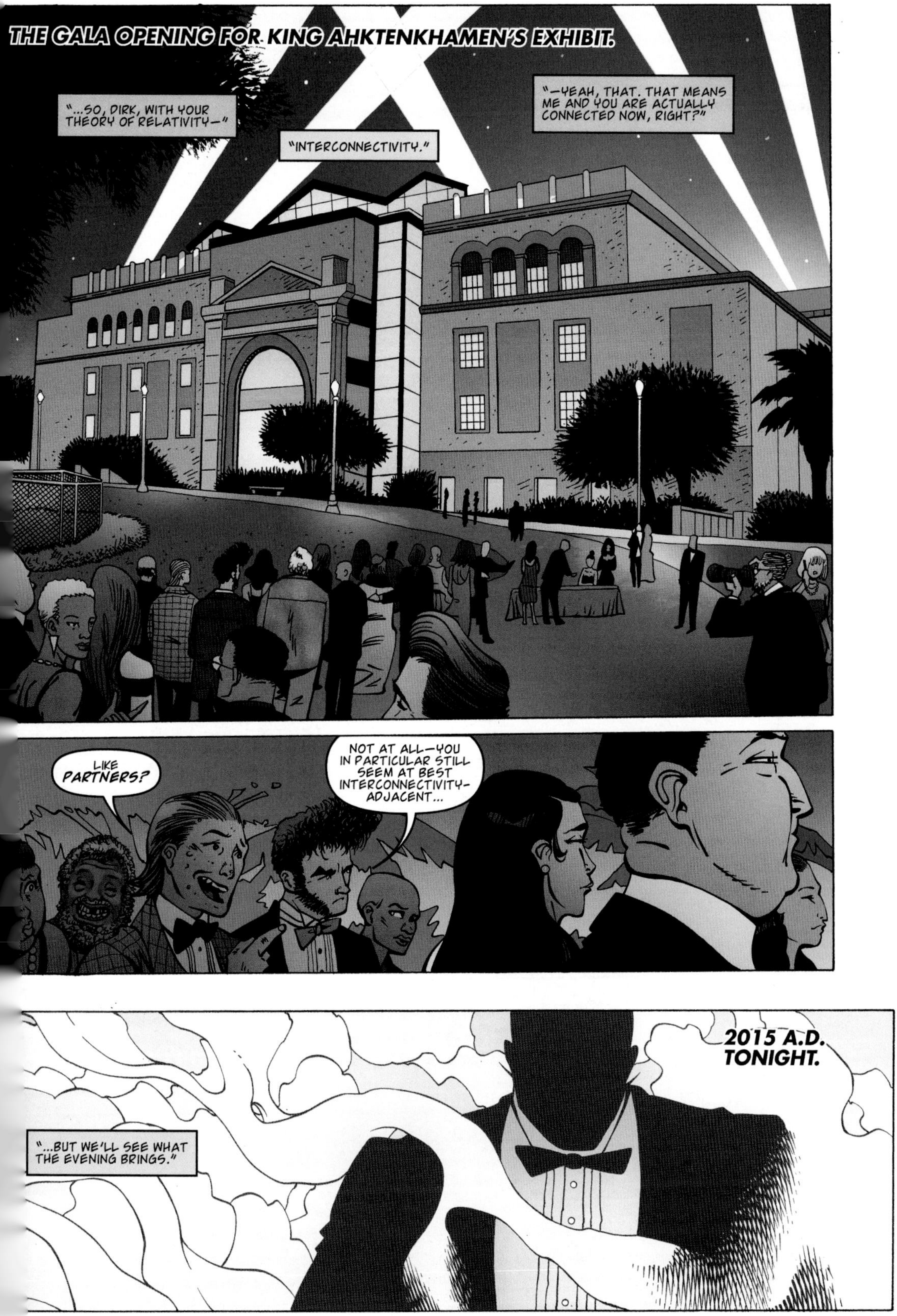
THE GALA OPENING FOR KING AHKTENKHAMEN'S EXHIBIT.
"...SO, DIRK, WITH YOUR THEORY OF RELATIVITY—"
"INTERCONNECTIVITY."
"—YEAH, THAT. THAT MEANS ME AND YOU ARE ACTUALLY CONNECTED NOW, RIGHT?"
LIKE PARTNERS?
NOT AT ALL—YOU IN PARTICULAR STILL SEEM AT BEST INTERCONNECTIVITY-ADJACENT...
2015 A.D. TONIGHT.
"...BUT WE'LL SEE WHAT THE EVENING BRINGS."

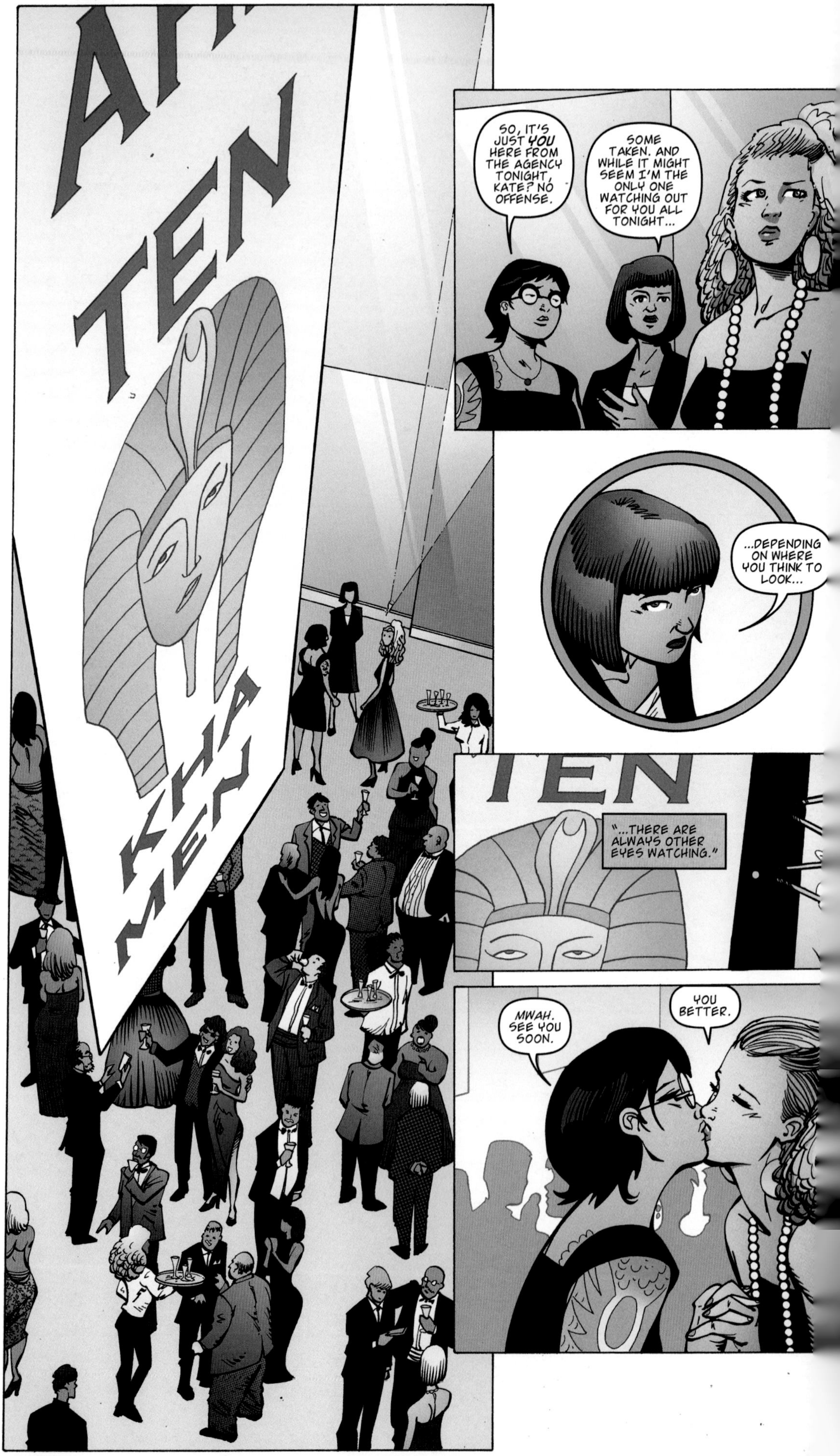
AT
TEN
KHA
MEN
SO, IT'S JUST YOU HERE FROM THE AGENCY TONIGHT, KATE? NO OFFENSE.
SOME TAKEN. AND WHILE IT MIGHT SEEM I'M THE ONLY ONE WATCHING OUT FOR YOU ALL TONIGHT...
...DEPENDING ON WHERE YOU THINK TO LOOK...
TEN
"...THERE ARE ALWAYS OTHER EYES WATCHING."
MWAH. SEE YOU SOON.
YOU BETTER.

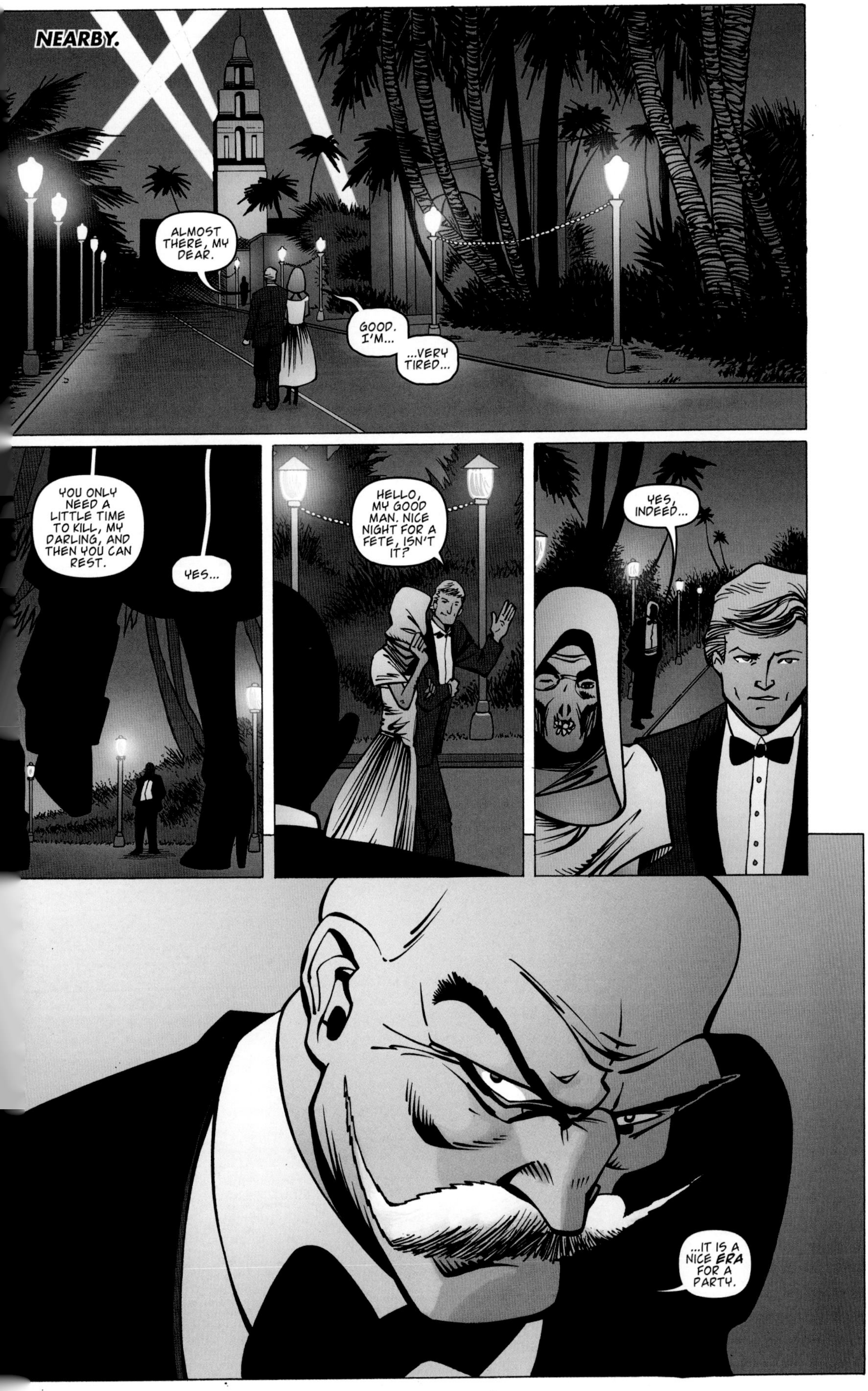
NEARBY.
ALMOST THERE, MY DEAR.
GOOD. I'M...
...VERY TIRED...
YOU ONLY NEED A LITTLE TIME TO KILL, MY DARLING, AND THEN YOU CAN REST.
YES...
HELLO, MY GOOD MAN. NICE NIGHT FOR A FETE, ISN'T IT?
YES, INDEED...
...IT IS A NICE ERA FOR A PARTY.

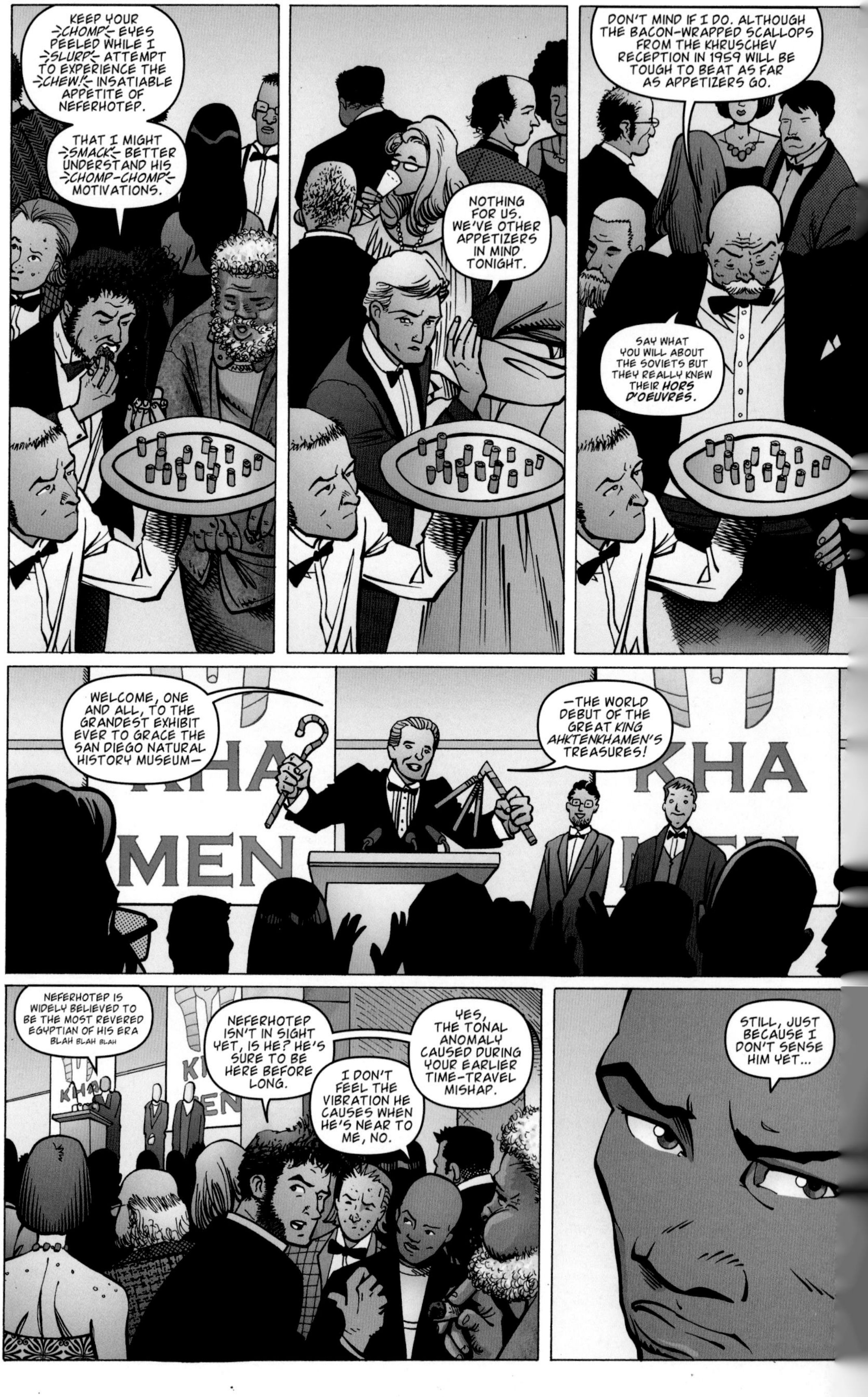
KEEP YOUR -CHOMP- EYES PEELED WHILE I -SLURP- ATTEMPT TO EXPERIENCE THE -CHEW!- INSATIABLE APPETITE OF NEFERHOTEP.
THAT I MIGHT -SMACK- BETTER UNDERSTAND HIS -CHOMP-CHOMP- MOTIVATIONS.
NOTHING FOR US. WE'VE OTHER APPETIZERS IN MIND TONIGHT.
DON'T MIND IF I DO. ALTHOUGH THE BACON-WRAPPED SCALLOPS FROM THE KHRUSCHEV RECEPTION IN 1959 WILL BE TOUGH TO BEAT AS FAR AS APPETIZERS GO.
SAY WHAT YOU WILL ABOUT THE SOVIETS BUT THEY REALLY KNEW THEIR HORS D'OEUVRES.
WELCOME, ONE AND ALL, TO THE GRANDEST EXHIBIT EVER TO GRACE THE SAN DIEGO NATURAL HISTORY MUSEUM—
—THE WORLD DEBUT OF THE GREAT KING AHKTENKHAMEN'S TREASURES!
KHA
MEN
KHA
NEFERHOTEP IS WIDELY BELIEVED TO BE THE MOST REVERED EGYPTIAN OF HIS ERA BLAH BLAH BLAH
NEFERHOTEP ISN'T IN SIGHT YET, IS HE? HE'S SURE TO BE HERE BEFORE LONG.
I DON'T FEEL THE VIBRATION HE CAUSES WHEN HE'S NEAR TO ME, NO.
YES, THE TONAL ANOMALY CAUSED DURING YOUR EARLIER TIME-TRAVEL MISHAP.
STILL, JUST BECAUSE I DON'T SENSE HIM YET...

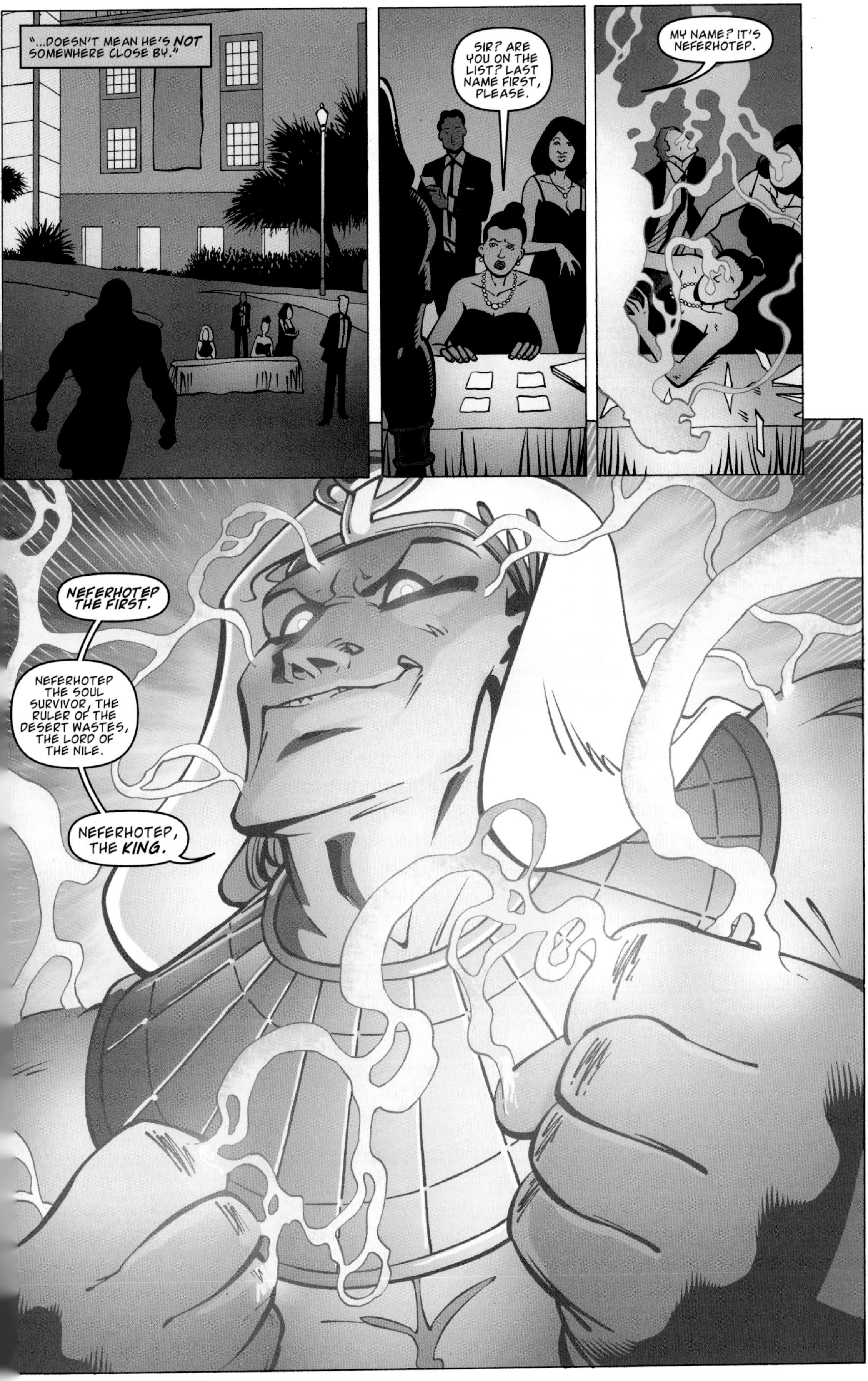
"...DOESN'T MEAN HE'S NOT SOMEWHERE CLOSE BY."
SIR? ARE YOU ON THE LIST? LAST NAME FIRST, PLEASE.
MY NAME? IT'S NEFERHOTEP.
NEFERHOTEP THE FIRST.
NEFERHOTEP THE SOUL SURVIVOR, THE RULER OF THE DESERT WASTES, THE LORD OF THE NILE.
NEFERHOTEP, THE KING.

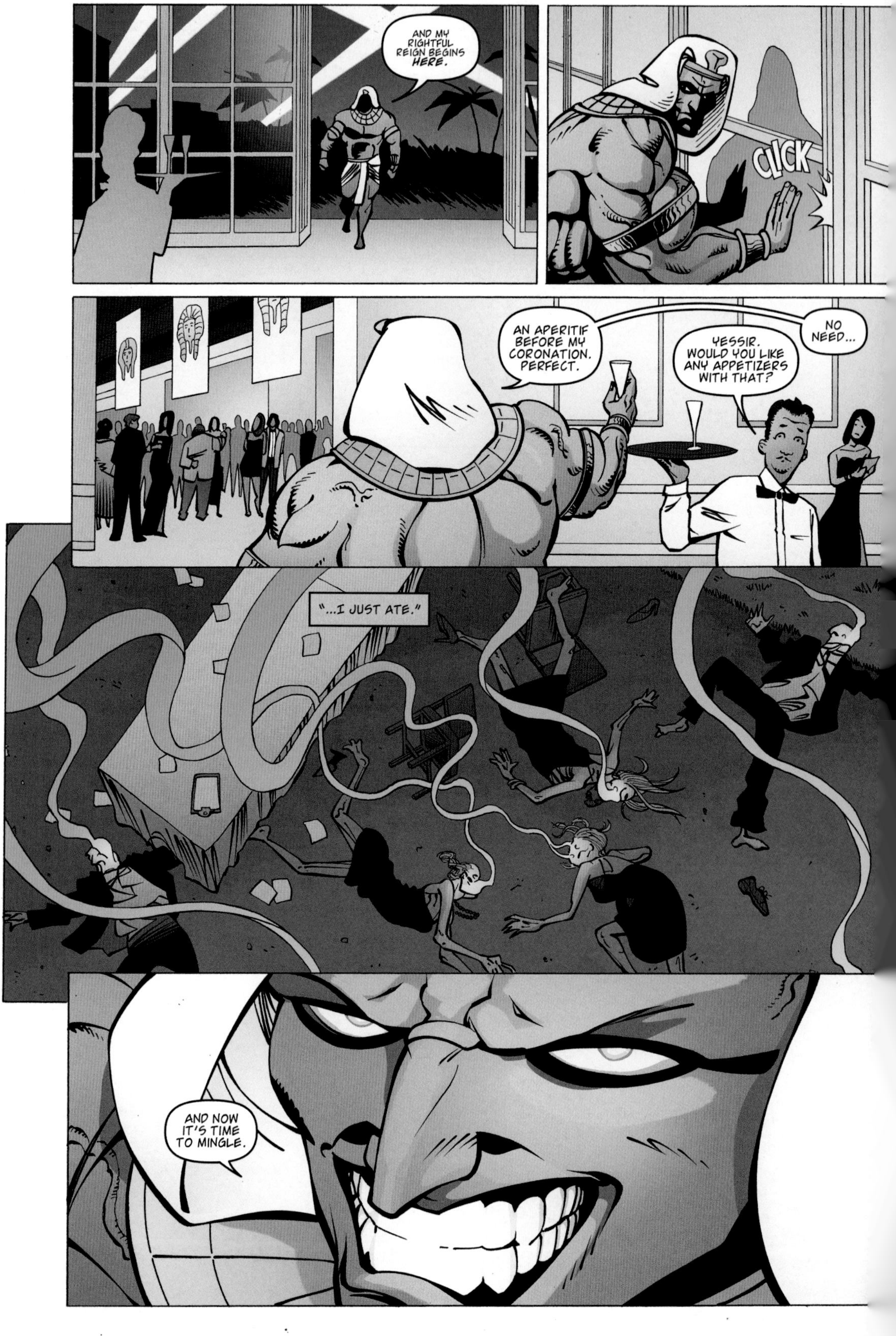
AND MY RIGHTFUL REIGN BEGINS HERE.
CLICK
AN APERITIF BEFORE MY CORONATION. PERFECT.
YESSIR. WOULD YOU LIKE ANY APPETIZERS WITH THAT?
NO NEED...
"...I JUST ATE."
AND NOW IT'S TIME TO MINGLE.

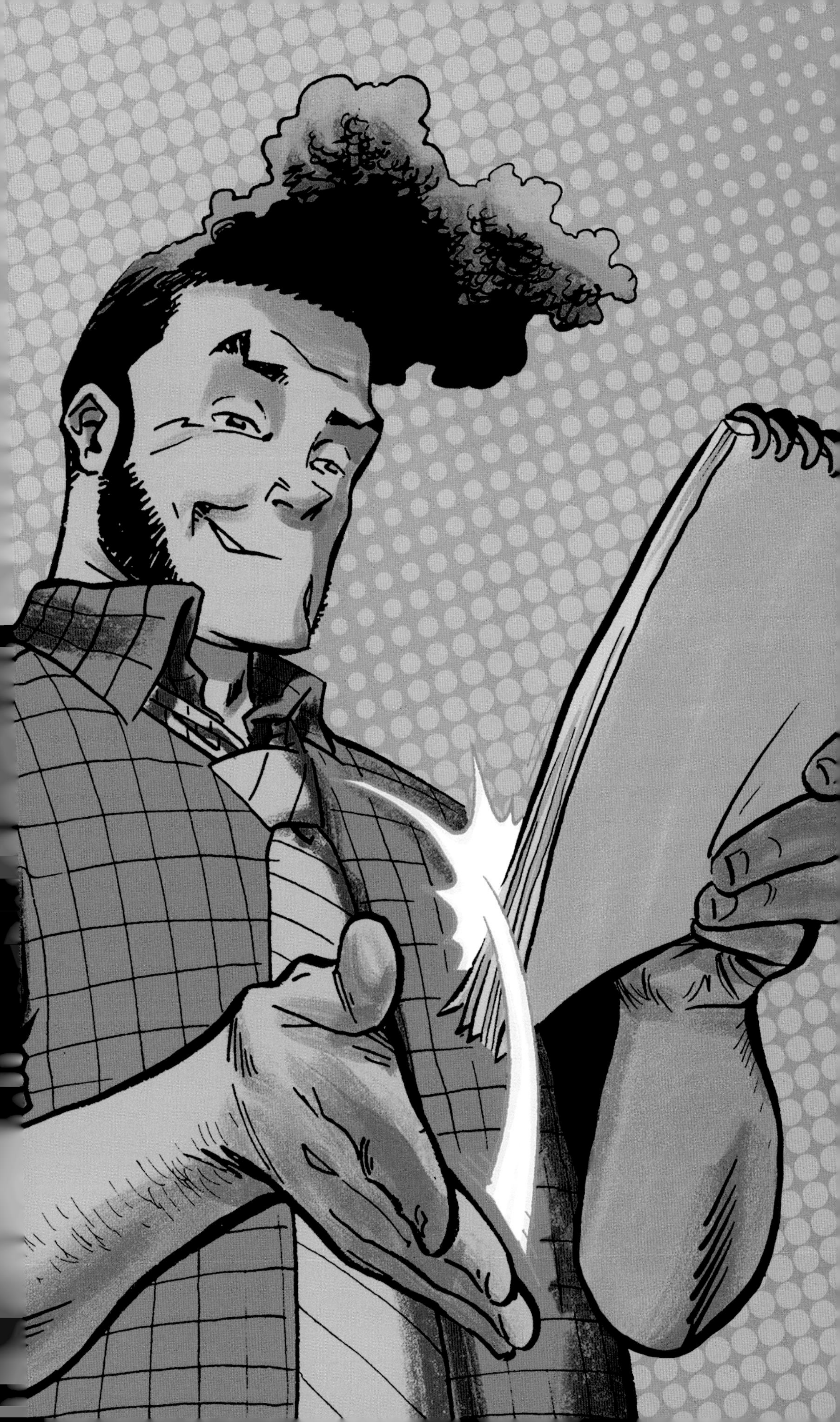

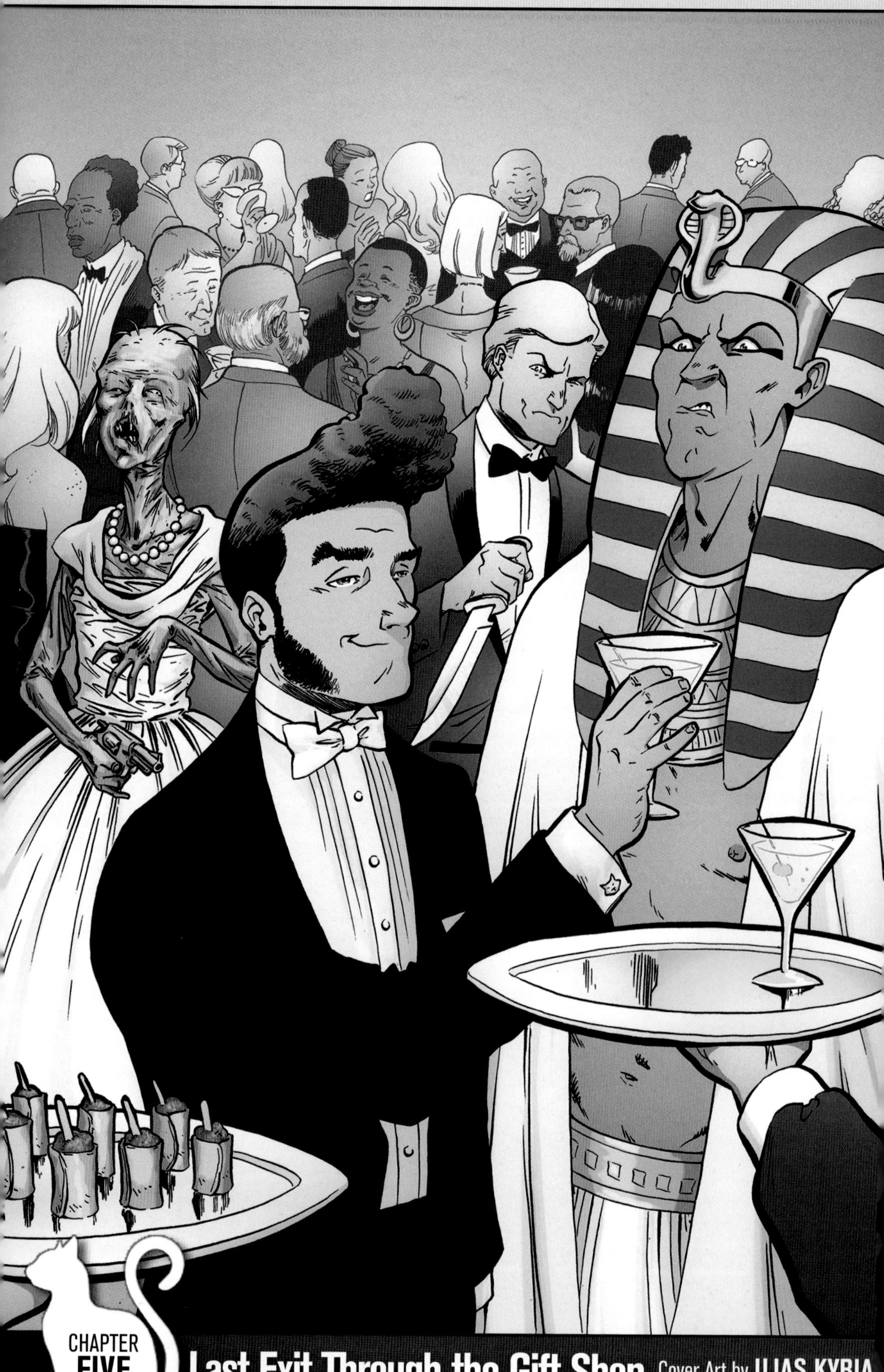

CHAPTER FIVE

Last Exit Through the Gift Shop

Cover Art by **ILIAS KYRIA**
Colors by **LEN O'GRA**

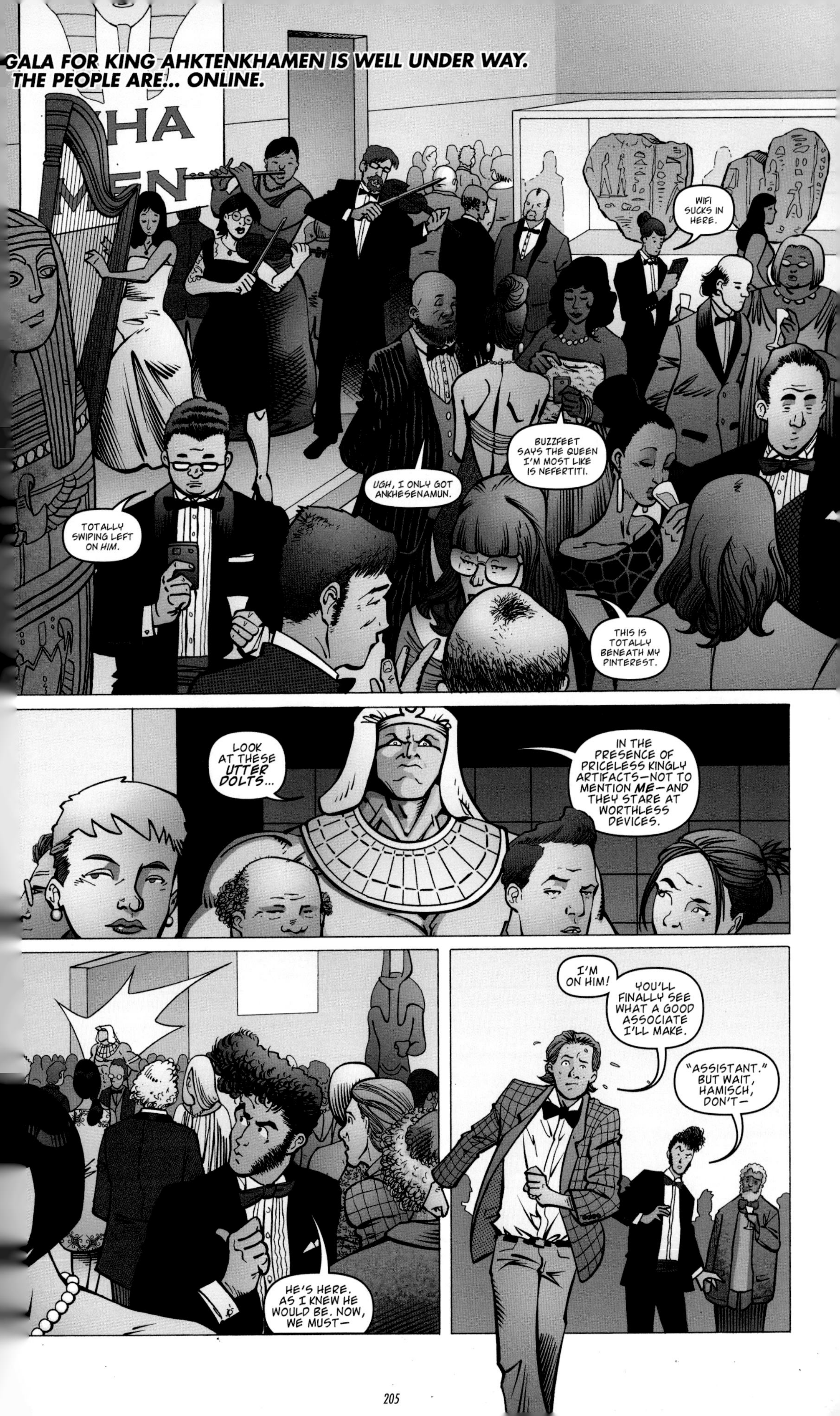
GALA FOR KING AHKTENKHAMEN IS WELL UNDER WAY. THE PEOPLE ARE... ONLINE.
WIFI SUCKS IN HERE.
BUZZFEET SAYS THE QUEEN I'M MOST LIKE IS NEFERTITI.
UGH, I ONLY GOT ANKHESENAMUN.
TOTALLY SWIPING LEFT ON HIM.
THIS IS TOTALLY BENEATH MY PINTEREST.
LOOK AT THESE UTTER DOLTS...
IN THE PRESENCE OF PRICELESS KINGLY ARTIFACTS—NOT TO MENTION ME—AND THEY STARE AT WORTHLESS DEVICES.
HE'S HERE. AS I KNEW HE WOULD BE. NOW, WE MUST—
I'M ON HIM!
YOU'LL FINALLY SEE WHAT A GOOD ASSOCIATE I'LL MAKE.
"ASSISTANT." BUT WAIT, HAMISCH, DON'T—

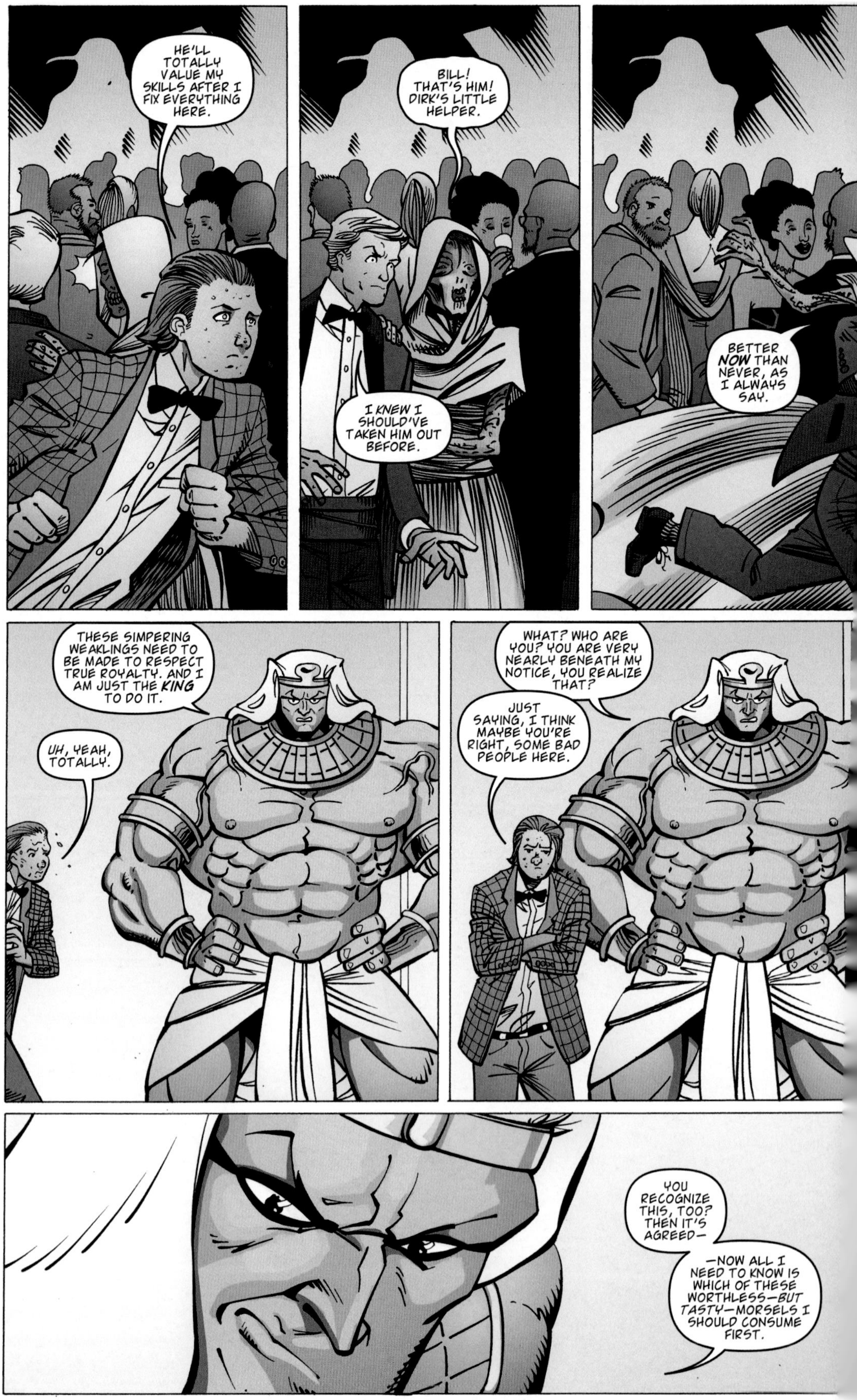
HE'LL TOTALLY VALUE MY SKILLS AFTER I FIX EVERYTHING HERE.
BILL! THAT'S HIM! DIRK'S LITTLE HELPER.
I KNEW I SHOULD'VE TAKEN HIM OUT BEFORE.
BETTER NOW THAN NEVER, AS I ALWAYS SAY.
THESE SIMPERING WEAKLINGS NEED TO BE MADE TO RESPECT TRUE ROYALTY. AND I AM JUST THE KING TO DO IT.
UH, YEAH, TOTALLY.
WHAT? WHO ARE YOU? YOU ARE VERY NEARLY BENEATH MY NOTICE, YOU REALIZE THAT?
JUST SAYING, I THINK MAYBE YOU'RE RIGHT, SOME BAD PEOPLE HERE.
YOU RECOGNIZE THIS, TOO? THEN IT'S AGREED—
—NOW ALL I NEED TO KNOW IS WHICH OF THESE WORTHLESS—BUT TASTY—MORSELS I SHOULD CONSUME FIRST.

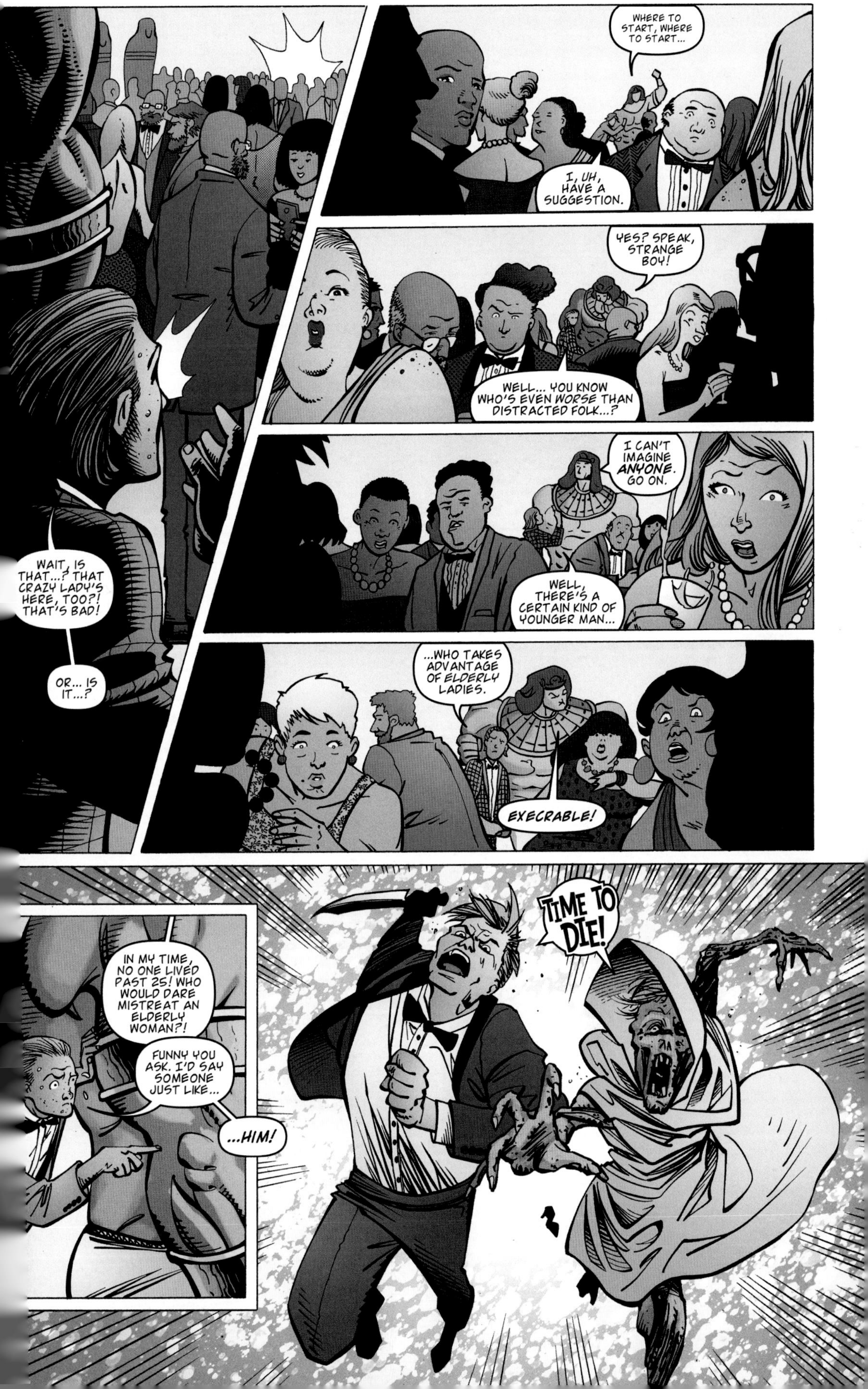

WHERE TO START, WHERE TO START...
I, UH, HAVE A SUGGESTION.
YES? SPEAK, STRANGE BOY!
WELL... YOU KNOW WHO'S EVEN WORSE THAN DISTRACTED FOLK...?
I CAN'T IMAGINE ANYONE. GO ON.
WELL, THERE'S A CERTAIN KIND OF YOUNGER MAN...
...WHO TAKES ADVANTAGE OF ELDERLY LADIES.
EXECRABLE!
WAIT, IS THAT...? THAT CRAZY LADY'S HERE, TOO?! THAT'S BAD!
OR... IS IT...?
IN MY TIME, NO ONE LIVED PAST 25! WHO WOULD DARE MISTREAT AN ELDERLY WOMAN?!
FUNNY YOU ASK. I'D SAY SOMEONE JUST LIKE...
...HIM!
TIME TO DIE!

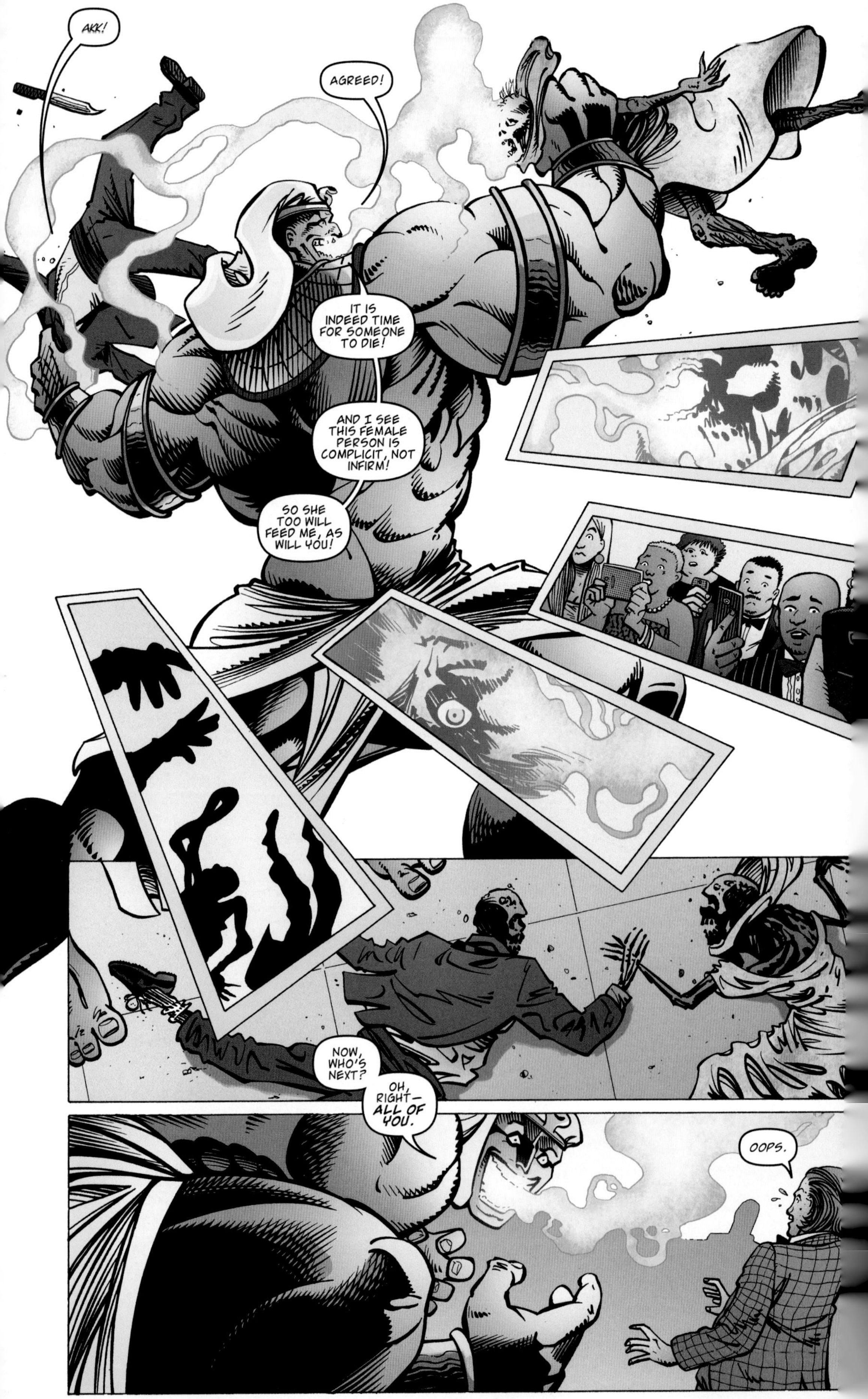
AKK!
AGREED!
IT IS INDEED TIME FOR SOMEONE TO DIE!
AND I SEE THIS FEMALE PERSON IS COMPLICIT, NOT INFIRM!
SO SHE TOO WILL FEED ME, AS WILL YOU!
NOW, WHO'S NEXT?
OH, RIGHT— ALL OF YOU.
OOPS.

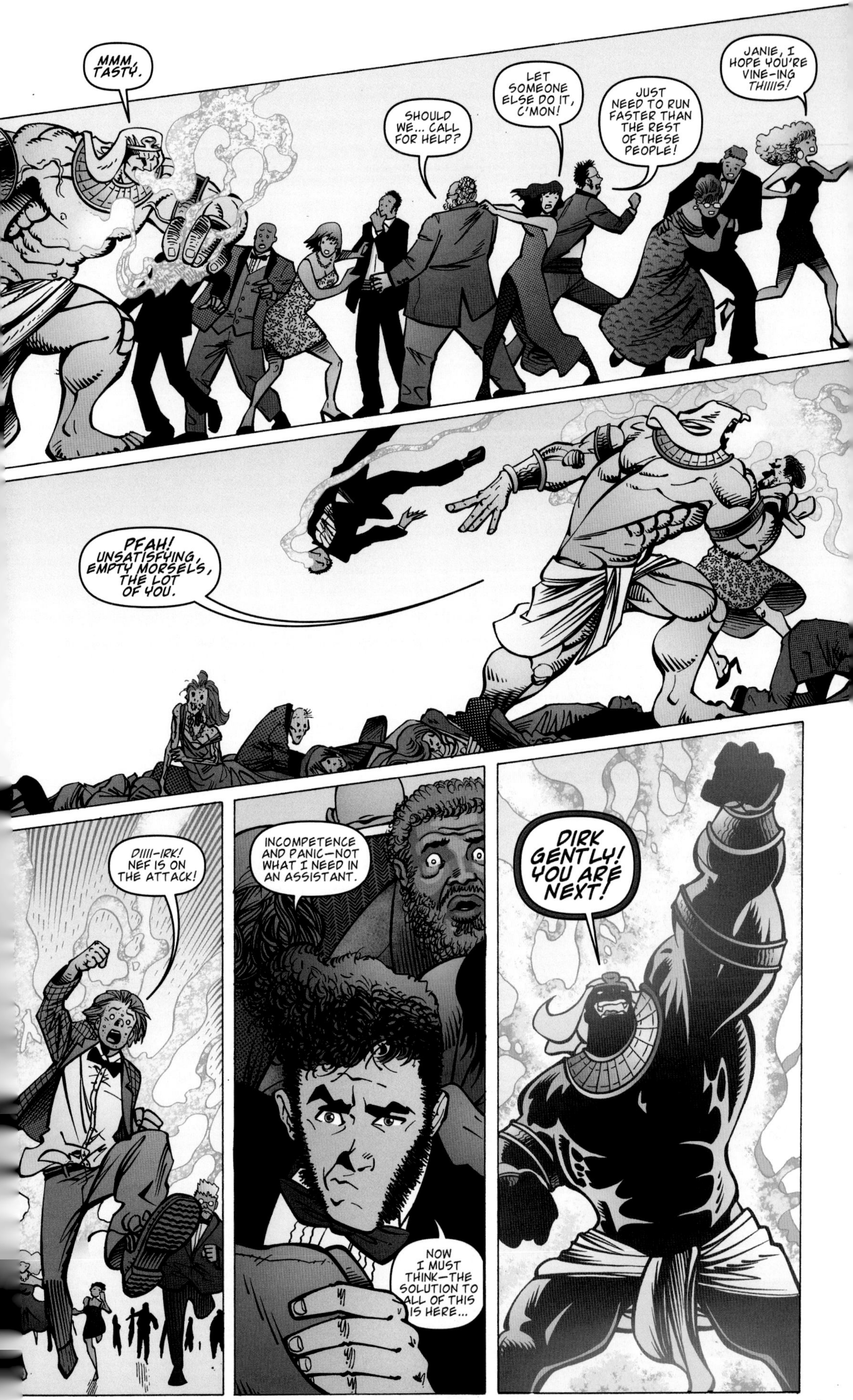
MMM, TASTY.
SHOULD WE... CALL FOR HELP?
LET SOMEONE ELSE DO IT, C'MON!
JUST NEED TO RUN FASTER THAN THE REST OF THESE PEOPLE!
JANIE, I HOPE YOU'RE VINE-ING THIIIIS!
PFAH! UNSATISFYING, EMPTY MORSELS, THE LOT OF YOU.
DIIII-IRK! NEF IS ON THE ATTACK!
INCOMPETENCE AND PANIC—NOT WHAT I NEED IN AN ASSISTANT.
NOW I MUST THINK—THE SOLUTION TO ALL OF THIS IS HERE...
DIRK GENTLY! YOU ARE NEXT!

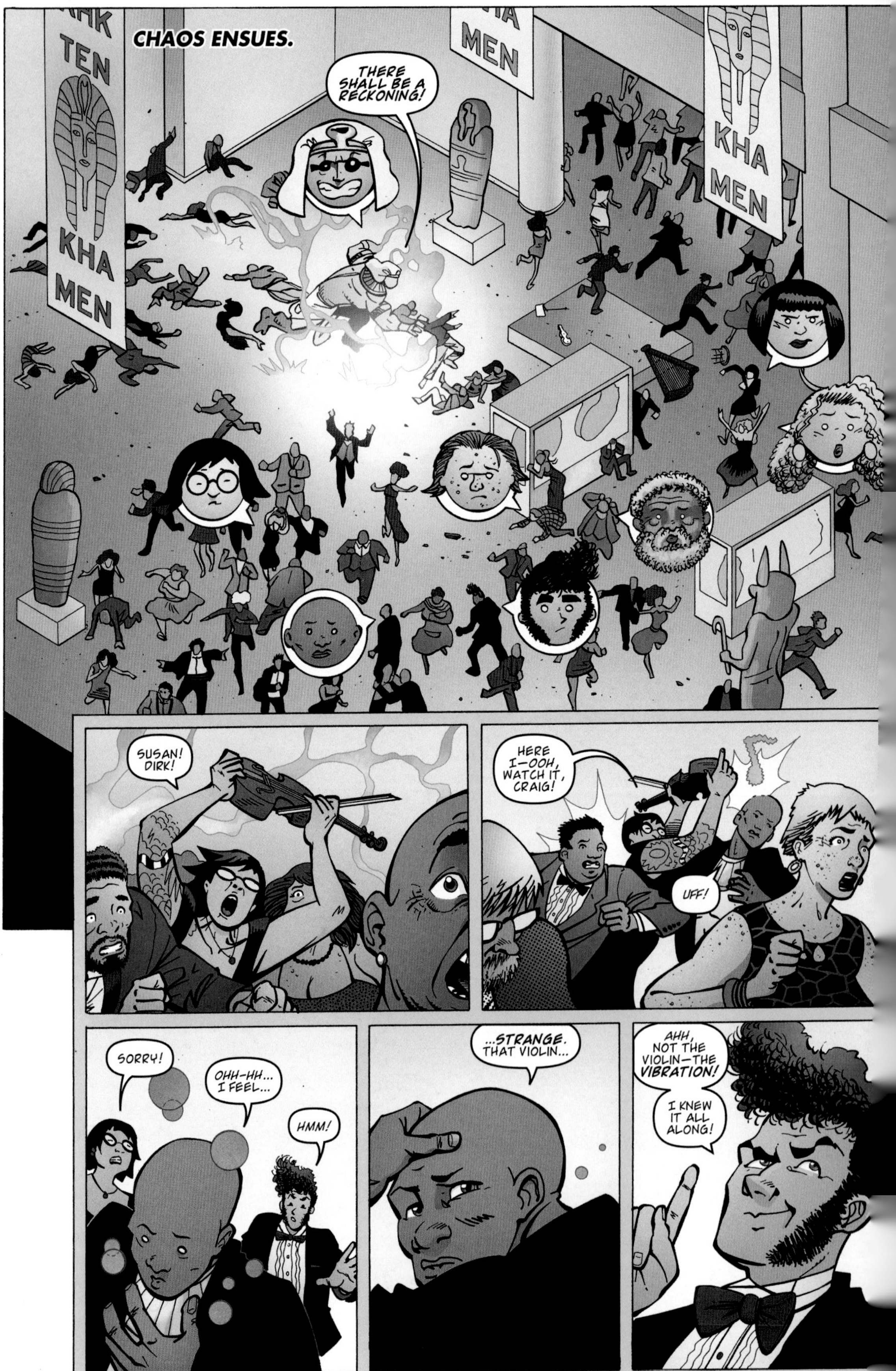
AHK TEN KHA MEN
CHAOS ENSUES.
THERE SHALL BE A RECKONING!
KHA MEN
KHA MEN
SUSAN! DIRK!
HERE I—OOH, WATCH IT, CRAIG!
UFF!
SORRY!
OHH-HH... I FEEL...
HMM!
...STRANGE. THAT VIOLIN...
AHH, NOT THE VIOLIN—THE VIBRATION!
I KNEW IT ALL ALONG!

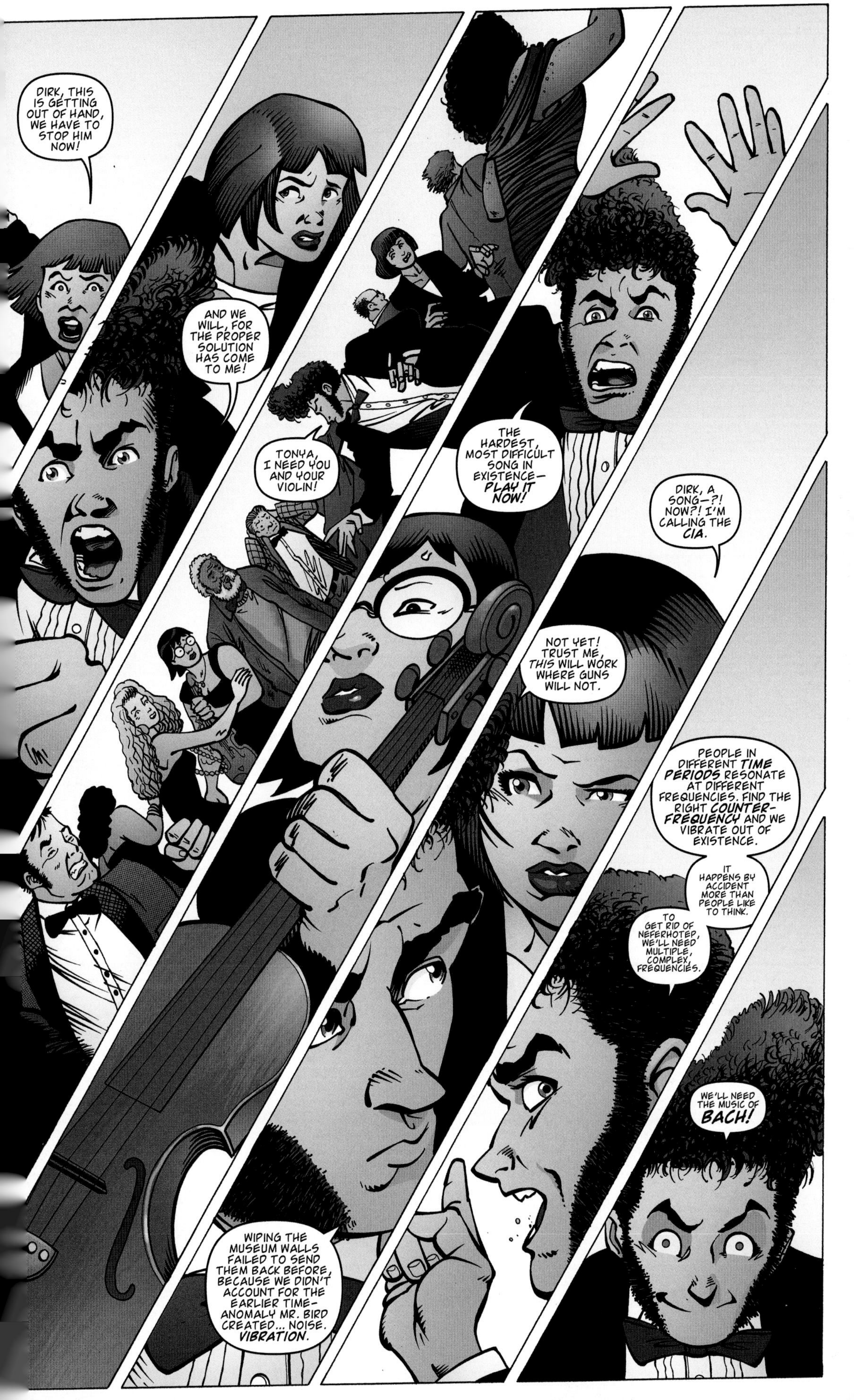

DIRK, THIS IS GETTING OUT OF HAND, WE HAVE TO STOP HIM NOW!
AND WE WILL, FOR THE PROPER SOLUTION HAS COME TO ME!
TONYA, I NEED YOU AND YOUR VIOLIN!
THE HARDEST, MOST DIFFICULT SONG IN EXISTENCE— PLAY IT NOW!
DIRK, A SONG—?! NOW?! I'M CALLING THE CIA.
NOT YET! TRUST ME, THIS WILL WORK WHERE GUNS WILL NOT.
PEOPLE IN DIFFERENT TIME PERIODS RESONATE AT DIFFERENT FREQUENCIES. FIND THE RIGHT COUNTER-FREQUENCY AND WE VIBRATE OUT OF EXISTENCE.
IT HAPPENS BY ACCIDENT MORE THAN PEOPLE LIKE TO THINK.
TO GET RID OF NEFERHOTEP, WE'LL NEED MULTIPLE, COMPLEX, FREQUENCIES.
WIPING THE MUSEUM WALLS FAILED TO SEND THEM BACK BEFORE, BECAUSE WE DIDN'T ACCOUNT FOR THE EARLIER TIME-ANOMALY MR. BIRD CREATED... NOISE. VIBRATION.
WE'LL NEED THE MUSIC OF BACH!

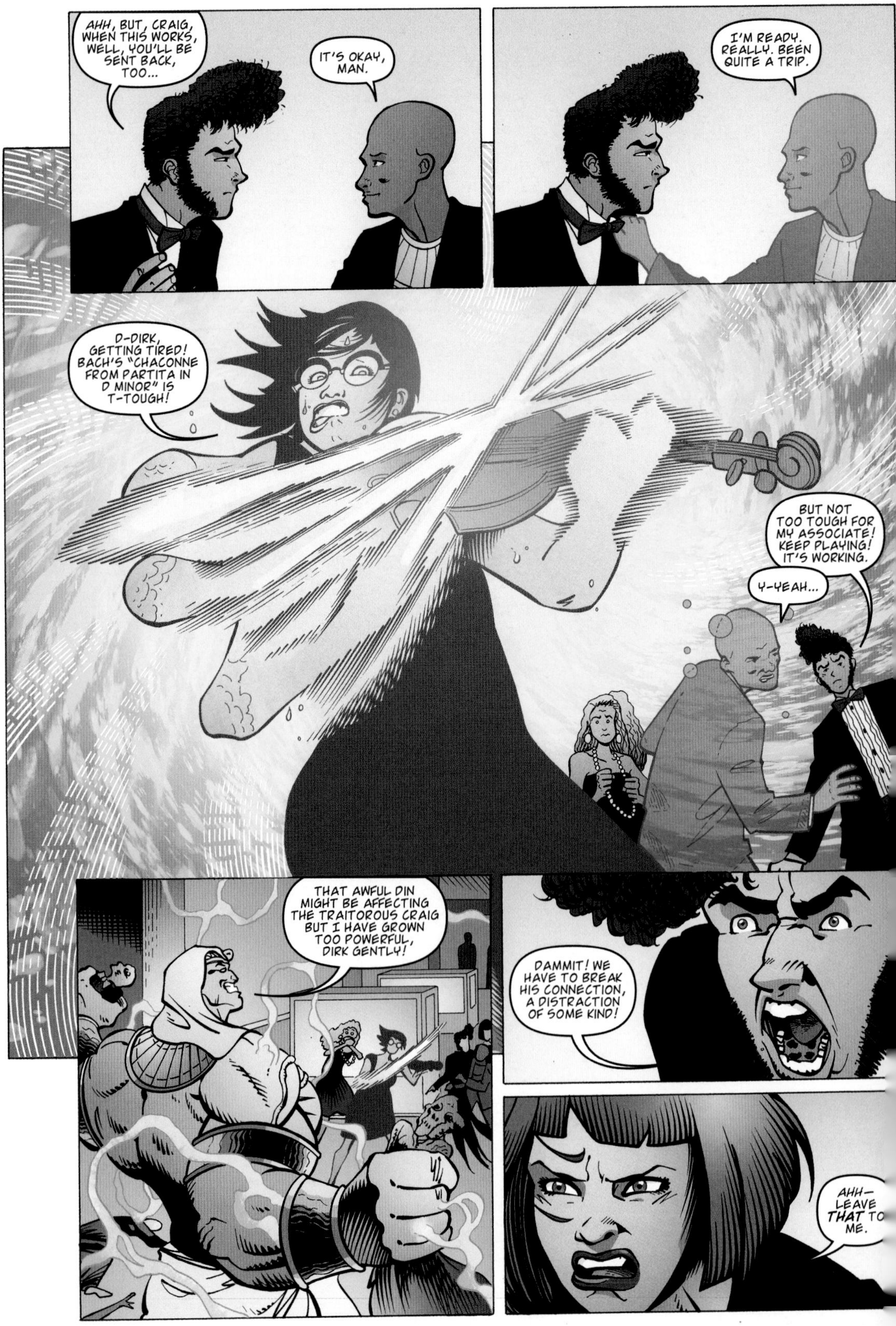
AHH, BUT, CRAIG, WHEN THIS WORKS, WELL, YOU'LL BE SENT BACK, TOO...
IT'S OKAY, MAN.
I'M READY. REALLY. BEEN QUITE A TRIP.
D-DIRK, GETTING TIRED! BACH'S "CHACONNE FROM PARTITA IN D MINOR" IS T-TOUGH!
BUT NOT TOO TOUGH FOR MY ASSOCIATE! KEEP PLAYING! IT'S WORKING.
Y-YEAH...
THAT AWFUL DIN MIGHT BE AFFECTING THE TRAITOROUS CRAIG BUT I HAVE GROWN TOO POWERFUL, DIRK GENTLY!
DAMMIT! WE HAVE TO BREAK HIS CONNECTION, A DISTRACTION OF SOME KIND!
AHH— LEAVE THAT TO ME.

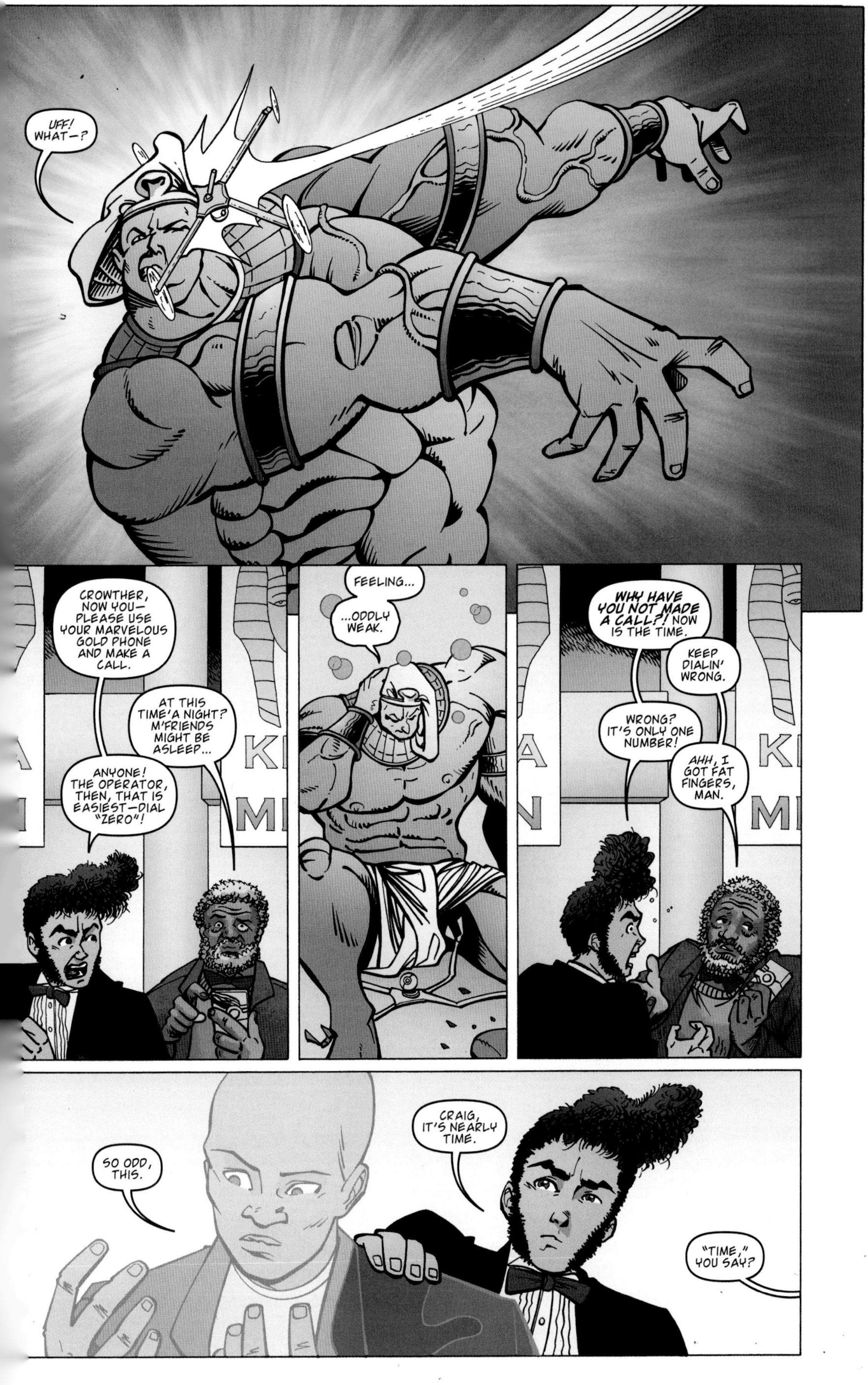

UFF! WHAT—?
CROWTHER, NOW YOU— PLEASE USE YOUR MARVELOUS GOLD PHONE AND MAKE A CALL.
AT THIS TIME'A NIGHT? M'FRIENDS MIGHT BE ASLEEP...
ANYONE! THE OPERATOR, THEN, THAT IS EASIEST—DIAL "ZERO"!
FEELING...
...ODDLY WEAK.
WHY HAVE YOU NOT MADE A CALL?! NOW IS THE TIME.
KEEP DIALIN' WRONG.
WRONG? IT'S ONLY ONE NUMBER!
AHH, I GOT FAT FINGERS, MAN.
SO ODD, THIS.
CRAIG, IT'S NEARLY TIME.
"TIME," YOU SAY?

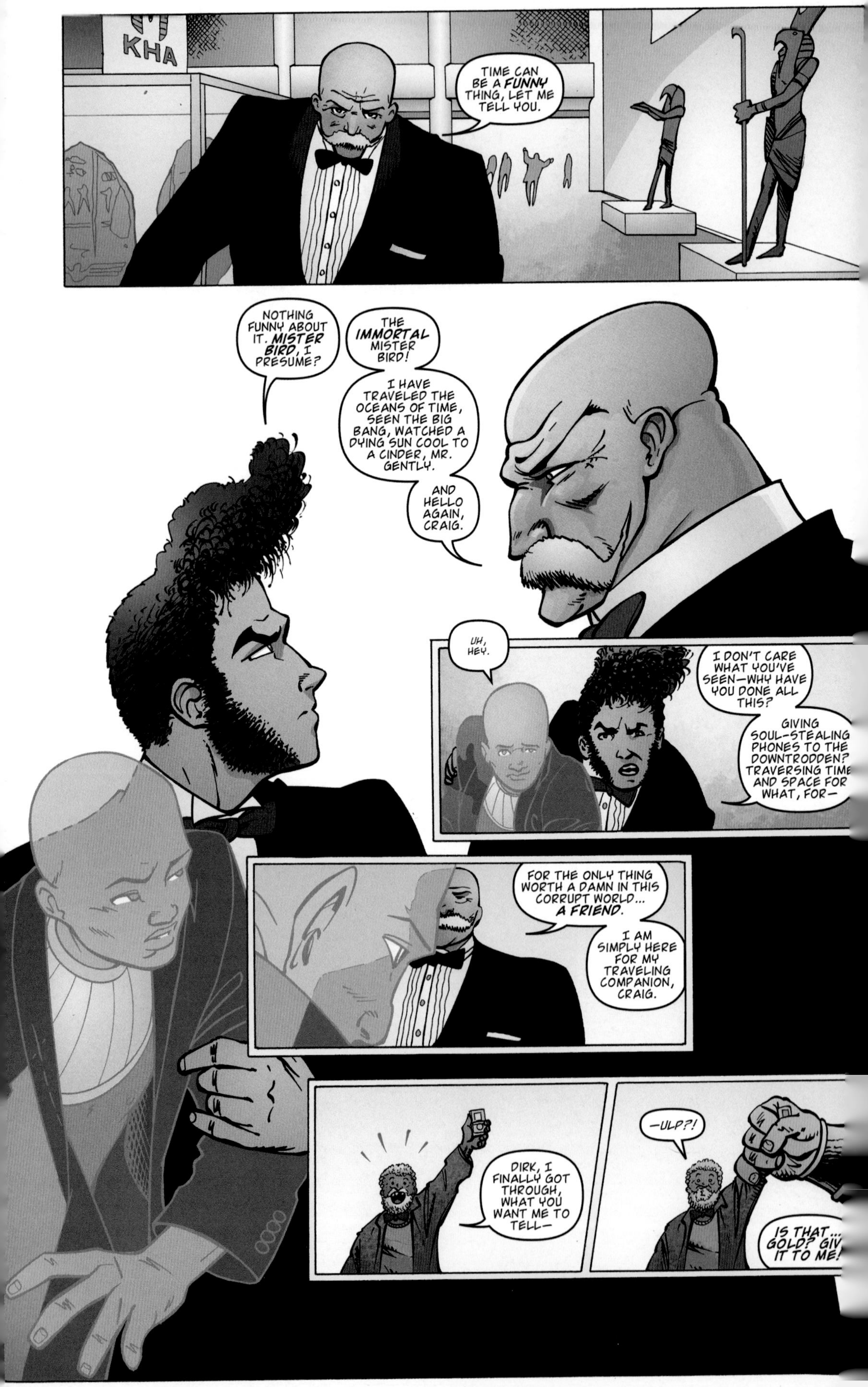
KHA
TIME CAN BE A FUNNY THING, LET ME TELL YOU.
NOTHING FUNNY ABOUT IT. MISTER BIRD, I PRESUME?
THE IMMORTAL MISTER BIRD!
I HAVE TRAVELED THE OCEANS OF TIME, SEEN THE BIG BANG, WATCHED A DYING SUN COOL TO A CINDER, MR. GENTLY.
AND HELLO AGAIN, CRAIG.
UH, HEY.
I DON'T CARE WHAT YOU'VE SEEN—WHY HAVE YOU DONE ALL THIS?
GIVING SOUL-STEALING PHONES TO THE DOWNTRODDEN? TRAVERSING TIME AND SPACE FOR WHAT, FOR—
FOR THE ONLY THING WORTH A DAMN IN THIS CORRUPT WORLD... A FRIEND.
I AM SIMPLY HERE FOR MY TRAVELING COMPANION, CRAIG.
DIRK, I FINALLY GOT THROUGH, WHAT YOU WANT ME TO TELL—
—ULP?!

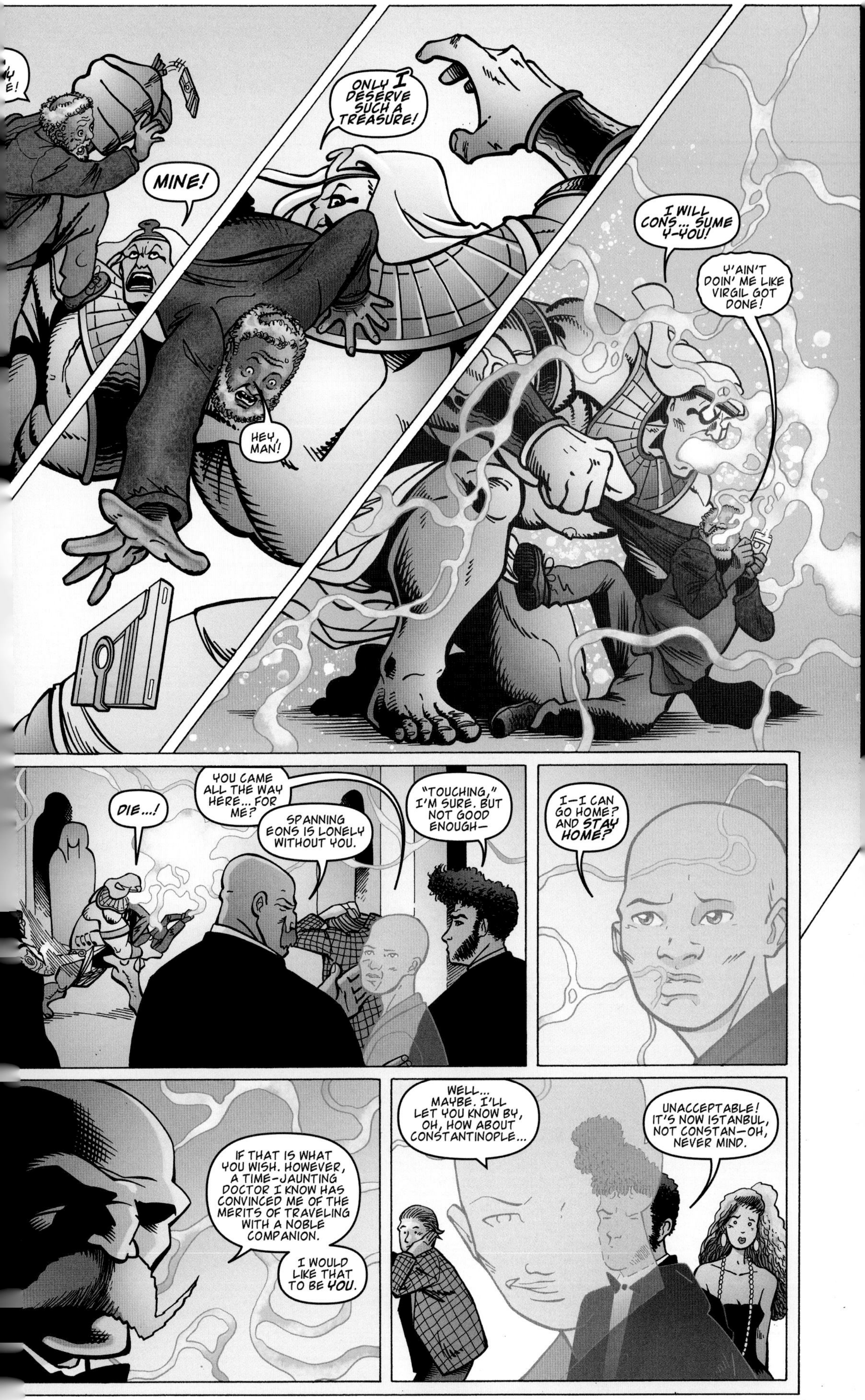
MINE!
ONLY I DESERVE SUCH A TREASURE!
HEY, MAN!
I WILL CONS... SUME Y-YOU!
Y'AIN'T DOIN' ME LIKE VIRGIL GOT DONE!
DIE...!
YOU CAME ALL THE WAY HERE... FOR ME?
SPANNING EONS IS LONELY WITHOUT YOU.
"TOUCHING," I'M SURE. BUT NOT GOOD ENOUGH—
I—I CAN GO HOME? AND **STAY HOME?**
IF THAT IS WHAT YOU WISH. HOWEVER, A TIME-JAUNTING DOCTOR I KNOW HAS CONVINCED ME OF THE MERITS OF TRAVELING WITH A NOBLE COMPANION.
I WOULD LIKE THAT TO BE **YOU**.
WELL... MAYBE. I'LL LET YOU KNOW BY, OH, HOW ABOUT CONSTANTINOPLE...
UNACCEPTABLE! IT'S NOW ISTANBUL, NOT CONSTAN—OH, NEVER MIND.

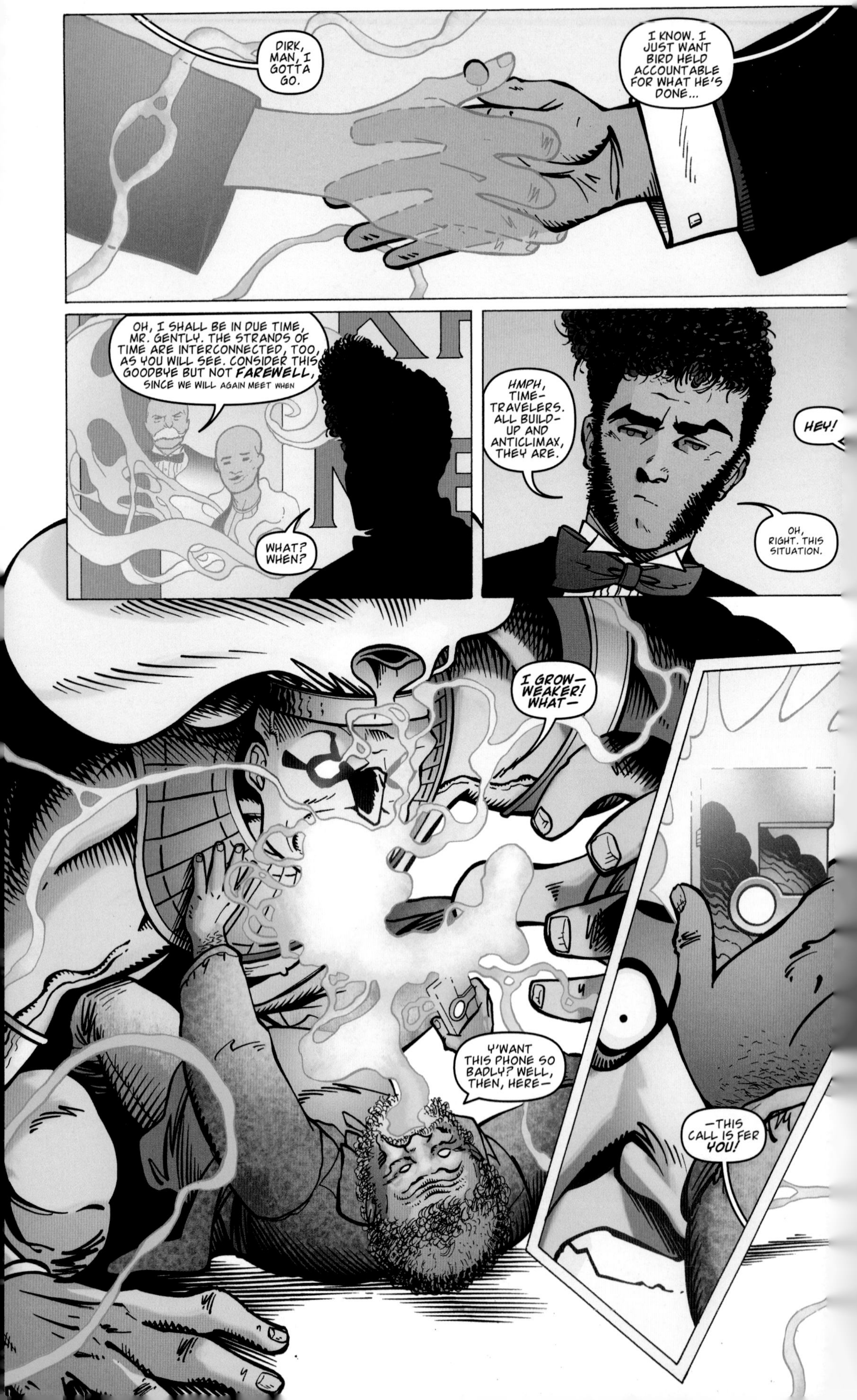
DIRK, MAN, I GOTTA GO.
I KNOW. I JUST WANT BIRD HELD ACCOUNTABLE FOR WHAT HE'S DONE...
OH, I SHALL BE IN DUE TIME, MR. GENTLY. THE STRANDS OF TIME ARE INTERCONNECTED, TOO, AS YOU WILL SEE. CONSIDER THIS GOODBYE BUT NOT FAREWELL, SINCE WE WILL AGAIN MEET WHEN
WHAT? WHEN?
HMPH, TIME-TRAVELERS. ALL BUILD-UP AND ANTICLIMAX, THEY ARE.
HEY!
OH, RIGHT. THIS SITUATION.
I GROW— WEAKER! WHAT—
Y'WANT THIS PHONE SO BADLY? WELL, THEN, HERE—
—THIS CALL IS FER YOU!

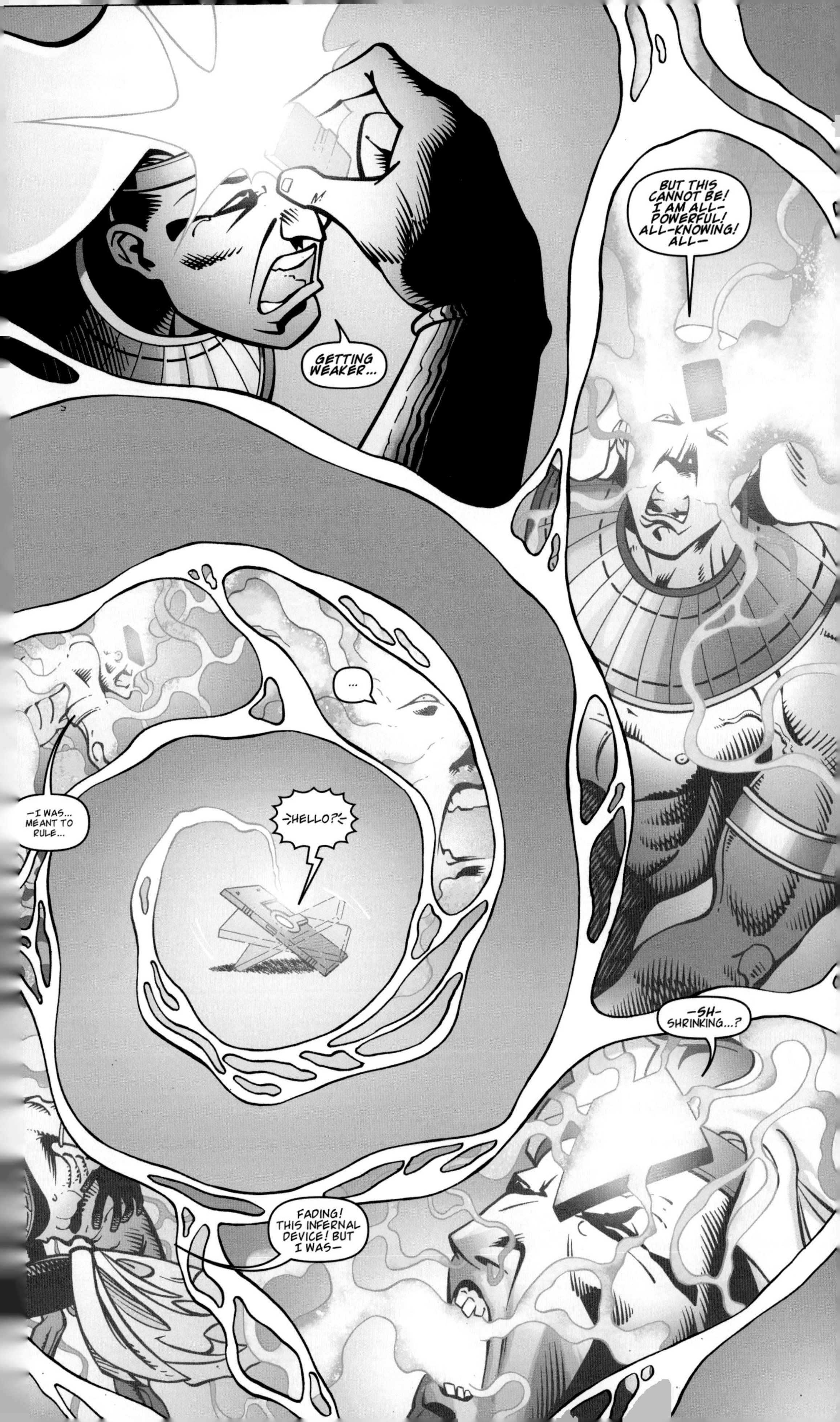
GETTING WEAKER...
BUT THIS CANNOT BE! I AM ALL-POWERFUL! ALL-KNOWING! ALL—
...
—I WAS... MEANT TO RULE...
—HELLO?—
—SH-SHRINKING...?
FADING! THIS INFERNAL DEVICE! BUT I WAS—

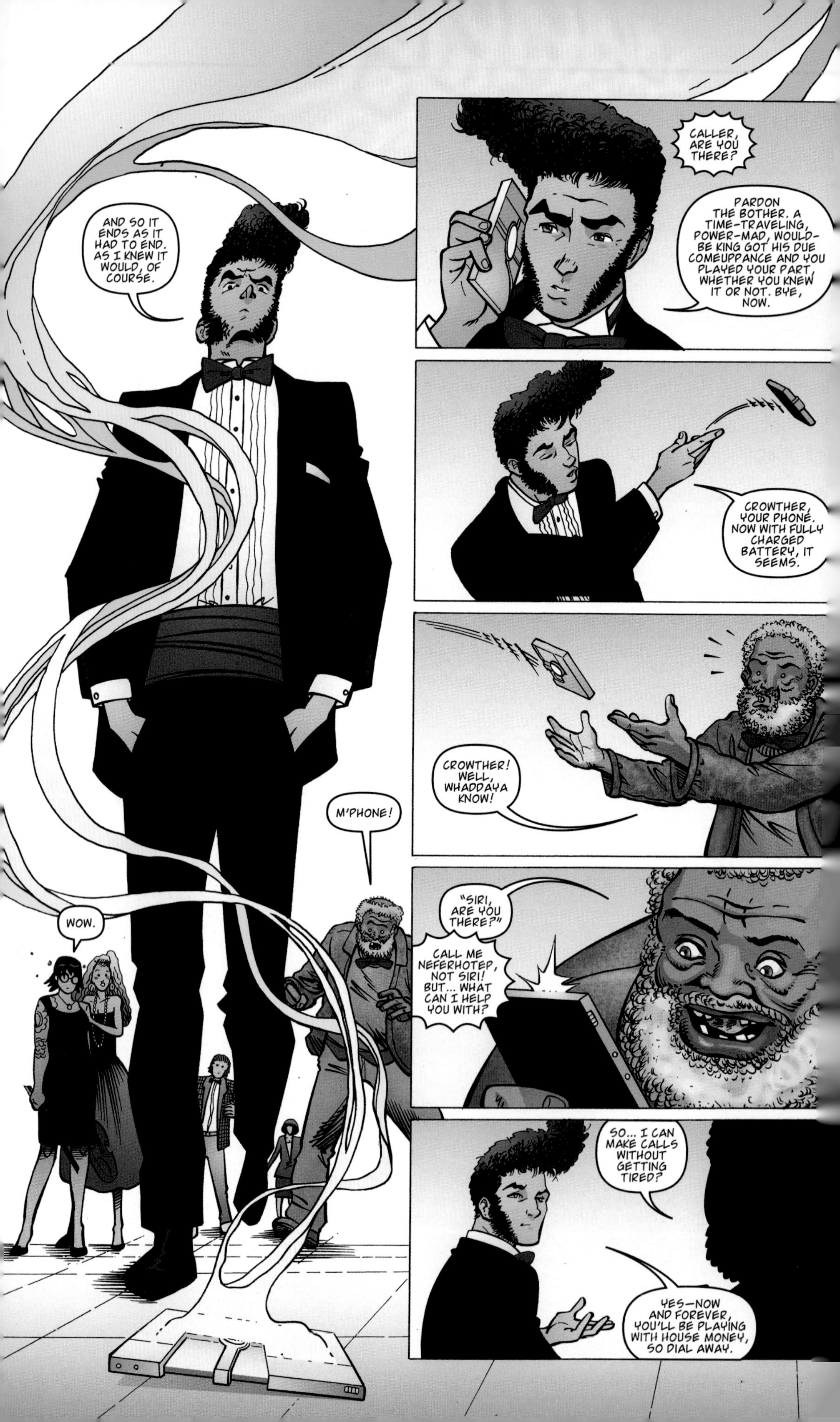
AND SO IT ENDS AS IT HAD TO END. AS I KNEW IT WOULD, OF COURSE.
CALLER, ARE YOU THERE?
PARDON THE BOTHER. A TIME-TRAVELING, POWER-MAD, WOULD-BE KING GOT HIS DUE COMEUPPANCE AND YOU PLAYED YOUR PART, WHETHER YOU KNEW IT OR NOT. BYE, NOW.
CROWTHER, YOUR PHONE. NOW WITH FULLY CHARGED BATTERY, IT SEEMS.
CROWTHER! WELL, WHADDAYA KNOW!
M'PHONE!
WOW.
"SIRI, ARE YOU THERE?"
CALL ME NEFERHOTEP, NOT SIRI! BUT... WHAT CAN I HELP YOU WITH?
SO... I CAN MAKE CALLS WITHOUT GETTING TIRED?
YES—NOW AND FOREVER, YOU'LL BE PLAYING WITH HOUSE MONEY, SO DIAL AWAY.

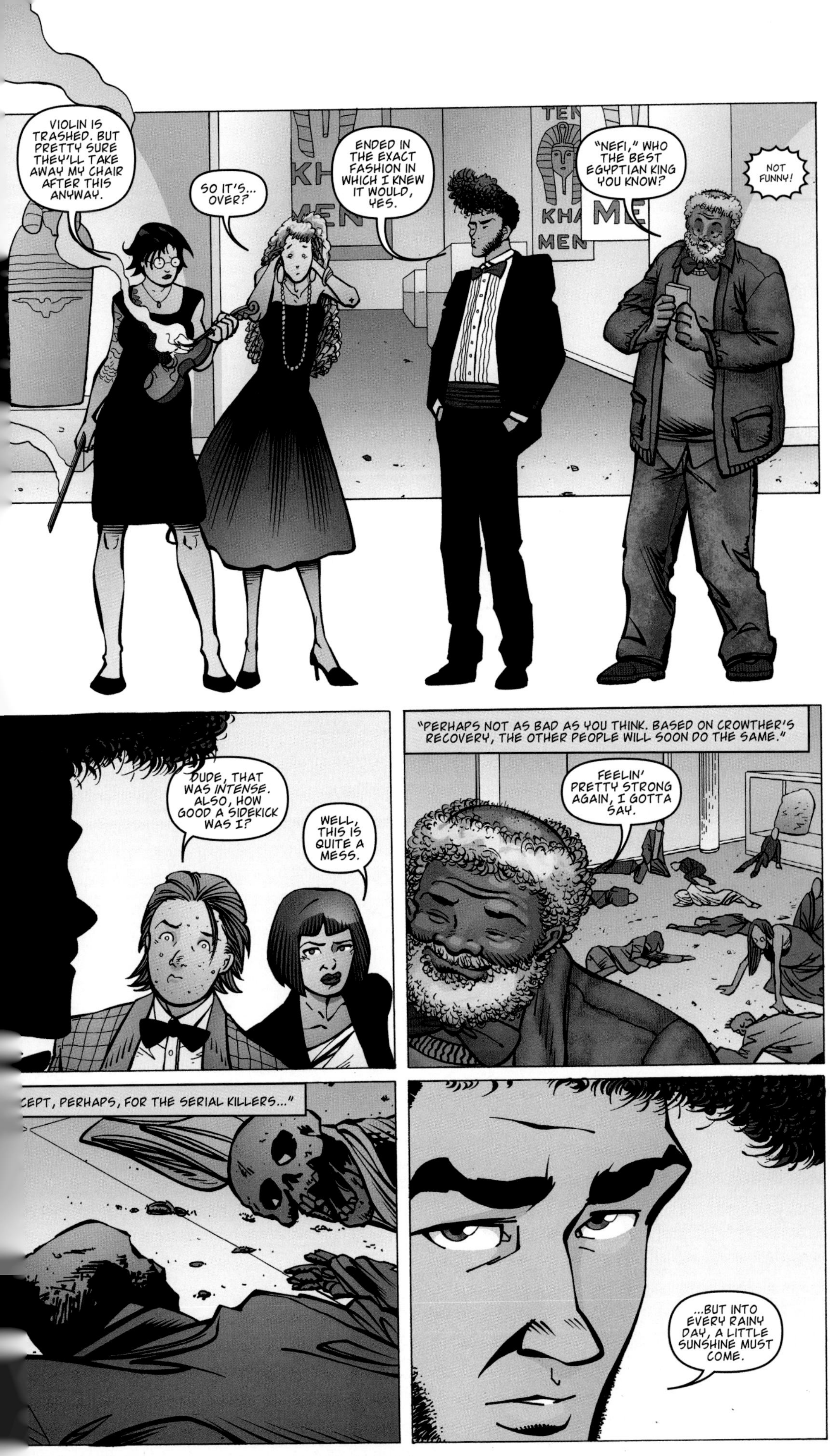
VIOLIN IS TRASHED. BUT PRETTY SURE THEY'LL TAKE AWAY MY CHAIR AFTER THIS ANYWAY.
SO IT'S... OVER?
ENDED IN THE EXACT FASHION IN WHICH I KNEW IT WOULD, YES.
"NEFI," WHO THE BEST EGYPTIAN KING YOU KNOW?
NOT FUNNY!
DUDE, THAT WAS INTENSE. ALSO, HOW GOOD A SIDEKICK WAS I?
WELL, THIS IS QUITE A MESS.
"PERHAPS NOT AS BAD AS YOU THINK. BASED ON CROWTHER'S RECOVERY, THE OTHER PEOPLE WILL SOON DO THE SAME."
FEELIN' PRETTY STRONG AGAIN, I GOTTA SAY.
CEPT, PERHAPS, FOR THE SERIAL KILLERS..."
...BUT INTO EVERY RAINY DAY, A LITTLE SUNSHINE MUST COME.

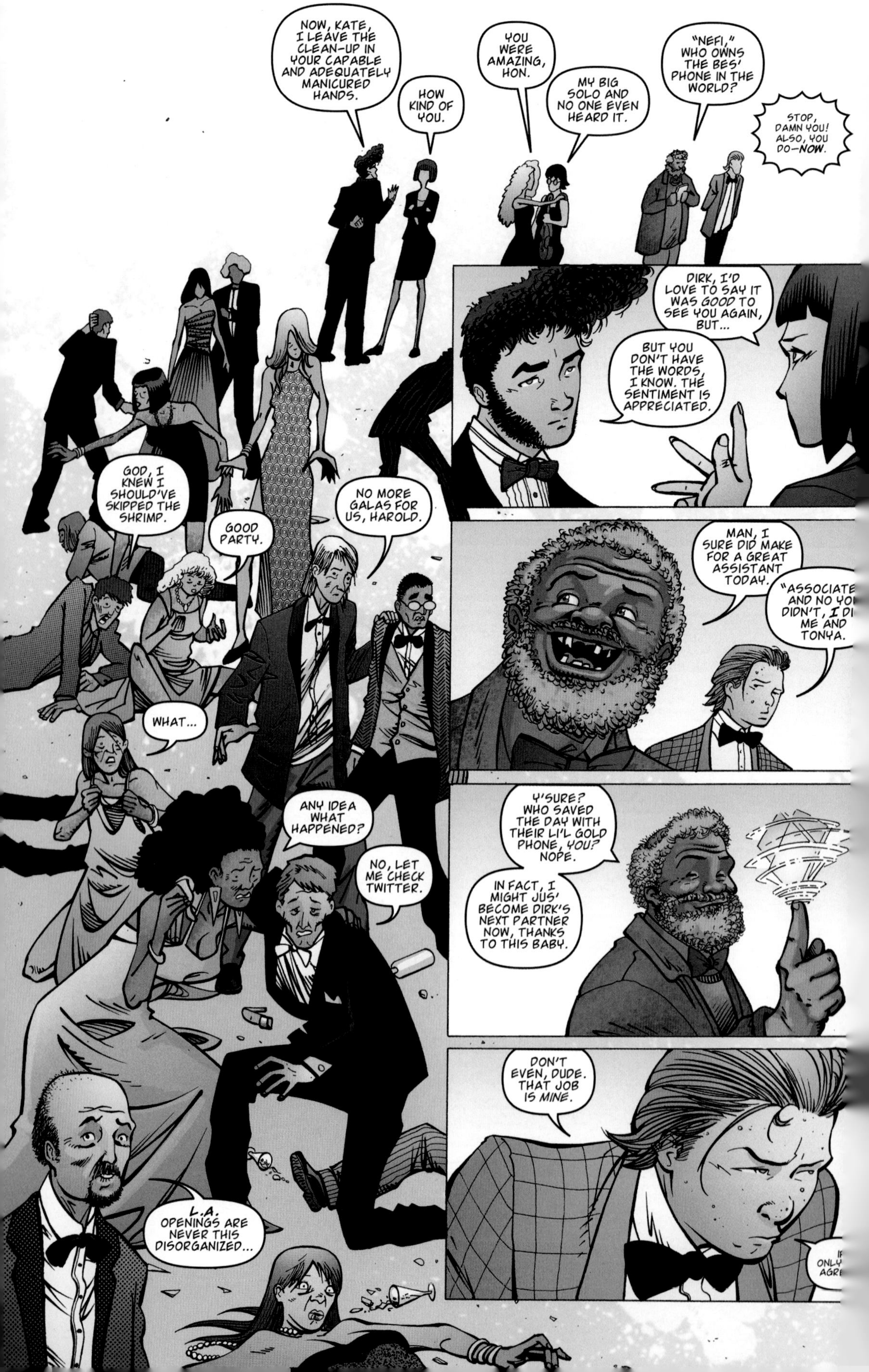
NOW, KATE, I LEAVE THE CLEAN-UP IN YOUR CAPABLE AND ADEQUATELY MANICURED HANDS.
HOW KIND OF YOU.
YOU WERE AMAZING, HON.
MY BIG SOLO AND NO ONE EVEN HEARD IT.
"NEFI," WHO OWNS THE BES' PHONE IN THE WORLD?
STOP, DAMN YOU! ALSO, YOU DO—NOW.
GOD, I KNEW I SHOULD'VE SKIPPED THE SHRIMP.
GOOD PARTY.
NO MORE GALAS FOR US, HAROLD.
WHAT...
ANY IDEA WHAT HAPPENED?
NO, LET ME CHECK TWITTER.
L.A. OPENINGS ARE NEVER THIS DISORGANIZED...
DIRK, I'D LOVE TO SAY IT WAS GOOD TO SEE YOU AGAIN, BUT...
BUT YOU DON'T HAVE THE WORDS, I KNOW. THE SENTIMENT IS APPRECIATED.
MAN, I SURE DID MAKE FOR A GREAT ASSISTANT TODAY.
"ASSOCIATE AND NO YO DIDN'T, I DI ME AND TONYA.
Y'SURE? WHO SAVED THE DAY WITH THEIR LI'L GOLD PHONE, YOU? NOPE.
IN FACT, I MIGHT JUS' BECOME DIRK'S NEXT PARTNER NOW, THANKS TO THIS BABY.
DON'T EVEN, DUDE. THAT JOB IS MINE.
IF ONLY AGRE

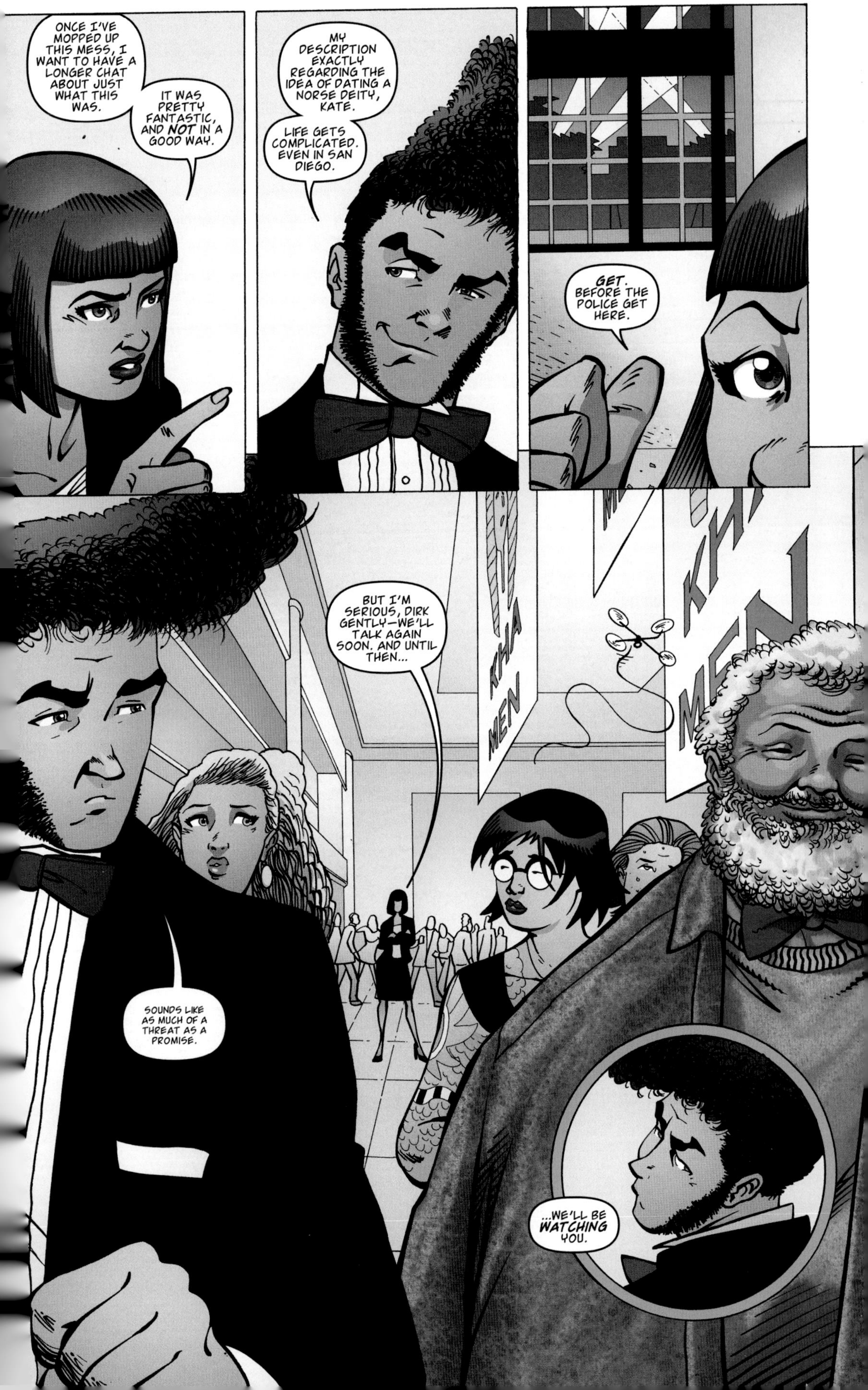
ONCE I'VE MOPPED UP THIS MESS, I WANT TO HAVE A LONGER CHAT ABOUT JUST WHAT THIS WAS.
IT WAS PRETTY FANTASTIC, AND NOT IN A GOOD WAY.
MY DESCRIPTION EXACTLY REGARDING THE IDEA OF DATING A NORSE DEITY, KATE.
LIFE GETS COMPLICATED. EVEN IN SAN DIEGO.
GET. BEFORE THE POLICE GET HERE.
KHA MEN
BUT I'M SERIOUS, DIRK GENTLY—WE'LL TALK AGAIN SOON. AND UNTIL THEN...
SOUNDS LIKE AS MUCH OF A THREAT AS A PROMISE.
...WE'LL BE WATCHING YOU.

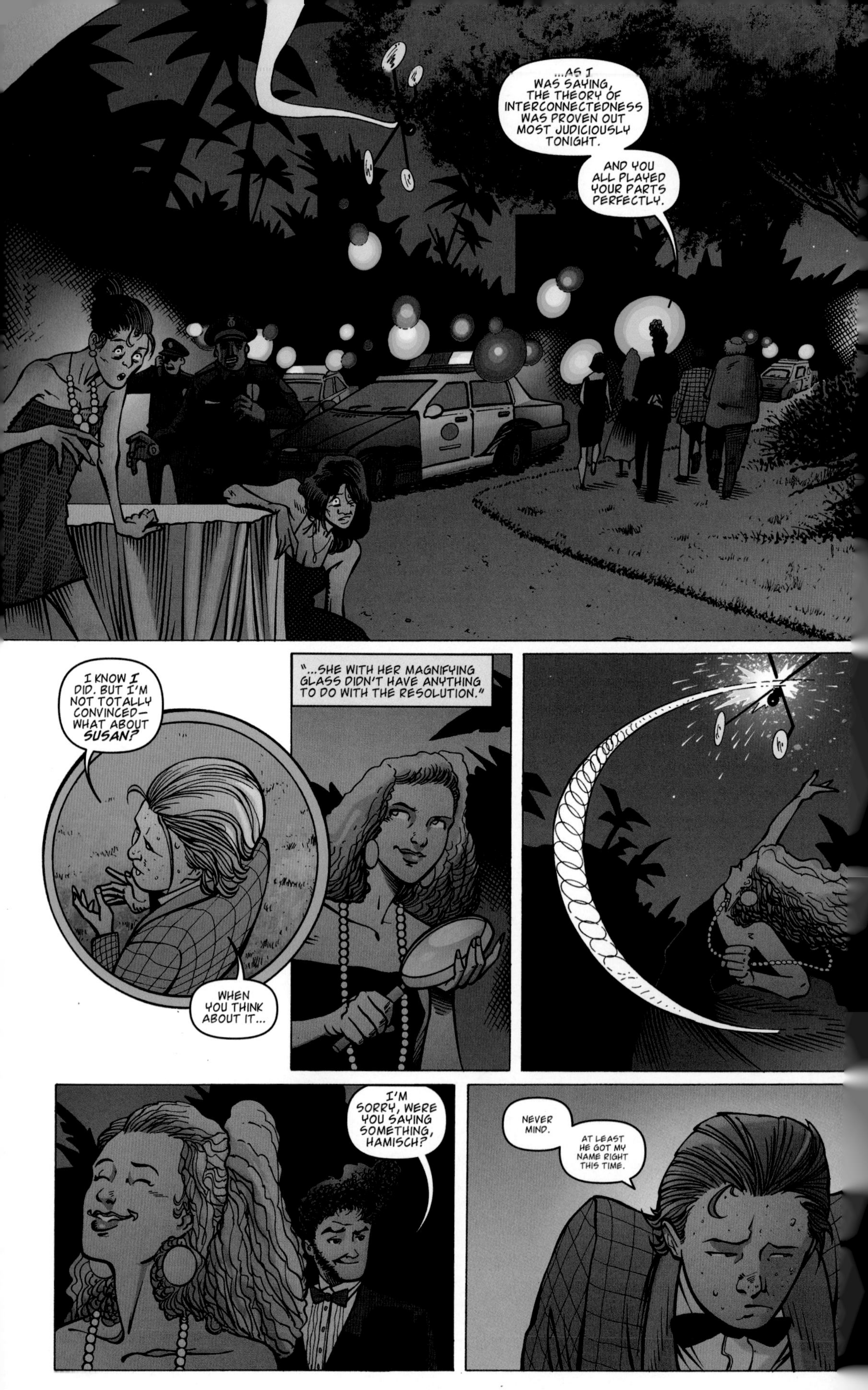
...AS I WAS SAYING, THE THEORY OF INTERCONNECTEDNESS WAS PROVEN OUT MOST JUDICIOUSLY TONIGHT.
AND YOU ALL PLAYED YOUR PARTS PERFECTLY.
I KNOW I DID. BUT I'M NOT TOTALLY CONVINCED— WHAT ABOUT SUSAN?
WHEN YOU THINK ABOUT IT...
"...SHE WITH HER MAGNIFYING GLASS DIDN'T HAVE ANYTHING TO DO WITH THE RESOLUTION."
I'M SORRY, WERE YOU SAYING SOMETHING, HAMISCH?
NEVER MIND.
AT LEAST HE GOT MY NAME RIGHT THIS TIME.

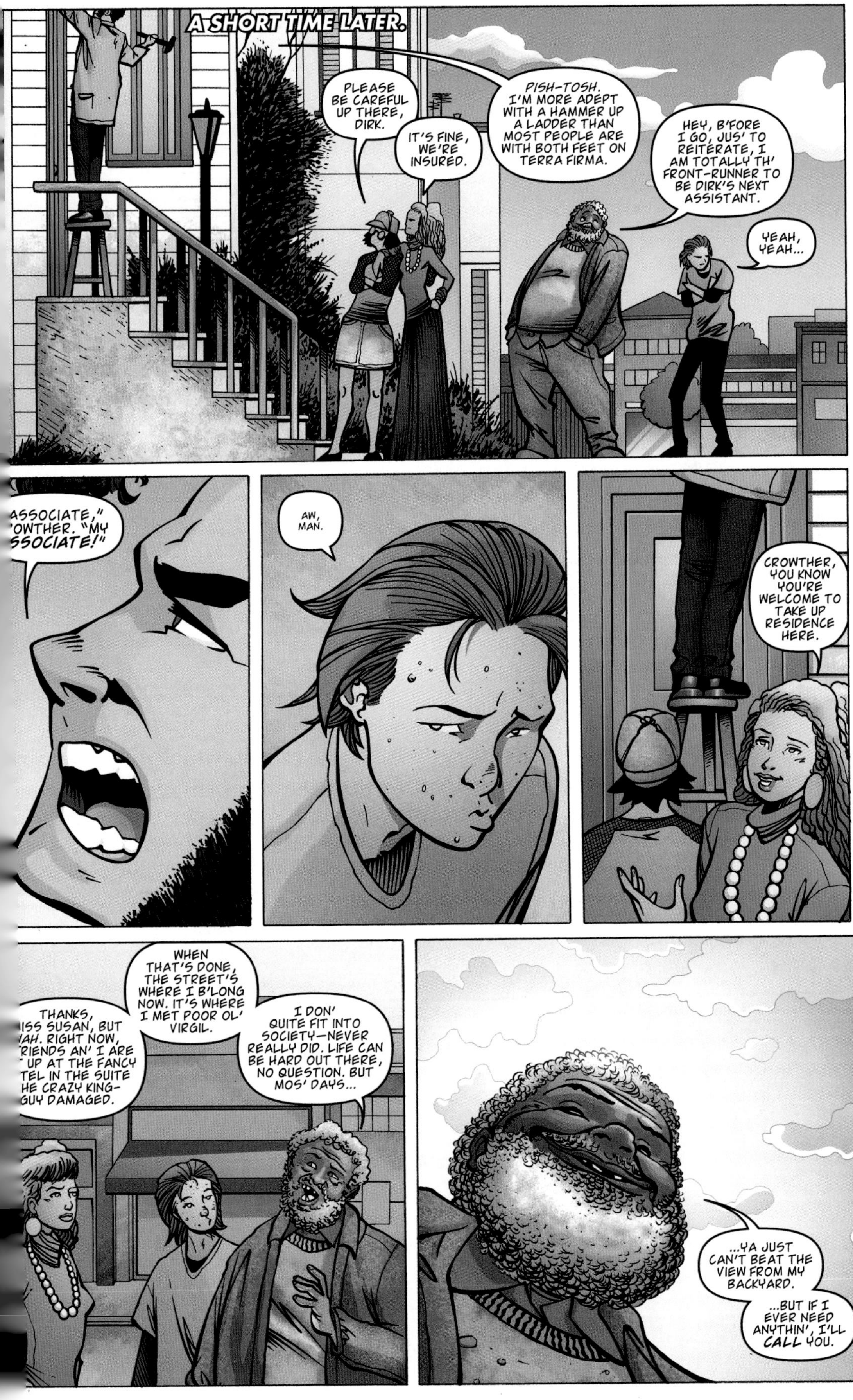
A SHORT TIME LATER.
PLEASE BE CAREFUL UP THERE, DIRK.
IT'S FINE, WE'RE INSURED.
PISH-TOSH. I'M MORE ADEPT WITH A HAMMER UP A LADDER THAN MOST PEOPLE ARE WITH BOTH FEET ON TERRA FIRMA.
HEY, B'FORE I GO, JUS' TO REITERATE, I AM TOTALLY TH' FRONT-RUNNER TO BE DIRK'S NEXT ASSISTANT.
YEAH, YEAH...
ASSOCIATE," OWTHER. "MY SSOCIATE!"
AW, MAN.
CROWTHER, YOU KNOW YOU'RE WELCOME TO TAKE UP RESIDENCE HERE.
THANKS, ISS SUSAN, BUT AH. RIGHT NOW, RIENDS AN' I ARE UP AT THE FANCY TEL IN THE SUITE HE CRAZY KING-GUY DAMAGED.
WHEN THAT'S DONE, THE STREET'S WHERE I B'LONG NOW. IT'S WHERE I MET POOR OL' VIRGIL.
I DON' QUITE FIT INTO SOCIETY—NEVER REALLY DID. LIFE CAN BE HARD OUT THERE, NO QUESTION. BUT MOS' DAYS...
...YA JUST CAN'T BEAT THE VIEW FROM MY BACKYARD.
...BUT IF I EVER NEED ANYTHIN', I'LL CALL YOU.

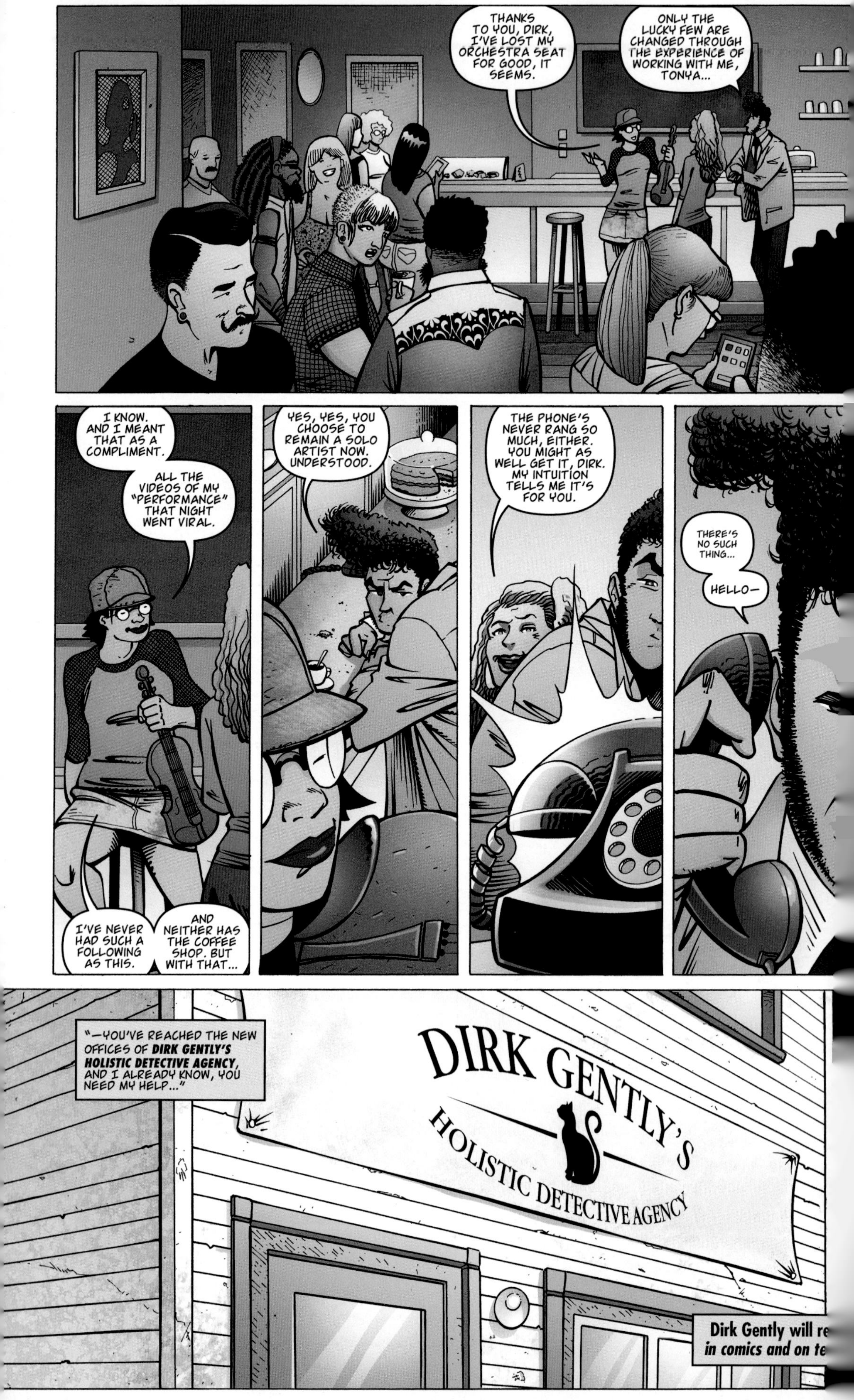
THANKS TO YOU, DIRK, I'VE LOST MY ORCHESTRA SEAT FOR GOOD, IT SEEMS.
ONLY THE LUCKY FEW ARE CHANGED THROUGH THE EXPERIENCE OF WORKING WITH ME, TONYA...
I KNOW. AND I MEANT THAT AS A COMPLIMENT.
ALL THE VIDEOS OF MY "PERFORMANCE" THAT NIGHT WENT VIRAL.
I'VE NEVER HAD SUCH A FOLLOWING AS THIS.
AND NEITHER HAS THE COFFEE SHOP. BUT WITH THAT...
YES, YES, YOU CHOOSE TO REMAIN A SOLO ARTIST NOW. UNDERSTOOD.
THE PHONE'S NEVER RANG SO MUCH, EITHER. YOU MIGHT AS WELL GET IT, DIRK. MY INTUITION TELLS ME IT'S FOR YOU.
THERE'S NO SUCH THING...
HELLO—
"—YOU'VE REACHED THE NEW OFFICES OF DIRK GENTLY'S HOLISTIC DETECTIVE AGENCY, AND I ALREADY KNOW, YOU NEED MY HELP..."
DIRK GENTLY'S
HOLISTIC DETECTIVE AGENCY
Dirk Gently will re
in comics and on te

COVER GALLERY

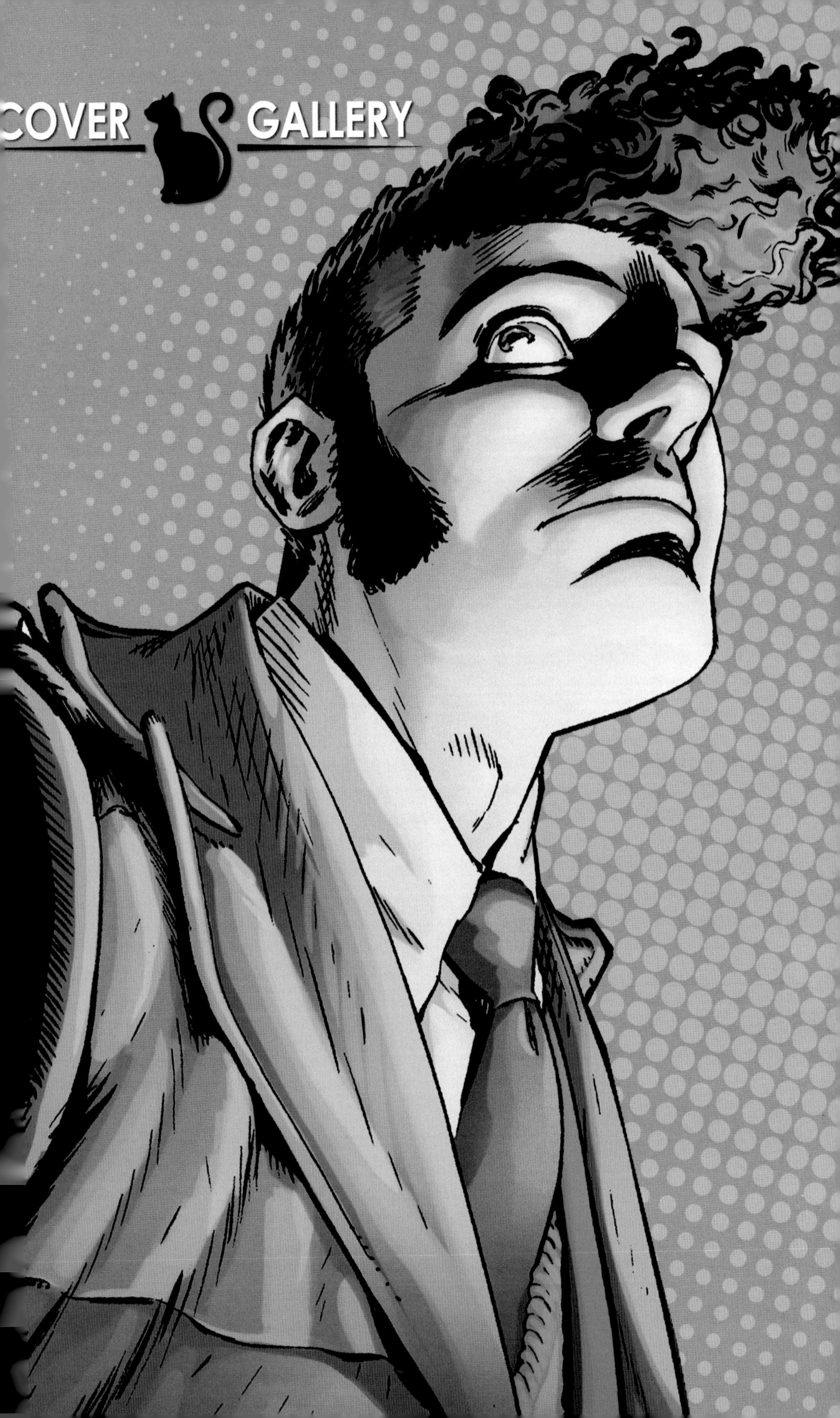

Cover Art by **ROB GUILLORY**

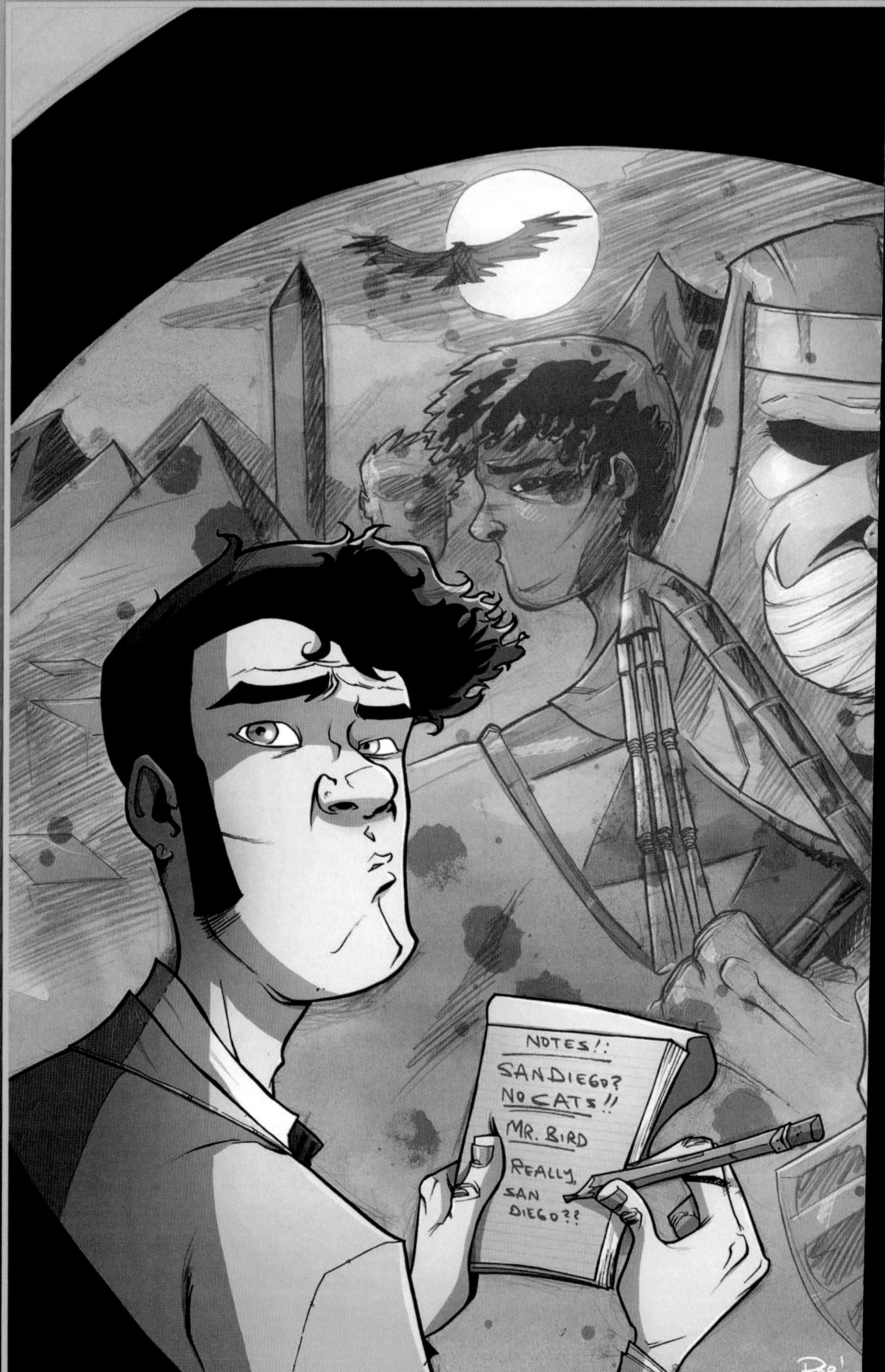
NOTES!:
SAN DIEGO?
NO CATS!!
MR. BIRD
REALLY, SAN DIEGO??
ROB!

Cover Art by **ROB GUILLORY**

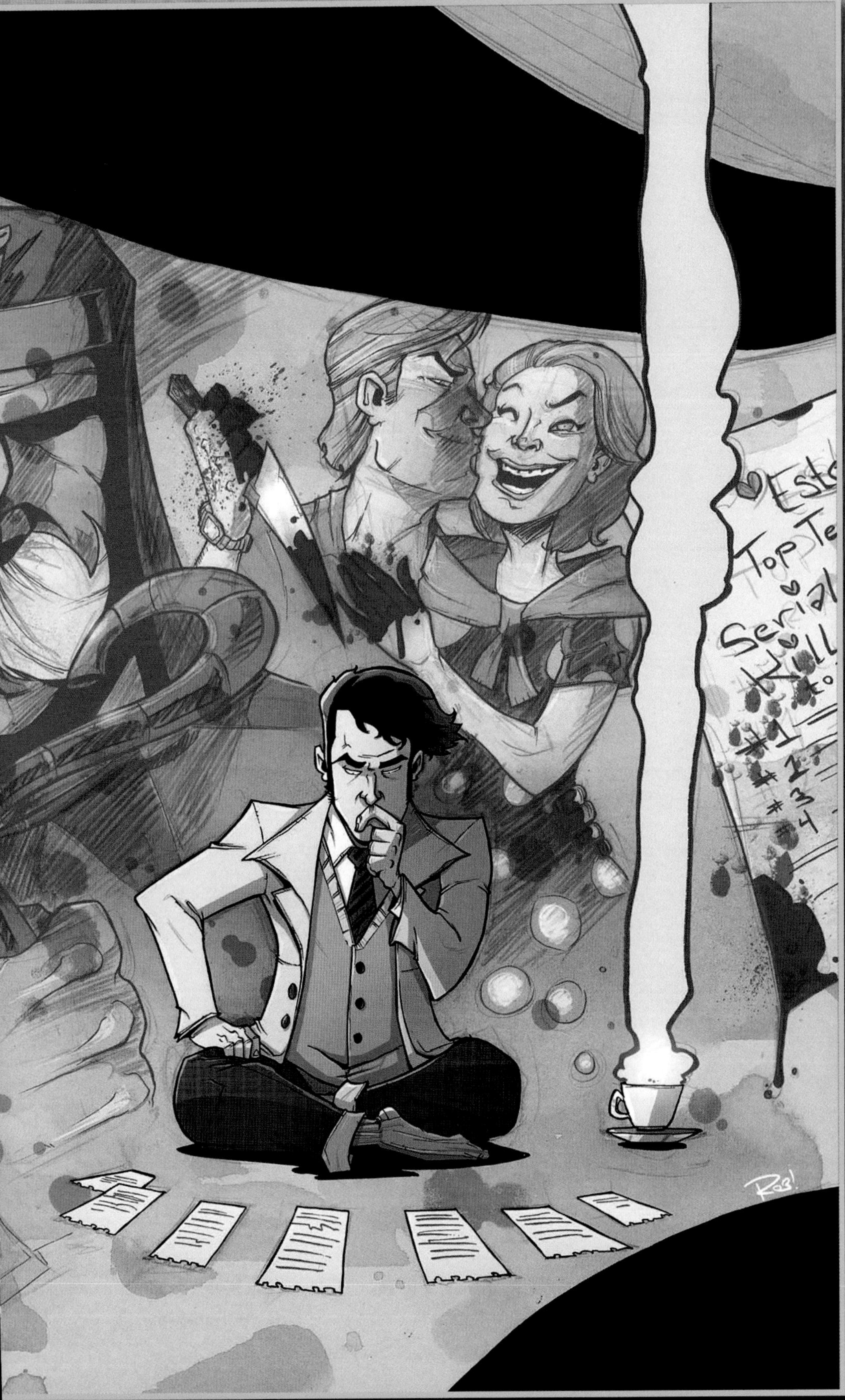

Cover Art by **ROB GUILLORY**

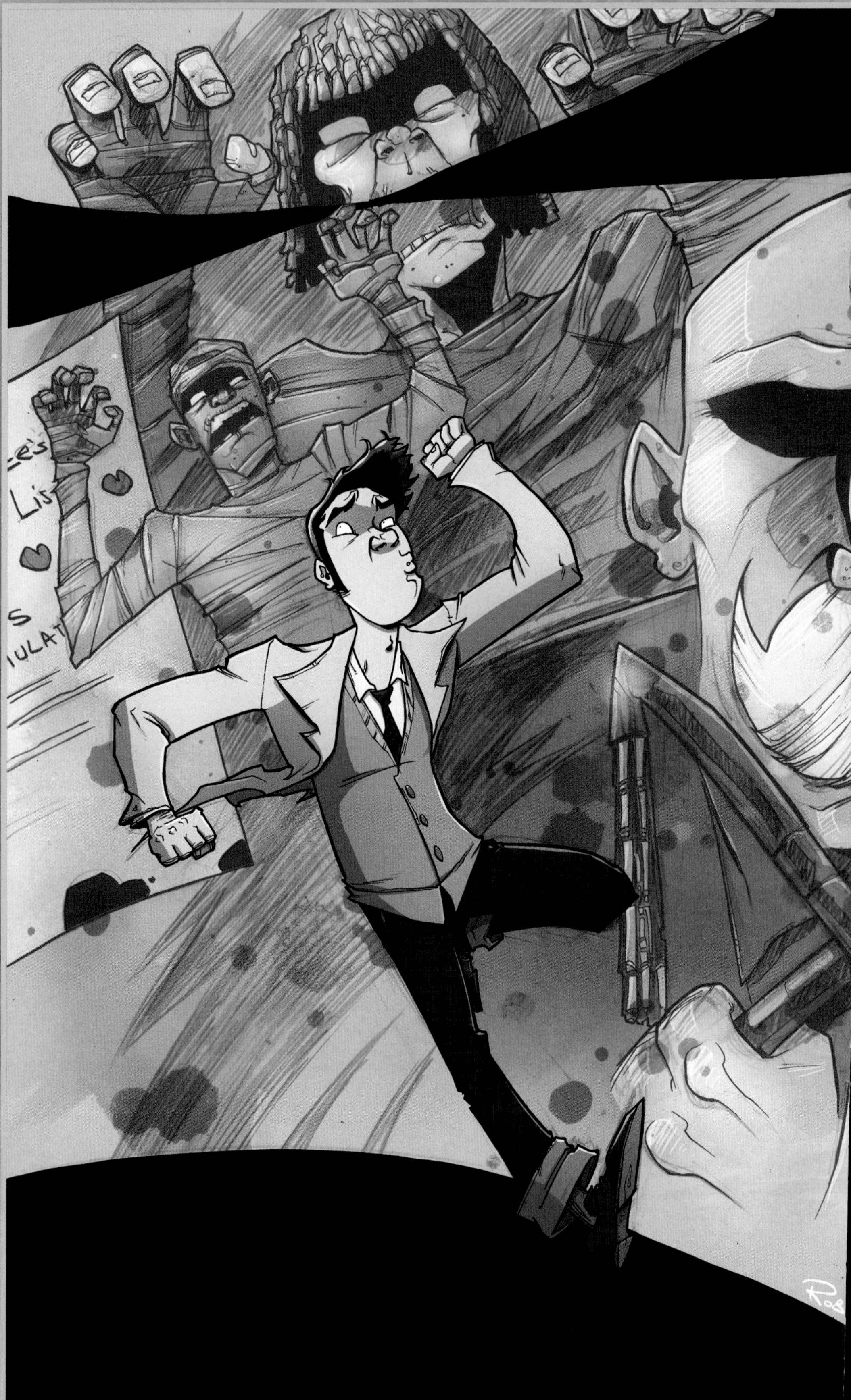

Rob

Cover Art by **ROB GUILLORY**

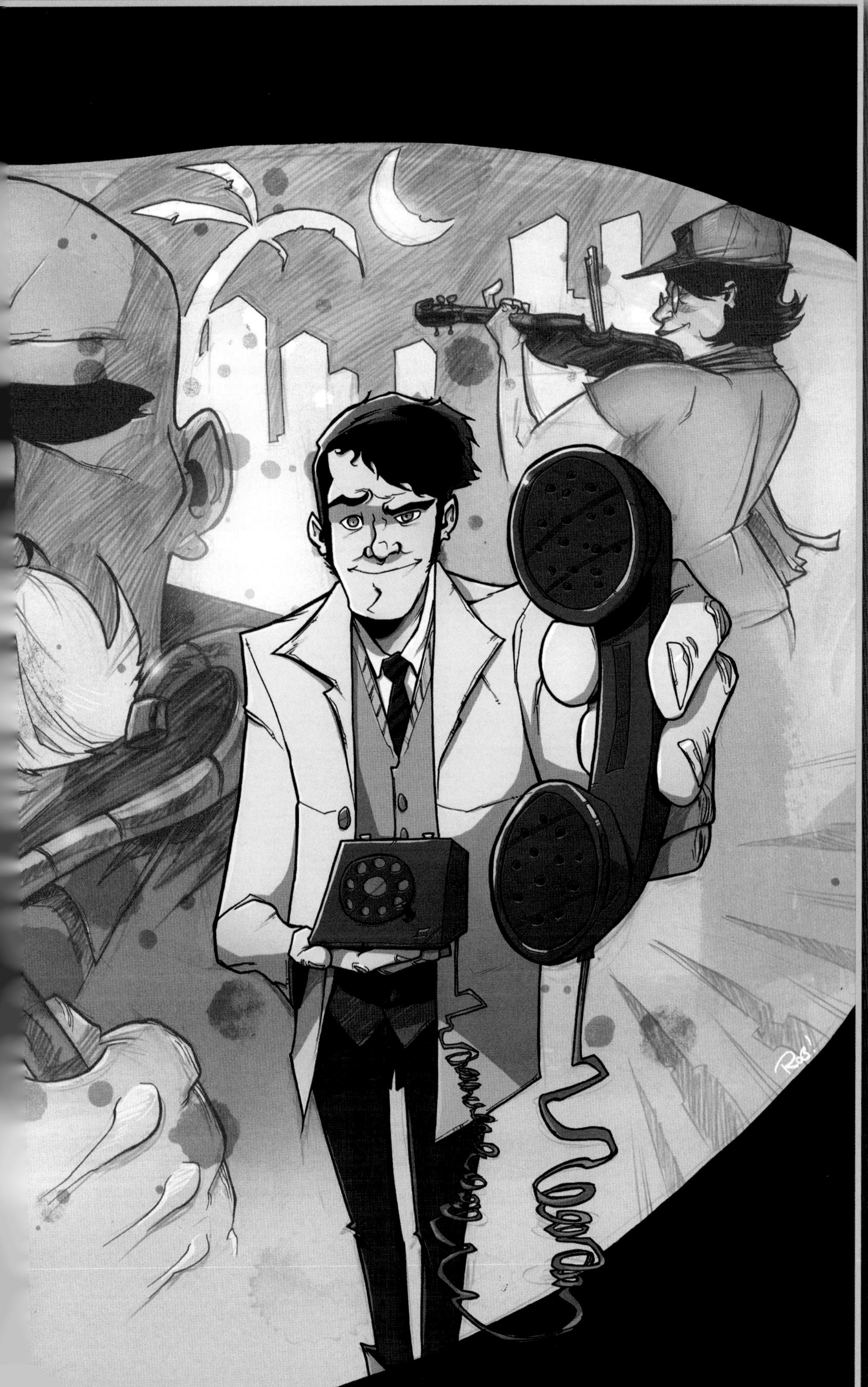
ROB!

Cover Art by **ROBERT HACK**   Colors by **STEPHEN DOWNER**

~A DOUGLAS ADAMS PUBLICATION~

HOLISTIC DETECTIVE

IDW
ISSUE No1

MYSTERY MAGAZINE

DIRK GENTLY

A SPOON TOO SHORT

by DAVID KYRIAZIS · KIRCHOFF

VARIANT EDITION
$3.99

AMBULANCE

O-0042

HACK
-steve.-15

Cover Art by **ROBERT HACK** Colors by **STEPHEN DOWNER**

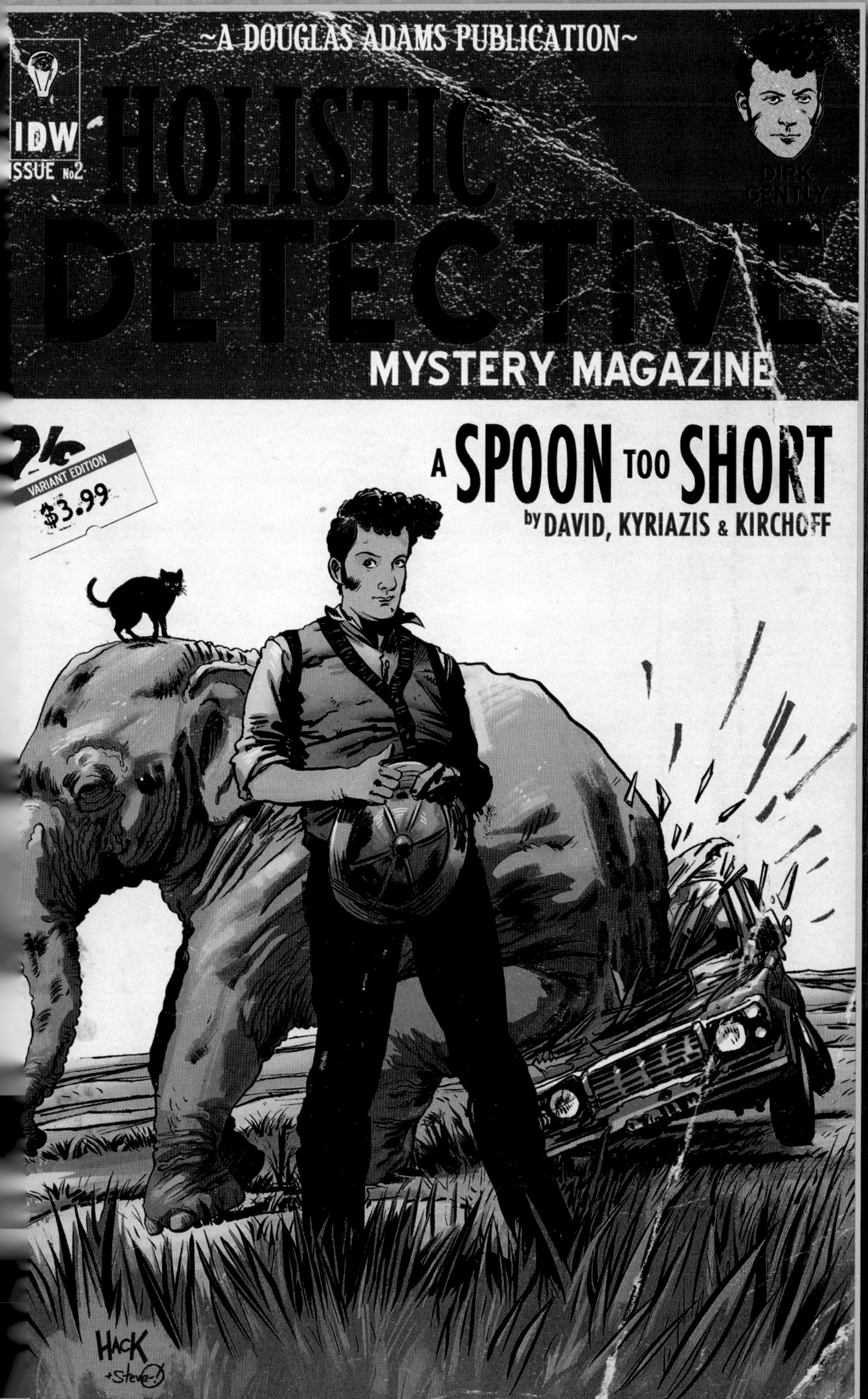
~A DOUGLAS ADAMS PUBLICATION~
IDW
ISSUE No2
HOLISTIC
DETECTIVE
MYSTERY MAGAZINE
DIRK GENTLY
VARIANT EDITION
$3.99
A SPOON TOO SHORT
by DAVID, KYRIAZIS & KIRCHOFF
HACK
+Steve-O

Cover Art by **ROBERT HACK** Colors by **STEPHEN DOWNER**

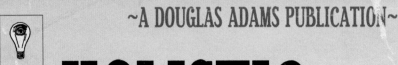

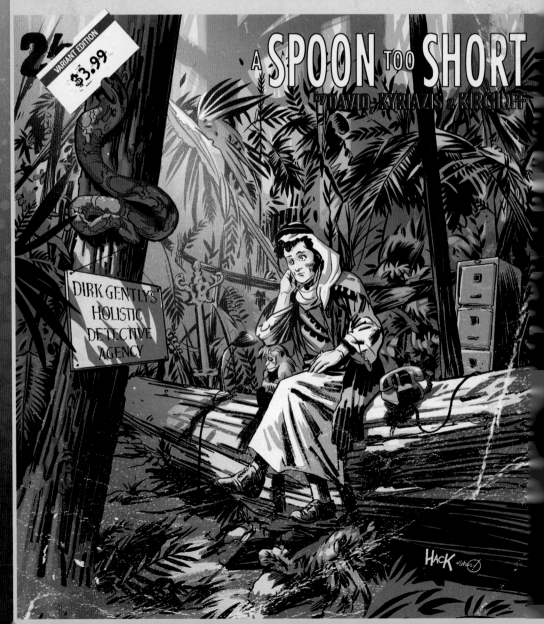

~A DOUGLAS ADAMS PUBLICATION~
IDW
ISSUE No 3
HOLISTIC
DETECTIVE
MYSTERY MAGAZINE
DIRK GENTLY
VARIANT EDITION
$3.99
A SPOON TOO SHORT
by DAVID, KYRIAZIS & KIRCHOFF
DIRK GENTLY'S HOLISTIC DETECTIVE AGENCY
HACK

Cover Art by **ROBERT HACK** Colors by **STEPHEN DOWNER**

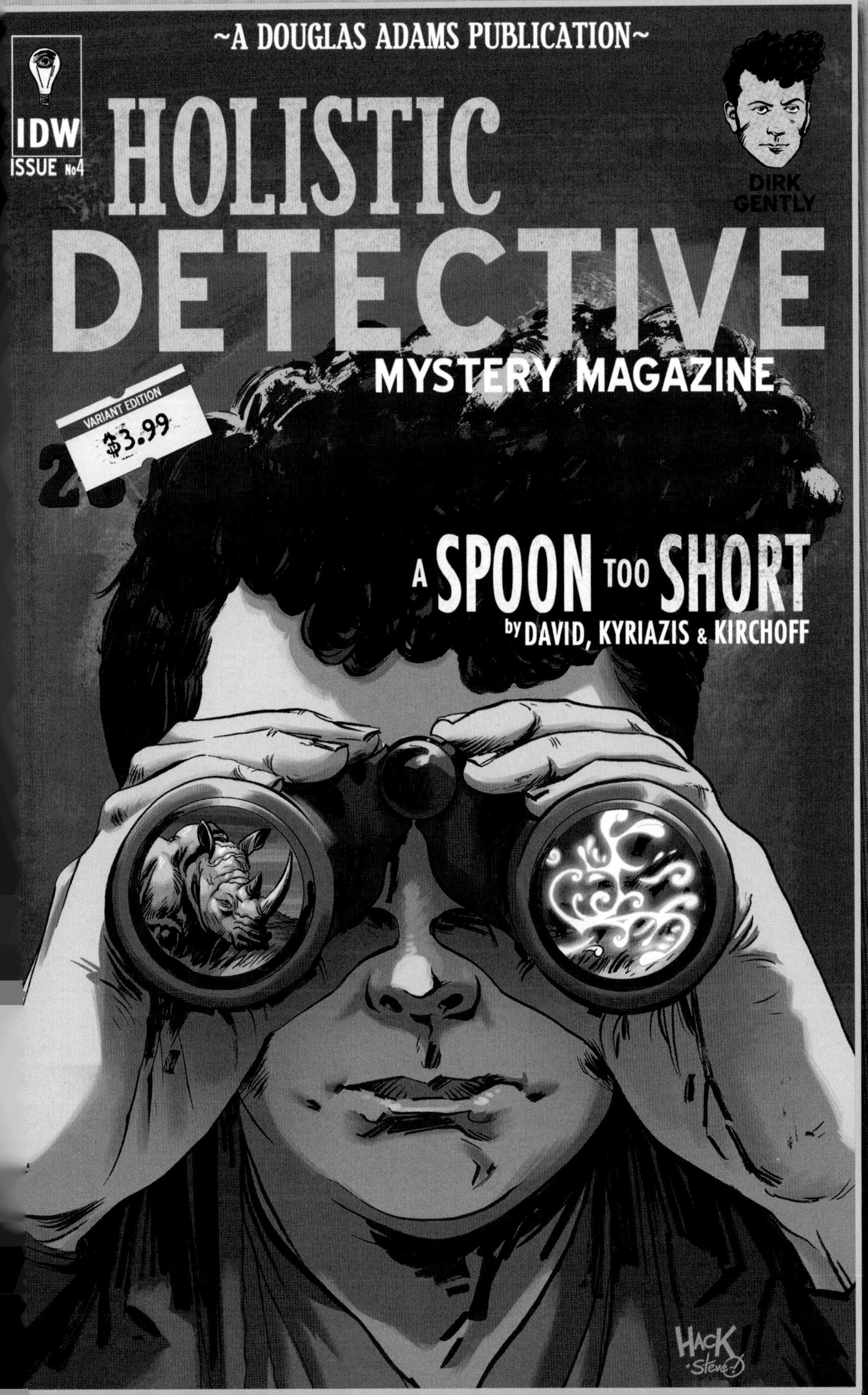

~A DOUGLAS ADAMS PUBLICATION~
IDW
ISSUE No4
HOLISTIC DETECTIVE
MYSTERY MAGAZINE
DIRK GENTLY
VARIANT EDITION
$3.99
A SPOON TOO SHORT
by DAVID, KYRIAZIS & KIRCHOFF
HACK

Cover Art by ROBERT HACK Colors by STEPHEN DOWNER

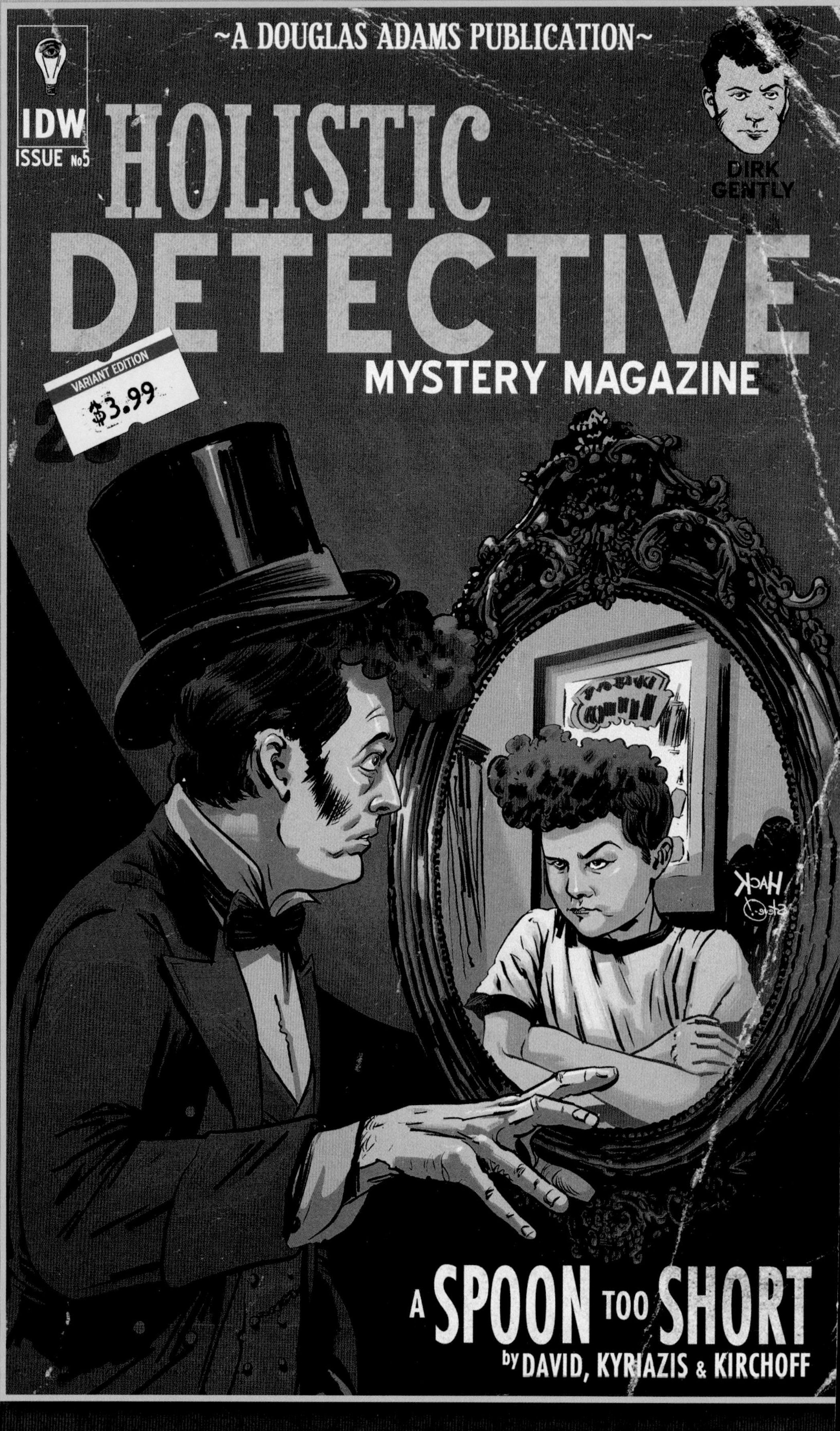
~A DOUGLAS ADAMS PUBLICATION~
IDW
ISSUE No5
HOLISTIC
DETECTIVE
MYSTERY MAGAZINE
DIRK GENTLY
VARIANT EDITION
$3.99
A SPOON TOO SHORT
by DAVID, KYRIAZIS & KIRCHOFF
HACK

Cover Art by **ROB GUILLORY**

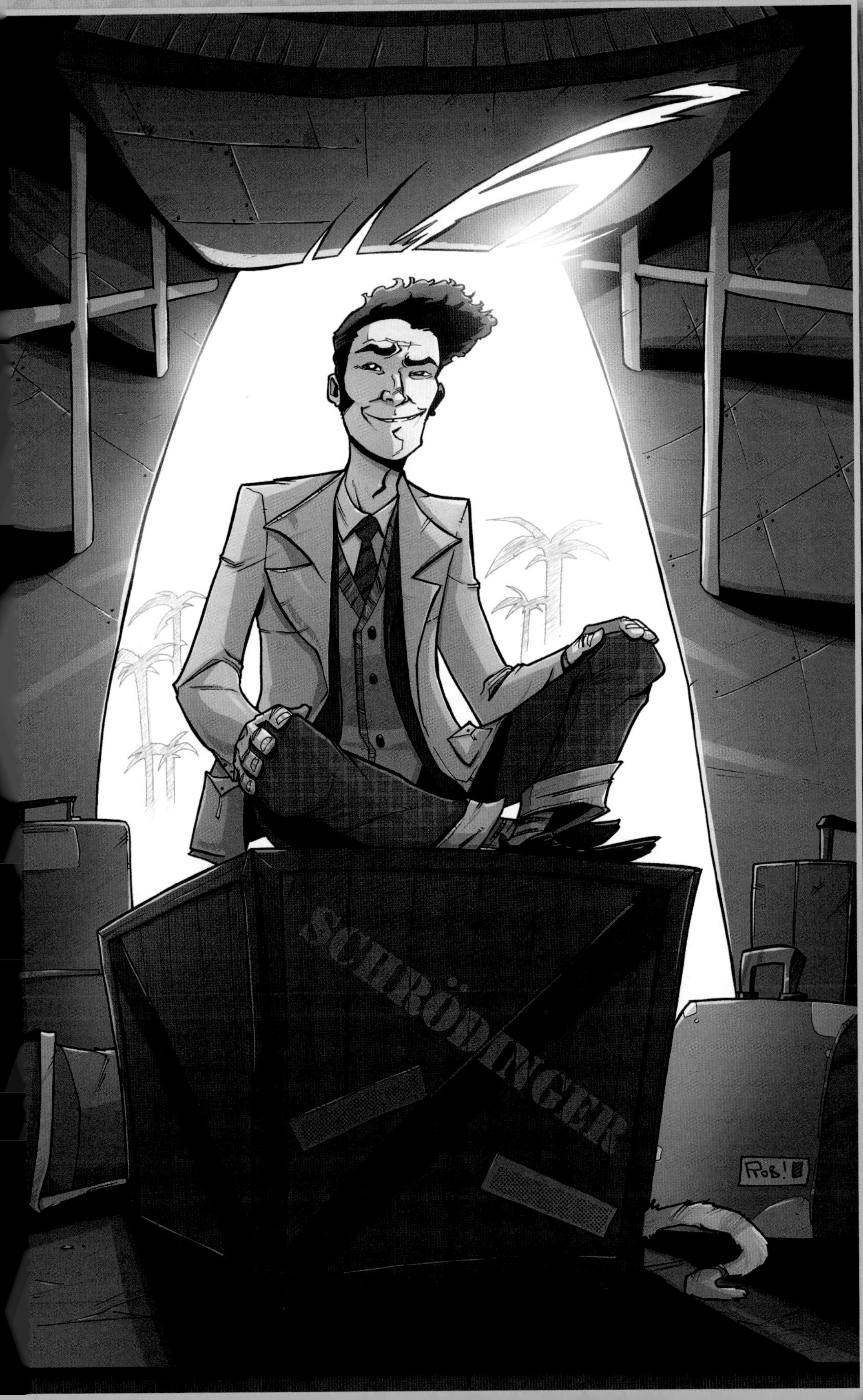
SCHRÖDINGER
ROB!

Cover Art by **ROBERT HACK** Colors by **STEPHEN DOWNER**

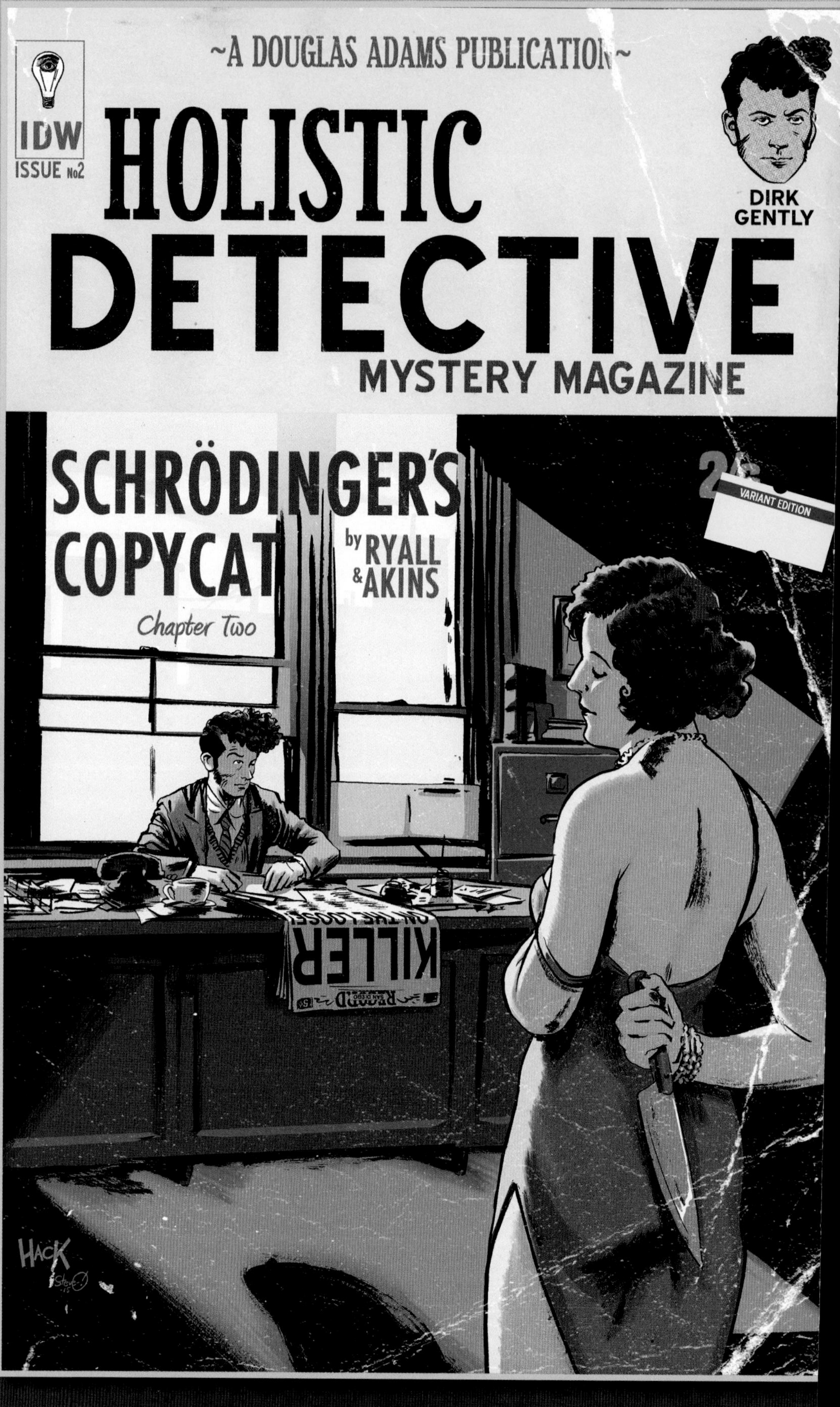
~A DOUGLAS ADAMS PUBLICATION~
IDW
ISSUE No2
HOLISTIC
DETECTIVE
MYSTERY MAGAZINE
DIRK GENTLY
SCHRÖDINGER'S
COPYCAT
by RYALL & AKINS
Chapter Two
VARIANT EDITION
KILLER
ON THE LOOSE!
HACK

Cover Art by **ROBERT HACK** Colors by **STEPHEN DOWNER**

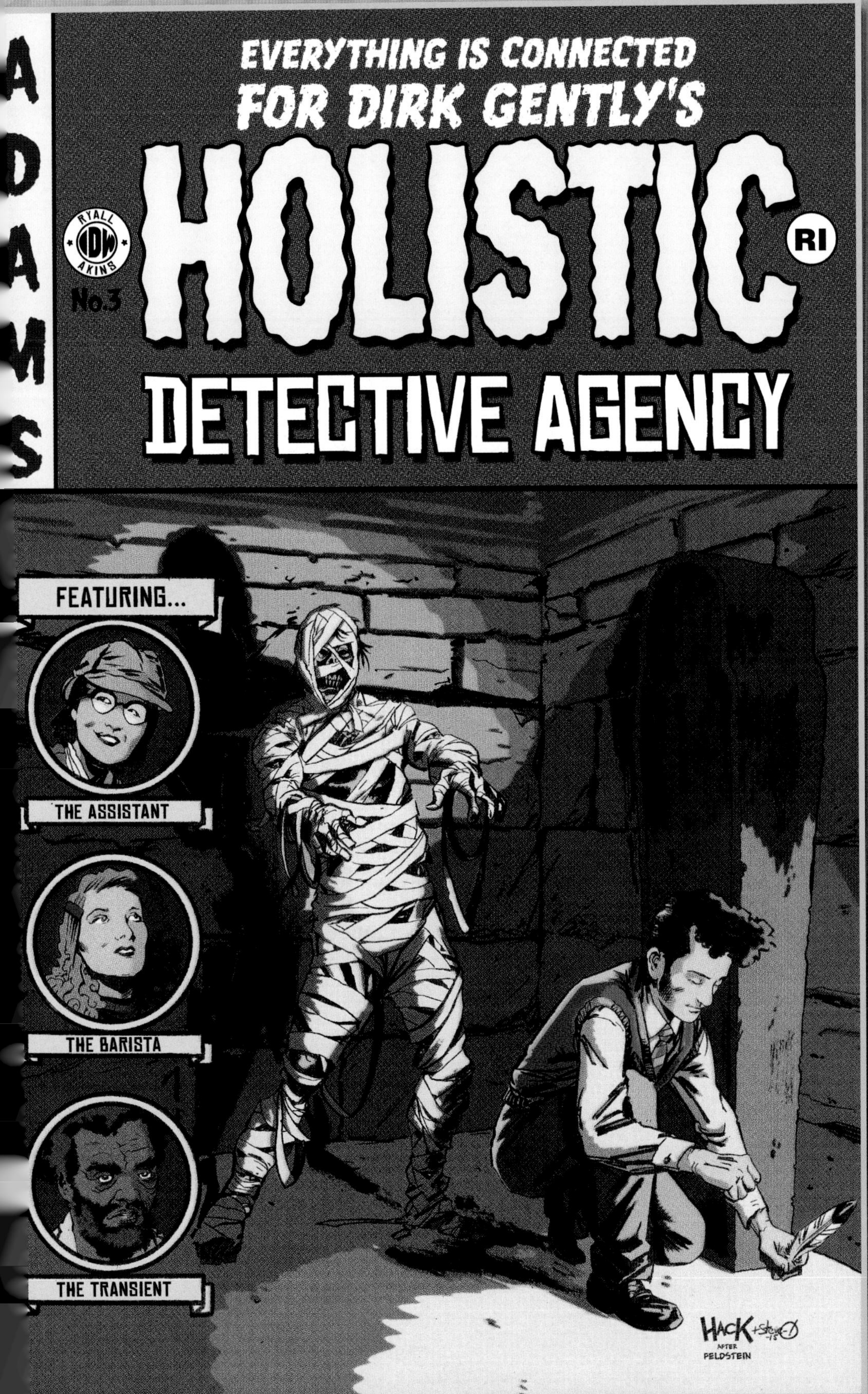

ADAMS
EVERYTHING IS CONNECTED
FOR DIRK GENTLY'S
HOLISTIC
DETECTIVE AGENCY
RYALL IDW AKINS
No.3
RI
FEATURING...
THE ASSISTANT
THE BARISTA
THE TRANSIENT
HACK
AFTER FELDSTEIN

Cover Art by **ROBERT HACK** Colors by **STEPHEN DOWNER**

~A DOUGLAS ADAMS PUBLICATION~
IDW
ISSUE No4
HOLISTIC
DETECTIVE
MYSTERY MAGAZINE
DIRK GENTLY
2/6
VARIANT EDITION
HACK
+Steve
-15
SCHRÖDINGER'S
COPYCAT
by RYALL & KYRIAZIS
Chapter Four

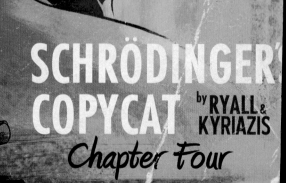

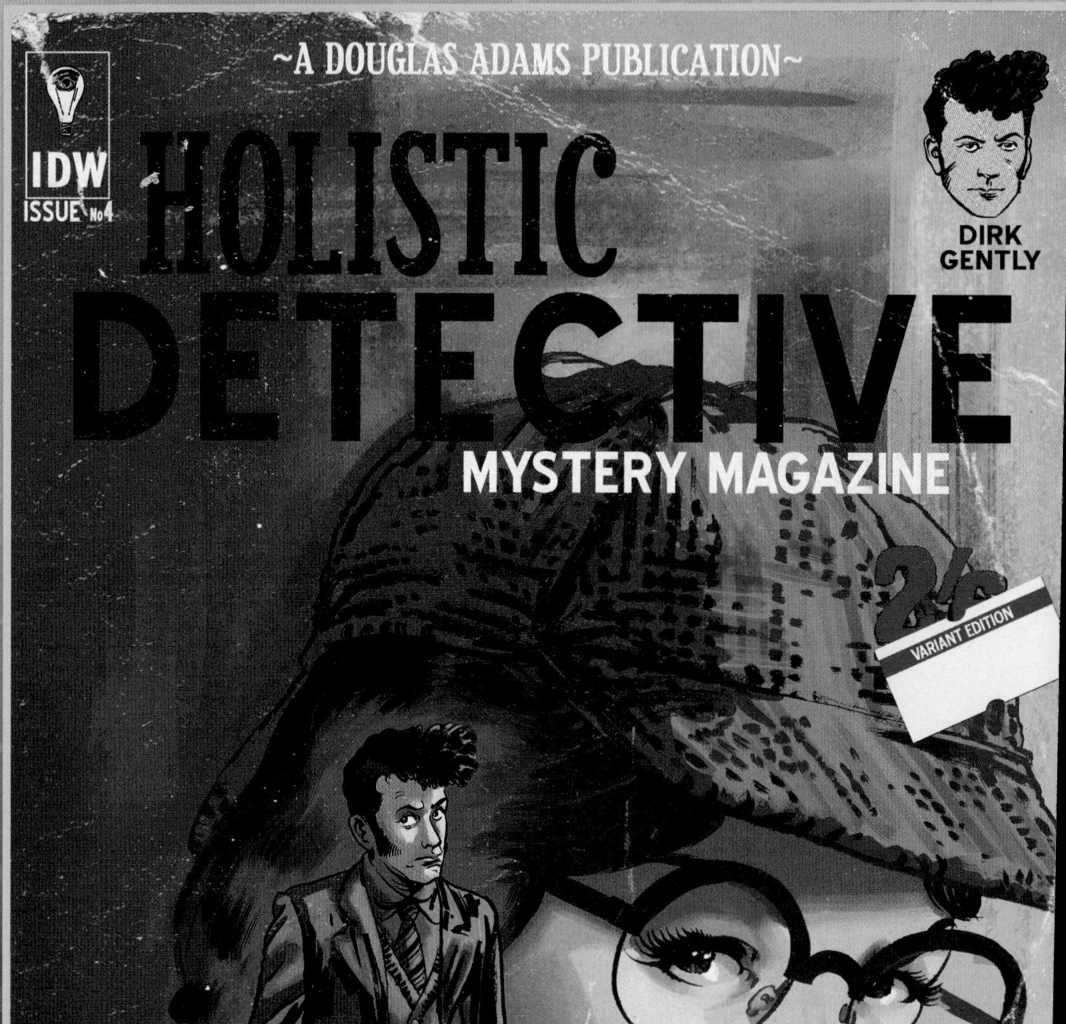

Cover Art by **ROBERT HACK** Colors by **STEPHEN DOWNER**

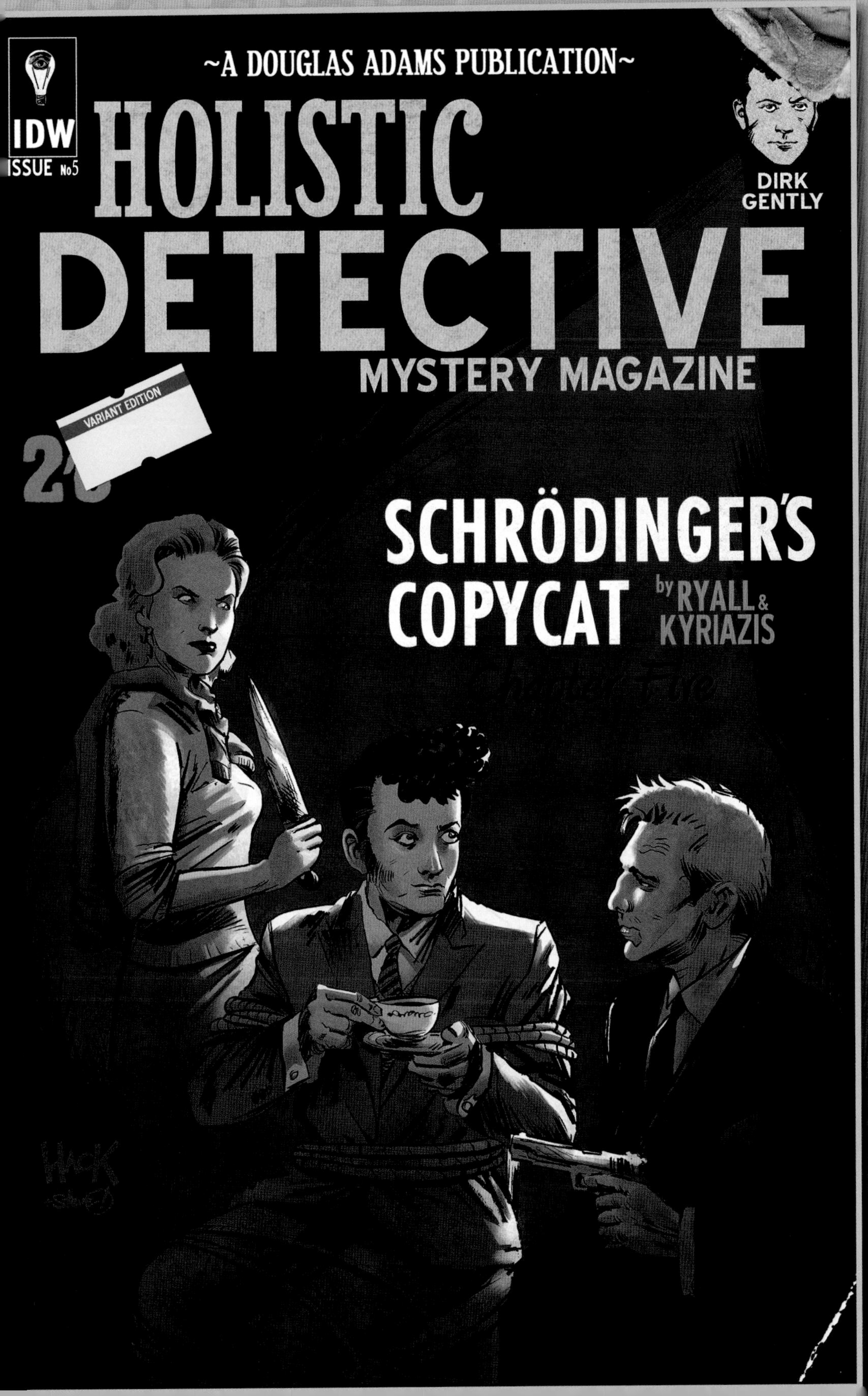
~A DOUGLAS ADAMS PUBLICATION~
IDW
ISSUE No5
HOLISTIC
DETECTIVE
MYSTERY MAGAZINE
DIRK GENTLY
VARIANT EDITION
SCHRÖDINGER'S
COPYCAT
by RYALL & KYRIAZIS
HACK

Cover Art by **BRIAN MILLER**

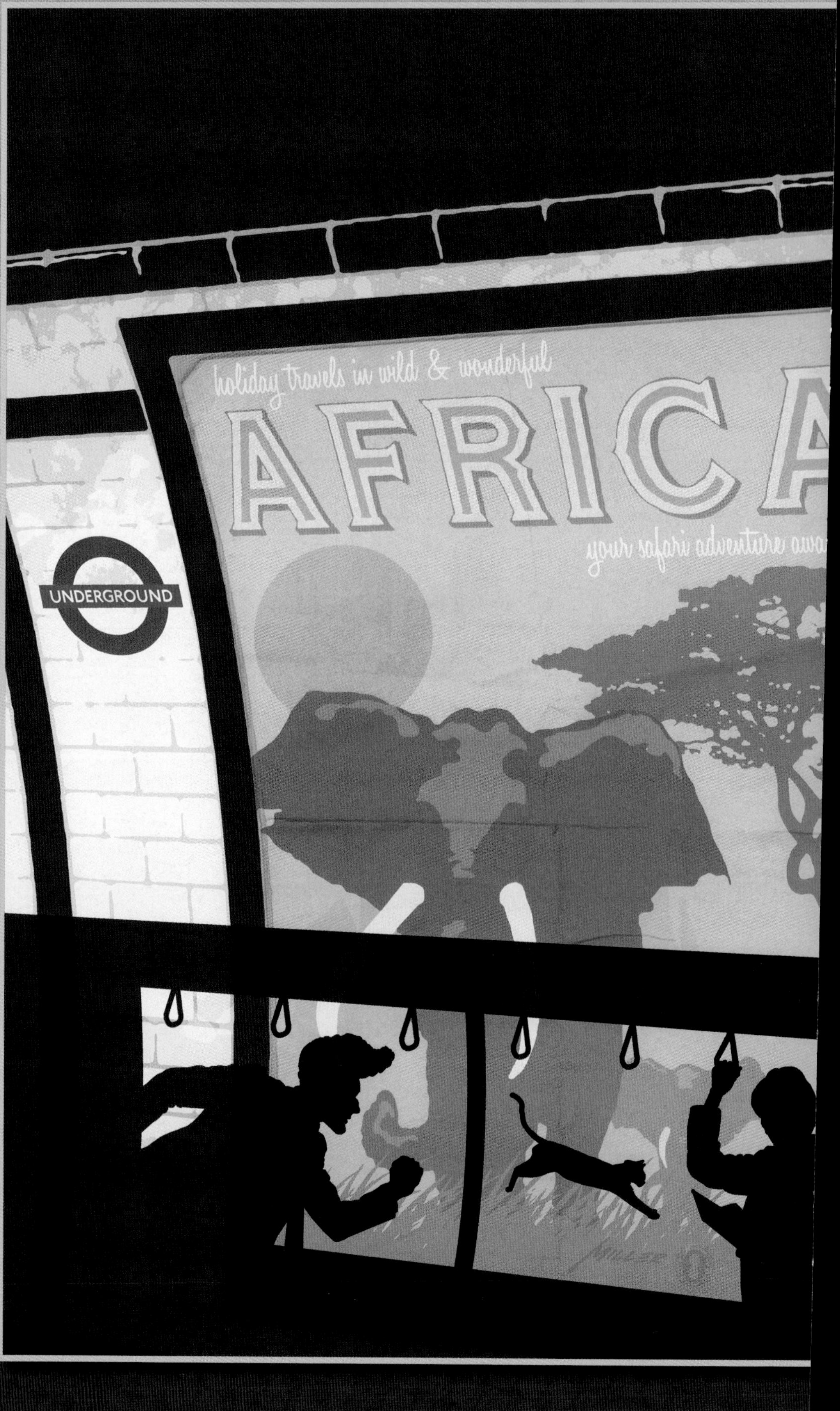
holiday travels in wild & wonderful
AFRICA
UNDERGROUND

Cover Art by **BRIAN MILLER**

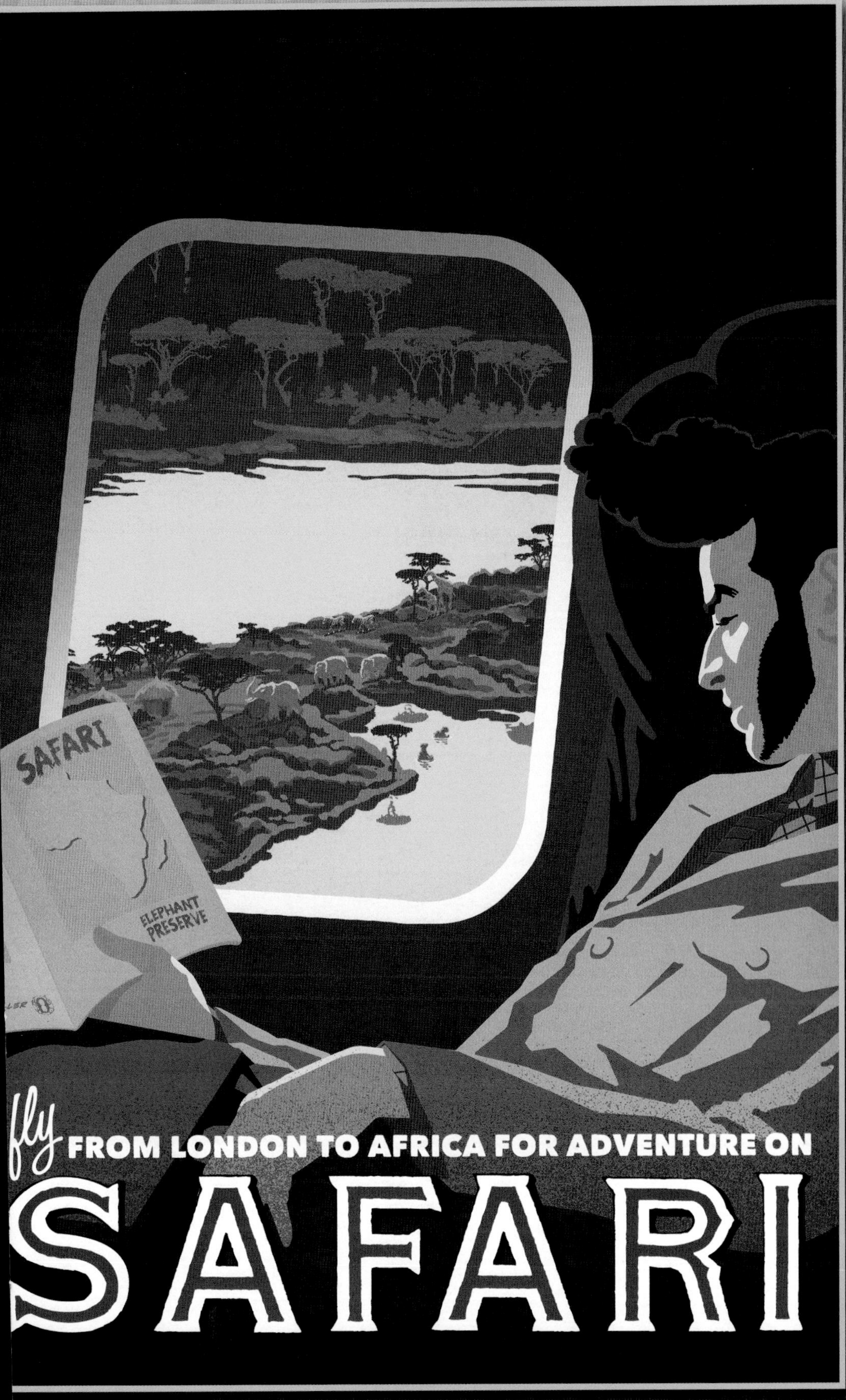
SAFARI
ELEPHANT PRESERVE
fly FROM LONDON TO AFRICA FOR ADVENTURE ON
SAFARI

Cover Art by **BRIAN MILLER**

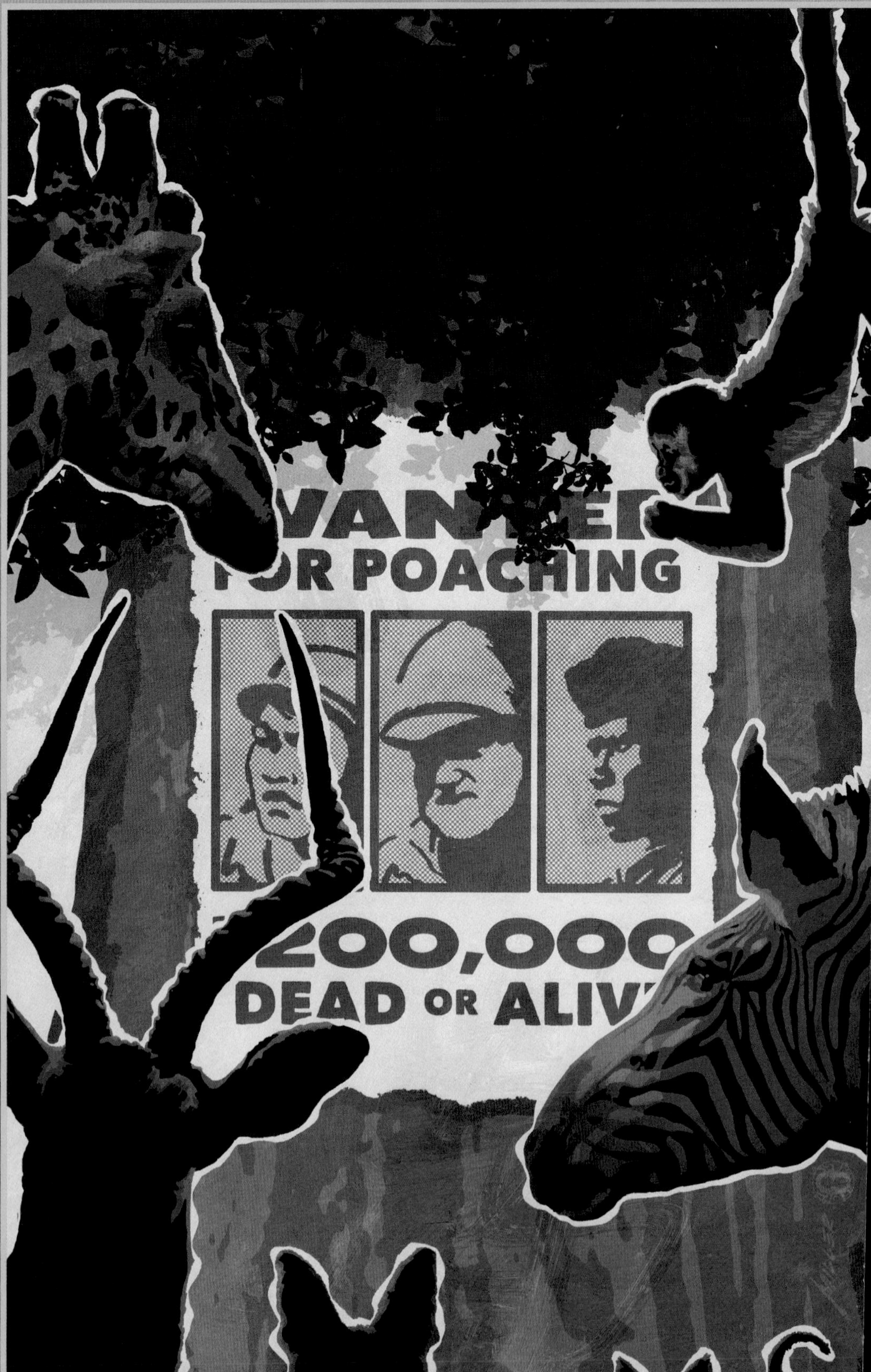

FOR POACHING
DEAD OR ALIV

Cover Art by **BRIAN MILLER**

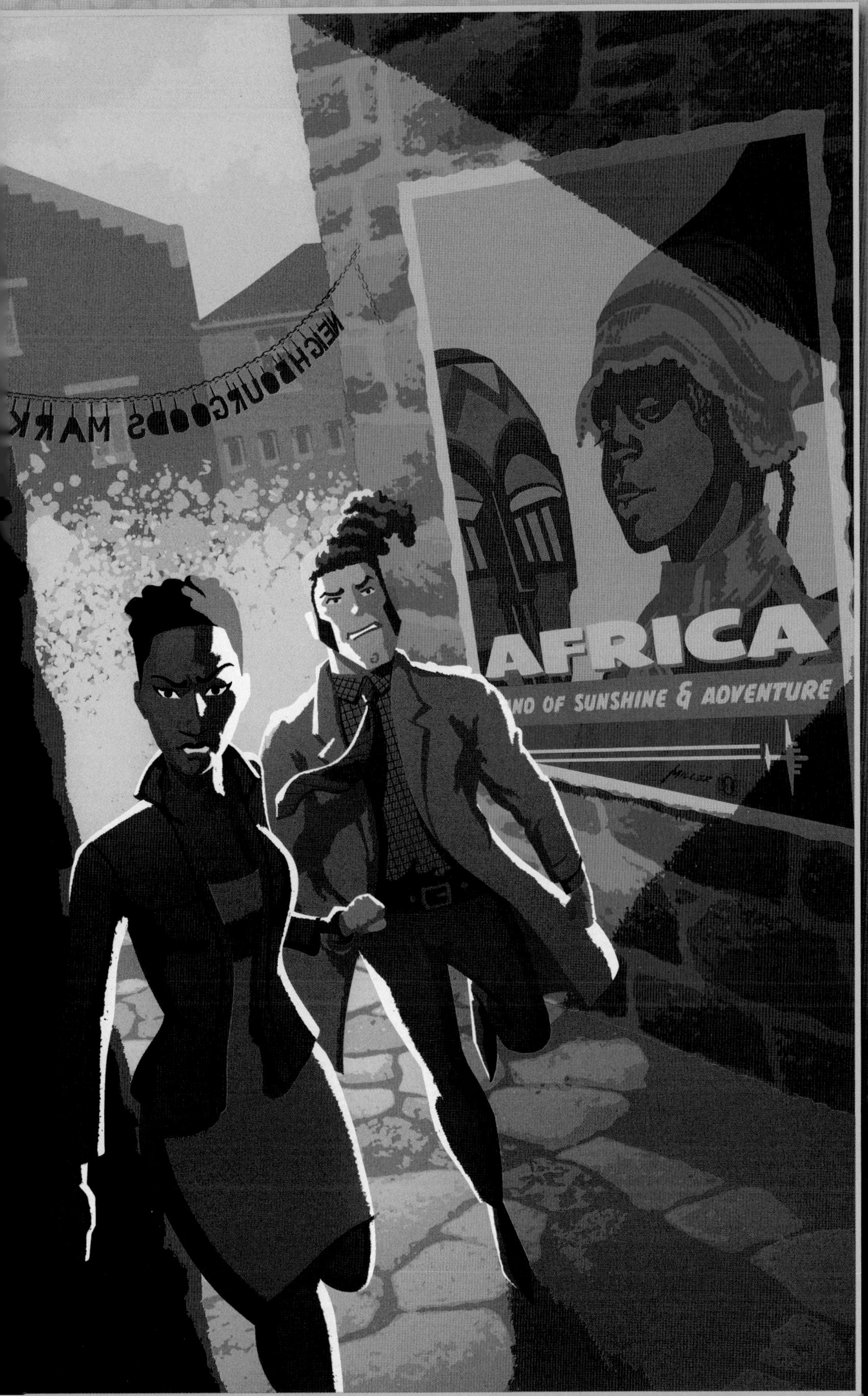

NEIGHBOURGOODS MARK
AFRICA
ND OF SUNSHINE & ADVENTURE

Cover Art by **BRIAN MILLER**

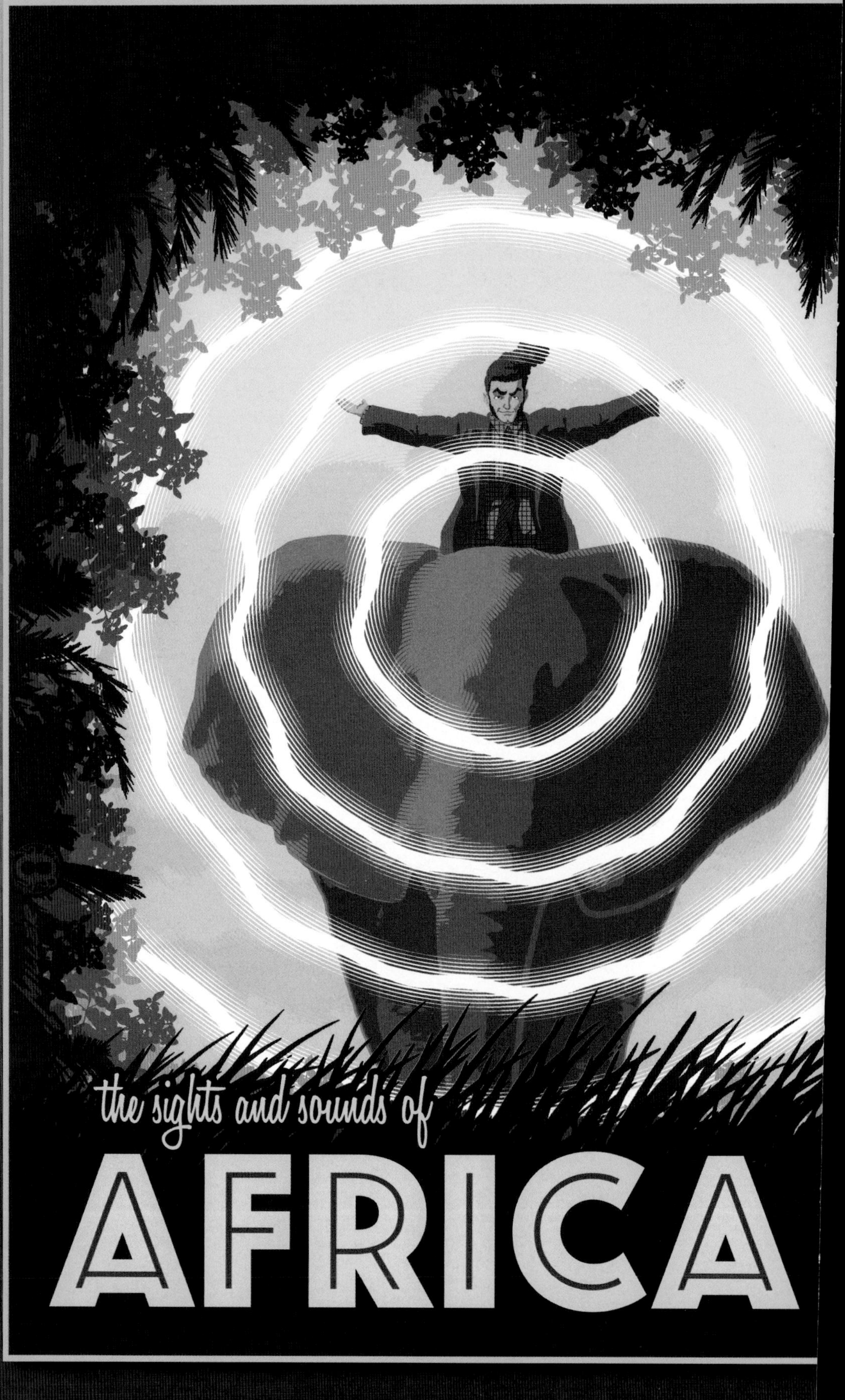
the sights and sounds of
AFRICA

PRODUCER'S GALLERY

PHOTOS FROM THE SET OF
DIRK GENTLY'S HOLISTIC DETECTIVE AGENCY

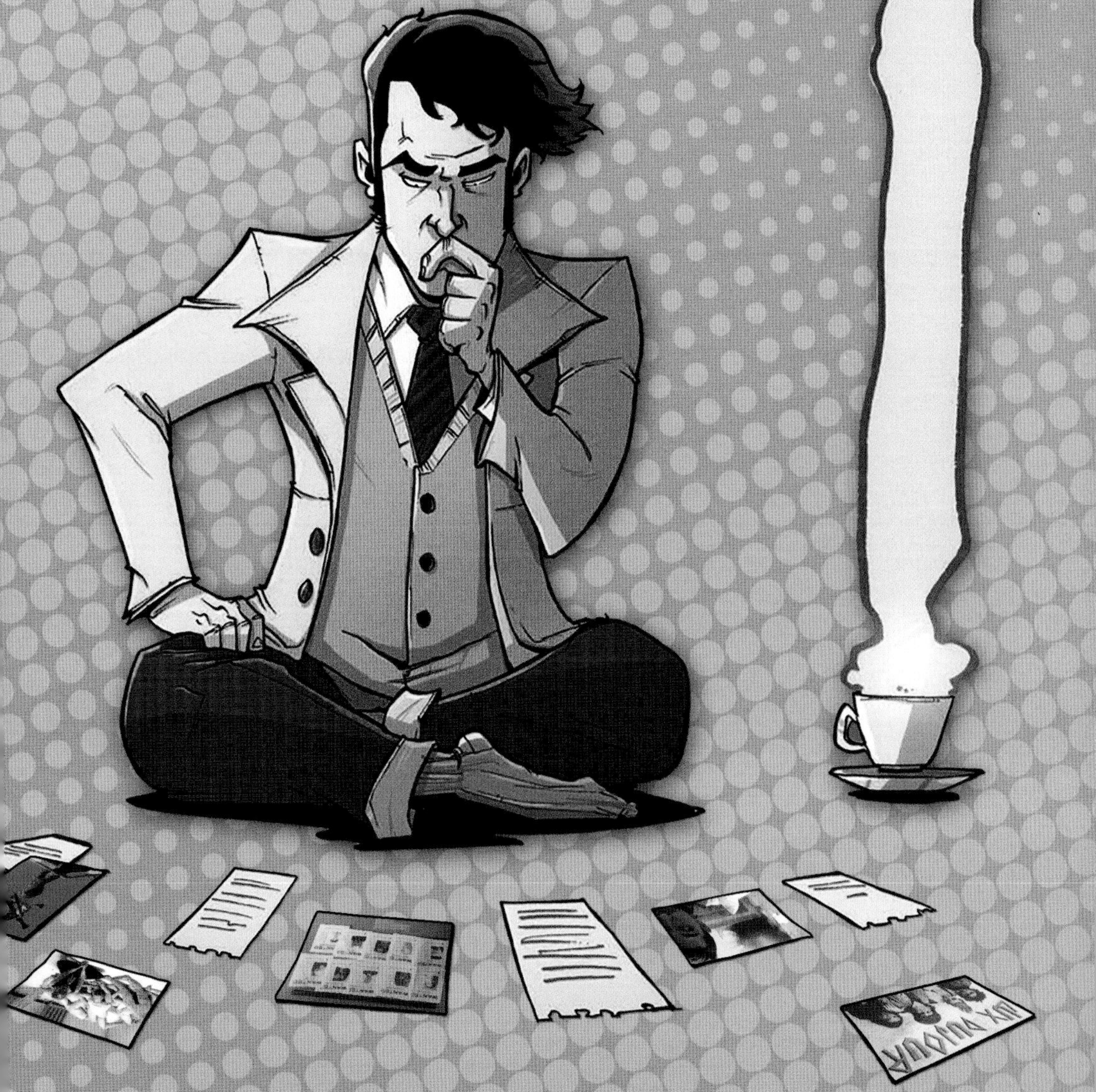

In the world of *Dirk Gently's Holistic Detective Agency*, very few things are certain. The light works (except when it doesn't), the gravity works (well, most of the time). The rest...?

Well, one thing is certain: Everything Is Connected.

One connection that has been especially fun to make is between the worlds of the Dirk of the origina Douglas Adams novels, the Dirk of these comic adventures, and the Dirk of the new television show. All three share certain characteristics, but are also in their ways, different.

Different, but connected.

Not least because the comics you hold in your hot hands were being written and drawn whilst we were simultaneously writing, shooting, and editing the TV show. It certainly made it easier for Ma (Landis, writer of the TV show and Executive Producer of the comics) and me (Arvind, writer of the comics and Executive Producer of the TV show) to share ideas and build the Gently-verse out acros both mediums.

Making a comic, though, is largely desk bound work. Making a TV show, by contrast, turns out t involve rather more... practical elements. A cast of dozens, a crew of hundreds, and a seemingl infinite range of ways that things could go wrong.

Fortunately, or rather, by the laws of Holistic Certainty, they didn't. Go wrong. Instead, we had one c the most intense but also most satisfying summers of our lives, working with a brilliantly talented an passionate group of people to bring Dirk to new audiences.

Here are some of the favorite momen from our scrapbooks: happy days wi a cast, crew and collection of anima stuffed and living, that we hope to b reunited with soon for new adventure

— Arvind Ethan David

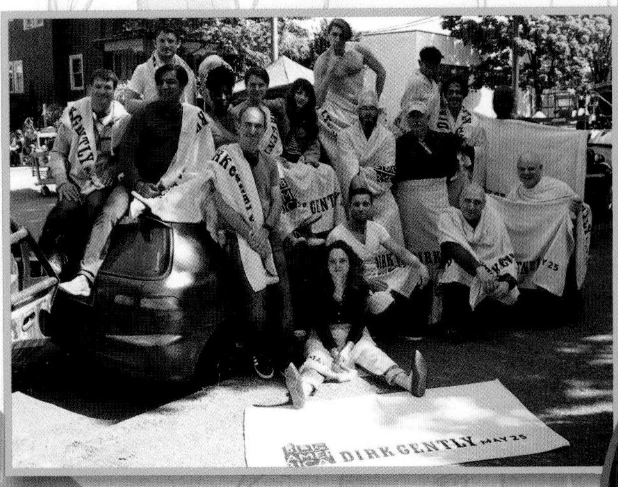
DIRK GENTLY MAY 25

By a wonderful – interconnected – co-incidence, the first day of principal photography was... TOWEL DAY, the day in which the world pays homage to the life and works of Douglas Adams. We donned bright Dirk-yellow BBC America towels to mark the moment.

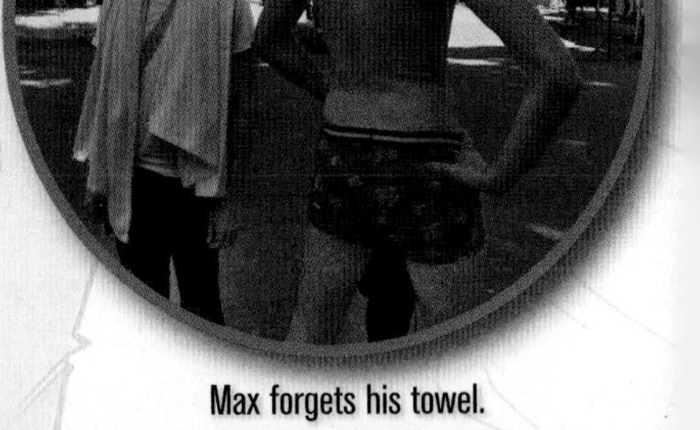

Max forgets his towel.

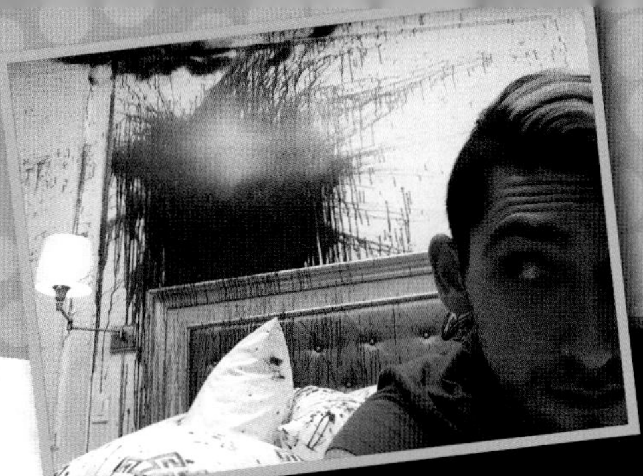

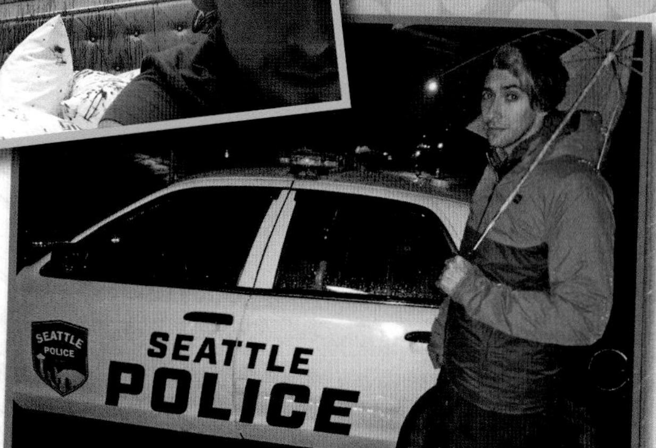
SEATTLE
POLICE
SEATTLE
POLICE

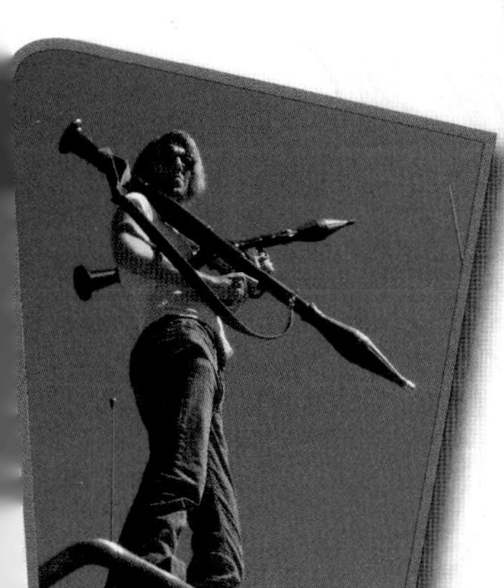

It was only a short period of time before our creator and ring leader, Max Landis, started getting in trouble on shoot.

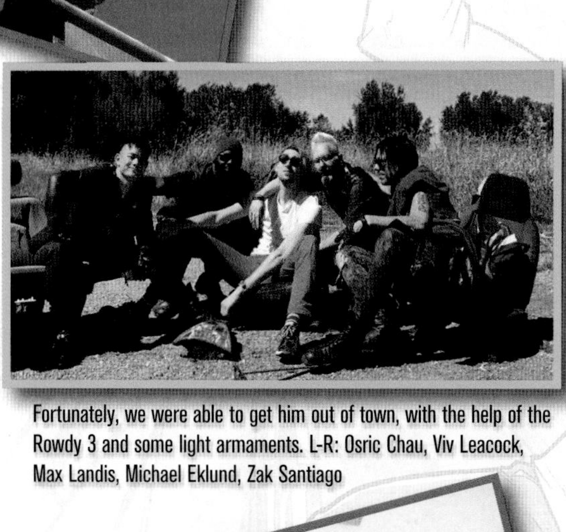

Fortunately, we were able to get him out of town, with the help of the Rowdy 3 and some light armaments. L-R: Osric Chau, Viv Leacock, Max Landis, Michael Eklund, Zak Santiago

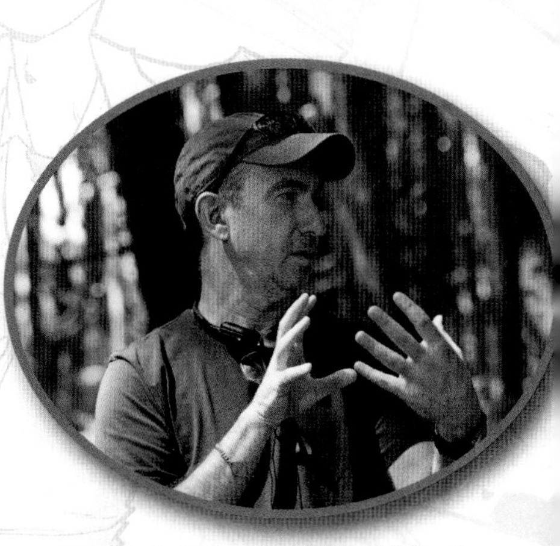

Our show runner, Robert Cooper of *Stargate* fame remains in calm charge whilst the rest of us are being murdered in our beds.

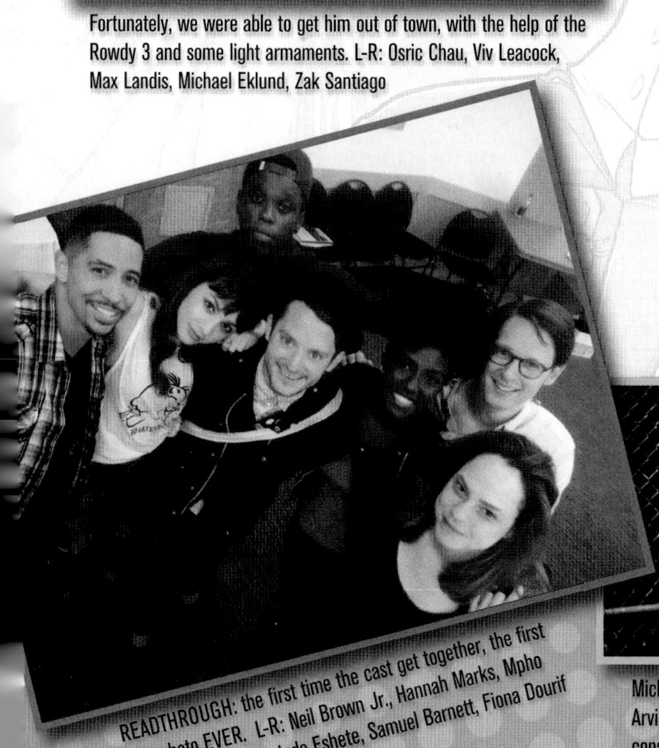

READTHROUGH: the first time the cast get together, the first cast photo EVER. L-R: Neil Brown Jr., Hannah Marks, Mpho Koaho, Elijah Wood, Jade Eshete, Samuel Barnett, Fiona Dourif

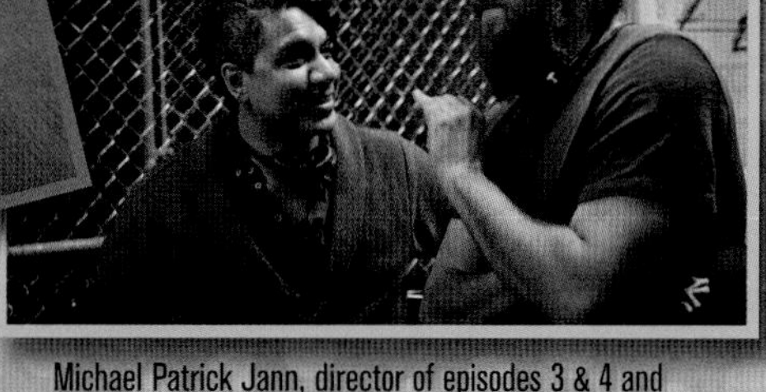

Michael Patrick Jann, director of episodes 3 & 4 and Arvind Ethan David discuss something very important and consequential. Seriously, they are solving the problems of the world.

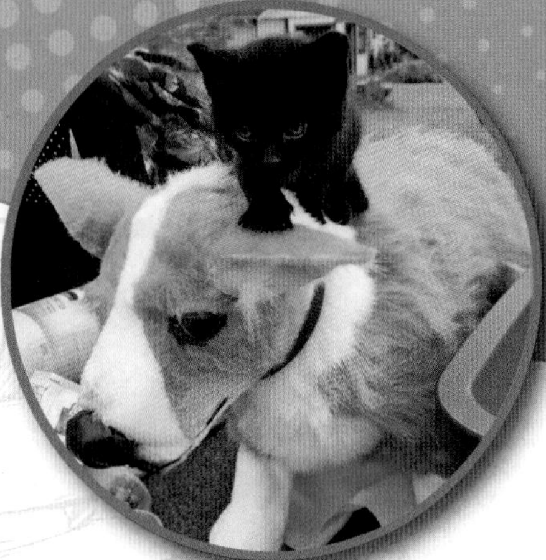

It's amazing how much money you can spend on really rubbish stuffed dogs and how cheap and amazing real kittens are.

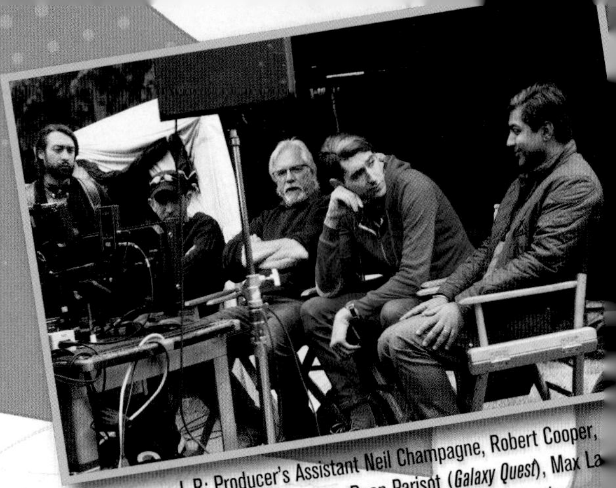

L-R: Producer's Assistant Neil Champagne, Robert Cooper, episode 1 & 2 Director Dean Parisot (*Galaxy Quest*), Max La and Arvind Ethan David on the first day of production.

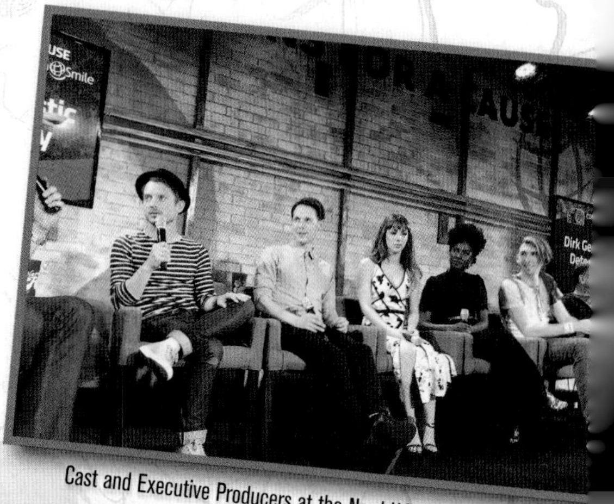

Cast and Executive Producers at the Nerd HQ Comic-Con panel.

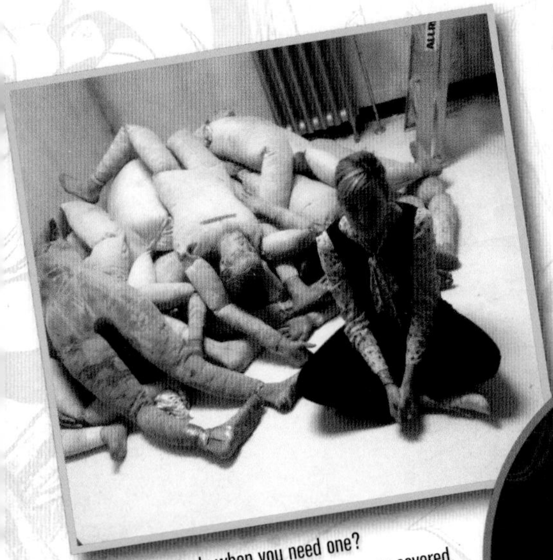

Where's a body when you need one? Production Designer Katie Byron has you covered.

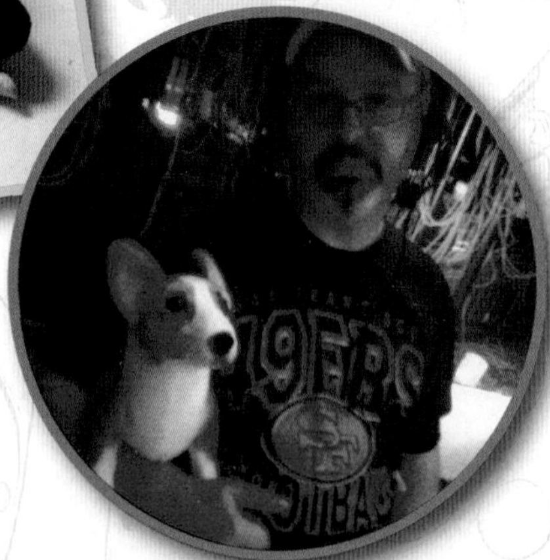

It's a dog and Assistant Direct Richard Worden.

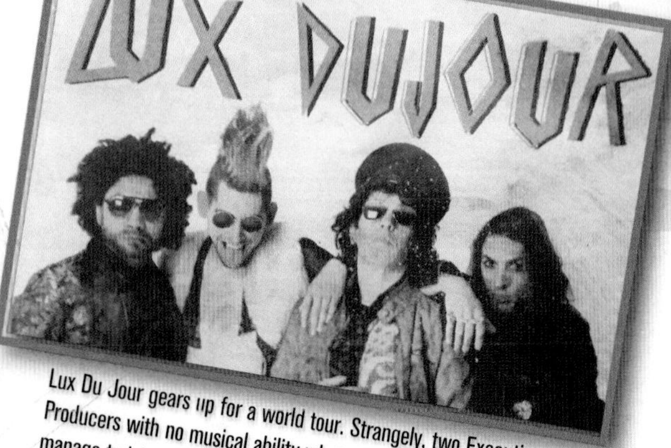
LUX DUJOUR

Lux Du Jour gears up for a world tour. Strangely, two Executive Producers with no musical ability whatsoever (but great hair) manage to join the band.

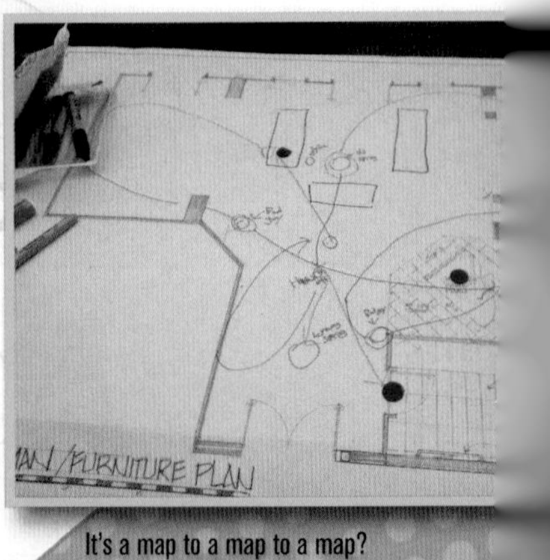
FURNITURE PLAN

It's a map to a map to a map?